Effective Organisational Communication

Companion Website

For open-access **student resources** specifically written to complement this textbook and support your learning, please visit **www.pearsoned.co.uk/ blundelippolitodonnarumma**

ON THE WEBSITE

Fourth Edition

Effective Organisational Communication

Perspectives, principles and practices

Richard Blundel
Kate Ippolito
David Donnarumma

PEARSON

Harlow, England • London • New York • Boston • San Francisco • Toronto • Sydney
Auckland • Singapore • Hong Kong • Tokyo • Seoul • Taipei • New Delhi
Cape Town • São Paulo • Mexico City • Madrid • Amsterdam • Munich • Paris • Milan

Pearson Education Limited
Edinburgh Gate
Harlow CM20 2JE
United Kingdom
Tel: +44 (0)1279 623623
Web: www.pearson.com/uk

First published in Great Britain as *Effective Business Communication* by Prentice Hall in
1998 (print)
Second edition published 2004 (print)
Third edition published 2008 (print)
This edition published 2013 (print and electronic)

© **Prentice Hall Europe 1998** (print)
© **Pearson Education Limited 2013** (print and electronic)

The Financial Times. With a worldwide network of highly respected journalists, *The
Financial Times* provides global business news, insightful opinion and expert analysis
of business, finance and politics. With over 500 journalists reporting from 50 countries
worldwide, our in-depth coverage of international news is objectively reported and
analysed from an independent, global perspective. To find out more, visit www.ft.com/
pearsonoffer.

ISBN: **978-0-273-77486-0** (print)
          978-0-273-77487-7 (eText)

British Library Cataloguing-in-Publication Data
A catalogue record for the print edition is available from the British Library

Library of Congress Cataloging-in-Publication Data
A catalog record for the print edition is available from the Library of Congress

10 9 8 7 6 5 4 3 2 1
16 15 14 13 12

Print edition typeset in 9.5/12.5 pt ITC Charter by 73
Print edition printed and bound in England by Ashford Colour Press, Gosport

NOTE THAT ANY PAGE CROSS REFERENCES REFER TO THE PRINT EDITION

For our families

Contents

Companion Website

For open-access **student resources** specifically written to complement this textbook and support your learning, please visit **www.pearsoned.co.uk/ blundelippolitodonnarumma**

Lecturer Resources

For password-protected online resources tailored to support the use of this textbook in teaching, please visit **www.pearsoned.co.uk/blundelippolitodonnarumma**

List of figures

List of tables

List of case studies

List of 'Face-to-face' cases

The authors

Richard Blundel is a senior lecturer at The Open University Business School. He is also co-author (with Nigel Lockett) of *Exploring Entrepreneurship: Practices and Perspectives* (Oxford University Press). He has worked in a number of public and private sector organisations, including periods as a corporate affairs manager in the European office of a large US industrial company and as a marketing research analyst in a specialist consultancy serving the computer industry. His research interests include commercial and social entrepreneurship, technological innovation and the role of communication in organisations. His work has been published in a number of journals, including *Entrepreneurship and Regional Development, Industry* and *Innovation, Management and Organisational History* and *Enterprise and Society*.

Kate Ippolito is an educationalist at the Royal College of Physicians and a sessional lecturer at Reading University. She previously worked as the Education Development Projects Manager in Brunel University's Learning and Teaching Development Unit and was the Oral Communication Learning Area Coordinator for the *LearnHigher* Centre for Excellence in Teaching and Learning project. Prior to that she was a trainer, working in the legal, financial and logistics sectors. Her research interests are the teaching and assessment of communication practices, including inter-cultural communication, and faculty development in Medical Education. Her work has been published in *Teaching in Higher Education* and *Reflecting Education*.

David Donnarumma is the Teaching Qualifications Manager at Trinity College, London. He has worked in the areas of English language teaching and communication skills teaching in both public and private organisations for 15 years. He has been a lecturer at the Open University, UK, and also led an academic skills team at Brunel University. He also spent a number of years working abroad teaching communication skills to senior executives in the telecommunications and pharmaceutical industries. His research interests are in English as a Lingua Franca, online communication skills and course materials development. He is currently working on a doctorate in Education focusing on the development of online communication skills in MBA students.

The contributors

Naveed Chaudhri has been a member of Oxfam's campaigns staff since 1999, following an earlier career in academic publishing. He has been engaged in grassroots campaigning with the Oxford Oxfam Group for over ten years.

Linda Clark is the founding partner of an executive recruitment and marketing consultancy, The Human Choice, specialising in the retail services sector. She has extensive marketing management experience in international retail organisations.

Jackie Clarke is a reader in marketing at Oxford Brookes University and Deputy Head of Research for the faculty of business. She is the co-author of two tourism marketing and management texts. Her research interests include tourism sustainability, branding, and consumer behaviour. She has marketing experience in a large aviation and tour operating company, and has conducted research and consultancy in Slovakia, Spain and for a UK-based museum consortium.

Tina Fawcett is a senior researcher in energy and environmental issues, working for the United Kingdom Energy Research Council (UKERC) and the Environmental Change Institute, University of Oxford. Tina is also the co-author, with Mayer Hillman, of *How We Can Save the Planet*, one of the pioneering guides to the implications of climate change, published by Penguin Books (UK edition) and St Martin's Press (USA edition).

Dan Herbert is the Programme Director BSc Accounting and Finance at the University of Birmingham. He has a background in accounting, both at the UK's National Audit Office and in local government. Dan's recent research activities have revolved around the use of open financial data to improve government accountability. He has contributed to spending analysis projects run by the Open Knowledge Foundation.

Elspeth Macfarlane is Head of the International Centre for Coaching and Leadership Development at Oxford Brookes University Business School. Her teaching and research are in the areas of management skills and human resource management. Elspeth also has extensive commercial experience in human resource management within an international retail chain.

Liz and Robert Robertson are the founders and directors of Robertson Languages International (RLI). Their company is a leading provider of integrated language services, ranging from translation services to large training programmes, serving a wide range of corporate clients.

Mark Saunders is Professor in Business Research Methods at the University of Surrey. He is also Director of Postgraduate Research Programmes. His research interests are Research Methods and Human Resource Aspects of the Management of Change, and these are reflected in his teaching. Mark is co-author of *Research Methods for Business Students* and *Strategic Human Resource Management*, which are published by FT Prentice Hall. He also undertakes consultancy in public, private and not-for-profit sectors.

Mitchell Sedgwick trained as a social anthropologist and has been engaged in ethnographic research on private and public sector organisations over the last two decades. He has held several long-term consultancies at the World Bank and the United Nations, including work on government institutions in Thailand and Laos, and state-owned enterprises in Burkina Faso. His research interests include cross-cultural dynamics at Japanese multinationals and headquarters–subsidiary relations.

Ian Wycherley worked as an accountant in the computer industry before lecturing in management at Oxford Brookes University. He has published research papers on environmental management and also on the management of relationships in industrial networks. Ian has an active interest in the role of storytelling in organisations.

Preface to the fourth edition

There can be too much communication between people.
Ann Beattie, writer

Who is this book for?

Effective Organisational Communication has a number of audiences, including under-graduate and postgraduate students taking courses such as communication, professional communication skills, management skills, international management and organisational behaviour. The book's combination of accessibility, up-to-date theory and practical application will also make it a useful resource for students from other disciplines, such as biological science, computing or engineering, which often include organisational and managerial themes in their course programmes. It is suitable for students who have English as a first or second language. It should also be of value to practising managers who wish to review and develop their own approach to communication, or to coach other employees in this vital and often neglected subject.

How has it changed?

The fourth edition of *Effective Organisational Communication* sees the arrival of a third co-author, David Donnarumma. In revising the book, the authors have retained many popular features of the previous edition, whilst also taking account of feedback from readers and reviewers. Our major revisions have focused on further enhancing the international and inter-cultural perspectives, incorporating more of a focus on language development and the use of social media tools and on creating more opportunities for readers to reflect on their personal experiences of organisational communication. Whether you are located in the UK, Scandinavia, or in another part of the world entirely, you are likely to be studying, working – or just spending time – in some diverse multinational and multi-cultural organisations. In the new edition we emphasise the practical implications of such diversity, with theoretical insights and compelling 'real-world' case studies that highlight contemporary challenges and opportunities, including those posed by continual advances in communication technologies. Here is a list of the key changes we have made to this new edition:

- **Key concepts**: We have continued to update and added more concise and easy-to-locate definitions of important communication concepts and terminology.

- **Case studies**: These have been updated and refreshed with current, real-world examples of communication challenges to support the development of your critical thinking.

- **Useful websites**: As websites are a dynamic source of information we have ensured that links are still 'live' and have added new, relevant online resources. This includes more links to web-based multimedia.

- **Internationalisation / globalisation:** We have strengthened this theme throughout the whole book.

- **Social media:** We have updated several chapters to include critique of social media tools such as *Twitter* and *Facebook* and we explore the challenges of using technologies such as video conferencing

- **Language development:** We have strengthened and included more information on language development skills particularly in the areas of verbal communication and report writing.

What is it trying to achieve?

The purpose of this book is to help you become a more effective communicator. It is concerned with the complex and dynamic mix of written, spoken and visual communication that takes place within and between organisations. We look at people's efforts to communicate in a variety of challenging organisational settings, including: multinational corporations, international aid agencies, local governments, scientific research teams and start-up ventures. In contrast to many popular texts in this area, *Effective Organisational Communication* is more than simply an instructional manual. Throughout the book, you are encouraged to identify connections between the development of skills in specific communication **practices** (e.g. drafting more focused and readable reports, communicating more clearly and persuasively in meetings), and a broader set of communication **principles**. The text also introduces contrasting research **perspectives**, expanding the scope of the subject and challenging some unspoken assumptions about the central theme of 'effectiveness' in communication. By exploring the links between perspectives, principles and practices, you can begin to generalise from your own experiences of communication, develop a more flexible repertoire of skills and refine your critical faculties. As a result, you will be much better placed to deal with new communication challenges.

How is it structured?

Chapter 1 provides a general overview of the book. It introduces the communication process, reviews a number of perspectives and insights and introduces some key themes that are developed throughout the text. It is therefore essential to read this chapter thoroughly, before proceeding. After Chapter 1, the rest of the book is divided into two closely interrelated parts.

Part 1 – Principles of communication

Chapters 2 to 7 establish a coherent framework for exploring the communication process, drawing on relevant research findings and real-life case studies. Chapter 2 identifies the principal barriers to effective communication and considers how they can be overcome. Subsequent chapters consider the role of words and images in various forms of communication; the communicator's key tasks of developing arguments; and the challenge of securing relevant feedback. The final chapter in Part 1 addresses the additional issues that arise when you attempt to communicate within and beyond the boundaries of organisations.

Part 2 – Communication in practice

Chapters 8 to 13 provide a comprehensive, practical and critical review of the main communication channels used in today's organisations. Each chapter follows a similar format, introducing the essential elements of the channel, including its strengths and weaknesses, showing how the generic principles of communication can be applied to improve effectiveness by working through examples of good and bad practice. Chapter 14 draws brief conclusions from the preceding chapters, discusses the challenge of evaluating (or 'auditing') organisational communication and points to some on-going challenges.

The Part 1 ('principles') chapters build on one another and are therefore best studied in sequence. Part 2 ('practice') chapters, with the exception of Chapter 14, are entirely

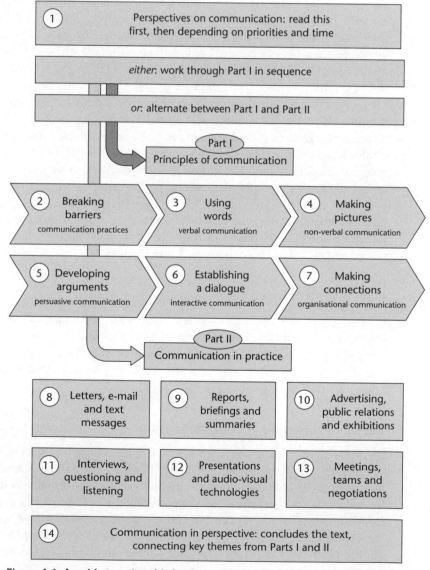

Figure A.1 A guide to using this book

self-contained, and can be worked through in any order, depending on your current interests and needs. Chapters 7 and 14 conclude each section, highlighting key themes and emerging issues. This flexible format allows you to explore the links between principles and practice by alternating between Parts 1 and 2 (see: Figure A.1 'A guide to using this book'). Each chapter contains several up-to-date case studies (including a 'face-to-face' example), practical exercises or discussion topics, annotated guides to further reading and useful websites, plus a full list of references. These features are designed to clarify your understanding, and to provide practice in applying what has been learnt.

How should I approach this subject?

'Effectiveness' in organisational communication is about the skilful application of knowledge. Just as in other fields, such as sports or the performing arts, the only way to improve your personal performance is to practise and the only way to *excel* is to keep on questioning your current approach, and to set yourself greater challenges. But there is more to this subject than simply enhancing personal capabilities. Organisations are strange and powerful beasts that have a profound impact on every aspect of our daily life. Though much of their impact is positive, organisations can also do a great deal of harm. The negative side is revealed in the controversies that we see almost every day in the media concerning organisations and their interactions with key stakeholders, such as employees, customers, suppliers and local communities. But is anyone learning from past mistakes? If organisations are to do less harm (and more good) in the future, part of the solution is to have a *better informed* debate about the ways that they communicate. We hope that this book encourages you to join in this argument by taking a continuing, *critical* interest in the communication practices of organisations and the people who inhabit them.

Richard Blundel, Kate Ippolito and David Donnarumma

Summer 2012

Acknowledgements

We would like to thank the many colleagues and friends who have contributed to the fourth edition of this text, including those who have drafted case studies and others who have helped with exercises, illustrations and ideas. We are very grateful to the international panel of reviewers who provided another set of detailed and perceptive comments. Also to all those who have helped by suggesting ideas, supplying materials, responding to questions, or helping with the artwork, including: Clare Allman; Abigail Ball; Michael Best; Chris Blackburn; Brian Brown; Ade Brownlow; Peter Clark; Emma Coles; John Colford; Andy Crane; Glauco DeVita; Stephen Duhan; Sandy Gordon; Jonathan Groucutt; Julie Howell; Jodi Ippolito; Bengt Johannisson; Yan Liu; T.C. Melewar; Phil Morgan; Tom Morton; Edward Mushinga; Abi Murray; Fiona Narburgh; Margaret Price; John Prior; Berry O'Donovan; Sonia Rees; Paul Rivers; Liz and Robert Robertson; Michael Rowlinson; Teresa Smallbone; David Smith; Richard Smith; Diane Smith Heather Summerfield; Alice Szwelnik; Richard Tallontire; Michael Thatcher; Heather Watters; Richard Weaver; Fiona Wheeler; Clive Wildish. Lastly, we would like to thank those involved in the production process, including our former editor Matthew Walker, current editor, Gabrielle James, and other colleagues at Pearson who have continued to support the project and provide helpful guidance.

Publisher's acknowledgements

We are grateful to the following for permission to reproduce copyright material:

Figures

Figure 1.1 and 1.2 from the *Mathematical Theory of Communication*. Copyright 1949, 1998 by the Board of Trustees of the University of Illinois. Used with permission of the author and the University of Illinois Press. Figure 4.4 from The Fairtrade foundation, **http://www.fairtrade.org.uk www .fairtrade.org.uk**, reproduced with permission;

Figure 4.12 from **www.hm-treasury.gov.uk/** Contains public sector information licensed under the Open Government Licence (OGL) v1.0.**http://www.nationalarchives.gov.uk/doc/**open-government-licence/open-government; Figure 4.13 from **www.bt.com**, accessed 1 April 2012, reproduced with kind permission of British Telecommunications plc; Figure 5.2 from The Advertising Archive Ltd 30540617 2002 UK Department of Transport Poster; Figure 5.4 from **www.oxfam.org.uk**, reproduced with the permission of Oxfam GB, Oxfam House, John Smith Drive, Cowley, Oxford OX4 2JY, UK **www.oxfam.org.uk.** Oxfam GB does not necessarily endorse any text or activities that accompany the materials; Figure 7.4 from http://photo.greenpeace.org/C.aspx?VP3=ViewBox_VPage&ALID=27 MZIF22TMQI&CT=Album Photo Ref. No. GPO3EJT, © Tim Dirver/Greenpeace; Figure 7.5 from 'Are you talking to me?: Stakeholder communication and the rewards of dialogue', *Unfolding stakeholder thinking 2: relationships, communication and performance* p. 42 (Crane, A. and Livesey, S. (Andriof, J., Waddock, S., Husted, B. and Rahman, S. (eds)) 2003), Greenleaf, Sheffield.; Figure 7.7 from 'Network evolution and the growth of artisanal firms: a tale of two regional cheesemakers – 1950–2000', *Entrepreneurship* and *Regional Development*, Vol. 14, No. 1, 1-30 (Blundel, R.K. 2002)

Figure 5.2 from The Advertising Archive Ltd 30540617 2002 UK Department of Transport Poster

Figure 7.4 from http://photo.greenpeace.org/C.aspx?VP3=ViewBox_VPage&ALID=27MZIF22TMQI &CT=Album Photo Ref. No. GPO3EJT, © Tim Dirver/Greenpeace

Text

Case Study 1.4 from 'For corporate IT chiefs, human interactions trumps technology', *Financial Times*, 08/07/2011 (Taylor, P.), © The Financial Times Limited. All Rights Reserved; Case Study 2.2 adapted from 'Groupthink, Iraq, and the War on Terror: Explaining US Policy Shift toward Iraq', *Foreign Policy Analysis*, 6, pp. 277–296 (Badie, D. 2010), © 2010, Wiley. Reproduced with permission of Wiley; Case Study 3.2 after *Research methods for business students*, 3 ed., FT Prentice Hall, Harlow (Saunders, M.N.K., Lewis, P. and Thornhill, A. 2003) pp. 300-1; Case Study 8.2 from 'OMG! I'm doing it all wrong,' *Financial Times*, 07/02/2012 (Maija Palmer), © The *Financial Times* Limited. All Rights Reserved; Case Study 8.3 from 'We rgrt 2 infm u yr fired. Hv nice day', *Financial Times*, 31/05/2003 (Harris, C. and Orr, R.), © The Financial Times Limited. All Rights Reserved; Case Study 9.4 from 'Getting the message across: shareholder communications', *Financial Times*, 04/12/2002, p. 14 (Payton, S.), © The Financial Times Limited. All Rights Reserved; Case Study 10.1 adapted from Marketing and advertising that respects children's rights, *The Guardian*, 12/03/2012 (Shrubsole, G.), Copyright Guardian News & Media Ltd 2012; Case Study 10.3 from 'Advertisers rush to master a fresh set of skills', *Financial Times*, 07/03/2012 (Gelles, D.), © The Financial Times Limited. All Rights Reserved; Case Study 11.1 after *Research methods for business students* 3 ed, FT Prentice Hall, Harlow (Saunders, M.N.K., Lewis, P. and Thornhill, A. 2003) p. 249; Case Study 12.2 from 'Anti-PowerPoint revolutionaries unite', *Financial Times*, 17/07/2011 (Kellaway, L.), © The Financial Times Limited. All Rights Reserved; Case Study 14.3 from 'Understanding the culture of collaboration: the art of joining different cultures', *Financial Times*, 29/06/2007 (Thomas, K.), © The Financial Times Limited. All Rights Reserved; Case Study 15.5 from 'Screen time: how video conferencing is gaining ground', *Financial Times*, 11/09/2011 (Palmer, M.), © The Financial Times Limited. All Rights Reserved.

Photographs

(Key: b-bottom; c-centre; l-left; r-right; t-top)

Age Fotostock Spain S.L.: 316b; **Alamy Images:** 85; **Bread & Butter GmbH & Co. KG:** 270; **FT.com:** 251; **www.CartoonStock.com:** 316

All other images © Pearson Education

In some instances we have been unable to trace the owners of copyright material, and we would appreciate any information that would enable us to do so.

Chapter 1

Perspectives on communication

The human mind is like an umbrella, it works best when open.

Walter Gropius, *Bauhaus* architect and designer

Learning outcomes

By the end of this chapter you should be able to:

- appreciate the nature and importance of effective communication within and beyond organisations;
- identify different elements in a simple model of the communication process and give a working definition of the related terminology;
- distinguish the principal dimensions of organisational communication, as used by researchers and practitioners;
- contrast several theoretical perspectives that may provide insights into different aspects of organisational communication;
- explore connections between theory, research evidence and 'real world' communication practices;
- assess your communication practices in the light of communication theory.

1.1   Introducing communication

This book looks at the ways that people communicate in organisations. Its main aim is to help you become a more effective communicator. As the chapter quotation suggests, one of the underlying themes is that effective communication requires an open mind (i.e. a willingness to take on new and unfamiliar ideas). The reason for this is simple. Unless you are open to the needs of your audience, and to the context in which the communication is taking place, your best efforts to communicate are very likely to fail. In today's organisations, you will encounter people from many backgrounds, whose life experiences are entirely different from your own. The context in which you communicate is also likely to be fairly complex and unfamiliar. For example, your employees, customers or suppliers may be located in several different countries, or you may be required to work in a 'virtual team', relying on web-based systems to keep in touch with your colleagues. But having an open mind is not enough. You also need an understanding of the broad principles of communication, a flexible set of practical tools, and some experience in applying them in different situations. The book is designed to help you develop your abilities in each of these areas.

This introductory chapter sketches a simple model of the communication process that will be critiqued, elaborated and applied throughout the text. It also provides working definitions of some of the more common terminology used in this subject area, including concepts such as, 'encoding', 'channels' and 'noise'. However, before we move into the theory of communication, it is worth considering two fundamental questions:

- Why is effective communication such a critical issue for organisations?
- Why is it so difficult to communicate effectively?

1.2   Communicating in organisations: issues and challenges

Human beings are social animals. In a complex technological society, our quality of life, even basic survival, depends on countless successful interactions with other people, mediated through markets, networks and various kinds of organisation. Without these intricate and largely unseen webs of communication, our economic prosperity, social welfare and cultural life would be undermined. Communication can be difficult; history reveals countless occasions when individuals, communities and nations have pursued simpler solutions to their problems, either avoiding the challenge altogether (i.e. 'flight') or resolving it by force (i.e. 'fight'). Communication can often seem a more demanding and time-consuming option than either 'fight' or 'flight'. This is because, in order for it to be effective, communication requires each party to make some effort to understand the other. However, though it may appear the more difficult option, effective communication does have its rewards. For example, it can help an organisation to achieve:

- satisfied repeat customers, rather than unhappy ex-customers;
- well-motivated employees, rather than expensive industrial disputes;
- a positive reputation in the wider community, rather than an international boycott of products;
- innovative and creative strategies, rather than inefficiency, indecision and resistance to change.

Organisations are complex phenomena. As a consequence, effective communicators need to be adept in handling challenges that simply do not arise in ordinary, day-to-day communication (e.g. in your immediate circle of friends). The kinds of challenges we need to consider include:

- formal organisation structures, reporting arrangements and procedures;
- cultural diversity, across countries, organisations, departments, employees and other organisational stakeholders;
- intense political, financial and time pressures, competing managerial priorities and demands.

Issues of this kind mean that communicating in organisations is often an uphill struggle. Moreover, the most common challenges are surprisingly similar, whether the organisation is operating in the private, public or voluntary sector. Hence, this book is concerned with communication in human organisations of all kinds. Practical issues are explored through a number of case studies of varying lengths, set in charitable organisations, government departments, small firms and international companies; there is also a 'face-to-face' case study in each chapter, which is related particularly to student experiences. Case study 1.1 looks at a frequent source of problems, when the communication process fails to keep up with the rapid growth of a new firm.

CASE STUDY 1.1

Communication breakdown – Victims of their own success?

Communication within an entrepreneurial start-up venture tends to be centralised, informal and face-to-face. The founding owner-managers have direct control over most aspects of the business and are able to keep in direct contact with a small team of employees. Everyone needs to be flexible and there is no need for detailed written procedures; if someone has a problem, they can simply call in and speak to the boss. However, over time, the firm grows in size and complexity. There is an increase in the volume of sales and in the number and variety of customers; more staff are recruited and people begin to specialise in particular tasks. At a certain point, the 'old' approach to communication can become severely stretched.

'Shooting Star' is a biotechnology venture, founded three years ago by two university scientists and a former school friend who worked for an investment company. Following a second round of venture capital financing, the firm has recently moved to a large science park, on the edge of the city. It now employs 15 people. Six of these are research scientists; the others comprise four laboratory technicians, a finance manager, an office manager, two administrative assistants and a marketing manager. Business is booming, but there are also serious communication problems: the administrators and the scientists are in a constant state of war – every other day the representative of one or other group makes complaints about unreasonable behaviour by the others. The team size has outgrown the meeting space, meaning that not everyone can fit around the meeting room table, and often there aren't even enough chairs for attendees! As a result, full departmental meetings have been abandoned in favour of smaller project-focused meetings. There is no formal opportunity for individualised feedback to be given, partly because all employees work in two open-plan offices and there is no private space for managers and employees to discuss such confidential matters. E-mail is the favoured communication channel, even by colleagues in the same office. The Finance manager, in particular, sends long, detailed e-mails explaining updates to important financial procedures, such as customer invoicing. Much to his annoyance these procedures are routinely overlooked and e-mails are unread or deleted by colleagues less passionate about finance! Two of the lab technicians have announced, via Twitter, that they are leaving for 'better jobs'; and yesterday there was a national newspaper report suggesting that the firm's first development project, a new medical treatment for babies, was experiencing problems during its pre-clinical trials.

Shooting Star's three original founders are spending almost all of their time travelling between meetings with investors, medical specialists and pharmaceutical companies. This evening they have at last managed to meet together for a meal. Looking round the table, one of the founders is shocked to see the exhausted faces of her colleagues. She comments, 'You know, I really thought things would get easier once we had got the business going, but things just seem to be getting more complicated. What on earth are we doing wrong?'

Case study 1.1 (*continued*)

Questions

1 Compile a list of the communication problems that are being experienced at 'Shooting Star'.

2 What do you think is the cause of each of these problems?

3 What changes might the founders make in order to deal with them?

Source: Shooting Star is a fictional organisation. Case prepared by the authors.

1.3 Stage one: a simple model of the communication process

Since earliest times, men and women have been speculating on the basic mysteries of human existence: our origins, the purpose of our lives and how we can gain a better understanding of ourselves and other people. Over the years, philosophers, theologians and artists have done their best to answer these questions, but it is only in the last few centuries that the process of communication in humans has been studied in a systematic way. Academic disciplines, including psychology, education, linguistics, sociology and anthropology, have contributed important insights, as has multi-disciplinary research in fields such as organisation studies, information systems, strategic management, human resource management and marketing. This wide-ranging research literature has also created a major challenge for students, teachers and textbook authors. First, because it is spread very widely, much of the published research on communication is quite difficult to locate. Second, many sub-specialisms have been created, each concerned with particular types of communication, to the exclusion of others. Third, there are several competing perspectives on communication, with their own research agendas and methodologies. In practice, this rich mixture of ideas is valuable because it reflects the real complexity of organisational communication in the twenty-first century. As we progress through the book, we will draw on many of these ideas in order to develop our understanding. However, we begin our journey with a very simple model of the communication process, and use it to introduce some key concepts that will be used throughout the text (see Figure 1.1).

This model was developed in the 1940s as part of a now largely-forgotten research project in the United States, which investigated the ways that technical information was communicated through telecommunications systems (Mattelart and Mattelart 1998, Shannon and Weaver 1955). The original authors did not intend their model to apply to human communication, and it has many limitations when it is used in this way (Maier et al. 2005). However, it remains relevant today as the source of several important communication concepts, because it has been so widely adopted by communication teachers and practitioners around the world. In its simplest version, the model describes a linear (i.e. 'one-way') process that comprises two individuals – a 'sender' and a 'receiver' – connected via a conventional telephone landline.

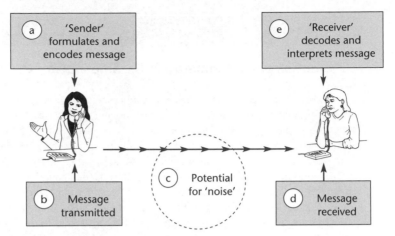

Figure 1.1 A simple linear model of the communication process
Source: Adapted from Shannon and Weaver (1955)

The **sender** is a person who constructs a message and attempts to convey it to somebody else. The communication process starts when the message is formulated in the sender's brain. Before the contents of the message can be transmitted, the sender will need to encode the contents. **Encoding** the message means that the sender converts it into a suitable format for transmission; in the case of a telephone message, this normally means that the person uses a series of spoken words. The choice of words is based on that person's chosen language and is influenced by many factors, including cultural background, level of education and emotional state. (Note: In practice, there are two encoding processes going on here, the first when the person speaks, the second taking place when the microphone converts the words into electrical impulses or binary code.) The encoded message is then transmitted through the microphone and along the telephone line. When the encoded message reaches the other end of the line, it has to go through a further conversion process. **Decoding** the message means that the transmitted signal is converted back into words and the meaning of the words is re-interpreted by the brain of the person at the receiving end. Again, this process is influenced by many factors, including the receiver's language skills, cultural background, level of education and emotional state. Once the conversion process is complete, the message is described as having been received. This sequence is repeated, with the positions of 'sender' and 'receiver' reversed, creating the basic outline of a telephone conversation.

In the pre-digital age, telephone conversations were sometimes affected by a random electrical crackle on the line, which the early researchers referred to as 'noise'. Today we have similar problems with mobile phones, where conversations can be cut short due to a weak or lost signal (e.g. when travelling in a train). In modern communication theory, the term **noise** is now interpreted much more widely and is used to refer to various kinds of barrier to effective communication that either distort or interrupt an encoded message so that it fails to reach the receiver in its original form. For example, taking this broader view of the communication process, even the temperature in a seminar room can become a source of 'noise' (see Case study 1.2).

CASE STUDY 1.2

'PromoCo': when temperature became 'noise'

'PromoCo', a Madrid-based sales promotions company, is giving a presentation that is meant to impress some of its most important clients. It is early afternoon in mid-July, and the guests have just enjoyed an excellent four-course lunch, provided by the company. They are directed into a well-furnished seminar room; the lights are dimmed and a digital projector is switched on. The presentation is delivered by a dynamic manager, who speaks clearly and has a well-produced set of slides. However, the air conditioning is not working properly and after a few minutes the room becomes very warm and airless. Members of the audience begin to feel uncomfortable. People shuffle in their seats and whisper to their neighbours. Some remove their jackets, look for windows to open and pass around bottles of sparkling water. One guest, who appears to have enjoyed the complimentary wine at lunchtime, is resting his head on the table and has closed his eyes. The temperature of the room has now become a source of 'noise', distracting the audience from the messages that the presenter and the company wish to convey.

Questions

1 Using the case as a starting point, identify six examples of 'noise' as experienced in a typical work or study environment. In each case, note how this kind of noise might distort or interrupt the transmission of a message between sender and receiver.

2 Discuss how you would reduce or remove the source of the noise in each of these examples.

3 From your discussion, does it appear that some forms of noise are more common, or more difficult to deal with, than others?

Source: PromoCo is a fictional organisation. Case prepared by the authors.

The simple model depicted in Figure 1.1 introduces two additional terms that we will be referring to throughout the text, the 'message' and the 'communication channel'. The **message** is what the sender has communicated to the receiver. One of the fundamental points to remember in communication is that there is always a degree of difference between the message that the sender intends to convey and the message that the other person actually receives. In other words, messages are always subject to a certain amount of noise. Achieving effective communication is in large part about trying to minimise noise. This is difficult enough in everyday communication (e.g. during a conversation involving two friends or neighbours); however, the challenges become even more complex in organisational communication, where there is a much more extensive and seemingly endless stream of criss-crossing messages involving larger numbers of people operating in diverse situations.

We need to begin to unpack some of the concepts introduced in this chapter. For example, the messages that we send contain a variety of different elements. These include straightforward things like raw data and factual information, but also less tangible things like our ideas, opinions, beliefs and emotions. These elements are sometimes difficult to distinguish, a point that is well illustrated by the examples in Table 1.1.

Table 1.1 The variety of different elements contained in our messages

Raw data	May include the results of scientific measurement, such as a series of temperature readings that has not been analysed or put into any meaningful context. Messages containing raw data can be readily transmitted by the sender, but cannot be effectively decoded or interpreted by the receiver, without establishing their context. For example, in the case of the temperature readings, this would include the temperature scale and the dates, times and locations of each reading.
Facts	Comprise data that are presented as objective information. They are meaningful and can claim to have some basis in truth or reality. For example, a recent report drew on published scientific research in order to state that the level of carbon dioxide in the atmosphere has risen by a third since the industrial revolution. Furthermore, the total temperature increase from 1850–1899 to 2001–2005 is 0.76°C (IPCC 2007).
Ideas	An abstract type of information, presented in the form of concepts, constructs, theories and models, which may have varying degrees of empirical support. For example, the 'enhanced greenhouse effect' is a widely-endorsed scientific theory that connects the burning of fossil fuels (e.g. coal, gas and oil), to an intensification of a natural greenhouse effect of carbon dioxide in the atmosphere, which in turn is leading to global warming (e.g. Fawcett et al. 2002: 11–13).
Opinions	Opinions, which may relate to facts or ideas, can be distinguished by their **subjectivity** (i.e. their authority derives from the individual or organisation expressing the opinion, rather than being founded on something that is already proven and more generally acknowledged). For example, in October 2011 the British prime minister of the time expressed his opinion that "Legislating now for a referendum, including on whether Britain should leave the European Union, could cause great uncertainty and could actually damage our prospects of growth." (BBC 2011)
Beliefs	Beliefs comprise a strongly-held set of opinions, which is usually linked to an individual's sense of identity, and influences daily behaviour. For example, in relation to climate change, some people have made radical lifestyle changes, based on their environmental concerns (e.g. switching from car to cycle journeys, avoiding air travel, offsetting carbon emissions by contributing financially to tree-planting initiatives), while others defend the right to drive fuel-hungry vehicles on the basis of a belief in personal freedom.
Emotion	Emotional energy can be contained in a message, expressing human feelings (e.g. love, anger, joy, bitterness, humour, passion, sentimentality, weariness, hopefulness), in conjunction with other elements, such as facts, or ideas. If this 'affective' element in the message is conveyed to the receiver, it may stimulate similar feelings, often adding to the overall impact. For example, a short television advertisement by the French environmental agency encouraged public support for action against global warming by challenging viewers with the question, 'Do you really want to kill polar bears?' This was followed by a statement to the effect that, by 2060, all of the world's polar bears are going to starve, because the Arctic ice pack will have melted, disrupting their food supplies. The powerful image of polar bears on melting ice sheets has since been used in several similar promotional campaigns.

In practice, organisations often exchange messages containing a rich mixture of facts, ideas, opinions and beliefs, often coloured by varying degrees of emotion. In later chapters, we consider how these elements can best be combined in order to deliver the kind of communication we are seeking to achieve.

The **communication channel** is the route or the technology that is used to convey the message to a receiver. Shannon and Weaver's (1955) original model was based on research into a particular communication channel. Contemporary organisations make use of a number of different communication channels, including: face-to-face meetings and conversations, letters, telephones, e-mails, blogs, reports, posters, brochures and video-conferences. Recent technological changes have led to the decline of some channels (e.g. facsimile or 'fax' messaging), and the emergence of others (e.g. SMS or 'text' messaging) in organisational settings. Each of the chapters in Part II deals with specific communication channels. Messages are encoded in different ways, depending on the channel that is used. The form of encoding (e.g. as text, images or sound), is sometimes referred to as the 'medium' of communication. However, it is important to bear in mind that this term is also used to refer to communication channels and the way that we interpret information sent via these channels. For example, when advertising executives talk about different 'media', they are generally referring to television, radio, newspapers, poster sites, and so on.

The basic linear approach has introduced some useful terminology, but we need to recognise that it remains a very crude and simplified model of reality, even in the restricted field of the telephone conversation. In the next section, we take a first step in developing a more 'realistic' understanding of the communication process in organisations, by introducing the concepts of feedback, expectations and subjectivity.

1.4 Feedback, expectations and subjectivity

One of the initial modifications of the simple 'one-way' communication model was to add a feedback loop (see Figure 1.2). The term 'feedback' originated in cybernetics, the study of control systems (Boulding 1956, Buckley 1967, Wiener 1948), and introduced an influential 'systems theory' perspective into organisational studies. One very simple feedback mechanism is the thermostat. It regulates the temperature of a building by switching the central heating system on and off when it reaches a pre-set level. In human communication theory, **feedback** refers to the receiver's response to a message; it is a further message sent by the receiver, which gives the sender an indication of the way the original message has been received. It is important to note how human feedback differs from the smooth, automatic reaction of a thermostat. Humans are much more irregular and unpredictable. Individuals can respond to

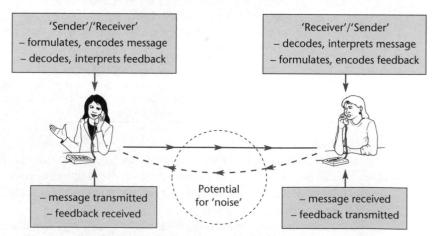

Figure 1.2 The linear model of communication with feedback

an identical message in a variety of ways, the reaction depending on the way they perceive it. There is a simple thought experiment that demonstrates this point. Imagine yourself walking down a street. Start smiling randomly at the strangers that you pass. How do they react? In all probability, a few people may smile back at you, several will appear rather hostile or suspicious, others will try to ignore you, while quite a few appear completely unaware of either you or your smile. (Note: In my own version of this thought experiment, the last group were mostly engaged in mobile phone conversations or texting.) In the revised model (Figure 1.2), the dotted line indicates that there is no automatic feedback 'loop' in human communication.

The key lesson from systems theory is that each sub-division of the organisation is affected by activity in other parts. Furthermore, the organisation itself is an 'open system', exposed to a wider environment in which it both experiences competitive threats and finds its collaborative partners (Child 2001, Luhmann 1995). In short, organisations do not operate like thermostats. Rather, their actions are the result of countless human decisions, each of which is based on *subjective* perceptions of the world in which they are operating and their pre-existing values and experiences:

> 'The behaviour of the organization […] must be interpreted as a result of the image of the executive, directed by his value system. […] He is a receiver of messages from the receptor of the organization, and his job is to transform those messages into instructions or orders which go out to the effectors. He cannot be regarded, however, as simply a sausage machine grinding out instructions from the messages received. It is more realistic to suppose that between the incoming and outgoing messages lies the great intervening variable of the image. The outgoing messages are the result of the image, not the result of the incoming messages.'
>
> (Boulding 1956: 27–8)

The subjective and unpredictable responses of human beings can certainly make life more interesting. For example, they have provided the basis for many cartoons and comedy sketches. However, because confused feedback gets in the way of mutual understanding, it can have disastrous effects in organisations. For example, it can contribute to industrial accidents, badly-designed products and services, mistreatment of internal and external stakeholders, lack of innovation and poor financial performance. One of our main concerns will be to find ways of overcoming the communication failures that feed these negative outcomes.

1.5 Organisational communication: key dimensions

Organisational communication is a wide-ranging field of study that spreads across academic disciplines (e.g. psychology, anthropology, organisation studies) and professional specialisms (e.g. marketing, public relations, human resources management), and makes use of many contrasting theoretical and methodological approaches. This section introduces something of the variety that is to be found in the communication literature. We begin by examining four of the more common distinctions: verbal and non-verbal, one-way and two-way, inter-personal and mass, internal and external.

Verbal and non-verbal communication

Verbal communication refers to messages coded in the form of words. This may be further sub-divided into spoken (or 'oral') and written forms. Written communication depends on established systems of grammar and punctuation, while spoken communication uses equivalents such as pauses and stress on particular words. Verbal forms of communication raise issues such as using appropriate vocabulary for an audience and translating meanings between different languages. There are also many forms of **non-verbal communication**. These include 'kinesics' (i.e. human posture, gesture, body language); 'proxemics' (the physical distance between people as they interact); the use of other visual media (e.g. pictures and signs); and other non-verbal sensory stimuli, such as sounds and smells; all of which can be used to convey a message. In practice, each of these forms can be used simultaneously. For example, text and images are combined in a business report, while presenters make use of words and gestures.

We also need to be aware of the power of meta messages (a term coined by lawyer Gerard Nierenberg, the author of *The Art of Negotiating* (Nierenberg 1995). Meta messages are those messages that are conveyed between the lines of what we explicitly say or write, possibly due to the purpose, context, or timing of the message and/or the relationship between the people communicating. For example, if a colleague asked you for assistance and you responded that you were working to meet a tight deadline that day, the meta message would be that you couldn't spare the time and, possibly, that your task was more important than theirs even though you did not explicitly refuse.

One-way and two-way communication

The distinction between **one-way** and **two-way communication** refers to more than the direction in which messages are travelling. Some communication channels are inherently 'two-way', such as face-to-face interviews and meetings, with instantaneous feedback. Other communication channels may appear to operate in one direction only, including posters and podcasts; but all forms of communication are normally open to some kind of feedback, using techniques such as communication audits or market research. Sometimes one-way communication is used inappropriately but for efficiency, such as in a lecture. The newer digital communications channels tend to be more 'interactive' than their analogue predecessors. For example, television viewers can now interact with digital broadcasts using their remote control keypads. Similarly, internet technologies, such as 'cookies', can provide organisations with feedback on the way their websites are being accessed. What technology does your university use to encourage two-way communication?

Inter-personal and mass communication

Inter-personal communication involves individuals interacting directly in relatively small groups, primarily through face-to-face channels such as meetings. This would have been the main type of communication experienced by people living in the pre-industrial era. In modern times, we are also exposed to **mass communication**, which refers to techniques for sending similar or identical encoded messages to large numbers of people, generally through the use of some form of technology. The origins of mass communication can be traced to the invention of printing technologies. Printed books, newspapers and advertising were the pioneering forms of mass communication developed in the eighteenth and nineteenth centuries. They were followed in the twentieth century by radio, television and the Internet. Today, organisations continue to engage in both inter-personal and mass communication, though the latter has tended to be under the control of professional specialists (e.g. broadcasters and web designers).

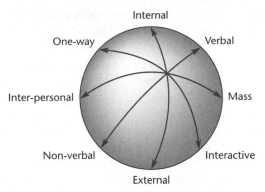

Figure 1.3 The multiple dimensions of organisational communication

Internal and external communication

There is a long tradition of distinguishing **internal communication**, which takes place *within* the boundaries of an organisation, from **external communication**, which involves the organisation and audiences in the wider world. This distinction is reflected in the different functional areas. For example, human resource managers have tended to focus on employee communication, while public relations, purchasing and marketing managers have dealt with external stakeholders. There has been a similar divide in academic circles, between researchers addressing internal communication processes, and others who are more concerned with corporate communication and media relations. Recently, however, there have been efforts to re-integrate internal and external communication issues, an approach that is also reflected in this text (Cheney and Christensen 2001, Zorn 2002). Researchers point to the increasingly 'blurred' boundaries of today's organisations, and argue that there is an underlying continuity between what have previously been termed 'internal' and 'external' communication processes (see section 7.3).

While these four dimensions of communication do not exhaust the ways that the field might be divided, they at least indicate some of the main areas that we need to address. Each dimension should be seen as overlapping and interconnected. So, rather than slotting them into one of the neat '2 x 2' matrices, often found in business textbooks, we have used the more holistic image of a globe (see Figure 1.3).

1.6 Different perspectives on communication

Our final task in this chapter is to conduct a brief review of some competing views of organisational communication. The aim is to give you a flavour of various perspectives that have informed academic debate in organisation theory and management studies over recent years, and which have also had an impact on everyday communication practices. Writing on the subject of communication ranges from highly instrumental, 'how to' (or '10 top tips') approaches found in many popular management texts, to some extremely abstract academic arguments regarding the nature of human discourse. So why do we need to consider more than one perspective on communication? Communication textbooks tend to emphasise practical techniques, helping students to make better use of particular communication channels (e.g. letters or meetings). In this book, we are aiming to combine the development of relevant skills with an opportunity to reflect on the wider challenges of organisational communication. To achieve this balance, we need to question conventional communication practices, including the assumptions on which they are based. By becoming more aware of the different perspectives used to study communication, we are also better positioned to question the tendency of writers to offer 'pre-packaged' solutions that take insufficient account of local circumstances. However, if the next section seems too demanding, you can always return to it later. In any event, we suggest that you re-read the next section when you have completed Chapters 7 and 14.

The following overview contrasts four broad academic perspectives on organisational communication: 'modern'; 'interpretive'; 'critical' and 'postmodern'. (Note: the terminology is adapted from Deetz 2001.) However, it is important to note the limitations of any exercise of this kind. Above all, there is little agreement amongst academics over the precise meaning of concepts such as 'modernism' and 'postmodernism' (Hassard 1999: 193). This means that the categories, descriptions and boundaries used in this summary remain incomplete and open to revision. Despite this, we think that they provide some useful reference points, illustrating some of the different ways we can approach the challenge of communicating in human organisations. You are likely to encounter a similar range of perspectives elsewhere in organisation theory, management studies and other areas of social science (e.g. Hatch 1997, Clark 2000, Westwood and Clegg 2001).

'Modern' perspectives

Modernism is associated with the rise of scientific enquiry in the Renaissance and Enlightenment eras; it remains a dominant way of thinking about the world, but faces challenges from other perspectives, including postmodernism (see below). Modernism's science-based framework emphasises objective measurement, decision-making based on rational calculations (i.e. 'utilitarianism') and progress towards an improved and more general understanding of real-world phenomena. Research in this perspective tends to treat organisational communication practices as being readily accessible to researchers, revealing some predictable features that make them open to a degree of managerial intervention and control. Research programmes have often followed the natural science model, seeking law-like generalisations through theory building and empirical testing, frequently making use of quantitative survey data as the basis for detailed statistical analysis of organisations (e.g. Thompson 1967, Pugh and Hickson 1976). Systems theory is another important strand in modernist research. This has tended to treat organisations as rather more complex phenomena that cannot be fully understood using the tools of natural science. For example, greater attention has been paid to the subjective perceptions of people in organisations, leading to more sophisticated explanations of processes such as organisational learning (e.g. Senge 1990, Weick 1979).

'Interpretive' perspectives

Interpretive research in contemporary organisations owes much to the ethnographic tradition in anthropology. In this subject area, it tends to be less concerned with general theory, but aims to reveal the complexity and richness of organisational communication. Ethnographic studies often involve researchers spending long periods 'in the field', using qualitative research methods such as participant observation to record conversations, stories, rituals and other routine events in offices, factories and other organisational settings (Van Maanen 1988). The results are often presented in the form of detailed narratives, accompanied by varying amounts of analysis (Pentland 1999). In contrast to natural science, where researchers can make direct interpretations of objects and processes (e.g. chemical compounds or weather systems), social science researchers are often required to interpret *other people's* interpretations of the world. This fundamental distinction, sometimes referred to as 'the double hermeneutic' (i.e. double interpretation) is an important feature of interpretivist studies. In general, they attempt to conduct research in ways that do not impose the researcher's interpretations of a situation onto the people they are observing.

'Critical' perspectives

The common feature of critical perspectives is their broader political agenda, which involves a radical critique of the way power is exercised under industrial capitalism (Alvesson and Willmott 1996). Hence, the subject area of organisational communication has been concerned mainly with ways in which communication channels are used to exercise power over employees and other stakeholders. Researchers have used a range of methods, including those associated with modern and interpretive perspectives, but their work can be distinguished by its more sceptical approach to established institutions. One of the central themes in critical management research has been the failure of ordinary workers and other stakeholders to defend their interests (e.g. not speaking up about health and safety problems, unethical behaviour or poor working conditions). Critical management researchers are concerned with the use and abuse of power in organisations. They have adapted earlier concepts such as 'false consciousness' (Gramsci 1971) to explain how particular 'discourses' (i.e. sets of arguments and ways of understanding issues) can become dominant, effectively blocking out minority views (Habermas 1984). For example, 'business process re-engineering' (BPR), an influential managerial fashion in the 1990s, was associated with some dramatic changes such as 'delayering' (i.e. in practice, removing whole tiers of management), and giving more responsibility to junior staff. Critical management research on BPR has highlighted the important role that language (e.g. the use of euphemistic terms such as 'empowerment') can play in overcoming employees' resistance to such changes (Knights and Willmott 2000).

'Postmodern' perspectives

Postmodernism is often presented as a challenge to the assumptions of modernism, including the way research is approached. For example, postmodernist theorists have questioned whether it is possible for researchers to take a detached view of their research subjects, and whether there is a possibility of establishing general laws relating to real-world phenomena, such as organisations. The arguments supporting this perspective are complex, but at the core of postmodernism is the view that there is no neutral access to the world, as modernist researchers assume. Instead, our knowledge is always shaped by language, which is itself a product of society and open to a variety of meanings, depending on the context in which it is used. Consequently, postmodern research has focused on localised practices (e.g. Keenoy et al. 1997, Czarinawska 1998). In the field of organisational communication, postmodernists have argued that contemporary trends, such as globalisation and the rise of the Internet, have left people with multiple and 'fragmented identities', in the face of many competing discourses. This means that it is not possible to make any objective, generalised or unified statements about organisational communication. Instead, research tends to be directed at the deconstruction of particular communication practices. See for example, Livesey's (2002) study, which applies a technique called discourse analysis techniques to study the way that an oil company reported on environmental issues (see section 3.7).

Each of these perspectives has its supporters and critics. For example, the research aims of modern and interpretive studies are usually presented as apolitical and value-neutral, but critical theorists have argued that both have, to some extent, ignored the political dimension. Postmodernists have criticised interpretivists for representing cultures as unified wholes, rather than reflecting inherent tensions, while modernists have attacked both the interpretive and postmodern perspectives for the absence of coherent theoretical frameworks or sufficiently rigorous research methods. One of the more significant developments in recent years has been the introduction of feminist perspectives on organisational communication. Feminist studies have addressed several issues that had been excluded from much of the earlier work in this area, including 'the complexities of sex and gender, race and ethnicity, and sexual–social orientation' (Buzzanell 2000) and the persisting impact of micropolitics on the under-representation of women at the senior management level of organisations (Morley 2000). The feminist research agenda can be seen as part of a more general trend towards rethinking the standard approaches to organisational communication (e.g. Wright 2001, Grimes and Richard 2003). Another important feature of this reassessment is the emergence of critics who are pointing to the way that Western cultural assumptions and values have dominated the published work on communication and arguing that greater attention needs to be paid to cultural diversity (Munshi and McKie 2001, De Vita 2001). In other chapters of the book, we consider how diversity is influencing communication practices in a variety of settings.

We have now reviewed four contrasting perspectives on communication, and have developed some provisional ideas about their implications for studying this subject. Case study 1.3 revisits these perspectives, highlighting the different ways in which they can shape our understanding of the term 'effective', when it is applied to organisational communication.

CASE STUDY 1.3

What do we mean by 'effective'? Comparing perspectives

The title of this textbook includes the word 'effective'; similar titles can be found in other subject areas (e.g. 'effective financial management'). But what do we really mean by the word 'effective', firstly in general terms and then when it is applied to organisational communication? The *Concise Oxford English Dictionary* offers the following definition:

effective /ɪˈfɛktɪv
▶*adjective*

1 successful in producing a desired or intended result: *effective solutions to environmental problems*. ■(of a law, rule, or policy) operative: *the regulation will be **effective from** January*. **2** [attrib.] existing in fact, though not formally acknowledged as such: *she has been under effective house arrest since September*. ■ assessed according to actual rather than face value: *an effective price of £176 million*.

▶*noun* a soldier fit and available for service.

- ORIGIN **late Middle English**: from Latin effectivus, from efficere 'accomplish' (see EFFECT).

Case study 1.3 (*continued*)

So, which of these explanations applies to the title of this book? It seems that the first and second definitions are closest to the apparent purpose of the text, which claims that it is 'designed to help you develop your abilities' in various aspects of the communication process. In the first definition, 'effective' communication suggests that you (and other readers) can achieve your intended aims through skilful application of the relevant knowledge and techniques. The second definition goes a little further, so that being effective also means achieving a 'powerful' or 'impressive' result. Both suggest a very 'instrumental' purpose. In other words, that the book is concerned only with helping its readers to achieve what they want to achieve personally, using communication as a tool. So how might the four perspectives on communication broaden our basic understanding of 'effectiveness'?

Modern

In this perspective, we are searching for general rules or principles governing the communication process. By applying these rules in practical situations, we can become more 'effective' in achieving our aims. The underlying assumption is that the process is fairly objective. Communication problems can be defined by the 'sender', who then selects and applies an appropriate solution. For example, Chapter 2 discusses some inherent physiological barriers to communication, such as selective attention and memory loss. Having become aware of this information, the 'sender' is able to design and implement communication channels in ways that seek to overcome the barriers and deliver the message.

Interpretive

In this perspective, we recognise that communication is as much about the meanings constructed by 'receivers' as it is about our performance as a 'sender'. It has been particularly influential in the field of cross-cultural communication, where efforts have been directed at better understanding local customs. In other words, our attention becomes focused on the context in which the interaction is taking place. For example, Chapter 6 considers how organisations secure relevant feedback by becoming more sensitive to the diverse characteristics of their various stakeholders. This perspective can be very revealing, giving us a much better understanding of our own communication practices, including their inherent values and norms. However, it can still be consistent with a rather narrow interpretation of 'effectiveness', based ultimately around our own communication aims.

Critical

In this perspective, we start to raise more radical (i.e. deeper) questions about the communication process. For example, what does effectiveness mean for other actors? What is the impact of choices regarding message content, or between communication channels, on the relative power of different groups within or beyond the organisation? Critical theories challenge (or 'contest') the apparent objectivity of everyday communication practices. For example, in Chapter 7 we consider the changing relationship between organisations and their multiple stakeholders. In this perspective, 'effectiveness' becomes politicised, so we see our own communication aims as being in competition with those of others.

Postmodern

In this perspective, we draw on a combination of interpretivism and critical theory, in an effort to understand what 'effectiveness' might mean in specific organisational settings. As noted in the text, there are many strands of postmodern thinking. However, common themes include the notion that our own communication practices form part of a web of competing narratives, and that these narratives, or 'discourses', are fragmented, socially constructed and have

---

Case study 1.3 (*continued*)

real consequences in the world. By examining, or 'de-constructing', these narratives, we can understand more about the ways in which power is exercised in organisations. For example, in section 3.6 we see how researchers studied a corporate takeover in Singapore by analysing the texts that were produced in and around each organisation. Our understanding of 'effectiveness' has expanded beyond a narrow concern with our own practices. Communication itself has become the raw material for researching the organisation, its activities and their effects.

Questions

1 Outline the main differences between the four perspectives and their approach to studying a subject. Use the word 'organisation' to illustrate your argument.

2 Why might research in the *critical perspective* be of interest to someone studying communication in commercial businesses or other types of organisation?

3 What are your own views of the term 'effective' organisational communication? Compare them with those of other students and colleagues and try to prepare an agreed definition that could be applied to organisations of all kinds.

Source: Oxford Dictionary of English (3rd edition) (For dictionary definition only). Edited by Angus Stevenson. Oxford University Press, 2010.

Face-to-face 1 offers a more practical, applied perspective and illustrates the kinds of barriers that need to be overcome in our day-to-day practices for effective communication to take place. It is the first day of term at university, and everyone is asking, 'so where am I supposed to be now?'

FACE-TO-FACE 1

'So where am I supposed to be now?'

Cast your mind back to your first week at college, university or work and consider the following, possibly not too unusual, scenario.

Pearl arrives on her first day at university full of excited anticipation. Her first task is to get settled into her new room. She follows the instructions on her letter from the university accommodation office and locates her room in the hall of residence, only to find that it is already occupied by another newly arrived student, Jingsong. They compare accommodation office letters to find that they have identical details. With some difficulty and lots of gesturing Pearl persuades Jingsong, who is understandably exhausted and disorientated having spent the last 22 hours travelling from his home town in China, to accompany Pearl to the accommodation office to resolve the problem. The accommodation officer explains that they have a new online system for room allocation and there must have been an error. He does not apologise but does quickly arrange a new room for Pearl.

The next day is the first day of induction week. The first event on the schedule is an introductory talk. Pearl finds herself in a lecture theatre with 300 other students, straining to listen to a very quiet explanation of how the administration and computing systems work and who to see if they have academic, financial or emotional problems! Should they have problems, already? This talk lasts for an hour and there is no opportunity to ask questions. Pearl seriously hopes that this is not how lectures will be! She is looking forward to talking to other students and meeting her tutor at the 'Meet your tutor group' event, next on the

Face-to-face 1 (*continued*)

schedule. She gets to her department with some difficulty as, due to building work, the new signage has not been put in place, only to find that the 'Meet your tutor group' event has been postponed until tomorrow and that she should go to register. She thought she'd already done this online but joins the queue of several hundred students snaking around the sports hall. Having finally registered (again) she goes back to her room to take advantage of the WiFi connection and contact her friends on Facebook. She tries to log on but finds that she needs a password to access the network. The password has been e-mailed to her university e-mail account but she can't open that because she can't access the network! Defeated she heads to the bar and bumps into Jingsong with a group of new friends, that he did manage to meet through a 'Meet your tutor group' session. They all have tales of confusion to tell, and laugh about the idiosyncrasies of communication in large organisations.

Questions

1 What are the barriers to communication that Pearl faces during her first two days at university?

2 What would you recommend that the organisation does to address each of these barriers and improve the experience of new students?

3 What might Pearl have done differently herself to overcome them?

Summary

- Practising effective communication in different organisational settings requires an open mind, which means a willingness to take on new ideas and explore new perspectives.

- Communication in organisations is particularly challenging due to factors such as formal structures, cultural diversity, political, financial and time pressures, though efforts to improve communication practices can make a real difference to performance.

- The communication process is often described using a simple linear model, which features senders and receivers. Messages are encoded by senders, transmitted and then decoded by receivers; they are also subject to distortion, or 'noise'.

- Message content, including a mixture of raw data, facts, ideas, opinions, beliefs and emotions, can be conveyed through various channels, such as e-mail, interviews and video-conferences.

- Systems theory has been used to develop more elaborate models of the communication process, which include feedback loops, and highlights the importance of subjective perceptions.

- This book takes a holistic view of communication, seeking to integrate conventional dimensions, such as: verbal and non-verbal, one- and two-way, interpersonal and mass, internal and external.

- An emphasis on practical skills development is balanced by deeper reflection on communication practices in today's organisations. This is achieved by drawing on different perspectives – modern, interpretive, critical and postmodern.

Key terms

communication channel 7

decoding 5

encoding 5

external communication 11

feedback 8

inter-personal
  communication 10

internal communication 11

message 6

mass communication 10

noise 5

sender 5

verbal communication 9

PRACTICAL EXERCISES

1.1 'Effective' communicators? Assessing key strengths and weaknesses

Use this exercise to assess your own strengths and weaknesses as you begin this book. Keep the results on file and refer to them regularly during your studies, noting how far your personal 'strengths' develop and 'weaknesses' are being overcome.

(a) At the top of a new page, write down your description: 'An effective communicator is …' Try to sum up the main characteristics in a sentence or two, based on past experience and your reflections on this chapter.

(b) Below this description, divide the page into two columns and use them to list your 'Top Five' communication strengths and weaknesses. What do you do well, and where can you see room for improvement? Use the chapter headings from Part II of this book as a prompt. For example, how effective are you at letter writing, dealing with people on the telephone, giving presentations, being interviewed, 'socialising' informally and so on? Try to be as comprehensive (and honest!) as possible.

(c) Ask a trusted colleague or friend to review your description and comment on your 'Top Five' lists. How does their impression compare with your own?

Seminar option: divide into groups of four or five and discuss the differences between your descriptions of 'an effective communicator'. Draft a concise statement that incorporates each person's ideas. Finally, add together the ranking scores from each person's 'Top Five' list and calculate the averages. Use these to discover the 'Top Five' strengths and weaknesses for the group as a whole. Use a whiteboard or flipchart to present your results to the rest of the seminar.

1.2 Jan and Haluk – mis-reading the feedback?

Messages are vulnerable to noise and incorrect de-coding, even when they are delivered 'face to face'. Consider the following exchange, which involves a marketing manager, Jan (aged 26) and a sales manager, Haluk (aged 43), in the Copenhagen office of a Japanese electronics company:

Jan   (Walks into the office with a smile, waving several pages of computer print-out at Haluk, who sits at a desk covered with computer print-out paper, books and files, staring at a computer screen) 'Well, Haluk, I see that the regional sales report looks a lot better this month!'

Haluk   (Jumps up from the desk and folds arms) 'Is that so? "Looks better", does it? And what exactly do you mean by that?'

Jan   (Shakes head and laughs) 'Whoa! Take it easy Haluk, you do not need to be so aggressive!'

Haluk	(Leans back on the desk) 'I knew it. You're at it again, Jan, aren't you? Ever since that …'
Jan	'Look, Haluk, all I am saying is …' (Gestures with hands)
Haluk	'Alright. Look, just forget it … Jan. Believe me, I have just about had …' (A mobile phone on Haluk's desk starts to ring; Haluk turns away from Jan, picks it up and starts speaking) 'Hi Gary!' (pause) 'No, mate, that's not a problem. So, how was the skiing trip?' (Laughs and looks out of the window) 'Oh yeah? I bet she did!' (Laughs loudly) 'Yeah, yeah…' (Pause) 'So, what can I do for you, my old friend?'
Jan	'Well that's it!' (Storms out of the office)

(a) Draw up a list identifying what you consider to be the most likely causes of the unsuccessful exchange between Jan and Haluk.

(b) Using your list as a starting point, make suggestions as to how Jan might have avoided this outcome.

(c) Repeat the exercise for Haluk.

(d) Review your responses to the previous questions and try to identify any assumptions you have made about the two people in this exchange.

Seminar option: begin the exercise with two students role-playing the dialogue between Jan and Haluk. Repeat the role-plays, making use of the advice that you have generated in your answers to questions (b) and (c).

The final case study in this chapter illustrates many of the current issues raised in this chapter and highlights that sometimes the most obvious form of communication may not necessarily be the most effective.

CASE STUDY 1.4

For corporate IT chiefs, human interactions trumps technology

Every couple of months or so, the IT chiefs of some of the world's largest multinationals get together in the boardroom of a prestigious brownstone building on West 54th Street in midtown Manhattan that once served as the HQ of Fabergé. Today the brownstone with its marble foyer and bookshelf-lined reception rooms is headquarters for the Research Board, an invitation-only organisation founded in 1973 with a mission 'to inform, stimulate, counsel and connect the world's most senior IT executives.'

The Research Board's 100 members have each been interviewed for suitability and membership is restricted to only most senior executives responsible for IT within an organisation. IT vendors, telecommunications providers and consulting firms are excluded from becoming members to preserve the Research Board's objectivity.

While the Board does not publish its client list, some companies are known to be members. They include Bank of America, ExxonMobil, General Motors, GlaxoSmithKline, British Airways, Rio Tinto, Coca Cola. Think big. What they have in common is some of the largest scale IT deployments in the world and a willingness to learn from one another about how to do it better.

Not that you'd find this out from the Research Board's web site. It simply features a short business description and an address. Nevertheless, Peter Sole, the Research

Case study 1.4 (*continued*)

Board's chief executive, insists the organisation is not deliberately clandestine. He describes the Research Board as private, but not secretive, and the membership as elite, but not elitist.

'The business of technology is not getting any easier for CIOs, so the ability to cut through industry and vendor hype with their peers is invaluable to members,' says Mr Sole.

The Research Board's activity is organised around highly detailed research projects on subjects selected by the members, and small groups of members who meet to review a different topic three times a year.

Each meeting includes a collective examination of research conducted by the Research Board, external presentations by experts and a review of best practices. According to Mr Sole, 'each meeting is carefully choreographed to ensure members have a chance to engage fully with the topic, absorb new information, ask questions in a safe environment and think clearly about important topics that impact their organisations.'

The Research Board also shares feedback from its members with the sellers of IT hardware, software and services. Once a year the Research Board provides formal feedback from their membership – at no cost – to the CEOs of the largest enterprise technology vendors. 'We do it because improvements made by vendors based on the feedback we provide will ultimately benefit members because the products and services they buy will provide more value to their organisations,' says Mr Sole.

Not surprisingly, the chief executives of the largest enterprise technology vendors are keen to receive briefings from the Research Board because they know the quality and seniority of members represent a significant body of purchasing power and the views of CIOs in the largest end-user organisations.

'Meeting face to face and personal involvement are core principles of the Research Board,' says Mr Sole. 'Curiously, in the age of the ubiquitous technology communications devices, face to face interaction with peers at the Research Board meetings delivers a lot of value for CIOs in the largest companies in the world.'

Mr Sole suggests that part of the Research Board's appeal is that back at the office, members are expected to be experts on everything, always the smartest person in the room.

At the Research Board, everyone acknowledges that the collective intelligence in the room is much more powerful than any one individual. 'The experience is both liberating and humbling for everyone involved,' he explains. 'Technology is our raison d'être, but for this network of global CIOs, human interaction trumps technology'.

Questions

1 The chief executive claims that 'face to face interaction with peers at the Research Board meetings delivers a lot of value for CIOs in the largest companies in the world'. What are the benefits of face to face interaction for these Research Board members?

2 Why are human contact and physical presence still considered important to communication in today's organisations?

3 Imagine that you were conducting research on how people prefer to communicate across organisations. Outline a typical research question and the kinds of methods you might use when adopting the four perspectives outlined in the chapter (section 1.6).

Source: Taylor (2011). Copyright Paul Taylor. Reproduced with permission.

Glossary

sender The sender is a person who constructs a message and attempts to convey it to somebody else.

Encoding the message means that the sender converts it into a suitable format for transmission.

Decoding the message means that the transmitted signal is converted back into words and the meaning of the words is re-interpreted by the brain of the person at the receiving end.

noise The term noise is now interpreted much more widely and is used to refer to various kinds of barrier to effective communication that either distort or interrupt an encoded message so that it fails to reach the receiver in its original form.

message The message is what the sender has communicated to the receiver.

channel The communication channel is the route or the technology that is used to convey the message to a receiver.

Feedback refers to the receiver's response to a message; it is a further message sent by the receiver, which gives the sender an indication of the way the original message has been received.

Verbal communication refers to messages coded in the form of words. This may be further sub-divided into spoken (or 'oral') and written forms.

Mass communication refers to sending similar or identical encoded messages to large numbers of people, generally through the use of some form of technology.

Inter-personal communication involves individuals interacting directly in relatively small groups, primarily through face-to-face channels such as meetings.

Internal communication takes place *within* the boundaries of an organisation.

External communication involves the organisation and audiences in the wider world.

Further reading

Mattelart and Mattelart (1998) provide a useful historical overview of theories of communication; **Deetz** (2001) gives an alternative view from a broadly 'postmodern' perspective. Two of the most widely discussed approaches to international cultural difference are **Hofstede, Hofstede and Minkov** (2010) and **Trompenaars** (1994); the text by **Tayeb** (2000) includes some useful commentary and a critique of these theorists.

Hall and Hall (1990) is a widely-cited text on communication and cultural difference by two of the pioneers in this field.

Alvesson and Willmott (1996) introduces critical management studies.

Hatch (1997) is a more general introduction to organisation theory. The edited text by **Buzzanell** (2000) provides a broad overview of recent feminist perspectives on communication.

Jablin and Putnam (2001) is a wide-ranging academic review of the field, addressing many related specialisms, such as discourse analysis by **Putnam and Fairhurst** (2001) and the relationship between organisational communication and learning by **Weick and Ashford** (2001).

Adair's (2010) more practical approach aims to help managers understand the nature of communication in order to become better communicators.

Useful websites

Here are several websites which might be of interest to you. You might like to add some of your own too:

The University of Surrey's online Skills Unit Pack provides a useful overview of the communication cycle. (Available at **http://www.surrey.ac.uk/Skills/pack/cycle.html**)

The Health Knowledge website presents several principles and theories that underpin our understanding of effective communication. (Available at **http:www.healthknowledge.org.uk/public-health-textbook/organisation-management/5a-understanding-itd/effective-communication)**

References

Adair, J. (2009) *Effective Communication (revised edition): the most important management skill of all.* Pan, London.

Allen, R.E. (ed.) (1991) *The Concise Oxford English Dictionary.* Oxford University Press, Oxford.

Alvesson, M. and Willmott, H. (1996) *Making Sense of Management: a critical introduction,* 2nd edn. Sage, London.

BBC (2011) 'EU referendum: Government plays down vote rebellion'. (Available at: http://www.bbc.co.uk/news/uk-politics-15442765 (25th March 2012)).

Boulding, K.E. (1956) *The Image: knowledge in life and society.* University of Michigan Press, Ann Arbor, Michigan.

Buckley, W. (1967) *Sociology and Modern Systems Theory.* Prentice Hall, Englewood Cliffs, NJ.

Buzzanell, P.M. (ed.) (2000) *Rethinking Organizational and Managerial Communication from Feminist Perspectives.* Sage, Thousand Oaks, CA.

Cheney, G. and Christensen, L.T. (2001) 'Organizational identity: linkages between internal and external communication' in Jablin, F.M. and Putnam, L.L. (eds) *The New Handbook of Organizational a Communication,* 231–269. Sage, Thousand Oaks, CA.

Child, J. (2001) 'Trust – the fundamental bond in global collaboration'. *Organizational Dynamics,* 29, 4, 274–288 (Spring).

Clark, P.A. (2000) *Organisations in Action: competition between contexts.* Routledge, London.

Czarinawska, B. (1998) *A Narrative Approach to Organisation Studies.* Sage, London.

Deetz, S. (2001) 'Conceptual foundations' in Jablin, F.M. and Putnam, L.L. (eds) The New Handbook of *Organizational Communication,* 3–45. Sage, Thousand Oaks, CA.

De Vita, G. (2001) 'Inclusive approaches to effective communication and active participation in the multicultural classroom: an international business management context'. *Active Learning in Higher Education,* 1, 2: 168–180.

Fawcett, T., Hurst, A. and Boardman, B. (2002) *Carbon UK.* Industrial Sustainable Development Group, Environmental Change Institute, Oxford.

Gramsci, A. (1971) *Selections from prison notebooks*. Lawrence & Wishart, London.

Grimes, D.S. and Richard, O.C. (2003) 'Could communication form impact organizations' experience with diversity?' *The Journal of Business Communication*, 40, 1, 7–27.

Habermas, J. (1984) *Reason and the Rationalization of Society*. Heinemann, London.

Hall, E.T. and Hall, M.R. (1990) *Understanding Cultural Differences*. Intercultural Press, Yarmouth, ME.

Hassard, J. (1999) 'Postmodernism, philosophy and management: concepts and controversies'. *International Journal of Management Research*, 171–195 (June).

Hatch, M.J. (1997) *Organisation Theory: modern, symbolic and postmodern perspectives*. Oxford University Press, Oxford.

Hofstede, G., Hofstede, G. J. and Minkov, M. (2010) *Cultures and Organizations: software of the mind, third edition: Intercultural Cooperation and Its Importance for Survival*. McGraw-Hill, Maidenhead.

IPCC (2007) *Climate change 2007: the physical science basis, contribution of Working Group I to the fourth assessment report of the Intergovernmental Panel on Climate Change*. Cambridge University Press, Cambridge.

Jablin, F.M. and Putnam, L.L. (eds) (2001) *the New Handbook of Organizational Communication: advances in theory, research, and methods*. Sage, Thousand Oaks, CA.

Keenoy, T., Oswick, C. and Grant, D. (1997) 'Organisational discourses: text and context'. *Organization*, 4, 147–158.

Knights, D. and Willmott, H. (eds) (2000) *The Reengineering Revolution: critical studies of corporate change*. Sage, London.

Livesey, S.M. (2002) 'Global warming wars: rhetorical and discourse analytic approaches to ExxonMobil's corporate public relations'. *Journal of Business Communication*, 39, 1, 117–148.

Luhmann, N. (1995) *Social Systems* (Translated by Bednorz, J.). Stanford University Press, Stanford, CA.

Maier, A.M., Eckert, C.M. and Clarkson, P.J. (2005) 'A meta-model for communication in engineering design'. *CoDesign: International Journal of CoCreation in Design and the Arts*, 1, 4, 243–254.

Mattelart, A. and Mattelart, M. (1998) *Theories of Communication: a Short Introduction*. Sage, London.

Morley, L. (2000) 'The micropolitics of gender in the learning society'. *Higher Education in Europe*, 25, 2, 229–235.

Munshi, D. and McKie, D. (2001) 'Towards a new cartography of intercultural communication: mapping bias, business and diversity'. *Business Communication Quarterly*, 64, 3, 9–22.

Nierenberg, G.I. (1995) *The Art of Negotiating: psychological strategies for gaining advantageous bargains*. Barnes & Noble Books, New York.

Pentland, B.T. (1999) 'Building process theory with narrative: from description to explanation'. *Academy of Management Review*, 24, 4, 711–724.

Pugh, D.S. and Hickson, D.J. (1976) *The Aston Programme, volume 1*. Saxon House, London.

Putnam, L.L. and Fairhurst, G.T. (2001) 'Discourse analysis: issues and concerns' in Jablin, F.M. and Putnam, L.L. (eds) *The New Handbook of Organizational Communication*, 78–136. Sage, Thousand Oaks, CA.

Senge, P.M. (1990) *The Fifth Discipline: the art and practice of the learning organization*. Doubleday, New York.

Shannon, C.E. and Weaver, W.W. (1955) *The Mathematical Theory of Communication*. Illinois University Press, Urbana, IL.

Tayeb, M. (2000) *International Business: theories, principles and practices*. FT Prentice Hall, Harlow.

Taylor, P. (2011) 'For corporate IT chiefs, human interaction trumps technology.' *Financial Times* London Edition (25th October 2011).

Thompson, J.D. (1967) *Organizations in Action*. Wiley, New York.

Trompenaars (1994) *Riding the Waves of Culture: understanding cultural diversity in business*. Nicholas Brealey, London.

Van Maanen, J. (1988) *Tales of the Field: on writing ethnography.* University of Chicago Press, Chicago.

Weick, K.E. (1979) *The Social Psychology of Organizing.* Addison Wesley, Reading, MA.

Weick, K.E. and Ashford, S.J. (2001) 'Learning in organizations' in Jablin, F.M. and Putnam, L.L. (eds) *The New Handbook of Organizational Communication*, 704–731. Sage, Thousand Oaks, CA.

Westwood, R. and Clegg, S. (2001) *Point/counterpoint: central debates in organisation theory.* Blackwell, Oxford.

Wiener, N. (1948) *Cybernetics: or control and communication in the animal and the machine.* MIT Press, Cambridge, MA.

Wright, D.K. (2001) 'Editorial: communication research now focuses more on outcomes than outputs'. *Journal of Communication Management*, 6, 3, 206–207.

Zorn, T.E. (2002) 'Converging within divergence: overcoming the disciplinary fragmentation in business communication, organizational communication and public relations'. *Business Communication Quarterly*, 65, 2, 44–53.

PART 1

Principles of communication

Chapter 2

Breaking barriers: communication in practice

I talk to the trees, but they don't listen to me, I talk to the stars, but they never hear me.
(lyrics from the musical 'Paint your Wagon' by Lerner and Lowe)

Learning outcomes

By the end of this chapter you should be able to:

- recognise the importance of communication barriers, including the potential cost of unsuccessful communication;
- explore some important psychological, social, ethical, linguistic and cultural barriers to communication, using relevant research findings;
- evaluate the concept of the communication barrier through practical applications in a variety of channels;
- outline a generic approach to overcoming communication barriers, while also recognising potential constraints and limitations.

2.1 Introduction

Communication is about overcoming barriers, but failure is endemic. All over the world, individuals and organisations are attempting to interact, but the resulting messages are somehow lost or misunderstood. These failures are expensive; the 'cost' of ineffective communication practices is not simply in the time and resources wasted in preparing the message. There are also the cumulative effects, including those experienced by the intended receiver, who may have been relying on information contained in the message; and the sender, who assumes the message has arrived intact. Consider, for example, the true cost to an organisation of a poorly-executed public relations (PR) campaign. The initial cost includes both the PR agency's consultancy fee and the expenses associated with the campaign, but the longer-term damage inflicted on the organisation's image and reputation could be much more costly. As communicators, we are almost always over-optimistic about our messages, assuming they will survive unscathed, all the way from our own brains to those of the receiver. In fact, all messages are vulnerable to the phenomenon of 'noise' (see section 1.3).

This wide-ranging chapter explores a number of different sources of noise, each of which can become a barrier to inter-personal and organisational communication. We consider how insights from disciplines such as psychology, anthropology, linguistics and ethics have informed our understanding of human communication processes. Several practical illustrations are used to demonstrate how organisations have succeeded in overcoming sources of noise, facilitating more effective communication. The original concept of 'noise' in communication theory referred to technological problems (i.e. electrical interference resulting from the limitations of analogue telephone lines) (see section 1.2). However, as this chapter illustrates, communication barriers are primarily the result of human limitations. Consequently, the key to avoiding communication failure is increased self-awareness on the part of the sender, supported by feedback on the part of the receiver. If you reflect carefully on the needs of the people you are trying to engage with, and think about the characteristics of the channels you are using, you can begin to overcome these barriers to communication.

2.2 Barriers to communication? Identifying underlying causes

In order to overcome barriers to communication, it is essential to understand the underlying causes. Isolating the apparent explanations under separate headings is a useful first stage (see Table 2.1). Indeed, the rest of this chapter is structured around a similar set of headings, in order to draw on the relevant areas of research. However, it is essential to recognise that these causal sequences are rather more complicated in practice. For example, consider a situation where an organisation is seeking to communicate more effectively with its deaf employees. It might appear that the basic 'physiological' barrier can be readily overcome

Table 2.1 Common barriers to communication: probing for 'causes'

Apparent 'cause'	Practical example: a more complex explanation?
Technological	Message not delivered due to technical failure; but why was the failure allowed to develop and why are there no back-up systems?
Physical	Message cannot be heard and visual aids cannot be seen by some members of the audience; but why is the presenter not aware of or responsive to this?
Physiological	Message in an internal report not received due to blindness; but why was the message not encoded in a suitable format?
Psychological	Message from external stakeholder ignored due to 'groupthink' (Janis 1982); but why has this been allowed to develop in the organisation?
Cultural	Message from organisation misinterpreted by members of a particular cultural group; but why was organisation unaware of cultural diversity?
Linguistic	Message is misunderstood because of lack of shared expressions (e.g. jargon) or perhaps there was a misplaced emphasis (e.g. stress placed on wrong word); but why is jargon being used if not everyone understands it?
Political	Message from internal stakeholder not sent because individual is marginalised; but why is the organisation not encouraging a more open climate?
Economic	Message not available to a public sector organisation due to lack of resources; but why is it unable to exert pressure for additional funding?

through appropriate encoding of messages (e.g. by using a skilled sign language interpreter). However, research into the communication barriers experienced by deaf employees indicates that organisations need to address a much more complex set of social and cultural factors beyond those directly related to hearing loss (Luft 2000).

2.3 Technological over-optimism and 'blaming the tools'

In a world of mobile phone, video-conferencing and internet technologies, it is easy to assume that our communication problems are over. This kind of technological optimism is, of course, actively promoted by those whose job it is to market the latest hardware and software. However, while technology provides ever-faster and more portable communication channels, with increasing carrying capacity (or 'bandwidth'), the quality and effectiveness of communication flowing through any channel depends ultimately on the communicative practices adopted by users (Yates and Orlikowski 1992). Just as people tend to make overly-optimistic claims for new technologies, they also have a tendency to distance themselves from poor performance by interpreting the problem in technological terms. (In the words of an old saying, 'the bad craftsman always blames his tools'.) When technical failures do occur, the best solution is often to have an alternative technology to act as a fallback (e.g. preparing paper copies of a report to substitute for an electronic version, or having copies of presentation slides as overhead projector transparencies or handouts, as well as on a CD or flash memory). Other superficially 'technological' problems are generally a cover for human errors, such as selecting an inappropriate channel, or failing to use it effectively.

The following sections review some of the factors that influence the quality of interpersonal and organisational communication. We begin with human physiology and consider how our capacity to deal with information is affected by interaction between the brain, sensory organs and other parts of the human body. The purpose of these short, non-technical reviews is to draw attention to the complex and multi-layered nature of human communication. In doing so, we can marvel at the countless millions of messages that are successfully sent and received every day. (Note: Additional commentary on selected references is given in the further reading section at the end of this chapter.)

2.4 Physiological and neurological factors

Physiological and neurological barriers to communication are those that result from the performance characteristics and limitations of the human body and the human mind. Our sensory and information processing capabilities exceed those of the most advanced computers. However, because we are organic and self-conscious beings rather than unconscious machines, the underlying mechanisms are not as standardised and the results are less predictable. Research suggests that our ability to communicate with one another is profoundly influenced by three inter-related mechanisms:

- **alertness and attention:** affecting what data our senses manage to pick up;
- **perception:** resulting in different interpretations of the same sensory data;
- **memory:** affecting the messages we retain and those we can subsequently recall.

Figure 2.1 Human cognition: four linked mechanisms

This section explores these four processes – alertness, attention, perception, memory – in a non-technical way, highlighting the implications for communicators (see Figure 2.1). The key lesson is that the capabilities of different people will vary in each of these areas, affecting their ability to communicate. Furthermore, the *same* individual can display wide variations at different points in time.

Variations in level of alertness

Physiological and behavioural functions are influenced by a long-term cycle of alertness, known as the 'circadian rhythm' (popularly known as the 'body clock'), which traces the daily cycle of light and dark. Disturbances in these patterns can affect the performance of shift workers and air travellers, for example. People experience not only long-term changes in what is termed 'tonic alertness' during the day, but also a number of shorter-term variations in the level of arousal, which are stimulated by events in their immediate environment. The shorter-term change, known as 'phasic alertness', is a common feature of humans and other animals. For example, it can be observed when a cat's ears begin to twitch on hearing a new sound, or when a dozing student is startled into life on hearing his name called out in a seminar. When receivers are repeatedly exposed to the same stimuli, they become 'habituated' to it, the response is no longer activated, and the message blends into the background. For example, through repeated exposure we risk becoming desensitised to news of tragic events and fail to be shocked or to respond appropriately. This adaptation has important implications for communicators. It is one reason why advertisers are constantly searching for novel and more dramatic ways to deliver their messages, in order that their impact is maintained.

The role of selective attention

Since humans are bombarded by so many different stimuli, the brain has to ration its processing power. We can only 'pay attention' to a small fraction of this mass of incoming sensory data. People have also learnt to jump from one source to another – a common application of this skill is switching between rival conversations in a noisy bar. However, selective attention can work against communicators. Contemporary audiences have become accustomed to a world of electronically-mediated and visually-oriented communication, ranging from 'channel-hopping' through satellite television programmes to absorbing information in the form of ten-second 'sound bites' accompanied by equally short video images. There is evidence that these social and technological developments are influencing public expectations regarding the length and format in which messages are encoded. This represents a major challenge for organisations that need to convey long or complex messages, particularly where they are better suited to extended verbal or text-based argument. Some educational organisations are offering podcasts in addition to face-to-face sessions to help students study more effectively and flexibly. Might this threaten the traditional lecture? It seems that lectures and podcasts each have particular advantages and disadvantages from a student's point of view. Try listing the arguments 'for' and 'against' lectures and podcasts. Which is likely to be the most effective medium of communication? Which of the two do you prefer?

Powers of perception: constructing the world around us

We integrate information that is supplied by each of the senses in order to construct a meaningful interpretation of the world around us (Roth and Bruce 1995). Humans have very advanced powers of perception. In many cases we are able to re-construct a whole picture, or concept, from a tiny scrap of visual information. For example, it is often possible to recognise a friend's face, when it is glimpsed for a moment in the midst of a large crowd of people. We can also identify whole objects from fragmentary evidence (see Figure 2.2). This ability is useful to communicators, suggesting that it is not always necessary to spell out the entire message. Indeed, many of the most effective forms of communication rely on this imaginative capability for their appeal. For example, many of the greatest works of art are noted for the way that they leave the spectator to interpret missing or ambiguous elements.

However, it is also important to recognise the inherent limitations of this impressive sensory system. Research using simple optical illusions, such as those reproduced here (see Figure 2.3), has indicated that human perceptions are based on a hypothesis or 'best guess' from the evidence that the senses have managed to collect. If the evidence is ambiguous, people can misinterpret it and even 'see' things that do not exist. These misattributions are not limited to visual signals; inter-personal communication is also profoundly affected by our perceptions of other people. We make these judgements according to various cues, but research indicates that some have a particularly powerful effect. These 'central traits', such

Figure 2.2 Perception – object recognition

31

These three examples indicate some unusual features of our capacity to process visual stimuli.

(a) An ambiguous image: which way is the cube facing?

(b) An image that is 'impossible' in three dimensions.

(c) An implied image: we can 'see' a white, upward-pointing triangle, though it is not present on the printed page.

Figure 2.3 Three optical illusions

as a person's location on the 'warm–cold' continuum, lead people to infer other characteristics. For example, once we have identified someone as 'warm', they are also likely to be perceived as being 'sociable, popular, happy, good-natured and humorous' (Hargie 1997: 48). These perceptual limitations provide an important lesson for communicators, particularly in contexts where clarity of communication is the primary objective.

Memory

In some folk traditions, witches were accused of 'memory-snatching'; a crime that involved stealing the contents of people's minds. Today, we are more likely to explain the limitations of human memory with reference to stressful lifestyles, information overload, old age and the effects of alcohol. In any event, memory loss is clearly a major challenge for the communicator. In many cases, the primary concern is with ensuring that certain messages are retained, but there are also occasions when the purpose of a message is supported by people's ability to forget. Psychologists have identified three distinct processes of memory: registration, storage and retrieval. While there is considerable debate over the intermediate mechanisms, this relatively straightforward three-stage model has provided communication researchers with a useful framework for discussion (e.g. Argyle 1972, Hargie et al. 1994). We adopt a simplified model in order to address some of the practical implications of these processes (see Figure 2.4).

a) Selective attention and potential for 'information overload'

b) Information retained for further processing

c) Encoding of information for long-term storage

d) Retrieval of stored information and 're-processing'

e) Processed information generates a response

Figure 2.4 Human memory processes: a three-stage model

In some respects, the brain acts like the 'left luggage' office at a railway station. It accepts a message, holds on to it for you, and returns it when you return to request it some time later. Registration of an incoming message is closely related to selective attention, reviewed in the previous paragraph. The key lesson for the communicator is that this process is unlike the kind of storage available on a computer disc, where the encoded message is held indefinitely in an unchanged state. Research suggests that storage of a message in the human brain can occur at three distinct yet related levels, known as the sensory memory (or 'attention buffer'), the short-term (or 'working') memory, and the long-term memory. Each of these memories appears to have set 'time limits'.

The sensory memory acts as a kind of temporary collection-point for incoming stimuli of all kinds; this limit is often identified as either six or seven separate pieces of information. Once the 'attention buffer' is full, any additional information of the same type causes it to overflow, resulting in the loss of some of the original stored material. Communication specialists have argued that you can stretch this physiological limit by 'chunking' information into larger units (e.g. combining separate letters to form a word or a string of numbers in the form of a date). For example, you might use the mnemonic Roy G. Biv, to help you to remember the colours of the rainbow (Red, Orange, Yellow, Green, Blue, Indigo, Violet). A proportion of the in-coming messages may then progress to the part of the process, entering the short- and the long-term memory, but there appears to be a great deal of filtering at both intermediate stages. The whole process is also affected by the person's current state of mind. Again, it appears that 'chunking' the information can help with retention, because it imposes some kind of meaning on the information. However, it is important to note that each person processes incoming stimuli in a unique way. This uniqueness is the result of factors such as differences in prior experience, which lead to the recognition of particular patterns connecting new 'information' with that already held in the sensory, working or long-term memory. For this reason, it is difficult to work from someone else's lecture notes; in effect, the notes have been 'customised' to a particular set of memories and references.

These features of human memory raise a number of practical issues for the communicator. For example, it may be important to consider how long the receiver needs to retain your

Table 2.2 A simple activity to 'test' the sensory memory

Introduction	The limits of sensory memory can be demonstrated with a simple activity, which can also be conducted as a 'thought experiment'. Could you, for example, remember two minutes' worth of information long enough to record it on paper? Your level of recall should vary depending on the type of material conveyed. (Note: In a simpler variant of this activity, the first list of 20 random numbers may be re-presented as five 'chunked' dates, in the form: '1945, 2004 . . . '.)
Meaningless information, out of context	Read out a list of 20 random numbers, between one and 100. Speak clearly at normal speed; it should take no more than 15 seconds. Now ask people to write down as much of the message as they can remember. Compare these records with the original.
Meaningful information, in context	Record a weather forecast, as it is printed in a daily newspaper; this should take no more than two minutes. Ask ten prepared factual questions on *specific details* from the forecast. How much of the message is either forgotten or recalled incorrectly?
Information in narrative ('story') form	Read a short narrative, including lots of visual imagery (e.g. 'they crossed a rickety wooden bridge over a cool mountain stream . . . '). A children's story would be ideal for this purpose. Again, ensure the story lasts a maximum of two minutes, and follow it with ten prepared factual questions. Is recall any better than in the other examples?

message. Assuming that it is necessary to retain it for more than a few seconds, how can you increase the chances that it will pass through the intermediate filters and into the longer-term memory? Table 2.2 summarises a simple activity that can be used to assess your own abilities and those of friends and colleagues. (Note: Other exercises associated with this chapter provide an opportunity to explore the practicalities of engaging with the sensory, working and long-term memory.)

Case study 2.1 deals with a current issue that is related to physiological barriers to communication, the challenge of ensuring that web-based materials are designed in a way that makes them accessible to all users.

CASE STUDY 2.1

Responding to the challenge of web accessibility

The web has become an important communication channel, providing people with access to news, information, commercial markets, political debate and educational services. As a consequence, web accessibility has become a major issue for organisations of all kinds. A person's access to the web can be restricted for a number of reasons, including: physical disability, language differences, IT literacy levels and low bandwidth connections. Each of these will create a barrier to communication, unless organisations make an effort to design and implement their web presence appropriately. This case focuses on accessibility issues related to the ability/disability of users.

The World Wide Web Consortium (W3C) is an international not-for-profit organisation, based in North America. As part of its Web Accessibility Initiative (WAI), it has developed a detailed set of Web Content Accessibility Guidelines (WCAG 2.0), designed to ensure that websites provide improved access to people with disabilities. The accessibility guidelines are available from the W3C website (www.w3c.org). They deal with design requirements, including the provision of captions with audio content to overcome hearing-related disabilities; and described graphics, that can be read by screen-reader software, for those with visual disabilities. Many of the guidelines, such as consistent navigation features, will be beneficial for all users, whatever their ability/disability. The RNIB (The Royal National Institute of Blind People) advise that text-only versions of a website that have been used as alternatives to overcome accessibility issues in the past should be used only as a last resort (RNIB, 2009). The official language of the W3C site is English, but WCAG and related support documents have been translated into many other languages. WAI highlights the fact that at least 10 per cent of the population of most countries has disabilities, and that organisations cannot afford to deliberately miss out on this market. In addition to the ethical and equity-based arguments for constructing more accessible websites, WAI has identified a number of potential benefits for organisations. These include: increased market share and audience reach; more flexible and efficient websites, with lower development and maintenance costs; a public demonstration of corporate social responsibility, which should enhance the organisation's image; and reduced legal liabilities in countries with strong equal opportunities legislation.

Useability initiatives in the UK: RNIB's campaign for good web design

There are around two million people in the UK with sight problems. The Royal National Institute of Blind People (RNIB) helps anyone with a sight problem with imaginative and practical solutions to everyday challenges. This voluntary sector organisation also campaigns to change society's attitudes, actions and assumptions, so that people with sight problems can enjoy the same rights, freedoms and responsibilities as fully-sighted people. Since 1999, RNIB has run a Campaign for Good Web Design, in order to promote the creation of web products and experiences that could be used by everyone, regardless of ability/disability, technology and circumstance (www.rnib.org.uk). This has contributed to a lively debate, with some strong divisions of expert opinion on the question: is it possible to design a web interface that suits the needs of everybody? The following responses were quoted in a public debate, hosted by RNIB in 2002:

- If you research your user requirements well, you should find that everyone doesn't want the same thing. The web experience should be delivered in the way the users want.

- Although we're all different, people pretty much do things the same way. When we start to offer interfaces that work in different ways we start to force different groups of people to learn different ways of doing things. The aim should be to allow site users to do whatever they want while offering a user experience that is as consistent as possible.

- For me, the most successful design is that which allows the user to 'socialise' the design for their own needs.

Commenting on this debate, Julie Howell, leader of the RNIB's Good Web Design Campaign concluded that it was essential to involve users in the design process:

'It is becoming clear that adopting the W3C/WAI guidelines is not enough to ensure that visually impaired people will be able to make full use of a website. The inclusion of users with disabilities at every stage of the design testing cycle would seem to be the ideal way to ensure that any resulting website is both fully accessible to and usable by people with disabilities.'

Regulatory developments are increasing the pressure on organisations with poorly designed and inaccessible websites. In March 2003, the UK's Disability Rights Commission (DRC) announced that it would be investigating one thousand public and private sector

> ## Case study (*continued*)
>
> websites for their ability to be accessed by Britain's 8.5 million disabled people. Announcing the investigation, the DRC's Chair, Bert Massie, said:
>
> > 'The DRC wants to see a society where all disabled people can participate fully as equal citizens and this formal investigation into web accessibility is an important step towards this goal.'
>
> ### Questions
>
> 1 What is your own experience of website accessibility? Compare your thoughts with those of colleagues and draft a list of the most significant problems you have experienced when attempting to communicate using this channel.
>
> 2 Read the relevant guidelines, available from the W3C/WAI and RNIB websites – http://www.w3.org/WAI/ and http://www.rnib.org.uk/. Sample a selection of public, private and voluntary sector websites, assessing them against these guidelines.
>
> 3 Re-read Julie Howell's comment on improving accessibility. Why do you think it is 'not enough' for organisations to follow the W3C/WAI guidelines? What is the wider lesson for organisations seeking to overcome communication barriers?
>
> *Source*: RNIB (2002), RNIB (2009), DRC (2003), WAI (2010). Case prepared by the authors with acknowledgement to Julie Howell.

2.5   Social, cultural, linguistic and ethical barriers

The simple model of communication, outlined in Chapter 1, takes little account of the context in which the message is being sent and received. In practice, both senders and receivers are part of a wider social and cultural setting, which has an impact on the ways in which they communicate. In this section, we review three examples of the more important barriers to communication within and between social groups.

- **Social barriers** to communication include the social psychological phenomenon of conformity; a process in which the norms, values and behaviours of an individual begin to follow those of the wider group.

- **Cultural barriers** to communication often arise where individuals in one social group have developed different norms, values or behaviours from individuals associated with another group.

- **Linguistic barriers** to communication occur when individuals in a group lack the communicative skills to participate or they lack the understanding of some shared expressions and context, and so they are unable to interpret messages.

- **Ethical barriers** to communication; these occur when individuals working in an organisation find it difficult to voice dissent, even though their organisation is acting in ways they consider to be unethical.

Social conformity, cultural difference and ethical dilemmas are necessary features of social life. However, in certain circumstances (e.g. where there is an excessive degree of conformity, or where cultural differences are left unbridged), they can become both a symptom and a cause of communication failure.

Excessive conformity as a barrier to communication

In the mid-twentieth century, psychological research began to explore the pathological features of excessive conformity. In the shadow of major social evils of the period, including the Holocaust, researchers tried to discover why individuals were willing to take actions as part of a group that they would never contemplate as individuals. **'Groupthink'** is a term introduced by a North American psychologist, Janis (1982), to explain an extreme type of social conformity occurring within close-knit groups. Janis illustrated the argument with real-world case studies that drew on the example of US political and diplomatic crises (including: the 'Bay of Pigs' confrontation between the US and USSR in the early 1960s, the gradual escalation of the Vietnam War and the Watergate scandal of the early 1970s). These events were characterised by a number of managerial and communication failures, including: an incomplete survey of alternatives; inadequate reflection on strategic objectives; failure to examine risks of the preferred option; poor information search; selective bias in processing available information; failure to re-appraise alternatives; and failure to work out contingency plans.

Subsequent research has supported the view that groupthink can occur in any highly cohesive group that is insulated from the influence of others, has a single-minded leadership, is under stress and has no clear-cut solution to its problems. Unfortunately, these conditions can be found in many organisational contexts, ranging from defective decision-making in senior management meetings to situations such as a hostage-taking incident, where the participants may be exposed to real and imminent danger (Cohan 2002, Smith 1984). Janis's original research studies identified eight classic symptoms of groupthink:

1 An illusion of invulnerability, contributing to excessive optimism and risk-taking behaviour.

2 Collective rationalisation of the problem, which discounts negative feedback and neutralises problematic information.

3 An unquestioning belief in the inherent morality of the group and its cause, enabling it to ignore moral and ethical considerations.

4 Applying negative stereotyping to outsiders (or 'out-groups') and opponents, and to proposals that would lead to a change.

5 Direct pressure on dissenters to conform and reach consensus, so that any minority views are suppressed.

6 Self-censorship by group members, who suppress any personal objectives, concerns or areas of disagreement.

7 An illusion of unanimity, arising from the other factors, masking any underlying divisions.

8 Emergence of self-appointed 'mind-guards' to protect leaders, filter information, deflect opposition and exert pressure on dissenters.

A brief appraisal of the list indicates that each of these factors in isolation is a potential barrier to communication. The key contribution of Janis (1982) was to highlight the ways in which these symptoms can become self-reinforcing in an organisational setting, and connect that process to observed effects, such as poor decision-making.

Harvey (1988) outlines an interesting, and subtly different, case of communication barriers operating between members of a group, which he termed 'The Abilene Paradox' (AP). The Abilene Paradox takes its name from an incident in the life of his own family, which provoked him to reflect on the problem of communicating personal feelings to others. The following quotation summarises what took place during a miserable trip to Abilene, Texas:

> During a dust storm on a scorching 104-degree West Texas day, four adults piled into an unairconditioned car and drove 35 miles to eat at a cafeteria in Abilene. In the midst of a subsequent family argument during which each family member attempted to blame the others for the disaster, it was discovered that none of the four family members had really wanted to go to Abilene. No-one had vetoed the idea since each had thought, incorrectly, that everyone else had wanted to go.
>
> (Kim 2001: 169–70)

While there are many similarities between the processes identified as groupthink and AP, there are also some important differences. For example, under groupthink the cohesiveness of the group is the primary driver, and group members are actively involved in the reinforcement process. By contrast, individuals in the AP scenario appear to take a more passive role, simply 'going along with' a course of action out of a fear of upsetting other members of the group (Kim 2001: 175–6, 180–1).

Case study 2.2 presents a more recent case of Groupthink, which deals with the causes and consequences of groupthink in a past American president's (George Bush) administration and the Iraq war.

CASE STUDY 2.2

Groupthink, Iraq, and the War on Terror: explaining US policy shift toward Iraq

The Bush administration's decision to invade Iraq under the auspices of terrorism presented a significant departure from the rationales and strategies previously supported by members of the Bush administration. 9/11 did not simply provide an opportunity to implement a pre-existing policy; in fact, the chosen policy is surprising when considering previously held images of Saddam Hussein. In this context, the groupthink model explains the decision to incorporate Iraq within the War on Terror. Instead of viewing Iraq as an isolated threat that required a modest regime change policy – as the group advocated prior to 9/11 – the core group's adoption of the President's premise of a broad War on Terror, and the fixation with 'connecting the dots', forced a shift in their view of Saddam Hussein. This shift was primarily guided by the hawks within the administration who took it upon themselves to engage critics of the policy and convince them of an impending threat. Yet the administration's ideologues did not necessarily engage in duplicity; they in fact feared Saddam's threat in the wake of 9/11. In narrowing the scope of intelligence and quantity of information and analysis on Iraq, the administration's ideologues fostered groupthink while directing a shift in the group's image of Saddam Hussein.

These issues, along with the intelligence processing affair, neither implicate nor vindicate the core group as malevolent or rational. They instead highlight the drive to war that resulted in rushed, incomplete and inaccurate estimates that dealt with Iraq as a threat within the War on Terror. As the decision makers continued to argue long after the initial decision was made, the Bush administration decided to invade Iraq – within the War on Terror – based on the information available in March 2003. However, the presence of the foregoing symptoms showcases the administration's inability to critically evaluate information, resulting in poor information search, information processing bias and a failure

Case study 2.2 (*continued*)

to examine the risks of the policy. Using groupthink, the administration made the policy based on partial and inconclusive evidence, justified the morality of their policy, and dismissed warnings regarding potential setbacks. Internalisation of the information occurred during the evaluation process, moving policy makers toward a war stance. Because they were tasked with 'connecting the dots', members of the administration found evidence to perform this function and briefed decision makers accordingly. The timing of Powell's shift confirms that internalization occurred during the evaluation stage. He remained wary of the policy until new 'intelligence' was uncovered; his speech to the UN marked the shift. This shift explains the urgency with which the administration pursued the war policy.

Given the presently available documentation, it has become evident that the information available in March of 2003 justified the war policy insofar as groupthink infected the decision-making process and magnified Saddam's threat. The present case study illustrates that groupthink explains the shift in the Bush administration's perception of Saddam Hussein, from an oppressive dictator to a real threat to US security. Understanding the interconnected nature of the two outcomes of groupthink – defective process and changing images – prevents limiting the study of decision making within episodic bounds. That is, longer term shifts in perceptions can be considered in conjunction with flawed decision making. The 2003 Iraq decision-making process signified this type of ideational shift and defective process marked by the presence of groupthink.

Questions

1 Compare the summary of this case to the list detailing the symptoms of groupthink. Identify some examples of these symptoms.

2 In what ways was the decision-making by the Bush administration flawed?

3 In what ways did the Bush administration change their view of Saddam Hussein?

4 If you were responsible for coordinating communication in this context, what procedures would you put in place to reduce the risk of groupthink?

Source: Badie, D. (2010), adapted.

Moral silences? Barriers to ethical behaviour

Bird (2002) discusses three communication-related barriers to ethical behaviour in business organisations. These barriers can be summarised briefly in the following terms:

- **moral silence**, which means failing to speak up about issues that are known to be wrong;
- **moral deafness**, meaning a failure to hear or attend to moral concerns raised by others; and
- **moral blindness**, which is the failure to recognise the moral implications of actions.

The author summarises his thesis:

Many people in business fail to speak up about their moral convictions. They fail to do so in a number of different ways. As a result, many of the ethical issues and concerns facing business are not addressed as fully, as clearly, and as well as they would be if people voiced their concerns. Moral silence is occasioned and reinforced by the correlative phenomena of moral blindness and moral deafness as well as the quite contrary practice of giving voice to moralistic concerns.

(Bird 2002: 4)

There are strong parallels between the communication barriers identified in this study and the effects of excessive conformity, identified in the concepts of groupthink and the Abilene Paradox (Sims 1992). In both cases, organisations undertake actions that would not have been contemplated by the individuals operating independently. The interesting question from our perspective is the extent to which individual and organisational communication practices might overcome these barriers, so that opposition is voiced and concerns are attended to. We revisit this theme in our discussion of feedback mechanisms (see section 6.2 and Case Study 6.1).

Cultural difference as a barrier to communication

Cultures shape the way we think and behave. They can be seen as both shaping and being shaped by our established patterns of communication. However, people are often unaware of the profound impact of cultural forces. It is when we experience contrasting cultures at close hand that these forces become more apparent. Nations, occupations, organisations, teams and other social groupings all share a tendency to develop distinctive cultures. The influence of the classic definition by the anthropologists Kroeber and Kluckholm (1952) can be seen in the work of many later organisational researchers (e.g. Brown and Starkey 1994). It is rather convoluted, but remains of interest for its comprehensiveness and the emphasis placed on communication:

> Culture consists of patterns, explicit and implicit, of and for behaviour. [It is] acquired and transmitted by symbols, constituting the distinctive achievements of human groups, including their embodiments in artefacts; the essential core of culture consists of traditional (that is historically derived and selected) ideas and especially their attached values; culture systems may, on the one hand, be considered as products of action, on the other as conditioned elements of further action.'
>
> (Kroeber and Kluckholm 1952: 181)

Cultural diversity is clearly a valuable feature of human societies. However, when people from dissimilar cultures get together, they can encounter powerful barriers, limiting their capacity to communicate. We all have our own anecdotal examples of what is sometimes termed 'culture clash'. In some cases, the consequences can be simply amusing, or at worst, mildly embarrassing. However, a failure to deal appropriately with cultural difference can also lead to disastrous outcomes for individuals and organisations.

Organisations are increasingly accepting the need for their employees to participate in inter-cultural training, designed to increase their awareness about others', and their own, cultures and enabling them to overcome cultural barriers, avoid culture clashes and communicate effectively across cultures. The **Iceberg Metaphor** (see Figure 2.5) is often referred to in such inter-cultural training because it usefully highlights how the explicit and tangible aspects of culture, such as food, costumes and music, which are visible to us (i.e. above the waterline), are far fewer than that large proportion of invisible, unarticulated aspects of culture such as assumptions, understandings, beliefs, values and judgments, which are hidden below the waterline. Furthermore, in many cases, it is the invisible aspects of culture that actually influence and explain the visible ones. For example, religious beliefs influence how food is prepared and eaten, and notions of modesty affect styles of dress. This image also illustrates that it is the hidden aspects over which people from different cultures are more likely to clash. In this way, it highlights the need to increase our inter-cultural awareness, through sharing and exploring each other's hidden aspects of culture, if we are to avoid clashes and misunderstandings.

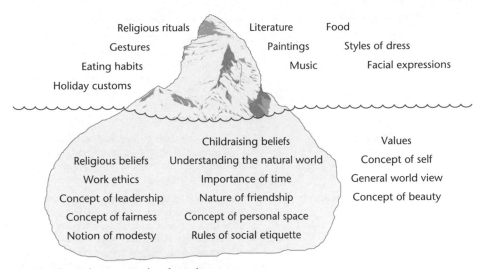

Figure 2.5 The iceberg metaphor for culture
Source: http://www.indoindians.com/lifestyle/culture.htm

So how else can we begin to make sense of cultural difference? One approach is to try to categorise the most important dimensions of culture, and relate them to people's behaviour in organisations. The most influential research study in this area was conducted by the Dutch researcher, Geert Hofstede, who drew on the work of earlier cultural researchers such as Kroeber and Kluckholm (1952) in order to test the so-called 'convergence thesis'. The convergence thesis suggested that the world's population is becoming more alike, with national cultural difference being squeezed out by the process we now refer to as 'globalisation', symbolised by universally-available consumer products such as Coca-Cola and MTV. Hofstede's original study, which was conducted in the 1970s, involved a large questionnaire-based survey of employees of the international computer company IBM. The findings were published in 1980, with a second edition in 2001 (Hofstede 2001). The survey respondents included several different occupational groups, located in the company's various national subsidiaries. Using a statistical clustering technique, Hofstede was able to distinguish four key dimensions that appeared to characterise particular cultures. A fifth dimension, relating to time orientation, was added in subsequent extensions of the research (Hofstede 2001: 351–72). Table 2.3 offers a brief commentary on the original dimensions.

Hofstede's famous definition of culture highlights the differences that are measured across these dimensions. He treats culture as 'the collective programming of the mind that distinguishes the members of one group or category of people from another' (Hofstede 2001: 9). His work, along with that of other researchers, including Trompenaars (1994), is grounded in the perspective of culture as an enduring source of difference. As such, it has contributed strongly to the convergence debate (e.g. Hickson 1997, Tayeb 2000: 441). It is certainly the case that 'culture clash' remains an important barrier to communication, but there are increasing doubts about the continuing relevance of this perspective in the multi-cultural settings of many contemporary organisations (Holden 2002), particularly as Hofstede's research defined culture in terms of national culture, yet cultural homogeneity is not a reality in any nation.

Table 2.3 Hofstede's taxonomic approach to cultural difference

Dimension	Comment
Individualism/collectivism	This dimension is reflected in the ways that managers communicate. In collectivist cultures, there is a stronger emphasis on reaching consensus but may be less room for individual initiative. Individualist cultures appear more argumentative but, arguably, may be more likely to generate collaborative, creative solutions.
Power distance	This dimension relates to inequalities between senior managers and subordinates, and possibly lecturers and students. Power, distance and status affect the way that information flows up and down the hierarchy, and the levels at which decisions are made.
Uncertainty avoidance	This dimension reveals differences in how willing managers are to tolerate unstructured, unclear situations. Managers from 'high' uncertainty avoidance cultures tend to plan activities in more detail, which can be associated with rigid, inflexible procedures. Those from 'low' uncertainty avoidance cultures tend to put less energy into assessing risk.
Achievement/relational	This dimension affects the core values of and practices of organisations rooted in a particular national culture. For example, 'achievement' cultures (referred to as 'masculine' in Hofstede's original study and retained in the 2001 edition) emphasise material gain and aggressive competition, while 'relational' (or 'feminine') cultures are higher on creativity and mutual support.

Towards a deeper understanding of cultural difference?

Before moving on to consider an alternative perspective, it may be useful to analyse a typical 'culture clash' scenario, described by the British writer Handy (1996); similar examples can be found throughout the international management literature. The case describes problems experienced when two teams of engineers were drawing up the contract for a collaborative project involving a French and a British company. Members of the French team wanted each part of the contract signed before moving on to the next one. The British team interpreted this as a lack of trust on the part of the French and resisted their request. However, the French team saw reluctance to sign the documentation as displaying a lack of commitment on the part of the British. Fortunately, someone eventually spotted the cultural obstacle and defused the situation; otherwise, the negotiation could have broken up, resulting in a costly delay.

This kind of mutual incomprehension across national cultures is a potential barrier to communication. Consequently, the 'lesson' of the story, that is, the need to improve inter-cultural awareness, remains an important one. However, there are some problems with this kind of analysis. Above all, there is the danger of relying on shorthand, stereotypical accounts of culture that ignore local- and individual-level factors and the reality that cultures are dynamic and constantly changing. Much popular writing on intercultural communication falls into this trap, reducing the complex and subtle issues of cultural difference into over-simplistic anecdotes or comparative tables.

Reliance on these crude characterisations as a basis for doing business across cultural boundaries can be compared to the use of a foreign language phrasebook when travelling abroad. The phrasebook might help you to undertake basic tasks (e.g. booking a hotel, ordering a meal), but would be of no help whatsoever in more demanding tasks (such as reading a novel or listening to an opera). This argument is developed by the authors of a text highlighting the complexities of intercultural communication from a 'Chinese' perspective:

> Many paradoxical statements are made [by Westerners] about Chinese society. This is partly because authors are not being clear about just which Chinese society they are talking about. It is common, unfortunately, to mix up quotations from ancient classics, observations made about overseas Chinese immigrants in the UK or North America, and observations made in Taiwan and in Mainland China. This makes as much sense as trying to describe what the 'English' are like by quoting Chaucer and mixing observations made in London, Capetown, and Peoria, Illinois.
>
> (Pan *et al.* 2002: 118)

For this reason, Pan et al. note that their own research was conducted in the southern Chinese city of Guangzhou (Canton). They see it as providing well-researched statements that cover this narrower geographic scope. They avoid making claims about China as a whole, on the reasonable basis that 'it would be very difficult to generalise meaningfully about what is approximately one fourth of the world's population' (ibid: 118).

There are many problems with the way that culture is interpreted, both in popular discussion and in the research literature. Difficulties that often arise include: a failure to explore underlying assumptions; a tendency for perceptions of 'the other' to become distorted; and an under-emphasis on the ambiguities associated with multiple cultural identities:

- **Hidden assumptions**: Many research studies are themselves 'culture-bound', containing implicit assumptions regarding key issues such as gender and disability. Here is an example of how such assumptions can cause confusion: a researcher was presenting the results of a detailed statistical study into transport and personal mobility. The figures he had presented were then challenged by a member of the audience, but the researcher could not understand why the other person was disputing his findings, '[T]hen suddenly the light dawned. 'Oh', he exclaimed to general guffaws [laughter] from the audience, 'you're including *children*' (Ashe 2001: 12).

- **Subjective perceptions**: The ways that we interpret other cultures is subject to distortion, in the sense that people tend to focus attention on those areas that most differ from, or most resemble, their own experience. This phenomenon is exemplified by the Victorian explorer's command, 'Take me to your leader!', which superimposes domestic assumptions about a hierarchical social organisation onto another, unknown culture. Interpretivists have argued that, because perceptions are bound to differ, according to the nature of the observer, cultural difference must be re-interpreted as a subjective construct. This tendency to interpret other cultures through our own cultural lens is manifested in a perceived hierarchy of civilisation, whereby a British person may describe other nations as 'driving on the wrong side of the road'. Hence, it is misleading to represent cultural systems in an 'essentialist' framework, such as a typology, which implies that categories are stable, homogeneous and can be measured objectively (Holden 2002: 27–9).

- **Multiple dimensions**: Many of the existing characterisations of cultural difference give a misleading impression of universality. This ignores the many sources of ambiguity, including multiple cultural identities (e.g. where people may regard themselves simultaneously as French, black, Catholic, female and European), and the ways that these are negotiated over time. The preoccupation with 'culture clash' gives a misleading impression of the real experience of today's international organisations, because it emphasises confrontations between two unitary cultures. The reality is that most international organisations are multi-cultural.

Multi-cultural organisations consist of people from many different national, social and economic backgrounds, who bring their multiple identities to work; such organisations are increasingly common in the twenty-first century, largely as a result of economic globalisation. As Tayeb (2000: 323) has noted, 'confining behaviour to a handful of dimensions presents a simplistic and unidimensional picture of reality' in organisations of this kind. We need to consider many other factors in order to explain how people behave differently under different conditions.

So what are the implications of these developments for our approach to culture and communication? How do we currently operate in our multicultural organisations? It would be unrealistic to claim that we can engage in a truly multicultural approach to organisational communication, given the limitations of a concise textbook with an unavoidably 'Western' focus. However, we can begin to take a more critical approach to our communication practices and to the principles that underpin them (e.g. Yates and Orlikowski 1992, Holden 2002, Pan et al. 2002). In order to achieve this aim, our critical survey of communication practices and principles includes a number of case-based illustrations drawn from some of the newer multicultural contexts. A useful starting point for this process is to reconsider the story of the blind men and the elephant, which is often used to highlight the challenge of understanding a multi-faceted problem.

The blind men and the elephant: a helpful analogy?

This classical Indian story is frequently used as an analogy for the task of understanding complex and multi-faceted phenomena, such as human organisations and cultures. It concerns a group of blind men who encounter an elephant for the first time. One man grabs its tail and says, 'so an elephant is thin, like a rope'. Another man touches its hide and says, 'You are wrong, an elephant is rough and flat like a wall.' A third feels for its leg and says, 'Not at all, it is tall and round like a tree . . .', and so on. The men are unable to agree on the true nature of the elephant. Since each man is aware of only one part of the animal, they are left with different perceptions of the whole. The analogy goes some way to explaining the obstacles faced by those researching human organisations and their communication practices. However, if we reflect on the story for a moment, it is clear that one important perspective is missing. Case study 2.3 recounts another typical story of mutual misunderstanding arising from 'culture clash'. This time our task is to de-construct the barriers from both sides, in order to get a deeper understanding of the resulting interactions.

CASE STUDY 2.3

The missing tourists of Suzhou: de-constructing cultural barriers

Two English women were visiting Shanghai and decided to sign up for a guided tour around Suzhou, a neighbouring city famous for its gardens and canals. The tour was organised by a local travel agency that catered primarily for Chinese speakers. The travel agent did not speak English, but one of the English women had a basic grasp of spoken Mandarin. After an extended conversation, involving a lot of repetition, double-checking and occasional miming, the trip to Suzhou was confirmed. The travel agent was unfamiliar with

Case study 2.3 (*continued*)

catering for foreigners, but he was confident that the arrangements would work out well. The women were given train tickets from Shanghai to Suzhou and badges that included the name of the travel company. The travel agent told them that they were to be met by a guide. She would identify herself by holding up a board that listed members of the tour party. The two women carefully wrote down their full names for the travel agent, in what was (to him) an unfamiliar western alphabet. The plan was that he would fax the names to the guide in preparation for the tour.

The following day the two women arrived at Shanghai railway station. The women were not sure whether the guide was going to meet them at Shanghai or Suzhou, but since there was nobody at Shanghai who looked like a tour guide, they got on the train. On arriving at Suzhou an hour later, badges prominently displayed, they could not see anyone holding a board displaying their names. Being the only foreigners getting off the train, the two women were immediately surrounded by a crowd of local traders trying to sell maps and taxi rides. After several fruitless minutes wandering around Suzhou station forecourt, local traders in tow, they noticed a woman holding a board with some Chinese characters written on it. They approached the woman, hoping she might be able to help them. It was quickly established that she was the guide they had been looking for. The guide was rather irritated with the English women, as they were holding up the rest of the party, who had already assembled near the tour minibus.

In their defence, the English women pointed out that their names were not displayed on the board she was holding. In addition, none of the other members of the party appeared to be wearing the tour company badges, which they had assumed were some kind of back-up system. The tour guide was amazed at these comments. She pointed to her board. It contained several lines of Chinese characters, one of which included the phrase:

两个英国女士

LIANG GE YING GUO NU SHI

Figure 2.6 'Two English women'

In translation, the phrase means, 'two English women' (see Figure 2.6). As the tour guide gathered everyone into the bus, the two women shook their heads and reflected on the experience. After all, who could have possibly failed to spot something as obvious as that?

Questions

1 This story exemplifies several common communication barriers, some of which have multiple causes. Prepare a list of these barriers and the associated causes.

2 Suggest how each of the participants might have helped to overcome the barriers you have identified. Why do you think they failed to take the relevant actions?

3 Cross-cultural communication issues are often presented from a predominantly 'Western' viewpoint. Why is it important to address cultural difference from multiple perspectives? How might this case be re-drafted to give equal emphasis to non-Western perspectives?

Source: Co-authored with Tina Fawcett.

A Linguistic barrier

Communicative problems may be a result of different social or cultural roles. For example, Deborah Tannen (1991) describes the difficulty of understanding and communication between men and women, but as a linguist she looks at language. In this short section, we will focus on language as a barrier.

The most obvious linguistic barrier to communication is individuals having different first languages so that they cannot understand each other. Clearly, if an organisation employs speakers who have Swedish as a first language, but all communication is given in French, then there is an obvious problem. With changes in global higher education over the last ten years or so, English is increasingly the main language in many educational settings, acting as an international language between speakers. In the business world, 80% or more of the daily English business communication in the world takes place in non-native English (Kankaanranta 2008). However, in an environment where we constantly have to shuttle between different varieties of English, we will have different levels of proficiency and hence communication will become ever more complex (Canagarajah 2006). If individuals share the same language, be it as a first, second or even third language, what barriers to communication can there be? How can misunderstandings take place?

The first breakdown in communication may occur because of the lack of a shared knowledge or understanding. For example:

Peter: Will you let HR know there is a problem?

Khalid: HR? A problem?

Peter: Yes, HR – Human Resources – that there is a problem

Khalid: Oh right, Human Resources, but I didn't realise there was a problem . . .

In this example, Peter assumed Khalid shared the same knowledge of what HR stands for, but Khalid did not know. In addition, Khalid did not understand that there was a problem, because in his context there was not a problem, so there was no reason to contact HR. Communication often suffers because individuals make assumptions about what is shared knowledge or understanding.

A second barrier to communication is called the Illocutionary force of the utterance, which was first introduced by a North American philosopher of language, John Austin (1975). The illocutionary force of an utterance is what an individual means when they say an expression. As individuals, we don't always say what we mean. For example, you might say *It's cold in here*, when really you mean *Can you close the window please?* When you say *How are you?* to a co-worker, you as the sender of the message don't expect a fifteen-minute discourse on how ill the receiver has been feeling. This may be quite common in discourse between first and second language speakers of a language who do not necessarily know the 'internal' understanding of a language. Can you think of any other examples?

There are different strategies that can be used to make communication clear and help resolve the issue. These may include repeating a message or rephrasing the message to make it clearer. Another option is to ask 'check questions' at the end of a message, such as *Is that ok?* or *Did you get that?* In communication, where the language of communication is not the sender's and receiver's first language, research has suggested that individuals tend to maximise the simplicity of their expressions because their command of the language of communication is far from perfect (Mauranen 2006). The next section will look more closely at ways of overcoming barriers to communication.

2.6 Overcoming the barriers

Having reviewed some of the main barriers to communication, it is time to develop some constructive proposals for overcoming them. In doing so, we necessarily move into a more practical and instrumental way of thinking. Throughout the book, the emphasis is on active questioning, rather than learning pre-packaged solutions. However, it is possible to outline our approach in very broad terms. This can be summarised as three connected activities: taking the receiver more seriously; thinking more clearly about the message; and delivering the message skilfully. The following paragraphs introduce these activities at a generic level. They will be elaborated in later chapters, when we take a more detailed look at different aspects of communication, and their application in specific channels.

Taking the receiver more seriously

There are a number of things that the sender can do to minimise the risk of communication failure. Firstly, the sender can take responsibility for ensuring that messages are delivered, rather than losing interest at the point at which they are 'sent'. As this chapter has indicated, the outcome of any communication is ultimately dependent on the receiver. Therefore, when framing any message, it is important to consider the receiver's pre-existing attitude, expectation and degree of involvement. In some cases, this could involve some background research. For example, it may be necessary to discover what the receiver already knows about the content of a message, how they feel about the topic (for example, is it likely to interest, frighten, annoy or bore them?), and their perceptions of the sender – that is, does the organisation, or its representatives, have sufficient credibility to convey or to reinforce the message? Table 2.4 illustrates the challenge of understanding a receiver's needs. Read through the remarks made and try to suggest the likely reason for communication failure and how it might have been avoided, bearing in mind that the reasons for non-communication are often more complex than they might at first appear.

Thinking more clearly about the message

Young children have a refreshingly honest tendency to express the first thing that comes into their minds. For example, a child travelling on a bus has few inhibitions when confronted

Table 2.4 Exploring communication barriers: interpreting the receiver

Receiver	Surface evidence (a sample statement)
Information services manager, US-owned software company	'Believe me, Jack, that young woman from the Hamburg office just has no idea. I've been in the computer software industry 25 years and I've never heard such garbage . . . '
Foreign aid-agency worker in a post-conflict country	'You know, I'm sure he said first right and then take the second turning on the left after the road junction, then left at the third round about . . . but we seem to have ended up on a construction site!'
Investment analyst at an after-lunch company presentation	'Did she say sales were up by 25 per cent in the last 12 months? I thought it said 20 per cent on the projection slide. I could really do with a break; this presentation has gone on so long I've almost lost the will to live!'

by something unfamiliar, prompting questions such as, 'Mummy, why is that man wearing a funny hat?' Adults tend to take more care over their communication. For example, they may anticipate a negative reaction and adjust their message in order to avoid this outcome. As a former head teacher used to say, 'Engage brain before mouth!' A great deal of inter-personal communication, including casual everyday conversation, is spontaneous. In other words, it is not prepared in advance. This is not the case for a large part of the communication that takes place in organisations, where many messages need to be thought out carefully before being delivered. This preparation is necessary for a variety of reasons. Perhaps most commonly, it is because the message content is either complex or contentious, or because the audience is widespread and diverse. There are various useful techniques for generating and organising ideas, before attempting to communicate them. One of the simplest is to make use of diagramming techniques; for example, the use of Mind Mapping, invented by Buzan (1995). The guiding assumption is that it is often easier to express, share and structure ideas if they have been presented in a visual format (see section 3.2). For example, by using large sheets of paper or a whiteboard, a whole group of people can become involved, working through the problem together. Diagrams can also be used to work out a logical order in which to present the material to an audience, an important factor in many communication channels, including written reports and verbal presentations (see Figure 2.7).

Delivering messages skilfully

There are three general rules for effective delivery of any message, whatever media and channels are used. The first, focusing your attention on the receiver, rather than on yourself as the sender, is particularly relevant to inter-personal communication, but also has implications for other channels. The second is concerned with the way messages are coded, while the third returns us to the receiver, and the key issue of securing appropriate feedback:

● **Focusing on the receiver**: Self-consciousness is a common barrier to inter-personal communication. For example, a very nervous presenter will find it difficult to convey credibility, or to deliver a message that is both coherent and engaging. Failing to focus attention on the receiver can also contribute to the mis-interpretation of any feedback that is received (e.g. a hostile response at a press conference may be interpreted as a personal attack, and the underlying source of the hostility may be left unexplored).

● **Using multiple channels and encoding**: If the receiver is likely to find a message difficult to absorb, the likely solution involves using more than one communication channel (e.g. sending an e-mail and making a follow-up telephone call), and on encoding messages in several ways (e.g. including both text and graphics in a report). The use of multiple channels and encoding can have the effect of reinforcing a message, which is particularly important when the task involves a degree of persuasive communication (see section 5.1). This also increases the likelihood that the message will be in an appropriate format, when an organisation is engaging with diverse audiences. However, in multiplying these variables, there is also an increased scope for inconsistency between the different channels and forms of encoding (e.g. where a spokesperson's words are contradicted by a written statement). Organisations often exert tight operational controls on their communication channels in an effort to minimise this kind of problem. However, there are difficult trade-offs between the degree of control exercised and the organisation's ability to engage more flexibly with its multiple stakeholders (see section 7.3).

● **Securing appropriate feedback:** Given the open system characteristics of human communication, it is essential to check for any responses from receivers. Feedback allows the sender to make adjustments to the content and format of messages. As noted above, it is important to assess 'negative feedback' in as objective a manner as possible; for example, by taking into consideration the context in which feedback is given. However, it is generally difficult for individuals and organisations to avoid taking criticism personally.

Using spider diagrams

Simple sketch (or 'spider') diagrams can help in various communication tasks, from note-taking to the analysis and presentation of a complex problem. Our minds appear to work by association, and the diagram provides a visual link between different words and ideas. Firstly, to generate ideas: instead of simply listing points down a page, write your main subject word in the centre of a blank sheet of paper. Begin to draw a series of lines from it, labelled with linked ideas. The simple example in Figure 2.7 is based on the topic 'Holidays':

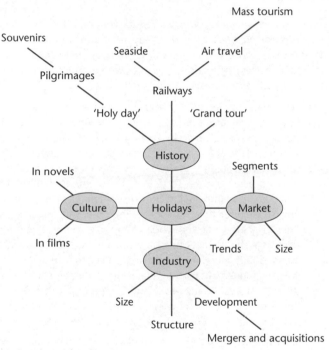

Figure 2.7 A simple spider diagram

   Now, to structure those ideas into a report or presentation, consider the logical links between them. The material can be organised in various ways, including: importance, urgency, simple to complex, and chronological order. This is always a matter of judgment, based on the material you need to communicate and the needs of your audience. As a practice exercise, imagine that you have been asked to give a talk, with five minutes' notice, on a topic about which you know virtually nothing. Experiment with diagramming to generate related ideas on the topic, and use a second diagram to order these ideas. If possible, deliver a talk based on what you have prepared. Did the diagrams help in this task? Were you surprised at how much was stored away in your mind?

Even with thorough preparation, there are bound to be some communication failures. However, it is possible to learn from the experience and seek to avoid making a similar mistake in future. Poor communication practices are difficult to rectify, whether they occur at the individual or the organisational level. The most effective communication practitioners, like those in other fields, are never satisfied with their most recent effort. Rather, they strive for *kai-zen*, or continuous improvement. Given a reasonable level of self-confidence, self-awareness and determination, it is possible to make use of constructive criticism and 'un-learn' past practices. Face-to-face 2 illustrates the issues that arise when differences in communication practices and preferences are not discussed, thus preventing self-awareness and mutual understanding from developing.

FACE-TO-FACE 2

'What planet are you from?'

Consider a situation when you have had to work on a task or project with another person that you did not previously know. What difficulties did you face, if any? What, in particular, were the barriers to communication? Now read the following extract from these two students' learning journals and assess whether there are any similarities or differences compared to your experiences.

Alisha: 'This week our lecturer gave us the brief for our next project and told us that we have to complete it in pairs. Cool, I thought, I'll work with Stan again as he's a good friend and I've worked well with him before. The problem is that this time the lecturer has selected the pairs that will work together so that we get to work with people we wouldn't otherwise. I've been paired up with this guy called Ji Chen who I'd never spoken to before. He seems friendly enough but he doesn't say much and it seems like I'm the one coming up with all the ideas. I hope his written English is better than his spoken English because we've got to write a report and I'm not going to do the whole thing! We've met a few times already because he thinks we should meet twice a week and he's always waiting for me, looking a bit stressed, but then he expects me to lead the meeting. He keeps suggesting that we go for lunch but I've already explained that it's Ramadan and I don't eat during the day, at least I think I told him . . . Then the other day he announces he's going home for the break and will miss the first week of term, so he'll be away right up until the deadline. Everyone knows that's the busiest time on a project!'

Ji Chen: 'This term we are working on a project in pairs with a person we do not already know. I thought this would be a good experience because when I study and socialise with friends we tend not to speak in English, so we're not getting as much practice as I'd hoped. I've been put with quite a young student called Alisha. She seems nice but she is very talkative and I find it difficult to follow when she speaks very quickly, with lots of slang, and I feel rude if I try to interrupt her. I suggested that we meet regularly because I don't like rushing close to a deadline and I am going home for a family wedding over the break. The problem is she is always late for our meetings and doesn't apologise. I think maybe it's a cultural thing but if we agree that we will meet at 10am how do I know what time she means? Then when we meet she just wants to talk and I think we need to get our ideas down on paper! I think it would be good if we got to know each other better so I suggested that we went to eat lunch together but she says that she doesn't eat or drink anything until she gets home. I'm not sure why.'

Face-to-face 2 (*continued*)

Questions

1 What seem to be the barriers to communication for these two students?

2 Drawing on ideas from Chapter 2, and your own experience, what do you suggest that they do to resolve these issues?

3 What are the similarities and differences between this case and your own experience?

Summary

- Communication failures are endemic, often resulting in significant costs and harm to the organisation and its stakeholders.
- It is important to understand the underlying causes of communication failures, which may involve a range of factors: physiological, psychological, cultural, political, economic, technological and physical.
- Communicators need a basic understanding of physiological processes including differences in alertness, selective attention, powers of perception and memory, and their potential impact on communication.
- It is also important to consider social and cultural barriers, including a tendency towards excessive conformity in social groups ('groupthink'), moral silence, and the complex issues arising from cultural diversity.
- While it is dangerous to rely on pre-packaged 'solutions', there are a number of simple techniques, such as diagramming, that can help people to overcome particular communication barriers.
- In more general terms, barriers can be overcome by taking the receiver more seriously, and by thinking more clearly about the content, format and delivery of messages, including the use of multiple channels and forms of encoding.

Key terms

Physiological and neurological barriers 29

Iceberg Metaphor 40

Multi-cultural organisations 44

PRACTICAL EXERCISES

2.1 The art of listening

Writing in the *Harvard Business Review* back in 1952, the American management writer F.J. Roethlisberger identified listening as a key factor in effective inter-personal communication:

'The biggest block to personal communication is man's inability to listen *intelligently*, *understandingly* and *skilfully* to another person.' (emphasis added)

(a) Do you agree with Roethlisberger's assessment? Give examples to support your argument.

(b) Roethlisberger refers to 'skilful' listening. What do you consider to be the main skills of a good 'listener'? Draw up a list and compare yours with those prepared by colleagues.

(c) How is the 'art' of listening affected by factors such as cultural difference and technological innovation? Give examples to illustrate these influences.

(d) Assess your own capabilities as a listener, by reflecting on recent occasions when you have been in this role. Compare your own assessment to that of a friend or close colleague. How well do they match?

2.2 Avoiding the question: deliberate communication barriers

In some situations, receivers may construct their own, deliberate barriers to communication. For example, in a broadcast interview, the tactic of pretending not to hear or to misunderstand the sender is often used as a defensive shield against unwelcome questions. Professional politicians and corporate spokespersons may make more or less 'artful' attempts at avoiding the questions that are being posed. Sophisticated media training, often provided by former journalists, helps them to replace a meaningful answer to the interviewer's question with their own pre-prepared statement, an essentially meaningless remark, or a carefully-worded 'sound bite', designed to catch the attention of other media organisations. These 'pseudo-answers' can sound very convincing. For this reason, both interviewers and audiences need to be alert if they are to identify examples of deliberate non-communication. The exercise is designed to improve your skills in detecting these behaviours.

(a) Make a recording of an interview on radio and/or television. Replay it several times, so that you are familiar with the exchanges. (Note: If possible, obtain a written transcript of the programme; these are sometimes available from the broadcaster's website.)

(b) Try to identify examples where the interviewee's response ignores the question, answers a different question, or fails to give a meaningful reply.

(c) What tactics does the interviewer use in order to obtain answers to the original questions posed? How successful are these tactics?

(d) Can you think of any other situations where people put up deliberate barriers to communication? How are these barriers challenged?

CASE STUDY 2.4

Translating the Japanese manufacturing model in Thailand

This case study is based on a larger research project, which investigated the ways that multinational companies attempt to transfer their domestic working practices to foreign subsidiaries (Sedgwick 1999, 2000). The extract focuses on Japanese automobile and consumer electronics manufacturing plants in Thailand and assesses their efforts to introduce concepts such as quality circles, job rotation and on-the-job training.

The Japanese manufacturing model
Organisational style in Japanese manufacturing stresses task flexibility and dependency between organisational segments of the manufacturing process. The system is based on

Case study 2.4 (*continued*)

strong information flows throughout the organisational hierarchy generated by a workforce capable of communicating efficiently and accurately. Ideally the system devolves authority – over a limited sphere of activities – down to lower levels than would be the case in a traditional 'Fordist' model associated with Western manufacturing systems. Thus workers, who are generally highly trained both at school and at the company itself, appear to have a high degree of autonomy over their specific tasks while at the same time pushing a great deal of information about those tasks into the system. [Note: 'Fordist' refers to a highly rationalised approach to mass-production, based on assembly lines, that was first pioneered by the Ford Motor Company and similar organisations, in the early 20th century.]

The Japanese manufacturing model draws on many years of hands-on experience and long-term knowledge building. In addition, many of its practices have been adopted by manufacturers across the world. The broad acknowledgement of the strengths of the Japanese model has reinforced the confidence of Japanese managers, especially at firms with strong manufacturing traditions, such as those reported in this case. This process has also been encouraged by the Japanese media, where a vast array of publications target an avid audience of business managers and engineers. As a consequence, Japanese managers carry a fairly stable model of management to their assignments overseas. They also have an understandable expectation that this home-grown, and internationally-praised, model should be perpetuated in their companies' foreign subsidiaries. So, how successful are Japanese multinationals in transferring this model to Japanese subsidiaries in Thailand?

Life on the shop floor

Industrial managers do not spend any significant amount of time pondering either the contents or boundaries of models; they are relevant to the extent that they provide guidelines for action. Let us have a look then at some specific activities associated with Japanese management. The most convenient place to find readily observable action is on the shop floor itself. In industrial production, 'quality control' (QC) has a wide breadth of potential meanings, but the activity most closely tied with quality control in Japan is **QC circles**. These are small group activities in which, typically, assembly line workers share ideas about how to solve minor problems on their lines. Ideas are tested by gathering data from the line that can be analysed using simple statistical measures. 'Circles' are based on the intuitive logic that a worker who is thinking, while he is doing, can make valuable suggestions regarding how work can be conducted more productively. As such, QC circles constitute perhaps the best-known application of non-Fordist manufacturing concepts. In the process of participating in circles, workers are assumed to become more interested in their jobs, more engaged with their colleagues, and more highly committed to the company.

While there are of course variations in Japan, QC circles tend to meet regularly once or twice a week near the shop floor, after work, for 30–40 minutes. Workers are not paid for their participation. By contrast, in Thai plants, QC circles were conducted in overtime pay conditions. In many plants they were dropped altogether, or were never present, because of heavy production deadlines. In all plants with active QC circles comparatively rudimentary analytical tools were utilised to identify the sources of production difficulties. Through job rotation, a typical worker at a large firm, who is likely to spend an entire working career in that firm, will change tasks and learn new skills. Over the course of a career this broad, hands-on knowledge of the factory should generate more competent managers, as workers rise through the ranks. Job rotation and on-the-job training (OJT) combine to form a system in which workers in Japan are given early responsibility for learning new tasks on a functioning line – where mistakes immediately affect output – with guidance from more

Case study 2.4 (*continued*)

experienced co-workers. Awareness of the effect on all line members of a worker's failure to quickly learn new tasks is deliberately used to motivate new line members. By contrast, in Thailand, the researcher observed very few cases of job rotation among workers in the factories studied. Thai workers were reluctant to change tasks. They interpreted such changes as an indication that they were judged incompetent in their current jobs. In addition, they did not want to separate themselves from the social relationships they had established with their co-workers.

Japanese managers were satisfied with this arrangement as it generated stability on the production line and did not require that they retrain workers for new tasks. Meanwhile, the calculation by Japanese managers on how intensively to rotate Thai engineers was based essentially on whether it was best to spread out limited engineering manpower by frequent rotation or keep good engineers focused on tasks they could manage consistently. The latter option was viewed as safer, and prevailed overwhelmingly. On-the-job training predominated in Thai factories. However, this was explained in interviews with Japanese managers as a response to high demand for output, as opposed to the 'best choice' for training as it would likely be articulated in Japan. The managers also took more time in moving new workers onto production lines, so that mistakes could be more tightly controlled. They felt that Thai workers had plenty of potential but were inexperienced and poorly trained when they were first employed. On-the-job training was therefore supplemented by limited classroom work, covering assembly methods.

In the automobile plant, classes were conducted by Japanese foremen flown in from Japan with a Thai manager acting as translator; the written materials in the classroom were in Japanese or English and the whole experience appeared frustrating for all involved. In the consumer electronics plant, manuals had been translated into Thai, and most of the training was conducted by Thai engineers. However, observations of the training sessions suggested that the tutors were insecure in their knowledge of Japanese methods.

Muda-dori (time and resource management) is highly valued among Japanese manufacturers as a general paradigm under which waste, defined both in physical terms and in terms of time, is cut out of the production process. It includes **just-in-time** (JIT) delivery of parts by both external and in-house suppliers. In Thailand, plant lay-out reflected the JIT scheme. For example, every tool, machine, and supply bin was positioned in a designated spot so it could be used most efficiently in the production process. However, more complex measures, such as making additional calculations to identify waste on production lines – a common QC circle activity in Japan – were avoided. Instead, waste reduction on the lines in Thailand was the responsibility of production engineers, as in traditional Western systems. The notion of earlier segments of the production line creating products 'just-in-time' for their 'customers' further along in the production process was poorly developed. Just-in-time delivery by outside suppliers, even Japanese-owned suppliers, was not attempted. Indeed, Japanese managers joked among themselves that they knew of one Japanese automobile assembler that had a year's worth of supplies stockpiled on its huge lot.

Translating working practices – just a matter of time?

The research suggests that Japanese managers in Thailand either chose, or were forced, to limit the use of Japanese shop floor practices. This may, in part, be due to the fact that the plants were start-ups, in operation for around five years, with a largely inexperienced labour force. Many of the Japanese managers in these plants said that they fully expected shop floor and production systems to match those in place at 'sister plants' in Japan within 10 to 15 years. This was not the case, however, in another Japanese subsidiary, which had

Case study 2.4 (*continued*)

manufactured motor vehicles in Thailand for over 30 years. Whereas the average age of workers in the start-ups was 24 years, most workers in the older plant had 'grown up with the company'. They had joined young and stayed – the average age was now 37 years. The president of this company told the researcher that, try as he had, he simply could not get these production systems in place in Thailand to any degree that approached their level of use in Japan.

Since no product may be released from the factory at below-standard quality, intense production pressures, combined with human and physical resources on the ground, have produced a set of manufacturing methods in Thai subsidiaries very much at odds with the Japanese ideal. Production systems in Thailand are managed from above, with decisions controlled tightly by a centralised cadre of managers and engineers oriented to a top-down flow of information. From the evidence of this study, it appears that large-scale Japanese manufacturing multinationals in Thailand have reproduced those traditional 'Western' practices that they learned to avoid at home.

Note: gender difference in the case study firms
The case study does not address gender issues specifically. However, over 98 per cent of the Japanese, Western, and Thai engineers in these companies were male, as were assembly line workers in motor vehicle plants. By contrast, in the consumer electronic plants, women accounted for around 45 per cent of assembly line workers. An interesting distinction between Japanese plants in Japan and the subsidiaries in Thailand was the relatively high proportion of Thai women among non-engineering, 'white collar' staff, typically in jobs involving accounting and data management. Japanese managers often commented that compared with their male counterparts, female Thai staff were highly 'reliable'.

Questions

1 Review the case and identify the main 'messages' that describe the Japanese manufacturing system.

2 List what you see as the main barriers to communicating these messages in the Japanese subsidiary plants in Thailand. Try to support your points with examples from the case material.

3 Compare your list to the types of barriers identified in the chapter, commenting on any patterns that emerge.

Source: Written by Mitchell Sedgwick.

Glossary

Physiological and neurological barriers to communication are those that result from the performance characteristics and limitations of the human body and the human mind.

'Groupthink' is a term introduced by a North American psychologist, Janis (1982), to explain an extreme type of social conformity occurring within close-knit groups.

Iceberg Metaphor highlights how the explicit and tangible aspects of culture are far fewer than that large proportion of invisible, unarticulated aspects of culture.

Multi-cultural organisations consist of people from many different national, social and economic backgrounds, who bring their multiple identities to work.

Further reading

Gross (1996) includes several chapters that offer an accessible introduction to the cognitive and social psychological aspects of communication.

Cooper and Locke (2000) is an edited text that illustrates how psychological research is applied in particular aspects of organisational life.

Janis (1982) is the classic work on 'groupthink' and Bird (2002) is an interesting analysis of 'moral silence'; Sims (1992) brings these two aspects together. There are many studies on cross-cultural barriers to communication and related issues.

Hofstede (1991) and Trompenaars (1994) reflect the dominant approach, while Tayeb (2000), Kirton and Greene (2000) and Holden (2002) are examples of more critical interpretations.

English (2001) reports another approach to breaking down barriers in an international context.

Sedgwick (1999, 2000) develops themes introduced in Case Study 2.4.

Useful websites

Here are a few websites which might be of interest to you. You might like to add some of your own too:

Geert Hofstede's website explores the impact of cultural difference on business communications. (Available at
http://www.geert-hofstede.com/)

The INCA project website provides tools to enable you to assess, develop and record your intercultural competence. (Available at
http://www.incaproject.org/).

Tony Buzan's website offers ideas for how you might use Mind Mapping® to extend and organise your thought processes. (Available at
http://www.buzanworld.com/)

References

Argyle, M. (1972) *The Psychology of Interpersonal Behaviour*, 2nd edn. Penguin, Harmondsworth.

Ashe, A. (2001) 'From Anne Ashe' in *Ahead of time: birthday letters to Mayer Hillman*. Policy Studies Institute, London (11–20).

Austin, J. (1975) *How To Do Things With Words*, 2nd edn. Oxford University Press, Oxford.

Badie, D. (2010) Groupthink, Iraq, and the War on Terror: explaining US policy shift toward Iraq. *Foreign Policy Analysis*, 6, 277–296.

Bird, F.B. (2002) The Muted Conscience: moral silence and the practice of ethics in business. Quorum, Westport, CT.

Brown, A. and Starkey, K. (1994) 'The effect of organisational culture on communication and information'. *Journal of Management Studies*, 31, 807–828.

Buzan, T. (1995) *Use Your Head*. BBC Books, London.

Canagarajah, S.A. (2006) Changing communicative needs, revised assessment objectives: testing English as an international language. *Language Assessment Quarterly*, 3 (3), 229–242.

Cohan, J.A. (2002) '"I didn't know" and "I was only doing my job": has corporate governance careened out of control? A case study of Enron's information myopia'. *Journal of Business Ethics*, 40, 3, 275–299.

Cooper, C. and Locke, E.A. (2000) *Industrial and Organizational Psychology: linking theory with practice*. Blackwell, Oxford.

DRC (2003) 'Press release: First DRC formal investigation to focus on Web access'. Disability Rights Commission, London (28th March).

English, T. (2001) 'Tension analysis in international organizations: a tool for breaking down communication barriers'. *International Journal of Organizational Analysis*, 9, 1, 58–83.

Gross, R.D. (1996) *Psychology, the Science of Mind and Behaviour*. Hodder & Stoughton, London.

Handy, C.B. (1996) *Understanding Organisations*. Penguin Books, London.

Hargie, O.D.W. (ed.) (1997) *Handbook of Communication Skills, 2nd edn. Routledge, London*.

Hargie, O., Saunders, C. and Dickson, D. (1994) *Social Skills in Interpersonal Communication*, 3rd edn. Routledge, London.

Harvey, J.B. (1988) 'The Abilene Paradox: the management of agreement'. *Organizational Dynamics*, 17, 16–34 (Summer).

Hickson, D.J. (1997) *Exploring Management across the World*. Penguin, London.

Hofstede, G. (1991) *Cultures and Organisations: software of the mind*. McGraw-Hill, Maidenhead.

Hofstede, G. (2001) *Culture's Consequences: comparing values, behaviours, institutions and organizations across nations*, 2nd edn. Sage Publications, London.

Holden, N. (2002) *Cross-cultural Management: a knowledge management perspective*. FT Prentice Hall, Harlow.

Janis, I.L. (1982) *Groupthink*. Houghton Mifflin, Boston, MA.

Kankaanranta, A. (2008) 'Business English Lingua Franca in Intercultural (Business) Communication'. *Language at Work – Bridging Theory and Practice*. Danish Society for LSP and Professional Communication, 4/Spring 2008, 22–27.

Kim, Y. (2001) 'A comparative study of the "Abilene Paradox" and "Groupthink"'. *Public Administration Quarterly*, 25, 2, 168–189.

Kirton, G. and Greene, A-M. (2000) *Dynamics of Managing Diversity: a critical approach*. Butterworth-Heinemann, Oxford.

Kroeber, A.L. and Kluckholm, C. (1952) *Culture: a critical review of concepts and definitions*. Harvard University Press, Cambridge, MA.

Luft, P. (2000) 'Communication barriers for deaf employees: needs assessment and problem-solving strategies'. *Work*, 14, 51–59.

Mauranen, A. (2006) Signalling and preventing misunderstanding in English as lingua franca communication. *International Journal of the Sociology of Language*, 177, 123–150. Special Issue, ed. by C. Meierkord.

Pan, Y., Scollon, S. and Scollon, R. (2002) *Professional Communication in International Settings*. Blackwell, Oxford.

RNIB (2002) 'Press release: RNIB debate sees web usability experts divide over "one size fits all"'. RNIB, London (8th July).

RNIB (2009). Text only websites. Available at: http://www.rnib.org.uk/professionals/webaccessibility/designbuild/text/pages/text_only_websites.aspx. Last accessed: 14.10.11

Roth, I. and Bruce, V. (1995) *Perception and Representation: current issues*, 2nd edn. Open University Press, Milton Keynes.

Sedgwick, M.W. (1999) 'Do Japanese business practices travel well? Managerial technology transfer to Thailand', in Encarnation, D.J. (ed.) *Japanese Multinationals in Asia: regional operations in comparative perspective*. Oxford University Press, New York.

Sedgwick, M.W. (2000) 'The Globalizations of Japanese managers', in Befu, H., Eades, J.S. and Gill, T. (eds) *Globalization and Social Change in Contemporary Japan*. TransPacific Press, Melbourne.

Sims, R.R. (1992) 'Linking groupthink to unethical behaviour in organizations'. *Journal of Business Ethics*, 11, 9, 651–664.

Smith, S. (1984) 'Groupthink and the hostage rescue mission'. *British Journal of Political Science*, 15, 117–123.

Tannen, D. (1991) *You Just Don't Understand: men and women in conversation*. William Morrow Paperbacks, London.

Tayeb, M. (2000) *International Business: theories, policies and practices*. FT Prentice Hall, Harlow.

Trompenaars (1994) *Riding the Waves of Culture: understanding cultural diversity in business*. Nicholas Brealey, London.

WAI (2010) *Developing a Web Accessibility Business Case for Your Organization: Overview*. Available at: http://www.w3.org/WAI/bcase/Overview. Last accessed: 14.10.11.

Yates, J. and Orlikowski, W.J. (1992) 'Genres of organizational communication: a structural approach to studying communications and media'. *Academy of Management Review*, 17, 299–326.

Chapter 3

Using words: verbal communication

Prose is words in their best order; poetry is the best words in the best order.

Samuel Taylor Coleridge, poet

Learning outcomes

By the end of this chapter you should be able to:

- appreciate the importance of written and spoken words in organisational communication;
- apply principles of plain English, in order to produce clear and concise language;
- identify the most common sources of misunderstanding in the use of language, and how they may be avoided;
- explore the ways that the interpretation of spoken language is influenced by paralinguistics;
- develop a more self-aware and flexible use of words, adapting styles to meet the needs of different business situations.

3.1   Introduction

This chapter looks at the ways that words are used, and frequently abused, in organisational communication. The task of constructing text-based messages, whether they are written or spoken, is often very demanding. This is particularly true for people who are attempting to make use of less familiar languages. Getting more of the right words in the right order is not sufficient to transform prose into poetry. However, it should increase the chances that important messages will be conveyed effectively. The chapter covers written and spoken English. It begins by outlining the principles of plain English, and comments on the issues of spelling, grammar and punctuation. (The companion website includes an introductory guide to English grammar and punctuation, with a number of additional practical exercises.)

There is a discussion of the difficult balance between clarity, conciseness and the desire to make language compelling and meaningful. We also consider the issue of translation between languages, noting some implications for international organisations, where English is often the adopted language. There is also a review of issues specific to spoken English and a reflection on the use of language as a matter of style. The final section addresses a related topic, the ways that language is used to construct organisational 'stories', and how they influence the communication process.

3.2 Clarity: using plain English

Plain English is a term used to describe clear, concise use of the English language that avoids unnecessary jargon or complication. The use of plain English is essential for effective written and spoken communication that takes place in organisations. It is often tempting to elaborate or extend the text, in order to provide additional information. For example, a researcher who is drafting a report based on the findings of a survey may have access to an enormous amount of raw data, providing the basis for many different arguments and reflections. However, the researcher's intended audience, perhaps a marketing director or small sub-committee, is more likely to want a summary document taking up no more than one page of text. The reality is that most senior managers simply do not have time to read large amounts of written material, or even to listen to extended verbal reports. Consequently, the communicator is always required to focus attention on the most important points, and to cut back any superfluous language. Applying plain English principles is good for the writer or speaker. It forces you to think more clearly about the content of the message, including the central arguments that are being developed (see Chapter 5). (There is even an environmental benefit. Imagine the paper and ink cartridges that would be saved if all of the world's written reports were five per cent shorter!) The plea for plain English is something that you are sure to hear from over-burdened managers around the world. It can be reduced to two basic rules: using fewer words; and replacing words with pictures, an under-valued technique that can provide more concise messages, without sacrificing content. In isolation, these rules may seem obvious, but applying them across a wide range of communication channels requires practice and commitment. At first, time taken to re-draft and refine text might seem wasted. However, the streamlined results are likely to repay that effort many times over. This is also true of the process of editing, pruning and fine-tuning essays, which is necessary if you are to present a strong argument within the imposed word limit.

Using fewer words

It is easy for an unnecessary word to slip into a sentence. Like any intruder, it will do its best to hide, so writers need to be vigilant. How can text be condensed without losing the essential messages? Writers often find it difficult to believe that their text is open to further editing. Consider the following extract, from an imaginary company based in the Netherlands, which demonstrates the process of achieving plainer English. While the language has been exaggerated for effect, similar cases have been reported in many 'real world' organisations (see Case study 3.1).

> ### Chief Executive's Annual Address to Shareholders: First Draft
>
> Of course, it is indeed extremely heartening and reassuring to be in a position where our current shareholders' attention can be drawn to the absence of any seriously negative repercussions affecting active corporate-wide operations. This outcome is one that has arisen as a direct consequence of a not inconsiderable diminution in the principal influential macro-economic indicators over the preceding annual financial reporting period. Moreover, during the course of the period in question, a significant enhancement in the company's overall sales turnover performance and financial profitability measures in the markets of southern continental Europe has been achieved, with a particularly significant and notable improvement in the various countries of the Iberian peninsular region, where it operates. A relatively optimistic trend extrapolation can be forecasted at this stage, suggesting a full realisation or modest improvement on prior-year forecast projections for the indigenous market in those non-alcoholic beverages destined for domestic consumption. A significant and pro-active commitment to the development of our corporate human resources is seen as a necessary and vital pre-requisite for the continued upward increase in the company's future fortunes.

This paragraph contains 180 words. The best way to develop your editing skills is through practical exercise. See how far you can shorten this word count without losing the essence. A shortened version is included below, but make your own attempt at sub-editing before reading on.

There are three main techniques for shortening an existing draft.

- First, writers can remove fillers, hedges or redundant words. For example, fillers, such as, *of course* are fine to use in conversation as they give you some extra time to think about what you want to say, but they can be omitted without affecting the message. Hedges such as *quite* or *fairly* can soften or boost what you want to say. However, they are meaningless without a reference point. What, for instance, is meant by, 'a relatively optimistic trend…'? Editors should also delete cosmetic and redundant words, such as '*pro-active* commitment …' and 'an *upward* increase …'.

- Second, the writer needs to replace any long-winded (or 'verbose') word groups with shorter noun groups. Long word groups can be a sign of insecurity on the part of the writer or speaker. People try to compensate for their lack of confidence in the message content by expressing it in grandiose terms. For example, the Chief Executive's reference to '… a not inconsiderable diminution in the principal influential economic indicators over the preceding annual financial reporting period …'. This can be replaced with a shorter noun group - 'the recession last year'.

- The third technique is to switch from passive to active voice. The original address is written entirely in the 'passive' voice. This means that it takes the form 'object–verb–subject', rather than the active form, 'subject–verb–object'. Some organisations make extensive use of the passive form. For example, it is the conventional language of most scientific reports. One of the advantages of the passive voice is its ability to suggest objectivity, by removing the author. However, it also requires additional words, is usually less interesting to read and can sound as if the author is distancing themselves from any decision. For example, 'It was decided that the deadline would be extended' (passive) rather than 'The project manager decided to extend the deadline' (active).

Here is one way of condensing the Chief Executive's statement, using the simple techniques described above. The text is reduced by more than 50 per cent to just 80 words, with no loss of meaning and with some useful details added. As a bonus, the text has a livelier and more direct tone, which is more appropriate for its intended audience.

> **Chief Executive's annual address to shareholders: edited version**
>
> I am pleased to report that the company is thriving, despite the recession last year. Sales in southern Europe are up 20 million Euros from 2007–8, with margins improving to 15 per cent. Spain and Portugal are stronger, with turnover increasing by 60 million Euros and margins of over 17 per cent. We forecast even higher 2008–9 sales, including 140 million Euros in the Dutch retail market. We believe that investing in people will help us to improve our performance.

Using 'pictures' if possible

There is a popular saying that 'A picture paints a thousand words'. This is true of many organisational messages, where it is more effective to substitute images for spoken or written words. The term 'picture' can be interpreted very loosely for this purpose. For example, in a market research report, you might replace a long and difficult section of text, summarising the results of a survey, with two simple pie charts (for example, a typical extract suitable for replacement might read, 'We found that 16.5 per cent of respondents "agreed strongly" with the proposition, compared to 17.6 per cent who expressed this opinion the previous year; a reduction of 1.1 percentage points. In addition, 28.4 per cent of respondents "agreed" with the proposition, in contrast to a figure of 32.6 per cent the previous year; a reduction of 4.2 percentage points. The figure for the respondents who were "undecided" was 32.8 per cent, representing an increase of 3.6 percentage points from the previous year …'). Similarly, a long written description of how to get to a particular location can be replaced by a well-drawn route map. Chapter 4 considers how various types of manufactured image, and other non-verbal codes, can be used alongside written communication to make our messages clearer and more effective.

Times New Roman 18pt	Tahoma 18pt
Book Antiqua bold 18pt	**Helvetica bold 18pt**
Monotype corsiva 18pt	Arial Narrow 18pt

Continuous text is often printed using fonts like Times New Roman that have *serifs* (i.e. small projections or curls) at the end of each stroke; *sans serif* fonts, such as Tahoma, are more commonly used for titles and headings.

Figure 3.1 Selecting a suitable font

Case study 3.1 reviews the activities of an organisation called the Plain English Campaign, which has achieved some notable victories in its efforts to promote principles of the kind outlined in this section.

CASE STUDY 3.1

The Plain English Campaign

'We are an independent organisation fighting for crystal-clear language and against jargon, gobbledygook and other confusing language.'

The Plain English Campaign (PEC) is a self-funding organisation, which promotes the principles of plain English from offices at New Mills in the English Peak District. It was founded in 1979 by a social rights campaigner called Chrissie Maher. Her campaigning activities were first prompted by the deaths of two elderly women, who had been unable to understand the text of an application form that would have provided them with housing benefit. Today, PEC has over 12,000 members in 80 countries, who can access its services by e-mail, telephone and via its website. PEC defines plain English on the basis of its effectiveness in communication:

'Plain English is something that the intended audience can read, understand and act upon the first time they read it. Plain English takes into account design and layout as well as language.'

Activities and resources

PEC is financed through its commercial services, which include training courses, editorial work, books, magazines and corporate memberships. The organisation also provides a number of free guides, including 'How to write in Plain English', which can be obtained via the website. PEC is probably best known for its annual 'Golden Bull' award for particularly bad examples of written English. The awards achieve a good deal of media coverage, and the offending organisations are usually required to explain the reasons for their poor writing practice. For example, one of the 2011 awards went to Flybe for the following extract:

'I believe that what has not been explained to you is that it is not a £4.50 card charge, in the process of booking a flight, you will have a booking fee which is for a Credit Card (return journey), booking fee £4.50 and Credit Card supplement £1.00, for a (one way) booking fee £5.50 and credit card charge £1.00.

Concerning a Debit Card (return flight) booking fee £4.50 and there is no additional fee for a Debit Card. for a (one way) booking fee £5.50 with no additional Debit Card charge. If you which any more details about our charges, you can call our call centre on 0871 700 2000 / 01392 268500 (from outside the UK) (calls cost 10p per minute; calls from mobiles and some networks may be higher) and one of our agent will be happy to assist you.

Regards

Flybe' (PEC, 2012)

The 'Crystal Mark'

In 1990, PEC introduced the Crystal Mark as a seal of approval for organisations that would encourage organisations to communicate more clearly with the public. The Crystal Mark has become well established in the UK and is also used in some other English-speaking countries, including the United States, Australia and South Africa. Among PEC's criteria for securing the Crystal Mark are: an average sentence length of about 15 to 20 words; 'active' rather than 'passive' verbs; everyday English; use of 'we' and 'you' rather than 'the insured' or 'the applicant'; conciseness; clear, helpful and consistent headings; appropriate type size; and a clear typeface. Documents that meet the required standards can be identified with the Crystal Mark symbol, subject

Case study 3.1 (*continued*)

to verification by PEC. The organisation has also launched an Internet Crystal Mark, which applies similar principles to website design. Public, private and voluntary sector organisations are becoming increasingly aware of the importance of plain English, both for the purposes of more effective communication and as a defence against legal action. For example, the UK's Unfair Terms in Consumer Contracts Regulations 1999 state that all consumer contracts must be drafted 'in plain and intelligible language.' Unclear or ambiguous contract terms can be challenged in court, prompting warnings from the Office of Fair Trading. Similar legislation operates in other European Union countries.

Questions

1 Why do you think organisations continue to generate poorly-worded documents, despite the efforts of campaigners such as PEC?

2 Review the PEC website, including the examples of bad practice, and the 'translations' into plain English. Try to find three additional examples, from corporate websites, and produce your own translations, using the guidance provided.

3 What do you see as the additional challenges, if any, when drafting plain English text for use:

   a. in HTML, i.e. web format (e.g. a corporate intranet)?

   b. in cross-cultural settings (e.g. the Olympic Games)?

   c. to promote an artistic event (e.g. a theatre or gallery)?

   d. in an oral presentation (e.g. a politician's conference speech)?

Source: Plain English Campaign (PEC 2012); case prepared by the authors, with acknowledgements.

3.3 Style, grammar, presentation

Organisations often use different types of communication for different purposes. For example, e-mail may commonly be used for communication among employees, but official communication may need to take the form of a printed letter. The style of these written forms of communication will vary. Among colleagues it may be fine to send an e-mail which is written informally, with abbreviations and emoticons (e.g. ☺); however, in communicating to external organisations a more formal style may be required. In some organisations, short e-mail messages are routinely written in an informal style, with many grammatical errors, and presented with no punctuation and all written on the same line with no spacing. Style can also be the use of the appropriate vocabulary. The efforts it requires to achieve correct English are time-consuming and unnecessary. The implication is that errors do not matter, so long as the essential message is clear. Does it matter if little or no punctuation is used? Would it make a difference if the message was written in an informal style and was used as a legal contract?

Some grammatical errors have a very limited effect on communication. For example, a few years ago there was a vociferous campaign to change the wording used on signs above the 'express' checkouts in British supermarkets. The wording was changed from '10 items or less' to '10 items or fewer'. The protesters had argued, correctly, that the adjective 'less' referred to a single item (e.g. 'I have less mashed potato than you'), while 'fewer' referred to several separate items (e.g. 'I have fewer chips than you'). Hence, for the checkout signs, 'fewer' was the correct word to use. But was this protest worthwhile? In this instance, the meaning remained clear despite the grammatical error. However, if the wording had been changed to *'It's 10 things or less, innit'*, some people would not have understood because the wrong style had been used. Sometimes, using the wrong style, incorrect grammar or wrong presentation can result in misunderstanding, which can lead to costly and unnecessary problems in organisations. Furthermore, inaccuracies send meta messages (section 1.5), in addition to the main message that you are aiming to convey. For example, grammatical errors and omissions indicate that you, and the organisation that you represent, are careless and lack credibility and that you do not respect the recipient enough to check correspondence (Thompson 2003). Table 3.1 presents a few examples of text where grammatical errors and presentation issues can make the content ambiguous or difficult to read. Readers who are confident in this area can demonstrate their abilities by correcting these examples; additional guidance is provided in the 'Further reading' at the end of the chapter, and on the Companion Website.

Table 3.1 Style, grammar and presentation

Error	Example
A confused dependent clause	Welsh Rugby Union chiefs gave their full backing to a judge after he jailed a violent player who stamped on an opponent's head for six months.
Too many connectors and the absence of punctuation	We sell a range of products to the wholesale market because it is profitable to do so and also since there is the prospect of growth with signs of improvement in the Northern area and some opportunities in the West though we only have one sales representative located there at present whilst the warehousing issue is being resolved and we are rushed off our feet therefore I really do hope that you will be able to bear with us in the meantime because for some reason or other we seem to barely have time to take a breath.
Faulty grammar and presentation issues (punctuation)	Our company were very pleased, to have done the presentation for your office, yesterday. As you would have clearly seen the best feature, of our services are, above all their very top qualified technicians. Each one of them have been awarded, full industry certification, and commitment to the job with also an extensive two years training programmes. I hope we can therefore be looking forward, to have heard from you in due course.

3.4 Beyond plain English? Using language creatively

Languages are living phenomena, and the English language is particularly vibrant, as it is in such widespread use across the globe (Crystal 2003b). Today, approximately four times as many people are communicating in English as a second language as English as a first language, and increasingly communications in English involve no native speakers (Jenkins 2000). New words (or 'neologisms') and expressions are created all the time, while others are becoming redundant, losing their original meaning and fading away. For example, the last two decades have seen the arrival of terms such as 'collateral damage', 'global warming', 'snow-boarding', 'road rage', 'spin doctors', 'spamming', 'text messaging' and 'virtual business'. In many cases the terms are associated with technologies; consequently, they tend to fall into disuse and their original meanings are being forgotten once the technology is superseded. The sheer richness and variety of expression can be of great value to the communicator; however, it also poses major problems. As we have already noted, the essential requirement in effective communication is to generate shared meanings between 'sender' and 'receiver' (see section 1.3). The dynamic nature of language lends it additional richness, but can also be a source of confusion. **Pragmatics** refers to the study of how we use language in social situations and how our choice of certain words influences how the receiver interprets our meaning. This includes the exploration of how we know what forms of language are appropriate and acceptable (Thompson 2003). Is appropriateness and acceptability as dynamic as language itself? How do we know, for example, when we can use slang or swear words? Face-to-face 3 towards the end of the chapter explores these issues.

Metaphors, figurative expressions and idiom

Metaphors are words that are used in a creative rather than a literal way. They are often used as part of a figurative (or descriptive) expression. For example, someone who is busy at work might be described using the expression, 'having a mountain to climb'. Metaphors are also used to make abstract ideas more concrete. In a speech given in 1947, the British statesman, Winston Churchill, described the post-1945 division of Europe as 'an iron curtain' descending across Europe 'from Stettin in the Baltic to Trieste in the Adriatic'; his expression passed into history with the symbolic demolition of the Berlin Wall in 1989. Churchill suffered from occasional bouts of depression and created another evocative image, 'black dog', to describe the real physical threat posed by his otherwise intangible illness (Jenkins 2001: 466, 810, 819). Metaphors are often found in the language of organisations. For example, the 'glass ceiling' is a vivid metaphor that originated in North America, where most of the large corporations are housed in 20- or 30-storey skyscrapers. The top floors of these buildings are commonly reserved for the spacious offices of the chief executive and other senior staff. Hence, 'the glass ceiling' captures the idea that women, in particular, face an unyielding but invisible barrier, blocking their promotion from middle management positions. However, it is important to balance the use of these expressions against the needs of the audience. For example, imagine the challenge if you had to explain the concept of the glass ceiling to an audience that had no prior experience of skyscrapers. Can you suggest any alternative metaphors that would convey a similar meaning in a world of single-storey buildings?

You can see how metaphors of the kind we have discussed can be used to give your messages greater impact. However, they are also a potential source of confusion if audiences are unfamiliar with the resulting figurative expression. **Idiom** refers to distinctive ways in which ideas are expressed in a particular language. The English language, which has spread to many different parts of the world, now includes a rich variety of local idioms. The expressions that people use and (more importantly) those that they understand, depend largely on where they acquired the language in question. For example, the meaning of a phrase such as 'their comments were met by a stony silence', or 'they had a frosty reception' will be self-evident to people who learnt to speak English in the United Kingdom, but may be unfamiliar to people who learnt it elsewhere. Similarly, the expression, 'I am another one' makes perfect sense to a Ugandan English speaker but probably means very little to English speakers from elsewhere. The expression is used by a person who has done something interesting or unusual; it implies that there is another part to this person's life, previously unknown to others (Mushinga 2003). Indian English has produced many wonderful visual expressions, which may also sound unfamiliar to users of English in other parts of the world:

Another characteristic of Indian English is the literal translation of idiom, echoing the earlier medieval tradition of translation from French into English of phrases like 'a marriage of convenience' and 'it goes without saying'. Today, there are several such Indian English translations that have become part of a shared vocabulary: 'may the fire ovens consume you', 'a crocodile in a loin cloth', and comparisons like 'as good as kitchen ashes', 'as helpless as a calf', and 'as lean as an areca-nut tree'. Abuse in Indian English is a particularly rich source of idiomatic translation. From masters to servants: 'you donkey's husband'. From parents to children: 'Why did I rear a serpent with the milk of my breast?'

(McCrum et al. 1992: 362)

Sometimes idiomatic language becomes more widely adopted. For example, the imagery of gold has long been used metaphorically to describe how people are paid. This has given rise to several expressions that are now widely used in international business English. For example: encouraging people to join a company ('golden handshakes'); allowing them to leave a troubled company painlessly ('golden parachutes'); or using financial inducements to ensure that they conform and remain with the organisation ('golden handcuffs', 'golden collars' and 'gilded cages').

Before leaving metaphor and figurative language, it is worth noting the powerful, sometimes amusing and often persuasive effects that you can achieve by adapting or embellishing an existing expression. For example, the British politician, Dennis Healey, was famous for the way he used language to attack his opponents; he once compared another politician's skills in political debate to being 'savaged by a dead sheep'. If this kind of language game is to be effective, it is essential that it makes sense to the intended audience. Take, for example, the idiomatic expression 'Pigs might fly', which the British use to refer to something that is not likely to happen or to be practical. Another British politician, Ken Clarke, once elaborated on this phrase in a speech attacking the opposition party's policies. He suggested that, 'It is not just a matter of pigs flying. It is a whole farmyard on a mission deep into space.' Clarke's remark was very effective when it was delivered to a British parliamentary audience and reported in the domestic media. However, the same words would be completely ineffective if used on an audience that was unfamiliar with the original idiom.

Clichés and empty language

Cliché refers to words and expressions that have become so over-used that they lose their original meaning. Empty language consists of words, often including clichés, which are used purely for effect. The business community is particularly prone to adopting and then over-using fashionable terms, which are often slipped into a sentence for cosmetic effect rather than to convey anything meaningful. For example, 'empowering', 'going forward' and 'synergies' are popular terms, but they have become ill-defined and vacuous due to over-use. Irritating over-use of such terminology has resulted in the invention of 'buzzword' (or, less politely, 'bullshit bingo'), a game played by employees who avoid boredom in meetings by trying to collect a certain number (or 'full house') of these clichés. One of the symptoms of empty and clichéd language is that unrelated expressions are sometimes combined to create bizarre mixed metaphors. For example, a politician once attempted to highlight the greed of company directors with two idiomatic phrases (i.e. 'having a snout in the trough' and 'riding on the gravy train'). However, he inadvertently combined them, creating the entirely meaningless phrase, 'having their snouts in the gravy train'.

Euphemism – the deliberate disguise of meaning

A **euphemism** is an innocuous word or phrase that is used to disguise or reduce the impact of an unpleasant reality. Hence, instead of saying that people have died, people may refer to them as having 'left us' or 'passed away'. Similarly, when governments drop bombs on cities, resulting in the death of civilians, official statements contain euphemistic phrases such as 'forces engaged in a number of surgical strikes against enemy targets', acknowledging the killing of non-combatants and of their own forces with military terminology such as 'collateral damage' and 'friendly fire'. Euphemisms are a common feature in all forms of persuasive communication (see Chapter 5). However, if the primary objective is clear expression, they are best avoided.

Jargon and specialist terminology

Jargon refers to distinctive vocabulary or specialist terminology that is used by specialist groups, but which may be unfamiliar to wider audiences. All kinds of groups, from trainspotters and salsa dancers to economists and brain surgeons, tend to develop their own jargon. Jargon can act as a useful shorthand for terms the group uses regularly; however, it can also become a serious obstacle to communication with non-specialists. Because the words are either unintelligible, unfamiliar, or difficult, people tend to lose interest in the written or spoken message. This distancing can also lead to some hostility between groups. For example, the former British Prime Minister, Margaret Thatcher's low opinion of the economics profession was once revealed in the comment that, 'you and I come by road or rail, but economists travel on *infrastructure*' (Howard 1988: 9 – emphasis added). Even if the audience remains engaged, its attention will be distracted, as people attempt to unscramble the meaning of the jargon. The lesson for communicators is to assess their audience before making use of any kind of specialist language. In the same way, unexplained abbreviations and acronyms create barriers to those less familiar with a topic. If your audience is likely to be unfamiliar with particular words or abbreviations, be sure to provide a clear explanation (e.g. by including a glossary in a report), or use language that non-specialists can understand.

Each of these elements of the living language, from figurative expressions to technical jargon, becomes more problematic when communication involves speakers who do not have English as a first language. This is due to the added complication of translating meanings between languages. Case study 3.2 deals with this practical challenge: how can we retain the original meaning of a message when it is translated into a number of different languages?

CASE STUDY 3.2

Translating questionnaires in international research

Translating questions and associated instructions into another language requires care, if your translated or target questionnaire is to be decoded and answered by respondents in the way you intended. This is extremely important for international research if the questionnaires are to have the same meaning to all respondents. For this reason, Usnier (1998) suggests that when translating the source questionnaire attention should be paid to:

- **Lexical meaning:** The precise meaning of individual words. (For example, the French word *chaud* can be translated into two concepts in English and German, meaning 'warm' and 'hot'.)

Case study 3.2 (*continued*)

- **Idiomatic meaning:** The meanings of a group of words that are natural to a native speaker and not deducible from the individual words. (For example, the English expression for informal communication, 'grapevine', has a similar idiomatic meaning to the French expression 'téléphone arabe', which translates literally as 'Arabic telephone'.)

- **Grammar:** The correct use of language, including the ordering of words and phrases to create well-formed sentences. (For example, in Japanese the ordering is quite different from English or Dutch, as verbs are at the end of sentences.)

- **Experiential meaning:** The equivalence of meanings of words and sentences for people in their everyday experiences. (For example, terms that are familiar in the source questionnaire's context, such as 'dual career household', may be unfamiliar in the target questionnaire's context.)

Usnier (1998) outlines a number of techniques for translating your source questionnaire. These, along with their advantages and disadvantages, are summarised in the table below. In this table, the *source questionnaire* is the questionnaire that is to be translated, and the *target questionnaire* is the translated questionnaire. When writing your final project report, remember to include a copy of both the source and the target questionnaire as appendices. This will allow readers familiar with both languages to check that the equivalent questions in both questionnaires have the same meaning.

Table 3.2 Translation techniques for questionnaires

	Direct translation	Back-translation	Parallel translation	Mixed techniques
Approach	Source questionnaire to target questionnaire.	Source questionnaire to target questionnaire to source questionnaire; comparison of two new source questionnaires; creation of final version.	Source questionnaire to target questionnaire by two or more independent translators; comparison of two target questionnaires; creation of final version.	Back-translation by two or more independent translators; comparison of two new source questionnaires; creation of final version.
Advantages	Easy to implement, relatively inexpensive.	Likely to reveal most problems.	Leads to good wording of target questionnaire.	Ensures best match between source and target questionnaires.
Disadvantages	Can lead to many discrepancies, including those relating to meaning, between source and target questionnaire.	Requires two translators: one a native speaker of the source language, the other a native speaker of the target language.	Cannot ensure that lexical, idiomatic and experiential meanings are kept in target questionnaire.	Costly, requires two or more independent translators. Implies that the source questionnaire can also be changed.

Source: Developed from Usnier (1998)

Case study 3.2 (*continued*)

Questions

1 The case identifies four key aspects of language that need to be addressed when translating documents such as questionnaires. Identify or draft examples of text to illustrate each of these issues.

2 The case highlights a number of practical problems faced by an organisation that operates in multiple languages. Which problems do you consider the most difficult to manage?

3 Can you identify any additional challenges for the multi-lingual organisation, including universities? How might they be resolved?

Source: this case is based on an extract from Saunders *et al.* (2003: 300–1) – reproduced with permission.

3.5   Spoken English: additional communication issues

Most of the language issues discussed in previous sections can be applied equally to written and spoken English. This section introduces two additional issues that are particularly relevant when English is spoken: the importance of emphasis and its connection with paralinguistics; and the non-verbal behaviours that are associated with the process of speaking.

Inflection and emphasis

Inflection in spoken English is where the speaker changes the pitch of her voice to place emphasis on particular words. Authors may achieve a similar effect in written language by altering the typeface (e.g. using *italicised*, **bold**, UPPER CASE or <u>underlined</u> text). However, the adjustments used in spoken English may be less apparent. People who are very familiar with a particular spoken language are able to detect subtle variations in emphasis, and therefore in the meaning that the speaker is trying to convey. However, non-native speakers may miss some of these signals. The differences in meaning can be dramatic. For example, consider the simple sentence, 'We don't want your money.' How would different inflections change the message when it is spoken aloud?

(a) *We* don't want your money …

(b) We *don't* want your money …

(c) We don't *want* your money …

(d) We don't want *your* money …

(e) We don't want your *money* …

In each case, the meaning of the statement is 'qualified' by the emphasis given to a particular word. The inflection signals that the listener is to expect a pause, followed by a clause beginning, 'but …'. Thus, example (d) might continue, 'but we do want hers', while example (e) suggests, 'but we do want your support'. Watch out for this type of mis-interpretation of your intended message when you are speaking in presentations, meetings and even in one-to-one conversations.

Paralinguistics: the role of non-verbal signals

Paralanguage refers to the range of sounds and other signals that people use to surround their spoken words. This includes sounds that are similar to actual words (e.g. 'mmm', 'huh'), intakes of breath, sighs, pauses and silences. Paralanguage has a very important function in all kinds of spoken language, including speeches, oral presentations and conversations. For example, in the case of a conversation, it can be used to indicate that a person is listening, to encourage the speaker to continue, or to signal agreement. Paralanguage is one of several forms of non-verbal signalling, including eye contact, facial expression and gesture, that are used to reinforce words, and to introduce subtle differences into their meaning. These signals are also subject to cultural variations, which can on occasion lead to the mis-interpretation of oral messages. The wider role of non-verbal signals is discussed in more detail in the next chapter (see section 4.7).

Face-to-face 3 illustrates how confusion ensues when idiomatic language is used instead of plain English.

FACE-TO-FACE 3

'What are you on about?'

The following examples show how idiomatic and colloquial language are used in discussions with non-native speakers and how this can be inappropriate, inconsiderate and unsuccessful, as it means that the conversation will require rephrasing and the different meanings will need to be worked out by the speakers.

Example 1: The following extract is from an interaction between M, an American English as a native language speaker, S, a German, and H, a Chinese speaker, reported and discussed in Roberts (2005).

M:	Let's say we need decorations and we need it cleaned up. What's your bottom line?
S:	What's my what?
M:	What is the bottom line. What, what's the –
H:	bottom line, yes
M:	least you can do it for? The least it can be done for?
S:	The lowest, uh –
M:	Yeah.
S:	price? Four thousand.
M:	Four thousand.
All:	hahaha

(Roberts 2005: 151)

Example 2: The following extract is of a British journalist interviewing a Chinese lawyer about human rights issues. The journalist uses the idiomatic expression *in my book* which the lawyer does not understand. What happens is that both parties misunderstand and there is a communication breakdown.

Journalist:	… but that makes it a criminal offense, in my book!
Lawyer:	eh sorry?
Journalist:	well don't you think this is criminally wrong?
Lawyer:	eh you mean if it was (secret) – yes

(Seidlhofer, 2009)

> **Face-to-face 3 (*continued*)**
>
> **Questions**
>
> 1 What are the idiomatic expressions misunderstood by the participants?
> 2 Can you think of any colloquialisms that you use?
> 3 How could the speakers in the above conversations make the communication more cooperative or make their messages more easily understood? What would you say instead?
> 4 How do we know when it is appropriate for us to speak more formally or informally? What is the relationship between the language we choose to use and the context or audience?

3.6   Language and organisation: narrative and discourse analysis

The final section of this chapter moves from a concern with the form of the language to the 'stories' that it can convey. The interest in organisational stories, and the broader role of narrative in research, is shared by the interpretive/ethnographic and dialogic/postmodern perspectives, as discussed in the opening chapter (see section 1.6). The late twentieth century saw an increased interest in the way that language influenced organisations. Researchers in these traditions treated language as more than just a tool for achieving managerial objectives; it became a subject of study in its own right, with research focusing on the ways that language was used to create and shape the organisation, its underlying meanings, identities and practices.

> The significance of narrative data lies not just in their richness and new universal availability, but in the fact that they are the same kind of data that organizational members use to plan, enact, interpret, and evaluate their own actions and those of others.
>
> (Pentland 1999: 716)

Empirical studies of organisational narratives have made use of a variety of theoretical frameworks and qualitative research techniques (Livesey 2002a). In contrast to functional approaches to communication, which focus on abstracting general principles, this kind of research tends to concentrate on the complexity and richness that is found when language is used in particular settings. However, it can also provide insights into the ways that 'stories' are shaped and deployed in order to achieve strategic purposes (Boje et al. 1999: 354). Two recent examples from the management and business communication literature illustrate the kinds of insight that can be obtained by studying communication in this perspective. The theme of story-telling in organisations is discussed further in Case Study 3.4 and in the guide to further reading at the end of this chapter.

Battle in the boardroom (Ng and De Cock 2002)

The researchers study the hostile takeover of one of Singapore's best-known companies ('Cleo') by another long-established business ('Antony'). They make use of multiple sources, including internal company documentation, such as board minutes and draft minutes, in order to 'craft' their own account of these events. The resulting narrative reveals how a key protagonist, the chairman of the acquired company, 'Cleo', made use of language to secure overall control of the strategic agenda. For example, it shows how he exploited language to present a convincing set of causal connections (i.e. establishing a sequence of causes and effects, that board members and other stakeholders began to accept as the most likely explanation). The 'Cleo' chairman's performance was also strengthened by his ability to draw on selected Chinese cultural themes, such as personal loyalty and fraternal (i.e. brotherly) piety, in order to play the traditional role of the wise patriarch (ibid: 41). This resonated with the board members of both companies, who shared these conventions. By contrast, the chairman of 'Antony', an Indonesian, was seen as less effective in presenting his ideas. He also appeared to suffer from a preconceived view of Indonesians as 'short-term traders' (ibid: 33). The authors warn that the narrative 'should not lead us to see storytelling as automatically dissolving facts' (ibid: 42). 'Cleo's' chairman did not rely on words alone, he also surrounded himself with loyal managers and took control of information flows. However, it does indicate how this exercise of power was only possible because he had established 'discursive legitimacy' through his story-telling performances (ibid: 42).

Global warming wars (Livesey 2002b)

This paper analyses texts published by the US oil company ExxonMobil, as part of its response to the debate on climate change, following the negotiation of the Kyoto Protocol in 1997. In contrast to European oil multinationals, notably BP and Royal Dutch Shell Group, which modified their strategies in response to evidence from the climate scientists, ExxonMobil maintained an isolationist stance, shared by the US government, which downplayed the threats of global warming and maintained the primacy of fossil fuels (ibid: 125–6). The researcher analysed a series of advertorials (i.e. sponsored articles) published in The New York Times newspaper during March and April 2000. The research was conducted using two methodological approaches: rhetorical analysis, which explores how texts frame meanings, create understanding and make connections with audiences; and discourse analysis, which is concerned with the broader relationship between the texts and the sociological context in which they are employed (see section 5.3). The following extract illustrates how rhetorical analysis was used in this study:

> The texts achieve their effect by altering linguistic meanings and relationships in ways that reshape ExxonMobil's own and other actors' identities. 'Prudence' and 'responsibility' (and their implied opposites) are moral terms used in the ads rhetorically to characterize/construct the agents (scientists, economists, environmentalists, government regulators, energy suppliers and consumers), acts (government regulation, production of energy-efficient fuels), and agencies (science and technology, climate science, economics, public policy) variously interposed in the dramatic scene.
>
> (Livesey 2000b: 126)

For example, an Exxon advertorial entitled 'Do No Harm', published on 16th March 1997, begins with what looks like an early attempt to undermine scientific evidence on the potential 'harm' associated with climate change. It does this by likening what it calls 'different views of the climate change debate' to regular weather forecasts that are constantly being revised and updated. The advertorial suggests there is no proven link between the activities of the company and harm to the environment, and argues that changing current business practices would impose costs and threaten to 'harm' the economy. This careful use of language has the effect of shifting the idea of 'harm' away from the environment to the economy, at the same time presenting the corporation as the responsible (or 'prudent') actor:

> ExxonMobil's argument here produces the conclusion that the problem is not global warming, but the wrong-headed, if not arrogant, views of the climate scientists (and the misguided government representatives and public that trust them), who 'believe they can predict changes in climate decades from now.'
>
> The paragraph [in the advertorial] continues, 'Advocating "precaution," and despite scientific uncertainty, they believe actions should be taken immediately to reduce carbon dioxide emissions by mandating severe restrictions on energy use.' The ironic quotation of the word 'precaution' here signals the inversion of terms about to take place.
>
> 'Precaution,' usually associated with conservative and measured approaches, and in the climate change debate characterized by environmentalists as necessary to safeguard the 'health' of the planet, suddenly becomes hasty, if not hysterical action, and an instrument of 'harm.' Rather than precaution, the company calls for a *prudent* approach, saying: 'a prudent approach to the climate issue must recognize that there is not enough information to justify harming economies and forcing the world's population to endure unwarranted lifestyle changes by dramatically reducing the use of energy now.' (*ibid:* 128–9 – emphasis in the original).

Both of these studies take a critical approach to the ways that individuals and organisations exploit language, in order to pursue their sectional interests. Narrative studies can provide valuable insights into these processes. In particular, they can help us to grasp the complex challenges that confront organisational stakeholders, as they seek to convey their own messages in the face of the competing 'stories' of other actors. We return to this theme in Chapter 5, which tackles aspects of persuasive communication, including the use of verbal and non-verbal codes.

Summary

- In general, organisational communication is improved through the consistent use of plain and unambiguous language.
- The basic principles of plain English are: use fewer words and use pictures in place of words, where appropriate.
- Editing and summarising text is a key management skill. It involves the removal of fillers, hedges or redundant words, replacing long-winded word groups with shorter noun groups and switching from passive to active verb forms.
- Plain English means avoiding words and phrases that have lost their meaning, euphemisms that deliberately disguise meaning, and technical terminology, or 'jargon' that is not readily understood by the relevant audience.
- Correct use of style, grammar and presentation is also an important discipline that can reduce the scope for misunderstanding and increase the speed of communication.

Summary (*continued*)

- The widespread use of the English language has created a great deal of colour and variety. However, it is important to use local idiomatic expressions with a combination of sensitivity and imagination, ensuring that they are appropriate to the audience.

- In spoken English, communicators also need to be aware of the ways that emphasis on particular words and 'paralinguistics' (e.g. the use of pauses and 'ums' and 'errs') can influence the interpretation of verbal messages.

- Language is both a medium of communication and a framework for understanding human experience; techniques such as discourse analysis can be used to deconstruct narratives, revealing their constitutive role (i.e. in establishing shared meanings).

Key terms

cliché 67	inflection 70	paralanguage 71
euphemism 68	jargon 68	plain English 60
idiom 66	metaphors 66	pragmatics 66

PRACTICAL EXERCISES

3.1 Drafting simple instructions

(a) Prepare a draft set of written instructions for someone carrying out one of the following tasks for the *first* time:
  - log onto a computer, compose and send an e-mail;
  - withdraw £50 from a cash-point machine;
  - write an essay.

(b) Ask someone to test your instructions and to point out any faults or ambiguities.

(c) Re-draft the instructions to make them clearer and more concise. Use a red pen to mark the changes on the old draft, then write out your revised version on a separate sheet. Compare your final draft with the original.

3.2 Jargon-busting

(a) Prepare a list of the 'Top Ten' worst examples of jargon in one of the following fields, or in your own specialist area, presenting them in a poster format:
Accountancy, Business, Medicine, Computing, Economics, Engineering, Finance, Law, Marketing, Personnel, Purchasing, Sales.

(b) For each jargon word or expression, suggest a sensible alternative that can be understood by a non-specialist. Did you find any jargon words that do not have any 'layperson's' equivalent?

(c) Consider how the problem of jargon and other specialist terminology may be complicated by factors such as translation and cultural difference. How might you overcome these difficulties in an international organisation?

CASE STUDY 3.3

'Story-telling': researching organisational narratives

The nature of stories

Oral histories, captured in the form of myths and legends, have long been used to store the collective knowledge of tribes and nations. They allowed knowledge to be passed down between generations, before reading and writing became a widespread channel of communication. A story is often a simple tale of how a character desires something – a promotion, for example – meets a difficulty, and struggles to overcome it, using internal resources, such as persistence, luck, or outside help. Human interest arises from the ensuing struggle between a desired outcome and reality (McKee 2003). The management writer, Boje (1991: 111), has defined a story as 'an oral or written performance involving two or more people interpreting past or anticipated experience'. This definition highlights the active role of the receiver, who reads or listens to the story. Good story-tellers employ various techniques to interact with the receiver, increasing their motivation and enjoyment. For this reason, it is generally more effective for stories to be told face to face, rather than through indirect channels, such as e-mail. A 'good' story is an accessible and immersive experience that can exclude other thoughts in the mind of the receiver (Denning 2000). Stories are more vivid, engaging and entertaining than most types of organisational communication, such as formal policy documents, memos or statistical reports (Swap et al. 2001). For this reason, they can be used to communicate more memorable and persuasive messages (Morgan and Dennehy 1997). An often-overlooked characteristic of stories is that the 'truth' lies in the meaning that they convey to the receiver, rather than in the accuracy of the events that are portrayed (Gabriel 2000).

How stories are used in organisations

In some fields, like journalism, education and sales, stories have an especially significant role. However, stories are told and passed on in organisations of all kinds. People are natural story-tellers, and the stories they tell help employees to give meaning to their work. Management educators and writers also use stories, adapting old myths for inspiration or drafting case studies to communicate practical examples (Greco 1996). Most of the stories found in business settings are relatively short, taking less than five minutes to tell (Boje 1991, Swap et al. 2001), yet these short stories can still be effective. For example, they can be the turning point in a long meeting, where people have been considering large amounts of factual data and statistical charts. If someone says, 'I think that's similar to what Sally did when…', the quality of attention changes, as other members of the meeting engage with this narrative. In these situations, even if other people disagree with the point of the initial story, they are likely to respond with a story of their own (Cohen and Prusak 2001, Collinson and Mackenzie 1999, Greco 1996). Stories from respected executives have become a preferred approach in teaching leadership effectiveness in many of today's companies (Ready 2002). They can be useful in explaining how the political process works in an organisation, and to pass on tacit knowledge. Stories are used in training courses in organisations to improve the recall of the message (Snowden 2001), and as a more relaxing alternative to traditional exercises such as ice-breakers and role-plays (Parkin 1998). They can also be used to establish social norms and values in an organisation, as the following example illustrates:

> Bill Hewlett used to work for General Electric (GE) and observed that the company had lots of security systems to protect their materials and equipment. Many employees felt that this showed that GE did not trust them. Some people wanted to teach GE a lesson, so they stole from the company, despite the security systems. Later, after starting his own company, Bill

Case study 3.3 (*continued*)

Hewlett once discovered a locked store cupboard at one of his own factories. He broke it open using a bolt-cutter, and left a note saying, 'don't ever lock this door again'. As the story was repeated around the company, it had the effect of reinforcing more general levels of trust between managers and employees (cited in Dennehy 1999).

The next story also conveys organisational values, but with more threatening or negative connotations:

Ryan was a senior manager who had two fishbowls in his office. In one were goldfish, in the other, a piranha. Ryan asked each of his staff to pick a goldfish that was most like themselves (spotted, dark, etc.). Then, when Ryan was displeased with someone, he would ask the person to take his or her goldfish and feed it to the piranha (cited in Frost 2003).

Most current stories are negative or neutral about the organisation, while positive ones tend to refer to the past (Gabriel 2000). Some researchers have argued that 'good' stories, whether positive or negative, are more believable than bad ones (Taylor *et al*. 2002). The implication of this idea, that a skilled storyteller can manage the meaning of events in an organisation, is exploited in various forms of persuasive communication, from sales to public relations. However, it also suggests that less powerful actors in an organisation – as well as external stakeholders, such as community groups – can gain additional power by telling a good story well. Consider the following examples of positive and negative stories, their sources and their effects on various audiences:

UPS is an international parcels delivery company, based in the United States. There are many stories circulating within the company concerning drivers who have delivered parcels no matter what the weather. Similar messages were also presented in the company's public advertising campaigns. The stories had a strong human element. For example, in one case an eight-month pregnant manager was said to have covered for another employee in order to ensure that the deliveries were made on time (cited in Cohen and Prusak 2001).

The Union Pacific railroad company is also based in the United States. During the 1990s, various stories circulated amongst employees and customers relating to the company being unreliable. Employees had started to call it the 'Utterly Pathetic' railroad. Some stories had a dark humour, which added to their effectiveness. For example, it was said that a locomotive engineer got so fed up with the railroad's incompetence that he decided to commit suicide. He went outside, lay on the tracks – and starved to death (cited in Coutu 2003).

The implication is that, given their power and potential consequences, managers should take an interest in the kinds of stories that are being told in their organisation. They might also consider how best to influence these stories, though it is likely that heavy-handed intervention will prove counter-productive, encouraging a further outbreak of 'anti-stories'. The final story in this case was presented in a paper by the organisational researcher, Karl Weick (1996). It is based on real events, concerning 'Wildlands' (i.e. forest) fire-fighters. Read this re-interpretation of the story then answer the questions below:

Bob was a strong, experienced fire-fighter, working in the Wildlands. He had fought many different types of fire in ten years, and felt he had seen it all. One hot summer's day, he was fighting a fire with a new recruit called Jim. The two men worked hard, sweat streaming down their faces, their vision obscured by the smoke, and their mouths dry with the heat. Despite their efforts, the fire grew more intense. Jim lost his nerve, dropped his spade and backpack, and ran for safety. Bob called after him that the fire was nearly under control. A nearby tree exploded with a crash, and the wind blew flames towards Bob, nearly cutting him off. Bob turned and ran, still carrying his gear. Strong as he was, the equipment slowed

> **Case study 3.3 (*continued*)**
>
> him down in the dense undergrowth, and the fire caught up with him. He was trapped, and died of his injuries. (Adapted from Weick 1996).
>
> **Questions**
>
> 1 Reflect on your reactions to the story (for example, what pictures came into your head as you read it? Could you hear the characters talking? What feelings did you experience?). Consider what aspects of the story prompted these reactions.
> 2 What do you think is the basic message of the story?
> 3 How else could the message have been conveyed?
> 4 In what circumstances do you think that telling the story would be more suitable or effective than the other methods such as writing it in an e-mail?
> 5 Do you think that managers should be trained to tell stories? Give your reasons.
> 6 Try to identify five examples of how stories could be used effectively in the organisation that you work or study in.
>
> *Source*: Written by Ian Wycherley.

Glossary

Plain English is a term used to describe clear, concise use of the English language that avoids unnecessary jargon or complication.

Pragmatics refers to the study of how we use language in social situations and how our choice of certain words influences how the receiver interprets our meaning.

Metaphors are words that are used in a creative rather than a literal way. They are often used as part of a figurative (or descriptive) expression.

Idiom refers to distinctive ways in which ideas are expressed in a particular language.

Cliché refers to words and expressions that have become so over-used that they lose their original meaning.

euphemism A euphemism is an innocuous word or phrase that is used to disguise or reduce the impact of an unpleasant reality.

Jargon refers to distinctive vocabulary or specialist terminology that is used by specialist groups, but which may be unfamiliar to wider audiences.

Inflection in spoken English is where the speaker changes the pitch of her voice to place emphasis on particular words.

Paralanguage refers to the range of sounds and other signals that people use to surround their spoken words.

Further reading

Crystal (2003b), **McCrum et al**. (1992) and **Bryson** (1991) are informative and often entertaining tours of the English language, its history and development around the world.

Crystal (2003a) is a comprehensive reference; there are also many helpful guides to writing style, such as: **The Economist** (2001), **Urdang** (1991) and **Inman** (1994).

Lodge (1988) is a comic novel, written by a professor of English literature, which explores the communication problems between an academic and a factory manager, due to the different language that each employs.

Boje (2001) and **Gabriel** (2000) are academic overviews of current approaches to studying narratives and storytelling in organisations; **Tietze et al**. (2003) is an accessible introduction.

Denning (2000), **Swap et al**. (2001), **McKee** (2003) and **Snowden** (2001) discuss practical applications of storytelling in knowledge creation and other areas of communication.

Useful websites

Here are several websites which might be of interest to you. You might like to add some of your own:

The 'Academic writing' learning area of the LearnHigher project website provides a number of links to advice on developing your academic writing style. (Available at

http://learnhigher.ac.uk/Students/Academic-Writing.html)

The 'Report writing' learning area of the LearnHigher project website identifies resources that guide you through producing well-structured reports for a variety of audiences. (Available at

http://learnhigher.ac.uk/Students/Report-writing.html)

The Using English for Academic Purposes (UEFAP) website offers a comprehensive step-by-step guide to academic writing, including useful sections on rhetorical functions in academic writing and punctuation. (Available at

http://www.uefap.com/writing/writfram.htm)

References

Boje, D.M. (1991) 'The storytelling organization: a study of story performance in an office supply firm'. *Administrative Science Quarterly*, 36, 106–126.

Boje, D.M. (2001) *Narrative Methods for Organizational and Communication Research*. Sage, London.

Boje, D.M., Luhman, J.T. and Baack, D.E. (1999) 'Hegemonic stories and encounters between storytelling organizations'. *Journal of Management Inquiry*, 8, 340–360.

Bryson, B. (1991) *Mother Tongue*. Penguin, London.

Cohen, D. and Prusak, L. (2001) *In Good Company: how social capital makes organizations work*. Harvard Business School Press, Boston, MA.

Collinson, C. and Mackenzie, A. (1999) 'The power of story in organisations'. *Journal of Workplace Learning,* 11, 1, 38–40.

Coutu, D.L. (2003) 'Sense and reliability: a conversation with celebrated psychologist Karl E. Weick'. *Harvard Business Review*, 84–89 (April).

Crystal, D. (2003a) *The Cambridge Encyclopedia of the English Language*, 2nd edn. Cambridge University Press, Cambridge.

Crystal, D. (2003b) *English as a Global Language,* 2nd edn. Cambridge University Press, Cambridge.

Dennehy, R.F. (1999) 'The executive as storyteller'. *Management Review*, 40–43 (March).

Denning, S. (2000) *The Springboard: how storytelling ignites action in knowledge-era organizations*. Butterworth-Heinemann, Oxford.

Economist, The (2001) *The Economist Style Guide*. Profile Books, London.

Frost, P.J. (2003) *Toxic Emotions at Work*. Harvard Business School Press, Boston, MA.

Gabriel, Y. (2000) *Storytelling in Organisations: facts, fiction and fantasies*. Oxford University Press, Oxford.

Greco, J. (1996) 'Stories for executive development: an isotonic solution'. *Journal of Organisational Change Management*, 9, 5, 43–74.

Howard, P. (1988) *Winged Words*. Hamish Hamilton, London.

Inman, C. (1994) *The Financial Times Style Guide*. FT Pitman, London.

Jenkins, J. (2000) *The Phonology of English as an International Language*. Oxford University Press, Oxford.

Jenkins, R. (2001) *Churchill*. Macmillan, London.

Livesey, S.M. (2002a) 'Interpretive acts: new vistas in qualitative research in business communication. A guest editorial'. *Journal of Business Communication*, 39, 1, 6–11.

Livesey, S.M. (2002b) 'Global warming wars: rhetorical and discourse analytic approaches to ExxonMobil's corporate public relations'. *Journal of Business Communication*, 39, 1, 117–148.

Lodge, D. (1988) *Nice Work*. Penguin Books, London.

McCrum, R., Cran, W. and MacNeil, R. (1992) *The Story of English* (new and revised edn). Faber and Faber, London.

McKee, R. (2003) 'Storytelling that moves people'. *Harvard Business Review*, 51–55 (June).

Morgan, S. and Dennehy, R.F. (1997) 'The power of organizational storytelling: a management development perspective'. *Journal of Management Development*, 16, 7, 494–501.

Mushinga, E. (2003) Personal correspondence.

Ng, W. and De Cock, C. (2002) 'Battle in the boardroom: a discursive perspective'. *Journal of Management Studies*, 39, 1, 23–49.

Orwell, G. (1957) *Inside the Whale and Other Essays*. Penguin Books, London.

Parkin, M. (1998) *Tales for Trainers*. Kogan Page, London.

PEC (2012) 'About the Campaign'. Plain English Campaign, New Mills [accessed at: www.plainenglish.co.uk (26 March, 2012)].

Pentland, B.T. (1999) 'Building process theory with narrative: from description to explanation'. *Academy of Management Review*, 24, 4, 711–724.

Ready, D.A. (2002) 'How storytelling builds next-generation leaders'. *MIT Sloan Management Review*, 63–69 (Summer).

Roberts, P. (2005) Spoken English as a world language: International and intranational settings. Unpublished doctoral dissertation, University of Nottingham.

Saunders, M.N.K., Lewis, P. and Thornhill, A. (2003) *Research Methods for Business Students*, 3rd edn. FT Prentice Hall, Harlow.

Seidlhofer, B. (2009) 'Accommodation and the idiom principle in English as a Lingua Franca'. *Intercultural Pragmatics*, 6, 2, 195–215.

Snowden, D.J. (2001) 'Story telling as a strategic communication tool'. *Strategic Communication Management*, 28–31 (April/May).

Swap, W., Leonard, D. et al. (2001) 'Using mentoring and storytelling to transfer knowledge in the workplace'. *Journal of Management Information Systems*, 18, 1, 95–114.

Taylor, S.S., Fisher, D. and Dufresne, R.L. (2002) 'The aesthetics of management storytelling'. *Management Learning*, 33, 3, 313–330.

Thompson, N. (2003) *Communication and Language: a handbook of theory and practice*. Palgrave Macmillan, Basingstoke.

Tietze, S., Cohen, L. and Musson, G. (2003) *Understanding Organizations Through Language*. Sage, London.

Urdang, L. (1991) *The Oxford Thesaurus: an A-Z dictionary of synonyms*. Oxford University Press, Oxford.

Usnier, J-C. (1998) *International and Cross-cultural Management Research*. Sage, London.

Weick, K.E. (1996) 'Drop your tools: an allegory for organizational studies'. *Administrative Science Quarterly*, 41, 2, 301–313.

Chapter 4

Making pictures: non-verbal communication

'What is the use of a book', thought Alice, 'without pictures or conversations?'

Lewis Carroll, *Alice in Wonderland*

Learning outcomes

By the end of this chapter you should be able to:

- appreciate the role and importance of non-verbal communication in various aspects of organisational life;
- compare the many forms of non-verbal communication, ranging from human gestures to manufactured images;
- identify potential pitfalls associated with non-verbal codes;
- evaluate the effectiveness of financial and statistical graphics used in organisational reports;
- consider cross-cultural issues related to human gestures, body language and other communication practices;
- highlight the close connections between verbal and non-verbal forms of communication.

4.1   Introduction

Non-verbal forms of communication is a term that refers to any way in which we communicate our ideas, opinions and feelings to each other that does not involve using written or spoken words; including the use of signals, gestures and pictures. Most, though not all, involve encoding a message in some kind of visual image, hence the title of this chapter. We make use of a wide variety of non-verbal forms of communication in organisational life.

However, the 'pictures' reviewed in the following section are not limited to material artefacts, such as charts in a business report or photographs on a website. We are also concerned with the visual signals that people exchange, often unconsciously, as part of their everyday inter-personal communication: for example, the gestures and body language that re-inforce our

81

words, or express our state of mind, in meetings and presentations. Non-verbal signals can have a powerful effect. For instance, a well-designed reception area and smiling, smartly-dressed staff are likely to have a positive influence on a prospective customer, re-inforcing verbal statements about 'professionalism' and 'customer service' in a company's promotional literature. By contrast, a recruitment interview panel may be unable to avoid a negative assessment of an interviewee due to factors such as his untidy physical appearance, lack of eye contact, or what panel members perceive as a hostile facial expression. Our purpose, in drawing this wide variety of images together, is to highlight the important role of non-verbal communication in organisations, and to explore how non-verbal coding interacts with written and spoken forms. We explore the potential advantages and the most common problem areas, highlighting some of the ways that these difficulties can be avoided or overcome. Several of the themes are elaborated in later chapters, including a short section on the special problems of creating and maintaining a visual identity for your organisation, which is expanded in Chapter 10.

4.2 Using 'pictures' at work

In some situations, visual images can replace written or spoken words entirely. Their role in these cases is often to overcome context-specific barriers to communication, and the substitute images have been developed to meet the needs of the environment in which they are used. For example, traders on traditional commodities exchanges and bookmakers at racetracks overcome the twin problems of noise and distance with elaborate hand signals that instantly communicate information related to market prices. International organisations have also overcome barriers in the use of written language by replacing text with icons.

An **icon** is a simple symbolic representation of an object, which is used to communicate a message. For example, the scissors, pasting brush and printer symbols used in popular software packages direct users around the world to the routine processes of cutting, pasting and printing. Similarly, international airports and railway stations have adopted universally recognised icons on their direction signs, so that passengers can find restaurants, taxis, cash points and exits without needing to know the local language. Clear, internationally comprehensible signs are particularly important where failure to understand a message could result in an accident, for example on a motorway or a building site (Figure 4.1).

The other main function of visual images, in organisations as in other areas of life, is to reinforce written or spoken words. This reinforcement occurs in many different ways, for example:

- A skilled conference speaker uses an outstretched arms gesture to make the audience feel more directly involved in the presentation.
- A finance director giving a presentation to City analysts uses bar graphs and pie charts to display the raw data from a complex profit forecast in a clearer and more attractive way.
- A brochure designer searches photographic libraries to find a suitable image to support the central messages that appear in the text of an organisation's annual report.

Table 4.1 indicates something of the variety of forms in which people communicate without the direct use of written or spoken words. Specialist researchers in this field have introduced various terms to describe these activities. For example, the word 'kinesics' is sometimes used to refer to various forms of body language, including eye contact, facial expression, posture and gesture, while 'proxemics' refers to the role that personal distance

Figure 4.1 International signs and icons

and physical space play in communication (see section 4.8). In addition, the field of 'para-linguistics', introduced in the previous chapter, refers to the different ways that spoken language is modified by the actions that surround it, including the pace of delivery, tone of voice and use of silence (see section 3.5). However, it is important to note that any categorisation into different 'types' is necessarily artificial, since it does not reflect the 'holistic' reality of organisational communication (see section 1.6). In practice, messages are often communicated through a rich, flexible and simultaneous combination of verbal and non-verbal forms. Consider the kinds of messages that are being sent, consciously or unconsciously, in each of the following examples: is the meaning clear and unambiguous in each

Table 4.1 Categorising non-verbal communication: some practical examples

Human (primarily visual)	Practical examples
Eye contact	Interviewee does not look at interviewer while speaking.
Facial expression	Negotiator smiles at representative of other party.
Gesture	Chief executive folds arms during press briefing.
Posture	Members of a team lean forward during discussions around a table.
Personal distance and touch	Manager puts arm around employees' shoulders.
Personal appearance	Web design consultant arrives at company offices in casual clothes.
Manufactured (primarily visual)	**Practical examples**
Signs and symbols	Corporate logo is redesigned following acquisition.
Representational images	Photographs of all employees placed on corporate intranet.
Physical appearance and space	Offices re-painted in bright colours, with open-plan layout.
Use of other senses	**Practical examples**
Hearing	World music played by retail call centre as customers wait for service.
Smell	Hospital uses essential oils to counter smell of disinfectant and to relax patients.
Touch	Company selects thick embossed card covers for promotional brochure.

case? To what extent are the messages under the control of the sender? And what other factors might intervene to influence the receiver's interpretation of these non-verbal signals?

4.3   Potential benefits of non-verbal communication

The potential benefits of non-verbal forms of communication are most obvious on those occasions when people are forced to rely too heavily on bare words. For example, there are times when e-mail exchanges are inadequate, and it becomes essential for sender and receiver to meet face to face, or at least to gain some additional paralinguistic richness through a telephone conversation. 'Pictures' can be quickly assimilated. They can also help to simplify an otherwise complex message, attract the attention of an audience, motivate them to act, and help them to retain a message, once the original stimulus has gone.

Rapid communication of messages

People are all very adept at 'speed reading' visual messages. For example, if you ask someone a question, their facial expressions (such as a smile, raised eyebrows or a grimace), can communicate the answer instantaneously, and long before the spoken reply. The more subtle human signs can only be detected in face-to-face settings, but some can be employed in technologically-mediated forms of communication, such as video conferencing (see Chapter 13, Case Study 13.5), with the prospect of further applications as the quality of visual imaging is enhanced. Manufactured signs, such as those used on roads and motorways, also have the capacity to convey essential information quickly and easily.

Simplification of complex messages

There is a general requirement in organisations to simplify messages, so that they can be readily understood by non-specialists, and by people who do not have sufficient time to absorb a detailed verbal explanation. For example, the key findings of a research study may be displayed as bar charts, pie charts, cluster plots and so on, enabling an audience to *visualise* the information (see section 4.5). Flow diagrams can be used to summarise a manufacturing process, or to explain how a piece of furniture is assembled, without the use of extended verbal descriptions. For example, the dynamic Swedish furniture retailer IKEA has many years' experience in designing multi-language instruction leaflets for its 'flat pack', home-assembly products. IKEA leaflets are based on simple line drawings in a numbered sequence. The easily understood instructions, combined with good basic product design and manufacture, ensure that the same instructions can be readily understood by the company's customers, whether they are French, Saudi Arabian, Chinese or British.

Images aid communication where it might otherwise be impossible. In a similar way, if we are in a country where we do not speak the language we might resort to using gestures and drawing pictures and diagrams in order to communicate with people, and they might gesture and draw to communicate back, often to successful effect. Makaton is an internationally recognised communication programme that successfully uses symbols to support the written word, and signs to support the spoken word, to enable people with communication and learning difficulties to communicate (The Makaton Charity 2012).

Figure 4.2 Visual images can attract attention

Graphics can also be used to explain relationships and actions that would be difficult to convey in text or spoken words, due to their linear and sequential form (Sayer 2000: 149). For example, an organisational structure chart is used to describe a configuration, rather than a sequence of events; it would be very tedious and confusing to present this kind of information verbally.

Securing audience attention

A striking image can make us stop and look, exploiting 'phasic alertness' (see section 2.4). For example, Figure 4.2 (above) is likely to be one of the first things you noticed on turning this page. Dramatic or unexpected images can be used in many situations, including newspapers, advertisements, brochures, presentations and exhibition stands. Consider, for example, how an advertising agency might convey the following unpalatable message to an audience of young adults:

Though you are young now, you will need financial support in your old age. It is therefore time to start thinking about a pension.

In this case, the message was conveyed as part of a television advertising campaign by a pensions provider. The agency created a storyline involving an elderly man who attempted to dress and act like a teenager. It became evident that the man was engaged in a very belated attempt to enrol himself on a pension plan. The imagery was powerful, combining visual 'humour' with a sobering reminder to its intended audience that they too must start to face the realities of financing their retirement. However, in a world that is increasingly saturated with strong visual images, the ones that are used by organisations have to work ever harder to secure the attention of their audience. This often involves differing judgments. For example, in February 2012 critics accused the charity 'People for the Ethical Treatment of Animals' (PETA) of launching a campaign that encouraged people to become Vegan by promoting violence against women (Change.org 2012). The online campaign included disturbing images of a physically abused woman which people complained inappropriately made light of domestic violence and was insensitive to women who had suffered such abuse. PETA's associate director of campaigns and outreach defended the advert, saying that it was intended to be humorous and that 'the underlying message is a helpful one' (Yahoo News 2012).

Possibly at the risk of public over-exposure to shocking images (see section 2.4) the most recent UK-based campaign to discourage drink driving uses a more subtle, yet still persuasive, campaign, entitled *'Moment of Doubt'*. This features a barman reliving events that highlight the negative impact of drink driving on a *driver's* life (Directgov 2011). This marks a departure from a previous campaign's shocking images of a woman being hit by an invisible vehicle in an advert entitled *Crash*. Meanwhile Liverpool City Council incorporate children's drawings about road safety on their speed limit signs to remind drivers exactly why they should slow down in areas where children commonly play (Figure 4.3).

Following are examples of several quite different tactics that each rely on images to convey a more powerful message than words and numbers alone could.

Persuading and motivating

As we have already noted, non-verbal signals can reinforce a verbal message, adding to its persuasive power. For instance, the small business manager at a bank is likely to give your financing request a more sympathetic hearing if you arrive smartly dressed, rather than in a scruffy jumper and torn jeans. In the same way, an attractively packaged product or service can encourage repeat purchases, especially if its appearance is consistent with the prospective buyer's own values and self-image. This, however, could be changing as the public becomes increasingly aware of the harmful effects of waste on our environment and avoids products with non-essential packaging. Of course, negative images, such as a pile of rubbish outside an expensive restaurant, will have the opposite effect – particularly if the visual stimulus is accompanied by an unpleasant smell. (The role of images as persuaders is considered in more detail in Chapter 5.)

Making messages memorable

Lastly, non-verbal signals can help to get your message into a receiver's short-or long-term memory (section 2.4). Some of these 'pictures' remain potent over many years. For example, in the late twentieth century, IBM was using the enduring impact of the iconic image of the pioneering cinema comedian, Charlie Chaplin, in its advertising campaigns for personal computers. Other visual symbols, such as those associated with the major world religions, are even more enduring. Corporate and product advertising makes extensive use of visual 'hooks' to establish and build brand awareness and longer-term reputation. A **visual hook** is an image or picture that has enough impact to attract a

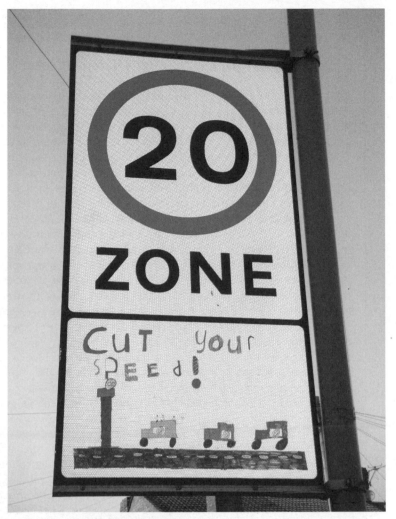

Figure 4.3 Children's drawings on speed limit signs
Source: Kate Ippolito

person's attention and enable them to remember the idea or product, often by relating it to (or hooking it to) previous knowledge or experiences. Auditory and kinaesthetic hooks also aid memory and recognition. For example, an advert showing a family having fun on the beach whilst drinking a brand of fizzy drink might lead to you associating that fizzy drink with having fun.

Repeated exposure to a strong image will increase the likelihood that the target audience will retain the connected messages. For this reason, organisations need to pay particular attention to aspects of their visual identity, ranging from trade marks and corporate logos to the face of a key spokesperson (see section 4.7).

Case study 4.1 reviews the recent evolution of a visual identity and the messages that it seeks to convey. It concerns a certification mark, which is being used to endorse fairly-traded products across Europe.

CASE STUDY 4.1

The FAIRTRADE Mark: creating a European identity

Consumers in the north [i.e. developed economies] rely on many products, such as tea, coffee and chocolate that are sourced from other parts of the world. These products have been exposed to large fluctuations in world commodities markets, and the producers – often including small farmers – have been unable to secure their livelihoods. Development agencies identified the role that consumers might play, if they were able to purchase products on a fairly traded basis. Inspection and audit ensures that producers meet agreed Fairtrade standards, which includes issues such as local participation and the reinvestment of Fairtrade premiums to improve social conditions or economic infrastructure. In 1989, the Netherlands introduced the first Fairtrade label, 'Max Havelaar', which acted as a seal of approval for products bought from registered suppliers according to Fairtrade criteria. The first Fairtrade product in the UK was launched in 1994. Fairtrade Labelling Organisations (FLO) International comprises national Fairtrade initiatives in 24 countries. The UK's original Mark consisted of two interlocked 'F's in upper case letters (facing one another, the right hand letter being inverted). A re-designed Mark was introduced in 2002 as part of a harmonisation initiative across Europe. According to The Fairtrade Foundation: "The symbol is open to interpretation – some see a parrot, others a green leaf, some see the black swirl at the centre as a road leading to a brighter future. The most popular interpretation is to imagine the blue as sky, the green as grass, and the black dot and swirl at the centre as a person holding one arm aloft. That figure represents the people at the heart of the Fairtrade system – it could be a farmer holding up their product, a shopper reaching to purchase, or a campaigner fighting for greater justice in international trade." (Fairtrade 2012) What do you see and what associations do you make?

According to the latest TNS report (2012) 78% of the UK public now recognise the Mark and associate it with helping producers in developing countries (Fairtrade 2012). In fact recognition of the Mark amongst British adults has more than tripled since 2003. Furthermore, there are more than 3000 Fairtrade products certified in the UK, including coffee, flowers and cotton clothing, and sales reached £1319 million in 2011. The latest initiative launched in February 2011 was for Fairtrade and Fairmined gold.

In the UK, the Mark is certified by the Fairtrade Foundation, which issues detailed guidance on the certification process and on the correct use of the Mark by users and licensees. For example, it specifies four ways in which the symbol and the qualifying statement (or 'strapline') can be presented, plus minimum sizes, acceptable colours and positioning on product packaging. In addition to the visual aspects, there are guidelines for copywriters, including the requirement that the expression 'Fairtrade' always be presented as a single word, with an upper case 'F' and lowercase 't'. The Foundation is part of an umbrella body, FLO International, which has the aim of establishing a single international Fairtrade label. Additional details on the Fairtrade Foundation can be obtained at: www.fairtrade.org.uk

The Mark illustrated in Figure 4.4 is one of the few available variations:

Questions

1 Were you aware of the Mark, in supermarkets, other food retail outlets, or high street coffee chains such as Starbucks?

Case study 4.1 (*continued*)

Figure 4.4 The FAIRTRADE Mark

2 Re-read the Fairtrade Foundation's suggested interpretations for their symbol. What do you see when you look at the Fairtrade logo and what associations do you make?

3 How would you assess the effectiveness of the Mark, based on the potential benefits outlined in the previous section?

4 The inverted 'F' mark was a simple but effective visual device. What do you think were the arguments for replacing it with the present symbol?

5 Can you identify any potential challenges for the Mark, as it is extended into new product areas (e.g. jewellery) and geographic markets?

Sources: The Fairtrade Foundation (2012). Case prepared by the authors.

4.4   Potential problems with visual media

In Chapter 3, we saw how inappropriate use of language is a source of problems for individuals and organisations. This section considers how non-verbal signals can also generate unintended and problematic results. There are three potential sources of difficulty:

● Inconsistency, in that a particular 'picture' may not be consistent with other aspects of the message that is being sent.

● Inherent unsuitability, in that it may not be suitable for the receiver that the sender is trying to reach.

● Context-related meaning, in that its meaning may be altered according to the context in which it is being received.

People often spend excessive amounts of time on the words and numbers that are encoded in their messages, but ignore or under-emphasise the non-verbal element. As a result, receivers' negative interpretations of the associated 'pictures' may undermine the effectiveness of the delivered message. Technological improvements in digital imaging, graphics software and colour printing have made it easier to integrate relatively sophisticated images into established communication channels, such as reports and presentations. However, these tools have created their own problems, as the task of design has transferred from technical specialists, such as graphic designers, to untrained and often inexperienced people. The following points cover some of the more common pitfalls, when we make use of 'pictures' in both their human and manufactured forms.

Inconsistency

Non-verbal communication can be a source of two types of inconsistency, which can reduce the effectiveness of the central message by confusing, and probably alienating, receivers. First, the non-verbal signals may not correspond to other forms of encoding, such as spoken or written words. For example, if a welcome message from an unsmiling hotel receptionist is interpreted, perhaps correctly, as superficial and insincere. Similarly a report or presentation, produced by the HR department and promoting health and safety issues, will be undermined if the authors inadvertently include old photographs showing scrap materials blocking a factory gangway, or workers not wearing protective clothing. In both cases, the inconsistencies may not be apparent to the sender. However, they can have a powerful effect on those receiving the combined message.

The second inconsistency is between the visual signal and the 'reality' that it is supposed to represent. Hence, even if the receptionist is smiling when welcoming the hotel guest, the facial expression may not be effective without substantiation, such as previous evidence of good customer service at this hotel. In the case of manufactured images, media researchers have pointed to the greater 'visual literacy' or sophistication of contemporary audiences. **Visual literacy** refers to our ability to understand and interpret cues in the form of images, pictures and body language. The idea is that, because people are routinely exposed to so many highly-processed images, they have become sceptical about their value (Klein 2000: 279–310). For example, in the late twentieth century, holiday brochures became notorious for their use of misleading photography, which gave a false impression of hotels and resorts; consumers became wary of these 'glossy' images, so that their use became counterproductive. Charts, maps and diagrams can also misrepresent their source data in various ways (see section 4.5).

Inherent unsuitability

Some 'pictures' are simply unsuitable for their intended purpose. For example, it is difficult to imagine how a dishevelled physical appearance would enhance a message within an organisation, except perhaps where the sender is trying to demonstrate that they have been working all night to complete a piece of work. One of the most common failings in representational images, such as photography and video, is the use of over-familiar or clichéd material. For example, almost every university prospectus includes pictures of tutors pointing earnestly at computer screens and of newly-graduated students throwing their hats in the air. Because they are so over-used, these images are less likely to attract attention. They can also send unintended messages to their audience. For example, an annual report that is full of 'stock' pictures of factory sites and smiling workers might convey an impression of the organisation as old-fashioned and uncreative. (**Stock pictures** are the name given to existing images or photographs that can be bought, often from agencies, and sometimes downloaded from the Internet for free, and are used to populate brochures, websites, etc. This saves individuals time and money but can result in a lack of individuality, creativity and authenticity.) Stereotypical images, including many popular representations of women, children, people with disabilities and people from less-developed countries have also been subject to criticism. Organisations, including charities and campaign groups, need to pay attention to the implied messages that these images convey.

Striking our target market!

- How do we increase the IMPACT of our multimedia promotional campaign?

Figure 4.5 Striking our target market

Context-related meaning

The meaning of 'pictures' can vary between contexts and over time, in much the same way as it does with words (see section 3.4). However, in the case of non-verbal communication, there is arguably an even greater potential for differences in interpretation, particularly in relation to human signals, such as gesture and eye contact. Consider, for example, the different implications of physical proximity between passengers standing in a crowded train, a group of friends celebrating at a party and two strangers involved in a verbal argument. These differences are further complicated by cultural factors. We are aware, from research and anecdotal observation, that regional and national cultures have generated contrasting approaches to common human signals, including the role of eye contact, the conventional meaning of particular gestures and the appropriateness of touching other people during a meeting or conversation (see section 4.8). These differences extend to the interpretation of manufactured images, including photographs, drawings and even physical artefacts like ceramics (Moeran 1997). Consider the following situation: you are sitting in a presentation on the subject of marketing strategy in an international consulting firm; the presenter decides to 'liven up' one of the slides by adding the image of a military jet firing air-to-surface missiles. The accompanying text reads, 'Striking our target market' (Figure 4.5). An illustration of this kind will have varying effects, depending on the background and nature of each member of the audience. For example, people with an interest in aircraft may simply try to identify the plane, those involved in recent anti-war campaigns will find the imagery offensive, while anyone unfortunate enough to have experienced a real bombing raid will be drawn into unpleasant recollections of past events. The implication is that communicators need to take care in their use of manufactured images, always considering how receivers might interpret them.

CASE STUDY 4.2

London 2012 Olympic logo: controversial or simply a grower?

Since its launch in June 2007 the 2012 Olympics logo has attracted a lot of attention, though not always the right kind. The graffiti-style logo, which cost £400,000 to design(Blitz 2011), divided opinion from the outset. Proponents, such as Shadow Minister

Case study 4.2 (*continued*)

for the Olympics, Tessa Jowell, praised its adaptability and suitability to be used in a variety of different contexts (Blitz 2007), but criticisms included claims that it resembled a swastika or set of beer mats (Blitz 2011)! The then-prime minister Tony Blair described it as 'brilliant or awful' (Blitz 2011), whilst then-mayor of London, Ken Livingstone, suggested that it might grow on people (ibid).

The official site of the London 2012 Olympic and Paralympic Games boldly claims that the logo:

> ...is universal and understandable worldwide. Our emblem is simple, distinct, bold and buzzing with energy. Its form is inclusive yet consistent and has incredible flexibility to encourage access and participation. It can communicate with anyone from commercial organisations to kids playing sport.
>
> It feels young in spirit. Full of confidence, certainty and opportunity. Not afraid to shake things up, to challenge the accepted. To change things. (London 2012, 2012)

Despite these intentions to be inclusive, in February 2011 Iran threatened to boycott the Olympic Games over the logo because they believed that it concealed the word 'Zion' and was racist (Blitz 2011).

Most recently there are concerns that the explosion of social media, that will make London 2012 the 'first truly digital Games' (Kortekaas 2011), will also make it easier for ambushers to associate themselves with the Games without paying the necessary sponsorship fees. And buying rights to use the logo doesn't come cheap, with some of the 55 Olympic sponsors for London 2012 having invested approximately $100m to use the Olympics logo in their marketing (ibid,).

So is London's 2012 logo the only Olympic logo to create such a stir? Apparently not. Rio's more recently unveiled 2016 logo stands accused of plagiarising the impressionist artist Matisse's work, 'The Dance'! (Rodrigues 2011). Whether too radical or too universal, Olympic logo designers, it seems, can't win. There are winners, though. Despite its contentious design the Rio 2016 logo, like the London 2012 one before it, is set to bring in the money, to the tune of an anticipated '3bn reais ($175bn) through the sale of merchandise and other marketing licenses connected to the symbol.' (ibid.).

Questions

1 List the issues that the 2012 Olympic Games logo has given rise to. Refer back to section 4.4 and identify the possible reasons for each of these problems.

2 What do you think of when you look at the 2012 Olympic logo? Do you agree with the message that the *Official site of the London 2012 Olympic and Paralympic Games* hopes that the logo will convey?

3 If you were responsible for designing the Olympic Games logo, what messages would you want to communicate? How might the merchandising opportunities influence you?

Sources: Blitz (2007), Blitz (2011), Kortekaas (2011), Rodrigues (2011), London 2012 Official website (2012). Case prepared by the authors.

4.5   The use and abuse of graphical data

Graphs and charts can be very effective ways to encode numerical information. However, it is easy to confuse an audience by selecting the wrong type of graphical image to represent your data, or by constructing an image incorrectly (Tufte 1990). Furthermore, research suggests that incorrectly designed graphics can influence the receiver's decision-making, raising a number of broader policy issues (Tufte 1997, Arunachalam et al. 2002). The inclusion of charting tools in popular software packages (such as Microsoft Excel) means that the creation of charts and graphs is now easier than ever. However, just because it is possible to create a chart from a particular set of data items does not mean that the message it conveys is accurate or unambiguous. This section reviews a few of the more popular types of graphs and charts, noting some of the ways that they can be used and abused.

Pie charts

Pie charts are used to show the relative size of different items making up a total; for example, the breakdown of quarterly sales by region, or audience figures by age-group. Conventionally, the largest segment is placed at the 'top' of the pie, with other segments following in a clockwise direction. Each segment should be labelled, normally with figures indicating the value and percentage share. The overall total should also be stated. This usually takes the form of a separate label inserted below the graphic. If there is a requirement to emphasise a particular segment, it may be 'exploded' (Figure 4.6). Problems may arise when there are too many segments, making the graphic unclear. In these situations, it may be possible to aggregate some of the data into larger segments, so simplifying the graphical presentation. Component bar charts offer an alternative method of displaying data that has too many individual observations for a pie chart.

Total sample = 2,500 respondents, surveyed by telephone, June 2012

Figure 4.6 Pie chart with exploded segment

Bar charts

Bar charts are also used to compare the values of different items. They can be presented in either vertical or horizontal formats. The major advantage of bar charts over pie charts is that individual values can be read off easily against a scale, which should always be inserted

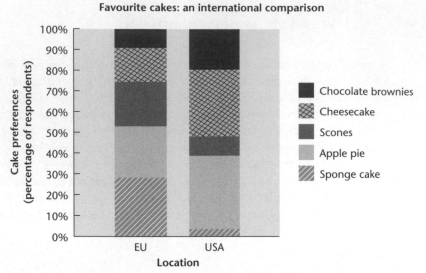

Figure 4.7 A component bar chart

on the appropriate axis. Bar charts are normally drawn with separated bars of equal width. Because each bar represents discrete data, it should not be linked to other bars using a line. More complex data can be presented using either multiple or component bar charts (Figure 4.7). In all cases, it is important to avoid distorting the data by introducing a 'false zero' in the vertical axis. The scale should run from zero, but in some cases (e.g. in order to highlight particular changes), the scale is broken. If this is done, it becomes essential to indicate the break clearly, to ensure that the reader interprets the data correctly. The convention is to mark the break with two 'zig-zag' lines through the axis.

Histograms

Histograms are sometimes confused with bar charts, but they can be differentiated according to the types of data they represent. Histograms are used for *continuous* data sets, such as a frequency distribution showing mortality rates by age of population; whereas bar charts

Figure 4.8 A histogram

are used for *discrete* or *non-continuous* data, such as a comparison of mortality rates in five different countries. Histograms should be drawn with the bars touching, reflecting the continuous nature of their source data (Figure 4.8). If there are large intervals in the data with low values, these can be combined to create some bars that are wider than others. In a histogram, the overall trend is sometimes shown by linking the tops of each bar with a curved line, or by superimposing a moving average.

Line graphs

Line graphs are often used to present continuous data, including various kinds of time series (e.g. tracking inflation or unemployment rates over the last 30 years). Typically, two or more lines are plotted on the same graph, so that comparisons can be made between variables, such as trends in personal disposable income and house prices. It is important to select suitable scales, line types and labelling so that each line can be distinguished (Figure 4.9). It is also possible to combine line graphs with histograms or even bar charts. Different data values can be presented on the same graph by using two scales on the left and right hand vertical axes. However, it is important to avoid overloading the graph with information. The better option is usually to break the data down into a number of simpler graphs, with suitable explanatory text.

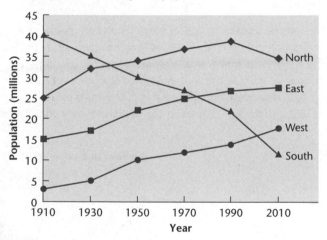

Republic of Utopia: regional population trends 1910–2010

Figure 4.9 A multiple line graph

Pictograms

Pictograms are based on the idea that data may be more appealing and informative if it is turned into a representative image. For example, a breakdown of the number of employees in different parts of an organisation may be illustrated using a picture made up of 'match-stick' people, each of which represents 100 employees. The most common pitfall associated with pictograms is the misrepresentation of quantities. The main source of distortion is a lack of clarity over the scale, which *may* be one-dimensional, like the linear scales used in graphs and bar charts, but can also take a two-dimensional form. For example, imagine that

Garden centre sales: roses by category (May 2012)

Figure 4.10 A simple pictogram

the finance director of a housing association wants to show that the average market price of houses has doubled between 1995 and 2012. The person preparing her presentation draws two houses, one twice the height of the other. The finance director rejects this pictogram, arguing that it distorts the argument. Why? Because it implies that house prices have quadrupled, since the *area* taken up by the 2012 house is four times that representing prices in 1995. At their simplest, pictograms may be little more than an elaborate version of more conventional graphics, such as a bar chart (Figure 4.10).

Maps

Maps can be used to represent all kinds of data that have a spatial or geographic dimension. For example, regional differences in sales revenues, average household income, crime rates or number of business start-ups are often indicated by colouring or shading the relevant national or administrative boundaries (Figure 4.11). However, maps can also be misleading. This is because the relative *size* of the areas shaded is usually unrelated to the data that are being displayed. For example, parliamentary constituencies vary in size according to

Our sales in Europe: 2012

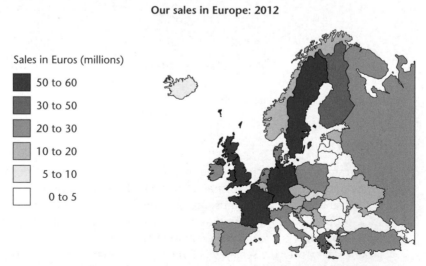

Figure 4.11 A map illustrating regional data

population density (i.e. rural constituencies are much larger than those in urban centres). A map that is coloured according to the political party holding each constituency would therefore tend to exaggerate the representation of those parties that were strongest in rural areas, while understating those associated with towns and cities.

The illustrations used in this section have been presented in a straightforward two-dimensional format. Computer packages now offer a range of supposedly 'three-dimensional' graphs and charts, which may appear to make data look more attractive. However, most of these are generally 'blocked-out' versions of the traditional two-dimensional formats (e.g. a conventional line graph is transformed into a series of ribbons). The cosmetic benefits of blocked-out graphs and charts are usually outweighed by the problems of interpretation. The most obvious obstacle is that the lines and bars in 'three-dimensional' graphics cannot be lined up against the relevant scale. This makes it difficult to determine the relevant data values.

Case Study 4.3 shows how graphics have been used in an effort to inform people better about government spending. This is a particularly demanding communication challenge, given the range of abilities in the use of numbers and the level of public interest in the details of public sector financial statements.

CASE STUDY 4.3

The challenge of communicating financial information

The UK government spends around £745 billion every year on providing services, welfare payments and other spending. As part of a wider effort to improve accountability for this spending, they have developed a set of accounting reports that shows the total income, spending, assets and liabilities of the UK government as a whole. The Whole of Government Accounting (WGA) reports (HM Treasury 2011) are large and complex reports, similar in format and content to the annual accounting reports of private companies. The accounts are intended for a wide audience of taxpayers and other stakeholders and show how the government has raised income, made spending decisions and managed its resources over the 12-month period covered.

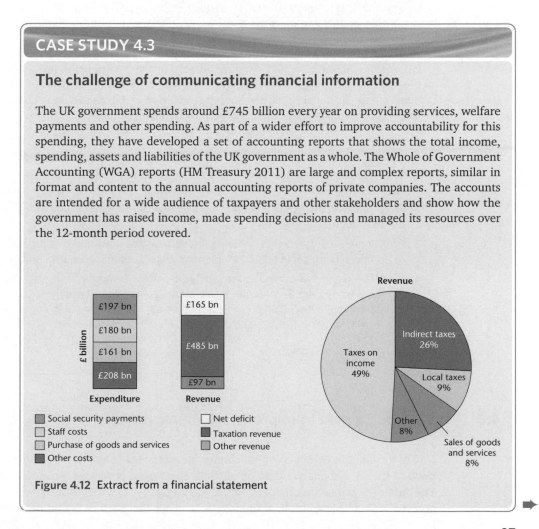

Figure 4.12 Extract from a financial statement

Case study 4.3 (*continued*)

The content of the reports is regulated tightly. To help ensure the reports are complete, accurate and useful the UK government has adopted a set of financial accounting standards based on the widely used International Financial Reporting Standards (IFRS). These standards set out what needs to be included in the reports and the technical details as to how the figures in the reports should be prepared. The standards are designed to ensure that reports are consistent year-on-year and that the figures included can be compared on a like-for-like basis with other organisations. These standards are set out in the Government Financial Reporting Manual (known as the FReM) (HM Treasury 2012).

The communication challenge

Whilst the FReM is very clear about the technicalities of preparing the accounts, it contains no guidance as to how the figures should be presented. The team preparing the WGA reports needed to decide how to convey the important messages contained in the reports to the target audience. The format and layout of government accounting reports varies widely between different bodies. In the worst examples the accounts are simply presented as large tables of financial data with a detailed technical commentary. By contrast, the best reports are designed to meet the needs of the users and present the information in clear and understandable ways tailored to their needs.

The WGA report presents accounting information in both tables and charts. The extracts below show information about the tax income of the government. This information is presented in three ways. The three extracts below show the different ways used to communicate the full details that users may be interested in. First a summary chart is used to show both income (revenue) and expenditure. Details of the revenue from tax are then presented in a pie chart. Finally the detailed figures are shown in the accounting statements.

Questions

1 What types of stakeholder might be interested in the information contained in the WGA report?

2 What problems might there be in communicating accounting information to each of the stakeholders?

3 Review the extracts from the WGA report. Discuss the advantages and disadvantages of using diagrams, pie charts and tables to convey accounting information.

4 The WGA report is a printed report. www.wheredoesmymoneygo.org is a project of the Open Knowledge Foundation that presents government spending information in an interactive website. Do you think this approach is a better way to communicate financial information to the stakeholders you identified in question 1?

Sources: HM Treasury 2011, HM Treasury 2012. Case prepared by Dan Herbert.

4.6 Visualising data to improve communication

One of the benefits of technological change in recent years has been the ability of organisations to gather and analyse data about their customers, processes, products and markets. The data they gather are often very detailed and there are often vast numbers of individual observations. The large scale of the data sets means that such data are often referred to as 'big data'. Making use of such data requires skill if the key messages contained are to be learned and communicated. One way in which this has been done is by using advanced data visualisation techniques.

Data visualisation is not new. One famous example of early data visualisation is Florence Nightingale's visual representation of the causes of death during the Crimean War (http://www.guardian.co.uk/news/datablog/2010/aug/13/florence-nightingale-graphics). The clarity of this representation demonstrated that most deaths were caused not by injuries in battle but by infection. She used the powerful diagram to argue for changes in nursing practices to reduce infection rates and thus reduce deaths. Another famous example from 1869 is Minard's visual representation of the deaths during Napolean's 1812 Russian Campaign. Minard's visualisation is often quoted as the best visual representation of data ever produced (http://en.wikipedia.org/wiki/File:Minard.png).

The advent of powerful data analysis tools has allowed large data sets to be analysed, visualised and communicated in very powerful ways. Specialist software is available that helps with the analysis and the design of visual representations. Two examples of such software are Google Fusion Tables and Tableau. Google Fusion Tables is a powerful analysis and visualisation tool that allows users to build maps and charts that present data in engaging and useful ways. In Case Study 4.3 an example of how financial data can be represented in static reports was considered. Using Fusion Tables a dynamic representation of this type of data is possible. http://lookatcook.com shows the data for one American county district presented to make it clear and engaging for non-specialist users. Tableau Software (http://www.tableausoftware.com/learn/gallery) enables the presentation of large data sets in ways that not only convey engaging messages but also allow users to focus on aspects of the data they are interested in.

The ability to analyse and present data in engaging ways assists organisations in making better decisions, communicating with stakeholders and understanding their operations better. The new analysis tools are also changing news media communications. Data Journalism is a new branch of journalism where stories are based on data items and analysis rather than on the more usual investigative journalism. Perhaps the most high-profile data journalism has been undertaken by the *Guardian* newspaper in the UK. Their Datablog (http://www.guardian.co.uk/news/datablog) relies entirely on data and analysis for its content.

The use of visualisations can also improve the quality of presentations. By using a suitable software tool alongside a data-projector, it is possible to make presentations that communicate complex numeric or statistical concepts in ways that are more understandable than would be possible in a normal, slide-based presentation. When combined with the skills of a great presenter such presentations can make incredibly powerful communication tools (for example, see http://www.ted.com/talks/hans_rosling_shows_the_best_stats_you_ve_ever_seen.html).

4.7 Visual aspects of corporate identity: an introduction

The image of a 'start-up' or one-person business is closely associated with the individual who runs it. However, larger organisations inevitably become more impersonal. As a result, there have been concerted efforts to manage the corporate 'image', that is, the way that human organisations, ranging from businesses to entire countries, are perceived by their various audiences or 'publics' (Olins 2000). This is reflected in a corporate visual communication industry that is currently valued in excess of £3 billion in the UK alone (International Visual Communications Association 2012). As organisations make changes in strategic direction, they find it necessary to review aspects of their visual identities. The most obvious visual elements open to managerial control are corporate symbols and logos. Some of these have very long associations (e.g. the simple red triangle associated with UK-based brewing company, Bass, since the eighteenth century). Shell, an Anglo-Dutch petrochemicals company, also has a long-established visual identity. Shell's distinctive symbol, also represented in the company name, was the choice of its founder, Marcus Samuel. It is a reference to his father's previous business activities, which included trading seashells in mid-nineteenth-century London. Organisations can also become associated with particular colours as a result of their historical development. For example, Shell's use of red in its colour scheme dates back to a tactical decision in the 1890s, when the company needed to differentiate its oil containers from the blue tins used by its international rival, Standard Oil (Yergin 1991: 63–70).

Many large corporations, such as BT, have undergone repeated changes of identity, reflecting shifts in strategic direction, changes in consumer fashion preference and a desire to escape previous associations. Recently, several of the more celebrated corporate 'makeovers' have attracted criticism, due to the high costs involved and to the perception that some of the changes were superficial, making little difference to the organisation's current performance or future potential. It appears that the more excessive spending programmes have been curtailed, reflecting the difficult trading conditions of recent years. There have also been examples of organisations redeploying their visual communication budgets in a more emergent or 'bottom-up' manner, opening up new channels of communication with employees. For example, Donaldson and Eyre (2000) report on a culture change initiative at the UK's second largest electrical retailer, Comet, which made extensive use of video interviews with members of staff and customers across the country. This simple example demonstrates how visual communication can be used in radically different ways, in order to address strategic issues regarding corporate identity and the more fundamental question of corporate image: how organisations are perceived by their key stakeholders.

The theme of visual identity and its complex relationship with corporate strategy and image is developed in the case study at the end the present chapter (Case Study 4.5). The implications for practice are explored as part of a broader discussion of corporate advertising (see section 10.3 and 10.4) and public relations (see section 10.5 and 10.6). In the next section, we return to the personal level and consider how individuals deploy visual signals, ranging from eye contact to physical appearance, to convey messages without necessarily making use of words.

4.8   Human signals: from eye contact to appearance

This section considers how human beings generate non-verbal signals, and the kinds of messages they convey. These 'human' signals are particularly evident in direct inter-personal communication, but many of them can also be conveyed through mediated communication channels, such as video recordings, photographs and even paintings. The received messages are often complicated by the fact that they are derived from a *combination* of intentional and unconscious non-verbal signs. Researchers have studied the ways that these signs are produced, through eye contact and behaviour ('oculesics'); facial expression, gesture and posture ('kinesics'); personal distance, use of space and touch ('proxemics'); and through the impression made by a person's physical appearance. In practice, senders are often unaware of how these combined non-verbal messages are being interpreted. Consequently, they may not recognise inconsistencies between these signs, their spoken words and any associated 'paralanguage' (see section 3.5). The potential for communication problems is further increased by the many different cultural conventions attached to the use of these non-verbal signals. The following categorisation illustrates the resulting challenges with some practical examples. You can probably add others from your own experience.

Eye contact and behaviour

Use of the human eye can have a powerful influence on inter-personal communication. For example, in most contemporary Western cultures, there is an automatic expectation that people engaged in a conversation will maintain a fairly constant degree of eye contact. While staring fixedly into the eyes of another person might be regarded as aggressive, looking away from their face during a conversation, even for a brief period, will generally be interpreted negatively. It signals either a lack of interest in the conversation that is taking place, or that the person averting their gaze is untrustworthy. This practice is in stark contrast to some cultural traditions, where withholding eye contact signals respect for the status of the person speaking. (It seems likely that similarly deferential practices once existed in Western societies, reflecting more hierarchical forms of social organisation.) The influence of these conventions is highlighted in the way that we interpret video images of an interview. If the interviewee is unfamiliar with television, she may continue to look at the person asking questions off-camera, rather than looking into the lens. For viewers accustomed to Western practices, the *apparent* lack of eye contact will stimulate negative connotations in much the same way as a 'face-to-face' interaction. Like the other non-verbal signals discussed in this section, national cultural differences have attracted considerable interest from researchers, and accompanying 'self-help' literature to guide unwary travellers and international managers (e.g. Hall 1959, Hall and Hall 1990, Harris and Moran 1996). The eye is also used in very subtle ways, often in conjunction with facial expressions, to convey various states of mind. These can also be conveyed in manufactured representations of the human face, including video images and photography.

Facial expression

Humans are capable of a great variety of facial expressions. As with other signalling systems, including human language, we learn these expressions from others, and their inherent meanings are shared within cultural groups. There is mixed research evidence on the ability of those outside a culture to make a correct interpretation of its facial codes. Facial expressions are sometimes difficult to interpret, even within the bounds of a culture. Consider, for example, Leonardo da Vinci's celebrated portrait, *Mona Lisa* (circa 1502). Popular fascination with the mysterious 'smile' of this Florentine woman has been explained as resulting from the artist's deliberate efforts to leave the corners of her mouth and eyes indistinct, and therefore open to interpretation (Gombrich 1978: 227–9). Some facial expressions are highly culture-specific. For example, raising an eyebrow has a sexual connotation in China, while smiling sometimes signals regret or embarrassment; the meanings of both signals contrast with those ascribed in other cultures, including those of the West (Dou and Clark

2002: 60). However, psychological studies have indicated a near-universal ability to recognise seven basic human emotions: anger, disgust, fear, happiness, sadness and contempt (Ekman and Friesen 1971). There is also strong anecdotal evidence for this phenomenon in the countless images of faces from around the world that we see in newspapers, television programmes and other mass media. Furthermore, it seems likely that with repeated exposure to other cultures, through working in international organisations or viewing global mass-media images, people do learn to make these interpretations.

Gesture and posture

Similar issues arise with respect to human gesture and other aspects of what is sometimes termed 'body language', including the way people sit and stand in relation to one another. Gestures can act as useful shorthand, conveying a simple message rapidly and overcoming other obstacles, including language differences. For example, the 'thumbs up' and 'thumbs down' hand gestures may be used by workers on a noisy construction site; or by tourists seeking confirmation that their hotel room is booked, or that they are taking the correct route. Problems can arise when culture-specific gestures are misinterpreted: travellers' tales are full of examples where seemingly 'innocent' gestures convey a different, and sometimes offensive, message in another culture. Gesture and posture, like facial expression, can also have different meanings *within* a cultural group. For example, putting an arm around the shoulders of another person can indicate personal affection or solidarity. However, in some organisational contexts it suggests a power relationship (e.g. a senior manager may feel permitted to make this gesture to a subordinate in some circumstances, but it rarely occurs the other way around). There are also close connections between the use of these signals and the ways that people position themselves in physical space.

Personal distance and touch

Cultural groups have different assumptions regarding the use of space between people and the appropriateness of physical contact during face-to-face communication (Hall and Hall 1990). Again, we can see that these norms are largely unconscious and highly context-dependent. For example, British people tend to retain a greater personal distance and engage in much less direct physical contact than their Italian or Spanish counterparts. However, these general conventions are superseded in certain situations, such as taking the elevator in an office building or travelling on the Underground in the rush hour. In both situations, conventional rules on proximity are modified and close contact is tolerated, with the strict proviso that people avoid any form of eye contact. Again, if a person experiences what appears to be an unnecessary attempt to break with their established norms for proximity and touch, the resulting signals are largely negative. For example, if other people get 'too close' or become too tactile (e.g. repeatedly touching the receiver's arm while talking), they will be perceived as over-familiar, 'pushy' (i.e. using excessive persuasion), or aggressive. Similarly, people who are 'not close enough' or insufficiently tactile, according to the receiver's normal expectations, will be perceived as cold, untrustworthy or hostile. International communicators can also 'learn' and adapt to these differences, though some of the subtleties may be more difficult to overcome. For example, where one group has prior expectations of another, it may be disconcerting to find that behaviour has been adapted to local norms.

Physical appearance

Receivers may be influenced by various aspects of another person's appearance, from the state of their hair to the style of their shoes. We signal various messages by our (largely inherited) physical features, and more deliberate, 'manufactured' aspects of our appearance, such as clothing, jewellery and other accessories. In an organisational context, these elements may be combined to signal valued attributes, such as personal status (e.g. displaying an ostentatiously expensive suit or wristwatch), professionalism (e.g. the white coat of a clinical specialist or research scientist), or other capabilities (e.g. the self-consciously non-conformist appearance of 'creative' staff in an advertising agency or a performing arts organisation). In some cases these signals are standardised, through the use of organisational dress codes or uniforms, both of which are designed to send out a consistent message about the structure of the organisation and its values. As in the other areas discussed, the most common communication problems related to physical appearance arise from differing expectations and conflicting norms. For example, some large corporations have experimented with a relaxation of their formal dress codes (in the so-called 'dress-down Friday'). In some instances these initiatives have proved problematic, with employees struggling to maintain their normal standards of professionalism and more formally-dressed visitors feeling isolated and uncomfortable. In certain contexts, clothing can still be a source of contention, often arising from differences in religious or ethical position. For example, women wearing the *burqa* or *niqab* have experienced resistance in some Western organisations, and particularly in France, where a law against covering your face in public was introduced in April 2011 (Crisafis 2011). However, like other non-verbal signals discussed in this section, dress codes and related signals are subject to change as international organisations begin to develop shared meanings and, in some cases, to acknowledge a greater diversity of practices (Holden 2002).

Case Study 4.4 outlines a novel approach to modifying cross-cultural communication practices, which has been applied successfully in various international organisations. It makes use of visual cues, ranging from product brochures to meeting agendas, in order to prompt interaction between groups of people from different cultural backgrounds.

CASE STUDY 4.4

CDP exchanges: a visual approach to cross-cultural interaction

Traditional approaches to dealing with cross-cultural interactions are modelled on the experiences of a traveller arriving in a foreign country for the first time. They focus on resolving the errors and confusion that arise from a lack of familiarity with local communication practices (see Hall and Hall 1990). As we noted in earlier chapters, confrontations of this kind – between two distinct cultures – are still relevant to communicators. However, many international organisations are facing a different challenge, as they seek to negotiate *new* patterns of behaviour that are suited to *multi*-cultural settings. Pan et al. (2002) outline an approach, described as the Communication Portfolio Display (CDP) exchange, that responds to this challenge. The authors argue that professional communication in international settings cannot be standardised around the practices of a single social or cultural group. They outline a method that encourages people to learn directly from those with whom they need to interact. This is based on the thesis that 'successful communication

Case study 4.4 (*continued*)

in the international workplace requires a *self-reflective* understanding of the processes of communication' (*ibid*: 5 – emphasis added). The core activity involves an exchange of 'best case' examples of professional communications materials, providing the basis for reflective discussion and feedback:

> 'To give an example, we could imagine that we have a small team of buyers based in Frankfurt who have established contact with producers of supplies in Guangzhou, China. The buyers will be going to China and the Chinese team will be visiting Frankfurt, as the relationship is expected to last over a period of at least several years. A traditional approach to the intercultural aspects of this program would be to provide training to the German team in Chinese communicative and cultural practices and also, if at all possible, to provide training to the Chinese team in German practices.' (*ibid*: 5)

The authors note that this approach is unlikely to be achieved, given the shortage of suitable training materials and consultants, particularly those whose technical expertise can be combined with language skills in Cantonese, rather than Mandarin Chinese. The alternative approach involves some or all of the team members compiling a professional CDP. The portfolio would include readily-available items, such as product brochures, business cards, letters, e-mails and CVs (or 'resumés'). Participants would also try to find materials that indicated how other communication channels, including formal meetings and presentations, were conducted. The portfolios would then be used to stimulate discussion within and between the teams:

> 'These CDPs would then be exchanged between the two teams. Each team would then conduct a "focus group" discussion of the materials from the point of view of their communicative effectiveness. That is, they would say what seemed confusing to them, what was missing, what seemed excessive or unnecessary, or whatever adjustments might be needed to improve their ability to understand. These comments and reflections would then be returned to the other team for them to consider and digest.' (*ibid*: 5–6)

The authors emphasise that the primary purpose of the exchange is not to isolate cultural, national or personal differences, but rather to encourage participants to reflect on the effectiveness of these practices, and to encourage a process of mutual learning. The desired outcome is that the people concerned are able to adjust their own practices to some extent, in order to achieve a better way of communicating within that particular setting.

Questions

1 How does the CDP approach differ from traditional work on cross-cultural difference? What do you consider to be their main advantages and disadvantages in a multi-cultural setting?

2 The portfolio of material provides a visual stimulus for discussion. How might it be extended to illustrate other, less-tangible communication channels, such as interviews or team discussions?

3 Experiment with creating your own CDP, which could include a recently-produced report, set of presentation slides and CV. Compare your portfolio to that produced by other students or colleagues, reflecting on the changes that may be necessary in order to meet everyone's communication needs.

Sources: Hall and Hall (1990), Pan et al. (2002). Case prepared by the authors.

Face-to-face 4 brings together discussion in this chapter about the everyday use of visual images and 'human' signals and explores, in practical terms, how they influence the effectiveness of the way messages are delivered, received and acted upon.

FACE-TO-FACE 4

Student elections: will they get the message?

Santanu is running for President of the Student Union and is trying to decide how best to 'market' himself to students at his university. How can he persuade such a diverse group of people to vote for him, rather than one of the other candidates? Santanu feels he is in with a good chance; he has been actively involved with the Student Union on a number of key campaigns including: calling for lower visa fees for international students; demanding increased night-time security on campus; and organising Fairtrade coffee, tea and chocolate at campus outlets. He thinks his manifesto is strong and gets across effectively who he is, what he stands for and why fellow students should vote for him. His message is popular but realistic; his headlines claim 'Vote for Santanu for a safer campus, more sports facilities and better personal tutoring'. But he knows that words are not enough. Furthermore, his campaign will need to rely on many votes from students who might never meet him personally. To be effective, his publicity manifestos and flyers need to have big visual impact – be memorable, persuasive and clear! Also, with so many images and signs vying for students' attention, including other candidates' publicity, he needs to stand out and encourage apathetic students to vote. His friend, Louise, thinks he needs a logo – a distinct, easily reproducible image that sums up: him, his values and his manifesto statements. Another friend, Ben, says that a photo showing him talking to other students is too serious and needs replacing with a picture that shouts 'I'm fun'. Santanu is not sure that 'being fun' is what he is all about, or that such images win President of the Union votes.

Despite relying heavily on flyers and posters, Santanu also recognises the importance of getting out there and telling would-be voters about his campaign. He also knows that when he is targeting people at club and society meetings, in the halls of residence and coffee bars, the non-verbal messages he conveys are crucial. He needs to come across as confident, not arrogant; friendly, but authoritative. Other candidates stand on tables to speak to student groups about their manifesto but Santanu finds this approach a bit disruptive, even aggressive! He has just two weeks to get out there and win the vote!

Questions

1 Imagine you are Santanu's friend, assisting him in his campaign. How would you recommend that he maximises the visual impact of his campaign? Consider both his use of visual images and 'human' signals.

2 Think about the images that you are surrounded by every day. Which visual stimuli around your university, or work place, have you found particularly influential?

3 In general, what kinds of images encourage you to:

 (a) take notice;

 (b) change your behaviour.

4 What do you think are the reasons for your responses to questions 2 and 3?

Summary

- Organisations make use of a wide range of non-verbal signals, including visual images, or 'pictures', both human and manufactured.

- There are many potential advantages of non-verbal encoding: messages are quickly assimilated; complex content can be simplified; the attention of an audience can be caught; and messages can be more memorable. In addition, images are often powerful persuaders and motivators.

- The most common problems arise when 'pictures' of all kinds are used carelessly (i.e. images are inconsistent, inherently unsuitable or inappropriate in a particular context).

- Graphs and charts can be used to present data in more informative and appealing ways. However, it is important to use the most appropriate type and format, ensuring that you communicate a clear and undistorted impression of the underlying figures.

- The visual identity of an organisation needs to be well thought-out and linked to its real values and activities. Managing the identity of a large business involves a complex mixture of strategic and practical issues.

- Communicators also need to be aware of how 'human signals', such as eye contact and gesture, influence the communication process. This is particularly important in multi-cultural contexts where there is a need to acknowledge diversity in the use of these codes.

Key Terms

Non-verbal forms of communication 81	icon 82 visual hook 86	Visual literacy 90 Stock pictures 90

PRACTICAL EXERCISES

4.1 Designing icons, symbols and diagrams

The meaning behind the images reproduced in Figure 4.1 can be absorbed 'at a glance', avoiding the need for a verbal explanation. The images are also designed to be understood instantly by people from a wide variety of cultures and language groups. With these requirements in mind, design your own images for the following purposes:

(a) a computer icon for instant access to a home shopping service;
(b) a directional sign indicating the police station at an international airport;
(c) 'No overtaking' and 'Cycle workshop ahead' signs for use on a cross-border cycle route.

Based on the discussion and illustrations in the chapter (section 4.3), sketch a suitable visual image to meet the following requirements:

(d) a diagram, which explains exactly how to carry out one of the following tasks without the use of words:

- log on to a computer, compose and send an e-mail;
- withdraw money from a 'cash-point' machine;
- research and write an essay.

(e) a visual identity for a new range of 'green' (i.e. environmentally-friendly) consumer products, either household detergents, paints or clothes. The manufacturer needs to build a distinctive and memorable image in the domestic retail market.

What aspect did you find most difficult in preparing each image? How should your rough drafts be improved, when re-drawn by a professional artist, to make them more effective?

4.2 Unacceptable images? The ethical dimension

Manufactured images can be powerful communicators. At one extreme, horrific war photography has forced national governments and the United Nations to change their policies; whilst at the other, beautiful landscapes have been used to promote everything from tourism to shampoo. Like any powerful communication technique, the application of these non-verbal signals is open to abuse. For example, in a notorious Nazi propaganda film of the 1930s, the anti-Semitic verbal commentary was reinforced through the use of close-up images of rats scurrying through the contents of an abandoned house. What kinds of ethical constraints should be placed on the way that images are used in organisational communication? Imagine that your objective was one of the following:

- to warn drivers of the serious dangers of speeding;
- to persuade young people not to start smoking;
- to persuade smokers to continue purchasing your brand;
- to inform schoolchildren about drugs or contraception.

Identify examples of the kinds of images you would consider both useful and acceptable to reinforce a verbal message in one of these cases. What kinds of images, if any, do you see as unacceptable for the stated purpose? Give a reasoned explanation for your choice. Supporting materials can be found in texts on business ethics, such as Bowie (2002).

Seminar option: This exercise requires all group members to pay particular respect to the views of others. Share your conclusions with the rest of the group. Discuss the issues arising, including any significant differences of opinion between individuals. Was there any consensus on the kinds of images that would be unacceptable in these circumstances? Were decisions based mainly on ethical judgements, or more practical concerns?

CASE STUDY 4.5

Visual identity, corporate image and strategy: the case of BT

The nature and dynamics of corporate visual identity are exemplified in the history of one of Europe's leading providers of telecommunications services: British Telecommunications plc (BT). A combination of technological innovation, market liberalisation and a changing socio-economic context have prompted changes in BT's corporate and business strategies, which have also been reflected in the organisation's evolving visual identity and its image in the minds of key stakeholders, including industry regulators, investors, customers and suppliers.

Case study 4.5 (*continued*)

From private enterprise to state monopoly

As in other countries, most of the UK's telephone network was once under the control of the state. BT's origins date back to the 1840s, when the first generation of telecommunications companies began to introduce electric telegraph services. Many new companies competed in the early burst of innovation. By the late 1860s this was already a thriving international business, with submarine cables connecting Europe with North America. The UK's inland telegraph system, including some related manufacturing businesses, was transferred to the state in 1870, a decade before Alexander Graham Bell's initial experiments with the telephone. The newly-emerging generation of telephone companies competed with the state-run 'General Post Office' (GPO). However, from 1912 until its privatisation in 1984, the state was the monopoly supplier of telephone services for domestic and business use, other than in a few municipalities.

Creating a new identity: privatisation and beyond

During its existence as part of the GPO, the precursor of BT had no separate identity. During the 1970s, telecommunications activities were separated from other parts of the Post Office, and in 1981 they came under the control of a separate public corporation, which operated under the name *British Telecom*. At this time, promotional materials used in display and television advertising featured a cartoon bird, named *Buzby*, whose voice was provided by a well-known British comedian. The company's partial privatisation in November 1984, when over 50 per cent of the company's share capital was sold to the public, was the first in a series of privatisations of state-owned utilities that continued into the 1990s. The privatised company, which adopted the legal title, 'British Telecommunications plc', was now actively traded on the London Stock Exchange and in other international exchanges. With its new commercial freedom, the company was positioned to respond to new competition in the UK, and to expand its operations globally. However, it was still popularly identified by the shortened trading name 'British Telecom', combined with a simple logo based on the initial 'T' in upper case, outlined by a circle. By the early 1990s, the company needed a more radical re-design to reflect its new strategic ambitions. The name and logo were still functioning effectively in its domestic markets, but problems arose when using this identity internationally. The main problem was the logo, which was almost identical to that of several other national telecommunications organisations, including the Spanish company, *Telefonica*. This restricted its potential as a registered trade mark, and made it unsuitable as a distinctive, international 'brand'. The adopted name *British Telecom* was also perceived in some markets as 'conservative and unexciting, reliable but not forward-looking'. Above all, it suggested that the company was national, rather than international in scope. Design consultants were asked to review the overall corporate identity. The subsequent re-design was more than simply 'cosmetic'. It followed a six-month research study, geared to the company's vision of becoming the most successful worldwide telecommunications group. It was also explicitly linked to changes in company structure, culture and operations. The new logo featured a 'piper', comprising a 'listener' (reproduced in red in the full-colour versions), and a 'teller' (reproduced in blue). This was meant to symbolise two-way communication, enabling customers to talk to one another: a central element in BT's business mission. The symbol was also seen as universal, conveying a similar message across different cultures. The use of a human figure was designed to highlight the personal element in the company's activities. On the practical side, the logo had to be suitable for a wide range of applications, from payphone kiosks to stationery. It had to be reproducible in monochrome and in full-colour format, and it had to look equally effective displayed on a computer screen or moulded into a plastic product. Other aspects of

Case study 4.5 (*continued*)

the re-design included improved typefaces and documentation. The new visual identity was accompanied by a change of name. The company adopted its initial letters 'BT' as a replacement trading name, while retaining the full corporate name for formal documents, such as contracts and share certificates.

'Connecting your world': BT in the twenty-first century

The 1990s saw further developments in BT's activities, including the expansion of Internet-related businesses, and the company entered the new century with four main lines of business: BT Retail, BT Wholesale, BT Global Services and BT Openworld. Its new strategic priorities include: putting broadband services 'at the heart of BT'; creating a 'media-enabled network'; and providing 'solutions and other value-added services for multi-site corporate customers in Europe'. This has contributed to a further re-assessment of BT's brand identity. In 2003, the company's 'piper' symbol was replaced by a multi-coloured globe, a design that had previously been adopted for BT Openworld. As with its predecessor, the logo is made available in full-colour and monochrome versions, in order to meet different applications (Figure 4.13). The new design was associated with a new brand vision that was summarised in the corporate slogan, 'Connecting your world'. The new identity makes bolder use of colour, intended to demonstrate characteristics such as 'dynamism' and 'freshness'. The designers have also selected photographic images that support the brand vision, for use in both consumer and business markets. Lastly, while the BT lettering is unchanged, the company has introduced new typography, to be used in all communication channels (such as brochures, advertisements or websites). The new typography is also designed to reinforce the identity in a consistent way.

Figure 4.13 The BT logo – monochrome version

Questions

1 Review the decisions made by BT in relation to its visual identity. How important do you think it was for the organisation to make these changes? What would the implications have been, had it made a different choice at each stage?

2 Compare the names and logos of three international telecommunications companies (or similar organisations operating in another sector), based on published materials (e.g. annual reports, websites). How effective do you consider these elements to be, in conveying a distinctive and appropriate identity for the organisation?

3 Draft a short report (maximum 800 words), outlining a proposed visual identity for BT or a similar organisation. Ensure that your proposal covers the relevant practical issues (e.g. use of colour) when reproducing the identity in various formats. Justify your choices, with reference to the strategic aims of the organisation.

Sources: BT (2003a, 2003b, 2012), BT logo reproduced with permission. Case prepared by the authors.

Glossary

Non-verbal forms of communication is a term that refers to any way in which we communicate our ideas, opinions and feelings to each other that does not involve using written or spoken words.

icon An icon is a simple symbolic representation of an object, which is used to communicate a message.

visual hook A visual hook is an image or picture that has enough impact to attract a person's attention and enable them to remember the idea or product, often by relating it to (or hooking it to) previous knowledge or experiences.

Visual literacy refers to our ability to understand and interpret cues in the form of images, pictures and body language.

Stock pictures are the name given to existing images or photographs that can be bought, often from agencies, and sometimes downloaded from the Internet for free, and are used to populate brochures, websites, etc.

Further reading

This chapter has covered various forms of non-verbal communication. Beginning with business graphics, **Tufte** (1990 and 1997) are beautifully-produced and inspiring source-books on this subject; other texts such as **Morris** (1999), **Richey** (1994) and **Saunders** et al. (2003) include more straightforward practical advice on presenting statistical data graphically. For ideas about how to present ideas visually, **McCandless** (2010) is a good source of inspiring ideas.

Arunachalam et al. (2002) is an example of empirical research into the impact of graphical information on decision-making.

Olins (1998, 2000, 2003) is a key source on elements of visual identity and its relationship to corporate image, from a leading practitioner. There are many research studies on aspects of non-verbal communication in inter-personal settings, mostly with a national cultural emphasis.

Hall (1959) was a pioneering anthropological study, with more recent sources including **Hall and Hall** (1990), and contributions to edited texts such as **Jackson** (1995) and **Joynt and Warner** (1996).

Useful websites

Here are several websites which might be of interest to you. You might like to add some of your own too:

Edward Tufte, an expert in the presentation of informational graphics, presents examples of effective visual representation of information via his website (Available at

http://www.edwardtufte.com/tufte/).

Find out more about the work of the Fairtrade Foundation and how they communicate their key messages via their website (Available at

http://www.fairtrade.org.uk/).

The 'Listening and interpersonal skills' learning area of the LearnHigher project website offers advice on how to interpret human signals (Available at

http://learnhigher.ac.uk/Students/Listening-and-interpersonal-skills.html).

The Makaton Charity website includes information on how Makaton is taught, learnt and used in everyday communications. (Available at

http://www.makaton.org/)

Test your ability to read human signals via the BBC's online 'Spot the fake smile' test. (Available at

http://www.bbc.co.uk/science/humanbody/mind/surveys/smiles/)

References

Arunachalam, V., Pei, B.K. and Steinbart, P.J. (2002) 'Impression management with graphs: effects on choices'. *Journal of Information Systems*, 16, 2, 183–202.

Blitz, R. (2007) 'Olympic organisers stand firm on using 2012 logo'. *FT Online* (June 13th 2007). (Available at: http://www.ft.com/cms/s/0/702da1d4-194a-11dc-a961-000b5df10621.html #axzz1aSgMp2GS (accessed 22nd March 2012)).

Blitz, R. (2011) 'Iran threatens Olympic boycott over logo'. *FT Online* (Feb 28th 2011). (Available at: http://www.ft.com/cms/s/0/a9a8f18a-4370-11e0-8f0d-00144feabdc0.html#axzz1aSgMp2GS (accessed 22nd March 2012)).

Bowie, N.E. (ed.) (2002) *The Blackwell Guide to Business Ethics*. Blackwell, Oxford.

BT (2003a) 'The company: BT group archives'. (Available at: www.btplc.com (accessed 6th August 2004)).

BT (2003b) 'Basic elements'. [Branding guidelines document, supplied by BT brand helpdesk]. British Telecommunications plc, London.

BT (2012) BT Homepage. (Available at http://www.bt.com/ (accessed 1st April 2012)).

change.org (2012) 'Tell PETA Violence Against Women is Never Okay'. (Available at: http://www.change.org/petitions/tell-peta-violence-against-women-is-never-okay (accessed 22nd March 2012)).

CIPFA (2003) *Code of practice on local authority accounting in the United Kingdom: a statement of recommended practice*. The Chartered Institute of Public Finance and Accounting, London.

Crisafis, A. (2011) 'France's burqa ban: women are "effectively under house arrest"'. *The Guardian* (19th September 2011). (Available at: http://www.guardian.co.uk/world/2011/sep/19/battle-for-the-burqa (accessed 25th October 2011)).

Directgov (2011) 'THINK! road safety'. (Available at: http://think.direct.gov.uk/index.html (25th October 2011)).

Donaldson, A. and Eyre, K. (2000) 'Using visual communication to drive change'. *Strategic Communication Management*, 32–35 (December).

Dou, W-L. and Clark, W.C. (2002) 'Appreciating diversity in multicultural communication styles'. *Business Forum* 24, 3–4, 54–61.

Ekman, P. and Friesen, W. (1971) 'Constants across cultures in the face of emotion'. *Journal of personality and social psychology* 17(2),124–129.

Fairtrade Foundation (2012) (Available at: http://www.fairtrade.org.uk/ (accessed 22nd March 2012)).

Gombrich, E.H. (1978) *The Story of Art* (13th edn). Phaidon Press, London.

Hall, E.T. (1959) *The Silent Language*. Doubleday, New York.

Hall, E.T. and Hall, M.R. (1990) *Understanding Cultural Differences*. Intercultural Press, Yarmouth, ME.

Harris, P.R. and Moran, R.T. (1996) *Managing Cultural Differences: leadership strategies for a new world of business*. Gulf Publishing, Houston, TX.

HM Treasury (2011) The whole of Government Accounting (WGA) Reports. HM Treasury, London.

HM Treasury (2012) Government Financial Reporting Manual (FReM). HM Treasury, London.

Holden, N. (2002) *Cross-cultural Management: a knowledge management perspective*. FT Prentice Hall, Harlow.

International Visual Communications Association (2012) 'What is the visual communications industry?' (Available at: http://www.ivca.org/about/about_the _industry.html (accessed 22nd March 2012)).

Jackson, T. (1995) *Cross-cultural Management*. Butterworth-Heinemann, London.

Joynt, P. and Warner, M. (1996) *Managing Across Cultures: issues and perspectives*. International Thomson, London.

Klein, N. (2000) *No Logo*. Flamingo, London.

Kortekaas, V. (2011) 'Digital "ambush marketing" threatens Games'. *FT Online* (Oct 9th 2011) (Available at http://www.ft.com/cms/s/0/f1879b92-ee78-11e0-a2ed-00144feab49a.html#axzz1aSgMp2GS (accessed 22nd March 2012)).

London 2012 Official Website (2012) 'Our brand' (Available at http://www.london2012.com/about-us/our-brand/ (accessed 22nd March 2012)).

Makaton Charity (2012) (Available at: http://www.makaton.org/ (accessed 22nd March 2012)).

McCandless, D. (2010) *Information is Beautiful*. Collins, London.

Moeran, B. (1997) *Folk Art Potters of Japan: beyond an anthropology of aesthetics*. Curzon Press, Richmond.

Morris, C. (1999) *Quantitative Approaches in Business Studies* (5th edn). Financial Times Prentice Hall, Harlow.

Office of the Deputy Prime Minister (2003) *Statistical Release: July 2003*. HMSO, London.

Olins, W. (1998) *Corporate Identity: making business strategy visible through design*. Thames & Hudson, London.

Olins, W. (2000) *Trading Identities: why countries and companies are taking on each other's roles*. Foreign Policy Centre, London.

Olins, W. (2003) *On Brand*. Thames & Hudson, London.

Pan, Y., Scollon, S. and Scollon, R. (2002) *Professional Communication in International Settings*. Blackwell, Oxford.

Richey, T. (1994) *The Marketer's Visual Tool Kit: using charts, graphs and models for strategic planning and problem solving*. American Marketing Association /AMACOM, New York.

Rodrigues, V. (2011) 'Olympic spirit under fire with Rio 2016 logo controversy'. *FT Tilt* (January 10th 2011) (Available at http://tilt.ft.com/#!posts/2011-01/10106/olympic-spirit-a-bit-under-fire-with-rio-2016-logo (accessed 22nd March 2012)).

Saunders, M.N.K., Lewis, P. and Thornhill, A. (2003) *Research Methods for Business Students,* 3rd edn. FT Prentice Hall, Harlow.

Sayer, A. (2000) *Realism and Social Science*. Sage, London.

Tufte, E.R. (1990) *Envisioning Information*. Graphics Press, London.

Tufte, E.R. (1997) *Visual Explanations: images and quantities, evidence and narrative*. Graphics Press, London.

Wychavon DC (2003) *Statement of Accounts 2002–2003*, Wychavon District Council, Pershore, Worcs.

Yahoo News (2012) 'PETA campaign director defends controversial vegan ad: "The underlying message is a helpful one" (Available at: http://news.yahoo.com/blogs/cutline/peta-campaign-director-defends-controversial-vegan-ad-underlying-214010566.html (accessed 22nd March 2012)).

Yergin, D. (1991) *The Prize: the epic quest for oil, money and power*. Simon & Schuster, London.

Chapter 5

Developing arguments: persuasive communication

> Only free men can negotiate. Prisoners cannot enter into contracts . . .
>
> Public statement by Nelson Mandela, February 1985 (Mandela 1994: 511)

Learning outcomes

By the end of this chapter you should be able to:

- appreciate the role of persuasive communication in various organisational contexts;
- identify the principal factors leading to successful and unsuccessful outcomes;
- review established theoretical perspectives regarding motivation and decision-making;
- apply verbal and non-verbal forms of communication in order to secure attention, develop arguments and secure agreement;
- address ethical aspects of persuasive communication.

5.1 Introduction

Everyone is involved in persuasion. Sometimes we are seeking to persuade others. For example, a manager needs a volunteer to work over the weekend in order to complete a project, or a trades union negotiator calls for improvements in working conditions. However, for much of the time we are on the receiving end of another person's efforts to affect, convert, convince, exhort, induce, influence, prompt, sway, urge or otherwise win us over. Many of these persuasive messages are highly sophisticated, the product of technical specialists, associated with advertising agencies, public relations consultancies and the emerging breed of political 'spin doctor' (Hollingsworth 1997, Michie 1998, Miller and Dinan 2000). A **spin doctor** is a person who provides a favourable slant to an item of news, a potentially unpopular policy, or similar, especially on the behalf of a political personality or party. These professionals are sometimes accused of exerting undue influence on, or even 'brain-washing', their audiences. In reality, the starting point for persuasive communication is that the receiver must have some freedom in responding to persuasive messages, and an underlying ability to choose between alternative courses of action. As the opening quotation suggests, without freedom, there is no scope for negotiation and therefore no need to persuade. In a relatively free and democratic society, audiences have some scope for accepting or rejecting the messages they are sent. As a result, even the professional communicators cannot guarantee the outcome of their efforts at persuasion.

This chapter focuses on the roles that persuasive communication can play within and between organisations. It reviews various types of persuasion that you are likely to encounter at work, plus some that everyone experiences as citizens and consumers. We also reflect on the key elements that people use to construct an argument, and apply the principles of rhetorical argument in a number of practical cases. Many messages contain degrees of persuasion, though they may be quite subtle and easy to overlook. For example, when an eager job applicant selects particular clothing for an interview, it is not purely a personal preference; it is a conscious choice, designed to influence the decision of the interview panel through non-verbal signals (see section 4.7). Similarly, as Case study 5.1 demonstrates, the purpose of a road traffic sign identifying a speed camera is not simply to provide information; it is a calculated attempt to change the behaviour of drivers.

CASE STUDY 5.1

Inform or persuade? The case for speed cameras

Driving at excessive speeds is a well-known source of accident and injury on the world's roads. There have been many initiatives from governments, transport departments and the police, designed to persuade drivers to comply with local speed limits; the most common being to penalise offenders with fines and endorsements on their driving licences. However, the traditional method, of using police vehicles to stop offenders, is costly and can create potentially hazardous distractions on multi-lane roads with heavy traffic flows; other drivers travelling in both directions tend to slow down for a short period, creating a 'ripple' effect in the traffic (Oesch 2002: 1). Speed cameras have been introduced in many countries since the 1990s, to record on film the registration numbers of vehicles travelling at more than the approved speed. There are average speed cameras which record a driver's speed over a given distance, and there are fixed speed cameras which record a driver's speed at one particular point. Research has demonstrated the effectiveness of these methods of speed control. For example, researchers in the Canadian state, British Columbia, reported a 7 per cent decline in crashes and up to 20 per cent fewer deaths in the year following introduction of cameras (Chen et al. 1998). In addition, research has shown that average speed cameras are more effective than fixed speed cameras with 54 per cent of those surveyed agreeing, and 51% agreeing that speed cameras save lives (Department for Transport 2012). A review of eight pilot schemes in the UK reported significant reductions in the number of fatal and serious injuries (Department for Transport 2003). Drivers are usually advised of the possible presence of speed cameras by warning signs, of the kind illustrated in Figure 5.1.

Case study 5.1 (*continued*)

Figure 5.1 Speed camera warning signs

However, there are many more signs than cameras. Consequently, one of the most contentious issues arising from the use of cameras has concerned their identification (Department for Transport 2003). Some have argued that it is more effective to publicise the location of each camera, using channels such as websites. There was a change of policy in the UK, so that cameras are currently painted in bright yellow, rather than the dull grey that was used previously. The effect is to highlight their presence to passing motorists, at least during daylight hours. Some people have questioned the logic of this approach, though it has the support of agencies such as the UK's Department for Transport. There has also been considerable debate regarding the emerging market in electronic devices to detect the presence of speed cameras, with some commentators seeing it as improving road safety, while others argue that it helps speeding motorists to avoid facing proper legal penalties. Most reports seem to suggest widespread public support for the installation of cameras. For example, there is an active campaign in the city of New York for the provision of additional speed cameras, plus 'red light' cameras at traffic intersections. It is also supported by groups such as Better Transport, who promote the interests of pedestrians and cyclists as part of their wider campaigning activities. However, there is also vocal opposition from some organisations representing the interests of drivers, which has also been reflected in driving magazines. Several independent websites have been set up to campaign against the use of speed cameras, and some motorists have taken direct action to undermine the process (e.g. people setting fire to speed cameras, or using imitation licence plates in order to avoid detection). While the overall number of cameras continues to increase, one of the original schemes, which operated in British Columbia, has since been terminated.

Further information on speed cameras is available at the following websites: www.dft .gov.uk and http://www.bettertransport.org.uk/. Details of other government sources and campaigning websites can be obtained via search engines.

Questions

1 Review the case and identify the persuasive elements in the 'messages' that are being sent by the speed cameras and the associated warning signs (see section 4.3).

> **Case study 5.1 (*continued*)**
>
> 2 Assess both sides of the argument regarding the identification and colouring of speed cameras. Which approach do you see as more persuasive?
>
> 3 Suggest other types of persuasive message, which might replace or complement those represented by speed cameras and warning signs (see section 4.3).
>
> *Source*: Chen et al. (1998), Oesch (2002), Department for Transport (2003, 2012). Written by the authors.

5.2   Persuasion in organisations

Though persuasive communication is used in all areas of organisational life, some functions are particularly 'persuasion-rich'. The basic dynamics of persuasion are evident in various types of inter-personal communication, such as the interactions taking place in meetings and interviews. However, in some of these, such as advertisements and press releases, the persuasive element is very explicit throughout. In other channels, including reports, letters and e-mails, persuasion may play a more subtle and intermittent role, forming part of the overall message. Consider the different ways that persuasive communication operates in the following practical examples:

- **Advertising**: Persuasive techniques are used to secure the attention of a target audience and to increase its subsequent recall of the message. Contrary to popular opinion, many adverts are concerned with ideas, such as building brand 'identity' and 'values', rather than action, in the form of an immediate purchase decision (see Chapter 10).

- **Public relations (PR)**: Public relations practitioners have not managed to secure themselves a very positive image. They are often portrayed as either not particularly bright people who enjoy lots of 'all expenses-paid' partying, or cynical, unethical people who spend most of their time distorting the truth on behalf of powerful corporate clients. Neither of these stereotypes is entirely accurate. Public relations is concerned mainly with managing the links between an organisation and the people outside, including customers, local communities and journalists.

- **Lobbying**: Lobbying means presenting an organisation's case to the key decision makers. Today, this is done mostly using briefing documents, lunchtime meetings and other PR tools, though the traditional meetings in the lobbies (i.e. corridors) of parliaments do still occur. These specialised forms of persuasion are used by all types of organisation, including companies, trades unions, single issue campaigners and charities (see Chapter 10).

- **Interviews**: Job interviews can often involve efforts at persuasion from both sides. Candidates are seeking to convince the panel that they are the right person for the job, while the organisation is trying to attract the strong candidates to accept job offers. Employers also want unsuccessful candidates to leave with a positive impression of their organisation, because this is essential to their longer-term efforts at recruitment. Persuasion can also be a factor in other types of interview, such as an employee performance appraisal. **An employee performance appraisal** is an annual or biannual meeting, usually between an employee and their line manager, at which the employee's performance is reviewed against previously set targets and targets are set for the next year's work performance (see Chapter 11).

● **Business meetings and negotiations**: In committee meetings and project team briefings, people often have to work hard, persuading others to accept their novel or controversial ideas and proposals. There are also those occasions when one party wants to deliver an effective counter-argument against another individual or group (see Chapter 13).

The next section introduces the underlying principles of persuasion, which draw on the concepts of rhetoric and argument. These principles are then applied to a series of practical challenges, indicating some of the ways in which organisational communication can be made more persuasive.

5.3   The essential principles: introducing rhetorical argument

The essential principles of persuasive communication have been understood for many centuries. They can best be summarised by returning to one of the sources of contemporary approaches to language, and the ways that it can be used in order to develop arguments. The term '**rhetoric**', meaning the art of using speech (including specific language techniques) to effectively persuade, influence or please, is used quite loosely today. However, its role in argument derives from the Ancient Greek term for an orator or speaker, where *têchnê rhêtorikê* referred to the skills required to construct an eloquent speech.

When the Greek philosopher Aristotle (384–322 BC) explored the structure of arguments, he managed to isolate three fundamental elements: *ethos*, or the credibility of the person presenting the argument; *logos*, the internal logic of the argument; and *pathos*, which equates with the emotional dimension. He defined rhetoric as 'an ability, in each particular case, to see the available means of persuasion' (Aristotle 1991: 36, Skerlep 2001: 180). These elements remain a useful framework for analysing persuasive messages. For example, if we reconsider the challenge of persuading people to refrain from drug abuse, it is clear that each of these elements has been exploited at various times (e.g. endorsement of anti-drugs messages by sports or music celebrities (ethos), publication of statistical reports detailing the consequences of abuse (logos) and personal appeals by parents and survivors (pathos)). In addition, we might also anticipate that communicating a message in a channel that combines these elements (e.g. a face-to-face presentation to school children, given by a former addict, who can present a clear and passionate case against drugs), has the potential to be more persuasive than messages that contain these elements in isolation (see Table 5.1).

Table 5.1 Three elements of a rhetorical argument

Element/type of argumentation	Practical example
Ethos: credibility of the person or organisation presenting the argument.	An organisation with a poor reputation appoints a new senior executive who is well-regarded by key stakeholders.
Logos: internal logic of the argument presented.	A government department issues a detailed research study that makes the case for its policy proposals.
Pathos: appeals to emotion in support of the other elements.	A police force asks the parents of a victim of crime to join in a televised public appeal for information.

Table 5.2 The basic components of an argument: Toulmin's model

Component	Description	Example
Claim	The assertion that is put forward for acceptance.	Research manager claims that the new product merits further capital investment.
Grounds or basis	Relevant data forming basis for the argument.	Research report highlights product's performance and market potential.
Warrant or explanation	Rules or principles for linking a claim to its 'grounds'.	What is generally regarded as relevant and strong research evidence.
Backings	Evidence supporting the 'warrant' in this particular case.	Details of the people who conducted the research, experience, methods used, etc.
Qualifiers	Phrases that place conditions or limits on the strength of the claim.	Report states that 'Product performance has been rated "excellent" in all applications tested *so far*'(emphasis added).
Rebuttals	Exceptional conditions, beyond the scope of the claim, that would otherwise undermine the argument.	Project will fail if a rival firm is successful in developing a product based on the next generation technology.

Sources: Toulmin (1957), Von Werder (1999: 674–8), Skerlep (2001: 185).

Analysing arguments: applying Toulmin's (1957) model

There are several approaches to the study of rhetorical argument, reflecting the broad social scientific distinctions outlined in section 1.6. This section focuses on work conducted within the 'normative/modern' perspective, which is primarily concerned with the ways in which speakers influence their audiences 'through the *intentional* use of speech' (Ovarec and Salvador 1993: 183 – emphasis added). Toulmin (1957) is one of the most influential figures in this tradition. His model of argumentation has been used to analyse the different components of an argument and their logical connections, both for research purposes and to help people improve their skills in presenting arguments. It begins from the idea that any argument consists of someone making an assertion or 'claim', with the aim of gaining general acceptance among a group of people. For example, the research director of an engineering company may be seeking board approval to invest in a research project involving a novel technology, which is currently at a development stage (see Table 5.2).

The potential value of Toulmin's model is in helping communicators to reconstruct and learn from previous arguments. It can also be used to encourage a more analytical approach to the managerial tasks of decision-making and presenting the outcomes to stakeholders (Skerlep 2001: 185). In the next section, we continue in this modernist perspective by considering the practical challenge of managing the process of persuasion in an organisational setting.

5.4 The challenge of persuasion: audience, message and context

In this section, we proceed with the simplifying assumption that persuasion is primarily a process of argument and counter-argument. Consequently, the main focus of the communicator's effort is on constructing a 'winning' argument. However, even in this narrow view of persuasive communication, we need to consider several broader questions. The answers to these questions are important, because they will inform the content of any persuasive message, its structure and the channels through which it is directed. The main issues to be addressed are: the nature of the audience; the nature of the message that is being conveyed; and the context in which the persuasive communication is taking place. (See Chapter 12 for further exploration of these ideas, specifically in the context of preparing and giving presentations.)

Assessing the nature of the audience

One of the most challenging tasks is to make a satisfactory assessment of your audience. The following list of questions indicates some of the more common issues that may require clarification or further research:

- What previous experience do they have, either of you as an individual, or the organisation that you represent?
- What do they already know, and how do they feel, about the subject matter of your message?
- What do you know about their personality and their current state of mind?
- Are you trying to persuade one individual or a large number of people?
- Are they able to act independently, or are they playing the role of representatives or agents of another organisation?
- What other factors might be persuading them in the opposite direction?

Researchers have explored the background to these questions at various levels of analysis. For example, a recent survey-based study distinguished five broad decision-making styles among senior executives. The authors suggested that these styles were relatively permanent characteristics of the individuals concerned and argued that persuasive communications would be more likely to succeed if they were tailored to the appropriate style:

'Executives make it to the senior level largely because they are effective decision makers. Learning mostly from experience, they build a set of criteria that guides them. Each decision is influenced by both reason and emotion, but the weight given to each of these elements during the decision-making process can vary widely depending on the person.'

(Williams and Miller 2002: 66)

It is certainly useful to gain a better understanding of individuals that you are seeking to persuade directly (e.g. the line manager with whom you are negotiating). Theories of human motivation may be of relevance here, though there is considerable debate over the relevance of classical 'content' theories, such as Maslow's (1943, 1987) 'hierarchy of needs', Alderfer's (1972) modified needs hierarchy and McClelland's (1988) categorisation of four key 'motives', often associated with its application in entrepreneurship research. Similarly, 'process' theories of motivation, many of which are based around concepts of 'expectancy', can be suggestive (e.g. Lawler 1973). However, subsequent research by psychologists has highlighted conceptual and methodological limitations when they are applied to organisational settings (e.g. Van Eeerde and Thierry 1996). Organisational theorists and strategy researchers, concerned with complex processes of persuasive communication and strategic decision-making, have also pointed out that these processes operate across many different levels of analysis, including the actions of individual managers; interaction between powerful sub-groups within the organisation; and wider economic, social and cultural influences (e.g. Barnett and Burgelman 1996, Lewin and Koza 2001).

Assessing the message: content and purpose

We now turn to some questions concerning the message that you are trying to convey. One set of questions relates to the content of the message. For example, does it comprise facts, ideas, opinions or a mixture of all three? Is it relatively simple or complex? Is the content likely to be surprising, or unwelcome or threatening to your audience, or to those they represent? In making this assessment, it is important to pay particular attention to the emotional (or 'affective') aspects of the message, since these can have a decisive effect on the outcome (see section 6.5). Organisational communicators often make the mistake of over-emphasising the cognitive aspects of their arguments, assessing them as logical and well-substantiated. This ignores the fact that audiences are human. In some cases, their powerful and sometimes unpredictable emotional responses will be fully capable of over-whelming the most impeccable logic and the evidence, carefully collected, that supports it. Non-rational aspects can become decisive when those you are attempting to persuade feel that their personal values, interests, security, or sense of identity is under threat. For example, during the international outbreak of SARS (Sudden Acute Respiratory Syndrome) in 2003, many public agencies, including local authorities in the Canadian city of Toronto, struggled to convince local populations that the threat had been contained. Popular fear of this previously unfamiliar disease proved more powerful than the dry statistics of reported incidents, and organisations that sought to persuade on the basis of their established reputation found their credibility being challenged.

There is a related set of questions concerning the underlying purpose of the message. Some persuasive messages have relatively modest objectives, but others are more demanding, requiring a corresponding increase in effort on your part. The following simple classification of objectives distinguishes between efforts to change what the receiver knows, what they believe, and how they currently behave.

Changing facts and ideas

If the relevant facts are clear and non-contentious, this simple form of persuasion is relatively easy, as the following dialogue makes clear. If senders have access to relevant supporting evidence (i.e. 'grounds', as identified in Toulmin's model), which they are capable of presenting in a straightforward manner, receivers will be persuaded to change their minds. Practise your skills in deconstructing arguments by analysing the following dialogue using the model outlined in Table 5.2:

Emily: 'So, Ifor, are you coming to the team briefing?'

Ifor: 'Are you crazy? It's only 9 o'clock.'

Emily: 'Sure, but didn't you know? Jay re-scheduled it yesterday.'

Ifor: 'You can't be serious, it's always at 11. Anyway, I'm sure someone would have told me.'

Emily: 'Yes, it's definite. I have checked with his PA, and there's an e-mail to confirm it – take a look if you don't believe me.'

Ifor: 'OK, you win. Well, let's get a move on then, or we'll be late!'

However, in some circumstances it can be far more difficult to persuade people to accept novel, complex or controversial facts and ideas. The pioneering scientist, Galileo Galilei (1564–1642), encountered violent opposition when he presented evidence that supported the 'heliocentric' theory of Nicholas Copernicus (i.e. the strange notion that the Earth revolved around the Sun, rather than the other way around). The new theory was seen as undermining the prevailing world view, which also legitimized the religious and political power structures of the time. First, Galileo's book was banned by religious authorities. He was subsequently forced to deny his 'revolutionary' ideas and spent the rest of his life under house arrest. Many examples from more recent history indicate that many people today remain unwilling to tolerate evidence suggesting that their world has changed.

Changing beliefs and values

Though they contain facts and ideas, a person's beliefs and values are bolstered by other powerful factors, such as self-image, cultural background and pressure exerted by a peer group (e.g. fellow scientists, or other members of a team, department or professional association). Therefore, if you are seeking to influence a receiver's beliefs and values, it is essential to consider more than the basic information content of the message. For example, imagine that you are working for an international retail organisation, which is re-positioning itself on the basis of enhanced customer service after many years pursuing a low-price, 'pile it high and sell it cheap' strategy. Many of the managers running local stores have been working for the company since graduation; their average age is 52 years. How can the regional operations director begin to persuade local area managers to implement the new strategy? Successful persuasion, in the face of such entrenched beliefs, may take some time. The pattern of communication is also likely to include a strong inter-personal and emotional dimension. In a dramatic example of this phenomenon, recorded as part of a television documentary, a member of a white supremacist group 'switched sides' and joined forces with an anti-racist campaign. For this individual, the catalyst for change was a close friendship with a work colleague who happened to be black. It required emotive pressure of a personal relationship, rather than the force of logical argument, to provide the energy needed to drive such a radical change.

Changing actions and behaviour

Influencing another person's actions can be very straightforward. For example, asking a colleague to send you a copy of her report, or asking someone to speak at a meeting, does not normally require much persuasive effort. Full-scale persuasion only arises where the receiver has an in-built resistance towards the proposed action or change in behaviour. These fundamental behavioural changes also require more than simply polite and rational discussion. For example, in countless public health campaigns, efforts have been directed at discouraging people from activities such as smoking, drug abuse and 'unsafe' sex. These campaigns have made use of posters, leaflets and other communication channels, containing messages that present frank and unambiguous information on the related risks (see Figure 5.2). Can this type of communication compete effectively against peer group pressure and slick commercialisation? In some cases, direct contact with people who have experienced the consequences has proved more persuasive.

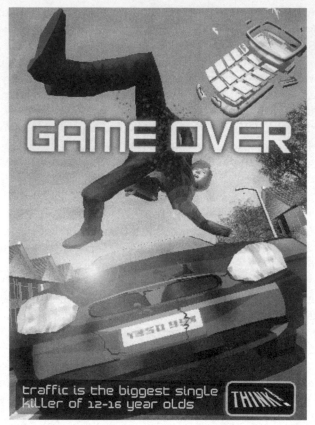

Figure 5.2 A warning poster
Source: The Advertising Archive Ltd. Reproduced with permission.

Assessing the context of persuasion

As in other forms of communication, ineffective outcomes may result from the sender's failure to fully grasp the context in which the persuasive message is being received. For example, is it happening *within* an organisation (e.g. encouraging employees to 'buy-in' to the new performance management system, seeking to overcome a conflict between rival departments), or in the *outside* world (e.g. attracting new customers to purchase a product, lobbying the government to increase spending on sports or the arts)? The approach to persuasion may also be affected by timescale and by the activities of other parties. Different strategies are required if you are under pressure to achieve a quick result, or where other actors are actively competing for the 'hearts and minds' of your audience.

The process of questioning should encourage the communicator towards creative solutions, designed to overcome the barriers that have been identified. For example, if the persuasive message involves a novel concept (such as a new technology, or unfamiliar work practice), the task of persuasion is likely to be much more difficult. Having identified this potential barrier, the communicator can take it into account when designing a message. In this case, the 'solution' may be to convey the novel content of the message using language and concepts that the audience already understands, and where there is already some common ground. The most persuasive communicators display a combination of awareness and flexibility, recognising and exploiting the fundamental self-interest of their audience:

> 'When what you have to say clearly intersects with what the other person wants or needs or cares about, you have given [them] a primary, compelling reason for listening. You're not actually demanding that he/she give up self-involvement. You're just piggy-backing on some part of the listener's own momentum . . . you're defining your message as another facet of his or her ongoing life concerns.'

(Hamlyn 1989: 38)

5.5   Persuasive practices: securing attention and arguing well

The communication practices most commonly associated with persuasion are efforts to secure attention (e.g. the salesperson's 'cold calling' technique or the advertiser's eye-catching design), and engaging in argument. In both cases, the result depends on the skill with which communication channels are selected and exploited. There are a number of generic 'recipes' for securing the attention of receivers, the secondary aim being to ensure the optimum pre-conditions for 'delivering' the message. While the appropriateness of particular techniques may vary depending on local circumstances, one or more of the following stimuli may generate a positive response:

- **Addressing people by name**: The use of personal names exploits the capacity for selective perception; it increases phasic alertness and can make people feel involved. Referring to a specific group in an audience, such as 'the team from our Zurich office', has a similar effect. Non-verbal cues, such as direct eye contact and gestures, are also used to attract attention in face-to-face settings, such as meetings and seminars.

- **Posing questions**: As problem-solving animals, humans find it difficult to resist a challenging question. For example, at the start of a presentation, the speaker might simply turn the opening statement into a question. (For example, 'Thank you for coming along this afternoon. Tell me, why do you think our main competitor has doubled its sales figures in the last six months?') Visual puzzles are another form of question that can attract attention in various communication channels, including display posters and television advertisements. The type of question that you choose to use can also have an impact on how successful you are in persuading your audience. Here are some suggestions on using various types of questions in ways that exploit their advantages and take account of potential limitations (see also section 11.4 for examples of using questioning techniques during interviews).

  (i) **Open questions** show you are genuinely interested in the receiver's response, as they allow people the freedom to respond in any way they wish. However, they can be time-consuming. Examples: 'What do you want to do when you graduate?'; 'What would you do to improve our corporate image?'

  (ii) **Closed questions** are used to seek confirmation and can be used to narrow down a receiver's response. These questions can normally only be answered with specific pieces of information, such as 'yes' or 'no'. Examples: 'Do you want me to go over that again?'; 'How many years have you been working for this organisation?'

  (iii) **Limited-choice questions** assist in controlling the conversation and saving time. They suggest to the receiver that one of the options you have given is correct. If

Table 5.3 Other forms of persuasive communication

Encoding/potential channels	Comments
Music and other sounds (e.g. soundtracks to advertisements, 'muzak' in retail outlets, 'on hold' music for call centres, hazard warning signals)	Music is sometimes described as 'organised sound'. Throughout history, sounds of all kinds have been used in persuasive communication. Songs have always been used to attract prospective lovers, whilst drums were beaten in order to terrify the enemy and lead reluctant soldiers into war. Because it is based on regular patterns, melody is readily absorbed and remembered. As a result, music provides a kind of mental 'hook' onto which other messages can be tagged. Advertising is often reinforced in this way. Ceremonial music at public events, such as the Olympic games, plays a similar motivational role.
Taste and smell (e.g. food outlets, perfume retailers, creating 'mood' in buildings and public spaces, warning of gas escape)	Though the sense of smell in humans is less developed than that of other animals, it remains an influential stimulant. As the smell of cooking emerges from a restaurant, passers-by begin to feel hungry and may decide to stop for a meal. The multi-million pound perfume industry prospers on the belief that its well-packaged aromas have a persuasive effect on users and those they want to attract. Smells can seduce, stimulate, warn and repel (e.g. bitter tastes are added to household chemicals to deter young children). The related sense of taste shares many of these attributes. However, there are obvious practical limitations on the use of these stimuli in organisational settings.
Direct action	People are often persuaded by actions rather than rational arguments. Direct action is usually associated with political protest movements, but it can also be effective in a business environment. A research scientist wanted to convince the materials company 3M that his invention had real market potential. Instead of using the conventional persuasion methods of formal presentations and feasibility studies, he produced a trial batch of his *entirely new* stationery product, distributing it to the secretaries of 3M's senior executives. The product proved very popular and supplies soon ran out. The secretaries, who were unable to obtain more stock, told their bosses just how useful the product was. Thanks to this direct action, the development project was approved and the 'Post-it note' became a highly successful product worldwide.

used insensitively, you may simply get the answer you want to hear. Examples: 'How many weeks of this timeshare holiday do you want me to reserve for you?'; 'Did you forget to attend the meeting, or did you just not feel like it?'

(iv) **Leading or value-laden questions** tend to enforce your own points of view onto the receiver with the aim of persuading them of your point of view. They are also quite likely to result in replies that do not reflect the respondent's real views or feelings. Examples: 'Why is your department so inefficient and badly-managed?'; 'How has this government helped you to improve your standard of living over the last three years?'

(v) **Probing questions** are used to gather additional information or to clarify the situation. If over-used they can become quite intimidating for the respondent. Examples: 'Why do you think that approach didn't work?'; 'What do you mean by your last comment?'

(vi) **Multiple questions** should generally be avoided; they can be ambiguous and lead to confusion rather than persuasion. Example: 'Can you please explain why you went there, who else attended and what did you say?'

- **Being provocative**: Persuasive communication often makes use of provocation. **Provocation** refers to the act of causing someone to behave in a certain manner: for example, stimulating anger or excitement in order to raise their initial awareness. This may be combined with other techniques, such as asking a question. For example, a British marketing consultancy once used a banner headline comprising the phrase, 'Are you bloody brilliant?' as the opening line of a job advertisement; it attracted attention and conveyed something about the distinctive culture of the firm. Non-verbal cues, including gestures and manufactured images, can also be provocative. For example, in the 1990s, Italian fashion company Benetton achieved high levels of awareness with a controversial poster and magazine campaign that included photographic images of an AIDS patient, a new-born baby and the bloodstained uniform of a dead soldier.

- **Using different channels and encoding**: We have considered how text-based argument and imagery may be used to construct and convey a persuasive message. These types of encoding lend themselves to conventional channels, such as presentations and promotional literature. However, organisations have access to other persuasive techniques, relying on different channels and forms of encoding. For example, imaginative communicators may be able to exploit other human senses. Sound, music, smell and taste can have a particularly strong persuasive impact, by-passing cognitive processes (i.e. the receiver's intellect), and making a direct impact at the level of the emotions and instincts. In some situations, they may also engage forms of 'direct action' in order to get their message across (see Table 5.3).

5.6   The other side of the argument? Persuasion as interaction

As the earlier discussion indicated, the heart of persuasion involves communicators in constructing a coherent argument, supported by credible evidence and addressing both cognitive and affective aspects. However, the simplified model that we have adopted up to this point has one major limitation. While it has taken some account of the audience, as part of the process of designing an argument, our approach remains locked into the linear (or 'one-way') model of communication (see section 1.3). This ignores the fact that persuasion is an *interactive* process, involving all parties in a negotiation of meanings. The classic error, repeated by many organisations, is in attempting to sustain an argument that is grounded in their own initial position rather than engaging in a *genuine* interaction with those they are seeking to persuade. Case study 5.2 highlights the need to take the other party's perspective more seriously.

CASE STUDY 5.2

'OK Biotec': science and the politics of persuasion

The environmental campaigning organisation, *Green Earth*, has alleged that an international biotechnology firm, 'OK Biotec', is polluting a waterway and harming wildlife, including the Bay Gull, an endangered sea bird (Figure 5.3).

Case study 5.2 (*continued*)

Figure 5.3 The 'Bay Gull'

The senior management of OK Biotec are mostly former scientists. They are justifiably proud of their technical innovation record. The company is internationally recognised as a centre of excellence in all of the technical issues relating to the supposed pollutant. It has also obtained independent scientific reports, stating that:

- the company's outflows have no measurable effect on local concentrations of the chemical concerned;
- the birds are indeed being harmed, but the culprit is a different pollutant, which is being released by a number of other companies in the area.

The chief executive officer of OK Biotec is Professor Katia Kleen, an experienced scientist who founded the company as a spin-out from her former university, which is the world-leading research centre in this field. Professor Kleen decides to take a direct approach. She issues a strongly-worded press release, dismissing the campaigners' evidence as 'amateur' and 'subversive'. Attached to the press release is a 15-page technical survey of the laboratories, incorporating all of the evidence from the independent researchers. Confident that the company is in the clear, Professor Kleen and her family leave town and enjoy a relaxing weekend at a country house hotel. And the result? Later in that same weekend, the *Sunday Inquisitor* publishes a front-page colour photograph of people in biological warfare suits, taking samples of a bright orange liquid pouring from an outfall pipe. Their headline blazes: 'Kleen says it's OK to poison the Bay'. The article continues on page two, illustrated with another large colour photograph of dead and dying Bay Gull chicks in a nest.

Television news teams from surrounding countries catch up with Professor Kleen in the early hours of Sunday morning. She is filmed in the luxurious surroundings of the country house hotel, surrounded by the aftermath of a champagne celebration. On Monday, the newspapers are filled with outraged comments from politicians and members of the public. Their perception, based on edited highlights from the television interviews, is that Professor Kleen and her company are acting in a complacent, incompetent, secretive and uncaring manner. The independent technical reports are completely forgotten. OK Biotec's share price collapses and trading is temporarily suspended. Two days later, a trespassing tabloid journalist is pursued by an OK Biotec security guard. In the ensuing confusion, he

Case study 5.2 (*continued*)

is accidentally savaged to death by an over-enthusiastic guard dog. The entire Board of OK Biotec is forced to resign.

Three years later, the pollution continues unabated, the Bay Gull has become extinct and OK Biotec continues to get the blame. Professor Kleen has just secured a deal with a magazine publisher, in which she intends to tell her side of the story. In retrospect, it seems that the company's senior management team could have been more persuasive in this situation, to the benefit of the Bay Gull and everyone concerned.

Questions

1 Identify what you consider to be OK Biotec's key communication errors.

2 Which messages had the greatest persuasive power for: (a) the OK Biotec management team; (b) the media; (c) the general public?

3 With the benefit of hindsight, devise an alternative communication strategy for OK Biotec. In doing so, suggest how the company should have responded at each stage, noting the likely media reactions.

Source: Written by the authors, based on real events. 'OK Biotec' is a fictional organisation.

FACE-TO-FACE 5

Involving others in your research: a matter of persuasion

Persuading people to participate in your research, even if it is only to get them to complete a questionnaire, can be one of the most challenging aspects. Read the following scenario and consider how this student seeks to persuade her audience to take part in her research project. Then, using the prompt questions below, evaluate her strategy and consider how you might approach this challenge.

Holly has come up with what she thinks is a great plan for her research project. She wants to explore students' and employers' perceptions of what makes a 'good' graduate employee. This will involve her surveying and interviewing a large sample of students and graduate employers, analysing the data, presenting and discussing her findings, and drawing conclusions and making recommendations. At the first meeting with her tutor he raised concerns that it was a bit ambitious given the time frame. So, first she needs to persuade him that it is a feasible project. She gets organised and works hard so that by her next tutor meeting she has drafted a logical schedule of work and has contact details of Human Resources (HR) managers in 10 locally based graduate employers. Her tutor is impressed.

Next she needs to persuade the employers to give up their time. Her tutor agrees to suggest some organisations in which he has contacts, and to write a letter to accompany the letter she will send to HR managers. She then plans to follow this up with a phone call. Her tutor suggests that she considers offering to share the findings with them, as those responsible for recruitment and trainee development may be interested in the results.

Holly now needs to get her fellow students on board to participate in her research. Again, if she is to persuade them to complete her questionnaires and to take part in interviews, she needs to think about what will make the process as effortless as possible for

Face-to-face 5 (*continued*)

them, and what she can offer this target audience in return. What might persuade or dissuade them? She decides that timing is important. She plans to ask them to complete her questionnaires at the end of a lecture, to ensure a good return, and to involve them early in the term, before they get anxious about and busy with their own projects.

What benefits can she offer other students? She could sell this as an opportunity to be on the other side of the interview situation, to learn about the interviewee's perspective before conducting interviews themselves. She could also offer to share her list of references. She could pay them but knows that there are ethical issues around this and that some researchers feel that this can affect responses; plus, she can't afford it. Of course ethics are another big consideration. She will need to assure participating students that their anonymity will be maintained and that the data collected will remain confidential. She is hoping that because she is a fellow student they will trust her and she will even get some candid, honest responses that they might not share with a lecturer or employer.

Questions

1 What strategies does Holly employ to ensure that she persuades her three target audiences to help her with her research project?

2 How does Holly apply the principles of rhetoric to persuade her audience to get involved?

3 Can you see any problems with the way in which Holly plans to persuade her prospective participants?

4 How might you persuade participants to take part in a project that you are planning? What might you do differently?

5.7 The ethics of persuasion

The circus promoter, P.T. Barnum, was known for the cynical maxim, 'There's a sucker born every minute'. This suggests that persuasion is a relatively straightforward task, and that its purpose is to win a 'one-off' victory against a gullible opponent. Hopefully, this chapter has demonstrated that 'effectiveness' in persuasive communication cannot be judged by our ability to mislead or deceive an audience. In organisational settings, this kind of 'win–lose' approach to persuasion is generally counter-productive, because the long-term reputation of the organisation will be damaged by repeated efforts to 'sucker' its various stakeholders. This lesson has become even more relevant in the era of the Internet, which provides an instantaneous channel for discontented stakeholders to communicate their dissatisfaction around the world. Consequently, the techniques of persuasive communication that have been outlined in this chapter will be effective only if receivers are taken seriously throughout the process. Of course, there are other reasons for behaving honestly, beyond this pragmatic concern with 'bad publicity'. Since the 1990s, many organisations have begun to take a more serious interest in business ethics and corporate governance. Under pressure from consumers, shareholders, journalists and governmental regulators, organisations of all kinds (including corporations, charities and public agencies) have begun to develop codes of conduct to regulate their activities. Persuasive communication raises a number of ethical issues. The most obvious of these is the use of lies and deception in areas such as advertising and selling (Carson 2002). Other areas include employee, supplier and shareholder relationships. In many cases, unethical persuasive practices are also likely to be either illegal or contrary to industry standards. Ethical issues relating specifically to persuasive communication can be divided into three broad categories, relating to the purpose, content and delivery of messages. Case study 5.3 considers some of the more contentious issues, using examples from the advertising industry.

CASE STUDY 5.3

The ethics of persuasion: examples from advertising

The advertising industry has long been the subject of criticism in ethical debates (e.g. Packard 1997). However, persuasive communication can also be regarded as unethical in many other contexts, ranging from job interviewing to the conduct of shareholder meetings. Consequently, examples from advertising are used here to illustrate issues that can be applied more widely:

- **Unacceptable purposes?** The intended purpose of certain messages may be considered unacceptable, but the picture is complicated by significant geographic and cultural variations in the ways that ethical standards are applied. For example, in the UK, television advertising targeted at children is closely regulated, but in some countries *all* advertising to children is banned. Similarly, it is illegal to advertise political parties and religious groups on UK television, though this practice is permitted in some countries, including the US. There have been increasingly stringent controls on the advertising of cigarette brands, again with some variation between countries.

- **Unacceptable content?** The previous section referred to Italian fashion retailer Benetton's advertising campaign, which featured graphic images of contemporary issues, including the bloodstained uniform of a soldier and a deathbed scene in a hospital ward. The campaign was criticised on the grounds that it exploited its sources in order to promote an unrelated and relatively superficial consumer product. Other frequent arguments have concerned nudity in advertisements, the portrayal of women and children, and comic stereotyping of other nationalities. These concerns also tend to be culture-specific, a factor that is normally taken into account by advertisers, on grounds of self-interest as much as ethics.

- **Unacceptable channels and encoding?** Some of the techniques developed to persuade audiences have subsequently been dismissed as unethical. For example, 'subliminal' techniques that fool the senses by projecting text or images for very short periods so that they are not readily apparent to the conscious mind. These forms of advertising have been outlawed for many years. However, technologies such as video text messaging are likely to present new challenges to the limits of acceptability. More traditional techniques, such as the 'hard sales' pitches perfected by unscrupulous dealers in double-glazing, time-share property and religion, are a continuing source of irritation and ethical debate. There is a degree of regulation of direct sales activities; the UK's 'Telephone Preference Service', for example, allows telephone subscribers to request their removal from the 'cold call' lists of direct sales firms. However, this service doesn't seem to operate when the source of the call is overseas, and in Indian and Far Eastern call centres especially there are specialists in cold calling the UK repeatedly for 'surveys' and 'com-

---

Case study 5.3 (*continued*)

puter warnings', etc., that seem to evade the authorities. Cases of undue pressure and mis-representation seem to be all too common.

Advertising and marketing professionals are often keenly aware of these ethical issues (e.g. Kotler et al. 2001). However, these efforts are not always communicated to external stakeholders. Reporting his research on marketing ethics, one North American academic noted with surprise that nearly half of the ethical codes in the organisations he studied were treated as *internal* documents. He concluded that ethical issues should be debated openly, across the boundaries of the firm:

'Since marketing is at the forefront of a firm's external communication, discussion of ethical issues should not be a foreign concept. Going forward, the necessity for clear and candid communication to surmount ethical problems seems mandatory . . . Further examination of what factors lead to candour/openness/transparency in marketing is needed.' (Murphy 2002: 175–6)

Questions

1 Find recent examples of advertising materials, of any kind, that might be regarded as 'unethical' under each of the three categories. Discuss your assessments with other students or colleagues, noting any differences of viewpoint and the basis of these arguments.

2 Why do you think that so many organisations appear to be treating their marketing-related ethical codes as internal documents? How would you suggest that an organisation communicated with stakeholders regarding these ethical codes?

3 Using the advertising examples as a guide, try to identify equivalent ethical issues that apply to other forms of persuasive communication (e.g. negotiations). Should these practices also be subject to ethical codes? If so, how might they be worded?

Sources: Kotler et al. (2001), Carson (2002), Murphy (2002). Written by the authors.

Summary

- Persuasion is an essential element in organisational communication, conveyed in all types of channels and present in many messages, which attempt to influence the ideas, beliefs or behaviours of receivers.

- While some organisational functions, such as marketing and public relations, are particularly 'persuasion-rich', persuasive communication plays an intermittent role in all areas of the organisation.

- The basic structure and content of persuasive messages, including the three fundamental elements of ethos, logos and pathos, can be related to established principles of argument (or 'rhetoric').

- The scale of the persuasive task depends on the nature of the sender, the receiver, the message and the context in which it is being communicated.

- Deliberate efforts at persuasion involve securing attention and developing a strong, coherent argument, which addresses the receiver's perceptions and feelings.

Summary (*continued*)

- Non-verbal signals, including images, music, smell and direct action, can act as powerful persuaders. Words alone may be insufficient; persuasive communication is often based on a creative use of multiple communication channels and forms of encoding.

- Persuasive communication raises important ethical issues for organisations, relating to the purpose and content of persuasive messages, and to the ways that they are conveyed.

PRACTICAL EXERCISES

5.1 Are you convinced?

We have all experienced being persuaded to do something, to change an opinion or alter our behaviour. Much of this persuasion relates to fairly trivial issues, but occasionally we are persuaded to make a more significant change. Spend a few minutes thinking back on an occasion when you were persuaded to change your mind:

(a) What type of change was involved? Was it concerned with facts, concepts, beliefs, behaviour – or a mixture of these?

(b) What persuasive techniques were used on you?

(c) How did you respond to this persuasive effort?

(d) What made you change your mind?

Seminar option: If you are working in a group, compare your answers with others. Does the type of persuasion appear to vary, depending on the subject matter? Can you reach any conclusions about the most effective persuaders?

5.2 The ultimate persuasion challenge?

(a) Divide into groups and spend 15 minutes devising the most difficult persuasive communication task you can imagine. It can involve a commercial business, a voluntary organisation, an educational organisation (including a university), or a public sector body. Write out the task on a large sheet of paper, specifying the message to be communicated, the sender, the receiver(s) and the general context. Use the following sample task as a model for structuring the information (see Table 5.4)). (Note: This example can also be used as an alternative group task, or by those studying independently.)

Table 5.4 A persuasive communication challenge: sample task

Sender	The city council.
Receivers	Local personal and business tax payers.
Message	Seeking agreement to increase local personal taxes by 45 per cent and business taxes by 24 per cent in the next financial year; the funds are needed for essential public services and economic development work.
Context	There is high regional unemployment, particularly among the under-25 and over-50 age groups. Local hospitals and schools are laying off staff due to budget cuts. It is also essential to encourage inward investment.

(b) Exchange your task with another group, and spend 30 minutes developing a communication proposal, designed to overcome the problem that you have been set. Try to be as creative and convincing as possible, whilst basing all your arguments on the perceptions of the *receivers*. If time allows, present your solutions and discuss how effectively you have made use of all available media and techniques.

CASE STUDY 5.4

Campaigning against poverty: Oxfam's persuasive communication

This case study is based on the reflections of a member of Oxfam's full-time campaign staff, based in Oxford. The author, Naveed Chaudhri, writes in a personal capacity and views expressed in the case study are not necessarily those of Oxfam GB.

Figure 5.4 The Oxfam logo

Background

Oxfam GB, a development organisation dedicated to finding lasting solutions to poverty and suffering, is one of the UK's biggest charities. Founded in 1942, Oxfam today works in more than 80 countries around the world. There is now a family of 12 Oxfams, which together form Oxfam International. The aim of Oxfam International is to maximise impact on poverty by co-ordinating the work of these individual members.

With wide public recognition, Oxfam GB undertakes a range of activities: it is a charity retailer, a responder to disasters, a funder of development projects, and a campaigner for change. Oxfam's mission statement gives a broad mandate for this wide range of activities, providing a clear moral message and a basis for all its public communications.

Oxfam is explicitly a campaigning organisation. It states: 'To overcome poverty and suffering involves changing unjust policies and practices, nationally and internationally, as well as working closely with people in poverty.' Recent Oxfam campaigns include seeking tighter UK arms-control legislation, pushing for funding for basic education for all, and arguing for the need to reform the world trade system. With limited resources, development charities can help only a tiny fraction of those in need, whereas improving policies and practices on these issues could potentially have a far wider effect on poverty.

Trust: the basis of Oxfam's legitimacy

It is important to put Oxfam's campaigning into perspective. Its core work is to put the funds of generous donors to good use in practical ways, to improve the lives of particular classes of beneficiaries. Without a continuing record of effective poverty relief, Oxfam would have no moral grounding for the opinions it expresses. This record is the basis both of enormous public trust, and, crucially for campaigning success, of widespread respect from politicians of all parties. Under UK charity law, Oxfam must ensure that its public statements are based on sound knowledge, and are necessary to achieve its defined charitable objectives. This is vital for any development charity seeking to campaign for change.

Inevitably, campaigners enter the political arena. The desire to speak out may conflict with the need to remain impartial, and with the need to retain broad-based public support. Campaigners must be able to communicate their concerns in a way which balances these competing pressures, in an often complex and rapidly-changing environment.

Ethical dilemmas: Iraq and Afghanistan

In early 2003, Oxfam recommended that there should not be US and British military intervention in Iraq. Although concerned not to be seen to be aligned with the anti-war movement (for the sorts of reasons outlined above), Oxfam's experience warned of the likely humanitarian situation following military action; a concern which was subsequently shown to be justified. A year or so earlier, however, Oxfam's call for a pause in the US bombing in northern Afghanistan to allow in food supplies before the onset of winter was unheeded, yet the feared widespread famine did not occur. Underlying these different concerns, justified or otherwise, was a single issue for Oxfam's credibility: whether entering publicly into the political arena would cause more harm or good. If the effect Oxfam could have on those particular situations was likely to be positive, would speaking out nevertheless have repercussions for its ability to work effectively in other parts of the world? Would the public's trust in the organisation be damaged?

Marshalling the arguments – and the support

Of course, it does matter very much that Oxfam gets the arguments right, and its 60 years' experience of working with poor people all around the world is perhaps its greatest asset. But campaigning is about far more than just lobbying at a policy level, and the knowledge Oxfam can bring to a discussion is just the starting point. Politicians need to be convinced that Oxfam's arguments are right; they also need to be given a reason to act. Thus the potential for bringing about the implementation of policy recommendations should be the measure of success when planning a campaign. This will rely on the different channels of influence that can be utilised, and, usually, on the level of popular support (or perceived popular support) for a campaign. Being right is of little use without some prospect, albeit sometimes over the long term, that one can change the political agenda for the better.

More than just 'marketing an idea'

Campaigning is seen by some as ultimately about marketing an idea, and campaigning organisations certainly have much to learn from the corporate sector about marketing tools and strategies. However, campaigning is much more than this. Far more than with any commercial product, people's loyalty to an idea is vital, and so the moral purpose underlying the campaign is paramount. Not only this, but the way in which one campaigns – the way in which one deals with people – is as important as the message itself. No matter how compelling the analogy with marketing, an organisation such as Oxfam, renowned for its humanitarian concern, would ignore this at its peril. And perhaps this is a lesson Oxfam can give to commercial companies: that a tangible concern for people should be at the heart of successful brands.

Case study 5.4 (*continued*)

Complex problems, simple messages? Understanding Oxfam's audiences

The problems with which Oxfam deals are complex, the factors affecting people living in poverty many and varied. Oxfam's recent '*Make trade fair*' campaign is a good example, in dealing with the labyrinthine details of the global trade system, yet needing to win the support of thousands, if not millions, of ordinary people in order to influence decision makers, in the face of very powerful vested interests.

Communicating these concerns requires a different approach for different audiences, with varying levels of detail required, depending on their levels of interest and knowledge. The largest number of potential supporters, perhaps motivated by a desire for the 'system' to be fair, but with a limited desire or opportunity to take action, needs convincing by very clear communications: setting out the moral arguments briefly and compellingly. This level of mass communication must be underpinned by the trust referred to above. It is also where the skills of mass marketing, including the increasing use of new technology (what is now termed 'e-campaigning') come into their own. Other audiences include: campaigns activists; politicians; trades unions; local, regional and national media; companies; and other non-governmental organisations. Our communications strategies need to be tailored to the needs of each audience, depending on the issues involved and how that audience is related to the relevant decision makers.

Not only do levels of engagement vary, but the motivations of these different audiences can be radically different. For example, an activist may be motivated to promote fairly-traded products by detailed explanations of the mechanisms by which the benefits to poor producers are guaranteed; yet average consumers will need to be convinced primarily of the quality of the product, coupled with a general belief that by buying it, they are making a positive contribution to the cause.

There are many other communications challenges for campaigners to face, including the need to address cultural sensitivities; to work alongside others living in very different circumstances; to work increasingly on a global scale for increased impact; and to use new technologies as campaigning tools. Nevertheless, the basic principles of campaigning remain the same, and to be successful, Oxfam needs to win the battle of both hearts and minds.

Questions

1 Re-read the case and identify examples of the ways in which Oxfam constructs and delivers persuasive messages, making use of relevant material from the chapter (e.g. Aristotle's fundamental distinction between the three elements of rhetoric: *ethos*, *logos*, and *pathos*).

2 What do you consider to be the main differences between persuasive communication in a campaigning organisation, such as Oxfam, and that taking place in a commercial organisation, such as a food retailer?

3 What are the main barriers to communication with Oxfam's various audiences? How are they being overcome?

4 Oxfam has developed a number of web-based resources, including the 'e-campaigning' activities referred to in the case. Review these resources (www.oxfam .org.uk)and prepare a short presentation (i.e. four bullet-pointed slides, plus notes) evaluating each resource in terms of its persuasive potential.

Source: Written by Naveed Chaudhri.

Key terms

An employee performance appraisal 116   provocation 125   rhetoric 117   spin doctor 113

Glossary

Spin doctor A spin doctor is a person who provides a favourable slant to an item of news, a potentially unpopular policy, or similar, especially on the behalf of a political personality or party.

An employee performance appraisal An employee performance appraisal is an annual or biannual meeting, usually between an employee and their line manager, at which the employee's performance is reviewed against previously set targets and targets are set for the next year's work performance.

Rhetoric The term 'rhetoric', meaning the art of using speech (including specific language techniques) to effectively persuade, influence or please, is used quite loosely today.

Provocation Provocation refers to the act of causing someone to behave in a certain manner.

Further reading

Much of the research on persuasive communication has been conducted within specialist disciplines, such as buyer behaviour, advertising, sales and public relations; additional references are included in Chapter 10.

Skerlep (2001) includes a reasonably accessible introduction to the theories of rhetorical argument, tracing it back to the classic study by **Toulmin** (1957). For more recent reading on argument, you could try **Andrews and Mitchell** (2001) which looks at argument in essays.

Von Werder (1999) also makes use of Toulmin's framework in a complex empirical study, exploring how Daimler–Benz reached an important strategic decision through argument.

Williams and Miller (2002) report a much simpler study, arguing persuasion techniques should be adapted to the decision-making styles of business leaders.

Cooper and Locke (2000) and **Warr** (1996) address some related psychological issues in work contexts.

Livesey (2002) is an interesting case study, analysing the persuasive communication of a large corporation using rhetorical and discourse analysis techniques.

Bowie (2002) is a useful edited 'reader' covering various aspects of business ethics, including those related to marketing, addressed by **Murphy** (2002), and selling and advertising, by **Carson** (2002).

Stott, Young & Bryan (2001) offer guidance on how you might use the art of rhetoric, amongst other techniques, to communicate your ideas persuasively in seminars and presentations.

Useful websites

Here are several websites which might be of interest to you. You might like to add some of your own too:

Bryman and Bell's online 'Research project guide' includes advice on ethical considerations. (Available at

http://www.oup.com/uk/orc/bin/9780199583409/)

The 'Listening and interpersonal skills' learning area of the LearnHigher project website allows you to assess your ability to use the right questions to achieve your purpose. (Available at

http://learnhigher.ac.uk/Students/Listening-and-interpersonal-skills.html

The Using English for Academic Purposes (UEFAP) website offers a comprehensive step-by-step guide to academic writing, including a useful section on rhetorical functions in academic writing. (Available at

http://www.uefap.com/writing/writfram.htm)

References

Alderfer, C.P. (1972) *Existence, Relatedness and Growth*. Macmillan, London.

Andrews, R. and Mitchell, S. (2001) *Essays in Argument*. Middlesex University Press, London.

Aristotle, ed. and transl. H. Lawson–Tancred (1991) *The Art of Rhetoric*. Penguin, London.

Barnett, W.P. and Burgelman, R.A. (1996) 'Evolutionary perspectives on strategy'. *Strategic Management Journal*, 17, 5–19.

Bowie, N.E. (ed.) (2002) *The Blackwell Guide to Business Ethics*. Blackwell, Oxford.

Carson, T.L. (2002) 'Ethical issues in selling and advertising', in Bowie, N.E. (ed.) *The Blackwell Guide to Business Ethics*. Blackwell, Oxford, 186–205.

Chen, G., Wilson, J., Mehle, W. and Cooper, P. (1998) *Interim Evaluation Report: photo radar program one year after introduction of the violation ticket phase*. Insurance Corporation of British Columbia, Victoria.

Cooper, C.L. and Locke, E.A. (2000) *Industrial and Organizational Psychology*: *linking theory with practice*. Blackwell, Oxford.

Department for Transport (2003) 'Speed Cameras'. Department for Transport, London.

Department for Transport (2012) 'British Social Attitudes Survey to Transport'. Department for Transport, London. (Available at: http://www.dft.gov.uk/statistics/releases/british-social-attitudes-survey-2011/). Last accessed: 20 March, 2012.

Hamlyn, S. (1989) *How to Talk so People Listen*. HarperCollins, London.

Hollingsworth, M. (1997) *The Ultimate Spin Doctor: the life and fast times of Tim Bell*. Hodder and Stoughton, London.

Kotler, P., Armstrong, G., Saunders, J. and Wong, J. (2001) *Principles of Marketing: the European Edition*, 3rd edn. FT Prentice Hall, Harlow.

Lawler, E.E. (1973) *Motivation in Work Organizations*. Brooks/Cole, Monterey, CA.

Lewin, A.Y. and Koza, M.P. (2001) 'Empirical research in co-evolutionary processes of strategic adaptation and change: the promise and the challenge'. *Organization Studies*, 22, 6, v–xii (Special Issue on Multi-level analysis and co-evolution).

Livesey, S.M. (2002) 'Global warming wars: rhetorical and discourse analytical approaches to ExxonMobil's corporate public discourse'. *Journal of Business Communication*, 39, 1, 117–148.

McClelland, D.C. (1988) *Human Motivation*. Cambridge University Press, Cambridge.

Mandela, N.R. (1994) *Long Walk to Freedom: the autobiography of Nelson Mandela*. Little, Brown and Company, London.

Maslow, A.H. (1943) 'A theory of human motivation'. *Psychology Review*, 50, 307–396 (July).

Maslow, A.H. (1987) *Motivation and Personality*, 3rd edn. Harper and Row, New York.

Michie, D. (1998) *The Invisible Persuaders: how Britain's spin doctors manipulate the media*. Bantam, London.

Miller, D. and Dinan, W. (2000) 'The rise of the PR industry in Britain, 1979–98'. *European Journal of Communication*, 15, 1, 5–35.

Murphy, P.E. (2002) 'Marketing ethics at the Millennium: review, reflections and recommendations', in Bowie, N.E. (ed.) *The Blackwell Guide to Business Ethics*. Blackwell, Oxford, 165–185.

Oesch, S.L. (2002) 'Statement before the Maryland House of Delegates, Commerce and Government Matters Committee: automated speed enforcement (5th February)'. Insurance Institute for Highway Safety, Arlington, VA.

Ovarec, C. and Salvador, M. (1993) 'The duality of rhetoric: theory as discursive practice'. in Poulakos, T. (ed.) *Rethinking the History of Rhetoric: multidisciplinary essays on the rhetorical tradition*. Westview Press, Boulder, CO, 173–192.

Packard, V. ([1957] 1997) *The Hidden Persuaders: the classic study of the American advertising machine*. Penguin, London.

Skerlep, A. (2001) 'Re-evaluating the role of rhetoric in public relations theory and in strategies of corporate discourse'. *Journal of Communication Management*, 6, 2, 176–187.

Stott, R., Young, T. and Bryan, C. (2001) *Speaking Your Mind: oral presentation and seminar skills*. Pearson Education, Harlow.

Toulmin, S. (1957) *The Uses of Argument*. Cambridge University Press, Cambridge.

Van Eeerde, W. and Thierry, H. (1996) 'Vroom's expectancy models and work-related criteria: a meta-analysis'. *Journal of Applied Psychology*, 81, 5, 575–586 (October).

Von Werder, A. (1999) 'Argumentation rationality of management decisions'. *Organization Science*, 10, 5, 672–690.

Warr, P. (1996) *Psychology at Work*. Penguin Books, London.

Williams, G. and Miller, R.B. (2002) 'Change the way you persuade'. *Harvard Business Review*, 80, 65–73 (May).

Chapter 6

Establishing a dialogue: interactive communication

Half of the money I spend on advertising is wasted; the trouble is, I don't know which half.

William Hesketh Lever, consumer product manufacturer

Learning outcomes

By the end of this chapter you should be able to:

- recognise the wide variety of responses stimulated by organisational activity and the importance of securing feedback effectively;
- identify the different characteristics of organisational feedback and the mechanisms that are used to collect and process this information;
- critically assess specific feedback mechanisms employed in relation to the organisation's employees, its customers and other stakeholders;
- make connections between feedback mechanisms and other organisational and managerial issues, such as knowledge management, organisational learning and emotional intelligence;
- develop your approach to giving and receiving feedback that supports professional development.

6.1   Introduction

As William Hesketh Lever recognised, it is not easy to find out what impact your organisation is having on the world around it. The communication challenge is not simply to obtain information but to secure feedback that is relevant, informative, and that enables us to make positive changes. Lever's problem was echoed more recently by the chief executive officer of Hewlett Packard, who commented, 'If HP knew what HP knows we would be three times as profitable.' This chapter is concerned with the ways that organisations secure feedback from their internal and external stakeholders, and from the wider environment in which they operate. **Feedback**, in this context, comprises the messages that organisations, or individuals working in organisations, receive from stakeholders in response to their own messages and activities. For example, comments about a company's customer service, posted on a review website, represent a type of feedback. Feedback is essential to any open system, facilitating interaction and enabling it to adapt and meet the changing demands of its environment (see section 1.4). In reviewing feedback mechanisms, we concentrate on the implications for communication, but also engage with a much wider debate concerning the ways that organisations manage knowledge and learn from their collective experience.

Stakeholders consist of individuals and groups who have an interest in, or are affected by, the activities of an organisation. They may include 'internal' stakeholders, such as employees, and 'external' stakeholders, such as members of the local community. An organisation requires feedback from all of its stakeholder groups if it is to continue to function effectively. The quality of this feedback depends, in turn, on the effective use of particular communication channels. For example, marketing departments have to maintain a close watch on qualitative and quantitative changes in demand (e.g. the emergence of a new fashion trend, or a collapse in consumer spending), in order that their company's products remain competitive. They do so using a number of channels, including survey questionnaires, focus group interviews, and the analysis of weekly sales reports. Organisational managers of all kinds need to obtain feedback from their colleagues and business partners. Failure to secure this feedback can lead to serious dysfunctional effects, such as under-achievement and internal conflict.

The sheer diversity of organisational feedback, and the many channels through which it is conveyed, make it difficult to generalise about the techniques for securing effective feedback. However, it is possible to identify some broad principles. The chapter begins with an overview of the main kinds of feedback, including their inherent characteristics and the form in which messages are received. It is followed by a closer examination of the feedback mechanisms that enable organisations to obtain information from one of their major stakeholder groups – their employees. We then consider the practicalities of form design: illustrating the challenges of constructing an apparently simple communication channel for the purposes of feedback. The chapter concludes with a brief discussion that highlights connections between the main themes of this chapter and related research, in the areas of knowledge management, organisational learning and emotional intelligence.

6.2 Organisational feedback: an initial overview

There is an astonishing diversity of organisational feedback mechanisms, but they are rarely subjected to systematic analysis. This section presents an initial critical review of the types of feedback that are secured in different parts of the organisation, highlighting their inherent characteristics and the communication channels through which they are typically conveyed. We have already noted that communication channels vary in the extent to which they facilitate feedback (see section 1.4). In the case of feedback, we can identify two distinct dimensions relating to the quality of the messages conveyed: their degree of urgency and their inherent complexity. Both dimensions need to be taken into account when designing and assessing feedback mechanisms:

- **Degree of urgency**: In some situations, the prime requirement is to secure *immediate* feedback on a particular organisational activity. For example, the engineers at a hospital need to know at once if there is a technical fault in a piece of medical equipment. The message is urgent because any delay is likely to affect service delivery, which could endanger the lives of patients. In other parts of the hospital (e.g. in the human resources department, where an employee's annual appraisal interview is processed), there is less urgency regarding the timing of the process.

● **Inherent complexity:** For some forms of feedback, the prime requirement is to convey very *complex messages* relating to the organisation. For example, at the headquarters of a restaurant chain, a dissatisfied customer's verbal complaint may be a mixture of factual information, subjective perceptions and strong human emotions. Complex messages of this kind can also contain a degree of ambiguity, requiring the organisation to interpret the meaning of the message (i.e. it may be difficult to identify the underlying cause of the complaint from the initial message; the customer may be upset about something else). In contrast, much of the feedback collected by the restaurant chain will comprise relatively straightforward data (e.g. standardised accounting reports sent to the finance department by each restaurant on a regular basis).

When these two dimensions are represented graphically, we are given some indication of the variety of feedback mechanisms employed in organisations. Figure 6.1 suggests the relative strengths of several common feedback mechanisms in terms of their information richness and immediacy of response. Many other examples could be added, and their position may be open to debate, depending on the particular circumstances in which they are being employed. Note that the categorisation 'low' degree of urgency in Figure 6.1 does not imply lack of importance, but only that the message contained in this feedback is not highly time-sensitive.

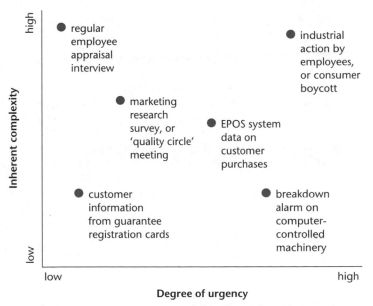

Figure 6.1 Characterising feedback mechanisms – urgency and complexity

Examining the diversity of feedback mechanisms

Organisational feedback is encoded in many different forms, ranging from numerical data on the management accountant's paper printouts to the spoken words and gestures of a protestor during the annual shareholders' meeting.

Collecting feedback

Feedback can be collected in many different locations, within and beyond the physical boundaries of the organisation. However, one of the challenges for communicators is to ensure that this collection actually takes place. We have seen how any message can be obstructed or distorted by powerful barriers, operating at the level of individuals, groups, the organisation and the wider environment. Consequently, the quality of the feedback obtained will depend a great deal on the context in which it is sent and the degree to which it is under organisational control. For example, statistical process control data, collected inside a company's production plant, may be highly reliable. By contrast, most organisations find it extremely difficult to gauge public reactions to their proposed or enacted strategies. In contrast to feedback from the production line, the latter involves less reliable types of data collection. Moreover, messages from the public are likely to be more complex and their responses are open to a variety of interpretations (see Table 6.1).

Table 6.1 The diversity of organisational feedback: some examples

Area of activity or stakeholder group	Typical feedback mechanisms	Comment
Suppliers	Bids from suppliers Informal contacts	Quantitative and qualitative data, collected via formal and informal processes in a purchasing department.
Production	Quality audits Production statistics	Quantitative and qualitative data, collected primarily via formal processes in a production department.
Employees	Appraisal process Job satisfaction surveys Staff turnover rates Response to job adverts 'The grapevine' Training evaluation forms	Mainly qualitative data, collected via formal and informal processes at a number of locations.
Customers	Sales data Market research Customer complaints	Quantitative and qualitative data, collected via formal processes in sales, marketing and customer service departments.
Local community/ general public	Stakeholder consultations Media coverage	Primarily qualitative data, may be collected formally by corporate affairs and informally by other members of staff.
Financial community	Accounting statements Analysts' reports Informal contact	Quantitative data (from accounts) and qualitative data, collected more informally by accountants, treasury managers and senior executives.
Management accounting	Accounting statements Variance reports	Primarily quantitative data, collected formally by cost accountants.

Sharing and using feedback

In the case of organisational feedback, one of the biggest challenges is to ensure that messages are conveyed beyond the point of collection, in order that other parts of the organisation are aware of any incipient problems. Like other messages, feedback may need translating across functional or departmental borders. Consider, for example, a Chinese manufacturer of hi-fi equipment who is exporting to international markets. Feedback received by the European sales team may indicate that there is resistance to some cosmetic features of the product design. However, unless this information is conveyed – in an appropriate format – to the company's research and development department in Shanghai, there may be a costly delay in remodelling the product. For senior executives, the main concern is to ensure their exposure to relevant streams of feedback from all parts of the organisation. Clearly, those at the centre of the organisation are not in a position to absorb all of the incoming information in detail. However, subject to appropriate filtering, their exposure to a diversity of feedback can enable senior executives to make important connections, informing their strategic decision-making (e.g. Grant 1996, Kay 2000, Spender 1996). For example, by synthesising feedback obtained from multiple stakeholders, the organisation will be better positioned to embark on a major acquisition, diversification or divestment. This is not a trivial task, and organisations often struggle to maintain an effective flow of information. Case study 6.1 considers how organisational feedback mechanisms can fail in respect of ethical issues, a form of 'moral deafness' that can have disastrous results for all concerned.

CASE STUDY 6.1

When feedback mechanisms fail: explaining 'moral deafness'

In his book *The Muted Conscience*, Frederick Bruce Bird explores an interesting and important question for all organisational communicators, which was first introduced in section 2.4. Given that all individuals have moral concerns, why do they so often fail to voice these concerns in the organisations where they work? Bird suggests that 'moral silence' is reinforced by various forms of 'moral deafness' and 'moral blindness'. In other words, people manage to ignore emerging ethical issues. Those who do speak out – the so-called 'whistle-blowers' – often face a great deal of hostility in their organisation. They can find their careers undermined and may even face threats of physical violence. The fear of experiencing these problems can act as a powerful disincentive to individuals. Also, at the organisational level, it seems that there are institutional obstacles to feedback of this kind. (Note: Although the author does not make this connection, these concepts can be linked to Janis's (1982) concept of 'groupthink' and the 'Abilene paradox' (see section 2.4), which suggest how social psychological factors might contribute to the process.)

Nestlé and infant formula: a case of 'moral deafness'?

In Bird's definition, 'People are morally deaf to the degree that they do not hear and do not respond to moral issues that have been raised by others' (Bird 2002: 55). He identifies the five types of moral deafness as:

- inattentiveness;
- not being ready to hear bad news;
- not seeking out bad news;
- not comprehending;
- not taking into consideration the accounts of others.

One of the cases cited as an example of moral deafness concerns Nestlé, one of the world's largest branded foods manufacturers. Nestlé has been engaged in more than three decades of argument with campaigning organisations over its strategy for marketing infant

Case study 6.1 (*continued*)

powdered milk formula in developing countries. In the early 1980s, the company was criticised publicly for promoting formula in situations where its use was bound to increase infant mortality, due to the poor quality of local water supplies and the risk that the product would be used incorrectly. Campaigners argued that advertising and sales promotion techniques were being used to persuade mothers to abandon breast-feeding in favour of the infant formula. The initial response from Nestlé's board of directors, which was captured in a televised international press conference, was widely regarded as both arrogant and defensive. Protests were organised in response to perceived inaction on the part of the company. Nestlé found its products boycotted by student unions, religious groups and other organisations involved with development issues.

Over subsequent years, Nestlé has made significant changes to its marketing and promotional practices. It has also engaged in a long and expensive public relations campaign, which has sought to engage in a dialogue with campaigners. The company has a separate section on its website (www.babymilk.nestle.com) addressing issues such as the company's compliance with international codes of practice. For example, it states that:

> 'Nestlé supports breastfeeding and believes that breast milk is the best start a baby can have in life . . . Nestlé learned a great deal from its experience concerning infant formula marketing in Africa, recognising our responsibility to go beyond what were accepted marketing standards at the time . . . We integrated the World Health Organisation's International Code of Marketing of Breast-milk Substitutes across our entire operations in developing countries in 1982, and continue to monitor its application, refining our instructions with experience'(Nestlé 2011).

However, campaign groups such as Baby Milk Action continue to exert pressure on the company, using its website (www.babymilkaction.org) to present a case against the company and to encourage people to boycott its products. This long-running debate has been given a new urgency in the context of the AIDS epidemic, which has created additional demand for infant formula and dietary supplements. The controversy has increased because breast feeding is one way the AIDS virus can be transmitted.

Questions

1 What factors do you think may have contributed to the apparent 'moral deafness' of Nestlé in the early 1980s?

2 What kinds of communication channel have operated to change the company's position since the initial protests? Can the current situation still be regarded as 'moral deafness' in Bird's definition?

3 Describe a recent example of an organisation displaying moral deafness, blindness or silence. This might be an organisation where you work or study. How might the development of technologies, such as e-mail and the Internet, have affected these phenomena?

Source: Baby Milk Action (2011), Bird (2002), Nestlé (2011). Case prepared by the authors.

6.3 Securing stakeholder feedback: the case of employees

This section considers some of the main feedback mechanisms used in relation to the key internal stakeholder group for all organisations – its employees. Similar exercises could be conducted for each of the main external stakeholder groups, including customers, students, suppliers and local communities. In selecting this stakeholder group, our aim is to examine the patterns of communication that underpin these feedback mechanisms, rather than to address them from a specifically human resources management (HRM) perspective.

There are many ways for organisations to obtain feedback from employees, relating to issues such as their performance in work tasks, their degree of satisfaction with the job, managers, colleagues and the work environment, and internal perceptions of the organisation. Feedback may be collected by line managers and human resources specialists, but it is doubtful whether these different sources are always integrated. In this section we consider four typical communication channels in brief, before focusing our attention on an increasingly popular channel: the '360-degree appraisal'.

- **Job satisfaction surveys**: Many organisations use questionnaire survey techniques to obtain feedback from employees. The questionnaires are sometimes presented in another guise (e.g. a 'communication audit'), and are often conducted by external research consultancies in order to overcome employees' concerns regarding anonymity. This channel is likely to generate a mixture of qualitative and quantitative data, relating both to specific issues (e.g. identifying problems with the catering facilities) and to employee attitudes (e.g. degree of support for a proposed organisational restructure). Data are analysed and summarised in order to provide feedback to senior managers and human resources departments, normally in the form of a written report or verbal presentation. Surveys can provide a broad yet concise overview, highlighting key differences between departments and types of staff, for example. An important, but sometimes overlooked, stage involves feeding results back to employees and then creating the opportunity to discuss the results' meaning and management responses to them.

- **Staff turnover rates**: This deceptively simple measure may be of more relevance in larger organisations, where there are enough employees to allow for the identification of trends. Such feedback, which is not deliberately collected but which results from statistics generated for other purposes, is a form of incidental feedback. **Incidental feedback** occurs as part of 'normal business' and, if observed, recorded and analysed, provides useful information that is not directly sought but which gives insight to particular trends. For example, falling attendance rates on a tennis course might indicate that learners do not find it useful. This might be complimented with collection of follow-up feedback to find out the reason why these trends are occurring. In another example, many students may get the same exam questions wrong, which might serve as incidental feedback to the lecturer that the questions were too difficult or ambiguous; or that students have not understood the topic sufficiently well. Increased staff turnover may indicate a number of things, including dissatisfaction with the job or the organisation, fears over its future, or a highly competitive job market. Similarly, reduced turnover may be interpreted positively (staff enjoy working for the organisation), or negatively (they are only staying on in the hope of large redundancy payments). To interpret the data correctly, it is necessary to complement statistical analysis of turnover rates (for example, between different time periods, or across departments and geographic locations) with qualitative data. This may range from informal feedback from managers to a more elaborate system of 'exit interviews' with departing members of staff.

- **Response to job advertising:** Organisations need to be aware of the state of the employment market, particularly when they are seeking large numbers of new staff, or have a shortage of people in a particular specialism. A decline in the level of interest in job advertisements may be measured in terms of number of initial enquiries, number of applications received, or quality of applicants. Each of these measures may indicate various possibilities. For example, the market may have become more competitive, the organisation may no longer be perceived as an attractive employer, or the pay and conditions for a specific post are not sufficient to attract good candidates. Also, in the UK, all employers are required by the Equality Act 2010 to be able to justify their approach to advertising a job vacancy (Equality and Human Rights Commission 2011). This is to identify and guard against discrimination against people with a protected characteristic (e.g. race, age, sex, disability, etc.). For example, indirect discrimination would include restricting advertising jobs to places that certain ethnic groups do not access.

- **'The grapevine':** This informal and unofficial channel can provide some of the richest feedback from employees. However, because messages pass primarily by word of mouth, in corridors, canteens and bars, senior managers find them elusive and difficult to assess. Even where they have access to these messages, the information may be transient, inconsistent and unreliable. Grapevines are a common source of mis-information, particularly when an organisation is facing threats or uncertainties. Rumours may flare up for a short period of time, and information received from one part of the organisation may be contradicted by that from another source. Despite the disadvantages, they may provide important insights into issues that need to be addressed with urgency. The Team Briefing is an effective, face-to-face method for communicating information (and responding to feedback) across all levels of an organisation. This typically involves departmental managers promptly cascading key information and Senior Management Team decisions to their departmental staff. Unlike using e-mail to disseminate such information, this method facilitates synchronous, two-way communication and creates opportunity for a dialogue. It is also effective for preventing rumours spreading via the grapevine, as misunderstandings and concerns can be tackled at the point of delivery. (Chapman/Businessballs 2011). See chapter 13 for more information.

Each of these channels provides feedback on employees, though the quality and format of the information varies significantly according to which channel is selected. The 360-degree appraisal has become a widely-adopted feedback mechanism, which tackles several limitations identified in earlier forms of appraisal. It integrates information from several different sources in order to provide a more reliable basis for appraising employees.

360-degree appraisal

The 360-degree performance review has grown in popularity as a result of the problems encountered with other forms of appraisal. The term '360-degree' refers to the idea that employees' assessments should be based on feedback from several sources, including their peers, subordinates, line managers and sometimes external stakeholders such as customers (Marchington and Wilkinson 2002: 329). From a communication perspective, the primary advantage of this approach is that multiple-rater assessments provide information that has greater validity, and that has the potential to be more persuasive when it is presented to the employee. The practice of giving and receiving 360-degree feedback should also generate valuable information at an organisational level, better informing strategic decision-making. It can also foster a climate of more open communication in the organisations where it is adopted, something that is particularly appropriate for new organisational forms (see section 7.3). Case study 6.2 illustrates how 360-degree feedback was implemented in one large organisation.

CASE STUDY 6.2

Modernising Medical Careers: multi-source feedback (MSF) in action

Figure 6.2 The NHS logo

Modernising Medical Careers (MMC) is a UK National Health Service (NHS) initiative that aims to improve patient care by reforming postgraduate medical education for doctors and developing a workforce of 'demonstrably competent doctors who are skilled at communicating and working as effective members of a team' (NHS, 2012). A key strand of the MMC initiative is the assessment and feedback activity. This includes observations of clinical procedures and interaction with patients; presentation and discussion of patient cases with experienced colleagues; and multi-source feedback (MSF). Here we will focus specifically on the MSF: a process which uses questionnaires to collect views from a range of co-workers that can be used for 360° assessment of a trainee doctor's workplace performance. Trainee doctors are required to nominate 12 assessors from amongst their co-workers, who should include a range of health professionals such as senior consultants, fellow trainees, nurses, physiotherapists, clerical staff and psychologists, and arrange for them to fill out a questionnaire. (See the Joint Royal Colleges Postgraduate Training Board website for examples – http://www.jrcptb.org.uk/assessment/Pages/WPBA-Documents.aspx) The questionnaires ask assessors and the trainee doctors themselves to rate their competence in areas such as: maintaining trust with patients; written and oral communication skills; working with colleagues; accessibility/reliability; ability to diagnose patient problems; ability to manage time effectively/prioritise; and ability to deal with stress. The assessment questionnaire should take approximately 10 minutes to complete. Once feedback from the questionnaires has been collated, the trainee doctor and their educational supervisor discuss it to identify strengths and areas for development.

Feedback on this Feedback Process

The Department for Medical Education at the Open University conducted an evaluation of the pilot of this assessment system to identify areas for improvement, based on trainee doctors' and their assessors' experiences and feedback (Open University Centre for

> **Case study 6.2 (*continued*)**
>
> Education in Medicine 2005). Timing was found to be the main issue; both trainees and assessors found organising and completing this number of assessments to be time consuming, with 34 per cent of trainees reporting that time constraints hampered implementation of the system. Feedback about the quality of the questionnaires was more positive; 63 per cent of trainees who completed an MSF self-assessment questionnaire found the paperwork 'easy' and 'self-explanatory' (ibid). These questionnaires are now distributed, completed and collated online via the trainee's e-portfolio, thus streamlining the process further. On the question of validity, almost one third of trainees felt that the assessments did not accurately reflect their level of competence ibid. It has been widely observed that, conversely, less well performing employees tend to rate themselves more highly than their peers assess them and highly performing individuals rate their performance less positively than their peers do. The 'feedback given' was the single most commonly identified benefit. Sixty-five per cent of trainee doctors and seventy-eight percent of assessors agreed that MSF provided trainees with useful feedback on their performance, but some trainees commented that there needed to be opportunity to discuss this with their educational supervisor ibid. Sargeant et al. (2009) argue that the value of feedback and the likelihood of advice given being acted on is seriously diminished if the recipient is not supported in making sense of and acting on feedback. The requirement for assessors to be better trained in giving feedback was also highlighted ibid.
>
> **Questions**
>
> 1 Why are trainee doctors required to seek feedback from a wide range of co-workers?
>
> 2 Why does the MSF involve trainees carrying out a self-assessment? What is the value of this?
>
> 3 Which additional stakeholders might complete the questionnaire?
>
> 4 If you were responsible for co-ordinating the MSF process for trainee doctors, what developments would you make on the basis of their feedback, and what additional areas might you want feedback on?
>
> *Sources*: NHS (2012), OU (2005), Sargeant (2009). Case prepared by the authors.

We return to the question of how individuals make use of feedback to improve their workplace performance in section 6.6.

6.4 Practicalities of feedback: designing a form

The preceding discussion has been concerned with the broad principles of communicating feedback. This section looks at one practical application of these principles: the task of designing a form. These humble documents can be an important communication channel, enabling the organisation to collect pre-specified information in a structured way (see Figure 6.3).

The form designer needs to address the following questions:

● **What do I really need to know?** There is a fine balance between asking too little and too much. It is a waste of resources to collect and analyse unnecessary information. In addition, an over-long form may alienate the person who has to complete it. On the other hand, missing out a key question can have disastrous results: for example, if a customer

'TrainCo' **Customer feedback form**

TrainCo would like to hear your comments on our services. Please take a few minutes to complete this simple online form. All feedback will be reviewed by TrainCo staff and we aim to respond to specific requests within 5 working days.

Which service did you use?
- ○ Local/commuter
- ○ Inter-city
- ○ International/sleeper

Which station did you travel from? [ALPHAVILLE ▲▼]

Which station did you travel to? [ALPHAVILLE ▲▼]

When did you start your journey? [01 ▲▼] [JAN ▲▼] Date

[01 ▲▼] [AM ▲▼] Time

What type of feedback are you sending?
- ○ Suggestion
- ○ Complaint
- ○ Request for information
- ○ Compliment

Please type your suggestion, complaint, request or compliment in the box below

[▲
                                         ▼]

Would you like a response from TrainCo?   ○ Yes   ○ No

If you have requested a response, please insert your contact details

Last name [   ]

First name (or initials) [   ]

Address [   ]

Town or City [   ]

Post or zip code [   ]

E-mail address [   ]

Phone number (day) [   ] please include area codes

Phone number (evening) [   ]

How would you like us to contact you?   ○ E-mail   ○ Phone   ○ Letter

Click here to send your feedback to TrainCo [SEND FORM]

Click here to clear the form and start again [START AGAIN]

TrainCo thanks you for your comments

Figure 6.3 Example of a form designed to obtain feedback

enquiry form fails to ask for a contact telephone number or e-mail address, essential for any follow-up calls or contact.

- **Are the questions clear, concise and acceptable?** Questions and instructions must be unambiguous and readily understood by anyone who might need to complete the form. The Plain English Campaign has fought a long battle with government agencies and businesses for clear language in forms and other documents (see Case study 3.1). It is also important to avoid questions that might upset the respondent, leading to a non-response, or even a complaint. For example, 'ethnic monitoring' questions that are now included in most job applications need to be worded carefully, accompanied by a written assurance that they play no part in the selection process. You should pilot your questionnaire before you begin your main study to check that it is clear and acceptable, and make any necessary changes.

- **Is the structure logical?** Again, it is important to focus on the needs of the person completing the form. If the layout is unclear, or the sequence of questions is unusual, it will lead to confusion and irritation. The result will be that the responses are either incomplete or, more seriously, may include errors and mis-representation. If there are questions that might put the person off completing the questionnaire, such as questions about their profile (age or ethnicity), then place them at the end of the form, as by then you are more likely to have gained their trust and interest.

- **Does the form encourage a positive response?** Taking care over the previous three points should help to increase the response rate and ensure that useful information is obtained. It is also possible to motivate the person who is *investing their time* in completing the document with an attractive form design and incentives for completion. It is relatively easy to produce a professional-looking document using standard word-processing software, particularly with the help of the templates provided with the more common computer programs. Some forms contain intrinsic incentives for completion. For example, a job application form holds out the prospect of employment, while a tax return comes with a threat of a financial penalty if it is not sent back by a certain date. In some cases, it may be necessary to provide additional incentives, such as free product samples, prize draws, competitions and charitable contributions. Will the group that you are asking to answer your questions ever benefit from the time they are giving to the study? For example, have you ever been asked to give feedback on a course that you have already finished, which means you will not benefit personally from any enhancements? Might you have put more effort into your responses if you had been asked for your feedback mid-way through the course with the possibility of benefitting directly? Even if any changes do not affect your target group, you should at least make arrangements to feed back to them your findings and any subsequent changes, if only for their information.

6.5   Feedback, knowledge and organisational learning

At the beginning of the chapter we noted that any discussion of organisational feedback mechanisms is bound to connect with a much broader debate concerning knowledge management and organisational learning. **Knowledge management** (KM) refers to techniques that organisations have developed in order to make better use of their intellectual resources. These resources range from knowledge held by people to data stored in information systems. By introducing KM (e.g. through training programmes and re-designed computer software), people are able to identify, create, represent and re-distribute knowledge in more efficient and effective ways. **Organisational learning** refers to the willingness and capacity of organisations and their employees to anticipate, learn about and respond to changes and uncertainty. For example, organisations can 'learn' to be more responsive to customers, or to improve their environmental performance. This section highlights three themes from that debate, which have a particular significance for the communication process:

- the distinction between single- and double-loop learning;
- the relationship between tacit and explicit knowledge; and
- the ongoing debate concerning individual- and organisational-level knowledge.

These brief introductions should also provide useful links for those studying related subjects, including organisation theory, strategy and change management. The chapter closes by returning to knowledge at the level of the individual, and the popular concept of 'emotional intelligence'.

- **Single- and double-loop learning:** This long-established distinction refers to the different levels at which feedback may be absorbed (Argyris and Schön 1978). In single-loop learning, the individual or organisation simply responds to the incoming message, while double-loop learning involves a deeper reflection on the reasons for the message, creating new perspectives and more substantial changes in activity. For example, a single-loop response to a decline in product sales might be to reduce production, whereas a double-loop response would be to re-think the whole marketing strategy.

- **Explicit and tacit knowledge:** Many writers have attempted to distinguish 'tacit' knowledge, which is a product of the direct experience of an individual or group, and 'explicit' knowledge, which has been separated from practice (e.g. in the form of a textbook). From our perspective, a key feature of tacit knowledge is that it is difficult to communicate, because it cannot be separated from the processes in which it was created and where it is being applied (Spender 1996: 67). For example, the practical knowledge of the game possessed by an expert, such as a leading football player (or a leading football team) can be observed in action, but the professionals concerned may find it difficult to transfer or communicate their knowledge to other people. By contrast, explicit data, such as the statistics recording number of goals scored by a team over many seasons, can be readily communicated.

- **Individual and organisational knowledge:** it is important to recognise that 'knowledge' operates in different ways at the level of an individual person, and at the level of an organisation comprising many different people. As individuals, we each have our store of memories, sets of skills, and personal ways of storing and accessing knowledge (e.g. in diaries, photo albums). By contrast, the knowledge held and used by an organisation cannot be reduced to that of its individual members; this is true even of relatively small organisations (e.g. a football team or a choir). Things become much more complex when you think about what large organisations, such as government departments, actually 'know'. The storing of knowledge is an important area in organisation studies; researchers explore how we use tacit, explicit and individual, as well as collective forms of knowledge (e.g. Penrose 1959, Spender 1996, Nonaka and Takeuchi 1995).

6.6 Individuals making use of feedback

Often the break in the feedback loop, particularly that which relates to an individual's performance, occurs between the receiver receiving the feedback and actually using it to improve their workplace practice. This might be because the feedback is not communicated from the sender to the receiver effectively. As Hattie and Timperley (2007) observe, 'Feedback involves the giving and receiving of feedback and there can be a gulf between the two.' A common issue at the sender end is that they lack skills in knowing what to give feedback on and how to do it (Pezet 2010). This results in not enough feedback being given or feedback being given that doesn't help the receiver act on it. Meanwhile at the receiver end, they may be unfamiliar with how to take on board and act on feedback. Receiving feedback, particularly criticism, is an emotional experience and may result in the receiver refusing to acknowledge and accept, and therefore act on the feedback, unless they are supported in this process (Sargeant et al. 2009).

Below are some suggestions for both givers and receivers of feedback.

Giving effective feedback

The BOOST model (Vitae 2012) is a useful aide memoire for clearly communicating feedback that the recipient can make practical use of:

Balanced – include both feedback on strengths and areas for improvement.

Observed – only include examples of what you have seen that individual do or say.

Objective – feedback should relate to facts about the individual's behaviour and not their personality, e.g. rather than saying 'You are so dismissive', you might say 'The way that you spoke to your team this morning was rather hurried and might have given them the impression that you weren't interested in their opinions or ideas.'

Specific – always use specific examples, e.g. rather than saying 'You're good at giving presentations,' you might say 'The presentation that you gave on Friday morning was very effective because you had clearly thought about what the client wanted to learn from it and included lots of up-to-date statistics and examples that were very relevant to that client.'

Timely – aim to give feedback as soon after the event as possible, so that it is fresh in the minds of the sender and receiver and relevant to the receiver.

Receiving feedback

Sargeant et al (2009) identify that when receiving positive feedback, which reinforces their existing working practices, individuals quickly accept and act on it. When feedback is not consistent with their self-perceptions, however, the process is more lengthy and emotionally charged and may result in the individual rejecting the criticism and making no changes to their behaviour. Anderson (2012) offers advice to the receiver on how to handle such criticism. This includes the 'AAAA' Approach to Responding to Criticism:

Step 1: **Acknowledge** what the sender has said with verbal and non-verbal communication (pause, nod), rather than disagreeing. This creates time for both of you.

Step 2: **Ask for more** information to ensure that you focus on exploring the facts rather than personalities and feelings.

Step 3: **Align** yourself with an aspect of the feedback that you do agree with and discuss this first to get off to a positive start.

Step 4: **Add your own** point of view. This may include agreeing with certain aspects of the criticism, apologising for the problematic behaviour being highlighted and explaining what you will do differently in response to the criticism. It would be useful to get the other person's response to this too.

A practical follow-up activity to receiving and discussing feedback is to devise an action plan to ensure that you do actually put the useful feedback into practice to improve your performance. Then solicit feedback again when you have had time to improve.

Case study 6.3 further illustrates the role that people can play in securing and acting on feedback, as we review the concept of 'emotional intelligence'. **Emotional intelligence** refers to the ability to be aware of, and to respond appropriately to, the emotional reactions of oneself and others. For example, a teacher who is emotionally intelligent will be able to support a group of learners who are anxious about an exam, without expressing his or her frustration that the learners should already be prepared for the exam. This idea emerged in the mid-1990s; a product of research into managerial cognition and its relationship with human emotion (Salovey and Mayer 1990). It has since become one of the most popular techniques for improving feedback at the level of the individual manager. Its proponents claim that, by paying greater attention to the emotional element in our communication, managers can enhance their own performance and that of their organisation. (Note: This theme is developed in the case study at the end of this chapter, which applies the concept of emotional intelligence to the experience of two placement students in an international firm.)

CASE STUDY 6.3

Constructing the concept of 'emotional intelligence'

Researchers have been taking an increasing interest in the role of emotion in organisations, including its role in communication (e.g. Shuler and Sypher 2000, Kramer and Hess 2002). One of the underlying themes in this work is that a focus on cognition (i.e. processes of rational thinking and expression) is insufficient; organisations need to take greater account of the emotional, or 'affective' dimension (i.e. how people process and express their feelings).

The concept of 'emotional intelligence' was first identified by two US-based researchers, Salovey and Mayer (1990), who were concerned with the way that people gain an understanding of emotion, as part of a larger project on the interaction between emotion and cognition. John D. Mayer has subsequently defined emotional intelligence as 'the ability to perceive, to integrate, to understand and reflectively manage one's own and other people's feelings' (cited in Pickard 1999: 50). He emphasises that this is not the same as simply having good 'social skills', or knowing how to behave in a particular situation:

> We are making visible the capacity of these people who think intuitively about emotion. You can have social skills but completely miss the emotional content of what's happening around you.' (Mayer, cited in Pickard 1999: 50)

Case study 6.3 (*continued*)

One of the implications of the term 'intelligence' is that the emotional dimension has a critical part to play in the information processing that takes place in humans. In short, we may be able to improve our thinking by managing this aspect more effectively. The concept of emotional intelligence was popularised by Daniel Goleman, a science writer on the *New York Times,* who has a background in psychology. Goleman's (1996) book, *Emotional Intelligence: Why it can matter more than IQ,* summarised the research evidence and provided practical examples, demonstrating its potential. Drawing on Salovey and Mayer's (1990) original 'domains' of emotional intelligence, he has identified four fundamental 'capabilities', each of which is composed of a specific set of competencies. The following listing was presented in an article that linked emotional intelligence to leadership skills (Goleman 2000: 80):

- **self-awareness:** emotional self-awareness, accurate self-assessment and self-confidence;
- **self-management:** self-control, trustworthiness, conscientiousness, adaptability, achievement orientation, initiative;
- **social awareness:** empathy, organisational awareness, service orientation;
- **social skill:** visionary leadership, influence, developing others, communication, change catalyst, conflict management, building bonds, teamwork and collaboration.

There are now several distinct approaches to emotional intelligence, each of which has its own methodologies. For example, UK-based researchers Dulewicz and Higgs (2000) have developed an emotional intelligence (EQ) measurement scale, which is based on psychometric testing in the form of questionnaire surveys, applied to managers attending training courses. The results were subjected to a principal components analysis (or 'factor analysis'), revealing independent factors. The authors have developed a model, relating 'EQ', 'IQ' (intelligence quotient) and 'MQ' (managerial intelligence) to personal performance. However, while adopting Goleman's EQ and MQ measures, they question whether the terminology is appropriate, given that IQ (or 'intelligence quotient') measures have resulted from a much longer and more thorough period of testing (ibid: 366). Meanwhile, Mayer and his colleagues have developed their own research scales, which are based on participants undertaking practical tests. For example, people are asked to identify a range of emotions from images of human faces. Another test comprises a statement such as 'Susan was angry, then Susan was ashamed.' Participants are asked to suggest what might have happened in between, based on a range of multiple-choice answers (Pickard 1999: 53).

Questions

1 Why might the concept of 'emotional intelligence' be of value to organisational communicators? What limitations (if any) can you identify in the concept? Illustrate your answer with five practical applications, from any area of organisational life.

2 Is emotional intelligence an exclusively Western concept? Consider its likely relevance to different national and organisational cultures.

3 Some writers on emotional intelligence suggest that the emotional intelligence of leaders is contagious, so that their 'mood' is quickly disseminated throughout the organisation (Goleman et al. 2001). How might you 'test' this idea? If it is valid, what are the practical implications for organisational communication?

Source: Goleman (2000), Goleman et al. (2001), Pickard (1999). Case prepared by the authors.

Face-to-face 6 explores practical application of the theory presented throughout this chapter, possibly in a more familiar setting, by presenting strategies used to collect and communicate feedback in a university.

FACE-TO-FACE 6

Course reps: repairing the broken feedback loop

Read the following scenario describing the experiences of two student course representatives (or 'reps') and consider how you might have carried out this role or a similar role.

Pippa and Errol have both volunteered to be the 'course reps' for their university's staff–student liaison committee. Their job is to form the link between staff and students on their courses and to make sure that there is communication between the two parties regarding the student experience. In the past there has been a breakdown in communication as a result of course reps not effectively communicating their fellow students' feedback and staff not appearing to take any notice of feedback that is communicated. Their first staff–student liaison committee meeting is coming up in a month's time and they want to be well prepared. They each volunteered partly because they thought that experience as a course rep would be a good thing to have on their CVs, but also because they wanted to try and bring about real, positive change.

Pippa and Errol begin by considering the needs of the groups that they will be liaising between. In some ways the groups will have very different agendas and yet they have similar expectations. They will want course reps to communicate facts and opinions, both effectively and ethically.

First they consider the most effective way to collect feedback from students. Errol remembers previous course reps coming into a lecture to ask for feedback when he was in his first year at university, and he knows that, like him, many of the students don't want to speak up in such a daunting environment. Both Pippa and Errol use a Virtual Learning Environment (VLE) on their courses so they decide to set up a questionnaire on that, to collect feedback. The questionnaire will be short and clear and will use an open question to ask students: *'What issues would you like the Course Reps to take to the Staff–Student Liaison Committee on your behalf?'* They also want to know how students would prefer to give feedback and receive responses to their feedback, so ask two further questions to find this out. Pippa recalls that she didn't even know what a course rep was; so they decide to upload to the VLE a short explanation of what they do and how they will communicate students' feedback (explaining that it will be treated with confidentiality and all comments will be anonymous) to try to gain the trust of those they are representing.

Next they consider how best to communicate with the staff, and decide to get hold of the minutes from the last meeting, so that they can see what kinds of issues were discussed. They also arrange to meet with a member of staff who is responsible for running the staff–student liaison committee meeting, who is happy to brief them, and makes suggestions on how to manage the feedback.

One week before the meeting and Pippa and Errol have a 45 per cent and 53 per cent return on their online questionnaires, respectively. Each reads through their questionnaires to identify key themes. Recurrent issues appear to be: not enough copies of core texts in the library; dissatisfaction at the short time-span between hearing about the work placements and the deadline for application; assignment deadlines all being on the same day; and lack of car parking spaces! The students who have completed the questionnaires say they are happy to do so online, which isn't surprising. (The reps might need to find another

Face-to-face 6 (*continued*)

way to elicit this information from those who didn't complete the online questionnaires!) The students don't mind how feedback on enhancements is delivered (online is fine); they just want some action as a result! Errol and Pippa both recall how frustrating it is to give end-of-module feedback, knowing that any subsequent changes won't be of benefit personally, and not even knowing what changes would benefit the year below. They admit to one another that they hadn't put a lot of effort into giving good-quality feedback in previous years.

The staff–student liaison committee meeting goes well. Pippa and Errol are both able to present (on paper and orally) figures and qualitative data that illustrate students' reasons for giving the feedback. Staff are surprised that they have received so much feedback to bring to the meeting. It is agreed that a staff member will liaise with the library to order more copies of core texts; that the work placement officer will be contacted about extending the application period for work placement applications; that they will conduct an audit of the deadline dates and if an unreasonable amount clash, will see what can be done to stagger them. Regarding the car-parking issue, the answer is 'sorry, we're all in the same boat', but as so many students from other courses have also raised this issue, the University has arranged for extra buses to run between campus and the local train stations.

Pippa decides to pass on to her fellow students these outcomes of the meeting straight away, via the VLE. Errol decides to wait until the relevant people have been contacted and decisions have been made and fed back to him.

Questions

1 Consider Pippa and Errol's different responses to feeding back to fellow students. Which approach would you have adopted, and why?

2 How do you like to give feedback? What is your reason for this response?

3 Based on your experiences, and suggestions in this chapter, how would you recommend that someone who was seeking to collect and use feedback from internal stakeholders (employees or students, for example) should go about it? Draft a list of ten key recommendations.

Summary

- Organisations make use of many different kinds of feedback, conveyed through a range of communication channels.

- Feedback can be assessed along two key dimensions: urgency and inherent complexity of the message.

- The major challenges for organisations are to synthesise information from multiple sources, and in a variety of formats, and to ensure openness to feedback, avoiding barriers such as 'moral deafness'.

- Various feedback mechanisms can be used to secure feedback from employees, a key internal stakeholder. These include employee appraisals, job satisfaction surveys, staff turnover rates, responses to job advertisements and organisational 'grapevines'.

Summary (*continued*)

- Even simple feedback mechanisms, such as forms, involve many practical questions. These include an assessment of the information needed, and issues related to the structure and content of the channel.

- The capacity to encourage interactive communication through feedback mechanisms is closely related to other organisational and managerial topics in the fields of: knowledge management, organisational learning and emotional intelligence.

- Being able to give, receive and act upon feedback is a key area of development for individuals in any organisation.

Key terms

emotional intelligence 153

feedback 139

incidental feedback 145

knowledge management 150

organisational learning 151

stakeholders 140

PRACTICAL EXERCISES

6.1 'Sun, Sea and Sand' – designing an evaluation form

You are the customer services manager at 'Sun, Sea and Sand' international holiday villages, which has several sites in Italy, Spain, Portugal, and Greece. You need to evaluate your customers' experience of the range of watersports, the restaurant–bar and children's daytime activities taking place at your sites. Your aim is to obtain this information by using an evaluation form that is distributed to each guest at the end of their holiday.

(a) Prepare an evaluation form, suitable for this purpose. What questions do you need to ask? What factors do you need to consider in designing the layout?

(b) Make a photocopy of your form and ask another person to complete it, taking on the role of a guest at one of your resorts. (Note: Copying your form onto an A3-sized sheet of paper and folding it on the longest side will give you a useful A4-sized brochure format.)

(c) Review the completed form. Did *the other person* find it clear and unambiguous? Did *you* get the information you expected and required? Consider any ways in which the form could be improved.

(d) Refer back to the opening sections of the chapter. How would you classify this method of collecting feedback? Would other methods be more appropriate? Give your reasons for this assessment.

6.2 Analysing organisational feedback mechanisms

(a) Re-read the opening sections of this chapter, which discuss the diversity of feedback mechanisms used in organisations.

(b) Conduct a review of the feedback mechanisms operating in your own university, workplace, or another selected organisation. Apply the frameworks in Figure 6.1 and Table 6.1 to analyse these mechanisms. (Note: You may need to focus on a specific part of a larger organisation, such as one department in a university.)

(c) Comment on your findings. For example: Is there any pattern to the kinds of mechanisms employed? Are there any apparent gaps in the information flows? If so, how might you rectify the situation?

Applying 'emotional intelligence': a tale of two placement students

This is a fictionalised case, based on the author's research. Students studying for a degree at 'New City University' have the option of taking a business placement during their third year. This provides students with experience of a graduate-like role, and the opportunity to practise and enhance their skills, thus increasing their employability at graduation. Many organisations offer such placements, and in doing so provide themselves with an opportunity to assess prospective graduate applicants 'on the job' in exchange for a fair salary. Prior to leaving the university to embark upon their placement, many students worry about their technical knowledge, organisational ability and time management skills. While these may be important, it is communication skills – including levels of emotional intelligence – that are more likely to result in a successful or unsuccessful year. Consider the case of two students, Theo and James, who are applying for a placement at 'Nova Communications', an international media communications company. The students have achieved similar marks in their university course so far.

Theo and James begin their placements

Following an application and two interviews, Theo and James are delighted to be offered a year's placement with this well-known and widely-respected organisation. The students are both assigned to the marketing division where they are to work within the e-marketing department and report to the same line manager, Josef Kant. Their new manager is 53 years old and has worked for the organisation for 15 years. Although technically and commercially very gifted, he is very demanding of his team and has a reputation for poor interpersonal skills and an exceptionally bad temper. Josef's outbursts are legendary and he prides himself that he has managed to breed a 'culture of fear' in his department. Colleagues and his line managers have told him in the past how his negative behaviour affects morale and productivity, but he usually replies that he 'couldn't care less'. Josef has refused to change and his attitude is summed up in the comment, 'Who cares? I can retire in five years' time.'

James and Theo appear to settle quickly into the department, and begin to produce work of a similar standard. However, it becomes obvious that the two students differ greatly in their ability to handle interpersonal relations. This is particularly clear from the very different ways that they deal with Josef, their 'difficult' boss.

James's story

James is the first to experience Josef's unique 'management style'. Josef calls him in to discuss some work that James has completed, but which does not meet with Josef's approval. Josef interrogates James, shouting and making threats to curtail the placement, 'if you don't get your act together'. James leaves the room upset, demotivated and confused but having no indication of how his performance could be improved. James expects the other team members to be supportive, but unfortunately Josef's culture of fear and bullying means that other team members either ignore what is going on, look after themselves or – worse still – adopt similar bullying techniques to Josef! The result is that James spends

Case study 6.4 (continued)

much of his time trying to avoid any contact with Josef. He also avoids completing tasks, has frequent days off sick and often 'goes missing' during the day.

Theo's story

Theo has similar encounters with Josef, but handles them very differently. When Josef criticises him, he is able to separate the content from the behaviour, listen to the arguments and understand what is required for improvement and acceptance. He also asks assertive questions until he is sure that he understands. Although Theo feels uncomfortable at Josef's behaviour, he does not allow it to affect his desired outcome, which is to complete the task on time and to the best of his ability. Although, like James, he is fearful of how Josef will react during these meetings, he works hard to develop some rapport with his boss, understanding that he has to succeed in this relationship in order to progress in his role.

The consequences for James and Theo

At first, James, clearly wanting to save face, pretends to Theo that he is coping with the situation. However as time goes on, Theo becomes aware of the despair that his colleague is suffering. Gradually, he persuades James to confide in him, so that he can offer some help. Theo tries to encourage James to deal more openly with the situation and confront the issues. However, James seems either unwilling or unable to do so. His performance is beginning to spiral out of control and he no longer has any real belief in himself. James struggles on to the end of the placement year, busying himself with non-threatening routine tasks. His only consolation is that Theo is willing to tackle most of the more demanding tasks, particularly those involving direct contact with Josef. The two students return to university with very different placement experiences. Theo has had a very successful year, enhancing both his technical knowledge and his transferable skills, whereas James is totally demoralised. The feedback that he receives from the company states that he is 'not a team player, lacks drive and motivation and does not handle criticism well'. Furthermore, James still has no idea how he might overcome the difficulties he has experienced. He looks forward to a return to university life, but is now dreading the prospect of a graduate job.

The sequel

Back at 'Nova Communications', it appears that Josef has finally overstepped the mark. The morale of his department is at an all-time low, trust has evaporated and Josef has lost any ability to motivate or develop his staff. To his delight, and that of his department, the company introduces a voluntary redundancy programme and Josef is pensioned off early.

Questions

1 Analyse the emotional intelligence of: (a) Josef, (b) James and (c) Theo, using the dimensions outlined in the main part of this chapter (see Case 6.3 in particular).

2 How could Josef have improved his communication with James?

3 Faced with similar circumstances in the future, what could James do to achieve better results?

4 Using the emotional intelligence framework, consider how you would assess yourself under each of the key dimensions. Try to identify at least two areas for further development.

Source: Written by Elspeth Macfarlane.

Glossary

Feedback in this context, comprises the messages that organisations, or individuals working in organisations, receive from stakeholders in response to their own messages and activities.

Stakeholders consist of individuals and groups who have an interest in, or are affected by, the activities of an organisation.

Incidental feedback occurs as part of 'normal business' and, if observed, recorded and analysed, provides useful information that is not directly sought but which gives insight into particular trends.

Knowledge management (KM) refers to techniques that organisations have developed in order to make better use of their intellectual resources.

Organisational learning refers to the willingness and capacity of organisations and their employees to anticipate, learn about and respond to changes and uncertainty.

Emotional intelligence refers to the ability to be aware of, and respond appropriately to, the emotional reactions of oneself and others.

Further reading

Brown and Duguid (2000) is a straightforward account of managerial techniques for handling feedback and other forms of organisational knowledge.

Pedler et al. (1997) and **Senge** (1990) are widely-cited works on the subject of learning organisations, a vast literature that coincides with our discussion of feedback mechanisms. **Lähteemäki et al.** (2001) offer a critique of organisational learning.

Baumard (1999) is a more demanding text for those interested in the way that organisations handle tacit knowledge. Other useful sources include **Nonaka and Takeuchi** (1995), **Grant** (1996) and **Spender** (1996).

Salovey and Mayer (1990) pioneered the concept of emotional intelligence (EQ).

Goleman (1996) popularised the concept and proposed techniques to improve emotional awareness and related skills, including (2000, 2001) on leadership.

Dulewicz and Higgs (2000) identify an approach to measuring EQ.

Duckett and Macfarlane (2003) apply the EQ concept in an empirical study. There are many texts on research methods, including **Saunders et al.** (2003). (See also, further reading in Chapter 9.)

Pezet (2010) provides a practical guide for developing your approaches to giving feedback to support development in organisations.

Useful websites

Here are several websites which might be of interest to you. You might like to add some of your own too:

The Businessballs website offers many models and ideas for understanding and improving organisational communication, including Team Briefing, a method of communicating information, such as responses to feedback, up and down the organisational structure, to overcome the negative impact of 'the grapevine'. (Available at

http://www.businessballs.com)

The Consortium for Research on Emotional Intelligence in Organisations website offers a wide range of articles and commentary about the importance of recognising emotional intelligence in organisations.

(Available at http://www.eiconsortium.org/)

The Higher Education Academy website includes video footage of students reporting back on how they receive and make use of feedback. (Available at

http://vimeo.com/9319496)

The Free Management Library offers techniques for giving and receiving feedback. (Available at

http://managementhelp.org/communicationsskills/feedback.htm)

References

Anderson, K. (2012) 'Handling Criticism with Honesty and Grace' (Available at: http://www.speaking.com/articles_html/KareAnderson_622.php (accessed 25th March 2012)).

Argyris, C. and Schön, D.A. (1978) *Organizational Learning: a theory of action perspective.* Addison–Wesley, Reading, MA.

Baby Milk Action (2011) 'Protecting breastfeeding – Protecting babies fed on formula.' (Available at: www.babymilkaction.org (accessed 8th November 2011)).

Baumard, P. (1999) *Tacit Knowledge in Organizations.* Sage, London.

Bird, F.B. (2002) *The Muted Conscience: moral silence and the practice of ethics in business.* Quorum, Westport, CT.

Brown, J.S. and Duguid, P. (2000) 'How to capture knowledge without killing it'. *Harvard Business Review*, 78, 73–80 (May–June).

Duckett, H. and Macfarlane, E. (2003) 'Emotional intelligence and transformational leadership in retailing'. *The Leadership & Organization Development Journal*, 24, 6, 309–317.

Dulewicz, V. and Higgs, M. (2000) 'Emotional intelligence: a review and evaluation study'. *Journal of Managerial Psychology*, 15, 4, 341–372.

Equality and Human Rights Commission (2011) 'Guidance for employers about their rights under the Equality Act 2010'. (Available at: http://www.equalityhumanrights.com (accessed 8th November 2011)).

Goleman, D. (1996) *Emotional Intelligence: why it can matter more than IQ.* Bloomsbury, London.

Goleman, D. (2000) 'Leadership that gets results'. *Harvard Business Review*, 78, 78–90 (March–April).

Goleman, D., Boyatzis, R. and McKee, A. (2001) 'Primal leadership: the hidden driver of great performance'. *Harvard Business Review*, 79, 43–51 (December).

Grant, R.M. (1996) 'Toward a knowledge-based theory of the firm'. *Strategic Management Journal*, 17, 109–122 (Winter Special Issue).

Hattie, J. and Timperley, H. (2007) 'The power of feedback'. *Review of Educational Research*, 77, 81-112 doi:10.3102/003465430298487.

Janis, I.L. (1982) *Groupthink.* Houghton Mifflin, Boston, MA.

Kay, J. (2000) 'Strategy and the delusion of Grand Designs', in *Mastering Strategy: the complete MBA companion in strategy.* Pearson Education, Harlow (5–10).

Kramer, M.W. and Hess, J.A. (2002) 'Communication rules for the display of emotions in organizational settings'. *Management Communication Quarterly*, 16, 1, 66–80.

Lähteemäki, S., Toivonen, J. and Mattila, M. (2001) 'Critical aspects of organizational learning research and proposals for its measurement'. *British Journal of Management*, 12, 113–129.

Marchington, M. and Wilkinson, A. (2002) *People, Management and Development*, 2nd edn. CIPD, London.

Nestlé (2011) 'Breastfeeding is best. Nestlé commitment'. (Available at: www.babymilk.nestle.com (accessed 8th November 2011)).

NHS (2012) 'Working Time Directive and Modernising Medical Careers' (Available at: http://www.healthcareworkforce.nhs.uk/working_time_directive/calling_time/working_time_directive_and_modernising_medical_careers/ (accessed 22nd March 2012)).

Nonaka, I. and Takeuchi, H. (1995) *The Knowledge-creating Company: how Japanese companies create the dynamics of innovation*. Oxford University Press, Oxford.

Open University Centre for Education in Medicine (2005) 'Foundation assessment programme qualitative evaluation for development of the assessment system'. (Available at: http://www.mmc.nhs.uk/download_files/Evaluation-of-the-assessment-system.doc (accessed 5th September 2007)).

Pedler, M., Burgoyne, J. and Boydell, T. (eds) (1997) *Towards the Learning Company*, 2nd edn. McGraw-Hill, Maidenhead.

Penrose, E.T. ([1959] 1995) *The Theory of the Growth of the Firm*, 3rd edn. Oxford University Press, Oxford.

Pezet, M. (2010) *Feedback Pocketbook*. Management Pocketbooks Ltd, Alresford, Hants.

Pickard, J. (1999) 'Sense and sensitivity'. *People Management*, 48–56 (28th October).

Salovey, P. and Mayer, J.P. (1990) 'Emotional intelligence'. *Imagination, Cognition and Personality*, 9, 185–211.

Sargeant, J.M., Mann, K.V., van der Vleuten, C.P. and Metsemakers, J.F. (2009) 'Reflection: A link between receiving and using assessment feedback'. *Advances in Health Science Education*, 14, 399–410, DOI 10.1007/s10459-008-9124-4.

Saunders, M.N.K., Lewis, P. and Thornhill, A. (2003) *Research Methods for Business Students*, 3rd edn. FT Prentice Hall, Harlow.

Senge, P.M. (1990) *The Fifth Discipline: the art and practice of the learning organization*. Doubleday, New York.

Shuler, S. and Sypher, B.D. (2000) 'Seeking emotional labour: when managing the heart enhances the work experience'. *Management Communication Quarterly*, 14, 1, 50–89.

Spender, J.C. (1996) 'Organizational knowledge, learning and memory: three concepts in search of a theory'. *Journal of Organizational Change Management*, 9, 1, 63–78.

Vitae (2012) 'Giving feedback' (Available at: http://www.vitae.ac.uk/policy-practice/14875/Giving-feedback.html (accessed 25th March 2012)).

Chapter 7

Making connections: organisational communication

Man is not the enemy of man, but through the medium of a false system of government.

Thomas Paine, political theorist

Learning outcomes

By the end of this chapter you should be able to:

- explore the relationship between organisations, inter-organisational networks and today's communication practices;
- evaluate well-established communication challenges presented by organisations, including the formal structures and managerial hierarchies, top management teams, organisational cultures, sub-cultures and unofficial communication channels;
- consider the impact of emerging challenges, including the inter-related issues of information and communications technology, the blurring of organisational boundaries and dialogue with multiple stakeholders;
- consider the use of different social media tools: blogs and Twitter
- reflect on the contribution of organisational theory and related research programmes, including more recent work on stakeholders and interorganisational networks.

7.1   Introduction

It is common to find individuals and organisations engaging in a sometimes uneasy mix of collaboration and competition (Lado et al. 1997, Child and Faulkner 1998). For example, two work colleagues may be collaborating on a major project, while also competing for a promotion opportunity. **Strategic alliances** are various types of collaborative relationship between two or more organisations, ranging from an informal distribution agreement to a joint venture or a consortium. These relationships may be formed in order to share knowledge, capabilities and other resources, or to develop new products and markets. Each party sees benefits from the collaboration, but as with the individuals who are collaborating, they may still be competing in other areas. For example, the Blu-ray Disc Association (BDA) is a consortium of electronics manufacturers, such as Sony and Philips, and other interested organisations (e.g. Walt Disney, Warner Brothers), that got together to develop the technology, establish format standards and promote it in competition with the main rival format, HD–DVD. Success or failure in these activities depends to a great extent on the quality of interaction between the relevant individuals and groups. Previous chapters have reviewed some of the broad principles of communication, primarily at the level of *inter-personal* interaction. This chapter concludes Part I by extending the scope to the level of *organisations* and the *inter-organisational networks* in which they operate.

Communication failures are a common feature of organisational life, and often create intense frustration for everyone involved. People tend to 'explain' communication failures through their most obvious symptoms (e.g. someone not returning a document on time, or angry exchanges in a meeting), but in reality they are usually the product of a much more complex set of organisational problems. Because people are focused on symptoms rather than underlying causes, their responses are often highly personalised and emotionally-charged. In such situations, a typical reaction is to attach all the blame to particular individuals and groups, rather than seeing them as part of a broader set of issues that need to be tackled. Of course, the capabilities and performance of individual managers can make a great deal of difference. However, it should be possible to distinguish weaknesses in 'management' from those that can be attributed to individual managers (Watson 1994). The value of organisational research is in helping us to probe beneath the surface level and to reveal more about the underlying causes of communication failure. With a better understanding of the relevant mechanisms, we have the potential to make more substantial improvements in communication practices, and to create healthier and more productive organisations.

This chapter begins with a brief review of the more common challenges faced by managers, focusing on formal structures, hierarchies, top management teams, organisational cultures and sub-cultures. The remaining sections respond to emerging organisational challenges, including the increasing use of information and communications technologies, the blurring of organisational boundaries and the additional complexity posed by recent developments in stakeholder thinking.

7.2   Five 'classic' organisational challenges

This section explores five themes from organisational research and practice that have had a particularly strong and lasting relationship with the way people communicate. The first three – **formal structures**, **hierarchies** and **top management teams** – are, to some degree, under the control of senior managers. The fourth and fifth – **organisational culture** and **the informal 'grapevine'** – are rather more elusive yet profoundly important influences on communication.

Organisation structure: always a compromise?

Every type of organisation, beyond the simplest sole practitioner or entrepreneurial start-up, needs a degree of formality in its structure and procedures. Formal structures or hierarchies are necessary for a number of reasons. For example, they help managers to allocate tasks and responsibilities between defined functions (e.g. marketing, finance, production), and they provide the basis for a clear chain of command. Formal structures are typically presented in the form of an organisational chart, showing the upward, downward and lateral connections between named individuals, job roles or departments. Managers can select from a number of different structures, which have been applied in different organisations in the past. **Hierarchies** are structures within organisations that, with varying degrees of steepness and rigidity, organise people into layers or levels, according to grade and role. Managers are ranked above their subordinates but below the top element (usually the chief executive officer (CEO)). Organisational researchers in the twentieth century identified a number of factors that were associated with the structures selected by organisations, including:

- size of organisation;
- technology used;
- type of activity;
- goals or objectives;
- competitive environment.

The **competitive environment** refers to all rival organisations who are trying to win customers in the same sector of the market. The guiding principle, which emerged from these 'contingency' approaches to management, is that an organisation's structure should 'fit' the functions it carries out and the environment in which it operates. At its simplest, this suggests two approaches to structuring a business: the 'functional' structure, which prioritised internal operations; and the 'product'-based structure, which was oriented around factors in the external environment – typically the organisation's markets (see Figure 7.1):

Functional structures have tended to be more efficient ways of organising 'production' but are less flexible in responding to changes in the 'market', whether it is a commercial customer or the users/consumers of a public sector service. By contrast, product-based structures can be more effective in meeting customer needs but are less well co-ordinated internally. In other words, each option represents an unavoidable compromise, which is signalled by the resulting communication flows.

Some organisations have attempted to get the best of both worlds, by introducing mixed or hybrid structures. Examples include the typical regional office structure, where each region has its own set of functions, with 'dotted line' links to head office (see Figure 7.2), and the 'matrix' structure, where functional and product reporting lines are combined in a cross-hatched pattern. (Note: The matrix structure is revisited in a practical exercise at the end of this chapter.)

Since the choice of formal structure contributes to distinctive patterns of internal and external communication, managers need to consider the potential trade-offs arising from their structuring decisions. The paradoxical implications of these decisions are highlighted in other research, which looks more broadly at how organisations are configured. For example, March (1991) contrasts the requirements for successfully 'exploring' (i.e. being innovative and entrepreneurial, creating new knowledge) and 'exploiting' (i.e. being cost-efficient, securing the maximum return from previously-acquired knowledge). In order to 'explore', the organisation needs to be structured in a way that allows for overlapping

(a) Functional

(b) Product

Figure 7.1 Functional and product structures

and fairly loose connections. However, a structure of this kind would be highly inefficient if it was applied to exploitation. Burns and Stalker (1961) also made reference to this fundamental dilemma, and used it to qualify their much-cited discussion of efficiency and innovation under 'organic' and 'mechanistic' management systems. In practice, some organisations have achieved a great deal of flexibility, adapting their mode of organising in order to meet these different demands. For example, a study of factories processing sugar

Figure 7.2 Regional offices – a 'hybrid' structure

beet revealed that they switched between organic and mechanistic forms of organisation at different times of the year. Furthermore, these changes in the management system followed a regular pattern, reflecting the highly seasonal nature of the organisation's core activities (Clark 2000: 241–5).

Managerial hierarchies: the case for 'delayering'?

The distances between people in organisations can be vertical, horizontal or geographic. Vertical distance is a measure of the degree of 'hierarchy', the number of levels in an organisational structure. Horizontal (or lateral) distance relates to the number of groupings at a particular level in the hierarchy. Together, these create the overall shape of the organisation. For example, large industrial corporations and government departments have tended to adopt 'tall' hierarchies, with many layers of management and relatively few staff reporting to the managers at each level. By contrast, high technology and consulting firms are typically 'flat' hierarchies, with few managerial levels (see Figure 7.3). Since the 1980s, large organisations of all kinds have been cutting out levels of management (i.e. 'delayering'), with the stated aim of reducing operating costs and improving information flow. In retrospect, many observers have noted that the overly aggressive delayering has created new problems, such as the loss of essential 'tacit' knowledge (i.e. situation-specific, experience-based knowledge, often built up over many years and difficult to communicate to others) (Nonaka and Takeuchi 1995). It also left certain managers over-burdened with too many lines of communication to subordinates.

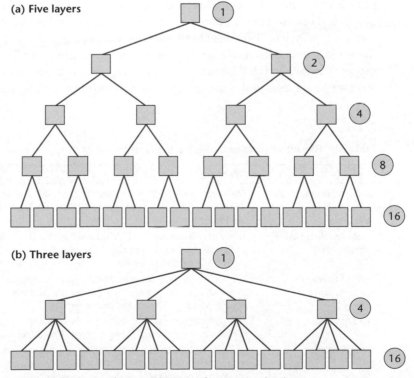

Figure 7.3 Tall and flat hierarchies: implications for communication

Top management teams: a block on communication?

The one person who really *should* be in touch with the entire organisation is the chief executive. The person in this role needs to deliver compelling messages to internal and external stakeholders, but also to be open to feedback on strategically important and urgent issues. However, many factors can conspire to block communication from flowing in either direction. Because of the complexity of a large organisation, the chief executive has to depend on others for feedback on performance, guidance on strategic direction and, in some cases, to convey messages from the centre. Incoming information is, of necessity, delivered in a highly summarised form. As a result, there is considerable scope for top management team (TMT) members to pursue internal political ambitions, furthering the interests of their own part of the organisation or attacking the performance of other areas, rather than addressing common strategic concerns. In short, TMTs form a critical link between the chief executive and the rest of the organisation. This has prompted a great deal of research on the composition and dynamics of these teams, focusing on issues such as decision-making capabilities, good governance and accountability. (Note: Chapter 13 includes a broader review of communication in teams.) These studies have pointed to serious problems experienced by many chief executives with respect to their TMTs. For example, Hambrick (1995) reports the results of in-depth interviews with 23 chief executives of major companies headquartered in the US and Europe. His research identifies five clear categories of problem, from the perspective of the chief executive: inadequate capabilities of an individual executive; common team-wide shortcomings; harmful rivalries; groupthink; and fragmentation (see Table 7.1).

The fragmentation problem in TMTs is partly due to the characteristics of organisations and to their strategic direction. For example, in large corporations with highly diversified operating units, based in unrelated industries (i.e. the traditional 'conglomerates'), there may be little need for interaction between members of the TMT. In contrast, the senior executives of a company engaging in intensive product–market (or internal process) innovation will need to meet regularly, often in face-to-face settings, in order to co-ordinate and make the many mutual adjustments that are required (Hambrick

Table 7.1 Five major problems with top management teams

Problem	Comment
Inadequate capabilities of an individual executive	The most common problem was the executive whose business area was delivering profits but whose short-sighted behaviour endangered its longer-term future.
Common team-wide shortcomings	The most commonly-cited limitation was that the team lacked relevant skills and experience for a radically-changed external environment, often reflecting the historic pattern of job advancement.
Harmful rivalries	These conflicts may seem inevitable, given the aggressive, achievement-oriented nature of many senior executives, and the tendency to build and defend personal 'empires' or 'fiefdoms'.
Groupthink	This pathological feature, which has been associated with overly-cohesive decision-making groups facing external threats, was discussed in section 2.4.
Fragmentation	In stark contrast to groupthink, there is an absence of cohesion in the top management team, with minimal interaction between senior executives, each of whom is operating in relative independence.

1995: 117–18). Other factors influencing the degree of integration/fragmentation are those relating specifically to chief executives, including the time they have been in post, their efforts to bring in new team members, and the prospect that they may be about to depart. The key point, from our perspective, is that communication patterns at the top of the organisation may be altered fundamentally over time as a result of the internal dynamics of the TMT.

Organisational culture and sub-culture: managing difference?

Organisations tend to develop distinctive cultures that are both signified and reproduced through communication practices, including initiation rites, myths/stories and symbols. People can quickly begin to identify with an organisational grouping, particularly when they have shared experiences, interests and goals. Equally, they can find it difficult to interact with others whose cultural associations differ. Organisational cultures cross-cut the national differences discussed in previous chapters. For example, it is evident that the organisational culture of IBM is different, in almost every way, from that of other computer manufacturers originating in the US, such as Dell or Compaq. Furthermore, these organisational cultures are to a large extent reflected in the companies' operations around the world. Cultures include self-perpetuating structures, leading like-minded people to be recruited into organisations, while encouraging those unsuited to move on. The picture is further complicated, because various departments and occupational groupings within an organisation are also likely to display their own distinctive norms, values and communication practices; these are usually termed organisational 'sub-cultures'. **Sub-cultures** are subdivisions within organisational cultures, involving the formation of groups made up of individuals with a distinct and well-integrated set of behaviours, beliefs and attitudes. For example in the organisational cultures of a university, academic staff and administrative staff may form distinct sub-cultures, based on their shared experiences and understanding. For communicators, one of the key challenges is how to manage the 'interface' between organisational cultures and sub-cultures in order to facilitate better internal and external communication. Case study 7.1 considers the impact that these sub-cultures can have on communication within the organisation.

CASE STUDY 7.1

'HeatCo': a clash of organisational sub-cultures

It is all-out war at 'HeatCo', a large European company manufacturing specialised heating and ventilation equipment. The accounts clerks are refusing to process invoices, customers are cancelling orders and the sales director is engaged in a 24-hour shouting match with the finance director in the main corridor. What has led to this crisis?

The accountants are responsible for producing accurate and reliable performance figures for all areas of the company. They follow their profession's 'conservatism' principle: always understating profits if the figures are uncertain. The accountants are scrupulous, methodical and insist on following procedures. Financial control is their top priority. They think that HeatCo's salespeople are flashy, disorganised loud-mouths. The accountants

169

Case study 7.1 (*continued*)

spend all their time in the office and have a suspicion that the overseas expense claims are being fiddled. The sales team is responsible for securing orders and achieving ambitious sales targets. Its members are natural optimists and extroverts, able to take the knocks when a big order falls through. They are flexible and energetic, always on the move in the UK and abroad. They hate paperwork. Creating business is their top priority, especially since the MD launched the company's new attack on the European market. The sales team thinks that HeatCo's accountants are sad, boring, bureaucratic nit-pickers. Sales figures were down in the previous quarter, and the sales team are under pressure to perform. In the rush to record details of new orders, salespeople are not filling in all the necessary details on the forms. As a result, the accounts department has been sending out incorrect invoices, and is having to handle subsequent customer complaints. Accounts clerks keep calling the sales office in order to check these forms, but the people they need are never around. The chief accountant has started sending warning memos to members of the sales team, but these have only exacerbated the problem: 'Who does that [expletive deleted] bean counter think he is?' complained one irate sales manager. 'He really should get out more,' added a colleague, as they marched briskly into the bar of the Budapest Hilton.

Questions

1 You are a communications consultant, hired by the MD of HeatCo. Discuss the possible short-term actions you could take to deal with the communication breakdown between these departments.

2 Prepare a short report (300 words maximum), outlining your chosen solution and arguing why it would be the most effective in overcoming the organisational problems identified in this case.

3 Organisational communication issues often mask deeper problems. Review recent news stories and identify an example of an organisation where communication problems proved to be the symptom of more serious organisational problems. What role did communication play in the outcome?

Source: Case prepared by the authors, based on real events. 'HeatCo' is a fictional organisation.

Case 7.1 describes a typical inter-departmental conflict, involving sales and accounting specialists. Divisions of this kind were once a very common phenomenon in many large organisations. However, there are signs that some of these traditional divisions, both of culture and knowledge, are being eroded. Faced with an intensification of external competitive pressures, companies have restructured their internal operations, removing many of the horizontal and vertical divisions that characterised the organisational hierarchies of the twentieth century. As a result of 'delayering', many employees have taken on additional roles. In the case of sales managers, there is now a general requirement for new recruits to demonstrate high-level accounting and finance skills, in addition to those previously associated with the sales professional. As sales departments become more fluent in the 'language' of accounting, there should be scope for more productive interactions with professional accountants. The more general transition from departmental 'silos' to multi-tasking project teams has the potential to reduce some long-established sources of communication problems in organisations. However, the emergence of more fluid and boundary-less organisational forms raises its own set of issues for the communicator (see section 7.3).

'I heard it on the grapevine': unofficial communication channels

Organisational grapevines consist of overlapping, informal networks of friends and colleagues who circulate information around an organisation, often during lunch breaks or social events. From an organisational perspective, grapevines can be very effective unofficial communication channels; this is because they are often considerably faster than conventional routes, are more likely to gain the attention of employees, and do not require any investment in communications infrastructure. For these reasons, managers occasionally make use of grapevines to release their official messages, by placing rumours that prepare the ground for a subsequent formal, officially-sanctioned announcement. However, grapevines can also become counter-productive. For example, in a time of uncertainty, such as restructuring or redundancy, harmless gossip is often replaced by misinformation. In these conditions, grapevines tend to distort and exaggerate messages as they are passed around. The best antidote to the exaggeration of unsubstantiated stories is for managers to act quickly and decisively. In some cases, organisations invest considerable resources searching for the source of negative stories (i.e. dealing with the symptoms rather than the cause). The more insightful approach, and that most likely to produce results, is to treat the material circulating on the grapevine as feedback, enabling managers to better interpret and respond to the underlying cause (see section 6.3).

7.3   Emerging challenges: organisations in the twenty-first century

While the 'classic' challenges outlined in the previous section continue to influence communication practices, many new issues are emerging, which are also having profound effects on today's organisations. Here, we review three closely-related developments: the mediating role of digital technologies; blurred organisational boundaries; and the rise of stakeholder thinking in public, private and voluntary sector organisations.

Digital technologies: transforming the pace and place of work

Information and communications technologies (ICTs) is the term used to describe computer-based technology, including computers, smart phones and tablet computers which are increasingly flexible in nature, allowing people to communicate more rapidly, more frequently and in remote locations. They have transformed the working lives of many people. Two of the key changes relate to the pace at which people work, and the places in which work is undertaken. For example, the widespread introduction of mobile phones from the mid-1990s introduced a new era of mobile computing, so that employees could remain in contact with corporate intranets, wherever they were located. More recent widespread use of wireless handheld devices means that people can literally send and receive e-mails, synchronise their office computers with their handheld devices, and access other web-based information whilst they are on the move.

Instantaneous interaction, via e-mail and other forms of data transfer, has had mixed results, however. From an employee's perspective, the positive outcomes have included the creation of new and more flexible ways of working, which have suited particular lifestyles. Against this, the new technologies have been seen as increasing managerial control over employees through computer-enabled monitoring of work activities. They have also intensified the pace of work in many situations (e.g. the intrusion of e-mails and text messages, often requiring immediate response, into the home environment). The introduction of remote working provides a useful illustration of these processes. Remote working is an increasingly common activity that, thanks to advances in ICTs, involves people carrying out work from locations remote to the office or usual workplace, including from home-based offices. With the expansion of broadband and other wireless connections (such as 3G networks), employees can obtain real-time access to corporate intranets in many locations, either on the move or from their home-based offices. It has also become cost-effective for organisations to provide their staff with the equipment needed to enable remote working; additional costs (i.e. capital equipment and line rental) are more than offset by the substantial reduction in corporate office overheads. In one of the pioneering remote working initiatives, a large computer company equipped all of its office workers to work from home. This enabled the company to manage some 13,000 employees from offices that could accommodate a maximum of 3,000.

The most widely-cited employee benefits relate to lifestyle issues. Home workers are able to spend more time with their families at important times of the day (e.g. before and after school). However, remote working has created a number of communication challenges requiring careful consideration and management. Cultural change is probably the biggest hurdle. The traditional, hierarchical management systems found in many large organisations represent powerful barriers to change. For example, removing employees from a manager's line of sight can lead to a perceived loss of power and status. The remote worker can also find that the initial novelty is replaced by a feeling of being distanced from the organisation, leading to loss of direction and motivation. It is easy for the employee to lose the sense of belonging that was present in the office environment, a perception that may be reinforced by other forms of marginalisation (e.g. in relation to internal politics and career advancement). Informal face-to-face communication and 'networking' (e.g. coffee machine conversations, impromptu meetings, after-work celebrations) add to the richness of office life and cannot be duplicated in the home office. In short, there is no technologically-mediated substitute for 'face time', a term that is itself a product of the 'virtual' era.

Despite reduced social contact being cited as a drawback of more flexible, technology-enabled approaches to work, advances in ICT are also creating challenges for organisations whose employees use technological developments to 'over-communicate'. One example is the current dilemma for organisations over whether to ban employees' use of internet-based social networking tools, such as *Facebook*. Employers fear that the growing popularity and addictive nature of these tools will prove a serious distraction for employees during working hours (Fenton 2007). Another is the issue of professionals, such as company executives and medical doctors, using **blogs**, with varying degrees of anonymity, confidentiality and professionalism, when discussing matters such as their company's future stock performance, or the condition of their patients (Financial Times 2007a, Hospital Doctor 2007). The term **blog** comes from the fusion of the words web and log and refers to a website that generally displays commentary, news or diary entries on a given subject or related to a specific person. Furthermore, French government officials were banned from using wireless handheld devices for fear that US spies might be able to infiltrate their e-mail communications (Financial Times 2007b). But perhaps the greatest challenge for organisations is the fast pace at which ICTs are developing and becoming obsolete, at least to members of certain sub-cultures within organisations. As the chief technology officer for Accenture commented: 'Younger people see e-mail as something older people do'. They prefer to use instant messaging (Cane 2007).

Communicating more rapidly and from anywhere has now reached another level, compared to the days of sending an e-mail, with new forms of social interaction and collaboration. Social media services enable users to swap ideas, or to participate in activities and events, while sharing their wider interests (ITU, 2010). These online services allow users to interact, collaborate and share in digital content using social networking tools such as Facebook, **Twitter** or online forums. In 2009, 800 million monthly visitors thought 'life wasn't worth living unless it was documented on Facebook and Twitter' (Clark, 2009, p.6; *The Economist*, 2010). Whilst we have already seen that some employers are banning the use of Facebook by employees in the workplace, the use of Twitter appears to be (at least for now) more acceptable. Twitter is a service, which lets users send 140-character texts, or 'tweets', to people who have signed up to follow them via the online environment. Twitter is a versatile tool, used for socio-political campaigns, citizen journalism and increasingly for marketing purposes, with companies like Dell reporting to have gained £1.9 million from sales and cost savings via Twitter (Campaign, 2009; Davidson, 2009). It has also proved to be an effective way to reach younger consumers and to help build a brand. As Lynne Franks, founder of SEED (Sustainable Enterprise and Empowerment Dynamics) (2011) said, **'one tweet can reach thousands of people in seconds'**. However, there is a flip side: the nearly six-year-old medium has become a very public complaint line, and ill-considered tweets or hacked Twitter accounts have caused plenty of embarrassment. In March, Chrysler Group LLP cut ties with an agency that handled its Twitter account after the agency sent a tweet that read: 'I find it ironic that Detroit is known as the motorcity and yet no one here knows how to f— drive.' (*Wall Street Journal*, 2011).

How should organisations address these communication challenges? One of the most important requirements is a programme of training and cultural adjustment, for managers and all those involved in remote working. Such training needs to cover every aspect of remote working, including technological and procedural aspects: for example, time management, arrangements for supervision, reporting progress, and obtaining additional support when it is needed. Perhaps the most important element is a code of conduct: an agreement of what is expected by both parties. Its importance reflects the fact that remote working is a relatively new communication genre (Orlikowski and Yates 1994, Yates and Orlikowski 2002), in which the ways of organising are still being resolved. Organisations may adopt different strategies with regard to 'face time', but it appears that regular visits to the office (e.g. at least once a week) may be valuable, providing access to informal channels and helping to reinforce a sense of belonging. Remote working has proved valuable for all parties, where it addresses issues of this kind. However, some tasks are more readily adapted to the remote working mode. The most straightforward tasks are those involving mainly bilateral communication (e.g. the remote worker receives the necessary information on a task from the office intranet, completes the task and sends it back to the point of origin). The communication issues become rather more complex in the case of 'virtual teams', where there is a need for intensive multi-lateral communication, requiring co-ordination of several people in different 'remote' locations (see section 13.7 and Case study 7.2).

CASE STUDY 7.2

Working online and at a distance

In this case study, the author, himself a 'homeworker', gives an account of working from home, its advantages and disadvantages and some of the types of communication he engages in.

I work for an organisation which provides distance and online learning materials to a wide range of students in the UK and abroad. As an academic, I have no set working hours, and I spend the majority of my time working from home. I go into the office on average about once a week. Before working here, I worked for a university in a face-to-face context, and I was at the university on most days, apart from when I was on leave or the university was closed. Coming to work for an institution whose employees are mainly home-based, and whose students are all home-based, was a quite a big shift for me. In terms of advantages, I find working from home a very relaxing and comfortable way to work. Although I have no fixed hours, I tend to work from around 8am to 7pm. The flexibility is great. I sometimes respond to e-mails in the kitchen in the morning, while making a cup of tea, or I might be responding to forum entries while having my lunch. There are also few distractions working from home – I am able to shut myself away and work with no other communication around me. I also have access to everything I need from home. The intranet means I can access internal documents, files and folders and the intranet means I can access more publicly available information. Of course, it also means I don't waste time commuting, and that time can be used to work or I can spend more time with my family. All of these advantages make me happier, and more productive and motivated.

However, saying all of that, there are some disadvantages. When I first started working, I spent large chunks of time at home working on course materials. This meant I didn't see or speak to anyone for long periods of time. This can be quite isolating and I struggled with this. I now make sure I call someone once a day, and this is not always about work, but is usually a social call, and helps me to not feel so isolated. The separation between home and work are very hard to manage, especially with a blackberry device, with e-mails coming in 24/7. This can be damaging to family life, and I have found myself responding to e-mails at all hours and in many different places. I think the final point to make here is that because all of the members of the team I work with are used to working from home, and away from colleagues, you have to work hard at creating and maintaining relationships to foster a team environment. I can easily see how this cannot work, but I try hard to touch base with colleagues every few days, and when I do go into the office, I make an effort to talk to everyone and have lunch with colleagues.

A lot of my communication with colleagues is done via e-mail. I find this takes up a lot of time, as e-mails need to be carefully worded. Often, a lot of miscommunication can happen, as you don't have any facial expressions, or immediate opportunities to correct or clarify what you want to say, as you would in face-to-face contexts. I also communicate with colleagues using video-conferencing software, which allows me to text chat, and share documents which we can view at the same time.

Some of the barriers to communicating can involve the technology if we are online, and this means we often have to allow extra time to communicate. I also think it is much easier when you are face to face and it is something difficult you want to talk about. This can mean some decisions have to be postponed until you can get everyone together. However, as the organisation is set up for homeworking, e-mail works quite well, and you can often receive responses, sometimes more quickly, especially as many people have smartphones

---

Case study 7.2 (*continued*)

such as blackberries or iphones. It is also useful to have this written record of what was communicated, or in the case of online communication a recording. I think all in all, some kind of blended approach, that combines working from home and in the workplace, is needed.

Questions

1 Looking through this case study, do the advantages outweigh the disadvantages for the author?

2 This was an employee's perspective. What do you think are the main advantages and disadvantages of homeworking from the employer's perspective?

3 Imagine you are a human resources (HR) manager in an organisation that is expanding its use of homeworking. Based on this account, draw up a bulleted list of recommended practice for employees working from home to ensure that they remain satisfied and productive.

Source: Case prepared by the authors.

Blurred boundaries?: inter-organisational networks

The borders of organisations are becoming increasingly blurred. A complex combination of factors, ranging from the introduction of 'total quality management' (TQM) concepts to the privatisation of public utilities and the out-sourcing of non-core activities, has transformed the industrial landscape. In the second half of the last century, many industries were dominated by large multi-divisional corporations, operating as discrete, vertically-integrated and relatively well-defined entities (Chandler 1962, Galbraith 1967). While 'big business' corporations and large public sector organisations have survived, they have increasingly made use of networks as a way of organising their operations (Birkinshaw and Hagström 2000, Child and Faulkner 1998, Ebers 1999, Jones et al. 1997). **Inter-organisational networks** are a distinctive way of organising economic activity across several independent organisations. Instead of relying on the internal hierarchy of the firm, or the 'invisible hand' of the market, activities are co-ordinated through a combination of formal contracts and more informal, trust-based relationships. For example, modern car manufacturing is based on complex networks of design consultancies, component suppliers, marketing consultancies, vehicle retailers and others, with the car companies acting as overall co-ordinators.

The tendency to organise activity across administrative boundaries raises some fundamental questions regarding the ways that organisations communicate. For example, researchers have focused on issues related to:

- trust (e.g. How is it established and maintained in networks?);
- intellectual property (e.g. How can information flows be protected from imitators?);
- knowledge creation (e.g. How is the process maintained when activities are outsourced?).

There are, as yet, only tentative answers to many of these questions. However, in broad terms we can conclude that managers need to invest time and effort in actively developing relationships. (Note: This issue is addressed in Case study 7.5 at the end of this chapter.)

They should also consider both the short and longer-term implications of any network connections that they make, including their likely impact on relationships with other stakeholders, and on the potential for organisational learning.

Case study 7.3 considers how one company made use of the Internet to organise an innovative 'virtual' business, which might be also characterised as an inter-organisational network. The case highlights the challenges and opportunities it faces as the company seeks to connect a number of different stakeholders, and to communicate an unfamiliar message in a clear and convincing way.

CASE STUDY 7.3

Making connections at Climate Care

Climate Care is an innovative company, founded in 1998 by Mike Mason, an entrepreneur based in Oxford, England. The company was set up 'To tackle climate change by reducing greenhouse gases in the atmosphere. We do this by offsetting – making CO_2 reductions on behalf of individuals and companies (Climate Care 2007). The primary cause of global warming, and global climate change more generally, is carbon dioxide emissions from the use of fossil fuels, such as coal, oil and gas. In the UK, individuals are directly responsible for about one half of national carbon dioxide emissions, from energy use in homes and personal transport. Climate Care offers to 'offset' these carbon dioxide emissions. This means that the company invests in practical projects, which aim to reduce carbon dioxide emissions, by saving energy or using renewable energy; the company also supports a rainforest restoration project in Uganda, which can help to absorb carbon dioxide from the atmosphere. This is quite a complex and unfamiliar marketing proposition, which requires careful communication. Because Climate Care is selling a service rather than a physical product, the web is an ideal channel for delivering supporting information and persuasive messages. We might imagine that what the end-customer needs is some reassurance that the proposition is genuine and that the offset projects are worthwhile. In addition, the interactivity of the website also allows people to calculate their emissions and make a payment quickly and easily. For example, if you select a return flight from Copenhagen to Sydney, the calculator indicates the distance (just under 20,000 miles), the resulting carbon emissions (5.21 tonnes) and the amount to be paid (approximately 46 Euros).

The virtual business: connecting Climate Care's partners

Climate Care sells carbon offsets directly to individuals and through a network of partner organisations, including the Co-operative Bank, the Environmental Transport Association, Explore Worldwide and Journey Latin America. Partners may offer services with 'built-in' carbon offsets (e.g. mortgages from the Co-operative Bank include an automatic annual offset), or as an optional feature. Many partner organisations are travel companies, providing offsets for the carbon dioxide generated by air travel. In most cases, the partner organisations are buying their own offsets from Climate Care, as well as recommending them to potential customers. The company's website (www.climatecare.org) provides an on-line calculator for estimating your carbon emissions, linked to pages where you can make a payment. Many customers buy their offsets directly from Climate Care through its website, but they also come via Climate Care's partners. The following illustration follows a prospective 'indirect' customer through the process.

Case study 7.3 (*continued*)

You are considering booking a flight to South America with Lastminute.com but are concerned about the environmental impact of your trip. When booking your trip, you simply select the button 'Offset emissions from this flight' and purchase a carbon offset through Climate Care. Elsewhere on the site, there is a series of pages headed 'Be carbon-wise with Lastminute.com' that provide information about Climate Care, explain the concept of offsets and the kind of projects that are supported through this scheme, and offer suggestions on 'more ways to go green'.

As they have become more well-known, carbon offsetting schemes have faced some strong criticism, with questions being raised over the effectiveness of the projects they support, and of the underlying principle of wealthy travellers being able to buy-off their responsibilities (Smith 2007). In August 2007, environmental campaigners visited the offices of Climate Care and another firm, the Carbon Neutral Company, dressed in bright red fish costumes: their message being that offsetting was a 'red herring' (i.e. something that distracted people from the real issue). Despite these criticisms, carbon offsetting is a rapidly-growing sector, attracting new players and posing new communication challenges.

Note: On 26th March 2008, Climate Care was acquired by the US investment bank JP Morgan, and in 2011 the company was bought back by its management team.

Questions

1 In what ways is Climate Care an interorganisational network?

2 What do you see as the major communication challenges facing Climate Care?

3 How might Climate Care overcome these challenges?

4 Can you identify another example of a virtual business, which connects a number of separate organisations/individuals using web-based technologies? In what ways is it similar or different to Climate Care?

Sources: Climate Care (2007), Lastminute.com (2007), Peskett et al. (2006), Smith (2007). Case prepared by Tina Fawcett and Richard Blundel.

The rise of stakeholder thinking

The concept of stakeholder thinking was popularised by the North American writer, R. Edward Freeman, in a book entitled *Strategic Management: a stakeholder approach*. Freeman's definition of stakeholders emphasises the idea that an organisation's strategy-making engages with many different actors:

'A stakeholder in an organization is (by definition) any group or individual who can affect or is affected by the achievement of the organization's objective.'

(Freeman 1984: 25)

The stakeholder approach to organisational strategy can be seen as complementary to network perspectives, discussed previously (Andriof and Waddock 2002: 39–41). Freeman's central argument was that an exclusive focus on a corporation's 'shareholder value' (i.e. a financial indicator based on the income yield and growth of its share capital) provided an inadequate guide for determining strategic direction.

'If in the past the focus was on enhancing shareholder value, now it is on *engaging* stakeholders for long-term value creation.'

(Andriof et al. 2002: 9 – emphasis in original)

This may seem a new, and perhaps rather idealistic, concept. However, its roots can be traced to the work of pioneering economists, Adam Smith's [1759] *The Theory of Moral Sentiments* and [1776] *An Inquiry into the Nature and Causes of the Wealth of Nations*, being important early sources. Smith connected economic and ethical issues in a holistic way, anticipating the 'open systems' view of organisations (Boulding 1956). However, this social and moral grounding was largely overlooked in the subsequent application of Smith's ideas (Skinner 1987, Andriof et al. 2002). Critics of 'free market' economics have argued that its narrow focus on shareholder value has contributed to negative outcomes for other stakeholders, including employees, consumers, local communities and the natural environment (i.e. poor working conditions, sub-standard products, damage to local economies, atmospheric pollution). Increasing concern over these effects has been reflected in an intellectual debate regarding the appropriate relationship between business and society (e.g. Galbraith 1967, Schumacher 1974). It has also sparked waves of activism by various stakeholder groups, including trade unions, consumer associations and environmental campaigners (see Figure 7.4).

There are several strands of stakeholder research. Many studies attempt to classify stakeholders into categories, representing their relationship with the organisation (see, for example, Figure 7.5). One popular application of these ideas is to 'map' the relative power and interest of different actors, including anticipated changes in these two dimensions, in an effort to guide public relations activities.

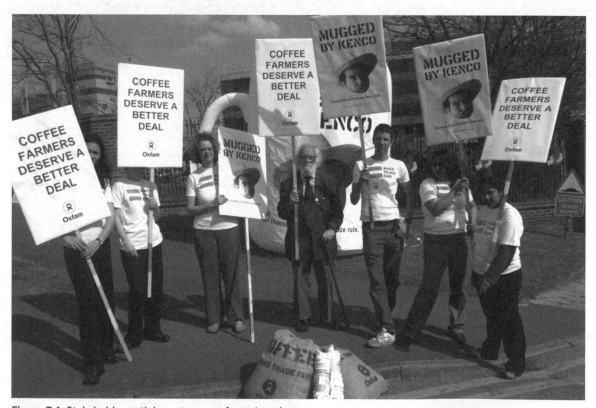

Figure 7.4 Stakeholder activism at a manufacturing plant
Source: Reproduced with permission form Oxfam GB. www.oxfam.org.uk

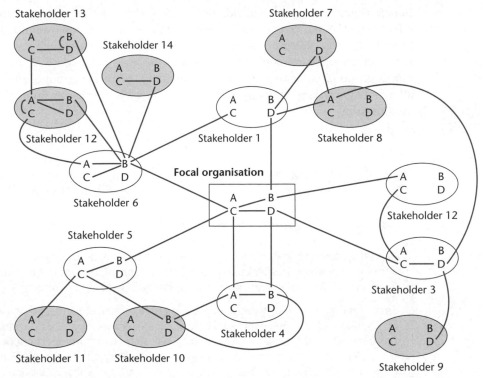

Figure 7.5 Differentiated network model of stakeholder relationships
Source: Crane and Livesey 2003:42. Reproduced with permission.

7.4 Organisational communication: reflecting on the challenges

Difficulties in communication can be both a symptom of an underlying problem in the organisation, and a contributory factor, perpetuating and even worsening the original problem. Unless the root cause of the problem is tackled, any communication-based 'solution' will be correctly perceived as purely cosmetic, and hence discredited. Senior managers often make the mistake of assuming that short-term solutions (or 'fixes'), particularly those relying solely on technology, are sufficient to deal with deep-seated structural problems (e.g. those arising from underlying economic, political or cultural factors). For example, they may organise a meeting or web presentation in the belief that this will be sufficient to 'get the message across' more effectively. Part I of this book, and Chapter 6 in particular, has emphasised the importance of two-way communication. However, it is also important to recognise that even the most sincere efforts at dialogue may have limited impact on more fundamental organisational problems. Indeed, increased contact between the parties may even exacerbate the conflict, due to 'noise', incorrect de-coding and distorted feedback (Newell et al. 2002). For this reason, managers also need to reflect on the broader pressures acting on their organisations, and to incorporate this understanding into their communication strategies and practices. Human organisations have always represented a compromise between differing requirements and objectives. As a result, a certain amount of tension is inevitable.

In fact, organisations and individuals actually *need* a degree of tension in order to work effectively. If completely freed of stress, they are likely to collapse into a kind of directionless inertia. However, when stress levels become excessive, everyone connected with the organisation begins to suffer and to under-perform. Face-to-face 7 explores how a group of students cope with the demands of carrying out a group project, with all members working remotely, which, as we have seen, is increasingly the case in many organisations.

FACE-TO-FACE 7

Group-working meets remote working: finding a way to communicate

Read the following scenario and, based on this group's experience and your own, as well as drawing on the real-life examples and theoretical explanations in this chapter, consider how you would have made a success of this remote working opportunity.

Thao, Anu, and Rosario, three Business and Management students, are working together on a group project. The deadline falls the week after their university's Christmas break and the three will find themselves collaborating remotely during the most important phase of the project. Thao will be returning to Vietnam on holiday and to attend a family wedding; Rosario will be visiting relatives in Italy; and Anu will be working full time. Initially their approach to working remotely works well. They enjoy meeting synchronously to use the 'chat room', and find it efficient to share research papers, and their opinions on them, via the discussion board.

Then they don't hear anything from Anu for a week. She misses the synchronous 'chat room' session and fails to post feedback on Thao's draft introduction on the discussion board, as agreed. Thao and Rosario feel frustrated and decide to wait for her feedback, but continue as best they can. Then Rosario starts to get connectivity problems; he can log on to their Virtual Learning Environment (VLE) only sporadically at first, and then not at all. He contacts his Internet service provider (ISP) but needs to wait for a technician to come to his house. Meanwhile, Thao is wondering where everyone is. She is very annoyed, as she is averaging an A grade and doesn't want this project to affect her average.

Finally Anu gets back in touch. She explains that she has been very busy at work and asks Rosario and Thao to feed back on her contribution to the group report. Both fail to feed back to her within 24 hours because Rosario can't log on and Thao is in a completely different time zone, and has already begun her weekend. Anu interprets the lack of feedback as meaning that they are happy with her ideas and spends the weekend steaming ahead with the project. Unfortunately she failed to find and read the work package allocation that Thao posted on the discussion board, which she negotiated and agreed with Rosario at the chat session that Anu missed. Without realising it, Anu has duplicated Thao's work, and has failed to carry out the tasks allocated to her.

With a week to go, the project is far from complete and the three partners are feeling demotivated and annoyed with each other. Thao thinks that if they had agreed ground rules by which they should have worked remotely and collaboratively, things would have been better. Rosario and Anu conclude that remote working isn't for them.

> **Face-to-face 7 (*continued*)**
>
> **Questions**
>
> 1 How would you have handled this situation differently to ensure more effective collaboration?
>
> 2 As Thao identifies, it is useful to establish ground rules for working together, especially if people are unfamiliar with working in a certain mode and with each other. Consider what factors they should have taken into account (including frequency of contact and contingency plans) and draft a list of ground rules by which they might have worked. (We will explore setting ground rules further in Chapter 13.)

This chapter has reviewed some 'classic' organisational issues, including decisions regarding structure, hierarchy, culture and sub-culture, and has explored their close relationship with communication practices. We have also considered the impact of emerging trends, including the proliferation of ICTs, increasing reliance on inter-organisational networks and a greater concern with stakeholder dialogue. Changes of this kind require us to reconsider established approaches to organisational communication, including the frameworks that we use to understand these phenomena. For example, Chapter 1 indicated one of the standard distinctions in the literature, between 'internal' and 'external' communication. In today's organisation, managers need to think in much broader terms, addressing the blurred boundaries of the organisation and the complex relationships in which it is engaged. Any meaningful communication strategy must take full account of an organisation's connections with multiple stakeholders, including suppliers, collaborative partners, consultants, contracted-out personnel and customers.

Summary

- Communication failures can be both a symptom of, and a contributor to, organisational problems. It is essential to get to the root cause, rather than relying on cosmetic solutions or technical fixes.

- Decisions regarding formal structures are always a compromise between factors such as efficiency and effectiveness, reflecting internal and external pressures. Like other structural changes, such as de-layering, they can have a significant impact on communication.

- Top management teams, which connect chief executives to the rest of the organisation, are vulnerable to communication failures: including 'groupthink' and fragmentation.

- Communication is often particularly difficult at the boundaries of organisational cultures and sub-cultures, due in part to their distinctive norms, values and practices. Such problems can be reduced using multi-tasking project teams.

- Digital information and communications technologies, blurred organisational boundaries and stakeholder thinking have posed new challenges; the common feature being a need for more flexible and interactive approaches to communication.

Key terms

blog 172

competitive
  environment 165

hierarchies 165

inter-organisational
  networks 175

organisational
  grapevines 171

strategic alliances 163

sub-cultures 169

twitter 173

PRACTICAL EXERCISES

7.1 Mergers and acquisitions: 'marriages made in heaven'?

Find a recent corporate merger or acquisition story from the *Financial Times* or other source. Based on the information that you have obtained about the companies involved, prepare a short report (maximum 1,000 words), outlining the communication strategy that you would adopt to ensure that the 'marriage' is a successful one. The kind of background issues you investigate will depend on the needs of the case, but might include some of the following:

- The history of each company – how did it grow?
- The cultural origins of each company – still tied to 'home' country?
- Technologies used by each company – degree of automation?
- Types of employee – professional, manual, craft skills?
- The nature of the products and services – innovative or traditional?
- Markets and customers – types and locations?
- Other key stakeholder issues – any significant sources of opposition?

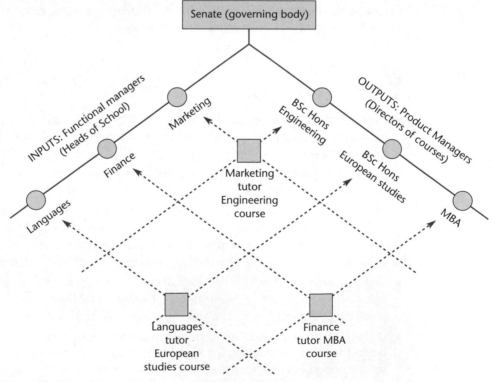

Figure 7.6 A matrix structure for a university

7.2 Communicating across a matrix?

Matrix structures are an attempt to combine the benefits of product-based and functional structures by operating both simultaneously, and with equal weight being given to each 'arm' of the matrix. Some universities, for example, have experimented with this type of structure; the 'products' are the courses and the 'functions' are the academic departments and other services. A typical matrix structure chart for a university is shown in Figure 7.6.

(a) What do you think the benefits of this structure might be?
(b) What communication problems would you envisage?
(c) How might these be resolved?

If possible, make contact with a manager who has experience of operating a matrix-type structure. See how far your assumptions prove to be correct in practice.

CASE STUDY 7.5

Entrepreneurial networking: communication as organisation?

This case reviews some of the evidence on networking activity in entrepreneurial ventures and considers the implications for organisational communication. Recent research is contributing to a change in our view of the entrepreneur, from the individualistic and solitary 'hero' to the collaborative communicator, who makes skilful use of network connections. Entrepreneurial networks differ, in many respects, from those surrounding most other small firms. The discussion focuses on the ways that entrepreneurs make use of personal networks in order to generate new ventures.

Entrepreneurship and networks: diverse influences

Entrepreneurs are widely regarded as playing a distinctive and often desirable role in the economy. An extensive research literature has built up, that seeks to understand entrepreneurship, often with the explicit aim of encouraging its development. Research into entrepreneurial networks is a relatively recent phenomenon, emerging as part of the upsurge of interest in the 'enterprise cultures' of the 1980s (e.g. Aldrich and Zimmer 1986, Birley 1985, Johannisson 1998). Consequently, it has been influenced by the diverse and sometimes contradictory theories of entrepreneurship that had already developed in economics, sociology and psychology (Swedberg 2000).

No more heroes? Re-assessing the image of the entrepreneur

One of the traditional images of entrepreneurship is of fiercely independent individuals, characterised by egocentric attitudes and behaviours (Gray 1998). At first sight, this might appear to contradict the more collaborative concept of social networks (Johannisson 2000). The focus on individuals is seen in many popular biographies of successful entrepreneurs (e.g. Dyson 1997), which help to reinforce a particular image of the entrepreneur as hero. However, recent work on entrepreneurial networks has prompted a re-assessment, putting the actions of individuals into a wider perspective and challenging the view of entrepreneurs as isolated individuals (Donckels and Lambrecht 1995; Jones and Conway 2000). Research on entrepreneurial teams supports this challenge; empirical studies have linked several variables with the emergence and growth of firms, including the size of teams, the prior experience of their members and their heterogeneity (Birley and Stockley 2000). There are strong, yet largely undeveloped, parallels between the entrepreneurial

183

Case study 7.5 (*continued*)

teams and entrepreneurial networks literature. These similarities are highlighted by recent attempts to probe beyond the artificial (i.e. legal/financial) borders of the firm, using a network perspective. The sharp distinction between internal and external connections is beginning to blur (Birkinshaw and Hagström 2000).

Entrepreneurial networking as a distinctive activity

Entrepreneurial activity is not synonymous with small businesses and start-up ventures. First, it is also found in other spheres, including large organisations (i.e. 'intrapreneurship') and community-based ventures (i.e. 'social entrepreneurship'). Second, most small firms display few entrepreneurial features (i.e. they are evident either to a very limited degree, or only intermittently). In terms of their activities, many firms are 'reproducers' rather than 'innovators', adopting well-established templates (Aldrich 1999: 80). In addition, most owner-managed firms harbour limited ambitions regarding growth and change, often choosing to remain 'micro' businesses (Johannisson 2000). Entrepreneurial ventures seek and exploit novel opportunities, often through some form of innovation, and under conditions of heightened uncertainty. They also tend to achieve higher levels of growth, relative to other ventures, often based on a modification of existing patterns of trade. Given these characteristics, it seems highly likely that entrepreneurial networks will also differ markedly from those of other small businesses.

Creating ventures: the role of personal contact networks

The process of *creating* a network is now identified as a key entrepreneurial activity, and has been the subject of many research studies (e.g. Birley 1985, Johannisson 1998, Larson and Starr 1993). One of the initial findings was that entrepreneurs rely largely on *informal* sources in their personal contact network (PCN) to mobilise resources before the formation of a venture (Birley 1985: 113). The unique connections between people in the PCN play an important communication role, enabling the entrepreneur to identify opportunities that are not evident to others. At the heart of this network, there are normally a small number of 'strong' ties that provide the entrepreneur with a shelter from the opportunism and uncertainty of the market. For example, one study found that most business owners reported between three and ten strong ties, primarily business associates, plus a few close friends and family members (Aldrich et al. 1989). The time and energy that entrepreneurs invest in these 'pre-organisational' networks appears to be converted into future benefits for their emerging firms. This includes 'human capital', in the form of relevant experiences, skills and knowledge, and 'social capital' (e.g. being known and trusted by others). Trust facilitates access to resources, through collaboration, and helps to overcome institutional barriers to entrepreneurial activity (e.g. local political resistance to a proposed development). However, the extensive personal ties used by entrepreneurs often lead to a blurring of business and social life, with mixed consequences. For example, reliance on particular individuals can sometimes lead to sudden, unpredictable and potentially disruptive structural changes. Furthermore, while all start-up businesses make some entrepreneurial use of their personal networks, most small firms settle into an established and fairly limited pattern of interactions. By contrast, entrepreneurs continuously develop their networks, with the more or less explicit aim of expanding existing ventures or establishing new ones. To achieve this, they maintain a broader 'latent network', parts of which are activated when required (Ramachandran and Ramnarayan 1993). Episodes of entrepreneurial networking can also be triggered by external events, such as the liberalisation of a market or the entry of new organisations into an industry (Blundel 2002). Figure 7.7 illustrates how an

Case study 7.5 (*continued*)

Figure 7.7 Entrepreneurial networks: changing connections over time
Source: Blundel (2002).

entrepreneurial network might develop, creating new connections (and breaking older ones) in response to changing industry conditions.

The shaded circle represents a manufacturing firm in a simplified supply chain. In the right-hand diagram, we can see three examples of entrepreneurial networking, where this 'focal' firm: (a) forms a new direct connection with a retailer; (b) forms a new alliance with another manufacturer; (c) encourages collaboration between two of its suppliers. The dotted lines in this diagram indicate network connections that have been discontinued as the firm pursues new opportunities.

What are the implications for policy?

The research suggests that entrepreneurial networks develop in distinctive and often unpredictable ways. Some networks 'crystallise' in the form of an organisation (Larson and Starr 1993: 7), while others appear to thrive in a repeated cycle of re-invention (Henry and Pinch 2000). Policy initiatives to support entrepreneurship need to recognise this inherent uncertainty and be flexible enough to allow for unanticipated outcomes. The implications for policy change will be clearer, once we start to look at entrepreneurial activity as an on-going process of communication. Turbulence at the level of an individual venture often masks a greater degree of stability at the level of the personal contact network (Johannisson 2000, Blundel and Smith 2001).

Questions

1 Entrepreneurs are often regarded as important actors in regenerating deprived regions, including those attempting to recover from conflict. How could entrepreneurial networking be supported, in order to encourage entrepreneurial activity in these situations?

2 How do you think the communication practices of entrepreneurs are likely to differ from those of other small business owners? For example, would particular communication channels be more heavily used when developing their PCNs?

3 Draft your own 'personal contact network', placing yourself at the centre and showing direct connections (or 'ties') and indirect ones (i.e. where the contact is through another person). Can you imagine a way of connecting members of your PCN as part of a commercial venture, or to provide an innovative service in the community (i.e. 'social entrepreneurship')?

Glossary

Strategic alliances are various types of collaborative relationship between two or more organisations, ranging from an informal distribution agreement to a joint venture or a consortium.

Hierarchies are structures within organisations that, with varying degrees of steepness and rigidity, organise people into layers or levels, according to grade and role.

competitive environment The competitive environment refers to all rival organisations who are trying to win customers in the same sector of the market.

Sub-cultures are subdivisions within organisational cultures, involving the formation of groups made up of individuals with a distinct and well-integrated set of behaviours, beliefs and attitudes.

Organisational grapevines consist of overlapping, informal networks of friends and colleagues who circulate information around an organisation, often during lunch breaks or social events.

blog comes from the fusion of the words **web** and **log** and refers to a website that generally displays commentary, news or diary entries on a given subject or related to a specific person.

Twitter is a service which lets users send 140-character texts, or 'tweets', to people who have signed up to follow them via the online environment.

Interorganisational networks are a distinctive way of organising economic activity across several independent organisations.

Further reading

There are many general texts on organisations, including **Huczynski and Buchanan** (1997), on organisational behaviour and **Hatch** (1997), which reviews approaches to organisation theory.

Watson (1994) is an interesting ethnographic study of managers in a UK-based manufacturing company. More specialised sources on organisation theory include **Morgan** (1986), **Aldrich** (1999), **Clark** (2000) and **Westwood and Clegg** (2001).

Andriof et al. (2002, 2003) are edited volumes covering recent developments in stakeholder thinking; **Friedman and Miles** (2002) review theory development in this field, and **Crane et al.** (2007) is a recent set of readings and cases on corporate social responsibility.

Best (2001), **Birkinshaw and Hagström** (2000) and **Ebers** (1999) tackle inter-organisational networks from various perspectives.

Wenger (2000) deals with networks of specialist practitioners, termed 'communities of practice', that may span organisational boundaries.

Nonaka and Takeuchi (1995) is a widely-cited source on knowledge creation, while **Spender** (1996) offers a contrasting view; **Newell et al.** (2002) is an accessible text on knowledge management.

Jay (1987) is an entertaining and insightful commentary on the key issue of organisational politics.

Swedberg (2000) is a useful reader on entrepreneurship. Several of the contributions to **Jablin and Putnam** (2001) are also relevant to the themes discussed in this chapter. If you are interested in reading more and finding out about the use of social media, then a good place to start is *The Economist* (2010) *A world of connections – a special report on social networking*.

Useful websites

Here are several websites which might be of interest to you. You might like to add some of your own too:

The Tomorrow's Leaders Report, commissioned by City and Guilds and the Institute of Leadership and Management (ILM) and accessible via the City and Guilds website, explores how the benefits of remote working may be being inhibited by outdated management. (Available at

http://www.cityandguilds.com/documents/ind_sport/Tomorrows_Leaders_Report_Kim.pdf)

The Google Blog Search is a search engine that specifically provides a portal to blogs on a myriad of topics. (Available at

http://www.google.com/blogsearch)

Wikipedia brings together an eclectic list of social networking websites with a description of their foci. (Available at

http://en.wikipedia.org/wiki/List_of_social_networking_websites)

References

Aldrich, H.E. (1999) *Organizations Evolving*. Sage Publications, London.

Aldrich, H.E., Reese, P.R. and Dubini, P. (1989) 'Women on the verge of a breakthrough: networking in the United States and Italy'. *Entrepreneurship and Regional Development*, 1, 339–356.

Aldrich, H.E. and Zimmer, C. (1986) 'Entrepreneurship through social networks', in Sexton, D. and Smilor, R. (eds) *The Art and Science of Entrepreneurship*. Ballinger, New York, 3–23.

Andriof, J. and Waddock, S. (2002) 'Unfolding stakeholder engagement', in Andriof, J. et al. (eds) *Unfolding Stakeholder Thinking: theory, responsibility and engagement*. Greenleaf, Sheffield, 19–42.

Andriof, J., Waddock, S., Husted, B. and Rahman, S. (eds) (2002) *Unfolding Stakeholder Thinking: theory, responsibility and engagement*. Greenleaf, Sheffield.

Andriof, J., Waddock, S., Husted, B. and Rahman, S. (eds) (2003) *Unfolding Stakeholder Thinking 2: relationships, communication and performance*. Greenleaf, Sheffield.

Best, M.H. (2001) *The New Competitive Advantage: the renewal of American industry*. Oxford University Press, Oxford.

Birkinshaw, J. and Hagström, P. (eds) (2000) *The Flexible Firm: capability management in network organizations*. Oxford University Press, Oxford.

Birley, S. (1985) 'The role of networks in the entrepreneurial process'. *Journal of Business Venturing*, 1, 107–117.

Birley, S. and Stockley, S. (2000) 'Entrepreneurial teams and venture growth', in Sexton, D.L. and Landström, H. (eds) *The Blackwell Handbook of Entrepreneurship*. Blackwell, Oxford.

Blundel, R.K. (2002) 'Network evolution and the growth of artisanal firms: a tale of two regional cheesemakers –1950–2000'. *Entrepreneurship and Regional Development*, 14, 1, 1–30.

Blundel, R.K. and Smith, D. (2001) 'Business networking: SMEs and inter-firm collaboration: a review of the literature'. *Research Report RR003/01*. Small Business Service, Sheffield (September).

Boulding, K.E. (1956) *The Image: knowledge in life and society*. University of Michigan Press, Ann Arbor, Michigan.

BT (2003) *Stakeholder Dialogue: Better World – BT's social and environment report*. British Telecommunications plc, London.

Bulearca, M. and Bulearca, S. (2010) 'Twitter: a viable marketing tool for SMEs?' *Global Business and Management Research*, 2, 4, 296–309.

Burns, T. and Stalker, G.M. (1961) *The Management of Innovation*. Tavistock, London.

Campaign (2009) Twitter, *Campaign–the annual 2009*, 11 December, p.21.

Cane, A. (2007) 'Where do we go from here?' *Financial Times* 11th July 2007 (Available at http://www.ft.com/home/uk (accessed 30 August 2007))

Chandler, A.D. (1962) *Strategy and Structure: chapters in the history of the industrial enterprise*. MIT Press, Cambridge, MA.

Child, J. and Faulkner, D. (1998) *Strategies of Co-operation: managing alliances, networks and joint ventures*. Oxford University Press, Oxford.

Clark, N. (2009) Top 5 Consumer Trends. *Marketing Magazine*, 16 December.

Clark, P.A. (2000) *Organisations in Action: competition between contexts*. Routledge, London.

Climate Care (2007) 'About Climate Care'. (Available at: www.climatecare.org (accessed: 27th September 2007))

Crane, A. and Livesey, S. (2003) 'Are you talking to me?: Stakeholder communication and the rewards of dialogue', in Andriof, J. et al. (eds) *Unfolding Stakeholder Thinking 2: relationships communication and performance*. Greenleaf, Sheffield, 39–52.

Crane, A., Matten, D. and Spence, L. (eds) (2007) *Corporate Social Responsibility: readings and cases in a global context*. Routledge, London.

Davidson, D. (2009) How to . . . put a price on your social media strategy. *Revolution Magazine* – 14605953, The Insider's Guide to Digital Marketing 2009, November, 29–33.

Donckels, R. and Lambrecht, J. (1995) 'Networks and small business growth: an explanatory model'. *Small Business Economics*, 7, 273–289.

Dyson, J. (1997) *Against the Odds: an Autobiography*. Orion Business Books, London.

Ebers, M. (ed.) (1999) *The Formation of Inter-organizational Networks*. Oxford University Press, Oxford.

Fenton, B. (2007) 'TUC backs online networking by employees'. *Financial Times* 30th August 2007 (Available at http://www.ft.com/home/uk (accessed 30th August 2007)).

Financial Times (2007a) 'Executive Blogging'. *Financial Times* 13th July 2007 (Available at http://www.ft.com/home/uk (accessed 30th August 2007)).

Financial Times (2007b) 'Blackberry Fool'. *Financial Times* 23rd June 2007 (Available at http://www.ft.com/home/uk (accessed 30th August 2007)).

Franks, L. (2011) *The secrets of social networking. Director (00123242)*, 65 (2), 50–54, October 1.

Freeman, R.E. (1984) *Strategic Management: a stakeholder approach*. Pitman, Boston, MA.

Friedman, A.L. and Miles, S. (2002) 'Developing stakeholder theory'. *Journal of Management Studies*, 39, 1, 1–21.

Galbraith, J.K. (1967) *The New Industrial State*. Hamish Hamilton, London.

Gray, C. (1998) *Enterprise and Culture*. Routledge, London.

Hambrick, D.C. (1995) 'Fragmentation and the other problems CEOs have with their top management teams'. *California Management Review*, 37, 3, 110–127 (Spring).

Hatch, M.J. (1997) *Organisation Theory*. Oxford University Press, Oxford.

Henry, N. and Pinch, S. (2000) 'Spatialising knowledge: placing the knowledge community of Motor Sport Valley'. *Geoforum*, 31, 2, 191–208.

Hospital Doctor (2007) 'Do medical bloggers compromise patient privacy?' *Hospital Doctor*, Elsevier Healthcare 26th July, 20–21.

Huczynski, A. and Buchanan, D. (1997) *Organisational Behaviour: an introductory text*. Prentice Hall, Hemel Hempstead.

ITU (International Telecommunication Union) (2010) The Rise of Social Networking. Available at: http://www.itu.int/net/itunews/issues/2010/06/35.aspx (Last accessed 12 March 2012).

Jablin, F.M. and Putnam, L.L. (eds) (2001) *The New Handbook of Organizational Communication: advances in theory, research, and methods*. Sage, Thousand Oaks, CA.

Jay, A. (1987) *Management and Machiavelli*. Hutchinson Business, London.

Johannisson, B. (1998) 'Personal networks in emerging knowledge-based firms: spatial and functional patterns'. *Entrepreneurship and Regional Development*, 10, 4, 297–312.

Johannisson, B. (2000) 'Networking and entrepreneurial growth', in Sexton, D.L. and Landström, H. (eds) *The Blackwell Handbook of Entrepreneurship*. Blackwell, Oxford.

Jones, C., Hesterly, W.S. and Borgatti, S.P. (1997) 'A general theory of network governance: exchange conditions and social mechanisms'. *Academy of Management Review*, 22, 4, 911–945.

Jones, O. and Conway, S. (2000) 'The social embeddedness of entrepreneurs: a re-reading of "Against the Odds"'. *Aston Business School Research Papers RP0023*, Aston University, Birmingham.

Kitchen, P.J. and Schultz, D.E. (2001) *Raising the Corporate Umbrella: corporate communications in the 21st century*. Palgrave, Basingstoke.

Lado, A.A., Boyd, N.D. and Hanlon, N.C. (1997) 'Competition, cooperation, and the search for economic rents: a syncretic model'. *Academy of Management Review*, 22, 1, 110–141.

Larson, A. and Starr, J.A. (1993) 'A network model of organization formation'. *Entrepreneurship Theory and Practice*, 4, 5–15 (Winter).

Lastminute.com (2007) 'Be carbonwise with Lastminute.com'. (Available at: www.lastminute.com (accessed: 27th September 2007)).

March, J.G. (1991) 'Exploration and exploitation in organization learning'. *Organization Science*, 2, 1, 71–87.

Morgan, G. (1986) *Images of Organisation*. Sage, London.

Newell, S., Robertson, M., Scarbrough, H. and Swan, J. (2002) *Managing Knowledge Work*. Palgrave, Basingstoke.

Nonaka, I. and Takeuchi, H. (1995) *The Knowledge Creating Company: how Japanese companies create the dynamics of innovation*. Oxford University Press, Oxford.

Orlikowski, W.J. and Yates, J. (1994) 'Genre repertoire: the structuring of communicative practices in organizations'. *Administrative Science Quarterly*, 39, 541–574.

Peskett, L, Luttrell, C. and Brown, D. (2006) *Making voluntary carbon markets work better for the poor: the case of forestry off-sets*. Forestry Briefing no. 11, Overseas Development Institute.

Ramachandran, K. and Ramnarayan, S. (1993) 'Entrepreneurial orientation and networking: some Indian evidence'. *Journal of Business Venturing*, 8, 513–524.

Schumacher, E.F. (1974) *Small is Beautiful*. Sphere Books, London.

Skinner, A.S. (1987) 'Smith, Adam (1723–1790)', in Eatwell, J., Milgate, M. and Newman, P. (eds) (1987) *The New Palgrave: a Dictionary of Economics*. [4 vols] Macmillan, London (Volume 4, 357–375).

Smith, A. [1776] (1993) *An Inquiry into the Nature and Causes of the Wealth of Nations*. Oxford University Press, Oxford.

Smith, A. [1759] (2002) *The Theory of Moral Sentiments*. Oxford University Press, Oxford.

Smith, K. (2007) *The Carbon Neutral Myth: offset indulgences for your climate sins*. Transnational Institute / Carbon Trade Watch, Amsterdam.

Spender, J.C. (1996) 'Making knowledge the basis of a dynamic theory of the firm'. *Strategic Management Journal* (Special Issue), 17, 45–62.

Swedberg, R. (ed.) (2000) *Entrepreneurship: the social science view*. Oxford University Press, Oxford.

The Economist (2010) A world of connections – a special report on social networking. *The Economist*, 30 January.

The Wall Street Journal (2011). Tweeting Without Fear. How Three Companies Have Built Their Twitter Strategies. *The Wall Street Journal,* December 9.

Watson, T. (1994) *In Search of Management*. Routledge, London.

Wenger, E. (2000) 'Communities of practice and social learning systems'. *Organization*, 7, 2, 225–246.

Westwood, R. and Clegg, S. (2001) *Point/counterpoint: central debates in organisation theory*. Blackwell, Oxford.

Yates, J. and Orlikowski, W.J. (2002) 'Genre systems: structuring interaction through communicative norms'. *The Journal of Business Communication*, 39, 13–35.

PART 2

Communication in practice

Chapter 8

Letters, e-mails and instant messaging: written communication

A person who can write a long letter with ease cannot write ill.

Jane Austen, writer

Learning outcomes

By the end of this chapter you should be able to:

- assess the advantages and disadvantages of the letter as a communication channel;
- select and apply appropriate formats, including structure, content and style, and consider legal, practical and promotional aspects of letterhead design;
- assess the advantages and disadvantages of e-mail as a communication channel;
- select and apply appropriate e-mail formats, including headings, content and style, and consider related practical issues, such as the archive storage of e-mail;
- evaluate potential applications for other communication channels, such as text messaging and instant messaging.

8.1 Introduction

This chapter considers four text-based communication channels that are widely used in organisations. It begins with the traditional channel of letters, which have remained an important vehicle for internal and external communication, despite the expansion of electronic alternatives. This chapter also conducts a similar review of the role computer-mediated communication channels such as email, instant messaging and texting are playing in today's organisations. In each case, we assess the inherent advantages and disadvantages of the channel, note the different ways that it is used and highlight some of the major pitfalls. The examples given in this chapter illustrate British conventions regarding writing style and layout. More detailed advice on international usage, particularly in relation to letter-writing, can be found in larger dictionaries and specialist reference books, some of which are detailed in the Further reading at the end of this chapter. The companion website includes a more comprehensive set of sample letter formats, additional sources and useful links.

8.2 Business letters: principal uses and channel characteristics

For centuries, letters were the only practical form of long-distance communication short of dispatching an 'envoy' or travelling there yourself. Today, there are many faster and sometimes more reliable technologies for conveying text from one place to another, including e-mail, text messaging, and instant messaging services. Given these alternatives, why do organisations continue to send so many letters? Table 8.1 summarises some common types of business letters, noting some of their varied message objectives.

This long-established channel of communication has three main characteristics. As you review them, consider which of these characteristics has the potential to offer advantages over other text-based channels. Having noted the advantages, try to identify the circumstances in which they are most likely to occur. For example, what kind of messages and what type of receiver are involved?

Table 8.1   Some examples of widely-used business letters

Type of letter	Sender and receiver	Typical communication objectives
Promotional	Marketing department Prospective customer	Increase brand awareness, stimulate sales
Contractual	Purchasing department Supplier	Establish clearly defined contract terms
Credit control	Accounts department Customer (debtor)	Speed up customer payments – politely
Supplier payments	Accounts department Supplier (creditor)	Avoid conflict over firm's late payment
Adjustment/complaints	Customer services Customer	Keep customer loyalty by prompt action
Recruitment	Human resources Prospective employee	Inform and attract applicants
Employment contract	Human resources Employee	Provide clear and accurate information on pay and conditions
Disciplinary	Human resources Employee	Inform, meet legal obligations and encourage behaviour change
Redundancy	Human resources Employee	Inform, meet legal obligations and provide appropriate support
Legal	Law firm Client	Inform client about the progress of a case

'One-way' and non-interruptible

In contrast to a telephone conversation, for example, the letter is a 'one-way' channel. This means that receivers cannot, in the short term, request clarification or additional information. This is also how a letter may differ from an e-mail or texting. Consequently, the written message in a letter must therefore be well thought-out, clear and comprehensive. Hence, when writing a letter you should try and predict likely questions and ensure that you have explained anything that the reader is unlikely to understand. You should also think about who you are writing to and the purpose of your letter.

Asynchronous

Asynchronous communication means that there is a time delay between sending and receipt. The letter is an 'asynchronous' channel, for example. This can make it unsuitable for urgent (as distinct from important) messages, unless you make use of a motorbike courier, or send an advance copy by fax or as an e-mail attachment. As a sender, you are also unaware of whether the receiver has read your letter. With an e-mail, you can edit the options in your settings so that you request a 'read receipt' from the receiver of the message. When a rapid response is essential, consider a combination of telephone, plus either fax or e-mail. Despite the use of devices which allow you to receive and respond to e-mails on the move, there is no guarantee that you will receive a rapid response. This is in part due to the number of e-mails people send and receive each day, and their judgments about the urgency and importance of particular e-mails.

Provides a permanent record

The message contained in a letter can be retained by the receiver and kept as a permanent record. Legal matters are generally dealt with by letter, as this form of communication is still perceived to provide a more formal record, have more impact and because the transaction may require the use of special paper (for example, engrossment paper used by solicitors when typing out deeds, agreements or other official documents). Increasingly, however, legal documents are being sent by e-mail as PDF (Portable Document Format) attachments, which must then be printed off, signed and returned. E-mails also provide a permanent record as companies often back up their computer systems, which allow for the storing of e-mails on computer servers. Letters are more suitable than the telephone or face-to-face conversation when the message is long or complex. However, there is a down-side, since any hasty promises or 'spur of the moment' criticisms that you make in a letter cannot be retracted easily. This also applies to e-mail and text messaging, where it is even easier to make a hasty remark that you may later regret. Some online forms of written communication such as blogs or postings to forums do allow you to delete and edit messages, although some computer systems still keep a record of what you have written. So make sure you read through what you have written before you send it!

Case study 8.1 illustrates some of the more common examples of bad practice in letter-writing.

> ## CASE STUDY 8.1
>
> ### Letters and paper mail in a digital age
>
> A research study by the University of Surrey's Digital World Research Centre (DWRC 2001), 'The future of paper mail in a digital age', reported that e-mail would not replace all of the functions of paper mail in the near future. The report was based on an ethnographic

Case study 8.1 (*continued*)

study, which involved observing the ways that people interacted with paper mail in a domestic setting. The research suggested that letters have more than a simple communication function. Letters pass through a number of stages, from their arrival on the doormat until they are finally filed or thrown away. The researchers found that the progress of letters through these stages was dependent on the dynamics of family life in each household. For example, letters were left in prominent positions as visual 'reminders' (e.g. invoices awaiting payment); the parents of teenage children left mobile telephone bills outside their bedroom doors, with the intention of highlighting the costs or initiating a family discussion.

The visual characteristics of paper mail were also important at the initial stage in the process, when people skimmed through the incoming mail and sorted it intuitively. For example, they classified and prioritised letters by taking account of non-verbal cues, such as design and branding, as well as textual details such as the sender's address. The research suggested that the task of manipulating the flow of mail through the household was primarily undertaken by women:

'Women are the ones to first skim and sort the letters and it is women who actively position letters in strategic places in the home for other people to see. For example, they put bills in places where husbands will see them and then they keep track of whether the husband sees the bill. After a day or two the bill is taken away and paid by the women. In this way, men think they are in charge but in fact it is women who do all the work.'   (Royal Mail 2001)

The researchers noted that e-mail technologies could not currently replicate these communication practices. As the lead researcher commented:

'Letter mail is inherently shareable and supports domestic interaction, but e-mail is inherently private, focused on the individual's screen. In fact when householders were using e-mail, they printed off the messages and used them like letters around the house to remind them to do things and to share the information.'   (cited in Royal Mail 2001)

These findings reflect the concept of 'genre systems', in which patterns of communication and collaboration are shaped by the established technologies (Yates and Orlikowski 2002). It seems likely that developments in internet and e-mail technologies may transform these domestic behaviours in the coming years. However, for the time being, paper-based mail remains an important and influential communication channel. The head of future technologies group at Royal Mail commented on the implications of the study:

'Letters are used as an invaluable social tool. We have found fascinating relationships and roles that occur within the household when the mail arrives. Especially affecting women, these roles will be much more difficult in an increasingly digital age.'

Questions

1 Summarise the most important differences between paper mail and e-mail based on the findings of this study. Comment on these differences, noting any additional points from your own experience.

2 What are the implications of this study for organisations seeking to communicate with their various stakeholders:

a. via paper-based mail?

b. via e-mail?

> **Case study 8.1 (*continued*)**
>
> 3 The research study reported in this case is an example of trying to find out how people really make use of a communication channel. Suggest how you might research the use of e-mail in organisations.
>
> *Sources*: DWRC (2001), Royal Mail (2001), Yates and Orlikowski (2002). Written by the authors.

8.3   The mysteries of page layout and structure

There has been a radical simplification of page layout in recent years, based on so-called fully blocked page layouts and open punctuation. Fully blocked layout simply means that all text, including dates, recipient's address and subject heading, is aligned with the left-hand margin. Traditionalists regard this layout as unbalanced, but it is quick and easy for anyone to reproduce, especially when using word-processing software. Open punctuation means that all of the commas and full stops are omitted in the address section, greeting, and complimentary close of your letter. In a modern type font, open punctuation looks crisp and concise (see Figure 8.1). It also saves on the keystrokes required, saving time and reducing the risk of typing errors. Further examples of letter formats can be found on the companion website.

The basic framework for a business letter is logical and straightforward (see Figure 8.2). However, it is worth considering in a little more detail the main functions of each element, reflecting on how they may vary, according to the purpose of the letter and the cultural context in which it is sent and received.

The greeting/introduction

One of the first potential problems concerns the way that you address the person to whom you are sending the letter. There are many different local conventions regarding the way that you acknowledge a person's title and qualifications. For example, there is a British tradition of using a person's first name when writing to a Knight (e.g. 'Dear Sir John'), but most formal letters would begin with a person's surname (e.g. Dear Ms Patel). It is not always necessary to include the receiver's qualifications and professional memberships in the address section of the letter, but this can also cause problems for letter-writers. The normal order of precedence adopted in the UK is shown in Table 8.2. The following example shows how this works when addressing someone with a bachelor's degree, master's degree, doctorate and professional qualifications:

A.B. Starr PhD MSc BEng FRS

Local rules and practices of this kind may appear obscure and unimportant. However, in certain circumstances it can cause offence when conventions are broken, limiting the effectiveness of the message that is being conveyed.

The central paragraphs of the letter have three main functions: to establish the context, deliver the main messages and state any action required by the receiver.

Herberts Herbs
West Hill Farm
Malvern
Worcestershire
WR7 1AB

Our Ref PA/AJR

3 February 2013

Prof E.F. Gustavson
Box 1234
SE-405 999
Göteborg
Sweden

Dear Prof Gustavson

HERBERTS HERBS CATALOGUE

Thank you for your letter dated 29th January regarding our advertisement in the *Financial Times*, and for your kind remarks about our products. I am pleased to enclose a copy of our new catalogue and look forward to dealing with your order.

Yours sincerely

Patricia Anderson

Marketing Manager

Telephone 01234 567890
E-mail enquiries@herbertsherbs.com   Website www.herbertsherbs.com

Figure 8.1 A letter in fully blocked layout with 'open' punctuation

Establishing the context

It is always tempting to jump straight in with your main messages. Resist that temptation. Imagine your letter arriving on the receiver's desk. It may be half way down in a pile of other urgent correspondence. Three telephones are ringing and her marketing assistant has just poured a cup of coffee into his computer keyboard. How can you help this hard-pressed individual find her way into your letter in the simplest and most painless way?

● **Include a reference number:** If you have previous correspondence from her, copy that reference number onto your letter as 'Your reference: ...'. Most reference numbers today refer to computer filenames, sometimes incorporating the initials of either originator or typist, such as 'SAL72/LJH'.

● **Include a short explanatory heading:** This should be in bold text and/or capital letters, identifying the purpose of the letter as concisely as possible. For example: LASER PRINTER MODEL EXL345A – PAPER TRAY FAULT

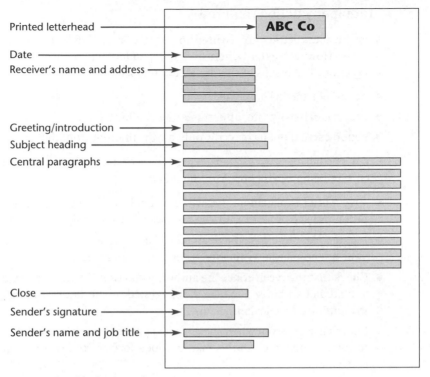

Figure 8.2 Structure of a business letter

- **Provide a link to previous correspondence:** Use your opening lines to refer to the most recent contact with the receiver regarding this topic. Typical openers include: 'Further to your letter of 14th January ...', 'Thank you for your fax dated 5th March ...' 'I am writing regarding yesterday 's meeting ...'.
- **Explain your reasons for writing:** You can assist the receiver by telling her at the start your reasons for writing the letter! By providing a sound rationale, you can help to establish the importance or the urgency of your subsequent main messages.

Delivering the main messages

Business-related messages typically consist of a number of inter-related points. These need to be strung together in a logical order, with any significant changes of subject area identified by inserting a new paragraph (see Chapters 1 to 3 for further advice on structuring messages).

Table 8.2 Listing qualifications and awards: a conventional approach

Order	Qualification or award	Examples
1st	Civil and military decorations and orders	OBE CBE VC DSO
2nd	Higher degrees	PhD MPhil MA MBA
3rd	Bachelor's degrees	BA BSc BEng
4th	Diplomas and similar	Cert Ed Dip M
5th	Professional memberships	MCIM ACA MIStructE

Stating any action required

Most business letters are written to achieve some kind of practical response from the receiver. However, letter-writers frequently under-emphasise or forget to include this essential section. The results of this are all too predictable:

- action not carried out at all;
- action carried out late, after numerous reminders;
- action carried out incorrectly, or in a way different from that envisaged.

In a hectic business world, your request for action must be stated clearly if it is to stand any chance of being acted upon. You should also:

- Give a brief explanation of why the action is important and/or urgent. For example: 'In order for us to proceed with this case, we need you to sign and date the appropriate form.'
- Include clear and realistic deadlines. For example: 'We would like to have you confirm your attendance in writing by the end of September.'
- Check that the receiver has the authority and capacity to act as required. For example: 'If you are not authorised to take the suggested or alternative action, please could you pass my letter to the relevant person.'
- But in all cases, even when chasing an unpaid bill, remain polite. For example: 'Thank you for your cooperation in this matter. I look forward to hearing from you at your earliest convenience.'

The close

The closing section of the letter is often used to highlight any action points, as noted above. It can also be used to express a positive, cordial and helpful impression. For example, a conventional closing sentence might be, 'Please do not hesitate to contact me, should you have any questions or require additional information.' The closing phrase varies between countries. For example, in Britain, the convention is to end a letter addressed to a named person with the phrase, 'Yours sincerely', while the phrase, 'Yours faithfully' is used when the person is not named (i.e. if the letter begins with an expression such as 'Dear Madam' or 'Dear Sir').

8.4	The style and content of a letter

The previous section provided an outline or skeleton, which we now need to flesh out in words. In doing so, it is useful to bear in mind the special characteristics of the letter. Receivers cannot easily question you about anything that they find ambiguous or unclear. They have to interpret your message based on the words used and what they already know about you and your organisation. The style of a letter is the product of a number of factors, including: vocabulary, grammar, overall length and appearance (see Chapter 4). Ideally, the style should be adapted to suit both the receiver and the purpose of your message. However, since receivers are not visible and may often be unknown, writers are in danger of 'speaking' to them inappropriately. This can result in anger,

Middleburg Bank ®
Making money a pleasure …

15th May 2008

Colonel JK Wilson
Dunmarchin
12 Castle Street
Avebury
Wiltshire SN99 PDQ

Dear Colonel Wilson

CURRENT ACCOUNT NUMBER: 78901234 – OVERDRAFT

It has come to our attention that this account is at present overdrawn by a sum of £104.46. This overdraft has not been authorised. Please note that in accordance with current regulations governing this account, an administration charge of £25.50 has been debited. Full details are available on our website at www.middleburg-bank. com. Please take immediate action to correct this situation. If you have any difficulty in making the necessary payment, please contact Middleburg's automated Financial Helpline on 01234 567890 as soon as possible.

Yours sincerely

IM Younger

Credit control assistant

www.middleburg-bank.co.uk

Figure 8.3 Example of an ineffective letter

confusion and less credible messages. An example of this occurs when 'Middleburg Bank' sends out its standard letter to a current account customer who has an overdraft (see Figure 8.3).

Colonel Wilson is a retired soldier and respected magistrate. It later turns out that the bank overdraft was caused by a bank employee's clerical error on this customer's standing order payments. He is therefore outraged at the tone of a letter that 'totally ignores my unblemished record of loyalty and prompt payment'. After 38 years with the same bank, Colonel Wilson decides to move his account to one of Middleburg Bank's main rivals. He also uses his homepage to start a campaign, revealing other examples of the bank's incompetence and bad manners to the wider world. How might Middleburg Bank have avoided this upset, and the subsequent bad publicity?

In the following paragraphs, we highlight some of the more common pitfalls for the business letter-writer, and note the kinds of questions that need to be asked when drafting an effective business letter. These can be used in conjunction with the exercises at the end of the chapter, and on the companion website.

Initial questions about the receiver and subject matter

The first questions to ask concern the person who is going to receive the letter. What is your relationship to this person or organisation (e.g. are they a long-standing customer, a key supplier, a charitable donor, an industry regulator or tax authority)? Are there related factors you should take into account (e.g. any pre-existing issues between you and the receiver, or any known differences of culture and language)?

Length, tone and use of words

In the light of these questions, consider whether your letter is of an appropriate length, assess the overall tone and check on any words that could be problematic. The following checklists can help to structure this assessment. Firstly, in relation to length:

● Does the letter contain any unnecessary information?
● Does it include everything that is essential?
● Are the sentences clear and concise?
● Is there any repetition (other than intentional repetition for impact)?

You might ask a colleague who knows less about the matter to check it for clarity and errors. The aim, as with other communication channels, should be to match the overall tone of the letter to the purpose of the message and the nature of the audience. One of the most important issues is the degree of formality. For example, you might write a letter to a friend or close colleague using informal expressions such as, 'Hi Mike', 'How's it going?', 'Take care', similar to those you would use in a conversation. This tone would be entirely inappropriate in other circumstances, such as direct-mail letters distributed by organisations for promotional or campaigning purposes (see Case Study 8.4 at the end of this chapter, and Chapter 10). The following questions may be helpful when assessing the letter at a draft stage:

● Does the tone of the letter appear appropriate? (Note: If you are unsure about the tone, it may be useful to read it out to a colleague.)
● What is the letter trying to achieve (e.g. is it seeking to inform, persuade, criticise or apologise)?
● Could the wording of the letter be misinterpreted (e.g. could it appear discourteous, unhelpful or over-familiar to the reader)?
● If the roles were reversed, how would you react to the letter?

It is particularly important to consider the use of words in a letter, including any technical language, specialist terms or abbreviations that might be unfamiliar to the reader. Decide whether it is better to explain these words in simpler language, or to replace them altogether with more common equivalents (see section 3.2). You should also avoid clichés and idiomatic phrases, which can be a source of confusion for readers who are unfamiliar with the language (see section 3.4). While expressions of this kind may be acceptable in face-to-face communication, they are generally perceived as unprofessional when incorporated into formal letters. For similar reasons, it is important to proofread outgoing letters, ensuring that spelling, punctuation and grammatical errors have been corrected. Many people rely on the grammar and spelling checkers provided with word-processing software.

However, these are far from infallible, and often generate unsuitable substitutes. The final checking process should include a search for any factual errors, including incorrect dates, prices or contract terms. One of the other common pitfalls of wordprocessed letter-writing, particularly in an organisational setting, is for someone to save the wrong version. Before posting any heavily revised letters, it is worth checking that the printed version is the final draft, and not an earlier one that has somehow remained on file.

8.5   Business stationery and letterhead design

Picture yourself in the process of opening a letter. What are the first things that you notice about it? Before reading the first word, you will have handled the paper and absorbed the graphic design of the letterhead. Business stationery conveys important first impressions about an organisation and gives you an opportunity to convey a positive, consistent image. This section considers some promotional, practical and legal issues regarding the design of business stationery.

Promotional and practical aspects

The letterhead contains factual information, including: company name, business address, telephone, fax and e-mail address. However, the receiver can also be influenced by design aspects, such as: the organisation's logo, use of colour, typeface and the overall visual impression that these elements convey (see Chapter 4). When preparing or selecting a letterhead design, it is important to keep some basic practical points in mind:

- Is adequate space left for the letter, especially when used with window envelopes?
- Is the font size large enough (i.e. are the address details still legible if a letter is scanned, photocopied or faxed)?
- Are the organisation's postal address, telephone, fax, e-mail or website details likely to change in the near future?
- Is the letterhead design consistent with other stationery and signage used in the organisation?
- Will the design look out-dated in five years' time?

It is also essential to consider printing costs. The key factors here are the number of colours used, size of print run and the choice of paper. Small print runs remain prohibitively expensive, despite advances in print technology. Against this, there is the danger of writing off large amounts of unused stationery when your address details change. Some large, multi-site organisations print only the corporate logo on their stationery, with all the other details being added when the letters are printed out. In some cases, this is a more flexible and cost-effective solution.

Statutory requirements

It is essential to ensure that business stationery meets the legal requirements of the countries in which it is being used. For example, much of the relevant British legislation can be found in the Business Names Act 1985 and the Companies Act 1985. The law covers

Table 8.3 Statutory disclosure requirements: some practical examples

Sole trader	**Red Revolution Records** (proprietor: F Smith) 99 High Street Manchester M0 3QG
Partnership	**Lewis, Singh & Jones** (Dental Surgeons) (Partners: P Lewis, J Singh and K E Jones) 654 Market Street Manchester M0 8YP
Limited company	**Molto Bene Pasta Houses** Molto Bene House 56 New Lane Expressway Manchester M0 9LZ ALSO, in smaller type at the bottom of the page: Molto Bene Pasta Houses Limited Registered in England and Wales Registration Number: 1234567 Registered Office: 45 Lion Terrace, London SE44 2XY

business signs, letterheads and other formal documentation, including written orders, invoices, receipts and demands for payment. Similar legislation applies to registered charities. Regulations of this kind are designed to protect those who deal with an organisation from being misled or obstructed should they need to take subsequent legal action. For example, certain words cannot normally be used in the name of a business. These include 'Royal', 'National' and 'University'. There are also various disclosure requirements for business stationery and signs, depending on the business's legal structure (see Table 8.3):

- Sole traders and partnerships: If you trade under your own name, the Business Names Act 1985 does not apply. If using a different business name, your own name(s) and address must be included on all documentation. Large partnerships, with more than 20 partners, are allowed to omit names of partners from their stationery, so long as a full list is available for inspection. You may not list only some of the partners: all must be included.

- Companies: The Companies Act 1985 requires that the following are disclosed on the letterhead: the full corporate name (indicating whether it is a public or private limited company); the country or countries of registration; the company registration number (issued by Companies House); and the registered office address.

Directors are not usually listed on the letterhead. If they are included, then all must be included, as for partnerships. In practice, the necessary details are normally printed, in a small font size, at the bottom of the letterhead page. The registered office address is often different from the business address. It may be the corporate headquarters or, in the case of a smaller business, the office of its solicitor.

8.6 E-mail: channel characteristics, formats and applications

E-mail is often referred to as a hybrid; a mixture of text-based and conversational communication. This is due to the characteristics of the channel, some of which are the same as paper-based alternatives, such as the letter, and others which are the same as 'real time' channels such as the telephone. E-mail is like a letter in that it is non-interruptible (i.e. the receiver cannot ask for clarification mid-way through the message, as in a conversation) and leaves a permanent record of what has been said. It also relies mainly on one form of coding (i.e. written words), so lacks the richness of verbal communication and the additional cues that come from face-to-face exchanges. However, the electronic nature of the channel does allow for a much greater degree of interaction between sender and receiver, and if both sender and receiver are online and engaged at the same time, exchange of messages can become almost synchronous. **Synchronous communication** happens in real time, without any time delay, so that the sender sends the message and the receiver instantaneously receives it, without the kind of time delay that occurs with an exchange of letters, for example. In many cases, these real-time exchanges might be better handled using other channels, such as the telephone or instant messaging services such as is used by Blackberries or Facebook. However, given many people are now always online, and do not go anywhere without their mobile devices, this form of communication may be becoming more acceptable.

E-mail is an essential tool for any asynchronous communication. It is used as a communication tool in many e-learning programmes (although online forums and discussion boards are now also used) as an important part of the tutoring process. Students located in different time zones around the world can post queries on discussion boards, or e-mail them to tutors at any time of the day or night. Tutors can then respond relatively quickly and easily (i.e. in comparison with conventional airmail letters), and the response can, in turn, be read at a time convenient to each student. As is the case with letters, there is also the option of sending out multiple copies (i.e. 'block e-mails') of the same message to named individuals. The danger is that because of the ease of sending multiple copies by e-mail, individuals may be copied in unnecessarily. In online courses, block messages are often posted to the online forums, which tends to avoid this form of block e-mailing and copying people in unnecessarily.

Many of the features of letter writing are applicable to e-mail writing: it depends on who is writing the e-mail, who you are writing to, and the purpose of the e-mail. For example, if you are applying for a job, then you can send a letter in an e-mail. In this case, the format and structuring will be very similar to a letter sent in the post, but it will not contain the traditional address in the top right-hand corner of the mail.

Truly synchronous communication: instant messaging and texting

As discussed above, e-mail should really be considered asynchronous because the e-mail is composed and sent by the sender with no interruption from the receiver. The technology offers synchronous communication, characterised by face-to-face conversations or telephone conversations, online communication tools such as Skype or other video-conferencing software, instant messaging services such as are used in Facebook and BlackBerry messenger devices or texting via a mobile device. **Instant messaging** (IM) is a form of real-time, synchronous communication between two or more people based on typed text which is exchanged via computers or mobile devices connected over a network such as the Internet. Some examples of instant messaging include texting, using Skype chat or BlackBerry messenger. Although text is the main form of communication in IM, images and emoticons are often used to express different emotions (e.g. ☺ = happy). The Gartner Group predicted that 'by 2011, instant messaging will be the de facto tool for voice, video and text communications in business', replacing the relatively inaccessible e-mail (Cane 2007). Business has not quite reached this stage, as e-mail is still the main tool of communication, but other tools are being used for

'Header': subject title, date and time sent, sender's and receiver's e-mail addresses

Central messages

'Signature': sender's name, address and other contact details (optional)

Figure 8.4 Format of a typical e-mail

different messages. For example, texting may be used for a quick message to your boss to say you have won the project, and will follow up with an e-mail. However, the relationship you have with your boss, and how formal that is, will determine if such use of communication is appropriate. Instant messaging is limited by the number of characters, but does have the advantage of the expectation of a quick or instant reply. See the list of useful websites at the end of this chapter for tips on how to use instant messaging for business purposes.

In the next section we consider the basic format of the e-mail, noting how it may be adapted for various purposes and highlighting a few common pitfalls, including the often-ignored social and cultural issues that surround this computer-mediated channel (see Figure 8.4). Many of the same errors may be made when using instant messaging, particularly as use of this medium has extended beyond social communication and become more widely used in commercial and organisational interactions.

E-mail subject heading: a useful cue, often ignored

E-mail subject headings serve the same purpose as those used in business letters. However, in an e-mail, they have particular value because the subject appears in the receiver's in-tray, along with the name of the sender and the date of sending. Many writers fail to include a subject line in their e-mail; an unhelpful habit that may result in their message being ignored, or left until all of the other recent arrivals have been dealt with. A short but informative subject heading, possibly written in capital letters, is all that is required. The original heading becomes the default that is inserted by e-mail software when the receiver replies to an incoming message (e.g. 'AGENDA FOR MONDAY'S MEETING' becomes 'Re: AGENDA FOR MONDAY'S MEETING'). People rarely update their e-mail subject heading to reflect the way that the topic has changed following a series of exchanges, but doing so can help to clarify and emphasise the current message.

Specifying deadlines

If you require a response from the receiver, always state a reasonable but specific deadline. This can be done politely, and may be re-inforced with a brief explanation or incentive. For example: 'To guarantee a place, please confirm before Wednesday 8th May whether you will be attending.' Avoid vague statements such as, 'when appropriate' or, 'in due course' as over-worked people are likely to interpret this as 'low priority' and your message may be forgotten. Setting your e-mail as 'high' priority and adding 'URGENT' to the subject heading might help to secure a response, but only if the claim is justified. Inappropriate or excessive use of these 'flags' will result in them losing their value.

E-mail language, style and accuracy: unresolved issues?

E-mails tend to vary in length and style depending on the purpose of your e-mail and who you are sending it to. Many e-mails tend to be used for short and relatively straightforward messages; however, others may contain more complex subject matter. In order for the information to be absorbed more readily, you should make use of short paragraphs, rather than long stretches of text. It is also helpful to break up the text, particularly where it includes a list of items or an important item of information, such as a date or an address, making it easier to read on screen. In order to make it easier for people to read e-mails, you should structure the key points, by signalling clearly how many key points you are making. For example, 'There are 3 key points' or 'I require you to complete 3 tasks' or list as numbered points: 1, 2, 3.

The language used in e-mails tends to be much more concise and direct than was the case in letters, although this will depend on who you are writing to. E-mails are sent to a wide range of people, including external stakeholders. The short and relatively informal language that is used in e-mails exchanged between close work colleagues and friends can sound over-familiar and discourteous if it is used in an e-mail to a senior executive or a customer. Consequently, your writing style needs to be very flexible, adapting itself to the needs of specific receivers. For example, informal e-mail messages are sometimes enhanced using improvised non-verbal cues (emoticons), such as ;-) to signify knowingness and :-(for unhappiness. These symbols would be regarded as unprofessional in more formal situations.

It is not easy to remember to adapt your writing style, particularly when the conventional practice is to sit in front of a computer and respond to a large number of assorted e-mails one after another. Some people have interpreted the speed and relative informality of e-mail communication as a justification for much lower standards of accuracy, in spelling, grammar and punctuation. Keying errors, or 'typos', may be left uncorrected and punctuation largely ignored. At a time when the medium is still without firm conventions, our view is that accuracy in typing is as important in e-mails as it is in business letters, and for precisely the same reasons. Obvious errors are distracting to the reader; they can lead to misunderstandings and are also likely to give a poor impression of the sender, and the department or organisation that they represent. The counter-argument, that it saves time to leave the message uncorrected, is difficult to sustain, especially as many e-mail programmes include spell-checker functionality. In practice, most keying errors could be avoided, and the whole process could be greatly accelerated, if people invested some time in perfecting the skill of touch-typing. In order to save time people sometimes type a whole e-mail in lower case, or more usually in UPPER CASE. This not only makes the communication difficult to read, as it is hard to see where sentences begin and end, but some people think that the use of upper case makes it LOOK LIKE YOU ARE SHOUTING and may see the e-mail as having an aggressive tone.

Common e-mail problems and pitfalls

Perhaps the greatest problems for this communication channel, from an organisational perspective, are the rise of junk e-mail (or 'spam'), and the general issue of overloaded in-trays. The sheer volume of e-mails received by many people in organisations has created stressful working practices, and workplace activities are now extended to any location where a person has access to the e-mail system. With the advent of mobile computing, this includes periods of business travel (e.g. dealing with e-mails during rail journeys or international flights) and a new intrusion into domestic life. For example, while it would have been unusual for employees to deal with work-related telephone calls at home during the weekend, it is becoming an established norm that people access work e-mails from a mobile device or from a home computer. From the sender's perspective, the overload problem means that you cannot always be sure that your message will be spotted amongst the dozens of other messages, particularly during times of absence, or circumstances of which you may be unaware (e.g. when they have accumulated during the receiver's vacation). Many senders have unrealistic expectations of the e-mail, assuming that their messages will be read, understood and responded to in a very short period. This ignores the fact that synchronous communication is a potential but not an inherent feature of the communication channel. The only way to ensure synchronicity and instant feedback is to select an alternative channel, such as the telephone or face-to-face meeting, where this characteristic is guaranteed.

Another problematic feature of e-mail has been highlighted by the practice of circulating supposedly humorous e-mail messages and attachments to friends and work colleagues. Recently, there have been several cases of disciplinary action taken against employees whose messages were interpreted as offensive by other work colleagues. The seemingly informal and instantaneous nature of the channel seems to encourage spontaneous and often poorly thought-out messages, that would not have been sent when organisations relied on paper-based systems. This is illustrated by another common source of embarrassment: when someone inadvertently copies or forwards material to the 'wrong' people, including earlier e-mail exchanges that may still be attached to the current message. Again, this human error is facilitated by the technology, which makes it easy to press a key without a great deal of thought or preparation. In the worst case, it can lead to an escalating cycle of retaliatory e-mails. This begins when an already stressed person receives what they interpret as a discourteous or unreasonable e-mail message. Instead of allowing himself to calm down, or checking his initial impression, the receiver responds immediately, sending a short and angry reply that provokes an even angrier response. If you know that you have written an e-mail in anger or frustration, it is worth saving it in draft form until after a lunch break or until the following day, when you can consider your message from a more objective perspective.

As this short review has indicated, e-mail communication still requires further clarifications around its code and what is acceptable practice. Case Study 8.2 looks at the issue of 'netiquette' and some of the issues indicated in this review.

CASE STUDY 8.2

The netiquette of working life

By Maija Palmer, technology correspondent

Vicki Walker made headlines in 2009 when she was dismissed from her job as financial controller of a New Zealand healthcare company for writing e-mails to co-workers in all capital letters. The company claimed the communications, which included

Case study 8.2 (*continued*)

sections highlighted in red lettering, were 'confrontational' and said she had 'caused disharmony in the workplace by using block capitals, bold typeface and red text in her e-mails'.

An employment tribunal later found that Ms Walker had been unfairly dismissed and awarded her $11,500 in compensation, but the case highlighted the need for a code of etiquette when using newer forms of communication such as e-mail, social networking and instant messaging.

Whether or not it should be seen as a sackable offence, etiquette experts almost universally agree that people should avoid writing e-mail in capitals.

'It just looks shouty,' says Patricia Fitzpatrick, founder of the Etiquette School of New York. 'It is best not to do it.'

Understanding the etiquette of new technology is becoming increasingly critical. Employees and businesses are struggling to define what is correct, resulting in many misunderstandings. Some 8 per cent of companies with more than 1,000 employees have fired someone over their use of social media, according to a 2009 study by Proofpoint, the internet security firm.

Etiquette experts say they are fielding more questions on technology than ever before. The latest edition of Emily Post's book *Etiquette*, considered the ultimate authority on correct societal behaviour in North America, included a section dedicated to the dos and don'ts of modern communications. A separate book on technology etiquette is due to be published soon by the Emily Post Institute.

'Business etiquette is becoming more difficult as our methods of communications become more complex. It's not just letters and phonecalls, it is e-mail, Twitter, text messages and so on,' said Lizzie Post, the great-great-granddaughter of Emily Post and co-author of the latest etiquette book. 'We get a lot of questions about it from people now. A lot of people aren't sure how to navigate certain parts of our world.'

Both the Emily Post Institute and Debretts, its UK rival, have Twitter feeds with more than 5,000 followers each, and both offer advice about technology and etiquette on their websites.

'There is growing interest. If I ever tweet about technology etiquette, I always get an instant and lively response,' says Liz Wyse, expert at Debretts.

Corporations are also becoming big customers for etiquette experts. Banks often hire in etiquette consultants to help brush up the manners of new employees and Cancer Treatment Centres of America, the healthcare organisation, for example, regularly works with the Emily Post Institute.

'Companies want their employees to have the people skills that are often lacking these days. It is easy to hide behind a computer screen and avoid confrontations, so people may not have the skills to deal with conflict in a constructive way,' says Ms Post.

Ms Fitzpatrick says she works with a mix of corporations, universities and individuals. About half her business is training 20-something employees who have just entered the world of work.

Tech tips from the etiquette experts

- Don't communicate electronically at the expense of personal interaction. There is a reason people often need to discuss things face-to-face – human contact still matters. (Emily Post Institute)

Case study 8.2 (*continued*)

- Avoid typing your message in capital letters because CAPS ARE THE EQUIVALENT OF SHOUTING. Also beware of anger and frustration in the choice of words. (Emily Post Institute)

- People in the flesh deserve more attention than a gadget, so wherever possible turn off your phone in social situations. (Debrett's)

- Don't put your phone on the dining table, or glance at it longingly mid-conversation. (Debrett's)

- Think of your texting as a conversation: if you would respond in the conversation, then respond in the text. (Emily Post Institute)

- Don't post minute-by-minute updates to your relationship status. Out in the real world, relationships are subtle, complex and dynamic. (Debrett's)

- Unlike in e-mail messages, it can be permissible to write real-time messages entirely or mainly in lower case. (Matthew Strawbridge, author, *Netiquette*)

- It is acceptable to use standard IM abbreviations, but be prepared to explain any that the other person doesn't understand. (Matthew Strawbridge)

'They are the texting generation, who don't necessarily spell every word out when they send communications. Most colleges are more informal than they used to be. Students are on a first-name basis with their professors, so when they graduate and come into the world of work, no-one has taught them about the increased level of formality they will need,' Ms Fitzpatrick said.

The most common complaint, the experts say, is about people constantly checking their smartphones during meetings, mealtimes and other social occasions. There is plenty of evidence to suggest the smartphone does go everywhere with us. A study by Ofcom (the UK communications regulator) last summer, for example, found that UK teenagers were so addicted to their mobile phones that they used them while eating, in bed and even on the toilet. These are definite no-nos. Calls from inappropriate places are disrespectful, and focusing on a phone rather than a companion is rude, says Ms Wyse. 'Ideally you would never prioritise a gadget over a person.' 'If you are expecting a very important call, announce that you may have to answer your phone in the beginning, and then keep your phone in your pocket on vibrate until the call comes. You shouldn't have the phone on the table. Don't keep fiddling with it, it is the constant interaction with the phone that irritates people,' she says.

Another tricky issue involves answering e-mails. Etiquette experts say it is polite to respond to e-mail within 24 hours of receiving it. But they admit that can be hard to do when inboxes are deluged with hundreds of messages a day.

'You really should try to get back to people quickly, even with the shortest note. But who can answer 300 emails?' Ms Fitzpatrick says. She suggests that new norms may have to be defined in this area.

Already, some elements of informality have crept into communications with the use of e-mail. The exclamation mark, used so sparingly in business communications and good literature, is allowed in e-mails and text messages.

Academic studies, such as the work of Justin Kruger of New York University and Nicholas Epley of the University of Chicago, have shown that e-mail conveys emotion very poorly. Sarcasm, for example, does not come across easily in e-mail.

Case study 8.2 (*continued*)

Thus, says Ms Post, an e-mail sometimes needs to be overly enthusiastic to appear friendly.

'I sometimes send email out with a smiley face on it,' she said. 'I always defer to the formal at first, but over time a certain rapport develops and it is fine to be more casual. The direction seems to be towards informality.'

There are limits, however. E-mail is simply not appropriate for every situation.

'Never send bad news by e-mail. You should never fire someone by e-mail, for example. It is clearly better to have that conversation face to face,' says Matthew Strawbridge, author of *Netiquette: Internet etiquette in the age of the blog*. Nor should e-mail or text messages be used to send condolences or to end a relationship.

Social networking is another area where technology etiquette is still evolving. Tricky questions include whether employees should accept requests from the boss to be friends on Facebook, and if it is ever acceptable to 'unfriend' someone on a social networking site.

The answers are 'no' and 'no'. The experts suggest politely declining requests from the boss with an explanation about keeping personal and professional lives separate. Letting a boss see social networking updates will only mean trouble later, if there are embarrassing photos posted by friends, or unwise remarks made about a bad day in the office.

The question of unfriending is harder. It can never be done with delicacy, the experts say, so the best solution may be to close down the account and start again if someone really must be removed from a friends list. It is better to be more selective about accepting friends in the first place than to deal with pruning them later.

The experts themselves admit they are still feeling their way in these areas. Etiquette is ultimately about respect and consideration for others, and the same rules of courtesy should apply online and offline. But it can take a little while to firmly establish norms with anything very new.

'When you have a fast-growing group of users, like on Facebook, you will get lapses,' says Mr Strawbridge. 'Everyone inevitably does something that upsets other people online.'

Questions

1 What are some of the main suggestions of netiquette from the experts?

2 Which of these tips do you already know? Which ones do you need to start using? Can you think of any more?

3 How does your writing style vary according to the type of message and receiver?

4 What lessons can we draw about the way this communication channel is being used at present and how it might be improved in the future?

Source: Palmer/*Financial Times* (February, 2012) http://www.ft.com/cms/s/0/94239bbe-4dae-11e1-b96c-00144feabdc0.html#axzz1pZBO5Mk5

Face-to-face 8 further illustrates the use and abuse of e-mail as a communication medium by providing an example that is not wildly different from e-mails that have, on occasion, been received by the authors and their colleagues!

FACE-TO-FACE 8

Falling foul of e-mail faux pas

Read the following e-mail communication (see Figure 8.5), sent by a student to members of staff at a university, and consider the likely reaction of the recipients to the message (or messages?) that it conveys:

To: brenda.smith@springfield.ac.uk
From: lovegod777@hotmail.com
CC: Director of Studies, Head of School
Subject:

HI

HOW R U DOIN? I'M WRITING TO ASK AGAIN FOR AN EXTENSION FOR MY ASIGNMENT THAT IS DUE IN TOMORRO. I SENT YOU E-MAIL YESTERDAY BUT YOU HAVEN'T REPLIED. THE THING IS THAT I HAVE BIN ILL AND HAVENT' BIN ABLE TO WRITE MY ASSIGNMENT. I ASSUME THAT IF I DONT NOT HEAR FROM YOU TODAY THAT IT IS OK.

CUL8R

Figure 8.5 Example of an email sent by a student

Questions

1 What are the reasons that this e-mail might not be as effective in conveying its message as the sender intends?

2 What amendments would you make to this e-mail before sending it?

3 How would you provide useful feedback to the sender of this e-mail, pointing out that it was not appropriate, explaining the reasons why this is the case and suggesting how to make improvements in the future? See Chapter 6 for more information on giving feedback.

8.7 Text messaging and beyond: emerging communication issues

Various commercial information providers are using text messages as a communication channel, for weather forecasts, sports results and traffic reports, for example. The channel has been used to provide online banking customers with immediate and automatic notification, when their current accounts either exceed or fall below a previously-agreed figure. It has also been adopted by household security firms, who can alert their customers when smoke or burglar alarms are sounded. In Chapter 10, we review another recent application of text messaging, which provides potential customers with marketing information by interacting with their personal computers (see Case study 10.2). However, as with any communication channel, problems occur when it is used inappropriately. Case study 8.3 opens with a reference to one of the more popular information services available via text messaging: supplying the latest football results. It goes on to report on a less attractive use for the channel: notifying people that they have been made redundant.

CASE STUDY 8.3

Texting redundancy: a communication perspective

You were promised Premiership goals on your mobile, but instead you learn you've been sent off. Staff at Accident Group, a Manchester-based personal injury specialist, were yesterday informed by text message that they had lost their jobs. The messages came from insolvency practitioners at accountants PricewaterhouseCoopers (PwC), administrators to Amulet Group, Accident Group's Luxembourg-controlled parent. Recipients were instructed to call a number, where a recorded message told them: 'All staff who are being retained will be contacted today. If you have not been spoken to you are therefore being made redundant with immediate effect.' While the growing popularity of text-sex is well documented, this example of text-sacking drew an angry response. 'Nobody should be given devastating news about their employment by text message. We desperately need more powerful provisions for proper workplace consultation,' said Brendan Barber, general secretary of the TUC. 'Sensitive matters of this nature should be carried out face-to-face.' The Department of Trade and Industry was equally critical, not least because PwC told employees to apply to the DTI to collect their May salaries, holiday pay, notice and redundancy pay. 'This shouldn't happen in future,' said the DTI, which, later this summer, plans to publish its proposals to incorporate the EU's information and consultation directive into UK law. While this is the first example of mass redundancies by text message, using alternative media to communicate bad news to employees is not new. Bill Morris, of the Transport and General Workers' Union, complained when Corus [a large steel-making firm] staff heard they had been made redundant on their car radios.

Questions

1 Why is text messaging an unsuitable channel for the purpose highlighted in this case?

2 What kinds of internal and external communication might be effectively undertaken using text messaging?

3 What are your own experiences of using this communication channel?

4 How do you think that existing texting conventions are likely to adapt, if this channel becomes more widely adopted in organisations?

Source: Harris and Orr (31 May, 2003). Copyright Financial Times Limited. Reproduced with permission.

Summary

- Letters remain an important communication channel for a variety of organisational purposes, and are associated with communication practices that differ from those of e-mail.

- Letters share three important communication characteristics: they are 'one-way' and non-interruptible; they are 'asynchronous' between sending and receipt; and they provide a permanent record of messages.

- Today, letters are normally prepared in a 'fully blocked' page layout with 'open' punctuation. They are typically structured around three tasks: establishing the context; delivering the central message; and stating any action required.

Summary (*continued*)

- As with other communication channels, the style and content of letters should reflect the relationship with the receiver and the purpose of the message. This can be problematic in the case of standard letters, where a polite, clear and concise approach is generally most appropriate.

- The fusion of database and text-handling technologies offers the opportunity to create customised letters in large quantities. However, such letters require careful targeting and drafting.

- Stationery can convey a positive image of your organisation, but it is also important to consider promotional, practical and legal aspects of the design.

- E-mail, text messaging and instant messaging are powerful communication channels, combining characteristics of text-based and conversational communication. However, inherent limitations, inappropriate usage, and a lack of consensus over communication practices mean that some of these channels remain problematic for business communication.

Key terms

asynchronous
communication 195

instant
messaging 205

synchronous
communication 205

PRACTICAL EXERCISES

8.1 Erskine Food Stores Limited

Consider the following exchange of correspondence between customer and retailer. This is an example of a letter of complaint (Figure 8.6), followed up with a letter of 'adjustment', that is, seeking to resolve the complaint or dispute (Figure 8.7). First, consider the customer's letter.

a. What do you detect from the style and tone of his letter?

b. What do you think he expects the company to do?

Now, note how the reply is structured, its general layout, use of language, tone, etc.

c. How would you feel on receiving the retailer's letter?

d. What messages do you think they have managed to communicate?

e. What changes would you make to improve its effectiveness?

8.2 Stationery and letterhead redesign: drafting an e-mail and letter

You are working for either a small high-technology manufacturing company or a voluntary organisation supporting children from deprived communities. Your manager has asked you to redesign the office stationery in order to meet current regulations and to project a more professional image of the organisation. She wants the work completed and the new stationery to be ready for use within the next eight weeks.

12th December 2013
Customer Services Department
ERSKINE FOOD STORES
545 Wroxeter Boulevard
Watlington
Herefordshire HE5 8WX

37 Wilson Street
Ickleston
Middlesex
UB22 8TX

Dear Sir/Madam

'ERSKWIK' BRAND SOUP: CHICKEN AND VEGETABLE WITH CROUTONS

I am extremely happy with our new Erskines branch in Ickleston, with its friendly staff and (generally) good products. However, the enclosed soup sachet comes as a big disappointment. Try it!

Having added your boiling water, see how rich and substantial it looks, a real improvement on the competition. Now sense the disillusion when you actually taste it. Regrettably, as I am sure you will agree, any initial flavour is over-whelmed by an excessive, lingering SALTINESS. On gastronomic and health grounds, your soup under-performs and does Erskine's a dis-service.

Do I have a duff batch, or do Erskine's have a duff Buyer?

Yours faithfully

Ronald Quincy-Smith

enc.
cc: Mr Bill Badger, *Consumer Watch*, Channel 7, XBC Television.

Figure 8.6 Example of a letter of complaint

11 January 2008

Mr R Quincy-Smith
37 Wilson Street
Ickleston
Middlesex
UB22 8TX

ERSKINES FOOD STORES
545 Wroxeter Boulevard, Watlington HE5 8WX
www.erskines-food.com

Dear Mr Quincy-Smith

We thank you for your letter and your kind comments about the staff and general standards at our Ickleston branch. However, we were sorry to learn of the problem you experienced with the Quick soup and apologise for the inconvenience caused when the product was found to be too salty. We examined the sample you kindly returned and it was tasted by our Buyer who agreed that it did have an excess of salt and was not according to the specification. As we were not sure if this was an isolated instance or a more general problem, it was necessary to obtain further samples from stock for checking and we regret the delay this caused when responding to your letter. Although the salt level in the stock packs was not as high as the one you purchased, there was more than the specified amount and therefore the supply was removed from sale pending further enquiries with our suppliers.

Meanwhile, we were concerned that this could happen and escape detection during the strict quality control procedures and we are continuing to monitor the situation closely to ensure there is no further lapse in standards. May we say again how sorry we are that you had reason to complain in this way. Occasionally, in spite of all the care taken, things can go wrong and we are grateful to be alerted so that we can take any action necessary to correct any shortcomings.

We hope you will continue to shop with us without further disappointment and you will accept our apologies together with the enclosed voucher towards the out-of-pocket expenses you have incurred.

Yours sincerely

B V Kelly (Mrs)

Customer Services

Enclosed credit voucher: 970987 £5.00

Tel: 01999 876543 Fax: 01999 876321 E-mail: service@erskines.co.uk
KW Erskine Food Stores Limited Registered in England 6789101112
Registered Office: 34 Victoria Avenue, Farebury, Wiltshire SN00 2JK

Figure 8.7 Example of a letter of 'adjustment'

a. Prepare an initial design to meet the promotional, practical and legal requirements discussed in this chapter. Invent a suitable business name and all necessary details, including your postal address, e-mail and website details. You may need to research the relevant legal requirements.

b. Draft an e-mail to your manager, Sarah Brown, requesting approval of the design and dealing with any production issues, such as the cost of printing and paper to be used.

c. Draft a letter to be sent to a number of companies, inviting quotes for printing your new design.

CASE STUDY 8.4

'Infant-plus' baby foods: direct marketing techniques

Many letters contain similar or identical information that needs to be reproduced for different receivers, including the routine letters sent out by banks, tax offices and education departments. Rather than redraft these each time, organisations used to generate standard (or 'form') letters, constructed from a series of model paragraphs. Inevitably, these letters sounded rather impersonal. As the 'Middleburg Bank' example in this chapter has indicated (see section 8.4), there are some obvious dangers in using standardised text, which ignores individual differences. However, by linking the way text is handled with an imaginative use of database software (a technique sometimes referred to as 'mailmerge'), it is possible to generate relatively personalised letters in large volumes. Mailmerge is used in many types of organisational correspondence, but one of the most common applications is communicating with current and prospective customers. It is one of the basic techniques of direct marketing, where databases are used to target particular individuals about products and services, rather than broad market segments (see Table 8.4).

Consider for example the imaginary food manufacturer, 'Infant Foods Inc', which specialises in bottled ready-meals for babies. The company wants to encourage new parents to trial *Infant-plus*, an up-market organic baby food brand. Several options are presented to the sales and marketing director. One suggestion is to run an extended series of adverts on breakfast television. However, the director points out that such a broad (or 'shotgun') approach would be largely wasted, since many of the viewers will not have babies, or have no interest in an organic product. After a long discussion, she decides to build the campaign around direct marketing. The first stage will be to purchase a list of prospects – the data set (see definition in Table 8.4) being captured from a competition that has run in a specialist magazine for pregnant women. This data will then be combined with lists already held by the company, to create a new data set. The plan is to generate approximately 200,000 personalised letters with money-off vouchers and a brochure insert. She hopes that, with the help of a high-quality data set, this 'direct' approach will be very closely targeted at people who are likely to be interested in *Infant-plus*. The initial promotional letter will be reinforced with other promotional tools, including a follow-up distribution of free samples and offers for related products and services.

Many different types of organisations, including charities and campaigning groups, are making increasing use of direct marketing techniques for fund-raising and member

Case study 8.4 (*continued*)

Table 8.4   Direct marketing terminology

Term	Comments
Mailmerge	This facility is offered by most wordprocessing packages, linking a database file containing names, addresses and other information to a text file containing a standard letter. Name, address and other data are drawn ('merged') into the standard letter in the appropriate locations, which are marked by keying in a code letter. The mailmerge is activated as the letters are printed out.
Database	A flexible electronic filing cabinet, often comprising a vast number of discrete items of data. Data can be sorted, filtered and extracted in ways that would be time-consuming and impractical using paper-based files. In addition to specialist software, spreadsheets and wordprocessing packages include useful database functions.
Data set	Raw data loaded into a database for subsequent manipulation. Widely-used data sets include: publicly-available statistical data, commercial lists of prospective customer contacts and confidential results from an in-house questionnaire survey. All forms of stored data are subject to data protection legislation.
Field	Within a particular record (see below), a single (i.e. 'discrete') item of information, such as one line of an address, a surname, date of birth or nationality. In the case of survey data, a field may contain the response to a question.
List	Data set containing names and addresses of consumers, sometimes with lifestyle and purchasing behaviour. Lists are created from market research surveys, competitions, returned product guarantee cards, etc. Lists are purchased by organisations in order to undertake focused direct mailing (e.g. 25,000 paraglider pilots, or 43,000 charity donors).
Record	Within a data set, a block of information relating to an individual person or organisation. This is the electronic equivalent of a file placed inside a filing cabinet.

recruitment, as well as in more traditional sales activity. Direct mail can be a powerful communication technique, but many people continue to dismiss it as 'junk mail'. Industry-sponsored research suggests that a high proportion of direct mail is opened, though this is not in itself a guarantee that the messages will be absorbed. When drafting communication in this form, it is essential to minimise the wastage rate. The following questions indicate some of the issues that need to be addressed:

- Have I targeted the recipients as closely as possible (e.g. filtering out existing customers when promoting introductory offers)?
- Is the style and content appropriate to all recipients? You may need to produce variants for different segments.
- Is the data set 'clean' and up-to-date? Have I considered using reply slips or other auditing techniques to assess the quality of the list?

One of the most important checks concerns the internal consistency of the data set. Ensure that the data fields are in a correct sequence and that all of them are drawn from the same record. When an organisation gets its 'name' fields and 'address' fields out of sequence, absolutely everyone – perhaps many thousands of customers – receives a letter containing someone else's details, undermining the effectiveness of any message it contains and potentially causing a loss of data protection and the release of classified information to the wrong person.

Case study 8.4 (*continued*)

Questions

1 Prepare your own direct marketing letters, using one of the scenarios below. Prepare two versions. In the first version, highlight each point in the letter where information would be merged from a database file. This will obviously include the recipient's name and address, but should also involve the main body of your letter. Try to be as creative as possible. Specify precisely the contents of each record and field. The second version of your letter should be addressed to a specific recipient, showing how a finished letter would look. Use the guidance on letter-writing contained in this chapter. Prepare a note to accompany the sample letter, suggesting how you might capture the data that has been used.

   a. You are a charitable organisation, providing accommodation and support for young offenders, and helping them to escape a life of crime. You want to launch a long-term national fund-raising campaign, entitled *Youth Action 2020*.

   b. You are a conventional retailer, moving onto the Internet to market your *Sandale* range of women's fashion shoes. You need to reach 20-to 35-year-old women in socio-economic categories ABC1.

   c. You are a government department, wanting to promote *Golden Age*, a new publicly-subsidised pre-retirement savings plan for 18-to 65-year-olds in regular employment. You want to reach both new and existing members of the workforce.

2 Comment on the potential advantages and disadvantages of direct mail as a communication channel in areas *other than* sales promotion and marketing. Identify examples where it would be particularly effective, and those where it may be counter-productive.

3 Consider the potential applications for direct mail techniques using electronic media, including e-mail and text messaging. Outline your proposals in a short oral presentation (maximum 5 minutes) or a one-page summary.

Glossary

Asynchronous communication means that there is a time delay between sending and receipt.

Synchronous communication happens in real time, without any time delay, so that the sender sends the message and the receiver instantaneously receives it, without the kind of time delay that occurs with an exchange of letters, for example.

Instant messaging is a form of real-time, synchronous communication between two or more people based on typed text which is exchanged via computers connected over a network such as the Internet.

Further reading

There are various guides to letter formats, giving 'model' examples of the major types of letter, including **Bond** (1998) and **Janner** (1989). Additional models and templates are available on the companion website. While it may be tempting to make use of popular guides to writing better letters and emails, the theme of this book is that the key to becoming a more effective communicator is to develop your own critical faculties, rather than relying too heavily on 'recipe book' solutions. Refer back to the reading recommended for Chapter 3, which deals more broadly with the use of language. Readers are also encouraged to consider recent research on the impact of emerging text-based channels, including work by **Minsky and Marin** (1999), **Yates and Orlikowski** (2002) and **Zack and McKenney** (1995). The broader implications for organisations are discussed in Chapter 7 of this book. **Newell et al.** (2001) provide a useful case-based analysis of intranet developments, while **Fulk and DeSanctis** (1995) explore the links between the new communication channels and organisational change. **Turban** (2003) is a good general introduction to e-business applications.

Useful websites

Here are several websites which might be of interest to you. You might like to add some of your own too:

The Ask Oxford website offers advice on letter writing and includes sample letters. (Available at

http://www.askoxford.com/betterwriting/letterwriting/?view=uk)

The Monster website focuses on applying for jobs, and provides advice on cover letters. (Available at

http://career-advice.monster.co.uk/cvs-applications/careers.aspx)

The Email Replies website explains why e-mail etiquette is important and offers a checklist of etiquette rules. (Available at

http://www.emailreplies.com/)

Debrett's provides a useful guide on etiquette in the workplace. (Available at:

http://www.debretts.co.uk/etiquette/work-life/office-etiquette.aspx)

References

Bond, A. (1998) *300 Successful Business Letters*. Barron's Educational Series, Hauppauge, NY.

Cane, A. (2007) 'Where do we go from here?' *Financial Times* 11th July 2007. (Available at http://www.ft.com/home/uk (accessed 19th March 2012)).

Digital World Research Centre (2001) 'The future of paper mail in a digital age'. DWRC, University of Surrey, Guildford.

Fulk, J. and DeSanctis, G. (1995) 'Electronic communication and changing organizational forms'. *Organization Science*, 6, 4, 337–349.

Harris, C. and Orr, R. (2003) 'We rgrt 2 infm u yr fired. Hv nice day'. *Financial Times*, London edition, 1 (31st May).

Janner, G. (1989) *Janner's Complete Letter Writer*. Century Hutchinson, London.

Minsky, B.D. and Marin, D.B. (1999) 'Why faculty members use email: the role of individual differences in channel choice'. *The Journal of Business Communication*, 36, 194–217.

Newell, S., Scarbrough, H. and Swan, J. (2001) 'From global knowledge management to internal electronic fences: contradictory outcomes of intranet development'. *British Journal of Management*, 12, 97–111.

Orlikowski, W.J. and Yates, J. (1994) 'Genre repertoire: the structuring of communicative practices in organizations'. *Administrative Science Quarterly*, 39, 541–574.

Palmer, M. (2012). The Netiquette of Working Life. *Financial Times*, London edition, (6th February). (Available at: http://www.ft.com/s/0/94239bbe-4dae-11e1-b96c-00144feabdc0.html (Accessed June 8 2012)).

Royal Mail (2001) 'Paper mail is here to stay' (press release). Royal Mail Group, London (6th March).

Strawbridge, M. (2006) *Netiquette: Internet Etiquette in the Age of the Blog*. Software Reference Ltd, Ely.

Turban E. et al. (2003) *Electronic Commerce 2003: a managerial perspective*. Prentice Hall, Upper Saddle River, NJ.

Yates, J. and Orlikowski, W.J. (2002) 'Genre systems: structuring interaction through communicative norms'. *The Journal of Business Communication*, 39, 13–35.

Zack, M.H. and McKenney, J.L. (1995) 'Social context and interaction in ongoing computer-supported management groups'. *Organization Science*, 6, 394–422.

Chapter 9

Reports, briefing papers and summaries

Perfection is achieved, not when there is nothing more to add, but when there is nothing left to take away.

Antoine de Saint Exupéry, writer

Learning outcomes

By the end of this chapter you should be able to:

- contrast the different types of reports used in organisations, relating these differences to their audience and purpose;
- identify and apply the principles for preparing a written report;
- tackle the process of report writing: briefing, preparation, drafting and completion;
- recognise the importance of summarising skills;
- develop summarising skills;
- reflect on the characteristics of this communication channel and its application in technologically-mediated and multi-cultural contexts.

9.1 Introduction

This chapter considers reports and briefing documents, two text-based communication channels that are widely used in organisations of all kinds. As was the case with shorter text-based channels, such as letters and e-mails (see Chapter 8), care and practice are needed to structure the report so that it is clear and appropriate for its purpose and context, and in an appropriate written style in order to meet the needs of particular audiences. The report should also be clear, accurate and concise. Our review of report-writing techniques includes a number of issues that influence the structure and content of a report. We trace the writing process, from the initial stages of obtaining a clear specification for the project, through to the final stages of editing and production. The final section of the chapter deals with an essential (and often under-rated) communication challenge, abstracting from complex source material and drafting concise summaries that focus attention on the most important evidence and argument.

9.2 Reports: principal types and purposes

Business reports come in all shapes and sizes. Our first task is to review the main options available, and consider which type of report best suits a particular purpose (see Table 9.1). One of the first issues to consider is how the report is to be delivered. This chapter focuses on written reports, but it is also possible to present an oral report, either in a meeting or as part of a presentation. (Chapters 12 and 13 deal with these channels.) Some reports are written in a formal style, while others are relatively informal. They may range in scale from a single page of concise argument drafted by one author to a multi-volume report compiled by a large team of researchers and editorial staff. There is a significant difference between the task of preparing a routine report, where the content and format tends to be pre-determined, and an original, one-off report, where there may be very little in the way of guidance from previous work. Many companies use standardised formats for routine internal reports, such as the 'weekly sales update' produced by a sales department, or the regular 'quality monitoring report' prepared by quality assurance staff in a manufacturing plant.

In the following sections, we focus on how to write an original report that makes use of relatively source-complex material, presented in a formal way. The subject matter might be, for example, a new strategy proposal, plans for an office relocation or an investigation into a recent industrial accident. The underlying principles of report writing are common to all types of document, so the advice can be adapted to suit your particular purpose. Whatever type of report you are writing, it is possible to identify four stages:

- obtaining a clear specification;
- research and preparation;

Table 9.1 Types of report: some practical examples

Type	Example of purpose
Executive briefing	The factory manager provides the managing director with a concise summary of the main issues and likely questions on health and safety prior to a shareholders' meeting when the issue is likely to be raised.
Research results	A market research executive at a medical charity is investigating the impact of a recent donor recruitment campaign. She presents the findings from a telephone survey to the charity's trustees and senior managers.
Regular update	On a weekly basis, the management accountant of a major retail chain advises regional managers of their profitability performances by branch and geographic area.
Business proposal	An entrepreneur contacts a venture capital company to offer a possible equity stake in her new leisure business. She provides them with a business plan to read before attending the presentation.

- drafting the report;
- editing and completion.

The process of any longer piece of writing, be it a report or some other document, is not linear. Often you will revisit drafts, making changes to the structure of the report or rewriting sections. This is all part of the process of report writing. The next section of this chapter will deal with the four stages identified above in sequence.

9.3   Obtaining a clear specification

A report is a kind of 'guided tour' through a jungle of ideas. It is important to plan your route in advance, but also to remain flexible; unforeseen changes are bound to arise once you get under way. To prepare successfully, it is worth asking some fundamental questions. Above all, clarify the report specification or **'Terms of Reference'** (TOR) and establish which items really need to be included to meet the needs of your audience. The Terms of Reference (TOR) should include information about what is to be achieved in the report (objectives), who should be consulted on the report, who will be reading the report, how it should be structured, and the time frame for its completion. The questions are bound to vary from case to case, but they can be summarised under four main headings: purpose, audience, source material and context.

Purpose, audience, context and source material

Before putting pen to paper, there are four basic questions to consider: what is the purpose of the report? Who are you writing the report for? What is the context surrounding the report? What source material will you use in the report? Let us now look at each of these in turn.

Purpose

It is essential to consider why you are drafting the report: its primary purpose plus any secondary aims. For example: is it designed to consult readers; to provide information; to explain a novel concept; or to persuade them to adopt a particular course of action? These questions, in conjunction with your research on the audience, can then be used to inform decisions on the kinds of language used in the report. Consider the previous example, of the GM foods debate. While academic language, with full Harvard referencing, would be strict requirements of any scientific report on the subject, the same features would become serious distractions in a more popular document, designed as part of a public consultation exercise. Similar issues arise when considering the use of images in a report. (For example, are photographs appropriate? Should data be presented in numerical or graphical formats?)

Audience

As with other communication channels, one of the most cost-effective ways of spending your time is to research and reflect on your 'target' audience. Find out as much as possible about the people who are going to read your finished report. Is it a specific person, a group of people with similar backgrounds, or a more diverse readership (i.e. multiple audiences)? What is their existing knowledge and experience of the subject matter of your report? Will they be familiar with any technical language that you intend to use? Are they likely to hold positive, negative or neutral views on the issues that you are discussing? For example, imagine how these points might apply if you were preparing a report on 'marketing opportunities' related to genetically-modified (GM) foods – a subject that raises a great deal of emotional energy on both sides of the argument.

Context

Report writing does not take place in a vacuum; it is essential to consider the wider setting in which your report is being prepared. For example: is there an urgent deadline for delivery, so that speed of delivery takes priority over perfecting the fine details of style and presentation? Is it a routine (e.g. weekly or monthly) publication that must follow a standard template, or – as we have assumed in this chapter – is it a bespoke piece of work that allows you to introduce a more original or distinctive style? Is the report designed to stand alone or is it designed to work with other communication channels, such as a series of oral presentations or an interactive website? Finally, if there are to be several channels, how will the authors ensure that the combined effect is both consistent and complementary?

Source material

There are always several preliminary questions to consider regarding the source material that will form the basis of your report. Again, these questions appear very straightforward but are easily ignored at the planning stages, leading to more serious problems later on. The most important questions concern availability and access:

- Where are the sources of secondary data that you will need to consult?
- Are they available in a compatible electronic format?
- If there are particular people that you need to interview, when are they going to be in the office, and are they willing to grant you a meeting?
- Is any of your source material likely to be either commercially or politically sensitive?
- Do any copyright regulations apply?
- Are there any other ethical issues regarding access or use of this information?
- Should sources be cited in the report?
- What is the quality of each available source (i.e. its credibility, accuracy, objectivity and currency)?
- Are there any information gaps that need to be filled?
- If so, is it necessary to conduct additional research in order to provide a comprehensive coverage of the issues?

Failing to ask these questions, and to deal with any resulting issues, can result in costly and embarrassing delays at a later stage.

As the previous points have indicated, there is a lot of groundwork to do before the writing can begin. You will also revisit some of them during the writing process. In some cases, the organisation may decide that it is more appropriate to commission external consultants to prepare a report. However, even in these circumstances, managers need to become involved in the process of briefing the consultants, who will also need answers to the questions raised in this section. Case study 9.1 highlights some of the difficulties that can occur when inadequate attention is given to this initial stage in the report-writing process.

CASE STUDY 9.1

'Nebulous Phones' and the under-specified reports

One of the most common causes of bad report writing is failure to obtain a clear specification. Though you may need to revise them as the work proceeds, it is still important that the main requirements are agreed with those commissioning the report. As the following case suggests, people often find themselves struggling to extract a clear specification (or 'brief') from senior managers or external clients. Sergey Nebulous is the founder and chief executive of Nebulous Phones, a large and successful mobile phone retailer. Sergey is notorious for his vague instructions to staff, and he invariably complains whenever they produce something that fails to match his requirements. Here is a selection, taken from Sergey's recent requests to his hard-pressed employees:

Extract 1

'Klajdia!, sorry to interrupt your lunch. I need a report on the Blue Whale acquisition. Lots of graphs and things. You know, something impressive-looking; it's for the analysts . . . don't you just HATE those people?!!! Anyway, enjoy the lasagne, I'll leave you to it.'

Extract 2

Subject: no subject
Date: Sun 12 July 2008 23:57:46 +0100
From: Sergey Nebulous <sergey@nebulous-elec.com>
To: Yusef Mugisha <ymugisha@nebulous-elec.com>
Priority: High
We need new supplier data interpreted. Include financial ratios etc. Sergey

Extract 3

'Is that Kay? Hello, Sergey here. Sorry to bother you at the weekend. Is it really that early? Anyway, have you seen that OUTRAGEOUS article in the *Sunday Inquisitor*? Loads of media hype about radiation and handsets! Kay, I want the FACTS. Can you please draft me a full-scale report, showing just how "green", you know, "sustainable" we are? Thanks a million, got to go. Bye now!'

Questions

1 Review the above three extracts and note the main limitations in Sergey's specification for each report, including any missing or ambiguous information.

2 Based on the faults you have identified, what kinds of problems do you anticipate arising from the reports prepared by Klajdia, Yusef and Kay?

3 Re-draft Sergey's report specifications to overcome the problems you have identified, inventing and inserting any necessary details.

4 What would your response have been, in practice, if you had been one of these three employees?

Source: Written by the authors. Nebulous Phones is a fictional organisation.

9.4   Researching and organising the source material

The second set of preparatory tasks is concerned with the research process and organising the source material you are going to use as the basis for your report. **Source material** refers to the data that you will draw upon to support your key points and to provide evidence on which to base your recommendations. It may be presented as graphics and images, as well as text. Research methods fall beyond the scope of this book, but detailed advice can be found in a number of specialist texts. Recent examples include Saunders et al. (2009) and Easterby-Smith et al. (2008); additional recommendations are given in the Further reading at the end of this chapter.

For the purposes of this chapter, our interest in the research process begins at the point when the main data sources have been identified. In the era of internet search engines and electronic access to official statistics, academic journals, newspapers and technical publications, selecting relevant information from an ever-growing pile of possibilities is often the main problem. **Diagramming** or 'Mind Mapping®' (Buzan 1995) can be a useful technique that helps the researcher to separate the 'wood' from the 'trees'. This process involves abstracting the main themes from the detailed background information that has been collected (see section 2.5). By writing out the topics to be covered on a whiteboard or large sheet of paper, you can begin to identify the most important sources and uncover logical connections between major topic areas. These connections are the basis for the development of arguments (see Chapters 5). They should also help in developing an outline structure for the report. Such plans can help identify gaps in the development of ideas, arguments, and sources of evidence. The structure of the report may be modified during the drafting stage, but this initial effort to organise the raw material can have a profound influence on the way that you think about the subject. Formulating a report is a creative process. It is generally advisable to draw on insights from a number of people, before committing to a particular approach. Much the same process occurs during the early stages of a student dissertation or thesis (Phillips and Pugh 2000). You should also remember that not all the approaches will work the same for all people. You may prefer to use a more linear approach, making bullet points, and this is fine. You should use whatever works for you.

There are generally several competing ways of tackling a research question and its associated body of evidence. The initial approach, which once seemed so promising, may reach a dead end. The prospective author becomes understandably downhearted at this point! However, students and supervisors often go through several cycles of proposals and counter-suggestions before the breakthrough occurs. As a result of discussion, someone stumbles upon the obvious 'solution', and the main stage of drafting the report can begin.

9.5   Report writing: drafting stage

How do you approach the task of writing? Some people can settle down and write out an extended piece of text from beginning to end. However, for most of us, writing is a more gradual process, with many corrections and a succession of drafts before arriving at the finished article. The task of writing a long report can be a source of concern, causing many writers to postpone the point at which they put pen to paper. In some cases, this is due to lack of prior experience and a fear of being exposed to external criticism (Ruderstam and Newton 2001). This, in turn, may flow from a person's lack of confidence in what they have to say. However, as many authors have commented, the activity of writing is itself a source of learning, as you engage with the subject and really begin to think about the ways that your information sources are connected (Phillips and Pugh 2000). This insight is reflected in the wider field of knowledge management, which has highlighted the essential relationship between knowledge creation and human action (e.g. Nonaka and Takeuchi 1995: 58–9). In this case, it suggests that authors may need to remain flexible, adapting their initial outline structures to accommodate the new ideas generated during the writing process. It is also important to recognise that different cultures show distinctive preferences in the way that logical arguments are constructed (De Vita 2001: 172, Zaharna 1996: 80). The guidance presented in the following sections is influenced by British conventions for structuring and presenting material. While it is not possible to represent the full diversity of communication practices, the broader principles of successful drafting (i.e. organising the source material, making the structure visible and using graphics where appropriate) may be readily adapted and applied to most organisational and cultural contexts.

King (2004) advises that when writing to communicate effectively for an international audience the writer needs to take into account:

- apparent cultural differences
- unspoken cultural differences and
- unconscious cultural differences.

We introduced this concept of apparent and hidden cultural aspects in Chapter 2 with reference to the Iceberg metaphor (see Figure 2.5). **Apparent cultural differences** in written business communication encompass aspects such as language, including use of US or British English, and format of numbers and dates. **Unspoken cultural differences** refer to business protocol, including preferred layout and inappropriate colours and logos. **Unconscious cultural differences** might include variations in the level of formality of interactions between managers and subordinates. For example, in some cultures managers, and subordinates, work collaboratively on tasks, with feedback and suggestions welcomed from both parties. In other cultures managers, and subordinates, roles are distinct, communication is more formal and there is a large power distance between them. These factors will impact on aspects such as: who reports should be targeted at, and the level of formality of language used. Another example of unconscious cultural differences is the level of individualism. A culture that takes a collectivist approach to life would welcome mention in the cover letter to a report of a personal aspect of the relationship (such as complimenting a recent achievement), whereas this might be seen as unnecessary and distracting in a more individualist culture (Hofstede and Hofstede, 2004).

Organising the report

A report is somewhat like a new building; a basic outline structure is required before you can work on the interior. In contrast to a building, report writers have some capacity to re-design the overall structure at a later stage. However, there is a close relationship between the way that the material is organised and the 'interior design' task of writing specific sections of text. Hence, it is advisable to draft an initial outline structure for the report as soon as the initial preparatory work is complete, but before drafting large amounts of text. There are two distinct elements to this process:

- identifying what the main sections and sub-sections are likely to be, and
- considering the order in which each topic should be placed.

The first element is an extension of the activities outlined in section 9.4 . At the drafting stage, we need to review the broad clustering of topics and loose connections that were identified previously, refining them into more concrete groupings of primary and secondary themes. For example, Whitley's (2000) text, *Divergent Capitalisms: the social structuring and change of business systems*, is divided into three distinct parts:

- the first gives an introduction to the concept of 'varieties of capitalism';
- the second outlines the 'comparative-business-systems' framework;
- the third applies the framework to business systems in East Asia and Eastern Europe.

While other structures may be conceived, the key point for the communicator is to ensure that there is an inherent logic, as indicated in this case. The actual order in which the sections are placed is always a matter of judgment. There are a number of logical alternatives to consider, as illustrated below (see Table 9.2). If you are unsure which order to adopt, it is worth experimenting with the alternatives; some are bound to work better than others. This choice should be guided by the standard concerns of the communicator. In other words, which sequence is most appropriate for the **material** being presented and which sequence is likely to be the most straightforward for the **audience** that has to absorb the message it contains? You should also think about whether the most important information you want to present should go early in the document or at the end.

The issue of structure raises questions regarding culture-specific approaches to writing. This can be a particular challenge for international managers and students, whose educational background has been in another national culture. For example, an Italian economist, now based in Britain, recalls the different expectations of British and Italian academics towards the essay format that is widely used in this discipline:

'In the Italian essay writing style, for example, a long and general introduction which illustrates the genesis of the issue to be examined and provides a retrospective analysis or historical overview of the issue is a must, regardless of the wording of the question. A British

Table 9.2 Getting a report in order: some alternative sequences

Logical sequence	Practical example
Importance	In a report entitled 'Ten challenges for the pharmaceutical industry', the most serious challenges are addressed first.
Urgency	The structural survey report for a newly-acquired building begins by identifying a leaky roof that needs to be repaired immediately and moves on to discuss longer-term maintenance work.
Date/Chronology	A progress report on computer system installation reviews events over the past month. Some reports, including the educational and employment sections of a CV, may be written in reverse chronological order, with the most recent items first.
Simple to complex	The documentation supplied with an accountancy training course begins with the basic concepts of book-keeping before explaining more advanced topics, such as accounting adjustments and ratio analysis.
Global to specific	A report into a company's absenteeism problems starts by looking at broad social factors, gradually narrowing down to causes within particular factories and departments. (Note: the opposite sequence, specific to global, may work equally well.)

reader, however, as the author learned at his expense during the early stages of his under-graduate study in England, would see this as lack of "convergence" to the point, or even "waffling" [i.e. engaging in a long and irrelevant discussion], and it might not be until the second page of the essay that concepts expressed are regarded as being really pertinent, and aimed at answering the question.'

(De Vita 2001: 172)

Experience with international students from many different backgrounds suggests that these kinds of cultural boundary can be crossed, given appropriate guidance and support. It also appears that there is a greater degree of convergence in the structuring of some text-based communication channels, including the academic dissertation and some varieties of business report, reflecting the internationalisation of the relevant organisations (e.g. universities, multinational companies and international consulting firms).

Table 9.3 compares the typical outline structure of an academic dissertation with that of a business report. This highlights two areas that tend to be down-played in business reports. The first of these is the review of earlier and related research in the area, that helps to locate a particular piece of work in its broader context (i.e. the 'literature review'). Business reports tend to have a much narrower focus on the immediate issue at hand. Second, the dissertation always includes a discussion of the wider implications of the findings. Again, this broadening out of the findings is often seen as beyond the scope of a business report, due to its shorter-term and more managerial focus.

The headings following Table 9.3 review the main sections of the business report, commenting on their main characteristics and some of the more common issues that can arise when drafting them.

Title page

Like the rest of the report, the title should be clear, concise and unambiguous. Writers commonly use a short 'main' title, followed by a colon and a more explanatory sub-title (e.g. 'Project Equinox: progress report for the period 2005–07'). The title page typically includes the author's name, organisational affiliations and the date of publication.

Table 9.3 Structuring academic dissertations and business reports

Academic dissertation	Business report
Title page	Title page
Abstract	Executive summary
Contents page	Contents page
Introduction	Introduction
Literature review	
Research methods	
Results or Findings	Results or Findings
Discussion	
Conclusions	Conclusions
Recommendations	Recommendations
References	
Appendices	

Executive summary

The **executive summary** is a section located at the front of a report that distils the entire contents of the document into a much more concise form. Its purpose is to provide busy executives with the essence of the report at a glance. It serves the same purpose as the abstract in an academic article, allowing the reader to make a rapid assessment of whether the report is relevant to their needs. Executive summaries usually emphasise the key recommendations of the report, which may be presented in bullet point format. The executive summary in a fairly short report may be a single paragraph or even just a few sentences, while longer reports tend to have longer executive summaries. A common error in report writing is to confuse the executive summary with the introduction; the latter serves an entirely different purpose.

Introduction

The purpose of an introduction is to lead the reader into the main body of the report. Like all reception areas, it should be welcoming to the new arrival. It may include the terms of reference, or state the reasons for writing the report and establish its importance. Introductions often contain a chapter summary, outlining how the topic is to be tackled in the following chapters. However, this should be brief, otherwise it could pre-empt the rest of the report.

Main section(s)

The main section comprises a number of sections and sub-sections, with appropriate titles, which may take the form of chapters. Authors can help their readers to navigate a way through the body of the report, by inserting some linking text at the end of each main section or chapter. This text should summarise what has been discussed and indicate how this relates to the next theme.

Conclusion

The conclusion is where the key arguments and/or findings of the report are drawn together and put in context. The concluding section should also relate back to the original objectives of the report. (Note: Writing the conclusion provides the author with a useful check that everything has been addressed.) The conclusion should not include any new, previously undiscussed material. Late findings or last-minute ideas should be either fully integrated into the text or reported separately. It may be tempting to simply 'tack them on' to the rest of the conclusion, but it is an unwise tactic. Audiences find it very confusing, and the resulting irritation can help to undermine the credibility and persuasive power of the report.

Recommendations

The new section is sometimes combined with the conclusion. In any event, the recommendations should always flow logically from the points made in the conclusion and the preceding argument. For example, this section might be used to suggest a preferred option from a range that was under consideration. Alternatively, it might make new proposals or recommend further research, based on the findings of this report.

References

Most business reports provide minimal referencing, the aim being to make the document as short and focused as possible. However, there is a trade-off between conciseness and evidence-based argument. Where external information sources are used, it may be helpful to provide some supporting details for the reader. Academic dissertations and research papers tend to have much fuller referencing, listing all of the sources. This is combined with extensive referencing in the text. Again, this reflects the trade-off between needing to substantiate the evidence, and word length and readability. For example, the 'Harvard' system of referencing, e.g. 'Kropotkin (2002) states that . . .' or ' . . . as suggested by recent studies (Schmidt 1999a). . .', has been widely adopted in academic writing. However, heavy use of referencing in this format can clog up the text, making it cumbersome to read. Where business reports do include references, the simpler 'Vancouver' numbering system is commonly adopted (e.g. ' . . . as suggested by recent studies,[23] . . .'), and the number of references is also kept to a minimum.

Appendices

Appendices are used for detailed data and analytical material that some readers are likely to need, but which would obstruct the flow of your argument if inserted earlier. In practice, they are rarely included in business reports, other than those presented as part of a detailed inquiry, involving large amounts of technical or statistical data. Appendices should never be used to 'pad out' a report or simply to indicate the amount of research material that has been collected – unlike the *human* appendix, they must serve a useful purpose!

Make the structure visible – 'signposting' the report

One of the most useful mental exercises for any report-writer is to consider how an audience is going to approach the task of reading the report. Most authors find it hard to accept that readers are unlikely to be sitting down with a nice cup of tea, working their way steadily from the opening sentence to the final full stop. In practice, a busy manager will begin by 'scanning' your report, absorbing the overall look of the piece and pausing over the occasional heading, paragraph, bullet point or illustration that catches their eye (see Chapter 4). You can increase the impact of your report, and assist the reader, by bearing this behavioural pattern in mind. Concise, informative headings, sub-headings and labels act as well-lit signposts, guiding the reader through the report. They also make a positive impression in the mind of the reader, suggesting that this is a competently drafted and valuable document. By contrast, poor signposting gives readers a poor initial impression of your report, even where the underlying content is strong. Signposting is also achieved by using appropriate language to link sentences or sections of the report together. This might be done by using linking words which connect sentences such as *in addition, however, therefore*. For example:

> *In December, the company's share price continued to fall and it was obliged to dismantle two of its partnerships.* **As a result**, *Nebulous holdings had to deduct $1 billion from its earnings for the third quarter of 2011.*

In these two sentences, *as a result* links the first sentence with the second. The first sentence is the cause, and the second sentence is the result. *As a result* helps the reader to understand the relationship between these two events. There are many more similar linking words. When linking words are used well, the writer does all the work for the reader, and the reader does not need to waste time trying to work out what the writer is trying to say. The reader can then focus on the information and critically assess this information in the report. Have a look at the Further reading section at the end of this chapter for further guidance.

The contents page, index, glossaries, section numbering and typography are also important signposting devices. Graphical items, such as charts and photographs, can help to identify the main subject areas, as well as being informative in their own right.

Contents pages and indexes

The contents page provides an overview of the entire report and is essential in all but the shortest documents. The conventional formats list section numbers and headings, with their respective opening page number indicated in a column on the right-hand side. Sub-section details may also be included. Accurate and detailed indexing is a fairly specialised skill, which tends to be restricted to longer reports and book-length publications. However, both tables of contents and more straightforward indexes can now be generated relatively easily with the help of standard wordprocessing software.

Section headings and numbering

The conventional approach is to keep headings short and to the point, the aim being to make the contents of that section or sub-section clear to the reader. In more formal reports, decimal numbering systems are normally used alongside the heading. Some legal and scientific reports may use up to four levels of sub-section, so that 'Section 1.9.3.1' is followed by 'Section 1.9.3.2', etc. This can be useful when it is necessary to refer to specific sections of text. However, multiple sub-sections can be confusing, for both the report writer and the reader. In business reports, numbering is best kept simple, using no more than three levels. If further levels are required, you can switch to bullet points or lists based on either lower case letters or Roman numerals (i.e. sequences running, 'a, b, c, d . . .' or, 'i, ii, iii, iv . . .').

Changing type

Bold text and larger font sizes can be used to identify the main section headings. You can also use upper case and lower case letters to create a logical hierarchy of headings and sub-headings. This hierarchy normally descends from larger font sizes to smaller, upper case to lower case and bold to ordinary text. It is important to use the structure consistently throughout the report, a task that is made easier by creating a template, or making use of those provided with your wordprocessing package. (Note: These are usually available as a 'drop-down' menu on the toolbar, or as part of the 'tools' menu.) In the days when most reports were produced on a typewriter, underlining was commonly used in titles and sub-titles. However, in wordprocessed reports this has been largely replaced by bold text, as illustrated in the following example (see Figure 9.1). The move away from underlining reflects the fact that text

Chapter title (20 pt bold, title case)	**12**	**Field Research**
Main headings (12 pt bold, upper case)	**12.1** **12.2**	**INTRODUCTION** **REGIONAL BREAKDOWN**
Sub-headings (12 pt, bold, title case)	**12.2.1** **12.2.2**	**South Asia region** **East Asia region**
Lower levels (12 pt, title case)		Consumer sample Producer sample
Bullet points (10 pt, title case)		• Increased demand for premium products • Dynamic new segments emerging • Limited impact of promotional campaign

Figure 9.1 Consistent use of typography: sample hierarchy of headings

can now be easily printed in bold. It is also partly because URLs (i.e. the 'Uniform Resource Locators' used to identify websites and web pages) are typically presented as underlined hyperlinks (e.g. www.pearsoned.co.uk), which could become confused with report titles.

Incorporating tables and figures

Wherever possible, summarise your analysis or findings in the form of tables or figures. Tables generally refer to numerical data, set out as labelled rows and columns, while figures can include anything from a photograph or line drawing to a pie chart summarising statistical data. A table is more concise than the same data presented as continuous text. However, a well-designed graphic can be even more focused and revealing (see Chapters 4). Tables and figures should be positioned as closely as possible to the relevant section in the report. However, to avoid confusing the reader they should always follow, rather than precede, the text to which they refer. The connection between them is made by including a brief reference in brackets at the end of the relevant sentence. For example, the text might state that 'An artist's impression of the new headquarters building indicates where the solar heating panels will be installed (Figure 18.3).' By connecting text of your report to the correct figure or table, you can assist the reader and reinforce your main arguments. (Note: Further advice on business graphics is included in section 4.5)

| 9.6 | **Report writing: completion stage** |

When you have been working on a report for a long time, it is difficult to judge it objectively. Be sure to get an independent opinion of the contents and format of your report before it is finalised. Ideally, you should ask a number of colleagues or friends to read it and make comments. If possible, your choice of reviewers should reflect the kinds of people that are going to be reading the final version. Your reviewers can provide constructive criticism on the content and advise on whether the writing style is readable and appropriate for the intended audience. One of the leading US software companies has described this review process, in somewhat patronising terms, as 'checking with Brad's mom'. In other words, the report authors ask themselves whether the mother of one of their executives would understand it. The next best alternative is to re-read the report for yourself. Indeed, this re-reading remains essential, even if the report has gone to external reviewers. Try to put it aside for a week, or at least a few days, since a period away from the material will give you a more realistic perspective. It will allow you to see gaps in the structure of the report, your use of source material and any odd wording you might have put in. Some writers take it a step further, find themselves a secluded location and read out sections of the report to an imaginary audience. This simple, if potentially embarrassing, technique is very effective at highlighting any unclear or long-winded passages.

Finalising a printed report

In some situations, the wordprocessed text of a business report may be typeset, in order that it can be printed professionally. For example, annual reports and other publications designed for external audiences may require this additional treatment. Copy editors use a standard set of symbols for correcting the page proofs that are returned by the typesetter

Alteration required	Mark to be made in margin	Mark to be made in text
Delete	⁊	/ or ⊢⊣
Delete and close up	⁊	∠ or ⊟
Close up (delete spaces)	⌒	⌒
Insert space (i.e. between letters)	Ψ	Ψ
Leave as set	(stet)	✓
Replace damaged letters	✕	encircle characters
Transpose	⌐⌐	⌐⌐
Move letters or words over to next line	(t.o.)	⊏
Run on (no new paragraph)	⌒	⌒
Change to lower case	(l.c.)	encircle characters
Change to bold type	(bold)	under characters
Change to italic type	(ital.)	under characters
Insert matter	⋏	⋏
Insert hyphen	⊢=⊣	⋏
Insert apostrophe	⸜ʻ	⋏
Insert quotation marks	ʻ ʻ	⋏
Insert oblique	①	⋏
Insert full stop	⊙	⋏
Insert comma, colon etc.	∩ʼ	⋏
Start new paragraph	(n.p.)	⌐
Insert superscript (i.e. powers in maths)	²ʻ	⋏
Change to upper case	(u.c.)	≡
Change to roman type	(rom.)	encircle characters

Figure 9.2 Proof correction symbols

(see Figure 9.2). These comprise marks that are made in the text, and a corresponding mark to be made at the same point in the margin. The symbols can also be helpful when editing your own wordprocessed printouts.

Finalising multi-authored reports

Multi-authored reports are those which draw on the expertise of several authors, and they require careful co-ordination, as is the case in many organisations. There are some intrinsic challenges to face when working on a large multi-authored report of this kind. For example, there is the task of co-ordinating the contributions of authors who may be located in different buildings, countries or continents. Above all, it is extremely difficult to produce a clear and consistent approach when the authors have different technical and cultural backgrounds. The following headings identify some common symptoms of this problem and suggest practical ways that they can be resolved or mitigated.

Variable grammar and writing style

Authors are likely to adopt the style with which they are most familiar. Such variation has its attractions and may be encouraged in some cases (e.g. where the purpose is to explore a range of views on a subject, held by a diverse group of people). However, if the report is aiming to express a collective voice (e.g. a statement setting out the organisation's ethical policy), it needs to be expressed consistently throughout. By anticipating this requirement at the planning stage, it is possible to minimise this variability and the need for excessive editing at the final stage. The authors should agree on grammatical and stylistic issues at the outset. For example, it is important to decide on using the present or past tense and the active or passive voice (see section 3.2). There also needs to be some agreement on the terminology used and any assumptions about the readership, including their level of understanding of such terms. As the writing proceeds, it is also advisable to exchange initial drafts between the authors, to ensure that everyone is following the agreed guideline.

Incorrect cross-references

When a section is added or deleted during the drafting process, it is easy to forget to change earlier references to numbered sections in the text. This becomes even more problematic in multi-authored documents. Most wordprocessing software includes facilities for sharing of files, within an overall 'master document'. The alternative is to leave the cross-referencing until the later stages, though this can become a very time-consuming task.

Inconsistent headings and labelling

This is another topic to address during the planning stages. The co-authors should adopt an agreed template, specifying variables such as the number of levels of heading and the relevant typefaces. In practice, many organisations have adopted standardised templates for their reports, minimising any potential for inconsistency. However, even where this software is being used, it is advisable to appoint one of the co-authors, or a third party, to act as the overall editor, tidying up any remaining differences in the heading formats, labelling of figures and tables, referencing and so on.

Grammatical and spelling errors

Today's wordprocessing packages contain very powerful spelling and grammar checkers. However, the editor cannot rely on these tools exclusively, since they are not yet intelligent enough to identify words where the spelling is correct, but the word itself is wrong (e.g. '**soul** trader' would not be corrected to 'sole trader'). Allowing a spell-checker to correct the text automatically is always a mistake, as the software is free to replace mis-keyed and unrecognised words with meaningless substitutes.

Case study 9.2 reviews how one application of technology, the use of editing tools, is influencing the drafting of business reports.

CASE STUDY 9.2

Using editing tools in report-writing: a critical assessment

Software packages, such as Microsoft Word®, include a number of tools that can help with the editing process, such as 'track changes', which tracks each author's changes in a different colour so that all authors can easily identify who made which amendments and can accept or reject them accordingly. These can be particularly useful in the case of multi-authored reports. In the past, the typical practice has been for authors to print out a paper copy of their report, with wide margins (i.e. 4 centimetres) on either side. The copy-editor then annotated the printed version, using a coloured pen. By contrast, the software-based tools enable editors to insert their comments directly into the text, while it is still in electronic form. This means that the file containing this annotated text can be circulated by e-mail to several authors for further comments and revision, whereas the paper version would need to be photocopied before distribution.

Some groups may prefer to work on shared documents using Google docs, which allows individuals to work on, edit, and make changes to the same document which is stored in the same place. It is even possible for individuals to work on the same document at the same time and make changes.

The following extracts illustrate: (a) how report text may be annotated (see Figure 9.3) and (b) the revised text (see Figure 9.4).

6.31.1 ~~Predictions of future effects of climate change~~ _From the regrettable to the tragic: predictions of future effects of climate change...(?)_

The IPCC's projection, published in 2001, is that the world's temperature is likely to increase by 1.4° C to 5.8° C over the period 1990 to 2100, depending on ~~the emissions scenario followed~~which forecast is closest to the truth . However, as this is a project ion for the average global surface temperature (which includes sea surface ~~temperature~~), it is very likely that nearly all land areas will warm to a greater extent, particularly in northern North America and northern and central Asia, where land temperatures could rise by 10ºC. Although these temperature differences may not sound very serious, the global temperature difference between the last Ice Age and the present time was around 5° C – 6° C. ~~Six~~ Ten(?) degrees of warming is therefore a ~~frightening~~ terrifying prospect.

The likely effects on humans and the natural environment of the high emissions scenarios range from the death of coral reefs to the creation of millions of environmental refugees. ~~Some~~ Many???? species will become extinct: it is expected that by 2060 Arctic pack ice will have melted so much that all polar bears will starve because the animals they feed on, such as seals, will become scarce. Infectious diseases will rise as the world gets warmer and, in addition, ~~diseases~~ they will sweep north into higher latitudes, infecting people and disrupting fragile ecosystems (this seems odd: are you talking about diseases that will affect animals and plants? In which case you should broaden the scope of 'Infectious diseases' at the beginning of the sentence.– Many countries will be under threat from rising sea levels, drought, storms, heat waves and extreme economic and social disruptions. Sea levels are predicted to rise by a metre over the next century, leading to huge delta areas of Bangladesh, Egypt and China ~~being inundated~~becoming submerged ????. The consequences of allowing the higher emissions scenarios to become reality are global, irreversible and ~~highly damaging~~catastrophic????. ~~It should be unthinkable when the cause can be attributed to the inadequacy of our current action and the lack of urgency in attending to it.~~(Make this blunter): How can we allow this to happen given that we know what needs to be done? Our lack of action and urgency are criminal and will be cursed by future generations.. (??)

Figure 9.3 Extract from a draft report: text annotated by an editor

Case study 9.2 (*continued*)

1.2 *From the regrettable to the tragic: predictions of future effects of climate change*

1.2.1 Higher temperatures

The IPCC's projection, published in 2001, is that the world's temperature is likely to increase by 1.4° C to 5.8° C over the period 1990 to 2100, depending on which greenhouse gas emission forecast is closest to the truth. However, as this is a projection for the average global surface temperature (which includes sea surface), it is very likely that nearly all land areas will warm to a greater extent. This is particularly true in northern North America and northern and central Asia, where land temperatures could rise by 10°C. The latest reports show that the effects of greenhouse gas emissions on temperature could be even more extreme than this. A new climate modelling approach, developed at the UK's Hadley Centre for Climate Prediction and Research, suggests that the twenty-first century could see more and faster warming than that estimated by IPCC. It is important to put possible temperature changes in perspective. The global temperature difference between the last Ice Age and the present time was around 5° C – 6° C. An increase of 10°C would turn the south of England into the Sahara desert. Five to ten degrees of warming is therefore a terrifying prospect.

1.2.2 Global impacts

The likely effects on humans and the natural environment of the high emissions scenarios range from the death of coral reefs to the creation of millions of environmental refugees. Many species will become extinct: it is expected that by 2060 Arctic pack ice will have melted so much that all polar bears will starve because the animals they feed on, such as seals, will become scarce. Researchers at Bristol University have shown that 6° C of global warming was enough to wipe out up to 95% of the species which were alive on earth at the end of the Permian period, 250 million years ago. Therefore, a huge wave of extinction could be set in motion before the end of the century. Human infectious diseases will rise as the world gets warmer and, in addition, they will sweep north into higher latitudes. Humans may not become extinct, but many more of us will die prematurely and we will run out of comfortable climatic zones in which to live. Many countries will be under threat from rising sea levels, drought, storms, heat waves and extreme economic and social disruptions. Sea levels are predicted to rise by a metre over the next century, leading to huge delta areas of Bangladesh, Egypt and China becoming submerged. The consequences of allowing the higher emissions scenarios to become reality are global, irreversible and catastrophic. How can we allow this to happen given that we know what needs to be done? Our lack of action and urgency are criminal and will be condemned by future generations.

Figure 9.4 The same extract with the editor's comments incorporated

Questions

1 Review the editor's annotations and try to classify the kinds of changes that have been requested.

2 Compare the two extracts. Do you think the revised version is an improvement over the original? What criteria did you use to make this judgment?

3 When editing your own written work, what are the most common changes that you need to make?

4 What do you see as the potential advantages and disadvantages of software-based editing tools, as outlined in the case?

9.7   Summarising written material: the vital art

One of the defining characteristics of successful managers is their ability to get to the heart of a complex issue and to make informed decisions. To achieve this, they must have a capacity to select and focus on key arguments and information. This has always been a demanding task, but it has arguably become more difficult, due to the rapid diffusion of information and computing technologies (ICTs). Access to potential data sources has expanded enormously, broadening the possibilities for research, but leaving people vulnerable to 'information overload'. In large organisations, strategic decisions are often informed by heavily summarised material, prepared by more junior staff or external consultants. Rather than finding time to read the full report, senior managers may rely on a combination of executive summaries and briefing papers, complemented by short presentations and skim-reading of material that they see as requiring further attention. Consequently, converting long pieces of text into concise yet accurate summaries has become a vital art. It is essential that organisations develop this capability, given their reliance on highly-summarised documents in strategic decision-making. For similar reasons, it is also an essential skill for anyone making their career in a large organisation. Like any art, it can only be learned through practice and reflection (see the practical exercises later in this chapter). However, the following checklist provides some initial guidance on drafting concise but accurate summaries:

- **Be sure of your brief:** Do you need to summarise everything in a document (or collection of documents)? Does your recipient have a particular focus or topic of interest that might influence the way you select and present material from the original source? What level of knowledge is assumed?

- **Read the source material thoroughly:** Do you understand the main themes and the structure of any arguments? Are you able to distinguish between reliable sources and more dubious ones (e.g. an objective, validated research study versus the unsubstantiated opinion of 'a person on a bus')?

- **Identify the key points in the original text:** If the material is well written, each paragraph should contain a number of clearly identifiable key points. Separate each major point from the supporting material (i.e. additional evidence or elaboration, often found in the subsequent sentences); a coloured 'highlighter' pen is a useful tool for this task. Mark only those points that are relevant to your brief. Consider using several colours to help you isolate different themes. Some of the material may be incredibly interesting, but if the person reading your summary does not require this information, leave it out. If you have several source documents, prepare 'key point' summaries of each, before moving to the next stage.

- **Compose a rough draft of the summary:** Prepare the text based around the key points and cutting out any supporting material (see section 3.2). This includes sentences beginning, 'For example . . .', detailed statistics and other data sources. Consider using simple graphics to illustrate the main arguments or evidence; this is a useful form of 'shorthand' that reduces the word length and makes material easier to assimilate (see section 4.5).

- **Check the rough draft against the source material:** Double check any facts and figures that you have copied from the source documents. Ensure that you have covered all of the areas specified in the brief and omitted any topics that were not specified. Re-read the whole draft summary. Does its overall balance reflect that of the original source document(s)? In other words, have you reflected the underlying arguments or perspectives equally?

- **Prepare a final version of the summary:** With careful editing you may be able to shave off a few more words, omitting any repetition or non-essential text. This process is much the same as that outlined for any report, but in this case you are paying even more attention than usual to the word length. It may be appropriate to present parts of the summary in bullet-point format. However, unless your audience has specified otherwise, it is advisable to retain full sentences: note format may be concise, but it is less readable than normal text and can be rather difficult to interpret. As a final check on readability, you may consider reading the summary out loud, to ensure that it flows smoothly.

9.8   Reflecting on the process of report writing

This chapter has presented an approach to report writing that is grounded in the cultural assumptions of Western, and specifically British, thought. While there is a good deal of common ground in some areas of international report writing, such as the structure of academic conference papers, and the official reports of the United Nations and its various agencies, there are also local variations. For example, despite the introduction of international standards, there are still significant differences in approach to financial reporting in various parts of the world. This closing section asks you to reflect on the kinds of adaptations (or transformations) that may be required if written reports are to meet the needs of today's diverse audiences. Though it might seem like a good idea to 'customise' reports to the needs of different readers, organisations face considerable practical problems, including resource constraints, in making their published reports accessible. Face-to-face 9 encourages you to think about the kinds of reports that you might be required to produce as a student, how the requirements differ from other types of writing that you have been engaged with, and therefore any challenges that this may pose.

FACE-TO-FACE 9

Writing a report, not an essay: understanding the differences

Anna is upset. She has just received from her lecturer feedback on a draft of her report entitled '*An analysis of the influence of culture on organisational communication*'. The feedback states that her assignment needs a lot of work because it is written too much like an essay and not enough like a report. The problem is that Anna, who is doing a degree in French and Spanish, has only ever written essays and assumed that an essay and report were pretty much the same thing! She calls her mother, who is an IT project manager for a global logistics company and writes a lot of reports for work, to ask her advice. The first thing Anna's mother asks is whether her report makes clear what its purpose is, who the intended audience is, and how it will help them to achieve their objectives. Anna admits that she hadn't even considered these things, let alone made them clear in the report. With her mother's help she drafts the following checklist to ensure that her report achieves its purpose:

Face-to-face 9 (*continued*)

Report writing checklist:

- Are the purpose and objectives of the report clear? i.e. Is it clear what the report covers and what the reader can expect to get out of reading it?
- Is it clear who the target audience is for the report?
- Is there an executive summary or abstract that a reader can read to get some understanding of what the report covers?
- Are there enough headings and sub-headings that indicate clearly what is covered in each section? (These titles can be quite detailed.)
- Can the information in the report be quickly and easily scanned by the reader? This may mean putting some key ideas in bulleted form.
- Is there any unnecessary repetition?
- Have graphs and illustrations been included to aid understanding and reduce unnecessary text?
- Are there recommendations listed at the end of the report to suggest action to take, based on the information in the report?
- Does the report present information objectively rather than trying to persuade the reader that 'my argument is valid' (the main purpose of an essay)?
- Will the report help readers make use of this specialised information?
- Is the report written in the third-person voice?
- Has the report been proof-read? (Of course this is important in essay-writing too!)
- Check with the tutor whether references and bibliography need to be included, as they may not be necessary.

Questions

1 Based on this checklist, guidance in this chapter, and your own understanding, consider how a report differs from an essay.

2 Imagine that you were helping Anna to write her report: '*An analysis of the influence of culture on organisational communication*'. Create a mindmap[d2] with some details to get you started.

3 Consider the next report that you plan to write: what are the aims and objectives, who is the target audience and what do you want your readers to do as a result of reading your report?

As outlined in Section 9.4, a mindmap is a strategy for planning and organising your ideas in preparation for writing a document, giving a presentation or preparing another task. It entails using a diagram to represent ideas linked to and arranged around the key words.

Case study 9.3 develops the theme of report-writing by concentrating on how reports are often delivered using non-traditional communication channels (i.e. in electronic formats, rather than as printed paper documents delivered by post). It describes how one leading international company has approached the challenge of presenting various types of company report on its website.

CASE STUDY 9.3

Incorporating reports onto a website: the case of Nokia

Nokia is one of the world's top companies in the field of mobile communications, boasting an estimated 36 per cent share of the global device market; it is also a major global brand. The company's origins are in Finland, but by the end of 2006 it reported sales in 150 countries, operation of 15 production centres in nine different countries, and research and development activities in a total of 14 countries around the world. Nokia has net sales of €41.1 billion and an operating profit of €5.5 billion (based on the 2006 year-end). The company employs 68,483 employees from more than 120 nationalities. All of the material on Nokia's international website (www.nokia.com) is in the medium of English, with a simple drop-down menu ('select a country') providing links to a number of national sites that display material in local languages. Nokia has made many different types of report freely available on its websites, including financial reports, environmental reports and 'white papers', each of which are reviewed briefly:

- **Financial reports and investor presentations:** it is possible to download the most recent annual and quarterly reports, plus those for previous periods, as pdf files. Recent presentations to Nokia investors are made available as webcasts on the Investors' pages. These presentations can be viewed using various media players and the accompanying slides can be downloaded as pdf files.

- **Environmental reports:** Nokia has made a number of reports available concerning its efforts to take care of the environment. These are generally in the form of pdf files, reproduced to a high standard with extensive use of colour, photography, etc. Another part of the site details the company's approach to dialogue with its internal and external stakeholders regarding environmental issues. There are also several case studies, accessible via hypertext links.

- **White papers:** these are commissioned research reports on a variety of current technology and product-related issues (e.g. 'Next generation mobile browsing' and 'Mobile video services'). These reports are also presented as pdf files and are freely available to download. As with other lists of pdf files, there is a short piece of explanatory text, with an icon that links to the website of Adobe, where users can download Acrobat® Reader® for free.

To find examples of these reports, type the title (e.g. *Financial reports*) into the search engine on the website. Nokia's various national websites carry a large amount of textual and graphical material, covering topics that are likely to be of interest to various audiences, including: product details, support services, investor relations, career opportunities and contact information. Almost all of the text on the national sites is in a local language. However, links to some of the more detailed reports indicate that some of these items are only available in an English-language version.

Questions

1 Some of Nokia's reports are presented on websites in HTML format (i.e. hyperlinked web pages), while others are available as pdf files, or even as webcasts. What kinds of communication issues would influence the choice between these formats?

Case study 9.3 (*continued*)

2 Review some sample reports in HTML format, from the Nokia site or that of another international organisation. In what ways would you need to adapt a 'conventional' approach to report writing in order to produce reports in this format?

3 Consider the main challenges and opportunities for international organisations like Nokia, in providing reports on their websites for diverse audiences around the world. Prepare a short (400-word) briefing document, outlining the opportunities and suggesting how the challenges might be overcome.

Sources: Nokia (2007), Turban (2003). Case written by the authors.

Summary

- Reports are an important text-based communication channel for complex and extended investigations and arguments. As a consequence, they require careful preparation and design.

- The key tasks at the preparation stage are to seek or develop a clear specification (or 'brief'), covering issues such as the nature of the audience, the intended purpose, context and sources.

- At the drafting stage, authors need to consider logical sequence, ways of making the structure visible, and use of figures and tables to summarise material.

- The process of writing can be a source of learning. Authors often make new connections as a result of engaging with the material, and may therefore need to remain flexible in response to emerging ideas.

- Proof-reading and an independent perspective are important at the completion stage. Authors and editors need to ensure that grammar and writing style are consistent and check cross-referencing, a particularly challenging task in the case of multi-authored reports.

- Organisations make regular use of summaries and briefing papers. It is important to practise the art of summarising text, which involves the identification of key arguments, elimination of superfluous detail and tailoring material to particular audiences.

- Organisations face new challenges in providing reports that are suitable for more diverse groups of stakeholders and for delivery using multiple channels, such as print and web-based formats.

Key terms

diagramming 226
executive summary 230

multi-authored reports 234
source material 226

terms of reference 223

PRACTICAL EXERCISES

4.1 Reports, briefings and bullets – summarising skills

Select a current organisational issue. Look through one of the chapters of this book and identify an issue, or you can use a topic provided by your tutor. Prepare the following documents, based on this topic:

a. A 2,000-word 'long' report, with contents page, executive summary, referencing and bibliography. Include tables and figures where appropriate.

b. A 500-word 'short' report, suitable for use as a briefing document. Imagine that your boss has to give a public talk on the topic and needs some background material.

Seminar option: Exchange your two reports with another student, and then provide comments on each other's reports. Suggestions for commenting:

What source material was used? Was the source material relevant to the topic? Was the source material appropriately referenced?

Was the report structured appropriately? Were headings used? Was there an introduction and conclusion?

Was the report written in the appropriate style? Did the report use informal words?

Did the report use correct grammar?

What did the report look like? Was all the spelling correct? Did it have the correct number of words?

Following this, you can then run a discussion around the following questions:

What was the most difficult aspect of the task? What kind of information is omitted in the shorter version of the report? What assumptions did you make about the audience in each case?

4.2 Presenting data – images replacing words

a. Obtain sufficient raw data for a short report from one of the following sources: results from a statistical survey (e.g. data from the UK's Office of National Statistics, which can be downloaded in pdf format); financial accounts from a company report (these are also available from many company websites in pdf format); technical data from a scientific report.

b. Write a short report (maximum 1,000 words, include a word count), summarising the data. The report should contain words and numbers, but no graphics or data tables. When writing a summary, your main task is to **reduce the original material. You may achieve this: by rejecting some points in the material, e.g. missing out any examples; and by rewording what was written in the original in fewer words. However, you should remember that when summarising you need to make sure that what you reproduce is accurate.**

c. Prepare a second version of the report, editing the text down to 500 words and inserting suitable graphics (e.g. bar charts, flow diagrams) to illustrate your main arguments.
(Note: The Further reading section in Chapter 3 suggests a number of suitable texts on statistics and data presentation.)

d. Prepare a third (and final) version of the report, containing only graphics, with explanatory titles.

Seminar option: Exchange your two reports with another student, and then provide comments on each other's reports. Suggestions for commenting:

What source material was used? Was the source material relevant to the topic? Was the source material appropriately referenced?

Was the report structured appropriately? Were headings used? Was there an introduction and conclusion?

Was the report written in the appropriate style? Did the report use informal words?

Did the report use correct grammar?

What did the report look like? Was all the spelling correct? Did it have the correct number of words?

Following this, you can then run a discussion around the following questions:

What was the most difficult aspect of the task? What options did you consider for representing the data graphically? Which version do you think would be most effective in communicating your arguments?

CASE STUDY 9.4

Getting the message across: annual reports in the Internet era

This newspaper article reviews recent developments in the world of investor relations. One of the traditional communication channels, the paper-based annual report, is being transformed by technological innovation and changes in the communication needs of investors, analysts and other stakeholders.

When you want to review an investment, do you reach for the glossy annual report sitting on your shelf? Or do you power up your computer and click your way through the same document online? If print is your preference, you are not alone. Technology evangelists may have predicted otherwise, but shareholders and analysts continue to favour printed material as a source of corporate information. The enduring popularity of print is, however, only one side of the shareholder communications story. The web is coming into its own, not as a replacement for traditional investor material, but as a source of additional, richer, more frequent and more time-sensitive information. As a result, investor relations are gradually being transformed.

There is plenty of evidence pointing to the continuing popularity of print among investors and analysts. Seventy-four per cent of sell-side and 63 per cent of buy-side analysts expressed a preference for printed annual reports over online equivalents in a recent survey by *Investor Relations* magazine. Furthermore, UK companies with large private shareholder bases think that 80 per cent of private shareholders would continue to ask for a printed annual report even if offered an online alternative, according to an October 2002 study by London-based consultancy Pauffley Creative Communication. 'The Internet is simply not a good medium for large chunks of text,' says Roger Burgess, a director at Pauffley. Indeed, the web is proving most popular as a distributed printing mechanism for annual reports, rather than a stand-alone medium: the Pauffley survey found that 96 per cent of companies that publish annual reports online do so in 'printer-friendly' PDF format rather than in the website language of HTML or a spreadsheet format such as Excel.

However, companies are finding the Internet to be a powerful complementary medium for investor relations, one that is slowly shifting companies' relationships with them. BP, the energy company, was an early adopter of online shareholder communications. 'The Internet helps us to disseminate information more rapidly and more cheaply on a completely global scale and opens up new opportunities to establish a dialogue with our shareholders,' says David Bickerton, head of external communications. The company uses the Internet to provide online broadcasts of presentations and speeches, corporate news

Case study 9.4 (*continued*)

announcements, electronic voting and other 'interactive' features. 'Print remains the best medium for reference material such as annual reports but the web brings wider coverage and greater efficiency,' says Mr Bickerton. 'In particular, it allows us to provide private investors with information and assistance in ways that simply wouldn't be possible off-line.' In 2001 the company launched New2BP.com, an online service for UK citizens unfamiliar with the stock market.

BP is seeing clear evidence that the web is bringing the company's corporate information to a larger audience: its *Statistical Review of World Energy* has a print run of 60,000 but is now downloaded electronically 300,000 times a year. With financial authorities and legislators in the US and Europe placing increasing demands on companies to provide greater transparency for all types of investors, the use of the internet in shareholder communications is set to grow. For example, 'web-casting' – the online broadcast of corporate meetings, presentations and speeches – is already being used as a means of complying with tighter disclosure rules.

Many believe that this is good news for investors and other stakeholders. 'Web-casts allow investors to see corporate management perform in front of a real, sometimes hostile audience, something that has previously been impossible for shareholders unable to attend physical meetings,' says Donald Nordberg, former financial editor at Reuters and current director of strategy for Raw Communications, an investor communications company. 'Downsizing has meant that many analysts now have far more stocks to cover,' adds Mr Burgess. 'Web-casts are extremely useful for them, since they cannot be in two physical meetings at the same time.'

Others believe that web-casts can also help companies to cultivate greater confidence and trust among their shareholders: 'As a species, humans are very receptive to audio and visual communications,' says Craig Moehl of Groovy Gecko, the London-based streaming media company. 'As such, web-casts allow companies to convey information in a far more personal and contextual way than text.'

Corporate web-casts are widely established in the US, where 83 per cent of the Fortune 100 companies now use them. They are also proliferating in the UK, where 30 per cent of FTSE 250 companies provide them, according to a July 2002 survey by *Investor Relations* magazine and European streaming media company Simplywebcast. The recent UK Company Law Review is likely to accelerate this trend: it recommended that annual reports should be made available online as soon as they are signed off – and at least 15 days before they are sent to shareholders – to allow investors to formulate and circulate questions before their annual general meeting.

Just over the horizon lies a more radical use of the Internet for serving professional investors. A new online standard for financial information, called 'eXtensible Business Reporting Language' (XBRL), promises to allow investors and analysts automatically to extract corporate performance data from multiple websites in a compatible format and compare, contrast, process and model it in any way they choose. A handful of companies, including Reuters and Microsoft, have already published financial statements in XBRL but the true value of the standard will be reaped only when – or if – it becomes widely established. 'At present, many buy-side analysts need to go to more than 100 different websites to keep track of information presented in a variety of different formats,' says Mr Nordberg. 'When XBRL becomes widespread, investors and analysts will be able to conduct automatic, global, real-time ratio analysis for the first time. And that really will be exciting.'

Case study 9.4 (*continued*)

Questions

1 Prepare two tables, summarising the potential advantages and disadvantages of annual reports, first for users and second for investor relations departments. The lists should compare the following formats:

   a. conventional 'hard copy' (i.e. full colour printed brochure);

   b. downloadable pdf file available via a website;

   c. HTML (i.e. hyper-linked web pages).

2 What do you consider to be the main factors driving the move to online reports in this area? Identify two other areas of organisational activity where online report writing is likely to become more important.

3 Sample an investor relations web-cast, either at the BP website or that of another large corporation. Comment on the effectiveness of this communication channel, in comparison with a text-based report, noting any significant advantages or limitations.

4 The article contained in this case study comprises approximately 980 words. Referring to the section on summarising in this chapter, prepare the following documents. Give each document a title and include a word count:

   a. an executive summary/abstract (250 words maximum);

   b. an outline (50 words maximum);

   c. a list of key words (five words maximum).

Source: Payton (2002). Copyright Scott Payton.

Glossary

Terms of Reference should include information about what is to be achieved in the report (objectives), who should be consulted on the report, who will be reading the report, how it should be structured, and the time frame for its completion.

Source material refers to the data that you will draw upon to support your key points and to provide evidence on which to base your recommendations.

Diagramming or 'Mind Mapping®' can be a useful technique that helps the researcher to separate the 'wood' from the 'trees'. This process involves abstracting the main themes from the detailed background information that has been collected.

executive summary The executive summary is a section located at the front of a report that distils the *entire* contents of the document into a much more concise form. Its purpose is to provide busy executives with the essence of the report at a glance.

Multi-authored reports Multi-authored reports are those which draw on the expertise of several authors, and they require careful co-ordination, as is the case in many organisations.

Further reading

For many students, the most demanding text-based document is the dissertation or thesis, written towards the end of a course of study. There are several useful guides to preparing dissertations and the broader issues of research, including **Easterby-Smith et al.** (2008), **Ruderstam and Newton** (2001) and **Saunders et al.** (2009).

Phillips and Pugh (2000) is designed for PhD students, but contains some helpful advice for those preparing undergraduate or masters dissertations. You'll also find **Lillis and North's** chapter on academic writing in Potter (2006) useful for any postgraduate writing. For further information on writing reports have a look at **Donohue et al**. (2009).

National Audit Office (2003) discusses the challenge of communicating in commissioned research projects. Students may also be interested in drafting business plans: specialised reports used to present a new business venture to prospective financiers. There are many texts setting out typical formats for business plan reports, including several published in conjunction with major banks and newspapers. Additional references on writing style can be found in Chapter 3.

Useful websites

Here are several websites which might be of interest to you. You might like to add some of your own too:

Tony Buzan's website offers ideas for how you might use Mind Mapping® to plan and structure your reports. (Available at

http://www.buzanworld.com/)

The Learnhigher website has a very useful section on all aspects of report writing. (Available at

http://www.learnhigher.ac.uk/Students/Report-writing.html)

References

Buzan, T. (1995) *Use Your Head*. BBC Books, London.

De Vita, G. (2001) 'Inclusive approaches to effective communication and active participation in the multicultural classroom'. *Active Learning in Higher Education*, 1, 2, 168–180.

Donohue, J., Adinolfi, L., Shrestha, P. (2009) *Professional Communication Skills for Business Studies*. Milton Keynes: Open University.

Easterby-Smith, M.P.V., Thorpe R. and Jackson, P. (2008) *Management Research: theory and practice. Sage, London.*

Hofstede, G. and Hofstede, G.J. (2004) *Cultures and Organisations: software of the mind,* 2nd edn. McGraw Hill, New York.

King, K. (2004) 'Is your written communication working (for an international audience)?' *Intercultural Management Quarterly* Volume 5, Number 2.

Lillis, T. and North, S. (2006) Academic writing. In: Potter, S. (ed.) *Doing Postgraduate Research (2nd edn)*. Open University series. Sage, London, 114–151.

National Audit Office (2003) *Getting the Evidence: Using research in policy-making*. Report by the Comptroller and Auditor General HC 586–1 Session 2002–2003 (16 April). The Stationery Office, London. [Also available at www.nao.gov.uk]

Nokia (2007) 'About Nokia'. (Available at www.nokia.com (accessed 16th September 2007)).

Nonaka, I. and Takeuchi, H. (1995) *The Knowledge Creating Company: how Japanese companies create the dynamics of innovation*. Oxford University Press, Oxford.

Payton, S. (2002) 'Getting the message across: shareholder communications'. *Financial Times*, London edition, 14 (4th December).

Phillips, E. and Pugh, D. (2000) *How to Get a PhD* (3rd edn). Open University Press, Milton Keynes.

Ruderstam, K. and Newton, R. (2001) *Surviving Your Dissertation* (2nd edn). Sage, Newbury Park, CA.

Saunders, M.N.K., Lewis, P. and Thornhill, A. (2009) *Research Methods for Business Students* (5th edn). FT Prentice Hall, Harlow.

Turban, E. (2003) *Electronic Commerce 2003: a Managerial perspective*. Prentice Hall, Upper Saddle River, NJ.

Whitley, R. (2000) *Divergent Capitalisms: the social structuring and change of business systems*. Oxford University Press, Oxford.

Zaharna, R.S. (1996) 'Managing cross-cultural challenges: a Pre-K lesson for training in the Gaza Strip'. *Journal of Management Development*, 15, 5, 75–87.

Chapter 10

Adverts, social media, news releases and exhibitions

Advertising is the cave art of the twentieth century.

Marshall McLuhan, media commentator

Learning outcomes

By the end of this chapter you should be able to:

- recognise how principles of persuasive communication are applied in the fields of advertising, public relations and campaigning;
- develop communication skills in commissioning advertisements, managing promotions, drafting news releases and designing exhibitions;
- explore the different ways that social media are being used in persuasive communication;
- examine how different channels can be combined as part of a co-ordinated communications strategy;
- reflect on the cultural and ethical issues arising from the use of persuasive communication in these channels.

10.1 Introduction

Every organisation is involved in some form of persuasive communication, whether it is to sell products and services, attract funding from donors, campaign against injustice or simply to improve their 'image'. So how can you ensure that you are communicating effectively when you are engaged in this kind of activity? The term **promotional mix** is often used to describe the combination of approaches that organisations use to communicate with the world around them. For example, the promotional mix might include: commissioning a newspaper advertisement, drafting a news release or helping to design an exhibition stand. It has always proved difficult to categorise the various channels for promotion, but the following components are commonly identified in the literature:

- advertising
- direct marketing
- public relations
- exhibitions and displays
- corporate sales promotion
- personal selling.

From the late twentieth century, there were strong trends towards integrating the various elements of marketing communication, with the aim of creating strong and coherent *corporate* brands, such as Apple, Google and Nike, as well as individual *product* brands. This has proved to be an ambitious goal, and many organisations have struggled to maintain their reputation. This is perhaps unsurprising, given the many barriers to communication discussed in the Part 1 chapters (NB: see, for example, Chapter 7 for the additional challenges faced by managers attempting to communicate across organisational boundaries). In the twenty-first century, we have also witnessed the rapid growth of **social media** which are transforming many areas of communication, including those discussed in this chapter (see also: Section 7.3 on blogs and Twitter, and Section 8.6 on instant messaging). In the second decade of the new century, conventional advertising campaigns are now looking more and more like Marshall McLuhan's 'cave art' (opening quotation). As a consequence, the next generation of managers will need to re-think these traditional communication channels and find ways of combining them with social media. The practical tasks required to *produce* promotional and campaigning materials are often contracted out to specialists, such as advertising agencies, public relations (PR) firms, web designers, social media specialists and exhibition consultants. However, it is still a good idea for managers to have a good understanding of these areas, so that they can work more effectively with these professionals. It is also the case that people working in smaller businesses, charities and campaigning organisations may find themselves directly involved in these activities, often as part of a small in-house team.

This chapter focuses on three conventional communication channels that still form an important part of the promotional mix: adverts, news releases and exhibition stands. However, given the pace and scale of change, there is also a strong emphasis on social media, and opportunities to examine their role as a channel for generating, and more importantly, *exchanging*, persuasive messages. The chapter contains several practical examples which provide you with an opportunity to apply many of the underlying principles of persuasive communication that are discussed in Chapter 5. There are also many practical exercises that will help you to prepare your own promotional materials. These activities are designed to make you better informed when preparing 'briefs' (i.e. project specifications) for an agency, comparing the sales pitches of competing firms or simply working with specialists from one of these areas. Vast amounts of money can be wasted if clients fail to give clear explanations of their requirements to external agencies or to their own in-house teams. These initial communication breakdowns have a knock-on effect, in the form of over-priced and unsuitable advertising, PR and exhibition materials. By taking a 'global' view of promotion, managers are also able to assess the overall effectiveness of the existing promotional mix, and to take action to reconfigure and enhance specific channels where necessary. We begin our review with the role of advertising, and its close relationship with techniques of sales promotion.

10.2 Advertising and sales promotion: an overview

Advertising refers to the process of one-way communication used by anyone wishing to sell a product or service. This may include exposing the target audience to their message via television, radio, newspapers, magazines, bill boards and the Internet. Markets have existed from the earliest times, and wherever people have sold goods or services, they have advertised. However, the advertising *industry* is a more recent phenomenon, a mid-nineteenth-century response to mass production (creating products and markets) and mass literacy

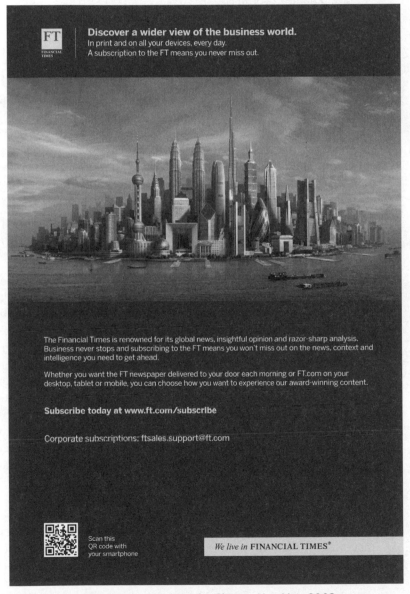

Figure 10.1 The Financial Times advertisement for Chinese New Year 2003

(creating the books and magazines in which adverts were placed), which has become a global industry. Most of the expenditure is on 'display' advertising, commissioned mainly by organisations to promote their goods and services. Other important categories include: recruitment advertising; financial and legal notices; and classified advertising (i.e. 'small ads', which are placed mainly by individuals). All this activity means that adults and children are exposed to hundreds of advertising messages every day. Many of these are both highly sophisticated and expensive to produce. However, there are less expensive forms of advertising, through regional newspapers, for example.

Advertising can serve a variety of communication objectives, including:

- creating or increasing awareness (e.g. informing the target market of a new service, brand name or social issue);
- informing or educating (e.g. explaining how to make better use of a service, advising members of risk groups of potential health threats);
- stimulating various types of 'purchase' decision (e.g. encouraging people to buy a product, switch between competing brands or donate to a particular charity).

Success in advertising requires the organisation to present persuasive messages to specific audiences. Individual advertisements can be very striking, but they rarely operate in isolation (see Figure 10.1). A **co-ordinated campaign** is the term used to describe the common approach of running a number of related advertisements alongside, together with other promotional devices. This combined effort is designed to reinforce the core messages through repeated exposure in various formats.

10.3   Planning an advertising and promotional campaign

Effective advertising is all about gaining exposure and having a measurable impact on your target audience. An isolated advert, however well-crafted, is unlikely to have any lasting effect because it is unlikely to reach enough people. In addition, those exposed to it may not absorb the message on the first occasion. To address these problems, advertisers have developed integrated 'campaigns' that run over an extended period. The language of the promotional campaign is often borrowed from the military, with terminology such as 'strategic targets', 'hit rates' and 'pre-emptive strikes'. The following fictional example illustrates some of the key elements of a typical campaign: imagine that you are a product manager responsible for your organisation's northern European sales territory. You have got the task of launching *Vegetale*, a brand new, vegetable-based, high-protein food that is being positioned as an attractive alternative to meat. How would you develop an advertising campaign, as the product moves from the development stage to its initial launch in this market?

Marketing research

You could begin by investigating the market, its principal characteristics and long-term potential. The following questions are indicative for the *Vegetale* case. Who buys food for the household? What are the recent trends in meat consumption? What are the existing alternatives to meat, and how are they perceived by both consumers and non-consumers? What do people already know and think of *Vegetale* and the company's other products?

Identifying target market(s)

Market research, together with your own instincts, should suggest how the market is segmented, and indicate the nature of your target customer. In the case of a product launch, the initial focus is likely to be on so-called 'innovators' and 'early adopters', the sub-groups who are first to experiment with an innovative product (Rogers 1995). In the *Vegetale* example, your research suggests that the demographic profile is likely to comprise females aged 20 to 35 from socio-economic groups A, B and C1 (professionals and skilled workers).

Developing campaign objectives

It is important to establish what the organisation is trying to achieve through its advertising campaign. Objectives are usually quantified, so that the success (or otherwise) of the campaign can be measured. Advertisers are particularly interested in the level of awareness of a product, and how far this is converted into trial purchases. In this example, you have decided to aim for a 25 per cent unprompted recall of *Vegetale* in your target market, by the end of a three-month media campaign. Unprompted recall means that, in a follow-up survey of the target group, respondents can describe the advertisement without being given a brand name or a similar prompt by the interviewer.

Planning and budgeting

In most organisations, budgets are tight, and campaigns have to be designed within these constraints. Planning decisions include the channels to be used (e.g. newspaper and television adverts, direct mail, in-store promotions), and the timescale of the campaign. Project management techniques are used to schedule and co-ordinate the different activities. The budget for *Vegetale* is sufficient for you to run the following: full-colour adverts in six women's magazines, with accompanying 'advertorials' (i.e. sponsored editorial articles that are used to provide more detailed information on the product); a social media campaign, based around a number of websites that are particularly popular with mothers of small children; a series of radio adverts on a regional music station that caters for the target age group; and a month-long programme of in-store tastings, run in conjunction with the three largest multiple food retail chains. In the second phase of the campaign you plan to run a 'buy one, get one free' (or 'BOGOF') promotion, supported by additional magazine advertising. You are considering whether to deliver single-portion samples of *Vegetale* to selected addresses, as part of an on-going market research survey (a technique sometimes referred to as '*knock and drop*').

Drafting material – key messages

Alongside the campaign planning, you need to recruit people to create the advertising materials. Individual adverts are built around 'key messages', and the real skill of advertising agencies is to convert these messages into memorable words, sounds and images. For example, your key messages might be that *Vegetale* is a new, nutritious, low-fat product, derived entirely from natural vegetable ingredients, which can be prepared much like meat and which has a similar texture to veal. How would you convey this to your audience? What would you do if the social media campaign generates hostile coverage from particular sub-groups, or if it suggests that people do not understand your key messages?

253

10.4   Communicating with an advertisement

An effective advertisement is likely to have two distinguishing features: messages summarised briefly, and messages reinforced using more than one medium. With an emphasis on the target audience and their creative approach, advertisements display many of the best features of effective communication, many of which can be applied in other aspects of organisational life. Advertisers can select from a wide range of possible formats, matching the style of delivery to the specific needs of the audience and the nature of the message (see Table 10.1).

The ways that advertising messages are formulated raise many interesting communication issues. For example, how do you deal with differences related to gender, or to the social and cultural backgrounds of your audiences? This challenge can be illustrated by a cross-cultural comparison of political advertising in Finland and the United States. The researchers identified some important differences in the non-verbal communication of male and female politicians when they appeared on television, as well as differences between the approaches adopted in each country (See section 4.7).

> '[T]he US female candidates' ads differ in a way that is statistically significant from the ads of their male colleagues. Thus, the female candidates project a "softer" image than the male candidates by assuming smiling facial expressions and making eye contact with the viewers more frequently. In Finland, eye contact is the rule for the candidates of both genders. However, this can be explained by the fact that the "candidate head-on" production technique — denoting that the candidate talks directly into the camera — is clearly dominant in Finnish candidate advertising. In the US, the production techniques are more varied. Regarding facial expression, the Finnish female candidates, as their US colleagues, smile more frequently than their male counterparts. This finding is statistically significant.'
>
> (Carlson 2001: 147)

What are the implications of this kind of research for advertisers? Firstly, it is clear that female politicians in the US face a real dilemma as they attempt to balance 'male' and 'female' styles in their advertising messages. In addition, we saw how approaches may be specific to one country or cultural group (e.g. Finland's technique of politicians talking directly to camera). As in other areas of cross-cultural communication, something that seems to work well in one place may turn out to be less effective when it is transplanted elsewhere.

As social media have become more widespread, advertisers have adopted **viral marketing** techniques, which exploit existing online social networks to enhance brand awareness. The 2006 release of the film Snakes on a Plane was accompanied by an early viral marketing campaign. The advertisers used fan blogs and a **wiki** to encourage discussion. While the campaign was successful in raising awareness of the film, there were some technical problems. For example, the designers of a 'value added' feature, which involved forwarding a personalised message spoken by actor Samuel L. Jackson, had failed to take into account the multicultural nature of their target audience. The software could not cope with names it did not recognise and generated error messages when they were entered.

Creating your own advertisement is one of the best ways to explore the different options available to advertisers, and to consider the associated communication issues (see the Practical Exercises section later in this chapter). When selecting the preferred treatment, it is essential to keep the target audience in mind, and to construct messages in ways that they are likely to find both meaningful and attractive. Above all, do not make the basic mistake

Table 10.1 Some popular advertising formats

Slice of life	This traditional format has been commonly used on television adverts for fast-moving consumer goods (FMCG) and domestic appliances such as washing machines. Short dramatised excerpts can be used to link a product with a lifestyle that is familiar to the target audience. They can also provide opportunities for the use of other formats, such as humorous, aspirational and demonstration.
Humorous	Visual and verbal humour secures audience attention and generates positive reactions. Humour is used for all kinds of products, including very 'dry' ones, such as financial services. For example, in the 1990s, the UK electricity industry ran a campaign called 'Creature comforts', which combined the voices of ordinary customers with an animated film featuring a 'family' of amusing plasticene animals. The campaign was a response to research suggesting that people perceived electric power as less 'friendly' than gas.
Aspirational	This is commonly used for premium and heavily-branded products. Imagery is used, either to enhance a brand identity, or to suggest that consumers can obtain some element of a fantasy lifestyle by purchasing the product. However, the credibility of aspirational messages can be undermined if they are not applied consistently, or where there is too stark a contrast between the aspiration and the actual experience.
Endorsement	This can work at various levels. At its simplest, the receiver is given an assurance regarding the message, because it is delivered by someone that they know and trust. Celebrities can also be perceived as 'humanising' a product or corporate brand. For example, in the early 1990s, the brewer Guinness used actor Rutger Hauer (star of the film *Bladerunner*) to re-position an 'old man's drink' for a new generation. Dressed in black and with bleached hair, he literally 'embodied' a younger and more sophisticated image of the product. Celebrities do not even have to be alive! Computer animation has been used to revive former celebrities, including Alfred Hitchcock, to promote products. Along with animated cartoons, these celebrities have three advantages over their living counterparts: they are immortal, they cannot become embroiled in a scandal and they do not demand repeat performance fees.
Demonstration	One of the most effective ways of introducing novel products, or ones that are difficult to understand, is to show them in use. Demonstrations are often used on television, but with some imagination they can be applied to other channels, such as newspaper advertisements. They can educate potential consumers, and reduce their fear of the unknown. For example, innovative technological products are often shown in the hands of non-specialists, highlighting their apparent ease-of-use.
'Postmodern'	There has been a recent increase in bizarre and self-parodying advertisements, sometimes given the inaccurate title 'postmodern', where the promotional message appears obscure, if not unintelligible. Tobacco companies pioneered this format when regulators began to restrict the content of their adverts. Over many years, the 'Silk Cut' campaign played on the brand name 'silk' and 'cut' in many different ways. Surreal advertising has been introduced because audiences are now so 'visually literate' that they can see through and de-construct traditional adverts. Hence, more sophisticated and puzzling content is needed to secure their attention. A more recent example in this self-parodying category is 'Cillit Bang', a deliberately garish advert featuring the larger than life character, Barry Scott. The success of this character and subsequent internet-based fan sites inspired the manufacturer to set up a blog for the fictitious Barry Scott to take advantage of a phenomenon known as viral advertising or marketing.

of developing material that appeals to *you*, the designer, rather than to the people that you are seeking to engage with.

During the era of mass communication, many have argued that large-scale commercial and political advertising has become too powerful. Organisations are under increasing pressure to behave ethically when engaging in this form of persuasive communication. Ethical issues have arisen in a number of areas, and may relate to the products being advertised (e.g. alcoholic drinks, tobacco or unhealthy food), or the techniques used to promote them (e.g. making use of language and images that may be regarded as misleading or offensive). Case study 10.1 addresses another important ethical issue, that of advertising to children.

CASE STUSY 10.1

Marketing and advertising that respects children's rights

'Every day . . . some businesses are dumping a waste that is toxic on our children. Products and marketing that can warp their minds and their bodies and harm their future.' Not the words of some zealous activist, but those of the British Prime Minister, David Cameron, just before the general election in 2010. They're worth recalling as UNICEF, the United Nations Global Compact and Save the Children launch a global manifesto, *Children's Rights and Business Principles*, in March 2012 (UNICEF 2012).

Principle 6 states that businesses should 'use marketing and advertising that respect and support children's rights'. That this ethic even needs spelling out speaks to the huge impact the commercial world increasingly has on children around the globe. Marketing to children is an increasingly lucrative industry – in the US, companies are estimated to spend $17bn a year targeting kids – and the means used to ensnare them in the consumerist net are increasingly pervasive. From online 'advertgames' that blur the boundaries between commercials and entertainment, to recruiting children as peer-to-peer marketers, companies' efforts at selling to kids are growing more insidious. The UN Principles recognise this concerning trend in stating that marketeers must 'consider factors such as . . . children's greater susceptibility to manipulation' when conducting their business. And with good reason: as marketing academic and children's campaigner Dr Agnes Nairn puts it, much marketing 'operates darkly, beyond the light of consciousness'.

Advertising has the potential to cause a wide range of harms to kids. Take health, for example. A study by Yale University researchers found that children exposed to junk food advertising during a trial ate 45% more junk food than children not exposed to the adverts (Harris et al. 2009). An extensive literature survey by the World Health Organization (WHO) in 2006 concluded that 'food promotion influences children's food preferences, and encourages them to ask their parents to purchase foods they have seen advertised'. Such concerns contributed to the UK's television regulator's 2006 decision to ban the advertising of foods high in salt and sugar during children's TV programming. Of course, this hasn't eliminated children's exposure to such ads – which increasingly come via the internet (check out McDonald's Bebo app, for starters).

Another trend that has piqued concern has been advertisers' role in the premature sexualisation of childhood. As UNICEF's Principles assert, companies should consider 'the effects of using unrealistic or sexualised body images and stereotypes' in their marketing. When the Bailey Review – set up by the UK's coalition government to investigate this very concern – reported in 2011, it found that 'We are all living in an increasingly sexual and sexualised culture . . . Many parents feel that this culture is often inappropriate for their children and they want more power to say "no".' But an area that UNICEF's Principles don't really touch upon is perhaps the one of greatest long-term concern. That is the creeping commercialisation of childhood overall. After all, as another recent UNICEF report showed, the UK's materialistic culture – coupled with our high levels of social inequality – is a key

Case study 10.1 (*continued*)

reason why Britain languishes at the bottom of the score table for children's wellbeing. The report, which surveyed children across several European countries, concluded that 'consumerism appears to have become inextricably enmeshed in children's relationships with family and friends . . . families in the UK, more so than in Sweden and Spain, use the purchase of new material objects (particularly new technology) in an attempt to compensate for relationship problems and social insecurity . . . in the UK parents and children seemed to be locked into a compulsive consumption cycle.'

The effects of this may reach beyond childhood. Other assessments have suggested excessive advertising moulds children's values to be more materialistic. In the US, some schools are given telecomms equipment in return for screening a daily 10-minute news programme, called Channel One, which also contains two minutes of advertisements. A study has shown that children enrolled at schools that used Channel One held materialistic values to be significantly more important than kids at a non-participating school. Worryingly, an emphasis on materialism has been demonstrated, time and again, to be associated with lower concern for environmental and social issues. So the launch of UNICEF's Principles for how businesses should better respect children's rights is welcome and timely. Yet in itself it is likely to do little to arrest the spread of marketing into children's lives. As UNICEF's earlier study of materialism and child wellbeing concluded: 'In 1991, Sweden banned television advertising aimed at children under the age of 12. Considering taking a similar step in the UK would go some way towards lifting some of the commercial pressures on children and families.' Perhaps the time has come not just for business to take children's rights very seriously, but also for the government to intervene.

Guy Shrubsole is director of the Public Interest Research Centre (www.pirc.info) and co-author of the report 'Think Of Me As Evil? Opening the ethical debates in advertising' (Alexander et al. 2011).

Questions

1 What different types of ethical issue can you identify from the case?

2 What practical lessons do you draw from the case, from the perspective of: (a) a marketing manager in an organisation that produces children's products?; (b) a campaigner against unethical advertising and marketing practices; (c) the parent of a young child who may be exposed to advertising of this kind?

3 Review the UN Global Compact website and identify one other ethical issue that an organisation may need to address as part of its advertising or public relations activities.

Source: This case is based on an article for The Guardian Sustainable Business (12 March 2012) (http://www.guardian.co.uk/sustainable-business). It was adapted by Richard Blundel and is reproduced with permission of the publishers.

Unethical advertising can often provoke complaints against the organisations concerned, which may result in lasting damage to their public reputation. In some cases, critics may even take direct action to undermine (or subvert) what they see as unacceptable messages. Perhaps the simplest and most widespread response is to add graffiti (i.e. hand-written messages) to display advertisements in public places, transforming the meaning of the original slogan. Case study 10.2 features an organisation that has refined this technique, using the power of the Internet to develop its own distinctive brand of persuasive communication.

CASE STUDY 10.2

Adbusters: challenging corporate advertising?

Adbusters describes itself as 'a global network of artists, activists, pranksters, students, educators and entrepreneurs who want to advance the new social activist movement of the information age'. Adbusters is probably best known for its professionally-designed parody (or 'spoof') advertisements, which reinterpret images and slogans associated with major global brands, such as Nike, Calvin Klein and McDonalds, in ways that subvert the original message. The advertisements form part of a wider array of persuasive and informational messages, supporting Adbusters' key stated aims, 'to change the way we interact with the mass media and the way in which meaning is produced in our society.' Adbusters Media Foundation also publishes a magazine from offices in Vancouver, Canada. Two-thirds of its magazine readership is based in the US, but the organisation reports having a diverse readership in many other countries around the world. Adbusters also operates its own full-service advertising agency, which is promoted for use by not-for-profit organisations wishing to develop a social marketing campaign.

The most important communication channel for Adbusters is probably its website (www.adbusters.org), which provides information on the organisation and its campaigning activities, contact details, useful links, magazine extracts, sample advertisements and materials that can be downloaded, including stickers to promote its annual campaigns, 'Buy Nothing Day' and 'TV Turnoff Week'. Most of the textual material on the website is in the medium of English, though the organisation's aims are also summarised in Spanish and French, under the headings: 'Cultural revolution is our business'; 'La revolución cultural es nuestro negocio'; and 'Notre affaire, c'est la révolution culturelle', and links to Swedish, Norwegian and Japanese versions of the website.

The Adbusters campaigns are an example of 'cultural jamming', a phrase coined by a San Francisco-based band called Negativland, who saw a skilfully reworked billboard as a way of encouraging viewers to reconsider original corporate strategy of the advertiser. Culture jamming has a long history that can be traced to the activities of French 'situationists' in the late 1960s, and many previous generations of graffiti artists and humorists. The writer Naomi Klein (2000) suggests that jamming has been enjoying a recent resurgence, resulting from a combination of technological advances and an underlying popular resentment against the overpowering commercialism of the leading corporate brands. This has stimulated a demand for counter-messages:

'The most sophisticated culture jams are not stand-alone ad parodies but interceptions – counter-messages that hack into a corporation's own method of communication to send a message starkly at odds with the one that was intended. The process forces the company to foot the bill for its own subversion, either literally, because the company is the one that paid for the billboard, or figuratively, because any time people mess with a logo, they are tapping into the vast resources spent to make that logo meaningful.' (Klein 2000: 281)

However, culture jammers also face challenges in conveying their persuasive messages. For example, Adbusters had to reconsider its promotional strategies after it was attacked for merchandising products associated with the 'Buy Nothing Day' campaign. The organisation has also been criticised for what some people regard as a patronising and puritanical tone in its 'adbusting' attacks on alcohol, smoking and fast food.

A more fundamental challenge to culture jamming is demonstrated by the ease with which corporate advertising and branding has been able to appropriate jamming

Case study 10.2 (continued)

techniques for its own purposes. Klein (2000: 298) cites the example of Nike's 'pre-jammed' advertising campaign, which carried the slogan, 'I am not/A target market/I am an athlete.'

Questions

1 Review some examples of culture jamming, from Adbusters or similar sites. What are these messages seeking to achieve, and what persuasive techniques do they employ? How might they respond to the appropriation of jamming techniques by corporate advertisers?

2 Consider the implications of culture jamming from the perspective of a large corporation, such as Nike. What communication strategy would you recommend in the event that key promotional messages were being jammed?

3 Select several examples of current corporate advertising. Analyse the material, identifying the key promotional messages and noting how these are reinforced (e.g. using words and visual signals). Suggest how a culture jammer might subvert these messages.

Sources: Adbusters (2003), Klein (2000). Written by the authors.

We close this section with a brief reflection on the complementary role of sales promotion, and the unique communication challenges presented by this channel.

Reflecting on sales promotion: when the 'receiver' bites back

In the introduction to this chapter, we noted that advertising and sales promotions are often closely connected channels. Conventional approaches to advertising reflect a one-way, linear model of communication, in which the primary aim is to code the persuasive message in a way that minimises the scope for noise (see section 1.3). While the advertising message may be thoroughly researched (e.g. by securing feedback from focus groups), the mode of delivery through mass media appears to leave the receiver in a relatively passive role. As we have seen, the underlying assumptions of the linear model are challenged by interpretivist and postmodern perspectives (see section 1.6). These emphasise that any communication activity is based on active engagement, requiring the negotiation of meanings with intended audiences (see section 1.6). In other words, it is their interpretations, rather than the intended goals of the advertiser, that determine the impact of a campaign. The importance of this insight is highlighted by the case of sales promotions such as product samples and special offers. These are widely-used promotional techniques, which do seek a direct engagement with the receiver. Typical applications of the product sample include trial-size shampoos, attached to magazines or delivered to the door, and software or apps that can be downloaded for a trial period. However, once the receiver becomes an active participant in the process, there is considerable scope for unanticipated effects, which can prove disastrous for the unwary communicator. In one extreme example from the 1960s, a company was forced to abandon its promotional campaign for razor blades when children began opening the product samples that were dropped through their letterboxes. Can you think of a similarly disastrous use of product samples?

Miscalculating the response of consumers is a common feature in promotional campaigns. In one high-profile example from the early 1990s, the domestic appliances company Hoover offered its UK customers two 'free' flights to European or US destinations if they spent more than £100 on its products. Many people saw this offer and made the simple calculation that it was worth buying a Hoover product, simply to secure the two free flights. However, the people responsible for promoting the offer do not appear to have anticipated this response. Consequently the offer was massively over-subscribed, leading to legal actions by disappointed customers, a public relations disaster, multi-million pound losses and the subsequent departure of several senior executives.

There is a general lesson from these cases of bad practice. When organisations try to engage directly with an audience, they need to consider their messages very seriously, and think about how people are likely to respond. The theme of interaction is continued in the next section, which considers the role of public relations. Linking the two sections, Case Study 10.3 looks at the way that advertising agencies are responding to the growth of social media, and developing the new skills that they need to survive and prosper in this new environment.

CASE STUDY 10.3

Advertisers rush to master a fresh set of skills

In this *Financial Times* article, David Gelles reports on the challenges faced by conventional advertising agencies as they seek to respond to the rapid growth of social media, and to incorporate it into their campaigning activities. It also looks at the changes of perception that are needed if marketers are to continue to get their message across in the new world of two-way communication.

Only a few years ago, digital marketers might have thought all was plain sailing. After a decade of disruption wreaked by the emergence of the popular web, companies and advertising agencies had finally understood the intricacies of placing online display and search ads. Yet in the past few years, a new generation of teachnologies has come along to disrupt once again the way advertisers operate. Led by Facebook and Twitter, and joined by behemoths such as Google and a bevy of start-ups, these Silicon Valley misfits have muscled into the ad business and upended traditional assumptions about how companies should allocate marketing budgets.

In addition to search and display advertising, big companies must now factor in social media, video advertising, mobile marketing and daily deals. 'We've gone from display and search to this much longer list,' says Nick Law, chief creative officer in North America for R/GA, the digital agency. 'These things are connected, and you can't do one without the other.' The promise of these platforms is tremendous. The new world of digital and social media marketing can give companies increased access to their customers, fresh insights into their preferences, a broader creative palette to work with, and additional data and metrics to study. Yet there are unsolved questions over how best to organise and execute digital and social campaigns. No single formula has emerged, leaving most companies and ad agencies in a state of constant experimentation. There is also lingering confusion over how best to measure the effectiveness of a campaign, and a company's return on investment. Ann Lewnes, chief marketing officer of Adobe, the software company, says she pushed the company into digital and social marketing early on. 'We saw the insights we could glean from customers, the iterations we could do on a campaign,' she says. 'We saw the ability to really, really measure results.'Adobe now spends 74 per cent of its more than $100m marketing budget on digital. Even for a digital-first company such as Adobe, each campaign is a fresh start of sorts. Ms Lewnes says 20 per cent of her budget is going towards experimental campaigns, and that each product launch requires a different mix of paid, earned and owned media.

Perhaps the largest shift in recent years has been the transition from the one-way, broadcast messaging of television, print and outdoor, to the two-way conversation that social options now allow companies to have with their consumers. "It requires a shift in your perception," says Maryam Banikarim, chief marketing officer of Gannett, the media company. "People find it hard to realise marketing is a two-way conversation rather than a one-way pushing out." Yet quantifying the effectiveness, and return on investment, of digital and social campaigns, remains a challenge. Rather than tracking click-through and conversion rates as with search and display advertising, marketers are trying to count followers, measure sentiment and analyse purchase intent. "A lot of people are just measuring their fans and followers," says Ms Lewnes. "But what's important are the insights you can glean from the data. Understanding if someone is happy or unhappy with something."

Social signals obtained from Twitter and Facebook can also give companies real-time insight. When MTV saw there was a spike in online conversations around the news that Beyoncé was pregnant, it added more pictures and stories about the story to its website. Yet many markers remain dissatisfied with the state of online measurement. Keith Weed, chief marketing officer of Unilever, the consumer products group that is the second-largest advertiser in the world, says: "Digital is in theory more measurable than anything else, in theory and in practice, but it's not broad enough yet. What we'll see is a significant maturation of ROI [ROI, Return on investment. In other words, we will develop better ways of measuring the financial return from investments in digital technologies.] in digital." More insights and creative opportunities mean more work for marketing teams, and can mean increased costs for marketers. In-house and at agencies, marketers are scrambling to acquire new skills, and add staff to monitor the exponential growth of online dialogue about companies. "You have to throw bodies at that," says Ms Lewnes. "There are people who have to monitor it all day." Myriad options are also forcing companies and agencies to change the way they work. "Twenty years ago there were templates," says Mr Law at R/GA. "Now, we don't have a typical client engagement. Because media are so flexible, we can get very specific."

One brand may need a robust Facebook page, while another may call for a strategy of engaging with consumers on message boards, blogs and elsewhere on the web. Such approaches are focing departments within organisations to collaborate in new ways. "It's brought the marketing teams much closer together," says Ms Lewnes. "They all used to be in their silos. PR was off operating by itself, advertising was operating by itself. Now they're working together." At its best, this can result in truly integrated marketing campaigns, with a unified message being pushed out across television, print, radio, and the web. "Things really are getting joined up," says Mr Weed. "The same creative is going to flow across

Case study 10.3 (*continued*)

multiple screens." Growing access to the web in emerging markets is also allowing for truly global campaigns.

"A few years ago I would be engaging much more of a national base on campaigns," says Mr Weed. "But Google and Facebook are truly global media companies in a way the world has never seen."

The amount of money being committed to digital marketing varies widely, with more developed countries seeing a higher digital spend. Unilever, for example, spends about 35 per cent of its US budget on digital, compared with 25 per cent in Europe, and just 4 per cent in India. Yet emerging markets could rapidly catch up, as they adopt digital media.

"In emerging markets they're going to go through these cycles much more quickly than us," says Mr Law. And digital advertising is still a small portion of global advertising, accounting for 16 per cent of total spend in 2011, according to ZenithOptimedia. That figure is growing fast, but television is set to remain the biggest advertising platform, accounting for 40 per cent of total spend through at least 2013.

Managing the growing array of digital and social initiatives has forced companies to revise their relationships with ad agencies, as well. Unilever reduced its roster of more than 400 digital agencies to fewer than 100, with just 12 lead global agencies, including Razorfish, AKQA and R/GA. "We're already fragmenting our spend across different media," says Mr Weed. "If you fragment the message, you're making it less cohesive and joined up." Technologies are changing fast, and few marketers would claim to know what new social platform might demand their attention a year from now. Pinterest, the online pinboard and sharing site, is the latest to draw a legion of users-and the interest of marketers– without having proved its business model or staying power.

How this shift in the marketing world plays out will help determine the winners and losers in the years to come. At stake are the valuations of companies such as Facebook, which earned $3.7bn last year, mostly from advertising, and is preparing to go public at a value of upto $100bn. Yet some basic trends are emerging, with mobile access to the web leading the pack. "If the first 1bn users connected to the internet through PCs, the next 1bn will be through mobile," says Mr Weed, who recently visited a family in the slums of Mumbai who nonetheless had two mobile phones. Unilever was the first and largest customer for Apple's mobile iAd marketing platform, and has renewed its contract for a second year.

"I want to get to the future first," Mr Weed says. "I don't want to be following my competitors."

If marketers continue to flock to new digital and social options, Facebook and its social media peers may prove their worth. Yet if a proliferation of online options fragments advertisers' spend, or if the promise of social media goes unfulfilled, this moment could one day be seen as another bubble. Regardless of that, it seems certain that new technologies are destined to change the way consumers interact with brands.

Just as the web reshaped the advertising world a decade ago, the new world of digital and social media marketing is forcing companies and ad agencies to re-evaluate where, how and when they engage with potential customers. "Ultimately, this concept of digital will disappear," says Mr Weed. "My 20-year-old son laughs at me when I talk about online and offline."

Case study 10.3 (*continued*)

Questions

1 Identify what you consider to be the main challenges facing marketers and advertising agencies as a result of the spread of social media

2 The writer of the article comments that 'new technologies are destined to change the way that consumers interact with brands'.

   a. From your experience, what are the main differences in the ways that younger and older people make use of social media?

   b. In either case, what are the practical implications for organisations wanting to advertise their products or services? (NB this article focuses on commercial organisations but you could also consider the implications for public sector organisations, social enterprises and charities – for example, how would it apply to a charity or a government agency that is trying to discourage drug abuse, or to encourage teenage volunteering?)

3 Does the use of social media for persuasive communication raise any ethical issues, given that these media may be used by impressionable teenagers and children?

Source: Gelles (2012). Copyright David Gelles. Reproduced with permission. Commentary and questions prepared by Richard Blundel.

10.5 Public relations: an overview

Public relations (PR) did not develop into a unified profession until the second half of the last century (Miller and Dinan 2000, Kitchen and Schultz 2001, Tench and Yeomans 2009). It draws on several specialist fields, involving people as varied as publicity agents and promoters from the entertainment industry, political lobbyists, analysts and advisors, newspaper and broadcast journalists, management consultants and advertising copywriters. Commentators have often noted, with some irony, that the PR profession seems unable to escape its reputation for engaging in disreputable practices. The main criticism is that PR is used to create a false impression of an organisation, individual or issue, in the minds of the public. It is also criticised for the kinds of activities that take place, the assumption being that it is all about 'corporate hospitality', meaning the provision of lavish, free entertainment for important clients and sleazy politicians. In reality, while it is possible to identify many examples of bad practice, PR can be a valid form of persuasive communication. It is used by all kinds of organisations, including charities, pressure groups and political parties.

The language of today's PR professionals reflects the concept of multiple stakeholders (see section 7.3). They talk in terms of developing a long-term dialogue with their various 'publics' (see Figure 10.2), each of which has different information needs. The UK's Institute of Public Relations (IPR) has defined this communication role as: 'The planned and sustained effort to establish and maintain goodwill and mutual understanding between an

Figure 10.2 An organisation's dialogue with its stakeholders

organisation and its publics' (IPR 2003). In the next section, we consider how this mutual understanding can be achieved and some of the potential pitfalls in communicating the relevant messages.

10.6   Successful PR: long-term commitment vs. short-term fix

The following discussion applies many of the principles of stakeholder theory, raised as part of our review of organisational communication. In particular, it draws attention to the concepts of stakeholder communication, including the distinction between asymmetrical and symmetrical dialogue (Crane and Livesey 2003) (see section 7.3).

For example, imagine that your organisation is running a large manufacturing site in a rural area. It is very scenic (i.e. is regarded as having high amenity value), but there are also few local employment opportunities and public services are in decline. The directors have agreed to an investment strategy that involves a major expansion of this factory site. It seems like good news for stakeholders in the local community. However, if the company has a poor record, with a series of pollution incidents, safety scares and arguments over planning controls, the local community may be unsympathetic to the expansion plans. This could turn to hostility and active resistance if, for example, a programme of automation at the factory is likely to result in local job losses. In such a situation, a typical short-term PR exercise, such as sponsorship of the local village carnival, would clearly be counter-productive. Everyone in the community would interpret it, quite correctly, as a cynical and 'cosmetic' (i.e. superficial, surface-level) exercise. Long-term PR requires a much greater commitment of time and effort, in communicating with a particular public. In practice, it would involve the organisation in a variety of activities, such as: hosting regular open days for local schools, residents and other interested parties; setting up consultative groups with representatives from the community; introducing planned and sustained initiatives to keep all members of the workforce informed and able to voice their opinions; and making a genuine and sustained investment in community activities. The investment is substantial, but long-term PR can also lead to significant benefits, as the organisation builds a kind of 'equity' in its employees and local community. The accumulated goodwill can provide it with a degree of protection during short-term crises, like a factory fire or a financing problem. However, this more substantial and ultimately more effective form of PR can only be successful if it addresses the following key principles.

Senior management commitment is essential

PR must be seen as a strategic concern, which rests ultimately with the chief executive or equivalent. Without top-level support, it is unlikely that the organisation will have the resources to make substantive changes in its day-to-day operations. The resulting lack of commitment, and competing pressures for resources, will lead to cynicism amongst stakeholders, including employees, and the often-criticised symptom of PR as a meaningless and cosmetic 'gloss'.

PR activity must be linked to strategic aims

This follows from the previous argument, regarding senior management commitment. Communication strategies must interact with the organisation's business and corporate strategies. However, few have grasped the radical implications of engaging in a real dialogue with stakeholders, in a way that informs strategic decisions, as opposed to a **'monologic' dialogue,** which is simply designed to control the area of debate in order to achieve pre-determined objectives. Now the challenge for organisations is to engage in a much more open discussion with stakeholders, with the genuine intention of sharing ideas and achieving collaborative goals (Crane and Livesey 2003: 47–8). This may sound rather idealistic. However, as we have seen in the case of advertising, the growth of social media has transformed the idea of 'real' dialogue into a central idea for people involved in public relations. In recent years, we have seen both large corporations and authoritarian governments struggling to keep control of 'the story', but being outwitted by the sheer numbers involved when social media are used to challenge their activities.

Organisations must understand and engage with its publics

The organisation must research and listen to its various publics or stakeholder groups. It is not simply a matter of seeking to express its messages in their terms; this may be a fundamental communication principle, but it remains rooted in the linear, 'one-way' model of communication. There is also a need to engage with their perspectives, and allow these to be reflected in public arenas, as part of a genuine dialogue.

PR strategies require plans, budgets and resources

Effective PR activity is an on-going managerial task, rather than simply a short-term project, to be introduced in a crisis. As a consequence, it must be organised effectively, with a degree of planning (e.g. allocation of roles, preparation of budgets and monitoring). In addition, senior management commitment must be reflected in the allocation of adequate resources to support these activities over the long term.

Feedback from PR activity should inform strategic change

PR activity should provide the organisation with a continual monitor on the environment within and beyond its administrative boundaries. By following these broad principles, it can be of great value to the whole organisation, helping it to interpret and adapt to changing situations. In this role, PR becomes much more than an exercise in presenting an 'image' to the outside world.

PR activities and communication channels

Organisations engage in many types of PR activity, which make use of particular combinations of communication channels. The choice of channel should be based on a combination of research into the needs of the various publics and an awareness of the organisation's objectives. Practitioners are also experimenting with emerging channels, notably the Internet and the new breed of trans-national television channel, such as MTV, CNN, Eurosport and BBC World. However, research evidence suggests that professional communicators have yet to grasp fully the nature and implications of these new channels (Aldísardóttir 2000, Chalaby 2002). The following summaries explain some of the more popular PR channels in use today.

Corporate advertising and brochures

Organisations sometimes promote themselves, rather than specific products or services. Brochures and annual reports are sent to major customers, suppliers, financiers and shareholders. These are often made available on corporate websites, either in an HTML version, as a series of hyperlinked pages, or retaining the original hard copy features by encoding it in pdf (portable document file) format.

Sponsorship

This can involve the organisation in supporting anything from an opera company to a baseball team, with the added incentive of prime seats for corporate hospitality (i.e. entertaining important clients). However, sponsorship can also take the form of a simple donation, based on employee interests or charitable activities, such as sponsoring a company team that is taking part in a fund-raising half-marathon or cycle race. Large corporations sometimes offer sponsorship to organisations with higher status or a perceived ethical stance (e.g. universities, schools, hospitals, charities), in the hope of enhancing a poor public image. However, if the contrast between donor and beneficiary is too stark, such initiatives can generate unwelcome media coverage for both parties. This is particularly likely if the funding is resisted, either by employees or other stakeholders of the beneficiary organisation.

Lobbying

Lobbyists have an important role, providing decision-makers with well-researched briefing materials, technical advice and arguments in support of their respective positions. Governments often make use of these expert briefings when drafting complex legislation. However, the activities of some lobbyists are highly suspect. For example, rewarding politicians for raising specific issues in parliamentary debates, or in specialist Select Committee meetings, is a morally dubious activity that has prompted several public controversies (e.g. the UK's 'cash for questions' scandal of the early 1990s), while bribing politicians to vote in a particular way is generally regarded as a corrupt and illegal practice.

Internal communication

It is essential to keep employees informed, involved and motivated, not only for the internal health of the business but because employees are an important channel to the outside world. Proud, satisfied employees will tell relatives and friends what an excellent organisation they are working for, whilst disgruntled ones will do the opposite. The views of insiders, whether positive or negative, will always carry considerable weight. Research into the use of employee communication has shown that it both increases the perceived external prestige of the organisation and is an important factor in explaining the extent to which employees identify themselves with their employer(Smidts et al. 2001).

Routine procedures

Seemingly routine activities, such as the time taken to answer an external telephone call, can have a big impact on the way that an organisation is perceived. For example, if incoming callers with simple queries are passed from department to department, they are likely to share their experiences with others; if these 'stories' accumulate, the organisation may find itself with a poor public image that is difficult to counteract. In this case, improved staff training programmes and better-constructed computer databases could reduce the problem. More generally, the lesson for all organisations is to monitor the effectiveness of all communication channels, however humble they might appear, take complaints seriously, particularly where a pattern is detected, and ensure that routine procedures are operating satisfactorily.

Other methods – briefings, news releases, exhibitions and events

Public relations practitioners make extensive use of press briefings and news releases, which are considered in the next section. They also communicate directly with stakeholders at exhibitions and by hosting special events (see section 10.8).

In the next section we experiment with drafting a news release, one of the most widely-used and cost-effective communication channels, with applications to public relations and other areas of promotional activity.

10.7   Media relations: planning a news release

The media, which in this context means television, radio, newspapers and magazines, can be seen as a kind of indirect route to the public. **News releases** are statements, often about the launch of a new product, service or event, used by organisations to brief media journalists and encourage them to write articles on the subject. Unlike news articles, press releases are biased towards the perspective of the organisation. Journalists research your business and listen to your briefings, including news releases, then report their findings to a wider audience as news stories. Many journalists also have their own blogs, where they expand on these stories and in some cases engage directly with their readers. News stories can deliver powerful messages. While some parts of the media are seen as politically-biased or sensationalist, many areas, including the trade press, are regarded as relatively impartial and well-informed. For this reason, media reports and editorials tend to be accepted more readily than the communications that come directly from an organisation. The other advantage of this communication channel is its cost-effectiveness. You have to pay for advertising or for exhibition space, but the messages that a journalist communicates are essentially free. However, there are two important issues to consider if you want to use this channel to communicate. First, you need to provide the kind of stories that journalists need. Secondly, once your story is out in the public domain, you will not have much control over the way it is presented.

So what makes a story newsworthy? One popular definition of a *non*-story is 'Small earthquake, nobody hurt'. Or, as a nineteenth-century writer, Charles Anderson Dana, noted, 'When a dog bites a man that is not news, but when a man bites a dog that is news.' In other words, a good news story needs to have some unusual, original, or surprising feature – and if the raw material of your story appears rather ordinary, the challenge will be to find a way of making it more interesting. The potential for securing coverage for a story also depends on the kinds of media organisations you are aiming for: the international, national, local or specialist media will have their own distinctive agendas and practices.

National and international media

Only the largest organisations are likely to be in a position to secure national or international media coverage on a regular basis. For example, the major publicly-quoted companies are of interest to the wider public as consumers, investors or employees. This would not be the case for a small enterprise with a limited client base, other than in exceptional circumstances. For this reason, it is not worthwhile issuing news releases to this audience, unless your story has a wider resonance (e.g. where a team of employees has made a major discovery, or the organisation has become involved with a more newsworthy partner). The national media tend to take a pro-active role, telephoning for comments on a particular issue and sending out their own journalists and photographers. This means that organisations generally have a very limited influence on the end-product. PR managers are often horrified to see a relaxed 45-minute interview with a broadcast journalist turned into what they regard as a 'wholly unrepresentative' 10-second clip that is inserted into a television news story. To overcome this problem, interviewees and writers of press releases often structure their words into 'sound bites'. **Sound bites** are short and memorable phrases used by presenters and interviewees that the journalist is more likely to use in an uncut form. The international and national media also monitor local media for suitable stories (see Figure 10.3). For example, the leading national newspapers make use of news agencies and local representatives (i.e. 'stringers'), to ensure that they have coverage around the world. These sources are ready to feed back any interesting news items, which may occasionally turn into major stories. These offer additional points of entry for organisations seeking more extensive coverage.

Local and regional media

The newspapers, television and radio stations that serve a local area may be hungrier for stories than their national counterparts. However, they do have strict selection criteria. For them, the main factor is the 'local angle'. For example: does the story, irrespective of where it takes place, concern people from this area? Does it refer to famous people who are visiting the area? Does it provide information on local events, proposals or controversies? Due to their limited resources, local newspapers may be more likely to reproduce the content of a

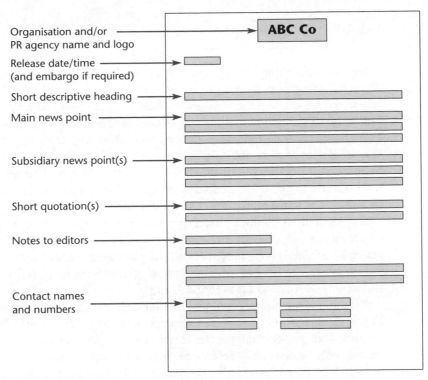

Organisation and/or PR agency name and logo

Release date/time (and embargo if required)

Short descriptive heading

Main news point

Subsidiary news point(s)

Short quotation(s)

Notes to editors

Contact names and numbers

ABC Co

Figure 10.3 The structure of a typical news release

news release, probably in the form of extracts, rather than originating their own story. They may also make use of photographs that are supplied to accompany a story.

Specialist media

Even the smallest organisations may be able to get into one of the many specialist media, including broadcast programmes, publications and websites. Consumer-oriented publishers cover a vast number of leisure and lifestyle interests such as yachting, football, music and cookery. There is also an extensive business or 'trade' press, which serves all kinds of industrial and professional interest groups (e.g. catering, quantity surveying, social work, mechanical engineering, medicine, farming). The main advantage of specialist media is that they enable an organisation to target messages at well-defined audiences, and to obtain informed feedback on subject-specific issues. However, for the same reason, these media may not be suitable for more general messages.

Figure 10.3 illustrates a typical format for a news release. The message content demonstrates a number of 'good practice' features, including:

- the provision of many concise and relevant facts, addressing the six fundamental news questions (i.e. Who? What? When? Where? Why? How?);
- placing the most important facts at the beginning, so increasing the chances that they will be included in an edited version of the story;
- presenting the information in a clear and simple format;
- providing relevant contact details for journalists wishing to clarify points, plus background notes for editors.

10.8   Exhibitions and events

Exhibitions and events enable organisations to interact intensively with various audiences. As such, these channels have great potential for persuasive communication. Organisations can attend a wide range of 'business to business' trade fairs and regular events, such as the film industry's international festival at Cannes. There are also many consumer-oriented exhibitions, covering industries such as house-building, food manufacturing and travel. Venues can range from 400-square-metre meeting rooms to the 158,000 square metres of floor space at the UK's National Exhibition Centre (NEC), near Birmingham. Many organisations invest in expensive exhibition stands, which require considerable staff time, both in setting-up and to maintain the exhibits. So is this an effective channel for promotional messages? Exhibitions do offer unique communication opportunities, arising from direct and simultaneous contact with many existing and potential customers (see Figure 10.4). For example, academic book publishers attend many international conferences, enabling their representatives to interact with customers, discuss book proposals with potential authors and monitor developments in research and practice.

Exhibitions are also a popular venue for new product launches. In some sectors, such as car manufacturing, companies sometimes invest in dramatic 'roll-outs' of their latest product, with musical fanfares, dry ice and laser displays. However, these high-budget performances have become something of an industry cliché, and there is an increasing interest in more focused and interactive alternatives. For example, the organisation may arrange a series of regional open days for an invited audience, drawn from its network of distributors or agents, existing customers and journalists. Exhibitions are also used to entertain key clients and suppliers, monitor competitor activity, build lists of prospective customers (or 'prospects'), obtain media coverage and foster relationships with journalists and commentators.

Staging 'events' – an alternative approach to persuasion?

Exhibitions are one form of 'event' which may engage the interest of the media, along with others. An alternative way to obtain media coverage is to stage an event that is designed solely for the purpose of creating a compelling news story. There is a long tradition of

Figure 10.4 Stands at an international trade show
Source: PA Photos/EPA

political protest, which has made use of this approach to overcome social and cultural barriers and ensure that marginalised voices are heard. For example, the civil rights activist Mahatma Ghandi led a number of protests, including the famous salt march, which highlighted inequitable trading conditions in colonial India (Ghandi [1927] 1993). Fathers 4 Justice (F4J), the civil rights group founded in the UK in 2002 to campaign for equality in family law, has perfected the technique with carefully-staged events that attract the media. These include scaling the walls of Buckingham Palace in a Batman costume and causing the National Lottery live draw to be taken off air while it was being watched by ten million viewers (F4J 2012). F4J, Greenpeace and other campaigning organisations also ensure that journalists are given access to photo-opportunities, increasing the potential for high-profile media coverage.

Managing exhibitions: a communication perspective

There is very little coverage of the subject of managing exhibitions in the advertising and marketing literature, but the principles appear similar to those outlined in our discussions of advertising and public relations. Exhibitions and events should be part of a coherent promotional strategy. The organisation's objectives need to be clear, and the whole exercise requires careful planning and budgeting. Examples that you may have experienced, from the perspective of an exhibitor or visitor, include careers fairs, which often take place on university or college campuses, and 'freshers' fairs where sports teams and other groups promote themselves to new students. It is worth thinking back to any events you have attended, and considering how far they achieved their stated objectives. Case study 10.4 highlights the kind of problems that can arise when this communication channel is not managed effectively.

CASE STUDY 10.4

'DozeyToys' – communicating at an international exhibition

The directors of DozeyToys, a new company specialising in wooden toys for young children, decided that it was the right time to start promoting their products to a wider audience. Jean-Paul Dozey, the chief executive, had spotted an advert for *SuperCadeaux 2013*, a major international trade fair for the children's toy industry, which was to be held in Marseille in two months' time. The company was pleased to secure the last available exhibition space and set to work constructing a world-beating stand. Arriving in Marseilles two days before the opening, Dozey Toys' marketing assistant was horrified to find that its display stand was 15 cm wider than the allocated space, so the stand had to be hastily redesigned. It was located in the centre of a section labelled *loisir-sportif*, which was devoted to children's sports equipment. This was unfortunate, given that the company's speciality was small wooden toys. On the opening day, there was no sign of the newly-translated product brochures. There were several frantic telephone calls to the printers, who claimed that the delivery deadline was not specified in the original order. When the courier finally reached Marseille, the marketing assistant found a number of embarrassing spelling errors in the German and English translations; it was now too late to get them corrected.

Case study 10.4 (*continued*)

For the first two days of the Fair, the DozeyToys stand was very quiet. This was not surprising, because none of the key retail buyers for this product area had been contacted or invited to the stand. Day Three was a complete contrast, and life on the stand became very hectic. The exhibition had opened to the public and a large army of school children descended on the stand. They scooped up the entire stock of promotional literature, including 10,000 brand new, full-colour French, German and English language brochures. The sales manager calculated that each brochure had cost approximately €5.50 to produce. At last, the fair was over and the display stand was dismantled. The managers of DozeyToys returned home sadder and wiser.

Questions

1 Review the case and identify the main strategic and operational errors that were made by the managers of DozeyToys.

2 Take each error in turn and analyse it from a communication perspective. What messages were sent and received? What were the main sources of noise?

3 Prepare a 500-word briefing document, consisting of practical advice for organisations attempting to stage their first international exhibition. Specify which items you think are most important, and which problems are most likely to arise.

4 Suggest how the company might recover the situation without a large amount of additional spending, by exploiting other promotional communication channels discussed in this chapter.

Source: Case written by Richard Blundel; while aspects of the case are based on real events, the individuals, organisations and events described are entirely fictional.

Face-to-face 10 looks at how you might use exhibitions as a promotional tool and asks you to evaluate a scenario that is set within the university context.

FACE-TO-FACE 10

Facing a dive in fortune

Read the following scenario and then use the questions below to guide your evaluation of Toni's experiences and to make recommendations for planning a similar promotional event.

Toni has been a member of his university student union sky diving society for two years and has recently volunteered as marketing director for the society; a particularly important role as membership of the society has been falling over the last few years. This decline is due partly to the fact that membership fees are relatively high, as they need to cover insurance costs, and also it seems that students would rather bungee jump than sky dive! His major channel for promotion is the Freshers' Week Fayre, when all the university societies set up exhibition stands in the sports hall and encourage new and returning students to join their club. The success of the society could depend on this event. As the student union has said that they can no longer afford to subsidise societies, they need to be self-funding and a major income stream is membership fees secured during Freshers' Week.

First Toni and his fellow members consider their communication objectives. Many students will not know that their society exists so one objective is to raise awareness. At the fayre they

Face-to-face 10 (*continued*)

need to stand out and be memorable. Then their job is to inform potential members how fun, well-organised and safe their society's activities are. Their third communication objective is to stimulate a 'purchase' decision; there is a lot of competition in terms of other societies trying to entice students to join and to spend their limited time and money with them.

Next they move on to identifying their target audience. Few people have sky dived before; however, every year the society hosts a big charity sky dive, so those interested in a new challenge, and who like raising money for charity, would be good targets. They decide to ask all current members how they heard about the society and what persuaded them to join, to try to get an insight into their potential members.

After that comes the planning stage, including budgeting. They decide to book a 'pitch' next to the bungee jumping and rock climbing societies, as they will be their direct competition. They want to face them head on and keep an eye on their recruitment success. They might even be able to share a proportion of their members – the real adrenalin junkies! As sky diving has high visible impact they decide to pay extra for a 'pitch' with audio-visual equipment, so that they can project videos of previous sky dives onto a big screen and play the sound through speakers.

Based on feedback from last year the two key reasons why people did not sign up as members was a lack of awareness of how thrilling sky diving can be – something that you can only really appreciate from doing it – and the expense – which Toni and fellow members think is well worth it. To overcome these barriers they decide to add weight to their promotional campaign by offering the first jump for free to those who sign up in the first hour. In order to appeal to the more cautious crowd, who would rather think it over than sign up on the day, they agree to produce and hand out DVDs of their sky dives.

On the day, Freshers' Fayre kicks off and things appear to be going well. A large crowd has formed around their video screen, the DVDs are being snapped up and the list of new members' names is long, given that they are only one hour into the Fayre. Toni decides to count the number of members that have signed up in the first hour and realises their error. They had completely underestimated the number of people who would do this. He also sees their miscalculation. As the cost of one jump is greater than the membership fee, it was worth signing up to jump once and never again! Worse still, people who have missed out on their offer this time assume that it will be the same next year and, rather than signing up, make a mental note to visit the generous sky diving society's exhibition stand next year, and this year cut their teeth with the bungee jumping society!

Questions

1 What do you think of the approach that Toni took to planning the promotional event at the Freshers' Fayre? Analyse his promotional campaign using relevant concepts (e.g. channels and media used, types of persuasive communication used) explored in this and previous chapters.

2 Having analysed Toni's approach, consider how you might have tackled this task differently. What are the reasons for your choices of approach?

3 At this point in the Freshers' Fayre, having realised their error, what would you suggest that Toni and his team do to salvage the situation?

4 Consider a team or group of which you are a member. How do you recruit new members? What are your communication objectives? Who is your target audience and what considerations do you need to take into account when planning a promotional event?

Summary

- Organisations engage in various forms of promotion and campaigning, using traditional channels, such as news releases and exhibitions, and emerging technologies such as text messaging. These activities often involve outside agencies, such as designers and media companies.

- Advertising messages are generally reinforced by other elements of a co-ordinated promotional/campaigning strategy. Strategies include well-defined objectives, reflecting organisational values and addressing the characteristics of target audiences.

- In promotional or campaigning activities involving direct interaction with customers or other stakeholders, there are more complex patterns of communication and an increased risk of failures. Managing these relationships has become even more important following the recent growth in the use of social media for promotional purposes.

- The concept of stakeholder dialogue challenges conventional views and practices and is increasingly important in the field of public relations.

- The news release remains an important communication channel, which needs to be seen as part of a broader public relations effort, involving other activities such as corporate advertising, sponsorship, lobbying and consultation.

- News releases, and the stories they contain, must be matched to the agenda, priorities and practices of the relevant local, national or specialist media organisations.

- Exhibitions and events provide organisations with an opportunity to interact directly with customers, or other stakeholders. However, they are also complex communication channels that demand careful planning and implementation.

- Organisations need to consider ethical issues across all of their communication channels. Advertising and marketing are forms of persuasive communication that have attracted particular attention in relation to business ethics.

Key terms

advertising 251	lobbyists 266	news releases 267	viral marketing 254
co-ordinated campaign 252	monologic dia- logue 265	promotional mix 249 sound bites 268	wiki 264

PRACTICAL EXERCISES

10.1 Creating the *Vegetale* campaign

1 Take up the role of the advertising agency designer (sometimes called a 'creative'), working on the promotional campaign for *Vegetale* (see section 10.3). Your brief is to address the following issues:

(a) Suggest a more appropriate alternative to the client's current product name, bearing in mind its target market and the benefits that the product offers to the consumer. Give reasons for your choice, identifying any important communication issues.

(b) Convert what you see as the key messages about the product into a concise and attention-grabbing slogan that can be used as the campaign develops. Again, give reasons for selecting this slogan, based on relevant communication issues.

(c) Draft an e-mail to your client, explaining your proposals and requesting a response.

2   The first phase of the *Vegetale* campaign has gone well, and the product is now in the shops, with a growing consumer base consisting predominantly of young ABC1 women. (Note: Insert your replacement product name for *Vegetale*, as selected in part 1(a).) The advertising agency has now been asked to design a new advert, targeting health-conscious, recently-retired people. The key messages are unchanged, but the client's own research suggests that there will be greater resistance to a novel food product amongst older people.

(a) Select a treatment from those outlined in Table 10.1. Prepare a short (maximum 200-word) justification for the client, explaining this choice. Feel free to combine two or more of these formats, or to introduce novel approaches of your own.

(b) Sketch out a rough, hand-drawn design for the proposed advertisement. Figure 10.5 identifies the main elements you are likely to find in a typical display advertisement, but these can appear in many different guises, so feel free to adapt it to meet your needs.

(c) Consider the options for introducing a social media campaign for your new target group.

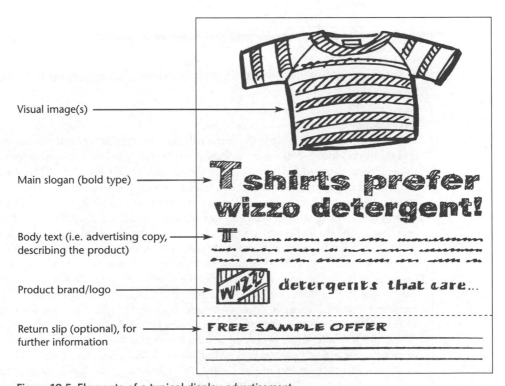

Figure 10.5 Elements of a typical display *advertisement*

10.2 Making news – drafting a news release

Based on the advice given in section 10.7, select, from the outlines provided below, material that can form the basis for a news story that is likely to interest:

(a) international/national media (e.g. television broadcasters and news agencies)

(b) local media (e.g. local newspapers or radio stations)

(c) specialist media (e.g. trade journals).

Draft different news releases for each story. The outlines are deliberately brief and mundane. However, in this exercise you have the great luxury, which is unavailable in real life, of inventing whatever additional details are necessary to turn something rather ordinary into a really newsworthy story. Follow the news release layout presented in Figure 10.3. To extend this activity, make additional notes on how you could use social media to increase the impact of your news story.

Outlines for the potential news stories
- Museum hosts a travelling exhibition
- New shop opens in city centre
- Company chief executive resigns
- Canteen manager retires
- Company launches a new product line
- Charity begins a new fund-raising effort
- Hospital threatens to close a specialist paediatrics unit
- Regional tourism strategy unveiled.

CASE STUDY 10.5

Communicating sustainability in tourism: 'sticking your head above the parapet'?

Background to the study

This case investigates the ways that sustainability messages are communicated in the travel and tourism industry. It draws on a research study conducted in six organisations, including in-depth interviews with the environmental managers at each company. These six travel and tourism operators host over 8.5 million leisure-focused visits (or 'trips') per year, including traditional sun and sea overseas package tours, long-haul cultural tourism, and all-inclusive resort breaks. Many tourism businesses are aiming to build sustainability into consumer perceptions of product quality and, over a longer time period, as a value associated with their corporate brand. In order to achieve this, communication to stakeholders is essential. Research into 'green' communication has focused on the micro, or managerial level, with green advertising as arguably the dominant topic (e.g. Banerjee et al. 1995, Carlson et al. 1993, 1996, Obermiller 1995, Polonsky et al. 1998). One of the common themes running through this research literature is consumer disillusionment. It seems that there is considerable confusion, and scepticism surrounding green communication (e.g. Kilbourne 1995, National Consumer Council 1996). Indeed, green communication from industry sources has been pin-pointed as the least credible with consumers (Coddington 1993, Linnanen et al. 1999). This is reflected in expressions such as 'greenwash', a play on the term 'whitewash', suggesting that the

Case study 10.5 (*continued*)

sustainability messages represent a superficial attempt to paint over a largely unchanged core product. However, from the perspective of the tourism businesses, engaging in green communication was perceived as generating significant risks for the company. This can be seen in the following quotations, which are from different tour operators, both large and niche, all with official awards and recognition for their programmes of environmental practice:

> 'We want to avoid putting our head above the parapet really . . . It's a bit like health and safety. We don't publicise that much at all either.'

> 'Once you start shouting about it, of course, you are sort of looking to be shot down because there is so much that you should be doing.'

> 'Building up credibility, but also to a certain extent it was based on the philosophy that if you stuck your head above the parapet and said we're environmentally friendly – say, for example, like the Body Shop did as a good example – you get your head shot off. Not for the hundreds and thousands of good things that you were doing, but for that one little thing that you weren't doing.'

Green communication can involve interaction with many internal and external stakeholders. In this case, we focus on communication with the consumer, the arena of marketing communications. Given the inherent problems, how are tourism businesses attempting to convey their messages on sustainability to consumers?

Communication in the tourism industry

The traditional framework for marketing communications comprises advertising, public relations, personal selling, and sales promotions. As they face the credibility, or 'sticking your head above the parapet', problem, tourism businesses might be expected to exploit most of these communication channels in order to get their message across. However, the research found that, with the possible exception of public relations, the companies made limited use of traditional approaches when seeking to communicate with consumers about sustainability. So how did they approach the communications task? The secret lies in the inseparable nature of the tourism product, a characteristic shared with many other service sectors. The product is inseparable because the consumer is a part of the production process. This connection lasts for the duration of the holiday, as the holiday-maker enjoys a 'product' that is rich in experiences, including their interactions with staff and with other features of the service environment that are created (or sub-contracted) by the tour operator. Inseparability provides the tourism businesses with an exploitable communication advantage that is not readily available to the manufacturer of goods, green or otherwise (Middleton and Clarke 2001).

A blueprint of the customer journey

It is possible to construct a flow chart, representing the main consumer/provider contact points throughout the service consumption process. This analysis, sometimes termed a 'blueprint' in the services-marketing literature, provides the skeleton onto which physical evidence and other communication devices related to sustainability can be attached (Lovelock 2001). Figure 10.6 presents the different stages of what one of the interviewees termed 'the customer journey', as analysed from the research interviews.

Each of these stages provides opportunities for consumer contact and communication, as mapped out and utilised by the tourism provider. Table 10.2 presents the actual

Case study 10.5 (*continued*)

communication channels and techniques used by the case study companies at each stage of the 'customer journey'.

Table 10.2 Consumer/provider contact points: the 'customer journey'

Stage in the 'customer journey' (Figure 10.6)	Communication channels and techniques
Pre-use Pre-purchase, Post-purchase	Brochures, website (traveller's tips, trip notes). Codes of practice, slide shows, newsletter, travel documentation and inserts, other printed documents (e.g. holiday hints guides/essential holiday guide/'making the most of your stay' leaflets, trip notes).
Transportation/flight To destination, From destination	In-flight magazine, in-flight video. In-flight magazine.
Destination/resort	Resort magazine/guide, participation in environmental initiatives, in-room TV channel, room information and folders, noticeboards, posters (e.g. environmental statement, codes of practice), display of environmental awards, staff (e.g. representatives, tour leaders), welcome meetings and printed information packs on arrival.
Post-use	Survey, newsletter.

Channels available at one or more stages in the journey
Annual reports, environmental reports, website (e.g. summary of environmental policy, environmental mission statements), newsletter, public relations (including media relations and sponsorship).

The communication methods adopted by these tourism companies emphasised the importance of physical evidence in the form of standardised literature. This counterbalanced the highly variable nature of the particular service product (e.g. experiences can vary due to changes in the weather, local travel problems, etc.). The communication strategies also made considerable use of front-line employees interacting directly with the consumer throughout the holiday (i.e. 'the personal touch'). According to one interviewee, 'the most effective way of getting all the information across is really through the [tour] leaders, because they have face-to-face contact with people and people listen to what they say . . . let's say they have a bigger role, which is why we're really concentrating on having the right people doing that job who understand the issues.' It is this direct staff/customer contact, so vital a communication tool during service usage, that is not generally available to most goods manufacturers.

Figure 10.6 Mapping the customer journey

Case study 10.5 (*continued*)

Other applications?

A similar 'customer journey' or blueprinting approach could be used by other categories of service providers, to convey sustainability messages to pursue other communication objectives. Based on the experience of these companies, there are a number of guidelines for achieving this aim:

- Set the parameters in terms of customer segment, product, location or brand.
- Map or flow-chart the different stages of the 'customer journey', from initial decision process through to post-use feelings.
- Identify all points of contact, both human and inanimate, between the provider and the customer. Information can be gathered by observation, or from key customer groups and employees.
- Identify the existing methods of communication at each point of contact, including any gaps, and consider appropriate ways to strengthen communication at each point.
- Assess the overall package of communication methods for consistency in presentation and reinforcement of the brand (i.e. beyond any immediate communication objectives), as well as for costing purposes and to deal with relevant issues such as staff motivation and training.
- Monitor and review the success or otherwise of the different communication methods post-implementation.

Questions

1 What do you see as the main communication challenges facing the companies in the case study?

2 Why do you think printed literature has proved to be such a popular communication tool for this and other service products?

3 Why might public relations activity, including the role of front-line staff, be more successful than advertising in communicating messages about sustainability?

4 What other messages might be communicated to consumers through use of flowcharts/ blueprints of the 'customer journey' and physical evidence at the points of contact?

Source: Case prepared by Jackie Clarke.

Glossary

Promotional mix is the term given to the combination of promotional approaches that an organisation uses to communicate with the world around it.

Advertising refers to a process that has traditionally made use of one way communication in order to promote ideas, products and services.

co-ordinated campaign A co-ordinated 'campaign' is the term used to describe the common approach of running a number of related advertisements alongside, together with other promotional devices. These campaigns are increasingly combining conventional and social media.

Viral marketing means exploiting existing online social networks in order to enhance awareness of a product, service or organisational brand.

wiki A wiki is software that enables users to quickly and easily create, edit, save and make links between web pages, and which is sometimes used to facilitate group discussions.

Monologic dialogue is that which is simply designed to control the area of debate in order to achieve pre-determined objectives rather than open discussion with the intention of achieving collaborative goals.

Lobbyists have an important role, providing decision-makers with well-researched briefing materials, technical advice and arguments in support of their respective positions.

News releases are statements, often about the launch of a new product, service or event, used by organisations to brief media journalists and encourage them to write articles on the subject.

Sound bites are short and memorable phrases used by presenters and interviewees that the journalist is more likely to use in an uncut form.

Further reading

There are many new books on the fast-moving field of social media, with recent examples including **Kerpen (2011)** and **Clapperton** (2009).

Looking back much further, **Packard** ([1957] 2007) is the classic study of mass market advertising, an interesting historical source that is still in print.

Another useful source of insights into advertising is the work of **Ogilvy** (1995), a leading twentieth century practitioner, and **Klein's** (2000) critique of corporate advertising and marketing.

Carlson (2001) is an interesting example of cross-cultural research in advertising, which also addresses gender differences, while **Alexander et al.** (2011) and **Carson** (2002) consider some important ethical issues.

Tench and Yeomans (2009) is a popular textbook on public relations.

Olins (2004, 2008) addresses corporate visual identity, and is written by a leading practitioner.

Melewar et al. (2005) is an interesting illustration of branding applied to France Telecom.

The debate between integrated corporate communications and the more open approach of stakeholder engagement can be captured by comparing **Kitchen and Schultz** (2001), who promote the integration, and contributions, such as **Crane and Livesey** (2003) in the edited volume by **Andriof et al.** (2003), which present leading ideas from stakeholder theory.

Belz and Peattie (2009) is a useful textbook on marketing and promotion, which concentrates on environmental sustainability.

Useful websites

There are many useful websites that can be used to support the topics addressed in this chapter. Here are some examples, which might be of interest:

The Adbusters website hosts a collection of parodies of well-known adverts from its base in Canada. (Available at

http://www.adbusters.org)

The European Commission publishes news and information on consumer and marketing law. (Available at

http://ec.europa.eu/justice/newsroom/consumer-marketing/news/index_en.htm)

The Advertising Standards Authority website contains information about maintaining advertising standards from a UK perspective, including rules for advertising. (Available at

http://www.asa.org.uk/asa/)

Friends of the Earth is one of many campaigning organisations that offer advice on drafting a press release (Available at

http://www.foe.co.uk/resource/how_tos/cyw_64_press_release.pdf)

The Influential Marketing Blog offers a series of reflections on current marketing, advertising and PR strategy from a US perspective. (Available at

http://rohitbhargava.typepad.com/weblog/)

References

Adbusters (2012) 'About Adbusters'. Adbusters Media Foundation, Vancouver BC. (Available at: http://www.adbusters.org/about/adbusters (accessed 19th March 2012)).

Aldísardóttir, L. (2000) 'Research note: global medium, local tool? How readers and media companies use the web'. *European Journal of Communication*, 15, 2, 241–251.

Alexander, J., Crompton, T. and Shrubsole, G. (2011) *Think of Me as Evil?: opening the ethical debates in advertising*. Public Interest Research Centre and WWF-UK, Machynlleth and Godalming: (Available at: http://assets.wwf.org.uk/downloads (accessed 31st March 2012).

Andriof, J., Waddock, S., Husted, B. and Rahman, S. (eds) (2003) *Unfolding Stakeholder Thinking 2: relationships, communication and performance*. Greenleaf, Sheffield.

Banerjee, S., Gulas, C.S. and Iyer, E. (1995) 'Shades of green: a multidimensional analysis of environmental advertising'. *Journal of Advertising*, 24, 2, 21–31.

Belz, F.M. and Peattie, K.(2009) *Sustainability Marketing: a global perspective*. Wiley, Chichester.

Carlson, L., Grove, S.J. and Kangun, N. (1993) 'A context analysis of environmental advertising claims: a matrix method approach'. *Journal of Advertising*, 22, 3, 27–39.

Carlson, L., Grove, S.J., Kangun, N. and Polonsky, M.J. (1996) 'An international comparison of environmental advertising: substantive versus associative claims'. *Journal of Macromarketing*, 16, 2, 57–68.

Carlson, T. (2001) 'Gender and political advertising across cultures: a comparison of male and female political advertising in Finland and the US'. *European Journal of Communication*, 16, 2, 131–154.

Carson, T.L. (2002) 'Ethical issues in selling and advertising', in Bowie, N.E. (ed.) *The Blackwell Guide to Business Ethics*. Blackwell, Oxford, 186–205.

Chalaby, J.K. (2002) 'Transnational television in Europe: the role of pan-European channels'. *European Journal of Communication*, 17, 2, 183–203.

Clapperton, G. (2009) *This Is Social Media: tweet, blog, link and post your way to business success*. Capstone, Chichester.

Coddington, W. (1993) *Environmental Marketing: positive strategies for reaching the green consumer*. McGraw-Hill, London.

Crane, A. and Livesey, S. (2003) 'Are you talking to me? Stakeholder communication and the rewards of dialogue', in Andriof, J. et al. (eds) *Unfolding stacendder Thinking* 2: relationships, communication a performance Green leaf, sheffield 39–51.

Fathers 4 justice (F4J) (2012) 'We are Fathers 4 Justice'. (Available at http://www.fathers-4-justice. org/f4j/(accessed 31 March 2012)).

Gelles, D. (2012) 'Advertisers rush to master a fresh set of skills.' *The Financial Times,* 7 March. (Available at: www.ft.com (accessed 10th April 2012))

Ghandi, M.K. ([1927] 1993) *An Autobiography: the Story of my Experiment with Truth.* Beacon Press, Boston, MA.

Harris, J.L., Bargh, J.A. and Brownell, K.D. (2009) 'Priming effects of television food advertising on eating behavior.' *Health Psychology,* 28, 4, 404–413.

Institute of Public Relations (IPR)(2003) 'Fact file'. Institute of Public Relations, London. (Available at: www.ipr.org.uk/news/factfile.asp (accessed 15th December 2011)).

Kerpen, D. (2011) *Likeable Social Media: how to delight your customers, create an irresistible brand, and be generally amazing on Facebook (& other social networks).* McGraw-Hill, New York.

Kilbourne, W.E. (1995) 'Green advertising: salvation or oxymoron?' *Journal of Advertising,* 24, 2, 7–19.

Kitchen, P.J. and Schultz, D.E. (2001) *Raising the Corporate Umbrella: corporate communications in the 21st century.* Palgrave, Basingstoke.

Klein, N. (2000) *No Logo.* Flamingo, London.

Linnanen, L., Markkanen, E. and Ilmola, L. (1999) 'Building environmental credibility: from action to words' in Charter, M. and Polonsky, M.J. (eds) *Greener Marketing : a global perspective on greening marketing practice,'* 2nd edn. Green leaf, sheffield 207–223.

Lovelock, C. (2001) *Services Marketing: people, technology, strategy,* 4th edn. Prentice Hall, Upper Saddle River, NJ.

Melewar, T.C., Hussey, G. and Srivoravilai, N. (2005) 'Corporate visual identity: the re-branding of France Telecom'. *Journal of Brand Management,* 12, 379–394.

Middleton, V.T.C. and Clarke, J. (2001) *Marketing in Travel and Tourism,* 3rd edn. Butterworth-Heinemann, Oxford.

Miller, D. and Dinan, W. (2000) 'The rise of the PR industry in Britain, 1979–98'. *European Journal of Communication,* 15, 1, 5–35.

National Consumer Council (1996) *Green Claims: a consumer investigation into marketing claims about the environment.* NCC, London.

Obermiller, C. (1995) 'The baby is sick/the baby is well: a test of environmental communication appeals'. *Journal of Advertising,* 24, 2, 55–71.

Ogilvy, D. (1995) *Ogilvy on Advertising.* Prion, London.

Olins, W. (2004) *On Brand.* Thames and Hudson, London.

Olins, W. (2008) *The Brand Handbook.* Thames and Hudson, London.

Packard, V. ([1957] 2007) *The Hidden Persuaders* (with new introduction by Mark Crispin Miller). Ig Publishing, Brooklyn, NY.

Polonsky, M.J., Bailey, J., Baker, H. and Basche, C. (1998) 'Communicating environmental information: are marketing claims on packaging misleading?' *Journal of Business Ethics,* 17, 3, 281–294.

Rogers, E.M. (1995) *Diffusion of Innovations,* 3rd edn. Free Press, New York.

Smidts, A., Pruyn, A.H. and van Riel, C.B.M. (2001) 'The impact of employee communication and perceived external prestige on organisational identification'. *Academy of Management Journal,* 49, 5, 1051–1062.

Tench, R. and Yeomans, L. (2009) *Exploring Public Relations,* 2nd edn. FT Prentice Hall, Harlow.

UNICEF (2012) *Children's Rights and Business Principles.* United Nations Global Compact. Available at http://www.unglobalcompact.org/docs/issues_doc/human_rights/CRBP/Childrens_Rights_and_ Business_Principles.pdf (accessed 31 March 2012).

Chapter 11

Interviews, questioning and listening

> Knowledge speaks, but wisdom listens.
> Jimi Hendrix, musician

Learning outcomes

By the end of this chapter you should be able to:

- compare the various ways that interviews are used in organisations, noting the differing requirements of each situation;
- make appropriate practical arrangements for successful interviews;
- enhance your listening skills and develop appropriate questioning techniques, reflecting the needs of the situation;
- prepare more effectively when attending interviews;
- appreciate related techniques, including those adopted in counselling interviews.

11.1 Introduction

Interviews have been usefully described as 'a discussion with a purpose'. They serve various purposes in organisations, ranging from recruitment and employee appraisal to marketing research and public relations. In communication terms, interviews are particularly rich in messages. The words spoken are often less important than the non-verbal signals that are exchanged. These include facial expressions, eye contact, gestures and posture (see section 4.7). As a result of this complex mixture of stimuli, interviews also offer considerable scope for misunderstanding and confusion. Hence, it is important for all managers to develop strong interviewing skills. Fortunately, there is considerable overlap between the knowledge and capabilities required by an interviewer and those that are needed to be a successful interviewee. Most people have had some experience of being interviewed. We will draw on these experiences as a useful starting point when discussing how to develop or enhance communication skills as an interviewer.

The chapter begins with a brief review of the main types of interview, which describes their distinctive characteristics. Two practical sections deal with the essential, yet infrequently practised, skills of listening and questioning. These are followed by suggestions on how best to prepare for an interview, looking from the interviewee's perspective. Finally, there is a short discussion on the role of counselling techniques at work.

11.2   Types of interview

Organisational managers and employees are routinely involved in the four broad categories of interview (i.e. recruitment and promotion; appraisal and performance management; coaching and mentoring; and disciplinary and grievance) that are reviewed in this section (see Table 11.1). In some cases, they may also find themselves being interviewed as part of the organisation's public relations, marketing or campaigning activities, which were the subject of the previous chapter. While it is possible to identify some 'ideal-typical' patterns of communication, each interview is a unique and dynamic situation, so that the results of a particular interaction may be difficult to predict at the outset. The level of formality (i.e. the degree to which the interview follows established procedures, with the associated paperwork) is likely to vary depending on the organisation and the individuals involved. However, some common features can be identified in each interview type.

Table 11.1   Main interview types and related communication practices

Type	Typical interviewer practice	Typical interviewee practice
Recruitment and promotion	Clarifies factual information regarding application; assesses inter-personal skills; makes conscious or unconscious subjective assessments of candidate; engages in persuasion.	Seeks to persuade interviewer(s); obtains additional factual information; makes conscious or unconscious assessments of organisation.
Appraisal	Listens to employee's self-assessment; probes for related problems and possible solutions; should be open, seeking to establish shared understandings and encourage employee.	Clarifies and reflects on challenges and achievements; raises outstanding issues and concerns; expresses preferences for future activity; should be open and not attempt to mislead employer.
Coaching and mentoring	Supportive questioning; clarifies mentee's next phase of activity; encourages mentee to reflect on previous phases of work experience and to generalise. Supports mentee in identifying future development opportunities.	Identifies perceived needs; reports on work experiences; responds to mentor's questions; reflects on previous phase of work experience; seeks coach's/ mentor's advice and guidance.
Disciplinary and grievance	Clarifies the problem and outlines any formal procedures; maintains objectivity and avoids personalising issues; seeks employee's agreement and commitment.	Explains the problem and/or mitigating circumstances; maintains objectivity and avoids personalising issues; may either seek agreement or engage in further persuasion.

Recruitment and promotion interviews

Interviews are normally used at the second or third stage of a recruitment process. Prior to this, applicants are 'screened' on the basis of information provided in *curriculum vitaes* (CVs) and application forms. **Screening** is essentially a *rejection* process. It is used to produce a 'shortlist', reducing the initial numbers to a more manageable size. Some larger organisations then ask shortlisted candidates to take part in psychometric tests, 'in-tray' exercises, etc. The final stage, where *selection* takes place, is almost always a personal interview. **Selection** , unlike screening, is about choosing the most suitable candidate from a shortlist, most of whom could probably do the job very well. Interviews can also be used to clarify and check up on the candidate's achievements and interests, as they are recorded on application forms or in a CV (e.g. 'So tell me, did you really cycle all the way from Moscow to Beijing?'). However, for many managers, the principal function of a face-to-face interview is to see whether the candidate would make a suitable colleague. In many cases, this draws on a more informal assessment, which seeks to establish whether the person would 'fit in' with existing members of the department or team. As a result, recruitment interviews can become highly subjective exercises, no matter how objective the rest of the process has been.

Recruitment interviews

Recruitment interviews involve both an individual, aiming to convince an organisation to hire them, and an organisation, hoping to find and convince the right employee to join them. As a result, both parties are engaged in various forms of persuasive communication (see Chapter 5). Interviewees make use of persuasive techniques with the obvious intention of getting themselves selected. However, prospective employers are also engaged in a more complex task of persuasion. First, they will be trying to ensure that the most promising candidates accept their job offer, knowing that these people may have attractive offers from rival firms. Second, recruitment interviewers should be ensuring that *all* interviewees, successful and unsuccessful, are left with a positive impression, perceiving the organisation as an efficient, fair and decent place to work. After all, it may be that the organisation wants to recruit some of the unsuccessful candidates on another occasion. They also have the potential to become important customers, suppliers or partners in the future. In any event, having had a direct experience of the organisation, they are bound to share their impressions with others. This kind of informal communication can contribute powerfully to the organisation's external image, particularly where there is a relatively small community of interest (see section 10.5).

Promotion interviews

Promotion interviews operate in a similar way to recruitment interviews, with internal candidates competing for a more senior post. The key differences are that interviewees are bound to know some members of the interview panel quite well, and that the applicants will continue to work for the organisation, whether or not they are successful at interview. Organisations also conduct interviews when employees are applying for changes in work task or location, which do not involve an increase in salary or status (i.e. a transfer or 'sideways move').

Appraisal interviews

Most large and medium-sized organisations operate a system of appraisal interviews. **Appraisal interviews** provide an opportunity for employees to review performance and progress with their line manager. They should include an open and honest discussion that highlights the person's achievements, probes the reasons behind any problem areas and identifies training or work experience needs. The interviewer or interviewee prepares a summary of the discussion and outcomes, and both parties agree an action plan for the next period. If the manager ensures a climate of openness and trust, the appraisal interview can be highly motivating. By reviewing the results of a number of interviews, it becomes possible to identify and correct underlying structural or procedural problems within the organisation. However, some organisations continue to link appraisals to performance-related pay schemes or bonuses. This combination is unlikely to encourage an open or self-critical approach in the employee, limiting the effectiveness of the appraisal as a feedback mechanism. Chapter 6 includes a more detailed discussion of the role of appraisal systems, including the technique known as '360-degree' feedback (see section 6.3 and Case study 6.2). Chapter 6 (section 6.6) includes advice, of use to both appraisers and appraisees, on how to give and make use of feedback.

Coaching/mentoring interviews

Coaching and mentoring interviews are a form of on-going developmental appraisal, which are often used with newly appointed and recently promoted staff. Ideally the coach or mentor will be someone other than the mentee's line manager, but possibly from the same organisation, to ensure an independent third-party perspective. The coaching model derives from the world of sport, where personal and team coaches help athletes to enhance their performance. It has become increasingly popular at board level (i.e. 'executive coaching'), where senior staff may be allocated a coach, normally recruited from a specialist consultancy.

Continuing with the sporting analogy, the pharmaceuticals company GlaxoSmithKline runs an employee development programme called *Corporate Athlete* which is based on the premise that people need to be physically fit and mentally focused and energised if they are to give high performance. The programme includes guidance in fitness, nutrition and self-awareness (GlaxoSmithKline 2006). In a coaching interview, the emphasis is on making the person more self-aware; encouraging them to discuss work-based projects, evaluate progress since the previous meeting and look forward to future challenges. Other people employ 'life coaches' to improve their well-being in all aspects of their lives. Here, the role of the interviewer is not primarily to instruct or to give detailed advice, but to develop the interviewee's confidence and capabilities by agreeing targets and encouraging reflection upon what has been learned.

Disciplinary and grievance interviews

Both disciplinary and grievance interviews are concerned with responding to problems. **Disciplinary interviews** are normally conducted in response to the problematic behaviour of an employee, while **grievance interviews** deal with problems that an employee has raised. Both raise considerable challenges in balancing the need for formality and objectivity, with a degree of human empathy and persuasive communication. Ideally, problems should be identified and remedied at an earlier stage (e.g. arranging an employee meeting to air and resolve a grievance, or tackling a disciplinary problem as part of the employee's appraisal or coaching session). In the case of disciplinary issues: isolated, minor incidents should be dealt with quickly and with minimal formality; in the case of a more serious, complex, or long-running problem, a more formal interview may be necessary.

Procedures for disciplinary and grievance interviews should be clearly stipulated in the individual's employment contract, and must be closely followed. In the worst case, you might subsequently need written evidence to defend against an unfair dismissal claim before an employment tribunal. During a disciplinary interview, the interviewer's main priorities are to establish the facts and to remain calm and objective. Both parties should avoid personalising the discussion, even if provoked. The employer is normally trying to secure some kind of commitment from the employee to acknowledge the problem and to overcome it voluntarily. Where the interview has been prompted by an employee's grievance (e.g. a junior member of staff has made a complaint about the behaviour of a manager), the interview follows a similar pattern, in which a participative, problem-solving style is generally the most appropriate. Though regulations vary between countries, there may be a legal requirement or a code of practice governing the way that the interview should be conducted (ACAS 2007). Disciplinary and grievance interviews raise questions concerning the relative power of employee and employer, which also influence the nature of the communication process. For example, research evidence suggests that supervisors and managers do not always adopt the most appropriate interview style to achieve the desired change in behaviour, with many of the disciplinary cases that are perceived as 'less serious' being handled in an autocratic manner (Hook et al. 1996, Rollinson et al. 1996).

Case study 1.1 considers another important application of interviewing, where it forms one of the data collection methods adopted for an organisational research project. You might use interviewing as a data collection method for your research. The case distinguishes between three types of research interview:

- 'structured' interviews, where interviewers follow a carefully worded script;

- 'semi-structured' interviews, where they typically make use of a checklist of topics to be covered, but are more flexible in the way that the questions are worded and the order in which they are raised; and

- 'unstructured' interviews, where there is minimal formality and the interviewee is encouraged to speak freely. This allows the researcher to explore issues in greater depth, and is based on a less directive style of interaction, which is guided by the interviewee's perceptions, rather than the interviewer's pre-determined plan (Saunders et al. 2003: 246–7).

CASE STUDY 11.1

Using interviews in an organisational research project

During a research project to survey employee attitudes in a public sector organisation, the use of interviews was considered for each stage of this undertaking. The first stage of data collection consisted of a series of unstructured interviews, which were undertaken with a representative cross-section of employees, to reveal variables to be tested empirically at the second stage of the research project. During the initial planning phase a number of decisions were made about these interviews, which included that they should:

Case study 11.1 (*continued*)

- obtain personnel data relating to job categories and grades, gender, age and length of service in order to select a representative sample;
- combine similar employee categories and use group interviews in order to overcome time constraints and assist the researcher's capacity to handle the data to be collected. As a result, six group interviews were arranged, consisting of about ten participants in each group, in order to cover all employee categories;
- not mix managerial and non-managerial participants within a group because this could mean that non-managerial employees would be reluctant to take part.

At the next stage of the research project a decision had to be taken about whether to use a questionnaire or structured and standardised interviews. Because the number of employees in the organisational sample to be surveyed exceeded 30, it was decided that it would be more efficient to use a questionnaire rather than interviews (Wass and Wells 1994). After the analysis of the questionnaire data, a further stage used a series of semi-structured interviews in order to explore and explain the findings obtained through the survey. These were also conducted as group interviews. Care was again taken in relation to the representativeness, size and composition of each group, as well as in relation to choosing the setting for the discussion to occur.

Questions

1 What kinds of information were the researchers seeking to obtain from the interviews that were conducted:
   (a) at the first stage of data collection?
   (b) after the analysis of the questionnaire?

2 Try to develop three or four of your own sample questions, in a format that might be suitable for each of these interviews. (Note: Review the content and format of these questions once you have completed the chapter, redrafting as necessary.)

3 In 'unstructured' interviews, the interaction is sometimes described as 'non-directive' (i.e. the researcher does not specify the questions). Can you identify other interview situations where a non-directive approach might be appropriate?

Source: Case based on an extract from Saunders et al. (2003: 249). Reproduced with permission.

11.3 Listening techniques

Our ears play an important role in the communication process, and as the opening quotation of this chapter suggests, listening underpins many forms of human interaction. (There is a long-established saying, to the effect that there was a good reason for providing us with two ears yet only one mouth.) Anecdotal evidence suggests that society places a relatively low value on the art of listening. For example, there is considerable coverage of 'effective speaking' in the popular communication literature, but very little material on 'effective listening'. Despite this, one of the best ways of enhancing inter-personal communication in interviews and other channels, such as meetings, is to invest some time in developing better listening skills. **Active listening** means more than simply using your ears; it also involves you observing the other person's behaviours, encouraging them to speak, ensuring that you do not become distracted from what the person is saying (e.g. by your own thoughts), and capturing what has been said for future reference. Active listening techniques include: summarising the person's words in your own mind, taking notes, using encouraging gestures, such as smiling, nodding, making eye contact, and positioning yourself so that you are facing the interviewee and able to give feedback. These techniques are explored further in the following section, which reviews six general characteristics of a more 'active' and effective listener.

Avoiding prejudice

Prejudice acts as a perceptual filter on the ear, cutting out those things that do not fit in with a person's original viewpoint, and reinforcing anything that does. In order to cope with a complex world we try to fit our experiences, and the people we meet, into pre-existing categories (see section 2.3). However, these rough and ready categorisations can become an obstacle to communication, creating 'noise' and distorting the more detailed information that we subsequently receive. In order to deal with our prejudices, they need to be recognised. One way of increasing awareness is to consider previous occasions when you have formed an inaccurate impression, based on an initial reaction to a personal characteristic, such as accent, age, disability, educational qualifications, gender, height, nationality, occupation, religious background or sexuality. The aim is to resist any simplified and pre-determined categorisation, and to pay greater attention to the individual person, and what they have to say.

Signalling interest in the person speaking

Interviewers and other listeners need to do more than simply pay attention. They need to demonstrate that they are receptive to the other person, showing that they are actually interested in what is being said. Interest can be signalled in a number of ways, mostly through non-verbal cues. For example, interviewers should adopt an 'open' posture with arms *unfolded*. They should also be facing towards the person speaking, and may also lean forwards slightly. Other non-verbal signals, such as degree of eye contact and facial expression, can be influential. Skilled interviewers combine these with verbal and paralinguistic cues, adjusting their tone of voice and using prompts (e.g. 'yes', 'I see . . .', 'good', 'mmm . . .', 'uh-huh'), to reinforce their support and encourage the speaker.

Being aware of feelings

Good listeners can operate simultaneously at two levels, picking up both cognitive and affective messages. (Note: in this context, 'cognitive' refers to processes of perceiving and thinking; 'affective' refers to processes involving human emotion.) At a 'surface' level, they need to extract and process information that the other person injects into the conversation (e.g. 'Yes, I have completed the report', 'No, we did not receive the training materials'). However, they also need to be alert to messages that are concerned with personal feelings and emotions. In some cases, national, organisational or departmental cultures discourage people from expressing their feelings in conversation, so that listeners are forced to interpret the messages more indirectly (i.e. they have to 'read between the lines'), in order to interpret the implicit meanings. National cultures are also thought to influence the extent to which people rely on cues from the overall situation when communicating. These range from 'high context' cultures, that draw a great deal of meaning from non-verbal cues, to 'low context' cultures, that rely more explicitly on the actual words that are used (Hall and Hall 1990) (see section 2.3). As we noted, the situation is rather more complex in today's more culturally diverse international organisations, which are often populated by people with several overlapping cultural identities. However, it remains the case that cultural factors can undermine communication during interviews (see Case study 11.2).

CASE STUDY 11.2

Jean-Jacques and the appraisal interview

It is 5.30 pm on a hot summer's day. We are in the administrative offices of a large city teaching hospital in northern Germany. Jean-Jacques, a talented computing technician, is in the middle of his six-monthly appraisal interview. He is trying to explain a series of problems to Petra, his immediate line manager. The main problem appears to relate to the contractors being used to install new computer cabling in part of the main teaching block: a nineteenth-century building in the centre of the hospital grounds. Petra asks Jean-Jacques to explain what is wrong:

J-J: (Folds arms across chest and sits back in the chair) You see, the contractors we hired have still not finished. I have spent five hours today trying to chase them up and the cabling is still not completed. (Sighs)

Petra: Will the computer suite in the teaching block be ready for the conference next week?

J-J: I hope so, but you know, it is not acceptable for private contractors to treat a customer in this way, simply because we are a not-for-profit organisation. I feel that hospitals like ours should make more intensive efforts in this direction.

Petra: But will the cabling be completed in time?

J-J: (Looks at the ceiling) I am not sure that I am making myself clear. We are experiencing a problem which is …

Petra: I don't need to understand the problem. I just need to be sure that the work will be completed in time.

J-J: You should understand that I am doing everything possible to ensure that the work will be finished (gestures with open hands and raised eyebrows), but I think perhaps there are wider issues here?

Petra: Good, so I will not expect a problem next week.

Petra continues with the appraisal interview, moving on to set Jean-Jacques' performance targets for the next six months. She is pleased to finish the interview on time, at 5.45 pm. Jean-Jacques is much less happy with the outcome. On the way home, he picks up a copy of his favourite newspaper and sits down at a pavement café to read through the job advertisements.

Questions

1 Review the case and the extract of dialogue. What do you think that Jean-Jacques is trying to communicate to Petra? Consider both cognitive and affective aspects of the messages.

2 What are the most likely barriers to communication operating in this interview? Consider the question from the perspective of both individuals.

3 Prepare a revised version of the dialogue, in which both Jean-Jacques and Petra have taken account of the issues you identified in the previous question.

Source: Case written by the authors. The characters and organisation are fictional.

Avoiding interruptions and distractions

One of the most difficult challenges for an interventionist (i.e. 'hands on') manager is to avoid interrupting other people while they are talking. By starting to speak, you will generally cause the other person to stop, and possibly lose their line of argument. Repeated interruptions are likely to cause irritation. In effect, the interruption signals that 'I no longer want to listen to what you are saying.' Consequently, interviewers should only interrupt when there is a good reason to do so. For example, it may be appropriate if the interviewees are either repeating themselves or digressing from the subject matter of the interview. Other gestures, such as shuffling paperwork or reading while an interviewee is speaking, are also distracting and should be avoided. However, interviewers may sometimes make use of non-verbal cues in a deliberate attempt to encourage the person speaking to be more concise, or to signal that they are bringing the interview to a close.

Signalling encouragement

There are various ways to maintain the momentum of a conversation without distracting the interviewee. As we have already noted, occasional nodding of the head, eye contact, smiling and the use of vocal cues can act as strong signals of encouragement. However, the reverse is also true. If the interviewer either fails to provide these cues, or stops using them during the course of the interview, the effect can be dramatic. This is particularly apparent in situations where the interviewee is nervous or has other reasons for being a reluctant speaker. On the contrary, if you really need a verbose interviewee to draw to a close, or to avoid the risk of over-running, you could use signals to encourage them to stop (e.g. remain silent, or even glance at your watch), and hope that they pick up on your cue.

Clarifying and summarising

If an interviewee is having difficulty expressing ideas coherently, the interviewer can assist by seeking confirmation: checking for a correct understanding of what has been discussed or agreed. One option is simply to ask the interviewee to clarify what they have been saying. Alternatively, the interviewer can attempt to paraphrase the discussion, and ask the interviewee whether this was an accurate representation. A similar interaction is required towards the end of an interview, when the interviewer draws the various points together in the form of a summary. Summaries are concerned with shared meanings. They help to ensure that all parties have a similar understanding of what has taken place during the interview. They also provide an opportunity to specify any agreements, decisions or actions. However, there is the danger of creating a false sense of agreement, particularly where the interviewer is overly-directive, or where the interviewee feels unable to challenge the way that the summary has been framed. Active listening requires interviewers to reflect carefully at this point, checking whether their clarifications and summaries accurately reflect the other person's contribution (Rogers and Farson 1976).

Effective interviews: the importance of practical arrangements

The practical preparations for an interview can make a significant difference in its effectiveness. These arrangements include the way the room is set out, avoidance of interruptions, and the way that interviewees are treated before and after the interview. It is also important to consider who is to do the interviewing, an individual or a panel.

- **Seating and room layout**: Layout does affect the atmosphere of the interview. It is often better to move away from your desk, with its distracting piles of work. Putting your interviewee in a lower or less comfortable chair sends out a message of superiority and distance. However, if you are aiming to retain some degree of businesslike formality, relaxing armchairs are best avoided (see Figure 11.1).

- **Interview panels**: Some interviews are conducted with a panel, comprising several people who may be from different parts of the organisation. For example, a recruitment interview panel may include a representative from human resources (HR) and one or more line managers. Panels are used in this case to ensure that different interests are represented, and to enable the interviewers to discuss the candidates after the interview. Panels can be particularly daunting for the interviewee, so seating arrangements become even more important. Panel members should remember to introduce themselves carefully at the start of the interview. It may also be appropriate to explain who will be asking questions first, and what areas each person will cover. These courtesies help to put the interviewee at their ease, and therefore enable the interviewers to make a more realistic assessment of their abilities.

- **Minimising interruptions and distractions**: Managers tend to have frequent telephone calls and visitors, so it is advisable to divert calls, switch off mobile phones and place a 'do not disturb' sign on the door. If the organisation's offices are open-plan, it is important to book a more private meeting room for the interviews. Interviewers often ensure that they are sitting in sight of a wall clock, so that they can keep track of time without disturbing the interviewee by glancing at their wristwatch.

- **Before and after the interview**: Some basic courtesies convey a positive image of the organisation, especially in the case of recruitment interviews, where the person is a visitor. For example, it is bad practice to leave people waiting in a busy corridor, fail to provide refreshments, or leave them unaware of where the toilets are located. It should be reasonably easy to obtain a suitable waiting room and offer the interviewees a coffee. Keep to stated interview times if possible and ensure that any agreed follow-up action is taken.

The next section takes us into the interview room and considers how questioning techniques and other aspects of behaviour might affect the quality of interaction between interviewer and interviewee.

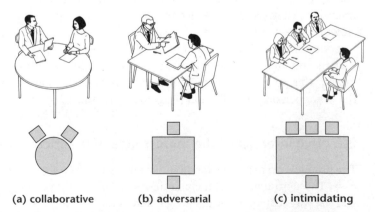

    (a) collaborative   (b) adversarial   (c) intimidating

Figure 11.1 Seating layouts for interviews

11.4   Questioning techniques and related behaviours

An interview is punctuated by questions and answers. The same question can be asked in many ways, and each style can generate a *different* response. By considering the types of questions people ask, and the related behaviours that they employ, it is possible to improve your questioning technique and encourage more useful interaction (see also section 5.5 for examples of how questions can be used in persuasive communication).

Open and closed questions

One of the most important distinctions is between 'open' and 'closed' questions. Closed questions demand a short pre-determined response: often a simple 'yes' or 'no' (e.g. 'Have you called the office this morning?'). Open questions, by contrast, encourage the respondent to think for themselves and thus allow for a wider range of responses. (For example, 'How should we tackle this production problem?') Consider how using a closed question limits communication in the following dialogue:

Jonas: 'So anyway, Helle, was that training course OK?'

Helle: 'Yes, I suppose so, though ...'

Jonas: 'Excellent, see you later!'

An 'open' version of the same basic question produces a much more informative (and therefore useful) answer from the interviewee, since it encourages them to speak for longer, and to give a more considered response:

Jonas: 'So, Helle, how did you feel about the training course?'

Helle: 'Well..., the tutor was excellent, but she was repeating a lot of the material we covered during our induction sessions in September.'

Jonas: 'Ah, that's unfortunate. Looks like we may need to revise the programme before the next run.'

Closed questions are useful for establishing the basic facts (e.g. 'How many people do you employ?'). You can also use them to 'close down' an overly wordy or rambling interviewee, forcing them to give more concise responses. Open questions, with occasional closed questions for clarification, are a very useful way to investigate complex issues, especially where your own knowledge of the area is limited.

Probing questions and clarification

Probing questions may be open or closed, and ask for additional information, based on the interviewee's previous responses. Clarification can play a similar role, but its primary purpose is to confirm that the questioner has understood the previous response correctly, rather than to ask for more. Probing and clarification need to be tackled carefully. These questions can easily sound aggressive, which typically prompts a defensive reaction from the 'victim', closing down the possibilities for further communication:

Jonas: 'So, Helle, how did you feel about the training course?'

293

Helle: 'Well, the tutor was excellent, but she was repeating a lot of the material we covered during our induction sessions in September.'

Jonas: 'Oh really, so which topics were repeated?'

Helle: 'The presentation skills, and the session on company organisation.'

Jonas: 'And did you tell the tutor about this?'

Helle: 'No, actually ...'

Jonas: 'Was there a feedback session for the trainees?'

Helle: 'Well, yes, but I wasn't about to say anything about it there.'

Jonas: 'So, what you're saying is, you could have spoken out at the feedback session, but you didn't?'

Helle: 'Hey, don't blame me, it wasn't my fault they got it wrong!'

Encouraging and summarising

These behaviours are useful tools that the interviewer can use to maintain momentum in the interview and to ensure that it achieves a degree of shared understanding. The interviewee may be encouraged by non-verbal signals, such as when the interviewer is nodding, smiling or displaying an open posture while the interviewee is talking. This is where the interviewer can make use of paralinguistic cues to signal encouragement (see section 11.3). However, as we saw in Chapter 4, many of these signals have highly culture-specific meanings. For the same reason, they are learned behaviours, so that people may be largely unconscious of making them (see section 4.7). Consequently, interviewers need to be particularly flexible and sensitive to the potential for misinterpretation in cross-cultural contexts. We have also discussed how summaries can be used to restate and encapsulate the interviewee's responses up to that point. They can clarify the interviewer's interpretation and enable the interviewee to confirm or challenge that interpretation. Both clarification and summarising are simple techniques, yet many interviewers make limited use of them, resulting in a less effective and more error-prone exchange.

Hypothetical questions

Hypothetical questions are an excellent way to make your interviewee reflect on things. This type of question is often used to test the mental agility and creativity of prospective employees (e.g. 'Imagine you're in charge of our Japanese export marketing operation. The local stock exchange has just collapsed. What would you do?'). Hypotheticals are also used in coaching and counselling, to help a person explore previously unconsidered options. (For example, 'So, if we could arrange that extra language tuition and the travel leave, how would you feel about spending two years in the Colombian regional office?')

Leading questions and interruptions

Leading questions direct the interviewee to respond with the answer that you either desire or expect. Leading questions are probably interviewers' most common fault. They are always communication failures, because they represent one-way messages masquerading as an exchange of views. They are often compounded by the use of frequent interruptions, so that the interviewee is unable even to complete the response to a question. An extreme example of both tendencies illustrates these dangers:

Jonas: So what did you think of our 'so-called' training course?

Helle: Well, it's difficult to say ...

Jonas: That tutor! A complete waste of space, don't you think?

Helle: I'm sure she ...

Jonas: Means well?

Helle: No, not really. It's ...

Jonas: Helle, I couldn't agree more. Be seeing you!

Leading questions are sometimes disguised, but they can be readily identified. Review the question and simply look out for any kind of prompt that would have the effect of directing the interviewee towards a particular response. In the first of the practical exercises at the end of this chapter, you are asked to monitor a 'live' interview. It is also possible to learn more about questioning techniques by analysing a recording of an interview, taken from a television or radio broadcast. The analysis grid illustrated below (see Table 11.2), can be used to record the type of question used, noting other interviewer behaviour, such as encouraging, clarifying and summarising. The use of an analysis grid allows for comparisons to be made between the performances of different interviewers, based on these or related criteria. It is only by exploring and practising these skills that you will discover whether, for example, you ask too many closed questions, fail to use clarification questions when faced with ambiguous responses, or have a tendency to ask leading questions. In any event, the keys to more effective interviewing are: to make a conscious effort to listen to the interviewee, focus on their responses and try to keep your opinions to yourself.

The process of questioning can be expensive and time-consuming, requiring specialist staff. Some organisations are experimenting with the use of web-based technologies in order to manage some questioning activities, including those used as part of the recruitment process. Case study 11.3 investigates how 'online recruitment' (OR) technology is being applied.

Table 11.2 Sample grid for analysing interview questions

Questioning techniques					
Open					
Closed					
Probing					
Hypothetical					
Leading					
Related behaviours					
Encouraging					
Clarifying					
Summarising					
Interrupting					

CASE STUDY 11.3

Online recruitment: an effective communication channel?

The use of online recruitment (OR) to attract and screen potential candidates has grown rapidly over the past 10 years, and the Internet is now a widely adopted medium by both recruiters and job seekers within the UK and across the world. Online agencies claim to be more efficient than their 'bricks and mortar' rivals. One chief executive, of the new breed of online recruiters, has argued that 'A face-to-face interview is often not necessary for temporary positions. More important is checking a candidate has the right experience' (cited in Ward 2000: 25). In the UK, online recruitment has become popular for both organisations and candidates. For instance, the CIPD (2006) found that 64 per cent of UK organisations used e-recruitment, suggesting that the growth of the Internet as a recruitment tool has been considerable. Online recruitment has begun to displace other more traditional recruitment methods (Parry and Tyson, 2008). Newspapers, who often depend heavily on this form of advertising revenue, are responding to the threat by providing customers with a combination of print and website advertising. Established recruitment agencies are also moving online, arguing that their combination of virtual presence and physical support services provides an advantage over the newer operators.

There are three main segments of the OR industry: the addition of recruitment pages to existing corporate websites; the creation of specialist web-based recruiters; and the extension of recruitment advertising onto the web. The early users of OR included the IT industry and universities, but this practice has now developed in many sectors. Monster Worldwide, the global leader in the online careers market, reported total revenue growth of 28 per cent overall to $329.0 million in the first quarter of 2007 from $257.0 million in the comparable quarter of 2006 (Onrec.com 2007). Many large public sector organisations use online recruitment and companies generally see online recruitment as being a successful method in the future (Parry and Tyson, 2008). Researchers have identified a number of advantages in OR as a communication channel, including (CIPD, 2006; Parry and Tyson, 2008):

- cost savings over conventional recruiting methods;
- more rapid responses and shorter recruitment cycles;
- access to a wider pool of potential applicants;
- access to higher-quality applicants (e.g. 'passive' job-seekers);
- access to highly specialised 'niche' markets;
- overcoming geographic constraints of international recruitment.

However, there are also possible disadvantages and dangers in adopting this communication channel for recruitment purposes, including:

- excessive response to website advertisements, requiring costly screening;
- under-representation of individuals and groups that are less familiar with web-based technology;
- poorly-designed or maintained websites/interfaces, resulting in the loss of good candidates and damage to corporate reputation;
- costs involved in implementing an effective system;
- ethical concerns arising from transfer of CVs and other personal information in electronic format (e.g. reselling of CVs to other organisations, potential for disclosure to existing employers, etc.).

Case study 11.3 (*continued*)

The limited research conducted to date suggests that for most organisations, the attractions of OR – notably its cost-effectiveness – are beginning to outweigh the disadvantages (e.g. Galanki 2002, Pearce and Tuten 2001). Furthermore, most of these negative factors can be addressed by careful preparation of web-based materials, for example, by providing realistic information in the job and candidate descriptions, and by using interactive tools to encourage self-screening by potential applicants. However, it appears that organisations are not prepared to discard the more traditional methods such as print media and employment agencies. The use of online tools for sifting and selecting candidates early in the recruitment process can allow an organisation to cope effectively with the increased volume of applicants that may result from the move online (Parry and Tyson, 2008).

Online recruitment also offers a number of advantages for the job-seeker, including rapid access to a wider range of job opportunities. The switch to electronic media can mean that a lot of information is stored electronically, and easier to transfer. However, application forms tend to vary between organisations, so there is still no end to the tedious and time-consuming task of filling them out.

Questions

1 Review the advantages and disadvantages of OR, as discussed in the case. Comment on how this technology could either enhance or limit an organisation's ability to communicate in each of the following cases:

   (a) A small or medium-sized enterprise (SME) that is not well known, seeking to recruit someone with very rare and specialist technical skills and knowledge.

   (b) An organisation seeking to ensure that its recruitment policies provide fair and equal opportunities, irrespective of age, gender, ethnicity and (dis)ability.

2 Find examples of the following:

   (a) a corporate website with OR pages;

   (b) an OR website;

   (c) a media website with OR advertisements.

   Compare the OR facilities on each site, assessing characteristics such as the quality of information provided, whether the site is easy to navigate, visual attractiveness and degree of interactivity (e.g. online screening questions).

3 Practise completing an OR application. Compare your experiences with those of colleagues or other students.

Sources: CIPD (2006), Galanki (2002), Parry and Tyson (2006), Pearce and Tuten (2001), Ward (2000), Onrec.com (2007). Case prepared by the authors.

11.5 The interviewee's perspective: making the best of it?

Interviews can be nerve-racking occasions. However, from the interviewee's point of view, the process is best viewed as just another channel of communication. Given practice and preparation, interviews can be handled effectively. In this section we consider everyone's favourite nightmare: the job interview; noting how communication principles can be applied to enhance the impression made by an interviewee. There are a number of things that can be done, both in advance of the interview and on the day itself.

Practice and review

It is worthwhile attending as many interviews as possible, in order to rehearse your interview technique. Mock interviews, ideally with a video recording, are also a useful technique for reviewing your own performance and that of other 'candidates'. The review should cover both the verbal interaction and any non-verbal signals. For example, the camera may pick up nervous habits, such as hand-wringing and ear scratching. There are also many interesting 'fly on the wall' documentaries that follow applicants through the job interviews process. Though the subject specialism may be different (e.g. many documentaries concentrate on the recruitment of doctors and veterinary surgeons), the basic principles are much the same. Use each interview that you go through as an opportunity for learning. This means reviewing your performance objectively. Do not waste time complaining about the way you were treated, but focus on how well you responded to the questions that were asked. If possible, try to get some informal feedback from the interviewer.

Prepare and organise

In a job interview, you are clearly involved in a process of persuasive communication (see Chapter 5). The interviewers are going to be looking for a range of personal attributes (e.g. enthusiasm, social skills, creativity, decisiveness), plus evidence to support your application. Prepare by finding out as much as possible about the subject of the interview, in this case the company and the job itself. Ensure that you are ready to reinforce the information contained in your written application. For example, if your form mentions that you are a keen mountaineer, be ready with anecdotes from expeditions that you have organised. If you have stated a particular ambition, be prepared to explain how you intend to realise it. There are also more practical aspects to consider:

- Do you know how to get to the interview address?
- Have you left sufficient time to cover a delayed train or traffic jam?
- What clothes are going to give the right impression?
- Have the interviewers asked you to prepare a short presentation (see Chapter 12)?

On the day

Always arrive in good time; you may pick up some useful information while waiting for the interview, or simply have a chance to chat to other candidates. When you enter the interview room, always remember to smile at the interviewer(s) and try, if possible, to shake hands. You should be aiming for that difficult combination of calmness and focused attention. When you are asked a question, take a few seconds to consider your answer; that pause always seems far longer to you than it does to the interviewer. Always answer honestly but concisely. Do not be afraid to ask the interviewer to repeat or clarify a question, but avoid doing this too often as it will look as if you are not concentrating. At an appropriate moment, try to insert a few questions of your own. Asking questions about the role for which you are being interviewed and the organisation is essential as it shows you have genuine interest. Make sure that you have some prepared questions; it is perfectly acceptable to have them written down to use as a reference. Good questions to ask of an organisation include: 'What sort of training can I expect to undertake in my first year?' and at later stages of the interview process, 'How will my performance be assessed?' These kinds of question demonstrate your interest, but also provide you with an opportunity to assess the organisation, and how seriously it is taking your recruitment.

If there is good dialogue during the interview, you will probably find that most of your questions have been dealt with. However, a good interviewer will usually close the interview by asking if you have any more questions, so it is a good idea to have another one in reserve; this ensures that you finish the interview with the last question. All the important areas should have been covered by this point, so your question may be something more straightforward. (For example, 'Please can you tell me what the next stage in the interview process is?') When the time comes to leave, do so with another smile and handshake. Avoid the temptation to scramble for your coat and make an undignified rush for the door.

Job interviews as two-way communication: 'taking control'

The idea of an interviewee 'taking control' of the process may sound aggressive and unlikely. However, it is important to see interviews as channels for a genuine two-way exchange of information. In this context, interviewees benefit by recognising that they are in control of their own responses. Interviewees who adopt this view often report that they feel less nervous about the process, and are therefore able to present their case more effectively on the day. Remember that interviewers are also human beings, and that most of them are not actively seeking to catch you out. Taking control means trying to 'help' interviewers to feel more positive about your application. Since they are likely to be meeting a number of other candidates, it is important to give them something – or ideally, several things – that make you stand out from the crowd. With suitable practice and preparation, plus a better understanding of the interviewer's task (see Case study 11.4 at the end of this chapter), the whole process of attending an interview can become more enjoyable as well as producing more successful outcomes. Face-to-face 11 follows the fortunes of a job applicant as he learns through experience how to handle job interviews.

FACE-TO-FACE 11

From 'interview nightmare' to 'dream interview': how I turned it around!

Read the first journal entry by recent graduate Joseph (Figure 11.2) and compare it to your own experiences of attending job interviews. Answer the first set of questions before moving on. Then read the second journal entry (Figure 11.3) and answer the second set of questions.

Face-to-face 11 (*continued*)

12th May 2008

Had a nightmare today! I had an interview for a job that I quite wanted and it went really badly. I think the main problem was that I didn't put enough effort into preparing. I'm studying for my finals at the end of this month and thought I should make them a priority. Also I thought it would be enough to have a good degree from a well-respected university and to know my subject, but they wanted to know all sorts of things about my experiences outside my studies, to find out how well I worked with other people and so on. I had some good examples of being in teams but couldn't provide the depth of evidence that they wanted, to prove that I was a successful leader or a good problem solver. I only realised this when I had a chat with the careers adviser who I bumped into on campus on my way home. I've made an appointment to go and get some advice before my next interview.

The other thing is that the train was delayed and I arrived 15 minutes late, so that got me off to a bad start! The actual interview was in this guy's office. The desk was overflowing with papers and he kept losing my application form and CV – which I'm sure he hadn't read in advance – in amongst other papers. His phone rang twice in the interview – the first time, he looked at the name on the display and ignored it. The second time he actually answered it! He didn't make much eye contact as he was reading my details and this made it hard for me to make eye contact with him. Not sure how else I could have shown I was listening. Then this woman from HR joined us. She really knew her stuff and seemed interested in what I had to say. She asked questions like 'Explain how you would be an asset to this organisation' and I knew that I should have had lots to say but my mind went blank and I couldn't get my ideas in a clear order. She also asked if I was applying for other jobs and I didn't know what to say. So I lied and said no. It finished in quite a hurry. The HR woman asked me if I had any questions and I'd thought of a few on the train but just couldn't remember them. What a disaster!

Figure 11.2 First journal entry by recent graduate, Joseph

Questions (part one)

1 Apart from the suggestions that Joseph makes himself, what other recommendations would you make for Joseph as he: (a) prepares for, and (b) attends his next interview? Compile your ideas in the form of a check list.

2 Look back at previous chapters and identify the main barriers to communication that were occurring in this scenario. You could present these in the form of a two-column list, with the barrier in one column and the scenario example in the other.

Face-to-face 11 (*continued*)

7th June 2008

I got offered a brilliant job today! I only went for the interview yesterday and I thought it had gone well. You know you just get that feeling. I arrived in time to have a chat with the other candidates and the HR woman who was looking after us and I felt quite relaxed. I think that was partly because I'd done a lot of preparation. The careers adviser suggested that I did a mock interview. He videoed it and I took the opportunity to discuss it with him. It was pretty tough, and I hated watching myself giving stupid answers, but it was really useful as things turned out. I realised that I needed to work on listening properly to the questions and taking my time to get my response out in a clear, logical and articulate way. This is because the interviewer would be looking as much at how I communicated as what I communicated – kind of obvious when you think about it! I also focussed on my body language and found that just by sitting up straight, leaning slightly forward, smiling and breathing slowly, I felt more confident and in control.

I realised that those difficult open questions were a chance for me to really impress and stand out from the other candidates, so I prepared responses to a few commonly asked questions like 'What have been your achievements?'. Because I'd spent some time thinking of lots of good examples with evidence to support them, I was confident I could answer other tough questions like 'What are your strengths and weaknesses?' and 'Why do you think we should offer you this job?' I also drew up a list of questions to ask them, and took that in with me. This also helped me to carry out my research on the organisation – I didn't want to ask any questions that I could easily find answers to on their website. I was able to ask questions about a new project that I knew two of my three interviewers were working on, and they seemed to really like that! At the end I asked if they had any reservations about me, and I'm glad I did, because they said they were concerned that I lacked experience. This prompted me to tell them about the experience I had gained on my work placement, which we hadn't really talked about before. It was great – worth all the work!

Figure 11.3 Second journal entry by recent graduate, Joseph

Questions (part two)

3 Identify the main approaches and techniques that Joseph employed to open up communication channels.

4 Do you have any further suggestions for Joseph?

5 Consider your own job interview experiences. (a) How do Joseph's interview experiences compare with yours, or those of your colleagues? (b) What have you learned from his experience, and what are the main action points you will you take away to work on?

11.6   Counselling techniques and the manager

Counselling covers a range of approaches to assisting people, through a process of listening and, in most cases, non-directive questioning. In some approaches, counsellors give specific advice, but in others, the emphasis is on enabling people to take responsibility for the issues they are facing. Counselling techniques are now widely used in organisations, with many training courses being aimed at both human resources (HR) specialists, and others with a general interest in supporting other people, including HR consultants and industrial chaplains (i.e. religious representatives). Managers are often criticised for taking insufficient interest in the problems faced by their staff, either due to time pressures or a reluctance to become involved in the private lives of their employees. While these objections are understandable, human resource specialists are keen to promote 'workplace counselling' as a positive development, benefiting the individual concerned, the manager, and the wider organisation.

Person-centred counselling: the interviewer as facilitator

In what is known as a 'person-centred' counselling interview, the role of the counsellor is simply to listen and to 'facilitate'. Above all, this means that a counsellor should *not* give advice (i.e. should not tell the interviewee how to solve the problem). Instead, the primary objective of counselling is to provide a climate in which the person is able to resolve problems for themselves. However, there are some important obstacles to successful counselling at work. Employees are understandably unwilling to share personal problems with line managers, whilst managers often find emotions difficult to handle, and (as professional 'problem-solvers') are unable to avoid giving advice. Hence, for many practical reasons, the following areas need to be distinguished:

- advice and instruction;
- befriending;
- workplace counselling;
- professional counselling.

During a counselling interview, the counsellor may make use of a range of 'active listening' techniques, of the kind outlined in this chapter. These have been summarised within the counselling field as displaying 'empathy', 'acceptance', 'congruence' and 'concreteness' (Rogers and Farson 1976). In other words, the counsellor seeks to: understand the problem from the other person's perspective (i.e. 'empathy'); avoid making judgments about the person's past actions or intentions (i.e. 'acceptance'); show genuine concern for the person's interests, above those of the organisation (i.e. 'congruence'); and encourage the other person to be more specific, rather than talking about situations that they find difficult in general terms (i.e.'concreteness'). Each of these actions implies particular styles of questioning and other aspects of communication that we have addressed. However, these may not always be present in a manager's repertoire of skills; they may also conflict with the political, economic and cultural climate of the parent organisation.

Counselling and the limits of work-related communication

Counselling is clearly different from giving advice or instructing employees. In practice, it is extremely difficult to switch between these roles, so managers may find their counselling sessions reverting to one of the other standard forms of interaction with employ-ees. Counselling is also a different role from that played by a close friend who takes time to share personal problems, acting as a 'shoulder to cry on'. Perhaps the key distinction for the organisational manager is between workplace and professional counselling. It is essen-tial for all concerned to recognise the dividing line between work-related personal issues, where the manager or human resources department has the relevant skills and experience to handle things, and those more serious problems (e.g. drug and alcohol abuse, clinical depression), which require urgent and professional support. Managers need to recognise the limits of work-related communication, referring cases of this kind to outside agencies.

Summary

- Interviews are a popular two-way communication channel that can help to create shared meanings, but their rich messages are open to misinterpretation. Interviewers can draw on their own prior experience as interviewees.

- Interviews are used within an organisation for a variety of purposes, including: employee recruitment, promotion, appraisal, coaching and mentoring. They are also used to deal with disciplinary problems and grievances.

- Listening is a skill that can be improved with practice. It is important for interviewers to focus attention on what is being said, avoid prejudice, signal interest and encouragement, be aware of feelings and emotion, clarify issues where necessary and summarise discussions.

- It is essential to recognise the differences between open, closed, probing, leading and hypothetical questions, and to make appropriate use of them during interviews. Interviewers should also be aware that interactions and responses are altered by the way they frame and express their questions. Interviewees can also take control in interviews with careful use of questions.

- Interviewees can reduce the inevitable tensions associated with interviews by practising how to handle this communication channel, and by exploiting its two-way features. This involves taking time to consider and respond to the perceived needs of the interviewer.

- Workplace counselling can be a helpful activity, using many of the listening techniques discussed in this chapter. However, counselling requires specialist skills and its use in an organisational setting demands careful consideration.

Key terms

PRACTICAL EXERCISES

11.1 The recorded interview

With the help of a video camera, tripod and recorder, you can practise the roles of interviewer and interviewee. Try to make the setting as realistic as possible by setting up desks and chairs, and by wearing appropriate clothes. Select one of the following scenarios, inventing any incidental details:

● a job interview;

● a promotion interview;

● an appraisal interview;

● a disciplinary interview;

● a research interview;

● a media interview.

Allow five minutes for the interview; play it back and discuss the outcomes with colleagues. Try to identify specific strengths and weaknesses. The interview grid provided in Table 11.2 can be used to record what occurred during the interview.

11.2 Where does it hurt?

The interviewer takes the role of a placement student or volunteer visitor in a hospital. The interviewee is a patient being visited, and takes one of the following roles, or others developed by the group:

● You have suffered a mild stroke.

● You have just had a baby prematurely.

● You are undergoing tests, having had repeated stomach pains.

● You have suffered concussion in an accident and have lost your memory.

The objective is for the interviewer to discover as much as possible about the patient's condition, without upsetting or annoying the 'patient'. Of course, the interviewee should try to be as reticent and unhelpful as possible, providing ambiguous answers or straying from the question. Observers should pay particular attention to the interviewer's use of open, closed, probing, hypothetical and leading questions.

CASE STUDY 11.4

A day in the life of a headhunter

This case study is based on a real-life assignment conducted by an executive recruitment consultancy (i.e. a 'headhunter') on behalf of an international client. It illustrates some of the communication issues that arise in selection interviews. Some of the incidental details have been changed to protect identities.

Setting the scene

My client is the Dutch subsidiary of 'Leisure Shops Europe', a British company looking to recruit an area operations manager. The role is based in the Netherlands and covers a wide geographical area, containing 25 retail outlets and leisure clubs across Northern Europe. The company is going through a major cultural change as it seeks to enhance the

Case study 11.4 (*continued*)

profitability of its retail and leisure portfolio. Consequently, it is in the process of bringing in experienced professionals across all functions. The initial recruitment, at board level, has recently been completed. Apart from the essential requirement of operations management experience in retail/leisure sectors, the candidates for the area operations manager role will need to show excellent people management skills and an ability to be flexible, while the organisation goes through inevitable pains of change. Today I have three candidates for face-to-face interviews. The fourth candidate is currently living abroad, so I will also be conducting a telephone interview this afternoon. We have used a combination of advertising – placed on a recruitment website – and executive search techniques to identify these candidates. I have already reviewed their CVs, which were sent either electronically or by post. Each candidate has been sent a detailed brief about the organisation and the role in advance of the interview. They have also received the ideal candidate profile, reproduced below.

Leisure Shops Europe

Area Operations Manager, Netherlands

The successful candidate will have a minimum of five years multi-site experience of operations management in retail and/or leisure organisations, ideally both. In addition to strong leadership and people management skills, they will be effective in motivating local managers to achieve high standards of customer service. Their personal maturity will enable them to be completely comfortable with the changing nature of the business, drawing on their own previous experience to implement change. They will also be conversant with computerised management information and budget planning/monitoring systems. Food experience (i.e. awareness of food hygiene, health and safety standards and regulations) is not essential, but would be preferred. While there is no requirement to speak Dutch, some language ability would be an advantage. A wide range of development opportunities are available, including free language courses and on-job coaching from language specialists.

Figure 11.4 Extract from an ideal candidate profile

One of the key challenges of this assignment is to find people who are prepared to relocate. There is an attractive benefits package and the company will pay for housing and schooling but I wonder whether the location will put off good candidates. There is no requirement to speak Dutch, but it will help if they have some knowledge or, at least, are prepared to learn.

The interviews begin

Candidate 1: David

David replied to the advert that we placed on the website. He has a background in retail operations together with some food service/catering experience.

David arrives on time at 9.30am. He is smartly dressed, well groomed and is carrying a fairly new leather briefcase. He has a firm handshake and looks me directly in the eyes. He

Case study 11.4 (*continued*)

responds to my questions about his work experience by giving clear examples of situations he has faced and how he has dealt with them. He gives enough detail but appears to be careful not to go on talking, preferring to wait for another question. One of our associates used to work with David's boss and we have been told that a potential area of weakness is in his people management, so I intend to probe this deeply.

He responds well to questions about his management style, dealing with poor performers and redundancy situations, and I am reasonably assured that there is no big hole in this area. Our dialogue is easy and relaxed and he tells me that he is very excited about this job opportunity. He asks me questions about something he has seen on the company's website and about the new strategy which he has read about in an article in a trade magazine. Finally he asks about the next stage of the interview process and I tell him that I have several other candidates to see and will get back to him at the end of next week. The interview has taken one hour and 20 minutes.

Candidate 2: Maeve

Maeve was identified through our executive search process. She has a strong leisure background and has held managerial roles in several international companies.

It is now 11.35am. Maeve arrives a few minutes late and is rather flustered, having got caught up in bad traffic. She is smartly dressed and is carrying a BlackBerry ® organiser, which she places in front of her on the interview desk. She speaks clearly and enthusiastically about her background and previous roles and enjoys telling me in great detail about the development project she is currently working on – how she identified the opportunity, hand picked the team of people she wanted to work with, developed good team spirit and set out innovative ways to set individual targets and incentives for each member.

She appears slightly concerned about the issue of moving her family to Holland, but is keen to stress that her partner, who is German, is very excited about the prospect. She asks a lot of questions about the location and, at the end of the interview, says she is very interested in being put forward to meet the client. I close the interview at 12.45pm. Maeve sends me an e-mail the next day to thank me for seeing her and to confirm an interest in the role.

Candidate 3: Thor

Thor appears on paper to be the perfect candidate. He has both retail and leisure experience, gained in large, well-respected organisations. He is German and speaks five European languages including Dutch. He is married to an English woman who also speaks Dutch, is available for immediate work and happy to relocate.

Thor arrives on the dot of 2.30pm; our appointed hour. He is dressed in a three-piece heavy wool suit and shirt with a stiff starched collar. He is very well groomed and his hair is immaculate. He has a strong (very strong!) handshake and asks for a cup of English tea (black). In asking him to tell me about the jobs he has held and why he moved from the leisure sector into retail, he responds in very short sentences preferring not to expand on any aspect unless I specifically ask him to. When I ask what has been his favourite job and why, he says he has liked all of them. His CV says that he left his last job two months ago. When I ask why (he has already told me he has a wife and four children under the age of five), he says, 'The role was not fulfilling and I needed the space to consider other options.' He also tells me that the area operations manager role is his 'perfect job'. However, what he omits to tell me – and I find out later from the human resources manager – is that he has already applied for a different role with my client's organisation and has been rejected

> ### Case study 11.4 (*continued*)
>
> due to poor perceived cultural fit. We shake hands at 3.35pm. I take a short coffee break and check my e-mails.
>
> *Candidate 4: Sasha*
> *Sasha replied to the advert we placed on the website. She has a managerial background in retail operations and food service experience specifically.*
>
> My telephone interview with Sasha lasts about one hour and ten minutes. She tells me about her background, highlighting why she has made certain career decisions in the past. She is very keen to point out that she enjoys working outside the UK and is looking to find another such position. She says that her current role in Istanbul is coming to an end because the division she heads up is merging with another and the entire management team is being made redundant. Sasha also tells me she is very happy to fly to the Netherlands for an interview at her own expense. She does not appear particularly concerned about the benefits package, which I mention briefly towards the end of the conversation. It is now just after 5pm: time to write up my interview notes and prepare a report for the client, proposing a shortlist of candidates.
>
> ### Questions
>
> 1 What do you think is the headhunter's impression of each candidate?
>
> 2 Identify which candidates more accurately match the job specification and suggest who should be put forward on the shortlist to the client.
>
> 3 How well do you think each candidate has prepared for the interview? Refer to the chapter and support your assessment with examples from the case.
>
> 4 Select one of the candidates and, based on what you know about the headhunter's requirements, prepare guidance notes covering the following points:
>
>   (a) Preparing for the headhunting interview.
>
>   (b) Conduct during the interview.
>
>   (c) Any follow-up actions after the interview.
>
> *Source*: Fictional case study illustrations prepared by Linda J Clark, and based on real-world experience of recruitment consultancy.

Glossary

Interviews have been usefully described as 'a discussion with a purpose'. They serve various purposes in organisations, ranging from recruitment and employee appraisal to marketing research and public relations.

Screening is essentially a *rejection* process. It is used to produce a 'shortlist', reducing the initial numbers to a more manageable size.

Selection unlike screening, is about choosing the most suitable candidate from a shortlist, most of whom could probably do the job very well.

Recruitment interviews involve both an individual, aiming to convince an organisation to hire them, and an organisation, hoping to find and convince the right employee to join them.

Promotion interviews operate in a similar way to recruitment interviews, with internal candidates competing for a more senior post.

Appraisal interviews provide an opportunity for employees to review performance and progress with their line manager.

Coaching and mentoring interviews are a form of on-going developmental appraisal, which are often used with newly appointed and recently promoted staff.

Disciplinary interviews are normally conducted in response to the problematic behaviour of an employee.

Grievance interviews deal with problems that an employee has raised.

Active listening involves observing the other person's behaviours, encouraging them to speak, ensuring that you do not become distracted, and capturing what has been said for future reference.

Counselling covers a range of approaches to assisting people, through a process of listening and, in most cases, non-directive questioning.

Further reading

Burley-Allen (1995) is one of the few straightforward guides to enhancing your listening skills. Most of the leading human resource management texts, including **Torrington** et al. (2010), deal with the operational aspects of recruitment, appraisal, mentoring, disciplinary and grievance interviews.

Healey and Rawlinson (1994) is a recommended contribution on the use of interviews in organisational research.

Galanki (2002) reports an exploratory study into online recruiting in the IT industry, and Parry and Tyson (2008) provide an analysis of online recruitment methods in the UK from an employer's perspective.

Caroll (1996) is a clear and helpful text on workplace counselling interviews. In addition, Chapter 6 includes several references to the concept of 'emotional intelligence' (EQ), which can be usefully applied to interviewing behaviour.

Useful websites

Here are several websites which might be of interest to you. You might like to add some of your own too:

The Skillswise section of the BBC website offers advice on developing effective speaking and listening techniques. (Available at

http://www.bbc.co.uk/skillswise/topic-group/speaking-and-listening
The British Council website provides access to an article, and further reading, that argues that observing and understanding body language is an important dimension of listening. (Available at

http://www.teachingenglish.org.uk/articles/listening-body-language)
The enotes website offers opinion and tips on developing and using listening skills in business. (Available at

http://www.enotes.com/business-finance-encyclopedia/listening-skills-business)

The Guardian Newspaper's Careers Advice section provides guidance on all stages of the application process, including preparing for and attending interviews. Available at

http://careers.guardian.co.uk/

The 'Listening and interpersonal skills' learning area of the LearnHigher project website provides a range of resources for developing active listening skills. (Available at

http://learnhigher.ac.uk/Students/Listening-and-interpersonal-skills.html

References

ACAS (2007) *Producing Disciplinary and Grievance Procedures: self-help guide*. Advisory, Conciliation and Arbitration Service, London. (Available at http://www.acas.org.uk/ index.aspx?articleid=820 (accessed 19 March 2012))

Burley-Allen, M. (1995) *Listening: the forgotten skill – a self-teaching guide*, 2nd edn. Wiley, London.

Caroll, M. (1996) *Workplace Counselling: a systematic approach to employee care*. Sage, London.

Chartered Institute of Personnel Development (CIPD) (2006) *Recruitment and Retention 2006*. CIPD, London.

Galanki, E. (2002) 'The decision to recruit online: a descriptive study'. *Career Development International*, 7, 4, 243–251.

GlaxoSmithKline (2006) 'Corporate responsibility report of 2006'. (Available at http://www.gsk.com/ responsibility/downloads/CR-Report-2006.pdf (accessed 19 March 2012))

Hall, E.T. and Hall, M.R. (1990) *Understanding Cultural Differences*. Intercultural Press, Yarmouth, ME.

Healey, M.J. and Rawlinson, M.B. (1994) 'Interviewing techniques in business and management research', in Wass, V.J. and Wells, P.E. (eds) *Principles and Practice in Business and Management Research*. Dartmouth Publishing, Aldershot, 123–146.

Hook, C., Rollinson, D., Foot, M. and Handley, J. (1996) 'Supervisor and manager styles in handling discipline and grievance: part one – comparing styles in handling discipline and grievance'. *Personnel Review*, 25, 3, 20–34.

Onrec.com (Online Recruitment Magazine) (2007) 'Monster Worldwide Reports First Quarter 2007 Results' (Available at http://www.onrec.com/content2/news.asp?ID=16456 (accessed 30 September 2007))

Parry, E. and Tyson, S. (2008) An analysis of the use and success of **online recruitment** methods in the UK. *Human Resource Management Journal*, 18, 3, 257–274.

Pearce, C.G. and Tuten, T.L. (2001) 'Internet recruiting in the banking industry'. *Business Communication Quarterly*, 64, 1, 9–18.

Rogers, C.R. and Farson, R.E. (1976) *Active Listening*. Industrial Relations Center, University of Chicago, Chicago, IL.

Rollinson, D., Hook, C., Foot, M. and Handley, J. (1996) 'Supervisor and manager styles in handling discipline and grievance: part two – approaches to handling discipline and grievance'. *Personnel Review*, 25, 4, 38–55.

Saunders, M.N.K., Lewis, P. and Thornhill, A. (2003) *Research Methods for Business Students, 3rd edn*. FT Prentice Hall, Harlow.

Torrington, D., Hall, L., Taylor, S. and Atkinson, C. (2010) *Human Resource Management*, 8th edn Pearson Education, Harlow.

Ward, A. (2000) 'Online job sites challenge dominance of traditional media'. *Financial Times*, London edition, 25 (15 March).

Wass, V.J. and Wells, P.E. (eds) (1994) *Principles and Practice in Business and Management Research*. Dartmouth Publishing, Aldershot.

Chapter 12

Presentations and audio-visual technologies

Your brain starts working from the moment you are born and never stops until you stand up to speak in public.

Sir George Jessel, politician and public speaker

Learning outcomes

By the end of this chapter you should be able to:

- identify the distinctive characteristics and requirements of oral presentations in various organisational settings;

- prepare yourself and your materials in advance of delivering an oral presentation;

- develop effective techniques for recalling the content of oral presentations;

- assess the advantages and disadvantages of audio-visual technologies and associated communication practices;

- deal with the practical challenges relating to the delivery of oral presentations, including timing, questions, disruptions and facilitating interaction with audiences;

- consider the additional communication issues raised by presentations delivered in culturally-diverse contexts, such as international conferences.

12.1 Introduction

People find themselves on the receiving end of all kinds of presentations. For example, you may have listened to various academic lectures, political speeches and team briefings. Presentations are also widely used by organisational managers and senior executives to brief various stakeholder groups, including employees, financial analysts and journalists. In larger international organisations, presentations are often relayed electronically, either as video recordings or as 'live' webcasts, in order to reach staff located around the world (Jones 2003, Turban 2003). Students also find themselves giving presentations as part of coursework exercises. They are also an increasingly common element in organisational recruitment programmes, running alongside more conventional selection techniques, such as interviews (see Chapters 11). However, despite its popularity, the presentation remains a very troublesome communication channel. Everyone has experience of sitting through badly-delivered presentations, while the prospect of actually delivering a presentation can often cause an otherwise self-confident person to collapse into a major panic. The dread of addressing an audience is also common amongst experienced managers, and is itself one of the primary causes of poor communication. Nervous presenters commonly resort to reading out pre-prepared scripts, and their audiences are forced to endure a dry and monotonous performance that communicates very little.

Many people owe their career success to their ability to give good presentations, despite the fact that they are a major source of anxiety for most of us initially. As with any behaviour-based skill there are those who are 'gifted', but that doesn't mean that effective and charismatic public speaking and presentation skills cannot be learnt. Through learning the techniques, you'll also develop the ability to understand how the communication process works, so that you can adjust your approach to suit your purpose.

This chapter aims to help you improve your own public speaking and presentation skills, and those of others in your organisation. It includes advice on preparing yourself and your materials in advance, using audio-visual equipment and handling an audience successfully. Case study 12.4, at the end of the chapter, deals with the additional challenges of presenting to international and culturally-diverse audiences. However, first we begin by considering the distinctive characteristics of this communication channel.

12.2　What makes presentations different?

In the past, the fundamental feature of this communication channel was physical presence; the sender and the receivers were together, in one room. With the expansion of electronically-mediated presentations, this does not necessarily apply to all presenters. However, in many cases, these also include a 'live' audience in the room where the presentation is being filmed. When confronted with a sea of faces, whose expressions are generally difficult to interpret, presenters may feel vulnerable and exposed; but giving a presentation can be seen as placing the presenter in a position of considerable power. There are few forms of communication where an audience is so entirely 'captive'. By **captive audience** we mean that, in contrast to people reading a report in their office or at home, those on the receiving end of a presentation have virtually no control over the process. More specifically, they cannot easily:

- stop or 'pause' the communication flow;
- return to or re-read an earlier part of the message;
- look up an unknown technical term in the dictionary;
- scan through and skip ahead to the end.

This means that you are even more responsible for orientating, guiding and taking care of your audience's needs because they are much less in control than when they are reading (Levin and Topping 2006). Also, because they are members of an audience, rather than solitary individuals reading a piece of written text, the receiver's power to take control is constrained by the disruption that it would cause for everyone else listening to the presentation. Consequently, most people, other than a few strong-minded individuals, experience group pressure to allow the presentation to continue. If they want to review or clarify parts of the message, this has to wait until the end of a talk. While this may seem to put the presenter at an advantage, the resulting lack of understanding, and related frustration, can become major barriers to communication. In short, it is not sufficient for presenters to rely on the fact that their audience is captive. Presenters also need to ensure that people are both willing and able to absorb their messages, and in many cases, to use the channel interactively:

- Willing to receive? This is a useful point to review the material on persuasive communication (see Chapters 5 and, in particular, section 5.3 on rhetorical argument). Consider the best ways of securing the attention of your audience and holding their interest through the presentation. Though presenters often want to avoid too many questions, particularly during the presentation itself, questions can be a useful way of maintaining interest and involvement. It can be helpful to advise your audience when you would like them to ask questions, for example, all the way through or at the end.

- Able to receive? Since audiences have little or no control over the information flow, it is important to allow pauses between your main points, avoiding information overload (see section 2.2). It is also important to provide appropriate signposting. **Signposting** is used to orientate your audience by reminding them of where you have just come from and where you are going next, and how your points link together. For example, you might signpost by saying 'Now that I have given a brief overview of the three key problems, let's move on to the possible solutions.' It offers the equivalent to the headings, sub-headings and contents page of a written report. Presenters can outline the overall framework at the beginning, include frequent reviews as they proceed, and summarise their key arguments at the end.

- Achieving interaction? There are a number of ways to stimulate two-way communication in a presentation. For example, the presenter can pose questions or ask for the audience to express its opinion through an informal vote (or 'show of hands'); or the presentation itself can be organised in a way that allows for a period of informal discussion. (In some academic conferences, this process is formalised by appointing a 'discussant', who comments on the preceding presentations, and may attempt to draw out some common themes).

The remaining sections of the chapter consider the practicalities of preparing and delivering a presentation. We begin with the task of preparing the necessary materials to convey the written and spoken messages that will be delivered in the presentation room.

Figure 12.1 The use of signposting is recommended

12.3   Preparing the presentation materials

Though it makes use of different media, the supporting materials for a presentation share many of the features of a written report, and both communication channels serve similar purposes (e.g. providing briefings, reporting results, making proposals). As a result, the overall process of preparation is much the same, whether you are communicating through a written report or combining written and spoken words in an oral presentation. For this reason, the following points are essentially a brief summary of the discussion in sections 9.3 to 9.6, which detail the main stages in researching and organising source material, and converting it into a suitable format for delivery. In preparing the materials, the presenter's main tasks can be summarised as follows:

- Answer four key questions: Who is your audience? What is your objective? What is the context? Which sources will you draw on as evidence?
- Clarify the terms of reference/project brief.
- Decide what to include and what to exclude.
- Decide how to organise the material.
- Make the logical structure visible.

You may need to repeat several stages of this process as you develop and refine your presentation.

Early on in the planning stage, Davies (2010) urges presenters to consider the audience's starting point, with regard to your topic, and the finishing point that you would like to get them to. Two key questions to ask are:

What do the audience think and feel prior to your presentation?

and

What do you want them to think and feel as a result of experiencing your presentation?

Davies (2010) recommends creating a *Micro-Statement;* a sentence that encapsulates the purpose of your presentation. This *Micro-Statement* should then be the foundation on which the content is built; all evidence presented should support it, or be excluded, and everything said to the audience should persuade them to accept and act on the *Micro-Statement*. For example, the Micro-Statement for my next presentation might be:

This organisation could increase its sales significantly if we began using social media tools, Facebook, Twitter and LinkedIn, to engage with existing and potential customers.

To test out your Micro-Statement ask yourself 'if the only thing that the audience remembered was this Micro-Statement, would that be a good enough result?' (Davies 2010: 50).

If the presentation is to be accompanied by a written report, it is important to ensure that the written version complements what is being presented in the oral presentation, rather than simply repeating it. The presenter needs to decide (or confirm) in advance whether the written report is to be circulated before or after the presentation, as this is likely to influence the content and structure of both elements. For example, if the audience has already had a chance to read the written report, the presentation provides an opportunity for discussion and focusing on specific issues of interest. However, if the written report is distributed afterwards, the presentation may work best as a 'broad brush' introduction to the topic, with the written version providing supporting detail. Incidentally, distributing the full written report at the start of an oral presentation is usually fatal; the audience will invariably become distracted, reading the report rather than listening to the speaker.

Sound preparation of the material is, of course, essential to the success of your presentation. However, presenters should put just as much effort into preparing themselves for the occasion. This is especially true if they are relatively inexperienced in this communication channel. Few of us are 'natural' presenters. Fortunately, as the next section discusses, there are some useful 'tricks of the trade' that can help to make the exercise more enjoyable, for presenters and audiences alike.

12.4 The presenter: posture, appearance, voice and memory

Many people, who are happy to spend hours working with a computer software package to perfect their presentation slides and graphics, fail to invest more than five minutes on the most important communication tool of all – themselves. Presenters are rather like athletes, needing a well-organised training schedule to reach competition standard. In this section we work on four of the most common areas where there is a need for improvement: the way people stand in front of an audience; their physical appearance; the way that they speak; and how they manage to remember what to say.

Exploiting non-verbal cues: improving posture

Presenters are sending out messages from the moment the audience first catches sight of them. These initial messages are based on your non-verbal signals (see section 4.8). Many speakers adopt a head down, round-shouldered stance when addressing an audience which may be because they are relying too heavily on their notes (see Figure 12.2). This has two powerful and wholly negative effects. First, the voice is projected into the floor, which makes it inaudible, particularly in a larger room or where the presentation is being relayed electronically. Second, a presenter adopting this posture is bound to have minimal eye contact with their audience. Both the posture and the lack of eye contact are often regarded as defensive responses, resulting from nervousness or lack of confidence in the material being presented. Other defensive gestures include:

- leaning on one foot;
- trying to blend in with the background, by standing at the side, or behind items of furniture; and
- folding the arms tightly across the chest, a symbolic gesture to protect the person's 'soft underbelly' from attack.

The audience may perceive these gestures in various ways. For example, they may be interpreted as suggesting that the presenter is ill-prepared, hostile or simply uninterested in the topic or the audience. To communicate clear, confident and positive messages, it is essential that presenters use non-verbal cues in ways that reinforce, rather than undermine,

Figure 12.2 An ill-prepared, disorganised presenter

their personal credibility. For example (see Figure 12.3), the appropriate posture is likely to be:

● upright and well balanced;

● stable, but not static, allowing for some movement around the room;

● moderately relaxed, but conveying energy rather than apathy.

Figure 12.3 A well-prepared, relaxed presenter

Achieving this kind of balance and flexibility requires considerable practice, in a number of different situations. It may also be necessary to consider the cross-cultural aspects of these non-verbal cues (see the case study at the end of this chapter). Practical exercises, and careful reflection on the outcome, can be undertaken in seminars, with colleagues, and as part of a 'real world' situation (see the practical exercises at the end of this chapter). Presenting is much like any sport or performing art, with gradual improvements, some stunning successes and the occasional unexplained disaster. Skills can only be developed and refined after repeated cycles of experience and reflection. However, over time, most 'reflective' presenters begin to feel more confident, positive and alert to the needs of their audience.

Physical appearance: clothing as a non-verbal signal

A presenter's choice of clothing can help to project the right image, as well as increasing self-confidence. However, there are no fixed rules regarding physical appearance. In the past, some organisations had notoriously strict dress codes, but today there is much greater diversity. As in all areas of communication, presenters may want to consider what messages their clothes are going to communicate to a particular audience. For example, the same expensively tailored suit could impress a group of overseas investors, make little impression on other executives, but completely alienate a group of employees who are being briefed on a major programme of cost-cutting and rationalisation. In this particular context, you need to balance your own comfort with playing the role that the audience expects of you. Clothing is relatively easy to change, so this non-verbal cue is at least worthwhile considering. However, having weighed up the arguments, presenters may simply decide to dress in the way that they feel most comfortable.

Developing the human voice

Though our voices are in regular use every day, they are not always ready for the tougher demands of an extended oral presentation. In contrast to informal one-to-one conversations, the presenter has to speak:

- for an extended period;
- in a fairly structured way;
- to many different people simultaneously;
- sometimes in a large venue, possibly with poor acoustics;
- louder and with more deliberate ennunciation.

Human voices are rarely inherently weak, but in many cases they are seriously underused in day-to-day activities. Speakers who attempt to address a large audience without practising their vocal delivery are in danger of mistreating their vocal system. If we made a comparison between this system and a sports car, they would be attempting to break the speed limit, without realising that it is necessary to get out of first gear. As Case study 12.1 suggests, in order to make more effective use of the human voice, we need a basic understanding of how it functions.

Having considered how the voice is generated, and how the basic delivery can be improved through physical exercises, presenters can begin to make tangible improvements in their public speaking. The next stage involves working on four main dimensions of vocal delivery – setting the volume, varying the pitch, pacing the delivery and exploiting the pauses.

Vocal mechanics: a practical introduction

The human vocal system involves a complex set of interactions, between the brain, which co-ordinates the activity, and various parts of the body, as illustrated below (Fig 12.4). The lungs are the real powerhouse, responsible for generating the human voice. When people breathe in, they are drawing fresh air into their lungs by tightening the diaphragm: normally an entirely unconscious action. Breathing out is a reversal of this process; the muscles relax and air flows out through the narrow trachea (or 'wind pipe'). The voice is created when air passes up the trachea and over the vocal chords, causing them to vibrate. These vibrations are amplified in the hollow areas of the mouth, the pharynx and the sinuses. They are formed into different words and paralinguistic sound, as a result of intricate movements made by the jaw, lips, tongue and teeth.

All of this activity is normally undertaken with little conscious attention being paid by the person speaking. Most voices can be improved, for public speaking purposes, by a combination of deeper breathing and a more active use of the mouth. Taking deep breaths ensures a better airflow, which converts into improved tone and greater projection (i.e. the voice 'carries' over a longer distance, so that it can be heard by everyone attending the presentation). Clear and well-projected voices are particularly important if the acoustics are poor, or if members of the audience are unfamiliar with your language (see Case 12.4 at the end of this chapter). Voice and singing coaches encourage students to breathe from the diaphragm (the area located above your stomach), an action that is much easier when the person is standing upright, with a relatively straight back. Opening and closing the mouth more deliberately helps to ensure that individual words are spoken clearly, as can greater movement of the tongue. Again, this can be practised, ideally with the assistance of a coach. The primary objective of vocal exercises of this kind is not to alter the normal speaking voice, or to remove a local accent, but simply to upgrade the voice for the greater demands of public speaking.

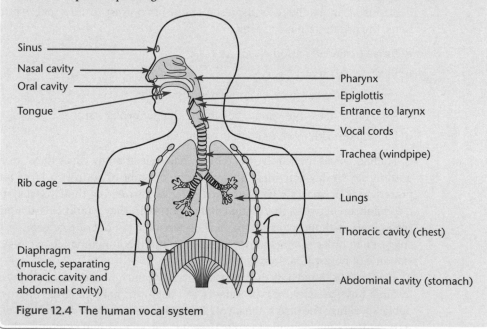

Figure 12.4 The human vocal system

Case study 12.1 (*continued*)

Questions

1 Do the physical aspects of vocalising really make such a difference? Read the following sentence out in your normal voice:

> 'Speech is an extremely complex cognitive and mechanical process, which appears to be unique to the human species.'

Now repeat the sentence three times, making the following changes:

(a) Do not allow your lips to touch.

(b) Do not move your tongue.

(c) Pinch your nostrils shut.

2 Comment on how these extreme cases might relate to some of the more common weaknesses found in what you would regard as ineffective public speaking voices.

3 It seems likely that vocal delivery styles are shaped by a number of different socio-cultural factors. Try to identify five likely influences on the employees of an international organisation. Would it be appropriate to encourage all employees to develop their voices in the ways outlined in this case?

Setting the volume

When members of the audience are unable to hear the presenter's words, there is a fundamental breakdown of communication. Yours could be the most interesting presentation ever, but if the audience cannot hear you they will lose interest. In practice, speakers are more often too quiet than too loud. Clearly, the volume level has to suit the venue and size of your audience. Ask a friend or colleagues to stand at the back of the room while you do a sound check. Some venues may provide electronic amplification, but it is ultimately the presenter's responsibility to ensure that everyone is able to hear clearly. Having established a suitable volume, the presenter should try to maintain it. All too frequently, an inexperienced person is asked to 'speak up', but after a few sentences the voice drops back to an inaudible level. While the volume level should be constant for most of the presentation, key points may be emphasised with either an increase or a decrease in volume. Variations of this kind, and others discussed in this section, serve a similar purpose to upper case letters or italics in a written report; they draw attention to specific words or phrases.

Varying the pitch

A speaker's natural voice may be a shrill soprano or deep bass, but it is still possible to use variations in tonal range to good effect. In general, presenters convey a more 'positive' message when sentences end on a higher note. However, this inflection can sound as if you are asking a question, rather than stating a point, and can suggest uncertainty. Doing the opposite tends to colour the message with a down-beat and depressing quality. Experience suggests that people find it very difficult to judge the way that they use pitch. In addition, some people have a lively and varied pitch in everyday conversation, but revert to either a constant high pitch or monotonous drone when they are speaking in public. Consequently, it is essential to obtain the advice of a colleague or friend, who has observed you during several presentations. Variable pitch makes for a much more engaging, and therefore persuasive, presentation. Pitch can also be used, in conjunction with the other variables discussed in this section, to underline particular points. For those with extremely monotonous delivery (i.e. with no perceptible variation in pitch) the answer is to make a special effort, with practical exercises, in order to achieve a greater variety.

Pacing the delivery

Everyone knows that the major fault of nervous and excited presenters is speaking too quickly. However, despite this high level of awareness, many presenters continue to make this mistake. Painfully slow delivery is an equally serious obstacle to good communication, especially when it is accompanied by a monotonous vocal style. To keep an audience interested, the best option is to vary the pace of delivery, avoiding either of these extremes. Almost all presenters, including the author, have made the mistake of including too much material in their presentations, and have then compounded the error by attempting to cover all of this material, even though there is clearly insufficient time. The best way to avoid this mistake is to plan ahead, ensuring that the content of the presentation is tailored to the time available. If it turns out that there is still too much to cover (e.g. if the start of the presentation has been delayed by a technical failure, or previous speakers have over-run their allotted times), it is always better to edit out some of the material. Unfortunately, most speakers are insufficiently flexible, and attempt to cover everything at a rapid pace, so losing their audience's attention. Having established a reasonable pace, it is also worth introducing a little variety in order to maintain interest and to highlight key points. Switching from longer to shorter sentences is one simple technique that can help to vary the pace of delivery.

Exploiting the pauses

The so-called 'dramatic' pause can work equally well in the theatre, comedy venue or conference room. Depending on its length, this little piece of silence is the oral equivalent of a comma, semi-colon or full stop. Pauses can be used to separate different ideas and to emphasise a particular argument. Longer pauses are very valuable, yet rarely used; they allow both audience and speaker some much-needed thinking time to absorb ideas or ponder questions. The silence created by a pause can have the effect of regaining attention. It is important to remember that a single pause will seem much longer to the presenter than it does to the audience. Consequently, presenters may need to force themselves to wait, before ending the silence and moving on to the next point. Skilled speakers can exploit (or 'milk') their pauses. Typical techniques include:

- using the pause to build eye contact with the audience;
- appearing to be lost for words, but then returning with a major piece of the argument;
- adding to the dramatic effect by simply walking silently from one part of the room to another.

Each of these elements can be used to introduce more variety into the spoken message. By using them in combination, presentations can be much more powerful, holding the attention of the audience and ensuring that the content is more persuasive and memorable. Aim to introduce vocal changes gradually, and record your voice, to monitor how your public speaking voice is developing.

Remembering what to say

A stage actor's greatest fear is 'drying', meaning to lose track of the script and forget what to say next. Humans have a great capacity for memorising information, but our capacity to remember can be undermined by the adrenaline rush that often accompanies the start of a presentation. There are four main options for ensuring that the presenter remembers what to say:

- reading a prepared script;
- memorising a prepared script;
- improvising on the day;
- using a prompting system, with key words, cue cards or similar devices.

It is worth reviewing these options and assessing them from a communication perspective. However, only the final option can be recommended for regular use.

Reading a prepared script

Nervous speakers often make the mistake of reading from a prepared script, on the basis that it gives them added reassurance and eliminates the risk of forgetting what to say. However, with rare exceptions, this tactic results in a very ineffective mode of delivery: the presenter's head is usually directed away from the audience, so the volume is inadequate; there is very limited eye contact and minimal use of gestures to reinforce the message; and the vocal style is likely to lack pace and pitch variation. Some politicians and business leaders have perfected the appearance of spontaneity when using prepared scripts. However, this is usually the result of extensive training. Scripted presentations can also be assisted by display technologies, in which words from an autocue are projected onto glass screens, placed either side of the podium. By glancing from one screen to the other, speakers can retain greater eye contact and give the impression of simply turning to address each side of the hall. However, this technology is not available in most organisations, and reading from a computer laptop is no substitute. With limited exceptions, such as brief introductory speeches, formal declarations and quasi-legal statements, it is best to avoid scripted presentations. If you do need to refer directly to text in a document, make sure the text is of a large font size, is well-spaced between lines and does not go to the bottom of the page, as this will result in you dropping your chin, restricting your vocal chords.

Memorising a prepared script

A few exceptionally gifted speakers can memorise the text of their presentation as though it was the script of a play. However, in an organisational context, a memorised speech can easily sound artificial. It is also a highly inflexible system, and you can be caught out when the presentation is opened up to questions or needs to be shortened due to time restrictions. Although it may be effective for short statements and introductions, unassisted memorising is not a practical option for most people. While Davies (2010) does not advocate writing a verbatim script he does recommend writing a *baseline text* that contains about 70% of the words in your presentation. He suggests that once written you should read this several times out loud, then prune it.

Improvising on the day

This is a valuable technique for informal occasions, such as making speeches at the office dinner. Some improvisation is also necessary, and occasionally very impressive, as part of a question and answer (Q&A) session, where the audience has an opportunity to respond to the presentation and the speaker needs to deal with unanticipated issues. In practice, while many contributions give the appearance of being an improvised response, they are often based on a great deal of preparatory work. As part of the planning process (see section 12.6), experienced presenters will prepare outline responses to cover all of the most likely questions or counter-arguments that are likely to arise from their presentation.

Using a prompting system

The use of key (or 'trigger') words combines the reassurance provided by a script with the flexibility of an improvised presentation. As a result, it is the most practical option for most presenters. It is still important to prepare the presentation material in a fairly detailed and structured way, particularly where there is an accompanying written report. However, prompting systems work on the assumption that, having become fully immersed in the subject, the presenter can 'trigger' recall of more extensive arguments using a fairly short list of key words or phrases. These are sometimes written on a series of cue cards, usually postcard-sized, which are tied together in case they are inadvertently dropped on the floor. Alternatively, some presenters rely on the key words that they have included as 'bullet points' on the slides that accompany the presentation. Additional notes (such as statistics or quotes) may usefully be typed into PowerPoint's Notes pane, directly beneath the slide and printed out for you to quickly consult during the presentation. In many cases, presenters find that they have very little need of the prompts, because the underlying messages are fresh in their minds. By contrast, if presenters spend too much time checking their prompts, the presentation begins to suffer from similar problems to those associated with reading a prepared script.

12.5 Audio-visual equipment and communication practices

As previously discussed (see Chapters 4), **visual aids**, such as photographs, diagrams and graphs, aid communication with your audience by attracting and maintaining their attention, aiding comprehension, evoking emotions and supporting memory retention. (The more senses brought to bear on a new idea the better an individual's ability to make sense of it.) In the case of oral presentations you might also exploit the use of audio recording and video to engage and stimulate your audience. Audio-visual (AV) equipment and materials should be considered as supporting technologies; they can enhance a good presentation, but they cannot cure a bad one. In addition, technical errors, breakdowns and crises can often undermine an otherwise satisfactory delivery. It is clearly important to plan and prepare AV materials in advance. However, as we noted previously, this should not be at the expense of preparing the presenters themselves (see sections 12.3 and 12.4). The following headings summarise the main AV technologies in use in organisations today, including their distinctive strengths, weaknesses and peculiarities. It is therefore worth experimenting with these technologies and associated communication practices, in order to become aware of the options available, and to develop the capability to select and employ them effectively.

Projectors (data and OHP) and visualisers

Traditional overhead projectors (OHPs) are occasionally used to present prepared transparencies containing text, illustrations and photographs. It is also possible to write directly

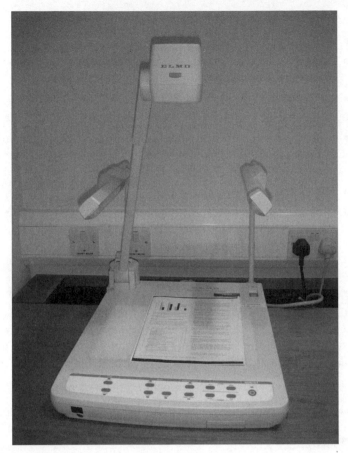

Figure 12.5 A visualiser

onto transparencies with a suitable pen during the presentation to capture the audience's ideas or to better explain a concept in response to questions. In most organisations, OHPs have been replaced by data projectors, which are used to display images directly from a computer system to a display screen. When it is useful for an audience to see text, images or diagrams from documents, visualisers are now often used for projection (see Figure 12.5). These work by projecting a videoed image and have the added advantage of being able to magnify text and allowing the presenter to project 3D objects and props.

Computer-based projection has many advantages, including:

- the capacity to insert hyperlinks in the presentation text, which allows the presenter to break from the conventional, linear format of the presentation;

- the option of linking to other computer-based sources, including web pages, video clips and spreadsheets, and the related possibility of incorporating presentation materials into a video-conference or webcast;

- the luxury of being able to make last-minute changes to a presentation.

However, there are inherent dangers in presenters becoming over-reliant on the presentation software that is used with this technology (see Case study 12.2).

Limitations and user errors include the following:

- standing in front of the display screen;
- using the slides as a script, meaning that the audience is ahead of you, as they can read faster than you can speak;
- talking to the projector or laptop, instead of the audience;
- displaying slides that do not coincide with, or contradict, the spoken delivery;
- using too many software features or too much text; it is important to keep slides simple, ensuring that the text is large enough to be visible from the back of the meeting room, and to use colour and graphics in moderation;
- not checking for spelling errors;
- technical failures: it is always advisable to have a contingency plan, an electronic copy of the presentation on an alternative data storage device (e.g. an extra, memory stick) and a paper copy of the presentation.

Whiteboards

These are a common teaching aid, also useful in organisational discussion and 'brainstorming' sessions, for building up spider diagrams and making rapid changes to the material presented. The presenter can make use of coloured pens to highlight issues (e.g. using alternate colours when listing points). Electronic whiteboards allow the presenter to capture written material, including the contributions of others, directly onto a computer system.

Limitations and user errors include the following:

- presenters turn their backs on the audience while writing on the board, making them difficult to hear; the solution is to practise writing from the side of the board while facing forwards;
- many presenters have illegible handwriting; this also requires practice;
- dried out pens: do not rely on those supplied at the venue, have a functioning set available;
- using indelible pens by mistake: a very common error that makes the presenter very unpopular with the next user.

Flip charts

These are a very simple, paper-based system that can be used for pre-prepared sheets or for writing 'live'. They are useful for group work (e.g. where your audience has an active role; where a small group gathers their ideas on a flip chart sheet that can be shared by the whole group); sheets can also be retained and pinned up around the room for future reference. You can impress an audience by preparing flip chart diagrams beforehand in pencil, so that you can quickly ink them in during the presentation.

Limitations and user errors: similar to those for the whiteboard, plus the challenge of removing paper and returning to previous flip chart pages; this is simply a matter of practice.

Using video

Short video clips can be very useful to illustrate a point. Showing longer clips (over 10 minutes) may have a role in communicating particular messages, but it can be counter-productive if it takes time away from a 'live' presentation; the video element can generally be made available for viewing at other times. You should download and save any internet-based video footage in advance, rather than relying on accessing it direct from the internet during your presentation. Remember that much video footage is subject to copyright, so you should check that you are permitted to play the selected video clips.

Limitations and user errors include the following:

- technical faults due to incorrect set-up or tampering by other presenters;
- incompatible playback formats or poor internet connection;
- inappropriate use during a 'live' presentation.

Props and 'take aways'

The term 'props' originates in the theatre; in a presentation it refers to additional materials that are used to enhance a presentation and reinforce key messages. Props come in all shapes and sizes, ranging from food samples to scale models of building developments. In some cases, the presenter may also wish to provide the audience with materials to take away after the presentation. These could include:

- an information pack containing supporting details;
- paper or electronic copies of the presentation slides, transcript or a related report;
- a product or design model; or
- simply a 'goodies bag' of product samples.

Limitations and user errors include the following:

- handing out material at the beginning of a presentation encourages the audience to look at it instead of focusing on the presentation;
- not letting your audience know that you will be circulating handouts, so that they feel frustrated and try to scribble down their own notes;
- lots of time taken up by audience passing the props around to examine, which distracts them from listening to you;
- inappropriate materials, including expensive brochures that the audience is not likely to read.

Case study 12.2 reports on a phenomenon that is sometimes termed 'death by PowerPoint', referring to the way that many presenters misuse this internationally known audio-visual aid, and in doing so manage to create some of the world's most tedious and unsuccessful presentations. Misuse of PowerPoint begins right from the planning stage. Despite the reputation in the digital world of former Apple CEO and renowned presenter, Steve Jobs, he was a strong believer in planning on paper, before even opening the presentation software (Gallo, 2009). Like many effective presenters he knew that it is the 'story' that you tell and the argument that you present that will engage the audience, not the presentation software (Gallo, 2009). So if you plan to use it, avoid the temptation to open the presentation software until you have fully explored your ideas, researched your material and organised your presentation's structure.

CASE STUDY 12.2

Anti-PowerPoint Revolutionaries Unite

This case is based on an article that is highly critical of the world's most popular presentation software package.

Last week I saw two women getting into a cab outside an office in central London. Both were in high heels and smart suits and were struggling with a flip chart, its pages flapping in the wind. The quaint sight of the large pad on aluminium legs filled me with longing for the days when people giving presentations wrote things down with felt pens on big sheets of paper.

I might have forgotten this scene, were it not for the fact that the very next day I was sent an invitation to join a brand new political party in Switzerland, the Anti PowerPoint party. "Finally do something!" its slogan says.

Actually I've been quietly doing something for years: I've been declining to learn how to use the ubiquitous piece of software. As a presenter, I'm a PowerPoint virgin, though as an audience member I've been gang raped by PowerPoint slides more times than I can count.

And what have I got from the experience? It is hard to say because my default reaction has been to blank it. I can't remember one single slide that I've ever been shown. And as I must have been shown hundreds of thousands of them altogether, a hit rate of zero seems rather on the low side. This doesn't mean I've never sat through a good PowerPoint presentation. But when I have, it has been because the person speaking managed to get a message across despite the distracting visual clamour going on behind them.

The Anti PowerPoint party has attempted to calculate the economic damage of gawping at all these slides and has concluded that Europe wastes €110bn a year from people sitting though dull presentations.

I suspect the true figure is even worse, as this ignores the secondary effects. PowerPoint must be the least enjoyable way of wasting time there is; a heavy slideshow can leave one feeling grumpy and passive and in no frame of mind for proper work.

Worse, it lowers the quality of discussion and leads to bad decisions. PowerPoint performs the miracle of making things simultaneously too simple and too complicated. It reduces subtle ideas to bullet points, while it encourages you to pad out a presentation with irrelevant data because cutting and pasting is far too easy.

The APPP is hoping to fight PowerPoint through peaceful means; it wants lots of journalists to write articles just like this one. Even if lots do, I hold out little hope of success. The seminal, devastating article on the subject, PowerPoint is Evil, was written by Edward Tufte in 2003 and published in Wired. And what has happened since then? Nothing, except that PowerPoint has gone on getting bigger.

Re-reading that article, I think Tufte was a bit soft on his target. He said PowerPoint presentations were "like a school play – very loud, very slow, and very simple". In fact they are far worse than that: school plays tend to be amateurishly charming and there is generally someone on the stage who you love.

Persuading everyone to stop using PowerPoint is going to be much harder than persuading them, say, to reuse plastic bags or get the loft insulated. People cling to it for three powerful reasons. First, because everyone else does. Second, because it is much easier than writing a proper speech, where you have to think carefully about what you are saying ahead of time. Third, and most important, PowerPoint assuages speakers' nerves – standing in a room with low lights, dumbly following prompts on a screen is not all that frightening.

To have any chance of success the APPP needs a terrorist faction, which would advocate cutting the wire in the middle of the table that connects the laptop to the projector.

Case study 12.2 (*continued*)

Or it could help people tamper with slides, inserting at random ones that said: "HERE IS ANOTHER DULL SLIDE" or showed a picture of people fast asleep.

Better still would be to campaign for an outright ban. In a world without the crutch of PowerPoint, presentations would be fewer in number – people would be put off by nerves and by the hard slog of preparation – and shorter. It might even mean that audiences listened. The human voice, especially when connected to a brain that has done some thinking, and a body that has done some rehearsing, can be a wonderful, memorable thing.

Ten days ago I went to a show in London called *True Stories Told Live* in which six people stood up and held forth without visual "aids". The subjects weren't promising – one spoke for 10 minutes about a cup of tea. But I can repeat his story to you now, which is much more than I could do about a PowerPoint presentation I saw the following day about women on boards, about which I remember only one thing: bone-crushing tedium.

Questions

1 Review the article and identify the criticisms of software-based presentation techniques.

2 Compare the list to your own experiences of similar presentations, either as the presenter or a member of the audience. Do you support the views given in the article?

3 What are the potential advantages of using software, such as PowerPoint, to support a verbal presentation?

4 Prepare and deliver two versions of your own five-minute presentation, covering the three previous questions. One version should make use of a software programme, while the other uses only 'manual' techniques. Look back at section 12.3 and create a Micro-Statement for your presentation. Compare audience responses to the two presentations.

Source: Kellaway (17 July 2011). Copyright Financial Times Limited. Reproduced with permission.

12.6   On the day itself: final preparations

This section assumes a 'worst case' scenario: you are giving the most important presentation of your life to a large audience of colleagues, senior managers and international visitors. The venue is an international hotel in a foreign country, neither of which you have visited previously. How can you maximise your chances of success and minimise the risks of a disaster? The scenario may not be typical for all presenters, but the underlying lessons would also apply more generally.

- **Checking the venue:** On arrival at the venue, you have a number of very basic practical questions to ask, including those on the following checklist: In which room is the presentation to be held? Is the room well sign-posted? Are there enough chairs for all of the expected attendees, plus a margin of error? Is there adequate lighting, ventilation, heating? Have the organisers scheduled refreshments, and at what time? If the venue is a large hotel or conference centre, there will probably be specialist staff to help with all of these issues. While liaising with these people can provide useful information and assurance, it is not sufficient. Even in the best-organised venue, you should always check the rooms in person, and at the earliest opportunity.

- **Checking audio-visual equipment and materials:** Again, experienced presenters learn that it is never a good idea to rely entirely on others, however competent and reassuring they may sound. It is good practice to request an early opportunity to check that the AV equipment is working properly, and that your own equipment can be combined with that provided by the venue. In an international setting, the most likely sources of technical problems include: incompatible hardware and software, translation errors and differences in power sockets and voltages (see section 12.5).

- **Checking your personal appearance:** All presenters should try to leave enough time for some last-minute grooming, especially if they have spent the previous hour carrying computers and audio-visual equipment between buildings. The key is to find a suitable mirror and assess whether you are still looking reasonably tidy and relaxed (see section 12.4).

- **Making a good entrance:** This is likely to be the time when you are most nervous, yet your audience's first impressions are likely to have a strong influence on their perceptions of the presentation. Some presenters recommend that you breathe deeply for a short period before taking up position. This simple technique can be remarkably calming and can also help to improve your vocal delivery (see section 12.4). It is tempting to rush into the opening sentence, but experienced speakers take their time to look slowly and calmly around the audience. This helps to establish eye contact with the audience, a positive signal that can be reinforced by taking up a confident stance and giving other non-verbal cues, including a smile. This initial activity may appear superficial, but it does help to create a perception of the presenter as a credible and potentially interesting source of information. It also allows the audience to settle down, and to adjust themselves to the person who is now centre stage. If you are being introduced, you then need to thank the person concerned, focus on the audience and begin your presentation.

The final section of this chapter reviews the four key elements of the presentation:

- creating an 'opener';
- signalling transitions and changing pace;
- closing the presentation;
- dealing with questions, interruptions and dialogue.

However, before moving into the delivery phase, Case study 12.3 considers the most common and problematic issue facing presenters on the day itself: dealing with stage-fright.

CASE STUDY 12.3

Beating stage fright: 'fight or flight' syndrome

Why do many people get in such a bad state before a presentation, and during other forms of public speaking (e.g. at a wedding reception)? The explanation can be traced to human physiology; greater awareness of the underlying cause can also help people to isolate and deal with the immediate symptoms. These physical and psychological experiences occur because the body is trying to prepare itself to deal with an imminent crisis. Much of this is driven by the body's release of adrenaline, though cognitive factors also play a part in this process (Schachter and Singer 1962, Parkinson 1987). The experience of 'stage fright', also referred to as 'fight or flight syndrome', occurs when a 'closed circuit' is set up within one

Case study 12.3 (*continued*)

branch of the autonomic nervous system (Gross 1996: 99–102). Fight or flight syndrome is an essential survival aid that we have inherited from our mammalian ancestors. However, this mechanism is of very limited value in the average presentation room. Its adrenaline-induced symptoms include:

- increased heart rate and higher blood pressure;
- heightened awareness, as the body gives priority to the sensory organs (e.g. dilation of the pupils to aid vision);
- dryness in the mouth, as the secretion of saliva is suppressed;
- excessive sweating and temporary memory loss, which may be a side-effect of these adaptations.

Perhaps the most inconvenient response is an urgent need to urinate, as the bladder muscles relax; this may also be explained as part of the body's preparation for dealing with the physical demands of defending itself against an attacker, or escaping to a safer location. With practice it is possible to overcome fight or flight syndrome, or at least to exert some control over symptoms. Presenters can minimise the fears that help to generate this response by ensuring that presentations are well-rehearsed and that they are familiar with any audio-visual equipment and materials. On the day, a combination of controlled slow breathing and positive thinking can be surprisingly effective.

It is advisable to avoid stimulants like coffee, and also to keep away from the bar. Alcohol is a depressant, reducing activity in the central nervous system. In small quantities it may help to relieve anxiety, but drinking also slows the reactions, impairing a person's overall performance. A better option is for presenters to find a quiet corner and spend a few minutes visualising themselves giving an excellent presentation; many professional performers have noted that establishing a positive mind-set can encourage the right kind of physiological response. There are also various training courses in which participants engage in a structured series of exercises, such as reciting poems, to overcome their fear of public speaking (Grenby 2003).

Questions

1 What is your experience of the 'fight or flight' response? Have you found it to be a problem in giving presentations, or in other forms of public speaking?

2 How useful do you think it is for people to be aware of the physiological causes? Can they really be overcome by using the suggestions given in the case study?

3 Can you identify any other contributory factors that might explain why some people experience stage fright to a greater extent than others? (Note: It may be interesting to compare your responses to these questions with those of colleagues or friends.)

Sources: Schachter and Singer (1962), Parkinson (1987), Gross (1996), Grenby (2003). Case prepared by the authors.

12.7 The presentation: four key elements

This section focuses on the delivery of the presentation, though the issues raised here need also to be considered at the planning stage. It suggests that presenters need to pay particular attention to four key elements. Three of these follow the structure of the presentation, from the opening words, to the way that transitions are made between each topic area, and finally to the best technique for drawing the presentation to a close. The fourth element concerns the way that presenters deal with questions, both during and after the presentation. Case study 12.4, at the end of the chapter, deals with some additional issues, relating specifically to presentations conducted in an international and culturally diverse setting.

Creating an 'opener'

How do you secure the audience's attention? As with all communication channels, the answer can be found by thinking from the receiver's perspective. In this case, the audience will want to be assured about two aspects of your presentation. First, that your message is relevant to them. Second, that you have the necessary credibility to deliver it. If either of these aspects is missing, the task of communication will be much harder. Imagine, for example, that your organisation is struggling to meet a 'sustainability' target, set as a result of discussions with external stakeholders. Your task is to talk to a group of office managers about reducing waste paper disposals across the organisation. They are all very busy people, the waste target appears marginal to their main work responsibilities, and they have attended the meeting reluctantly. What kind of opening statements (or 'openers') might you use in order to get this audience on your side? In reviewing possible solutions, it is important to remain flexible and sensitive to the local context. Many popular guides to delivering a 'winning' presentation claim to have identified the ideal recipe for this kind of communication challenge. In practice, it is always a matter of professional judgement, on the part of the presenter, drawing on the general principles developed in previous chapters.

The following examples illustrate some of the options available to the presenter in our scenario.

- **Pose a question that has relevance for the audience:** 'Let me begin by asking you all a question: how much do you think our organisation spends on waste paper, in one year?'

- **Create a powerful scenario, using visual imagery:** 'Imagine a warehouse about the size of a football pitch, and ten metres high. In six months, we will fill that warehouse with scrap paper.'

- **Quote a statistic that is likely to surprise the audience:** 'Last year, our organisation was spending in excess of £300 per employee on waste paper alone. This year we intend to halve that figure.'

- **Share an informal anecdote or narrative to surprise or entertain:** 'I was chatting to a manager from our Nairobi office last week. They have problems similar to ours, when trying to meet the sustainability targets. Eventually, we got around to this waste paper issue. "Yes" she said, "we were in a similar position, but now we've got the solution." "So tell me, what's your secret?" I enquired. "Well", she replied, "after considering a number of options . . . we bought bigger recycling bins!"'

- **Refer to a relevant and memorable quotation:** 'You probably remember our founder, Matt Schaebitz, saying "Saving a few cents in the organisation is better for business than taking the same money from our customers' pockets." So, making more money out of waste inside the organisation, and keeping our external prices competitive: that is exactly what we're here to discuss today.'

Presenters normally follow their opening statement with a brief explanation of who they are, if this is unclear to the audience, and what they are going to cover during the presentation. While this may seem like background information, it also has an important persuasive role, emphasising what members of the audience will gain by listening (see section 5.2). To recap an earlier point, there must be a perceived benefit for them and, in addition, the presenter must be perceived as having the relevant skills or knowledge to help them secure that benefit. For example, in continuing the waste reduction talk, the presenter might say:

> **'For the last three years, I have been working with each of the organisation's national subsidiaries to introduce our new environmental strategy. Of course there have been some teething problems, but we are now seeing a measurable reduction in waste. This morning I am going to discuss five simple and practical ways that you can reduce your office stationery costs, without affecting staff performance.'**

The purpose of this statement, in addition to setting out the structure of the presentation, is to secure the audience's attention. The presenter has calculated that the prospect of relatively painless cost savings should be sufficiently attractive to keep the office managers listening for the next few minutes.

Signalling transitions and changing pace

Presenters can easily lose their audience's attention by moving too quickly from one topic to another. It is essential to remember the inherent limitations of this communication channel and take time to emphasise transitions between each of the main points that you cover (see section 12.2). One of the most useful ways to guide an audience is to give a brief recap of the last topic. Having completed the recap, the presenter pauses for a few seconds before introducing the next topic. The signalling of transitions can be reinforced using non-verbal cues. Presenters can move to another part of the platform, make a symbolic gesture, or introduce an audio-visual prompt, such as a photographic image or an artefact. For example, in the waste paper scenario, we might imagine the presenter introducing the topic 'Practical solutions for reducing waste' by showing a short video extract that demonstrates a new recycling system. If there is more than one presenter, switching between you to signal a change in topic or focus can provide a powerful audio-visual cue for the audience. Regular transitions and frequent changes in the pace of delivery also help to keep an audience alert and interested.

Closing with a flourish

Closing statements are the equivalent to the concluding section of a written report, where the presenter draws the arguments together and attempts to ensure that the audience has absorbed them. It is an opportunity to remind everyone of the initial purpose of the presentation, and to summarise the key points, showing how they combine to achieve that purpose. In a live presentation (i.e. where interaction is either face-to-face or electronically-mediated in 'real time'), the presenter can make use of the distinctive features of this communication channel, discussed in section 12.2, to secure a degree of commitment and action from the audience. In communication terms, this requires a strong persuasive element, where the presenter injects energy and motivation (see Chapters 5). For example, in the waste paper scenario, the presenter might take the opportunity to interact directly with the office managers, challenging them to respond with proposals on how the new recycling system might be implemented in their own departments. In some situations, it may be appropriate to split the audience into groups, as in a traditional university seminar, setting a task and asking each group to report back. This modifies the primarily 'one-way' characteristic of the communication channel, and can allow for genuine dialogue, based on an agenda outlined by the presenter. The final element in the presentation discusses the ways that presenters handle questions from the audience, the most common basis for interaction in this communication channel.

Handling questions, interruption and dialogue

Presentations have a tendency to revert towards a 'one-way' channel, primarily because this is easier for the presenter to handle. Interaction, in the form of questions and other kinds of disruption, is more challenging for the presenter, but these can be essential if the channel is to operate effectively. Questions, whether during or after a presentation, provide presenters and audiences with the chance to engage in a dialogue. In some cases, presenters may decide to initiate the questions as part of their delivery. For example, the idea of opening the presentation with a single question can be expanded, so that the audience is asked to answer several questions in the form of a 'quiz'. (Note: Each person notes the answers individually, the 'answers' are not given at this stage.) The presenter has selected the quiz questions to highlight key points to be made during the presentation. After the quiz, members of the audience are already alert to these themes, and may also be eager to discover whether they have answered the relevant questions correctly.

Audience response systems, similar to those used by the studio audience in the popular television programme 'Who wants to be a millionaire', are being used increasingly by organisations to enhance presentations. Audience members, in response to a question displayed by the presenter, press a button on a handheld device, that corresponds to what they think is the right answer, or their preferred opinion. The systems are designed to encourage interaction, and enable presenters and audience members to identify response patterns.

Presenters need to make clear to the audience whether they are happy to take questions during the main period of delivery. The obvious advantage in deferring questions until the end is that the presenter can side-step unwanted interventions and keep the delivery on track. Unrelated or poorly-worded questions can disturb the presenter's train of thought and distract the audience. However, a few well-handled questions during the presentation can be valuable, confirming that there is a degree of shared understanding between presenter and audience. In a longer presentation, a series of intermediate questions can also be used to signal transitions, as well as bringing much-needed variety.

Sometimes presenters get the uncomfortable feeling that they are 'losing' their audience. This is usually signalled by a number of verbal and non-verbal cues. There may be some talking or whispering, and a distinctive pattern of body language and facial expression (i.e. several people are leaning back in their chairs, eye contact appears to lessen and presenters may detect a phenomenon that was once termed 'EGO', meaning 'eyes glazing over'). It is important not to ignore this kind of disruption, because it is signalling a communication barrier. Experienced presenters display flexibility in order to overcome this barrier, deviating from the 'script' and taking control of the situation. For example, they may decide that the best course of action is to pause at the end of a sentence, look around the room, and ask for questions or opinons.

Open questions are generally the most effective in stimulating audience participation and feedback (see section 11.4). It is also advisable to allow members of the audience to discuss the question first, rather than asking for an immediate response – and then facing an embarrassing silence. Returning to the waste paper scenario, the presenter might say, 'OK, I see a few sceptical expressions out there. What I'd like you to do now is to spend five minutes with the person sitting next to you, discussing the following issue . . .'. By altering the pattern of interaction, the presenter is allowing the audience time to recover, in the hope that this restores interest and brings the presentation back on course. The alternatives to using questions within the presentation are to introduce a short break, or to think seriously about shortening the remaining sections and bringing the delivery to a prompt but dignified close.

Many presenters find it difficult to switch smoothly from 'delivery mode' to engaging in an active dialogue with their audience. In part, this is due to a lack of self-confidence on the part of the presenter, who feels a need to retain control of the communication channel by maintaining its 'one-way' emphasis. Presenters can begin to resist the temptation to retain control through careful preparation. This involves trying to predict the kinds of questions that might come up and having a number of prepared answers in mind, and available through techniques such as 'cue cards' (see section 12.4). Handling questions from the floor can be particularly difficult in large audiences, where it may be difficult to provide microphones. One option is to ask questioners to stand up and introduce themselves. This gives the rest of the audience time to adjust to the person's speaking voice. The presenter should try to retain some control of the interaction, though this involves some difficult judgments. For example, at first sight it may seem reasonable to ask the questioner to stand up, to be brief and to speak clearly. However, the implication is that presenters are seeking to exclude those who lack the self-confidence or the language skills required to meet these requirements. In other words, they are opting for a rather narrow definition of 'effective' communication, prioritising clarity of expression over quality of interaction (see section 2.5). There is no easy solution to achieving an appropriate balance within the constraints of the organisational setting. However, presenters can make useful interventions, such as attempting to restate the question before giving an answer. This helps to ensure that the presenter has interpreted it correctly, and also gives other members of the audience a second opportunity to hear what has been said.

Question and answer (Q&A) sessions can pose three main problems for presenters. First, they may simply be unable to give an answer. Second, they may know the answer but consider that it is of little interest to other members of the audience. Third, they may know the answer but, for various reasons, be unwilling to give it. In each case, honesty is usually the best policy. In the first case, it may be sufficient for presenters to state that they do not have an answer to hand, but will obtain one if the person can provide contact details after the presentation. Alternatively, the presenter may be able to pass the question on to someone else in the room. In the second case, where the question is either highly specialised or of limited general interest, presenters can make it clear that they do have an answer, and will be pleased to discuss it with the questioner at the end. In the third case, where giving the answer would, for example, be embarrassing to members of the audience, or would breach some kind of confidentiality agreement, the best option is for presenters to state that they are either unable or unwilling to respond to that point at this time, giving whatever justification they consider to be necessary. Giving false information, or being 'economical with the truth' (i.e. using language carefully to encourage a false impression in the audience) in these situations may be unethical and also illegal. Given the free flow of information in most organisational contexts, the tactics of deception or distortion are also likely to be little more than a short-term fix, leading to greater difficulties in the future (Bird 2002, Bowie 2002).

Face-to-face 12 highlights some of the additional challenges involved in preparing and delivering group presentations at university. It also identifies some of the benefits that can be obtained, if the people concerned manage to get themselves organised before the event.

FACE-TO-FACE 12

Group presentations: getting your act together

Karin has just left her intercultural psychology lecture, where she and her fellow students were briefed on a group presentation that they need to prepare this term. She goes to the coffee shop, buys a coffee and begins e-mailing her old school friend, Lena, who is studying medicine in their home country, Sweden (see Figure 12.6). Lena then e-mails a reply (see Figure 12.7).

Hi Lena

It was great to see you over the summer! I hope your new term is going well. I have been enjoying getting back into my studies, until today, that is! We've just found out that we have to do a group presentation for our intercultural psychology module. This is my favourite subject and I know I could do a better job on my own!

My previous experience of doing a group presentation here was a bit of a disaster, with all the work being done by a couple of people (including me) and nobody turning up to the practices. Then we had arguments on the day when the pressure mounted up – people couldn't remember what they planned to say, or the order we would speak in, the audio-visual aids wouldn't work properly and I had to answer practically all the questions from the lecturer! Then in the end we got a worse grade than I could have got on my own! I'm really fed up!

You always have lots of good ideas! What would you do???

Take care
Karin

Figure 12.6 Karin's e-mail to Lena

Hi Karin

Sorry to hear that you are feeling down. I know what you mean about group presentations – it always seems to involve a lot of extra work just getting other people organised! My advice would be to take advantage of the fact that there is more than one presenter, rather than seeing this as a disadvantage, and do things that you couldn't do on your own. Having more than one presenter can make things more interesting for the audience because they get a variety of voices, faces and perspectives, which holds their attention and helps them to

Face-to-face 12 (*continued*)

distinguish between the separate sections. You need to get the transitions between presenters right though! It works really well if one presenter recaps their bit and then introduces the next person by making links between their two sections. This takes a bit of rehearsing!

Something else that works well with a few people is a role play. So you each act out a different character and use yourselves as audio-visual aids, I guess! For example, we have problems here getting our audience to discuss complex topics like medical ethics, so we use a role play to simulate a question and answer session, with one character asking another character the kinds of questions that the audience might have. This warms up the audience and then they ask some questions themselves!

I have also seen it used when people in the audience need to learn how to deal with sensitive situations, like breaking bad news to patients. This group acted out a scenario and it gave us, as the audience, a chance to get an insight into the different perspectives, and to begin to empathise with all the people involved. Then we evaluated how well we thought they'd handled it and offered suggestions for how we would act in such a situation. This is a serious example, but it can also be used to add humour too.

I found this useful handout on using role plays on the Internet – http://www.brunel.ac.uk/learnhigher/giving-oral-presentations/Roleplay.pdf

Hope this helps!
Good luck
Lena

Figure 12.7 Lena's reply to Karin

Questions

1 Do you agree with the advice that Lena has given to her friend Karin? What additional or different advice would you give to Karin about organising group presentations?

2 How might you make use of the advice that Lena has given when preparing and delivering your own presentations? What might you do differently on the basis of her suggestions?

3 What is your opinion of the use of humour in presentations?

Summary

- Organisations make extensive use of presentations, which range from informal face-to-face briefings to electronically-mediated webcasts.

- The oral presentation has the potential to be a rich, two-way channel, but presenters need to take account of its distinctive characteristics, including the inability of most audiences to stop, repeat or scan the flow of information.

- The content of presentations can be planned, much like a written report, taking into account factors such as whether the audience will have access to an accompanying report or hand-out, and whether to make use of audio-visual aids to reinforce verbal messages.

Summary (*continued*)

- Preparatory tasks include paying attention to physical issues, such as appearance, posture, voice and memorising information. In general, presenters should avoid both prepared scripts and pure improvisation. Cue cards or bullet points on presentation slides can help to trigger recall.

- It is important that the selection and use of audio-visual aids is appropriate to the type of presentation and the needs of the audience. Presenters should become familiar with their technical strengths and weaknesses, including their impact on communication practices.

- Practical arrangements at the venue – including rooms, equipment and refreshments – can have a major effect on the presentation. It is always advisable to check these details in advance.

- There are four key areas to address during the delivery of a presentation: establishing a compelling opening; signalling transitions and changing pace between major themes; concluding the presentation; and handling questions, interruptions and dialogue.

Key terms

Audience response systems 332

captive audience 312

Closing statements 331

Visual aids 322

Signposting 313

PRACTICAL EXERCISES

12.1 Presentation skills – self-assessment and critique

(a) Think back to the most recent talk or presentation you have *delivered*. Make notes on the following: How did it go? What do you feel were your main strengths and weaknesses? What areas would you most like to improve?

(b) Now think of the most recent talk or presentation you have attended as a member of the audience. Make a second set of notes on the following: How well did the speaker communicate his or her messages? Were you clear about the structure and objectives of the presentation? In what ways could the speaker's performance have been improved?

(c) Compare your two sets of notes. Identify examples where either you might learn something from the other presenter, or vice versa.

Seminar option: If you are working in a group, discuss your experiences, as outlined in questions (a) and (b). What are the major presentation strengths and weaknesses within the group? How do these compare to those of the presenters you have listened to recently?

12.2 Look confident, feel confident

This is a practical exercise, which should ideally be conducted in a small group setting. If possible, make a video recording to demonstrate the 'before and after' effect and to provide a basis for discussion and reflection. Some alternative exercises are included on the companion website and in the tutor's guide.

(a) The 'before' test: Walk to the front of a class or meeting room and introduce yourself to your colleagues as though you were beginning a presentation on a topic of your choice. (Note: A 30-second introduction will be sufficient.)

(b) The practice session: Make a conscious effort to stand upright, with both feet flat on the floor. Loosen up your head and shoulders; gently 'shake out' any tension in your neck and arms so that you are not standing there like a mannequin. Settle down with your shoulders back, your head centred and your chin up. Breathe slowly and deeply before you begin to speak.

(c) The 'after' test: Following the practice session, repeat the exercise adopting the upright stance and taking a few deep breaths before speaking. You should notice the following improvements:

- Your lung capacity is increased, so your voice is more resonant.
- Your voice projects impressively, and is not lost in the floor.
- You have better eye contact with your audience than the floor.
- You feel happier and more 'in control' of the situation.

(d) Consult the audience: Did they perceive you as more confident and competent, second time around? Check whether you over-did the upright stance. It will *feel* very strange to you at first, but should *look* perfectly normal to them. Continue practising until you reach a happy compromise.

12.3 Getting the foundation right

Next time you're required to prepare and deliver a presentation, refer back to section 12.3 on preparation. Begin by making notes on the following questions:

(a) What do the audience think and feel prior to your presentation?

(b) What do you want them to think and feel as a result of experiencing your presentation?

(c) What is your *Micro-Statement* (Davies 2010)? (In a sentence, sum up the purpose of your presentation and what you want the audience to do as a result of it.)

CASE STUDY 12.4

'LOGOS 2012': the diary of an international conference delegate

This case is a fictionalised account of experiences at an international research conference, 'LOGOS 2012', which attracts more than 800 researchers, policy-makers and practitioners from around the world. The conference runs over two and a half days, with presentations delivered in a number of 'parallel sessions', running simultaneously in different lecture rooms. It tells the story of Siobhán, a conference delegate from Dublin. It is her first major conference, and she has decided to keep a diary on her Smartphone, which she e-mails to her partner each evening.

Monday 14th: two nightmare presentations today . . .
This is a big conference! It's amazing how many people are interested in 'Learning organisations, governance and strategy'. The opening speaker was a local politician, who spoke

Case study 12.4 (*continued*)

mainly about what a really great city this is, and how we should all be considering the attractive foreign direct investment opportunities. 'What, on my salary?!' I thought, as I browsed through the conference handbook. (Note: They have also provided an electronic version on the conference website, containing all of the papers, but I haven't managed to download it to my Smartphone; so much for compatibility!)

I have sat through two *nightmare* presentations today, plus one that was really rather good. Yes, I quite enjoyed the first talk this morning. The speaker seemed very confident and managed to make a lot of bold statements. He also kept us amused with some humorous anecdotes about his old college professors. He was talking about the rivalry between the major 'Ivy League' universities and something about 'trophy' professors being traded like soccer stars. For some reason, he didn't have a copy of his paper in the conference proceedings, and there wasn't much information on his presentation slides. I managed to note down a few of the ideas, nothing very original, but it seemed to be in the same area as my own research. Perhaps I will e-mail him later to request a copy of the paper.

At the coffee break I got stuck in a long conversation with a social psychologist from Slovakia. My first attempt at 'networking' went quite well, but it meant that I had to run all the way to the next parallel session. I chose the session on the subject of 'Technology and learning', mainly because it was being held in the nearest lecture room. This proved to be a big mistake! The first speaker, who I quickly renamed 'The Whisperer', spent the entire 15 minutes of her presentation with her right hand over her mouth. She also spoke in a very quiet voice; so quiet that I could hardly detect her accent, though I guess from the contact details that she was probably Vietnamese. Fortunately, 'The Whisperer' had produced some fairly clear presentation slides, with plenty of paper copies, so I managed to get to grips with her basic arguments.

My final speaker was probably the worst. Professor Jangler is one of the most famous people in his field, and I was very keen to hear what he had to say about organisational learning and feedback processes. Unfortunately, this man has a nervous habit of playing with the keys and coins in his jacket pocket. It made a *terrible* noise that was picked up by his microphone and amplified very effectively around the room. Occasionally, it seemed as though he was going to stop rattling the keys. For a few precious minutes, everyone in the audience could relax a little and try to concentrate on what the professor was saying. But then there was another loud rattle and we all got distracted again. To make matters worse it sounded like he was reading his presentation word for word from the draft copy of his upcoming book, rather than delivering a purposely prepared presentation.

Tuesday 15th: the day war broke out!

Well, quite an exciting day, though perhaps for the wrong reasons. I was the second speaker in one of the early afternoon sessions. Fairly nervous, of course, but I was following your advice and trying to keep myself calm and focused. The first speaker in my session finished his presentation. I noticed that he had been speaking rather quickly, and when I looked up from my notes, all I could see was the back of his head. Of course, I was so busy doing my own last-minute preparations that I had no idea what he had been saying! Anyway, I was just about to get up and check that my presentation was loaded properly on the laptop when someone in the audience stood up and started to make an impromptu speech! I think the man was French, possibly Belgian, and this is roughly what he said:

'I am sorry, but I must interrupt. I think we need to remind everyone that this conference is an *international* event. The common language may be English, but for most of us this is a second, third or even *fourth* language. Some of the English-speaking presenters, especially some delegates from North America, Australasia and the UK, seem to have forgotten this

Case study 12.4 (*continued*)

essential fact. We are getting *very tired* of you speaking too fast, with not enough clarity, and using your local phrases and humour that nobody else can understand. You know, it is much easier to follow the other 'non-English' speakers; for example, the woman from Latvia, who spoke on Monday. I must say that this is extremely arrogant behaviour on your part; it is a kind of imperialism that you are showing towards us! We demand that you show other nations proper respect and courtesy.'

There was loud applause, then everyone became *extremely* quiet. Of course, I had to break the silence. I decided not to reply directly to 'The Speech', but was extremely careful to speak clearly, and to avoid those idiomatic phrases. I even cut out my little joke about the Irish pub at Moscow airport, just in case somebody was confused or offended. You know, it made me think again about that 'good' speaker I mentioned in yesterday's e-mail. Sure, I enjoyed his talk, with all of the humour and smart remarks. But now I am asking myself whether other people felt the same way, given what the French guy was saying earlier on. It's the conference dinner this evening, so I will try to get some informal impressions from some of the other delegates.

Wednesday 16th: the conference dinner

What a dinner! Far too much food, course after course, followed by what seemed to be an endless succession of very formal speeches, each of which had to be translated into English. I ended up on a table full of Brits and New Zealanders, who got very drunk and started passing notes around the table; it seems that someone was trying to form an escape committee. All very entertaining, no doubt, but it would have been good to find out what people really thought about 'The Speech'.

Questions

1 Prepare a list of what you consider to be the five 'worst' presentation practices referred to in the case.

2 Outline the main communication problems that you would associate with each of the practices on your list, and suggest how they might be overcome.

3 People often say that the most important form of communication at international conferences is the informal 'networking' that takes place during coffee breaks, or in the bar. Why do you think this may be the case?

4 Prepare a short (maximum 900 words) guide for LOGOS members, entitled: 'Advice to international conference delegates: the conduct of presentations'. The guide should pay particular attention to the issues raised in 'The Speech'.

Source: Fictional case prepared by Tina Fawcett and Richard Blundel.

Glossary

captive audience By captive audience we mean that, in contrast to people reading a report in their office or at home, those on the receiving end of a presentation have virtually no control over the process.

Visual aids, such as photographs, diagrams and graphs, aid communication with your audience by attracting and maintaining their attention, aiding comprehension, evoking emotions and supporting memory retention.

Closing statements are equivalent to the concluding section of a written report, where the presenter draws the arguments together and attempts to ensure that the audience has absorbed them.

Audience response systems are being used increasingly by organisations to enhance presentations.

Further reading

Most of the literature on presentations comprises 'how to' guides and lists of techniques, such as **Janner** (1989) and **DiResta** (1998).

Jay and Jay (1996) is an entertaining yet useful source.

Levin and Topping (2006) offer very comprehensive and friendly guidance covering all stages in preparing and delivering presentations.

Stott, Young and Bryan (2001) is particularly strong on the development of argument and the art of rhetoric.

Davies (2010) uses a motivational coaching style to present a systematic approach to preparing yourself and your presentation.

McCarthy and Hatcher (2002) and **van Emden and Becker** (2010) are useful for presenters delivering in educational contexts.

Murray (2003) focuses on preparing and performing in viva examinations.

There are also many practical manuals on the use of presentation software packages; these have not been listed due to their rapid updating. Research in this area has tended to concentrate on the use of particular technologies in presentations. There is also a great deal of research into the use of lectures in the teaching and learning literature. Beyond this, however, there has been rather limited reflection on the nature of communication in this channel, compared to that for meetings, for example. A review of literature on oral communication practices in universities can be found at http://learnhigher.ac.uk/Staff/Oral-communication.html in the *Theoretical Underpinning* section. Additional references are provided in other chapters, relating to particular aspects of the oral presentation. These include: Chapter 3 (use of spoken and written language in presentations and supporting materials); Chapter 4 (visual aspects of presentation, including graphics used for presentation slides and non-verbal communication related to both the speaker and audience); Chapter 5 (use of persuasive communication in a presentation); Chapter 6 (securing feedback from a presentation audience); Chapter 9 (combining oral presentations with written reports); Chapter 13 (using presentations as part of a meeting).

Useful websites

For this topic in particular, access to video footage offered by the Internet is invaluable for evaluating and learning from other people's presentation style. Here are several websites which might be of interest to you. You might like to add some of your own too:

Bradford University's Effective Learning Service offers a booklet 'Giving presentations' to help you develop skills for delivering effective individual or group presentations, including advice on controlling anxiety. (Available at

http://www.brad.ac.uk/acad/management/external/els/pdf/presentations.pdf)

Brunel University's website on 'Preparing and giving oral presentations' includes guidance on all stages of the process and an extensive collection of video footage of student presentations from a variety of subject areas and levels of study. It also includes suggestions on how to use PowerPoint effectively. (Available at

http://www.brunel.ac.uk/learnhigher/giving-oral-presentations/)

The LearnHigher 'Making groupwork work' project website comprises video footage, including video diaries, and practical tips and resources for developing group oral presentations. (Available at

http://www.learnhigher.ac.uk/groupwork/)

The Open University website includes a very comprehensive section on 'Giving presentations' with particularly useful suggestions for developing and using visual aids. (Available at

http://labspace.open.ac.uk/course/view.php?name=LDT101_10_2.9)

You will find examples of the inspirational presentation style of former Apple CEO, Steve Jobs, via YouTube (Available at http://www.youtube.com/). It's worth taking note, in particular, of the way he interacts with his visual aids, conveys his enthusiasm and engages his audience.

References

Bird, F.B. (2002) *The Muted Conscience: moral silence and the practice of ethics in business*. Quorum, Westport, CT.

Bowie, N.E. (ed.) (2002) *The Blackwell Guide to Business Ethics*. Blackwell, Oxford.

Davies, G. (2010) *The Presentation Coach: bare knuckle brilliance for every presenter*. Capstone Publishing Ltd., Chichester.

DiResta, D. (1998) *Knockout Presentations: how to deliver your message with power, punch, and pizzazz.* Chandler House Press, Madison, WI.

Flintoff, J-P. (2002) 'A case of visual aids disease'. *Financial Times*, London edition, 13 (9th October).

Gallo, C. (2009) *The Presentation Secrets of Steve Jobs: How to be insanely great in front of any audience*. McGraw-Hill, New York.

Grenby, H. (2003) 'Six ways to overcome your fear of public speaking'. *Harvard Management Communication* Letter, 6, 3, 3–5 (March).

Gross, R.D. (1996) *Psychology: the science of mind and behaviour*. Hodder & Stoughton, London.

Janner, G. (1989) *Janner on Presentation*. Random House, London.

Jay, A. and Jay, R. (1996) *Effective Presentation*. FT Pitman, London.

Jones, J. (2003) 'Using webcasts to inspire staff at the New York Times Company'. *Strategic Communication Management*, 7, 3, 14–17.

Kellaway, L. (2011) 'Anti-Powerpoint Revolutionaries Unite', *Financial Times* 17 july. Avilable at: http://www.ft.com/cms/s/0/059e

Levin, P. and Topping, G. (2006) *Perfect Presentations!* Open University Press and McGraw-Hill Education, Maidenhead.

McCarthy, P. and Hatcher, C. (2002) *Presentation Skills: the essential guide for students*. Sage, London.

Murray, R. (2003) *How to Survive your Viva*. Open University Press, Maidenhead.

Parkinson, B. (1987) 'Emotion: cognitive approaches', in Beloff, H. and Colman, A.M. (eds) *Psychology Survey: no. 6*. British Psychological Society, Leicester.

Schachter, S. and Singer, J.E. (1962) 'Cognitive, social and physiological determinants of emotional state'. *Psychological Review*, 69, 379–399.

Stott, R., Young, T. and Bryan, C. (2001) *Speaking your Mind: oral presentation and seminar skills*. Harlow: Longman.

Turban, E. (2003) *Electronic Commerce 2003: a managerial perspective*. Prentice Hall, Upper Saddle River, NJ.

Van Emden, J. and Becker, L. (2010) *Presentation Skills for Students*. Palgrave Macmillan, Basingstoke.

Chapter 13

Meetings, teams and negotiations

Talent wins games, but teamwork and intelligence win championships.

Michael Jordan, basketball player

Learning outcomes

By the end of this chapter you should be able to:

- contrast the different types of business meeting, their purpose and varying degrees of formality;
- identify the characteristics of meetings as a communication channel, assessing their advantages and disadvantages in particular situations;
- apply formal business meeting procedures, including relevant documentation, such as agendas and minutes;
- summarise the tasks involved in chairing a meeting, and identify the communication skills required in a successful chair;
- review the communication process in team meetings and assess the different team roles in communication terms;
- consider the distinctive communication challenges associated with virtual teams and video-conferencing;
- assess the effectiveness of 'win–win' negotiation techniques in an inter-cultural context;
- compare your experiences of working in teams to those situations presented.

13.1   Introduction

People are always complaining about them, yet we all spend much of our working lives in meetings of one kind or another. Meetings have the *potential* to be one of the richest and most creative communication channels (see Figure 13.1). However, they can also pose some

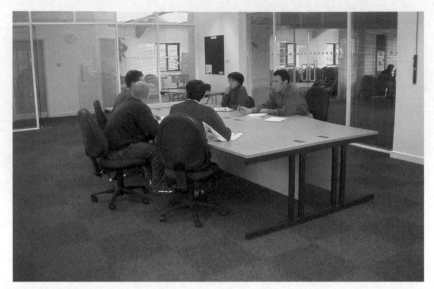

Figure 13.1 A meeting in progress

of the greatest challenges. This chapter considers why meetings often become so infuriating and unproductive, generating more heat than light. It argues that with careful preparation and management it is possible to minimise the downside and make the most of these gatherings, be it a top-level committee meeting or an ad hoc project team meeting. This section begins by reviewing the variety of meeting types and their different purposes, and addresses the general characteristics of this communication channel. The discussion then turns to the more formal types of meeting, their associated documentation, and the key role of the chair. This is followed by a consideration of communication in the more informal setting of the team meeting, and in the emerging world of 'virtual' team-working. The chapter concludes with a brief review of negotiation meetings, and the skills involved in securing a 'win–win' outcome. The chapter also reflects on the cultural and political factors that have shaped the diversity of meetings encountered in international organisations.

13.2 Meetings: principal types and purposes

Organisations are the venue for many types of meeting, serving a variety of overlapping purposes (see Table 13.1). These meetings may also operate with varying degrees of **formality** (i.e. the extent to which they keep written records and follow a set of rules and procedures). One of the most common sources of difficulty results from a mis-match between the meeting format and the nature of the communication being undertaken. For example, a management committee is set up with all the characteristics of an executive (i.e. decision-making) meeting, but its real purpose is to consult or to brief, rather than to decide. A related problem arises when the participants in a meeting have different views on its purpose. For example, imagine the potential for conflict when the sales director thinks she is giving a *briefing*, the regional managers are expecting to be *consulted* and the sales executives are hoping to *participate* in some real executive decisions. As we shall see, it

Table 13.1 Organisational meetings: overlapping types, purposes and styles

Type	Primary purpose	Formal example	Informal/internal example
Briefing	To deliver information	Chief executive presents financial results to investment analysts.	Project manager explains the task to a newly-formed team.
Investigatory	To gather information	Board of Inquiry interviews witnesses to a serious accident.	Architect and structural engineer visit construction site to resolve technical problem.
Advisory	To provide information	Panel of experts advise government department on new legislation.	Human resources manager consults two colleagues about a disciplinary case.
Consultative	To voice opinions	Community leaders speak at public inquiry into new airport runway.	Manager asks her staff how they feel about a proposed profit-sharing scheme.
Executive	To make decisions	Board of Trustees agrees a new strategic plan for hospital trust.	Emergency workers at the scene of a fire decide on the best course of action.

is difficult to separate the technicalities of communication in meetings from the broader political process in organisations.

13.3   Advantages, disadvantages and channel characteristics

Meetings share the benefits and drawbacks of any face-to-face communication. Benefits derive from instantaneous feedback and intensive flows of verbal and non-verbal communication (see Figure 13.2). These have the potential to offer a rapid exchange of ideas and

(a) Simple exchange between individuals   (b) Informal meeting/social event

(c) Intensive small group meeting   (d) Large chaired meeting

Figure 13.2 Contrasting information flows in a meeting

group synergies. In other words, combined efforts of a group can often generate better solutions than individuals working alone or communicating through less intensive channels, such as letters or e-mail. Successful meetings can both *inform* and *motivate* those attending. Unfortunately, business meetings rarely succeed in exploiting these opportunities to the full. To understand why, it is necessary to consider the kind of communication that is taking place.

Meetings involve a complex pattern of information flows. Messages criss-cross around the meeting room and are highly vulnerable to 'noise' and incorrect de-coding (see Chapter 2). Each attendee arrives with his or her own information, pre-conceived ideas, feelings and prejudices. As the meeting progresses, the limited attention spans and selective perception of each individual can lead to different interpretations of the material that has been discussed, the arguments presented and any decisions that may have been made. Discussions and arguments can become highly personalised as individuals 'play politics' or begin to identify themselves too closely with particular positions. Meetings often lose direction. In some cases, they may simply drift into unrelated topics, but can also be hijacked by one strong personality or by a faction that wishes to pursue its own agenda. The result is a misallocation of time; the meeting spends far too long on relatively minor agenda items, leaving insufficient time for the main business issues. As time rolls on, the most important issues are rushed through by an over-tired chair, who simply wants the meeting to end as quickly as possible.

The role of **the chair** is crucial, and we will return to it in section 13.5. For example, in a large formal meeting, the chair has the difficult task of co-ordinating information flows, ensuring that individuals are not excluded and closing down 'private' conversations (see Figure 13.2). Poorly-managed meetings generally make bad decisions, which is reason enough to seek to improve this vital communication channel. Equally serious is the demotivating effect of an unsuccessful meeting on everyone concerned.

13.4 The formal meeting

Many organisational meetings, notably those with executive powers, require a degree of formalisation if they are to operate effectively. The main features of a formal meeting are:

- established rules and procedures;
- written records of previous meetings;
- usually a specified membership who are invited to participate.

Many organisations operate through a system of **committees. Committee members** act as representatives for different departments or interest groups who may be appointed to their posts or elected by a wider group. The board of directors of a public company, for example, is elected by the shareholders, while charitable organisations are normally governed by a board of trustees. Universities are governed by a senate that is composed of elected members. Below the 'main board' (or equivalent) level may also be various sub-committees dealing with more narrowly defined subject areas, such as finance, social services or directors' remuneration. The decisions and recommendations of **sub-committees** are then reported to their 'parent' committee, representing a formal channel of communication (see Figure 13.3).

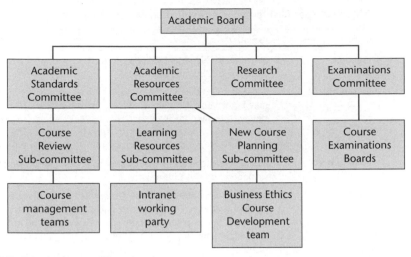

Figure 13.3 A typical committee structure

This section describes the main rules governing formal meetings and considers the task of producing two key items of supporting documentation: the agenda and minutes of the meeting. This model is then contrasted with recent research conducted on Chinese meeting practices, indicating the kinds of cultural variation that are encountered in the international organisation.

Rules and order

Most large organisations have a written constitution, or 'standing orders'. For example, in the British legal system, limited companies are governed by their principal legal documents: the Memorandum of Association and the Articles of Association. The company secretary is responsible for seeing that the rules are followed, and that statutory meetings (e.g. the annual general meeting) are held, with appropriate notice given. If the board of directors acts outside its rules or powers (i.e. in legal terms, *ultra vires*), the decisions are invalidated, and the individual directors find themselves in a vulnerable position; they have what is termed a 'fiduciary responsibility' to act in the best interests of the company's shareholders. Similarly, under British law, local government councillors can be fined, or 'surcharged', if their spending decisions exceed centrally-imposed limits.

There are a number of specialist terms used in and around formal meetings. As a general rule, it is advisable to become familiar with the procedures and the terminology used in any meetings that you attend (see Table 13.2). You might ask the secretary if there is a glossary of terminology for the meetings that you attend that you can refer to until they become familiar.

Preparing and circulating the agenda

The agenda, listing the topics to be discussed, provides a structure for the meeting. It may be a useful route map, but if poorly-constructed, it can lead everyone astray. A fortnight or so before the meeting, the secretary contacts members, requesting agenda items. The chair

Table 13.2 Specialist terminology associated with formal meetings

Term	Explanation
Agenda	Document which lists the topics to be discussed at the meeting, providing a structure for the meeting.
Adjournment	A break in the meeting before all of the agenda items have been covered. This may be because it is inquorate (see quorum below), to obtain information, or simply to allow participants to have a break. An adjournment is normally a temporary postponement with an agreed date and time for resumption. However, adjournment *sine die* means that it is for an indefinite period.
Amendment	Motions (see below) can be subject to amendments, which are also proposed, seconded and put to the vote.
AOB	Meaning – any other business. Committee members should submit items for the agenda in advance if possible; this allows them to be scheduled in a logical order. However, genuinely last-minute items can usually be notified to the chair at the start of the meeting. If time permits, they may be taken as AOB at the end of the meeting.
Ex officio	Ex officio members are individuals appointed to a committee by virtue of the office they hold, rather than by direct appointment or election.
Matters arising	This is a standard agenda item, referring to items from the previous meeting's minutes that require further discussion or clarification.
Minutes	Document that, once approved by meeting attendees, is intended to provide an accurate and unbiased record of the meeting.
Motion	Motions are part of the voting procedure used in some committee meetings. A motion is normally 'proposed' by one person and seconded (i.e. supported) by another, before being put to the vote.
Point of order	If someone thinks that the meeting is not following its written rules, they can point it out to the chair by calling 'point of order'. Examples include: quorum, *ultra vires*, and speaking on items which are not on the agenda.
Proxy	A proxy is someone acting on behalf of a person who is unable to attend the meeting. Proxies are most commonly used when a vote is called at an annual general meeting (AGM).
Quorum	This term refers to the minimum number of members or delegates required for a meeting to proceed. If attendance falls below that number at any time in a formal meeting, it is deemed to be *inquorate* and business must be suspended.
'Through the chair'	It is normal practice for all comments at a formal meeting to be addressed via the chair, rather than in direct exchanges between members. In theory, this rule enables the chair to exert some control over the meeting. The protocol is not always followed!
Ultra vires	This legal term derives from the Latin, meaning 'outside the powers'. It refers to decisions or actions that fall beyond the remit of a particular committee.

and secretary normally plan the 'running order', based on the items submitted. The following factors should be considered when deciding this order:

- **Logical sequence:** If the outcome of one decision is going to affect another, ensure that the 'dependent' topic is further down the agenda.

- **Simple items first:** It is often a good tactic to get straightforward items out of the way, before going on to more complex issues.

- **Consensus items first:** Uncontroversial items at the top of the agenda should be dealt with speedily. However, a seemingly bland item can cause unexpected controversy and time-consuming arguments. It is wise to check, before the agenda is finalised, whether the item really is as innocuous as it sounds.

- **Late arrivals and early departures:** There may be a topic that can only be discussed with a particular individual present. Hence, it may be necessary to defer or advance an item if that person is going to be late, or has to rush off to *another* meeting.

- **Less important/less urgent last?** The chair and secretary may be tempted to place 'minor' items towards the end of the agenda, but this is not good practice. If you have a full agenda, it is best to defer these items to a subsequent meeting or, better still, deal with them via another channel. For example, it is much less time-consuming to circulate a draft report, asking for written comments, rather than to review the whole thing, page-by-page, during a meeting.

Having established an appropriate order for the agenda, items of business may simply be numbered in sequence from 01 onwards. Many organisations use a slightly more complex referencing system comprising the current year, followed by number of the agenda item. For example, in 2012, the sequence would begin: '12/01, 12/02 …'. The sequence of numbers then continues from one meeting to the next (see Figure 13.4). The chair is often provided with an extended version of the agenda. The chair's agenda is annotated, with useful information to assist in running the meeting smoothly. For example, it might include a reminder to provide members of the meeting with a brief update on a rapidly-developing issue, before opening it to discussion. The chair is also likely to note provisional time allocations for each agenda item, to help with time-keeping during the meeting. Once the agenda is drawn up, the secretary sends out copies, normally including details of the date, time and venue. The agenda may be sent as a paper copy, or as an e-mail attachment.

Committees and boards usually have a regular pattern of meetings, which may be planned and notified up to a year in advance. This practice is supposed to increase the chances that members will be able to schedule their attendance around other commitments. However, in practice, 'extraordinary' meetings may also be needed to deal with urgent matters, while others may be re-scheduled or cancelled. It is important to ensure that everyone is included on the circulation list, particularly where the meeting has voting powers.

Greentek plc
FINANCE SUB-COMMITTEE

The next meeting of the Finance Sub-Committee will take place on
Monday 8th January 2012 at 15:00hrs in Room K383, Ryton Tower.

AGENDA

12/01	Apologies for absence	
12/02	Minutes of last meeting	
12/03	Matters arising	
12/04	Response to internal audit report	BJH
12/05	Capital investment proposal: project Alpha	ADR
12/06	Financial information system update	LPN
12/07	Software purchases: 2012/13	LPN
12/08	Any other business	
12/09	Date of next meeting	

Figure 13.4 Sample agenda and notice of meeting

Writing up the minutes

The minutes should provide an accurate and unbiased record of the meeting. They are presented to the following meeting for approval, after which they become the definitive record. If the previous meeting was contentious, members are likely to scrutinise the circulated minutes carefully, and may request corrections. In a formal meeting, the secretary is normally responsible for taking the minutes. Minute-taking is something of an art, balancing the requirement of recording proceedings accurately to produce a clear, concise account. There are three main types of minute, ranging from the highly detailed to the briefest summary: verbatim, narrative and resolution minutes.

Verbatim minutes

These are 'word-for-word' accounts of the meeting. The records of parliamentary debates and those of some public enquiries are verbatim. For example, *Hansard* is the official record of the British parliament, while the minutes of European Parliament meetings are first recorded in the languages in which members' speeches were given, then translated into the 23 official languages (i.e. Bulgarian, Czech, Danish, Dutch, English, Estonian, Finnish, French, German, Greek, Hungarian, Irish, Italian, Latvian, Lithuanian, Maltese, Polish, Portuguese, Romanian, Slovak, Slovene, Spanish and Swedish). Given the resources required for verbatim minute taking, it is not widely used in business organisations.

Narrative minutes

These are a more or less detailed summary of the discussion that takes place around each item, followed by a note of the decision taken. Narrative minutes usually include an 'action' column on the right-hand side of the page, with the name or initial of the person responsible for carrying out any matters agreed by the meeting. Meetings tend to agree things with little thought of how they are to be implemented; the action column counters by specifying a named individual. These actions are then reviewed at the following meeting, exerting some added pressure on the person concerned (see Figure 13.5).

Resolution minutes

These are the briefest type of minute, stating only what was agreed at the meeting. Resolution minutes are used primarily for statutory meetings (e.g. those required to form or make changes to the legal status of a company). The wording is normally in the form, 'RESOLVED: That Frederick George Wilson be appointed a non-executive director of Greentek plc, with effect from 1st January, 2012.' The alternative form is, 'It was resolved that Frederick George Wilson be appointed a non-executive director of Greentek plc, with effect from 1st January, 2012.'

13.5   On being a successful chair

The task of a chair is to manage the live flow of messages without either stifling useful discussion or showing obvious bias towards one or other viewpoint. This can be a challenging task, particularly when the meeting is affected by 'personality clashes' between members, or where controversial issues are under discussion. The role of chair is common

---

Greentek plc
FINANCE SUB-COMMITTEE

Minutes of the Finance Sub-Committee meeting
held on Monday 9th January 2012
at 15:00hrs in Room K383, Ryton Tower

		Action
Present:	Daniel Felton	
	Bridget Harris (Chair)	
	Jean Lafitte (Secretary)	
	Neema Patel	
	Lisa Nolan	
	Adrian Robertson	

		Action
12/01	Apologies	
	Received from Martin Smith and Kerry Jones.	
12/02	Minutes of last meeting	
	The minutes of the meeting held on 21st November 2011, previously circulated, were signed as a true record.	
12/03	Matters arising	
11/13	Computer security: Neema Patel reported that the anti-virus program was updated, effective from 1st December 2011. No further problems had been reported, but a review was to be carried out in June 2012.	NP
12/04	Response to internal audit report	KR
	A response was submitted on 20th December 2011, covering the substantive points made. Kay Rodgers of internal audit would formally report back to the next meeting.	
12/05	Capital investment proposal: project Alpha	AR
	Following Adrian Robinson's presentation, the sub-committee recommended that project Alpha go forward to the February board meeting.	
12/06	Financial information system update	LN
	A detailed report accompanying Lisa Nolan's presentation is appended to these minutes. It was agreed that regular updates be given in the development phase.	
12/07	Software purchases: 2012/13	LN
	The provisional list was agreed, with the addition of the updated virus-checker. Department heads would be asked to provide a list of their requirements by 31st March 2012 at the latest.	
12/08	Any other business	
	No other business was notified.	
	The meeting closed at 15:47hrs	
12/09	Date of next meeting	
	The next meeting is scheduled for 9th April 2012 at 15:00hrs in room K383, Ryton Tower.	

Figure 13.5 Sample narrative minutes

to formal and informal meetings, and is characterised by diplomatic, assertiveness and co-ordinating skills. The chair and secretary have complementary roles, which require close liaison over a number of tasks. These can be summarised under three headings, covering: the preparations required before the meeting, activity during the meeting itself, and follow-up action:

Before the meeting – tactical planning

Even where a meeting is scheduled on a regular basis, the chair needs to consider the *purpose* of the forthcoming meeting and establish appropriate tactics for achieving it. Sometimes, there are pragmatic decisions to make. For example, if there is insufficient business, or key personnel are unavailable, it is the chair's role to take the initiative and either cancel or postpone the meeting. Equally, if the proposed agenda is over-full, the chair can make a judgement that some items should be postponed, or dealt with through other channels. These early decisions avoid the depressing prospect of an impossibly long agenda, and the difficult task of rationalising it once the meeting is underway.

There are other practical issues, such as checking that the venue is suitable, with enough seats and reasonable heating, lighting and ventilation. If audio-visual equipment is required, such as flipcharts and data projectors, this needs to be in place and functioning before the meeting begins. The chair also needs to read all of the relevant background papers and reports, to be aware of the main issues under discussion.

During the meeting – diplomacy and time management

Above all, the chair needs to keep strict control of the time, ensuring that all business is covered adequately. The chair is also responsible for crowd control. For example, it may be necessary to stop someone who insists on repeating old arguments, jumping ahead or digressing from the current item. This requires a combination of tact and assertiveness. At the same time, the chair needs to be aware of those signalling a wish to speak, and ensure that everyone has a fair opportunity to contribute. By remaining calm and objective, the chair can help to set the tone for a meeting. Of course, they also have the power to undermine an otherwise successful meeting, by taking the opposite course.

The secretary should be able to assist the chair by having a sound knowledge of the formal rules and procedures; without this understanding, the meeting can become sidetracked by long and unresolved arguments over procedural issues and points of order (see Table 13.2). The chair also needs to ensure that the secretary has had time to record the details of a decision, before moving on to the next item. If a decision has not been expressed clearly, the chair or secretary may ask for it to be re-stated 'for the record'.

From time to time, the chair may also need to get a 'sense' of the meeting. This is often done by summarising the arguments that have been stated, and seeking or proposing a consensus view. In some cases, it is agreed in advance that a meeting will finish by a specified time. In these circumstances, it is even more important for the chair to keep a tight control on timing; otherwise, the tail-end of the meeting is likely to become disorganised and inquorate, as people drift away for other engagements. The chair should ensure that all the business is either dealt with in the meeting, passed on for action by named individuals, or held over until a specific date. It is important to avoid leaving ambiguities or 'loose ends', especially regarding those responsible for taking agreed actions after the meeting.

After the meeting – prompt follow-up

The secretary's main and most urgent task at this point is to ensure that the minutes are written up, checked and passed to the chair for review. They should then be circulated to all of those identified on the circulation list, including those giving 'apologies' at the meeting. (Note: This is one of the reasons for recording names formally in the minutes.) People become irritated if agendas and draft minutes are circulated a few days before the following meeting, as this gives them insufficient time to prepare for the meeting. One of the final tasks is to check the previous 'action' column before the meeting and to seek confirmation as to whether the named individuals have done what was required.

Practical arrangements for meetings

Practical issues, such as considering the seating arrangements and ensuring adequate ventilation, may sound trivial; however, as countless good and bad experiences have demonstrated, paying attention to these simple practical arrangements can have a significant effect on the success of a meeting (Case study 13.1).

CASE STUDY 13.1

Seating your meeting: the role of design

Seating arrangements have a major impact on the way people interact in a meeting (see Figure 13.6). When a meeting is being hosted by another organisation, you may have little influence over the layout of the meeting room. However, there are many good cases of design being used to facilitate improved communication. For example, when the British government's ministers meet in the Cabinet Room at 10 Downing Street, London, they sit around a long rectangular table that has a slight curve on either side. The design allows them to see the faces of colleagues on either side.

Figure 13.6 A selection of seating

353

> **Case study 13.1** (*continued*)
>
> **Questions**
>
> 1 Which of these seating plans have you used or experienced recently?
> 2 List the potential advantages and disadvantages of each seating plan.
> 3 Based on your assessments, identify the types of meeting where a particular plan would encourage effective communication, and those in which it would be counter-productive.
> 4 Are some of the seating plans undesirable whatever the purpose of the meeting might be?
>
> Test your conclusions by experimenting with different seating arrangements during your next meeting or team-based project.

More intractable communication problems in committees

We have seen that formal meetings, and the system of committees and sub-committees, are an important and unavoidable part of organisational life. This section has covered many of the potential pit-falls, showing how they can be avoided with the help of good documentation and well-prepared, competent people in the key roles of chair and secretary. These actions will improve the quality of communication in most formal meetings. However, some weaknesses in committee-based systems can prove more difficult to overcome. Among the most common are overlapping roles and the phenomenon of the 'talking shop':

- **Overlapping roles:** In large and complex organisations, there can be considerable confusion over the respective roles of particular committees or sub-committees. As a result of this, some issues will begin to 'bounce' from one meeting to another, delaying the decision-making process. At the level of the meeting, members are likely to become frustrated and the agenda will be over-burdened with items that keep reappearing with no sign of being resolved.

- **'Talking shops':** The authority of certain committees or sub-committees may be undermined by senior management, or in the case of subsidiaries, by decisions taken at the parent company headquarters. Other committees may be formed with the appearance of an executive role, which masks their real purpose. In both cases, those involved find themselves rubber-stamping decisions made elsewhere, which can be a very disheartening experience. It is likely to result in members 'voting with their feet'; in other words, attendances fall and the meeting may lose its identity altogether.

In these situations, any solution lies outside the meeting room. The chair and other participants will need to address the underlying structural or political problems that have resulted in these symptoms of poor quality communication (see section 2.3).

Using the chart below, consider which of the features described above you might usefully integrate into your meetings (see Table 13.3).

In the next section we focus on more informal meetings. However, as you will have found, communicative practices are dynamic, and so we often find that the distinction traditionally made between formal and informal meetings is increasingly blurred. This means that useful traditional practices, such as taking minutes and appointing a chair and secretary, might be adopted (and possibly adapted) for informal meetings.

Table 13.3 Improving your meetings: putting theory into practice

Feature	Suggestions for integration	Your notes
Rules and order	You might negotiate and agree ground rules according to how your group will work. For example, how often will you meet? Do you all need to be present to make a decision?	
Agenda	You might take it in turns to write, agree and circulate a list of items to be covered.	
Minutes	What format will these take? It might be enough to list decisions made, action points and the name of the person who is responsible for these being carried out.	
Appointing a chair and secretary	These are roles that you might rotate in order to spread the responsibility and the opportunity to develop useful skills.	
Considering room layout	Try sitting in a formation where you can't all make eye contact, then rearrange the furniture so that you can. How does each formation impact on communication?	

Team briefings

The **team briefing** potentially offers a way of linking formal and informal meetings by facilitating a cascade of information between the former and the latter. As explained in Chapter 6, team briefings are meetings at departmental or team level designed to allow a manager to pass on, or cascade, key information and Senior Management Team (SMT) decisions to their staff. They should also give team members opportunity to discuss and feedback on these messages. Ideally the team briefing should happen within several days of the SMT meeting. In order to maximise the time available for discussion during the team briefing, the Institute of Internal Communications (2012) recommends that employees be enabled to read the key information in bulletin format via e-mail, intranet or printed copy in advance of the team briefing. What do you see as being the advantages and disadvantages of adding this stage to the process?

13.6 Informal meetings: the benefits of team-working

Meetings come in all shapes and sizes. People often get together in less formal ways than those described in the previous section. However, the basic reasons for meeting are much the same, however informal the format may be. Reasons include carrying out tasks, such as tackling a complex problem, planning a future course of action, or generating new ideas:

- **The 'quality circle'**: At a manufacturing company, a small team of engineers, supervisors and production workers are sitting in a small meeting room, discussing how to redesign a component in order to overcome a technical fault that is affecting factory output.

- **The clinical discussion:** In the orthopaedic ward of a hospital, a clinical consultant, nursing staff and a physiotherapist are meeting to discuss their patient's recent progress following emergency surgery, with the aim of preparing a longer-term treatment programme.

- **The voluntary organisation:** In a local community hall, members of an integrated sports club for disabled and able-bodied people are planning their next fund-raising venture: a sponsored abseiling event.

Pre-determined agendas and detailed minutes may not be appropriate in these situations, though there is clearly a need for some degree of preparation and note taking. Even in the most informal business meetings, a little time spent on identifying the meeting's purpose and considering structure and procedures is likely to generate better results. However, the most important requirement is for the individuals concerned to work together as a team.

Some writers struggle with the distinction between a team and a group. Essentially a **team** is a group that combines a joint purpose and a shared sense of responsibility. Hence, there is a qualitative difference between a group of people in a park with a football and the same individuals, once they have formed into two competing teams that are beginning to play. In this section, our primary concern is with the kinds of communication that take place in these 'purposeful' teams.

Team-working as effective communication?

There has been a great deal of management writing concerning the nature and dynamics of organisational teams. While there are differences in presentation and emphasis, the underlying implication is that teams are more likely to achieve better outcomes than several individuals working independently (cf. Adair 2009, Belbin 2000, Hackman et al. 2000, Katzenbach and Smith 1998). More specifically, it is argued that an effective team can:

- **Solve complex problems:** Management problems are often wide-ranging and multi-disciplinary, requiring a combination of skills, knowledge and experience. Since these combinations are rarely found in one person, it is often necessary to create problem-solving teams that draw from different parts of the organisation, or spread across a number of related organisations. Increasingly organisations are moving beyond purely function-based teams to establish project-based teams.

- **Stimulate creativity and innovation:** Lively interactions between people can spark off new ideas and provide original perspectives. This often occurs when one person mentions something they have seen recently, prompting someone else to recall a related memory, and a third makes a link between the two. Organisations have sought to foster creativity by encouraging the formation of informal teams.

- **Increase motivation:** Most people have a need to belong (Maslow 1954), and enjoy mixing with others rather than spending all their time working alone. For example, a field sales force might theoretically spend all of its time on the road, communicating with the office through a laptop computer and mobile phone. Regular face-to-face meetings and social events may be used to build relationships, motivation and performance in these dispersed teams (see section 13.7 for a discussion of 'virtual' teams linked via e-mail and the Internet).

However, it is equally apparent that a poorly functioning team can cause all kinds of problems for organisations. The symptoms of dysfunction include: expressions of frustration and negativity; unhealthy competition (i.e. in-fighting) between team members; lack of involvement or commitment; loafing (Jackson and Harkins 1985) or freeloading (Kerr 1983), whereby individuals contribute less effort to achieving goals when working in a group than if they were working alone (possibly because they believe that their contributions will not be valued); dishonesty; a climate of revenge (i.e. 'back-stabbing') and a general lack of strategic direction. At this point, it may be useful to consider examples of such problems that you have experienced when working in teams, either at university or at work. What have you done to try to address them?

Both the positive and negative aspects of team-working can be investigated in terms of the communication taking place. For example, Tuckman's (1965) widely-cited model of team dynamics can be interpreted as an account of five distinct patterns of communication taking place during the assumed life-cycle of a team (i.e. 'forming', 'storming', 'norming', 'performing' and 'adjourning'). However, as critics have noted, an 'ideal-typical' stage model of this kind is unlikely to represent the variety of complex situations arising in real organisations. For example, where there are strongly-held norms in the wider organisation, individuals may be capable of making a rapid transition to the 'performing' stage. However, this may mean that important negotiation of and agreement on working practices between these individuals fail to take place within this team, resulting in problems further down the line. In contrast, pre-existing conflicts may result in a team being bound into a permanent condition of 'storming'.

Perhaps more interesting for our purposes are the contrasting patterns of intra-team communication taking place over time. Table 13.4 is a tentative re-interpretation of the Tuckman 'stages', highlighting these patterns. Without endorsing the Tuckman model itself, this simple extension indicates the inherent instability and dynamism of team-based communication. At one moment, it may involve intense exchanges between many participants (i.e. multilateral), but at other times it becomes dominated by bilateral exchanges. This phenomenon requires further empirical study, but is strongly supported by anecdotal evidence. Amongst other things, it highlights the challenges faced by a team leader, in managing transitions and handling the contrasting communication flows, to balance task, team maintenance and individual development goals (Adair 2009, Hackman et al. 2000).

Do you think that the Tuckman model is relevant to student teams? For example, it may be that you have been in a team that has got stuck in the 'storming' pattern of

Table 13.4 Indicative communication patterns in the Tuckman model

Stage	Outline of activity	Indicative patterns of communication?
'Forming'	Individuals meet and begin to establish team composition, purpose (task) and process (i.e. ways of working).	Fairly open and multilateral exchange of messages, as team members seek initial indication of capabilities and roles.
'Storming'	Disagreements emerge over task and process issues, potential for internal conflict and hostility.	Strong evidence of bilateral persuasive communication as arguments and counter-arguments are exchanged.
'Norming'	Team establishes agreed standards regarding purpose and process.	Greater attention to bilateral feedback as team leaders confirm consent and establish roles.
'Performing'	Team concentrates on achieving its common purpose, while maintaining process dimension.	Regulated multilateral exchanges between team members engaged in agreed roles.
'Adjourning'	Focus on completion of task and dissolution of the team.	Combination of intensified multilateral exchanges and some unilateral direction as task is pulled together, followed by bilateral leave-takings.

Source: Tuckman (1965 – adapted; indicative communication patterns added).

communication, or that never experienced the 'performing' pattern, perhaps because you reached the assignment deadline before having time to reach that stage. What do you think is the value of Tuckman's 'adjourning' phase? Why might it be particularly important in organisations engaged in project-based work, such as design engineers or consultants? (see section 13.7).

Communication and the concept of team roles

Another popular approach to the analysis of teams has focused on team roles. This strand of research has been based on the idea that performance can be enhanced by selecting an appropriately balanced team. Belbin's (2010a, 2010b, 2000) research originated in a series of experiments involving industrial managers who were attending short courses at a management school. The researchers compared the performance of different teams competing against one another in a series of business games. By measuring the behaviour of individuals and then experimenting with teams comprising different mixes of people, they isolated eight distinct team roles (see Table 13.5).

The higher-performing teams contained a balanced combination of these roles, whereas unbalanced teams tended to display signs of dysfunction. Each individual's 'primary' and 'secondary' team roles were identified using a self-perception questionnaire, which was based on an existing personality inventory. In real organisations, the task of constructing the optimum ideal team is complicated by a number of practical constraints. For example, an individual may be required on the basis of technical expertise, irrespective of any preferential team role. Some work-based teams are simply too small to be 'balanced'. The exercise of team roles may also be constrained by other obstacles, such as formal structures, political,

Table 13.5 The concept of team roles: a communication perspective

Team role	Primary contribution	Implied communication task
Chair	Organises, co-ordinates and seeks to retain team's focus and involvement.	Monitors and co-ordinates messages between team members.
Team leader	Initiates, provides leadership and drives team towards achieving task.	Generates persuasive bilateral and multilateral messages directed at team members.
Innovator	Creates novel ideas and solutions in support of the task.	Synthesises messages from diverse internal and external information sources.
Monitor-evaluator	Provides objective assessments of performance in relation to stated purpose.	Analyses primarily cognitive task-related messages within the team.
Team worker	Encourages other members, fosters team morale and reduces negative emotions.	Assesses and generates primarily affective, process-related messages within the team.
Completer	Maintains a check on outcomes in relation to project milestones and deadlines.	Analyses primarily cognitive task-related messages within the team.
Implementer	Carries out much of the practical work required to achieve stated purpose.	Receives bilateral messages (i.e. instructions) and avoids distraction from other internal exchanges.
Resource investigator	Establishes external contacts to secure resources in support of stated purpose.	Engages in bilateral exchanges of persuasive messages beyond the boundaries of the team.

Source: Belbin (2010a, 2010b – adapted; communication tasks added).

economic and cultural factors. As a consequence, team composition is usually something of a compromise. However, if you accept Belbin's counter-argument, that team members may adopt alternative roles when it becomes necessary, his initial conclusions remain of value. He argues that teams need to be balanced. That doesn't mean that each member needs to be well-balanced, but that collectively all the individuals in a team balance out each others' weaknesses and can make full use of everyone's strengths (Belbin 2010a). Furthermore, team building is an art, which managers can practise and develop (Belbin 2010b). Based on the descriptions of Belbin's team roles in Table 13.5, which do you think your 'primary' and 'secondary' team roles might be? You might like to learn more about your 'team role profile' by visiting the Belbin corporate web pages (see the useful websites listing at the end of this chapter).

The concept of team roles points to some interesting implications for communication within high-performing teams. The notion of a 'balance' between roles suggests that communication tasks are distributed. For example, the chair is concerned primarily with co-ordinating the intense flow of messages between team members, while the innovator synthesises new ideas from a more diverse range of sources, which may extend far beyond the team's boundaries. Similarly, the monitor-evaluator is engaged primarily with cognitive, task-related messages, while the team worker is more concerned with the exchange of affective (i.e. emotional) messages within the team. This interpretation would be consistent with much of the recent research literature in knowledge management, where teams and other forms of human organisation are depicted as purposeful, self-organising systems (see section 6.5).

Creative communication in teams: the case of 'brainstorming'

The term **'brainstorming'** was coined by advertising executive Alex Osborne in the late 1930s. It is a popular and well-established technique for creative problem-solving and generating novel ideas. However, it is often conducted wrongly, leaving people disappointed with the results. Building on our previous discussion, the activity taking place during a brainstorming session can be usefully analysed from a communication perspective. Consider the general principles for successful brainstorming.

- Appoint a 'facilitator' to write ideas on the board and encourage participation; ensure that this person can write quickly and legibly.

- Everyone else calls out any ideas that come into their heads, keeping them concise (insist on a maximum of two words); encourage everyone to participate.

- Do not reject or criticise any ideas at this stage, no matter how crazy they might appear. Accept, record and acknowledge every contribution.

- Once the initial flow of ideas is exhausted, move to the next stage; begin to link similar words on the board and draw out common themes, with the person at the board acting as a facilitator, attempting to consolidate the ideas.

- Finally, seek agreement on which of the new ideas is the most promising.

You may have noticed, from direct experience of engaging in brainstorming activities, how difficult it is to follow these guidelines. For example, it is hard to avoid the temptation to engage in a premature questioning of other people's ideas, particularly when the person concerned is less articulate than other members of the team. There is also a fairly common, task-oriented tendency to jump directly from ideas to solutions, without allowing time for the interim stages. From a communication perspective, the brainstorming 'recipe' comprises three stages:

- The first is designed to stimulate the collection of a diverse range of information.
- The second to encourage synthesis, or the creation of 'new combinations' from these sources.
- Third to refine the new information.

Researchers have failed to find evidence that brainstorming increases the quality or quantity of ideas, but the activity may make team members feel more motivated. Note the similarities between the stages of brainstorming and some of the team roles outlined in Table 13.5. The common feature in both approaches, which is also reflected in the Tuckman model, is that team-based activities depend on people managing complex and dynamic patterns of communication to achieve a stated purpose. The next section takes the idea a little further, by exploring the rise of 'virtual' teams, where a large part of the communication is electronically-mediated.

13.7   The rise of the virtual team

Modern organisations place considerable demands on individuals, who often find themselves needed in several locations at the same time. The symptoms of this trend are the increases in travel distances undertaken for work purposes (NTSU 2001). Transportation technology cannot overcome the basic laws of physics, but innovations in information and communication technologies have enabled cross-functional tasks teams to work together in real time, though team members are dispersed around the globe. Often referred to as 'virtual' teams, they exploit the full range of electronically-mediated communication channels, including text messaging, video conferencing (see Case Study 13.5), e-mail and instant messaging. As the reliability of these technologies has improved, the communication issues for virtual teams have become increasingly focused on people. Virtual teams tend to be formed where face-to-face contact is either impossible or not cost-effective. The reasons may be varied, but the underlying factor is the dispersed physical locations of team members. Virtual teams are often formed in high-tech industries, such as software development, where specialist expertise is spread widely. They are also used in alliance-based initiatives involving several organisations, located in different countries or regions. Virtual teams are, by their very nature, disjointed and somewhat artificial. As a consequence, they need particularly sensitive and capable management if they are to function effectively.

In Chapter 7, we reviewed the communication requirements of remote and home workers (see section 7.3). This suggested that some tasks, requiring limited bilateral communication, were particularly suitable for remote working. For example, much of the material for this book was prepared in the authors' home offices. The resulting communication flows (e.g. agreeing content between authors, exchanging e-mails with editors, occasional telephone or face-to-face conversations with other contributors, and specific information searches using libraries and the Internet) were mainly bilateral. In other words, they rarely involved more than two people at any one point in time. By contrast, virtual teams engaged in tasks such as developing software programs, economic development strategies or clinical treatments, will be involved in much more complex, multi-lateral interactions. The operating environment may also be more dynamic and uncertain, demanding spontaneous and simultaneous discussions and mutual adjustments. The resulting challenges are intensified where the team is international, and has to address time zone differences, different working practices and similar practical issues (Pauleen and Yoong 2001). Furthermore, different cultures have different understandings of acceptable and effective communication practices. For example, whereas in the UK the focus is often on saving time, including replacing business trips with video-conferencing, in China, face-to-face relationship building is an important process and is still central to business (Johnson 2011). Case study 13.2 illustrates how one company has made use of virtual teams to provide high levels of customer support to its global clients.

CASE STUDY 13.2

'Robertson Languages International': managing projects and virtual teams

'Robertson Languages International' (RLI) is a leading provider of integrated language services to a wide range of corporate clients (www.robertsonlanguages.co.uk). The company was established in 1989 by Liz and Bob Robertson and is based in the south of England. RLI's business structure is currently made up of two directors: Bob is in charge of language training, finance, marketing and IT and Liz is in charge of translation, personnel and quality systems, though there is considerable overlap between these roles. Two business development managers handle enquiries. A training manager deals with the course preparation and administration. Three project managers manage translation projects. Their work is supported by three in-house translators, IT support staff and a book-keeper.

In this case study, we take a look at two examples of RLI's work: organising a customised training programme, which illustrates some of the tasks involved in organising a new project; and providing specialist translation services, which highlights the particular challenges of virtual team working.

Indonesian language training

The client works for a UK government agency. He contacts RLI with a request for an intensive course in Indonesian, which needs to start immediately. The training can be delivered either at his offices in the north of England or as an intensive course (8 hours per day) at RLI's training centre. If it is to be at the training centre, he also wants to stay with an Indonesian host family in order to be immersed in the culture and to practise his language skills in the evenings. He requires basic skills, but the vocabulary needs to be focused around his work terminology. To meet the client's needs Bob Robertson and his team have a number of urgent issues to tackle:

1   Although RLI has a database of many trainers in many languages, it does not have one in the north of England. In view of the urgency of the course, Bob decides to carry out the training at the RLI centre.

2   The trainer, who has worked with RLI before on a freelance basis, is only available to teach the first week of the course as she is going on holiday. Using the trainer's professional contacts, the RLI database, web searching, contacts with universities and other sources, Bob and his team manage to find, interview and appoint a second teacher for

Case study 13.2 (*continued*)

the course. They also ensure that both trainers are happy to work on the same course. (The first trainer does not want work with someone from a different part of Indonesia because she regards the dialect as being 'less pure'.) The trainers are given a handbook and a briefing on the type of training that is required.

3 Bob's team finds a host family through some of the searching that has been carried out to find the second trainer. They ask the client about any special food requirements, allergies or other needs. As this is a new host family, RLI arranges a home visit to ensure that everything is appropriate, to agree on the meals to be provided and discuss how the client might be included in family life in the evenings.

4 Bob carries out a 'needs analysis' with the client. Sometimes this requires a language assessment to see how much the client knows already. In this case he is a complete beginner, so Bob's analysis focuses on the business functions and roles in which he will be using the language. They also agree some *realistic* learning goals. (Clients are often over-optimistic about what can be achieved in a 40-hour course!) After further discussions with one of the trainers, the team draft the course outline, purchase a published course book and CD, and get ready to greet the client.

It is now the first day of the course. Bob introduces the client to the trainer and gives an introductory talk on how to make the most of the training. This includes practical issues such as not taking mobile calls during the session – a common problem these days – and suggestions on language learning, such as ways to build up vocabulary. As the course proceeds, RLI's training manager ensures that the first trainer keeps clear records of what has been carried out in each session. This enables RLI to know exactly what progress is being made and also allows a smooth handover to the second trainer. Meanwhile, another client begins to learn a new language.

Specialist translation services

All translation projects require communication across languages and cultures, but some raise particularly complex challenges. For example, a project to translate clinical trials documentation into 13 EU languages requires RLI to select specialist medical translators and proofreaders, and to ensure that they all know the EU-approved terminology. RLI needs very careful selection procedures for translators in order to identify this kind of expertise. All of this has to be organised within tight deadlines, which means checking working hours in the various countries where translators are located. Marketing literature raises special cultural issues. RLI managers have to help companies to decide whether they are going to 'globalise' (i.e. use one message or brand around the world) or 'localise' (i.e. retain the same core message, but represent it in language and visual formats that appeal to audiences in each target country or cultural grouping). In practice, it is very difficult to transfer the meaning behind marketing literature into another language. For example a long and flowery (i.e. very elaborate) text in US English about a 'wonderful' cleaning product will look ridiculous to a reader in the Netherlands; the Dutch version needs to be much more concise and factual. This 'localisation' question can be very troubling for British and American companies, who prefer to stamp a uniform brand and style on their corporate literature.

RLI's projects involving China, now a very important market for translation services, require all of these cross-cultural communication factors to be taken into account. For example, there is an increasing demand for specialist translators who can work with Chinese regional dialects, and for additional advice on the localisation of materials. Over

Case study 13.2 (*continued*)

many years, RLI built a network of Chinese freelancers and other specialist companies to provide their translation services. Though UK-based managers were confident about decisions such as the choice between Simplified or Traditional Chinese, they were finding it difficult to advise on the use of particular dialects, or how to set up a website in Chinese that would appeal to a particular market segment. Recognising the huge potential of the Chinese market for both training and translation services, the directors decided in 2006 to focus attention on this part of the world, both to enhance RLI's business opportunities and to meet its clients' needs.

The first action was to research the Chinese market in as many ways as possible. Bob attended many seminars, read widely and became well-informed. Liz did some basic language learning, acquiring a few (out of more than 2,000) useful Chinese characters. The second phase was to consider how best to source Chinese translation services. Direct links with Chinese suppliers would provide RLI with lower costs and up-to-date language skills, but the challenge was how to find them and how to assess their expertise. RLI receives many hundreds of unsolicited CVs by e-mail every year, and a large proportion of these are from Asia. The problem is, when people are selling their services so strongly, how to differentiate and ensure quality? The outcome was a decision to approach China via Singapore, and the directors travelled there early in 2007. Setting up face-to-face meetings in Singapore provided an opportunity to meet prospective purchasers of English (training and translation), and prospective suppliers of Chinese and Malay. The meetings were very successful, and on their return, Bob and Liz decided to promote their capability in Chinese and support it in-house by recruiting a permanent in-house project manager. They were able to recruit a Chinese team member who had completed her translation studies at a UK University and was highly skilled in translation memory tools and other technical aspects of translation.

The UK-based Chinese project manager co-ordinates translation projects in order to overcome differences in time zones and to give clients a point of contact. When a new piece of work is identified, the project manager consults RLI's supplier database, identifies the best translators for the particular project, checks on their availability and makes sure that the work can be completed to fit the client's timescale. In some cases this can be very short – a client may have forgotten to translate leaflets or business cards for an exhibition that is taking place in the next 24 hours! In order to deal with the size, complexity and urgency of the task, the project manager may need to split the work between several translators; in effect creating a 'virtual team' linked by the Internet. Where there are several translators working on one project, the project manager also needs to ensure that everyone is absolutely consistent in the way they use language, including technical terms (e.g. 'shareholder value') and names (e.g. 'sales and marketing department'). This is essential in order to produce a document that reads seamlessly – as if it was translated by one person. She also needs to track the progress of her team and ensure that all of the translations are delivered on time. The final tasks, which are carried out in-house, are proof-reading; converting the text into a fully-formatted document (e.g. a brochure or booklet); ensuring that the material fits into the existing design (e.g. whether there is enough space to insert characters into headings and text boxes); and checking that the document will look right for the Chinese reader. RLI has a full desk-top publishing (DTP) capability (both PC and Apple Mac), though Chinese characters have always created challenges. Now that the company has an in-house project manager, she is able to assist the DTP team in making the subtle changes to layout and design that create a more attractive and accessible finished product for readers and an enhanced service to clients. For example, in the localisation of websites, RLI

> **Case study 13.2 (*continued*)**
>
> can advise on technical aspects (e.g. how to make browsers display characters correctly), improving design (e.g. which colours are most popular in particular markets), and use of images (e.g. why a picture of a chrysanthemum might be culturally inappropriate).
>
> **Questions**
>
> 1 Using *either* the Indonesian language training or the Chinese specialist translation services examples:
>
>   (a) list the main communication channels used at each stage;
>
>   (b) identify the key internal and external actors involved;
>
>   (c) note the kind of messages flowing through these channels;
>
>   (d) comment on the techniques that RLI managers have employed in order to communicate effectively throughout the process.
>
> 2 Based on the case illustration and the discussion in the chapter, what do you see as the major challenges facing RLI's in-house manager, in creating and managing a 'virtual' team of translators?
>
> 3 Prepare a list of the information and communication technologies that RLI is using to support its team-based working. (Note: you can make some assumptions about technologies that may be in use, though not mentioned specifically.)
>
> 4 Using the RLI case as a starting-point, draw up your own checklist of 'top communication tips' for a new manager who has been asked to co-ordinate an international project team.
>
> *Sources*: Robertson Languages (2007), Association of Translation Companies (2007). Case prepared by the authors, with acknowledgements to Bob and Liz Robertson.

13.8 Negotiation: applying persuasive communication

The essential nature and purpose of negotiations are much the same, whatever their scale or format. **Negotiation** is a form of persuasive communication, that may include anything, from two parties engaged in bilateral discussion, to a large number of participants engaged in many cross-cutting exchanges. The process of negotiation comprises periods of discussion and the presentation of proposals and counter-proposals. After some time, this may lead to an outcome that can be accepted by all sides. The basic 'give and take' interaction that characterises negotiation is first practised in early childhood, when requests in the form, 'Please can I have another biscuit?' are met with counter-proposals containing conditional statements such as, 'Yes, when you've put those toys away.' It is an activity that is found in many aspects of personal and organisational life. For example: when renting a flat; buying a new house or car; agreeing the terms of an employment contract; settling a complaint from a major customer; allocating office space between staff; or securing family agreement on a holiday destination. In this section, we treat the negotiation as a specialised type of meeting, which may take place in either a formal or informal setting.

Two main forms of negotiation: positional and principled

Traditional approaches to negotiation, generally described as 'positional' or 'distributive', have been extensively analysed using game theory and rational choice models (e.g. Raiffa 1982). In essence, each side is engaged in an attempt to maximise the outcome for themselves. The result is a 'zero-sum' game, where the resulting compromise is within the acceptable ranges of each side. In practice, positional negotiations are often undertaken by small teams of negotiators, with tightly defined mandates, giving them limited authority to act on behalf of their respective organisations or departments. The negotiation proceeds as a series of shifts in position, proposals and counter-proposals. If each party's ultimate point of compromise overlaps, an agreement may be reached. However, this form of negotiation often results in deadlock. Another common feature of positional negotiations is that one party may make a 'pre-emptive strike' against the other. For example, a politician can use selective leaks to the media in order to undermine an opponent, or a group of anti-road protestors may occupy a construction site before a public enquiry. This kind of tactical action, which can also be taken once face-to-face negotiations are underway, is designed to exert additional pressure. In practice, it is usually countered by the other party and can result in a breakdown in negotiations.

Responding to the perceived problems of positional negotiation, a group of Harvard Business School researchers developed an alternative approach, known as 'principled' negotiation (Fisher et al. 1991). This is based on the assumption that the goals of the parties are not necessarily incompatible. Hence, the bargaining process is 'integrative', involving a search for the objective principles underlying each party's position. The aim is to achieve creative and mutually-acceptable outcomes. A key feature of principled negotiation is the attempt to separate the issues and arguments from the personalities of those involved in the negotiations. Above all, it recognises the importance of achieving a 'win–win' solution.

Literature dealing with confrontation resolution offers a rich source of approaches for avoiding conflict when negotiating. The Interest-Based Relational (IBR) Approach is a conflict resolution strategy which acknowledges individual differences but can prevent people becoming too entrenched in a fixed position. The Thomas-Kilmann Conflict Mode Instrument (TKI) helps you to identify which style you tend towards when conflict arises – competitive, collaborative, compromising, accommodating or avoiding (Mind Tools 2012).

Advantages of 'win–win' negotiation

Since most organisational negotiations are part of an on-going relationship, a short term 'victory' over the other party may not be in your longer-term interests. For example, if you secure a deal that is highly unfavourable to a valued customer or key supplier (i.e. 'win–lose'), they are unlikely to do much business with you in the future. However, it is equally important not to be the victim of the other party (i.e. 'lose–win'). Hence, the best outcome for both parties is referred to as 'win–win' (see Table 13.6).

Table 13.6 Alternative negotiation outcomes

	A loses	A wins
B loses	Lose–lose	Win–lose
B wins	Lose–win	Win–win

Negotiation and power

Parties to a true negotiation will have some freedom of manoeuvre. However, this does not necessarily mean that they will come to the negotiating table as equals. In most cases, one party is in a stronger position than the other. For example, the large multiple retailers can exert substantial buying power over their smaller suppliers. However, as skilled negotiators recognise, it is the other party's *perception* of their power that is the key factor. By influencing these perceptions, an apparently 'weaker' party can alter the course of the negotiations in its favour. One approach to dealing with these inequalities is to manage the 'shadow' negotiation, the activity preceding the actual negotiation, but which can have a powerful influence on how the process unfolds (Kolb and Williams 2001).

The negotiation process

The skills required to manage a negotiation are similar to those used in other types of meeting, but the negotiation itself has a distinctive shape. Research on cross-cultural negotiation appears to support the established (i.e. Western) view that there is a common pattern comprising four phases:

- initial relationship-building activity;
- the exchange of task-related information;
- persuasion and bidding/counter-bidding;
- concession and agreement (e.g. Mendenhall et al. 1995).

Initial relationship-building activity

In all forms of negotiation, there are some ritual activities that serve the purpose of creating an appropriate climate. In 'principled' negotiation, this implies an effort to be cordial, collaborative, brisk and businesslike. However, there are cultural variations, notably in relation to the importance attached to fostering personal relationships, for example between Chinese and American business people (Chua et. al. 2009). Some negotiators emphasise physical location; for example, that it should be politically neutral and free from interruptions. (Many recent efforts at securing peace agreements have been hosted in quiet and relatively inaccessible locations.) Non-verbal communication can play an important role in these rituals. Hence, skilled international negotiators pay considerable attention to handshakes, appropriate eye contact and non-threatening gestures. This is also a period in which both parties engage in uncontentious 'ice-breaking' conversation. As the memoirs of many political leaders and diplomats have suggested, the formation of good inter-personal relations prior to negotiation can play a crucial role in the outcome.

Exchanging information

Negotiators prepare the ground for bargaining by collecting information, particularly in relation to the other party's situation (e.g. the power relations influencing decision-making in their organisation). In 'win–win' approaches, this phase is associated with efforts to assess your position from the other party's point of view. Cohen (2002) refers to this assessment process as identifying your BATNA (Best Alternative To Negotiated Agreement). According to Cohen, 'BATNAs are a measure of the balance of power among parties. If I need your help more than you need mine, you have a stronger BATNA and the balance of power to influence the outcome of negotiation favours you' (Cohen 2002: 24). As the negotiation progresses and you gain information about your partner's strengths (e.g. they have other alternative partners who they are also negotiating with), and weaknesses (e.g. they have a time pressure), and they gain information about yours, each party's BATNAs will change. They are now dynamic BATNAs, as the power shifts between parties. International negotiators sometimes make use of interpreters to obtain information surreptitiously from the other party; a tactic that is unlikely to generate a climate of trust.

Bargaining and persuasion

The bargaining phase is initiated when the parties begin to make tentative proposals. The 'win–win' emphasis in this phase is on reducing substantive differences between the parties. This is achieved by emphasising areas where there is already consensus, and by ensuring that any remaining disagreements are not personalised. Proposals should always be expressed in **conditional** terms (i.e. 'If you offer us X, then we could offer you Y'). The principle behind the bargaining exchanges is to identify factors that are most important to the other party, and to value every offer in *their* terms. For example, a busy customer may value door-to-door delivery very highly, even though it costs a supplier very little to add the customer to an existing delivery round. By contrast, the supplier's offer of 'instant credit terms' may be a costly concession, but be of little value to the customer due to the nature of their business (e.g. they may be a cash-rich retailer). It may require a truly creative team of negotiators to put together a proposal that offers a solution that satisfies all parties. This kind of creativity requires particular forms of communication, and rarely emerges from a confrontational approach.

Reaching and recording agreement

This phase marks the end of the tentative, conditional exchanges and a move to firm proposals. This transition may be influenced by cultural factors. For example, some may prefer to reach agreement on one issue at a time, while others take a more holistic approach. However, all negotiators emphasise the need to ensure that the terms of any agreement are entirely clear to all parties; this may involve a pause in proceedings to check that everything has been covered. Signifying agreement with a handshake appears to be a generalised ritual of negotiation. There is also a requirement to record the agreement and associated undertakings in writing. Many commercial and diplomatic agreements have broken down because the terms were drafted ambiguously and disputes subsequently arose over the small print. However, international negotiators are also sensitive to differences in approach. It appears that some cultures have tended to place particular emphasis on the formal (i.e. legalistic) aspects, while others may regard such behaviour as indicating a lack of trust.

Negotiation in a cross-cultural perspective: the case of China

Most texts dealing with 'cross-cultural' negotiation continue to emphasise binary oppositions between cultural groups (i.e. two cultural groups facing one another, each being fairly homogeneous). For example, Deresky (2003), a leading international management text, highlights an earlier study that compared Japanese, North American and Latin American negotiating styles (Casse 1982). This type of comparison, which is typical of many texts on the subject, has been summarised in Table 13.7. Similar examples of contrasting negotiating styles are reflected in the anecdotal accounts of business travellers, and in empirical

Table 13.7 Cultural difference in negotiation: an outdated approach?

Country/region	Indicative depictions of 'typical' styles
Japanese	Emotional sensitivity is highly valued; interaction involves hiding emotions; face-saving is crucial; decision-making is step-by-step; decision makers are openly influenced by special interests; the ultimate aim is the good of the group.
North American	Emotional sensitivity not highly valued; interaction is straightforward and imper-sonal; face-saving does not always matter; decision-making is methodical; special interests influence decision makers, though this is often considered unethical; the ultimate aim is profit motive or the good of the individual.
Latin American	Emotional sensitivity is valued; interaction is emotionally passionate; face-saving is crucial; decision-making is impulsive and spontaneous; special interests of decision makers are condoned; the ultimate aim of the group equates to that of the individual.

Sources: Casse (1982), Deresky (2003: 166).

studies that have investigated cultural difference (e.g. Buttery and Leung 1998, Graham 1985, Tse et al. 1994).

While it is important for international negotiators to appreciate the cultural backgrounds of others, there is increasing criticism of this kind of approach to cross-cultural manage-ment (Holden 2002). To begin with, there is a presentational problem; over-simplified summaries can help to reinforce crude cultural stereotypes, which may themselves present a barrier to communication. However, there is a deeper problem with the way that cultural difference is conceptualised in these frameworks. First, they tend to focus on confrontations between two unitary cultures, whereas much of today's international negotiation involves interactions between individuals and groups from many different cultural backgrounds. In addition, the people who work in today's international organisations often draw on mul-tiple cultural identities. For example, their parents may be from entirely different cultural backgrounds, and they may have had work and educational experience in several countries. Indeed, professional negotiators in international organisations tend to be selected on the basis of their multicultural experience and training. The traditional frameworks also take no account of variables other than national culture, such as organisational setting and techni-cal specialism, that may have a profound influence on interactions. International business negotiation is itself becoming a professional field, with its own set of cultural norms (Sheer and Chen 2003: 56). In summary, there is a danger in presenting national culture as static and determining, and so underplaying the complex ways in which cultures are actively recreated through human interaction (see section 2.5). Case study 13.3 considers recent research into Chinese negotiators and suggests that it is time for a fresh perspective on this vital communication issue.

CASE STUDY 13.3

The changing face of Chinese negotiation

Academic researchers from Hong Kong interviewed mainland Chinese and Western busi-ness professionals who had several years' experience in intercultural negotiation, rang-ing from commercial trading to technology transfer, joint ventures, real estate, cultural

Case study 13.3 (*continued*)

exchange and joint publishing contracts. A qualitative analysis of the interview transcripts revealed some conventional cases of cultural misunderstanding. For example, a factory director from Shanxi province described how he had 'learned' to maintain eye contact during negotiations with a Canadian investor:

> '[The] interpreter asked me privately whether I was really interested in the joint venture. I was surprised and asked why he asked me such a question. He replied that his boss (the Canadian investor) felt I did not pay attention to him and I always looked away. I learned the lesson. Afterwards, I made an effort to look at the "other side". I am still not very comfortable about this. But it helps negotiations. '(Cited in Sheer and Chen 2003: 61)

Both Chinese and Western interviewees identified other differences in communication style, such as a tendency for mainland Chinese negotiators to engage in 'empty rhetoric' (i.e. extended speeches) prior to the main negotiation. However, these factors did not have a decisive impact:

> 'Chinese interviewees conveyed that cultural differences in language, communication, and social etiquette influenced business negotiation in an *insignificant* way. Similarly, Western interviewees saw these as differences in "style", which were obstacles that could be overcome with relatively minor impact on negotiation. '(*Ibid*: 62 – emphasis added)

One-third of the Chinese interviewees believed that the nature of the negotiation (i.e. the supply and demand relationship) and the rituals of international business negotiation were the main driving forces, rather than national culture. The remaining two-thirds identified the *simultaneous* impact of professional and national culture. They gave four reasons for the reduced importance of national culture: the increasing Westernisation of China; increased exposure of Chinese business people to international negotiation practices; closer connection via the Internet and related technologies; and the priority attaching to business-related aims. This last point was summarised by a Chinese interviewee, 'Business first, other matters later.' The study concludes that Sino–Western negotiations are being influenced to varying degrees by national and professional cultures. However, it also suggests a rapidly *evolving* picture, as mainland Chinese negotiators engage more actively with the norms and practices of international business negotiation. For example, the Western interviewees made conventional comments on the Chinese concept of *Guanxi* (i.e. the use of personal relationships, often characterised as social networks), in the authors' terms, 'a necessary instrumental strategy to cope with the unstable and inconsistent political environments' (Ibid: 63). However, other studies have indicated that *Guanxi* is itself in a process of transformation, as part of the wider changes occurring in contemporary China (see Yeung and Tung 1996, Tsang 1998). That said, Chua et. al. (2009) found that *Guanxi* or social networks and an individual's degree of embeddedness within a social network still convey significant information about their trustworthiness. So much so, that when developing a business relationship, as well as socialising with their business partner, a manager will also want to interact with as many members of their counterpart's social network as possible. They also observed that due to the interrelatedness of socio-emotional and instrumental relationships in Chinese societies it is still 'neither uncommon nor inappropriate to achieve instrumental ends through personal relationships' (Chua et.al. 2009: 504). Therefore, it is important to remain aware that practices that take personal considerations into account when negotiating, which may be perceived as corrupt by Western business people, are not considered so by Chinese businesspeople. Despite the argument presented for reduced importance of national culture when doing business, Chua et. al.

Case study 13.3 (*continued*)

(2009) advise that an understanding of and ability to handle such cultural difference in negotiation styles is vital.

Questions

1 Why do you think both the Chinese and Western interviewees saw differences in language, communication and etiquette as of little importance in their negotiations?

2 How can this view be reconciled with the many popular anecdotes regarding 'culture clash' in international meetings and negotiations?

3 Why do you think the traditional concept of *Guanxi* may be changing in the new China? And, conversely, why do you think *Guanxi* is still important to some Chinese businesspeople?

4 What are the implications of these studies for the future of international business negotiation?

Sources: Yeung and Tung (1996), Tsang (1998), Sheer and Chen (2003), Chua et. al. (2009). Case prepared by the authors with acknowledgements to Yan Liu.

Case study 13.4 develops the theme of culture and negotiation further. It highlights the issues that can arise when multi-national deals are not carefully and sensitively negotiated and managed.

CASE STUDY 13.4

'Sharpo': cutting a deal with a blunt knife

Jane is managing director of 'Sharpo', a cutlery supplier. She is sitting in the executive boardroom sipping her coffee and waiting for her sales, production, HR and finance directors to arrive. She thinks back over the series of events that have led to this meeting.

In April 2004 Clive, the 'Sharpo' sales director, was approached by a buyer for a major UK high street retailer with the request that they supply a range of cutlery. The buyer explained that they wanted the cutlery to be to the same design as a market-leading range produced by a major European manufacturer. They insisted that the manufacturer should modify the design cosmetically to avoid copyright/design infringements and that they should produce to a much cheaper target cost by using less expensive materials. The retailer also demanded that the product should be supplied exclusively to them. Given the specific nature of these requirements, this brief could be met only by 'Sharpo' sourcing the product from overseas. To meet the cost criteria the product would need to be sourced in China, Pakistan or Thailand. Rather than discuss the brief with his colleagues, who were out of the office that week, at regional meetings and homeworking, Clive decided not to enter into negotiations as he normally would, but for speed and ease, to accept all the customer's demands. After all, they were too important a customer to lose!

Sharpo's production manager located a factory in China, machinery was specified, the product was developed and tooling produced. The HR department liaised with a local employment agency in China to recruit, train and house a workforce in a rented factory hostel, and production commenced. 'Sharpo' did not have any Chinese-speaking

Case study 13.4 (*continued*)

employees or anyone familiar with Chinese working practices and etiquette, so the company employed Ke Chen, a Chinese national with expertise in cross-cultural negotiation, to supply knowledge of Chinese regulatory authorities, handle the relationships, and negotiate locally on Sharpo's behalf. The cutlery range was launched in the UK market and the major high street multiple was extremely successful in marketing the product. Product design changes were made twice annually to ensure that the product remained 'fresh' and right for the market. Both supplier and retailer celebrated the success and further investment was made in China to support sales growth. Despite many invitations from the owner of the Chinese manufacturing firm, 'Sharpo' employees never actually visited the factory in China to meet, let alone congratulate, their collaborators or Ke Chen.

Four years later, the combination of a UK market downturn, overstocking, hugely opportunistic sales forecasts and policy changes have resulted in a collapse in demand. 'Sharpo' is left with no orders, a Chinese factory, a labour force and considerable investment liabilities. Relationships with their Chinese collaborators are non-existent and discussions about how to salvage their business venture is increasingly tense and uncooperative. Clive and his team prefer to communicate via e-mail, thus avoiding any oral communication that, they fear, may spark conflict. They argue that the cost of sending a representative to China to negotiate is not financially viable.

Clive is hoping that, over time, they will be able to negotiate to divert products into the USA market and to alternative UK retailers. He has learnt the hard lesson that major high street retailers can be ruthless, in this case copying others' products, securing major foreign investment on the back of poor business planning, and chasing the keenest possible prices at the expense of health and safety. However, so far he has failed to effectively share this lesson with his team, nor cascade the information to other teams in the organisation. At this point in time all links between the UK supplier and Chinese manufacturer appear to be irreparably severed, with both nationalities having failed to separate people from problems, and each being left with a bad impression of the other's national business practices.

Jane has been alerted to these issues and is keen to secure alternative sales streams and salvage relations with the Chinese manufacturer. She has called an emergency meeting with the board of directors to sort out the mess quickly.

Questions

1 Review the case and list the communication issues faced by each party that contributed to the crisis.

2 Suggest how Clive might have negotiated the business deal more effectively.

3 Draw up an agenda for the emergency board meeting.

4 What advice would you give to Jane about running this meeting?

Source: Case prepared by the authors; 'Sharpo' is a fictional company.

Time for a fresh perspective on negotiation?

This chapter has presented one of the most popular Western approaches to negotiation, the 'win–win' model. We have noted how the nature of international negotiation is changing as cultures interact and new practices and styles are created. The discussion points to the way that negotiation, like any form of organisational communication, is influenced by the context in which it takes place. This view is supported by recent research in large manufacturing organisations, which has shown how negotiation behaviour is influenced simultaneously by individual, relational and organisational factors. In other words, the ways that negotiations are conducted depends on the kinds of people involved, the ways that their parent departments are connected to one another, and the overall strategic goals of the organisation (Nauta and Sanders 2000). However, it would be wrong to conclude that we have no choice regarding the ways in which we negotiate or, more broadly, how we interact in other kinds of meeting and team-based activity. For example, Putnam and Kolb (2000) present a feminist critique of traditional and principled (i.e. 'win–win') negotiation. The authors argue for an alternative model, 'one rooted in feminist values and assumptions about social interaction' (Ibid: 80). This approach substitutes conventional assumptions regarding negotiation as a series of exchanges, for a process that the authors term, 'co-construction'. The pattern of communication replaces that of reciprocal concessions (i.e. 'if you do this, I will do that'), with a process of mutual inquiry, seeking to make connections and creating mutual understanding. The authors acknowledge that the approach sounds idealistic, but note that it is used in related areas, such as mediation and conflict resolution in the workplace. Like much of the earlier cross-cultural work (see Table 13.7), the authors tend to present their model as the polar opposite of traditional negotiation practice. For example, traditional relationships are 'Other [party] as distant', 'Instrumental' and 'Rational', whereas relationships in the alternative model are 'Other [party] as approachable', 'Expressive' and 'Emotional' (Ibid: 83 – Table 4.1). This does help to highlight the radical nature of their approach. However, it could be argued that much of its more socially-oriented, collaborative approach is already widely practised in existing forms of negotiation, beyond the dominant Western model.

Face-to-face 13 brings together and illustrates some of the issues around working as teams and organising meetings already identified in this chapter and highlights in particular difficulties faced by student teams working on assessed projects.

FACE-TO-FACE 13

Overcoming challenges of student team-working

A group of final year students has been allocated to tutor-selected teams of six members, and assigned the task of forming and operating as a profit-making enterprise for 12 weeks. Each team has been given a budget of £200 to get started, which they will need to repay from their profits. Anna, Baljit, Memo, Jake, Naz and Steve find themselves working together as Team 1. They get off to a great start and agree to call themselves Waste Not. They decide that they will offer a service, acting as a broker between local firms and the various agencies that recycle paper, cardboard, unwanted computing equipment and other waste. Problems begin at the second meeting when the two most vocal members – Baljit and Steve – clash over the decision of who will take the role of finance director, as both feel they have the necessary skills. The team had agreed not to appoint a leader but to take it in turns to chair meetings and to appoint roles of finance director, marketing director and sales director. They struggle and fail to agree upon who will take on which role by the end of the meeting. Anna, the person nominated to type up and circulate decisions and action points, is absent for the next three meetings, and all attempts to contact her by mobile and e-mail fail. By week four the team has split into two sub-groups, Baljit and Naz in one sub-group and Memo, Jake and Steve in the other. Both sub-groups appear to

Face-to-face 13 (*continued*)

be operating fairly successfully in terms of securing agreements with local firms. The situation erupts when members of both sub-groups – Jake and Baljit – call the same firm and begin to negotiate, unaware of what the other is doing. The firm finds out and terminates the deal on the basis that Waste Not is disorganised and incompetent. They are less than impressed by their internal communication! Team meetings cease. Baljit and Naz arrange to see their tutor to complain that certain members aren't pulling their weight (the 'absent member' and the 'loafer') and they don't think it is fair that the group grade is split. Finally Anna reappears and the team is forced to meet to agree on how they'll complete their final assessed report. The report is hurriedly written by Baljit and Naz and the team spends the last two weeks looking forward to the end of the project. A £300 profit is made and the team is given a C grade.

Questions

1 What do you think were the barriers that prevented this team from working effectively?

2 Based on ideas in this chapter and previous chapters, as well as your own experience, what strategies would you put into place to help the team achieve its true potential?

At this point it would be worth considering Face to face 7 (Chapter 7) which addresses the challenges of working in a virtual group, and Jaques and Salmon (2007) who explore the practicalities of working in virtual learning groups.

Summary

- Managers spend a large part of their lives attending meetings. Time invested in these rich but complex communication channels is productive only if they are used appropriately and managed competently.

- Organisations make use of many different types of meeting, which may have a briefing, advisory, consultative or executive role. These differences are also reflected in their procedures and associated communication practices.

- Formal meetings, such as committees, are characterised by rules, agendas, minutes, specific roles and memberships. Procedural aspects include the requirement to plan and circulate agendas in advance and to take accurate minutes.

- The chair of a formal meeting needs to be calm, objective, diplomatic and a good time-manager. The chair provides a structure for the meeting by planning the agenda, and manages the 'flow' of the discussion once the meeting is underway.

- The secretary also has an important role, assisting in the preparation of the agenda, advising on points of order, and ensuring that the minutes are clear and unambiguous.

- Organisations also engage in many informal meetings, which are often integral to the work of project teams. Given careful management and a sound understanding

Summary (*continued*)

of team roles and dynamics, team-working can be a creative and motivating form of communication.

- The rise of the 'virtual' team, connected through information and communication technologies, has extended organisational capabilities, while also creating a need for team members to deal with increased cultural diversity, and other practical issues, such as time zones and language differences.

- Negotiations are a specialised type of meeting. Many inter-organisational relationships are long-term, where principled and collaborative approaches are usually most effective. Negotiations in this form require a professional yet cordial atmosphere, where each party is able to evaluate offers from the other's perspective.

- Earlier models of cross-cultural negotiation, based on stereotypical assumptions about 'national' styles, are being challenged by the more collaborative and socially-oriented approaches of some feminist and non-Western writers.

PRACTICAL EXERCISES

13.1 Observing a meeting

Arrange to attend a local meeting that is open to the public (e.g. it may be possible to attend some of the meetings at your university or other organisation, such as the local council, chamber of commerce, trades union, voluntary or professional bodies). Observe the actions of the chair, secretary and other participants. In particular, look out for the following.

Does the chair:

- Start the meeting at the stated time?

- Ensure that each item received sufficient time for debate?

- Control anyone who strayed from the subject matter of each item?

- Allow those who wanted to speak to do so?

- Get clear and unambiguous decisions?

- Remain calm and diplomatic throughout?

- Close the meeting on time (if stated)?

Does the secretary:

- Distribute copies of all the reports and papers under discussion?

- Advise on any points of order?

- Ask the chair to clarify the wording of any decisions?

- Take any other part in the discussions?

Note: The precise role of the secretary will vary depending on the type of meeting; for example, the secretary of a trades union branch meeting may take more of a leadership role. Much of their work takes place 'behind the scenes' rather than in the meeting itself.

Do the other participants:

- Make positive and well-considered contributions to the discussion?
- Allow others to speak without interrupting?
- Appear to understand the arguments that were being put forward?
- Reach an agreement on items, or resort to a majority vote?
- Become agitated or visibly bored by the proceedings?
- Stay until the end of the meeting?

Take notes on these items at the meeting and discuss the findings with other group members on your return. What are the main lessons to learn from this experience?

13.2 The negotiation game

This exercise simulates a 'real-world' negotiation, following the approach outlined in the chapter as 'principled' negotiation. It depends upon all parties adopting a predefined role. The negotiation may be based on your own scenarios, or case materials provided by your tutor. For example, the issue for negotiation might be the opening hours at the university's computer facilities. One team represents the student union, which is requesting '24/7' access for all students. The other team represents university managers, who want to make a substantial reduction in current opening times. When the scenario has been identified, divide into two teams of four or five and spend 20 minutes preparing a position, using the 'win–win' guidance outlined in this chapter. Appoint one 'negotiator' to represent the rest of the team. The initial period of negotiation should run for about five minutes. During this time, other members of each team should act as observers, noting how the negotiation is progressing, but not making any interruptions. After five minutes, the negotiators may request a short 'time out', giving them an opportunity to consult in private with the rest of their team. Following a second period of five minutes, the negotiation is 'suspended', and the negotiators return to their teams to discuss the outcome. Each team prepares a short presentation structured around the following questions:

(a) What was the outcome? Did you achieve a 'win–win' solution, as described in the chapter? Check whether both parties have the same understanding of what has been agreed.

(b) Comment on the negotiation process. For example, did the discussions get bogged down at any point? If so, how was the obstruction overcome?

(c) Consider your own negotiation skills. For example, were both parties able to develop creative offers, valuing them on the other party's terms?

(d) Reflect on the wider issues discussed in this chapter. For example, how did your experience in this exercise compare to what has been said about the influence of culture and gender on how people negotiate?

CASE STUDY 13.5

Screen time: how video conferencing is gaining ground

The following article, written by Maija Palmer in September 2011, explores the extent of and reasons for the recent growth in video-conferencing usage.

If you can't beat them, join them, goes the adage. The fact that Sabre, one of the world's largest travel companies, recently started offering video conferencing as an alternative to

Case study 13.5 (*continued*)

flight bookings says a great deal about how much the use of telepresence has grown over the past few years.

A few years ago, the high-end telepresence room, equipped with cameras and big screens, was still something of a chief executive's toy – a status symbol to sit alongside the corporate jet.

Many of the systems were not bought on the basis of a return on investment calculation, but on a boss's whim.

"It was often the case that the chief executive had experienced it somewhere and just decided he wanted to install it – a bit like iPads for grown-ups," says Scott Morrison, analyst at Gartner.

For almost everyone involved, video conferencing was a jerky experience on a small screen that was widely dismissed as unreliable and unsatisfactory. The past few years, however, has seen the technology advance in a way that means users are finally able to experience the possibilities.

"We are in the middle of a fairly major transition," says O.J. Winge, senior vice-president of the telepresence business at Cisco Systems, one of the leading players in the sector.

"Five years ago, telepresence was in a couple of boardrooms," he says. "Now we have thousands of systems installed, and people are really starting to build their business models around this technology.

"We have full high-definition video calls, and interoperability all the way from a screen on an iPad to the big screen in a boardroom, and even between the systems of different vendors."

Interoperability has been one of the key recent developments.

"Even last year, a Cisco-Polycom call would not have worked," says Andrew Miller, chief executive of Polycom, the Nasdaq-listed telepresence group. "Video conferencing is at an inflection point with broadband, cloud computing, mobility and interoperability all pushing growth."

The ability to connect calls between different systems was a crucial point at which the mobile phone industry began to take off in the 1990s, and this could be a similar moment for video calls.

Cutbacks on business travel due to the recession, the grounding of flights by last year's Icelandic ash cloud and the global outbreak of severe acute respiratory syndrome are just some of the explanations for higher video-conferencing sales in recent years. Yet even as business travel has bounced back in 2011, telepresence sales have continued to rise.

According to the likes of Cisco and Polycom, growth rates in the sector are close to 30 per cent a year. John Chambers, chief executive of Cisco, has said that video conferencing is one of the three key growth areas for the business, while Ovum, the research group, has predicted the global video-conferencing market will be worth $3.8bn by 2016 – making it one of the fastest-growing segments in the technology sector.

There is, however, still some way to go on interconnection. Technological wizardry can link the systems – sometimes with complexity – but definitive agreements on how different telecoms networks should handle video calls and bill each other for them have yet to be reached.

In a typical technology-standards stand-off, Cisco and Polycom are both pushing their own consortiums. Cisco operates an exchange system with BT, AT&T and Tata Communications, while Polycom has set up the open visual communications consortium, which includes Airtel, AT&T, BT and Cable & Wireless.

Corporate video-conferencing systems offered by companies such as Cisco and Polycom are also not easy to connect with Skype, the internet video conferencing service now owned by Microsoft.

Case study 13.5 (*continued*)

"The problem is, who can you call on these video-conferencing systems?" says Mr Morrison at Gartner. "There are only a couple of million people connected and they are not on any directory. Compare this with Skype, which has more than 150m registered users who are easy to search for."

He estimates that about 95 per cent of video-conferencing calls are still between people at the same company. But gradually it is starting to be used for calls with clients and suppliers.

Indeed, he believes a cultural shift is taking place. "Video is still at the social-stigma stage. Doing video calls from a desk at work is still not so common and people can feel strange sitting there in an open office whispering at a screen. But this is changing – in the same way that now people think nothing of taking a mobile phone call in public."

Big banks, including HSBC, have thousands of video-conferencing systems installed in their offices. The technology is also starting to be a standard requirement on places such as oil rigs, which are hard to reach physically.

"Maintenance decisions on rigs used to take two months, but now it can take less than a week because you no longer have to fly an expert in on a helicopter," says Cisco's Mr Winge.

Companies are also making more use of the telepresence assets they have installed. Three four years ago, the system might have been used for just 45 minutes a day. Now it is more likely booked solidly for 4–5 hours.

"Telepresence has moved from being about travel savings to being about productivity," says Mr Miller. "The cost of an executive's time in an aeroplane means [that with telepresence] you are getting productivity at the push of a button."

A number of deals in the sector over the past few years show companies are also willing to stake big money on the technology. Logitech acquired LifeSize for $405m in cash in 2009, while Cisco paid $3.4bn for Tandberg of Norway. Most recently, Polycom bought Hewlett-Packard's telepresence business for $89m.

Indeed, many believe telepresence can one day be used far beyond corporate board meetings, such as for home tutoring or consulting doctors.

In South Korea, a new "technology city" being built in Songdo will have video conferencing built into every apartment, with the idea that residents would use this for all kinds of interactions, from education to dealing with government departments.

"The internet changed the way we do commerce, but it didn't really revolutionise service delivery," says Mr Winge. "Telepresence might be able to do that."

Questions

1 Review the article and identify the factors that have contributed to the recent growth in the use of teleconferencing as a means of communication.

2 What are the barriers still preventing the wider use of telepresence, particularly between organisations?

3 In addition to corporate board meetings, home tutoring and consulting doctors, what other 'meetings' could be facilitated by telepresence?

4 Imagine you are the Head of Communications for a multinational organisation. Draft a list of recommendations to enable colleagues to make effective use of telepresence. Revisit the advice earlier in the chapter on running meetings and consider how this could be applied to virtual meetings.

Key terms

Negotiation 364   Team briefings 355   The chair 346
Team 356

Glossary

The chair has the task of coordinating information flows, ensuring that individuals are not excluded and closing down 'private' conversations.

The agenda, listing the topics to be discussed, provides a structure for the meeting.

Team briefings are meetings at departmental or team level designed to allow a manager to pass on, or cascade, key information and senior management decisions.

Team A team is a group that combines a joint purpose and a shared sense of responsibility.

'Brainstorming' is a popular and well-established technique for creative problem-solving and generating novel ideas.

Negotiation is a form of persuasive communication, that may include anything from two parties engaged in bilateral discussion, to a large number of participants engaged in many cross-cutting exchanges.

Further reading

For further advice on the formal meeting, see **Armour** (2002) or **Martin** (2002). (Note: The British professional association, the Institute of Chartered Secretaries and Administrators (ICSA), is a useful source.)

Pan et al. (2002) discuss cultural difference in meetings. **Adair** (2009) develops a useful leadership philosophy, based on the task, team-building and individual development. **Bennis** (2000) is a retrospective collection of writings on leadership and change by an acknowledged commentator.

Aditya et al. (2000) offer a concise summary of the leadership field, including contemporary theories, albeit with a strong US orientation.

Belbin (2010a, 2010b) are useful updates and extensions of earlier work on team roles.

Pauleen and Yoong (2001) is a good example of research into multi-cultural virtual teams.

Jaques and Salmon (2007) offer guidance for learning from group work, including focus on online groups. It is also worth reading some practitioner accounts of team-working and leadership, such as **Harvey-Jones** (1994). On negotiation as a form of communication, see **Kolb and Williams** (2000) for a study of 'shadow negotiation', based on research conducted amongst female negotiators, and **Sheer and Chen** (2003) for an insightful empirical study on the complexities of cross-cultural negotiation.

Useful websites

For this topic in particular, access to video footage offered by the Internet is invaluable, for appraising and learning from other people's group working behaviours and interpersonal skills. Here are several websites which might be of interest to you. You might like to add some of your own too:

The Belbin website enables you to find out more about the Belbin team roles and obtain a Belbin team role profile. (Available at

http://www.belbin.com)

Brunel University's web pages on 'Participating in seminars' provide advice and downloadable tools for preparing for, contributing to and leading seminars and discussion groups. (Available at

http://www.brunel.ac.uk/learnhigher/participating-in-seminars/)

Harvard University provides a quick guide to 'Working in groups'. (Available at

http://isites.harvard.edu/fs/html/icb.topic58474/wigintro.html)

The INFED website contains information on the 'principles, theory, practice and development of work with groups'. (Available at

http://www.infed.org/groupwork)

The 'Group-work learning area' of the LearnHigher website offers a comprehensive series of resources and self-awareness activities that reflect the development of a group, including video footage and video-based analysis of student group working. (Available at

http://www.learnhigher.ac.uk/groupwork/)

The Listening and Interpersonal Skills learning area of the LearnHigher website includes guidance on active listening, using questions, giving and receiving feedback, and understanding nonverbal communication. (Available at

http://learnhigher.ac.uk/Students/Listening-and-interpersonal-skills.html)

The Mind Tools website contains information on aspects of negotiation such as conducting win–win negotiation and finding compromises. (Available at

http://www.mindtools.com/CommSkll/NegotiationSkills.htm)

The article on the Talarforum website entitled 'Are Swedes really that normal?' explores cross-cultural communication differences in meetings and highlights Swedes' behaviour as distinct from other nationalities. (Available at

http://www.talarforum.se/article/colin_moon/158/are_swedes_really_that_normal-colin_moon.pdf)

References

Adair, J. (2009) *Effective Leadership: how to be a successful leader.* Pan, London.

Aditya, R.N., House, R.J. and Kerr, S. (2000) 'Theory and practice of leadership into the new Millennium' in Cooper, C.L. and Locke, E.A. *Industrial and Organizational Psychology: linking theory with practice.* Blackwell Business Oxford, 130–165.

Armour, D. (2002) *The ICSA Company Secretary's Handbook* (4th edn). ICSA Publishing, London.

Association of Translation Companies (2012) 'About the ATC.' (Available at: http://www.atc.org.uk (accessed 18th January 2012)).

Belbin, R.M. (2010a) *Management Teams: Why they succeed or fail*. Butterworth–Heinemann, Oxford.

Belbin, R.M. (2010b) *Team Roles at Work*. Butterworth–Heinemann, Oxford.

Belbin, R.M. (2000) *Beyond the Team*. Butterworth–Heinemann, Oxford.

Bennis, W. (2000) *Managing the Dream: reflections on leadership and change*. Perseus, Cambridge, MA.

Bhagwati, J. (2001) 'A virtual meeting of minds'. *Financial Times*, London edition, 19 (20th September).

Buttery, E.A. and Leung, K.P. (1998) 'The difference between Chinese and Western negotiations'. *European Journal of Marketing*, 32, 132–146.

Casse, P. (1982) *Training for the Multicultural Manager: a practical and cross-cultural approach to the management of people*. Society for Intercultural Training and Research, Washington DC.

Chua, R.Y.J., Morris, M.W. and Ingram, P, (2009) 'Guanxi vs networking: Distinctive configurations of affect- and cognition-based trust in the networks of Chinese vs American managers. *Journal of International Business Studies*, 40: 490–508.

Cohen, S. (2002) *Negotiating Skills for Managers*. McGraw-Hill, New York.

Deresky, H. (2003) *International Management*. Prentice Hall, Upper Saddle River, NJ.

Fisher, R., Ury, W. and Paton, B. (1991) *Getting to Yes: the secret to successful negotiation*. Random House, London.

Graham, J.L. (1985) 'The influence of culture on business negotiations: an exploratory study'. *Journal of International Business Studies*, 16, 1, 81–96 (Spring).

Hackman, J.R., Wageman, R., Ruddy, T.M. and Ray, C.L. (2000) 'Team effectiveness in theory and practice' in Cooper, C.L. and Locke, E.A. *Industrial and Organizational Psychology: linking theory with practice*. Blackwell Business Oxford, 109–129.

Harvey-Jones, J. (1994) *All Together Now*. Heinemann, London.

Holden, N. (2002) *Cross-cultural Management: a knowledge management perspective*. FT Prentice Hall, Harlow.

Institute of Internal Communication (2012) 'Simplicity and commitment? the keys to team briefing' (Available at: http://www.ioic.org.uk/content/training/knowledge-bank/216-feature-simplicity-and-commitment-the-keys-to-team-briefing.html) (accessed 18th January 2012)).

Jackson, J. M. and Harkins, S.G. (1985) 'Equity in effort: An explanation of the social loafing effect'. *Journal of Personality and Social Psychology*, 49, 1199–1206.

Jaques, D. and Salmon, G. (2007), *Learning in Groups: A handbook for face-to-face and online environments* (4th edn.) Routledge, London.

Johnson, M. (2011) 'It's the networking that counts'. *FT Online* (25 September 2011) (Available at: http://www.ft.com/cms/s/2/83fd143c-e2d2-11e0-93d9-00144feabdc0.html#axzz1Z8yVzt9Q (accessed 18th January 2012)).

Katzenbach, J.R. and Smith, D.K. (1998) *The Wisdom of Teams: creating the high performance organization*. McGraw-Hill, Maidenhead.

Kerr, N.L. (1983) 'Motivation losses in small groups: A social dilemma analysis'. *Personality and Social Psychology*, 45, 819–828.

Kolb, D.M. and Williams, J. (2000) *The Shadow Negotiation: how women can master the hidden agendas that determine bargaining success*. Simon and Schuster, New York.

Kolb, D.M. and Williams, J. (2001) 'Breakthrough bargaining'. *Harvard Business Review*, 79, 88–97 (February).

Martin, D. (2002) *One Stop Company Secretary* (3rd edn). ICSA Publishing, London.

Maslow, A.H. (1954). *Motivation and Personality*. Harper and Row, New York.

Mendenhall, M., Punnett, B.J. and Ricks, D. (1995) *Global Management*. Blackwell, Oxford.

Mind Tools (2012) 'Conflict Resolution: Resolving conflict rationally and effectively'. (Available at http://www.mindtools.com/pages/article/newLDR_81.htm (accessed 18th January 2012)).

National Travel Survey Unit (NTSU) (2001) *Focus on Personal Travel: 2001 edition*. Department for the Environment, Transport and the Regions London.

Nauta, A. and Sanders, K. (2000) 'Interdepartmental negotiation behaviour in manufacturing organizations'. *The International Journal of Conflict Management*, 11, 2, 135–61.

Palmer, M. (2011) 'Screen time: how video conferencing is gaining ground'. *Financial Times* (11 September) (Available at: http://www.ft.com/cms/s/2/d5d696f4-d8a3-11e0-9089-00144feabdc0.html#axzz1Z8yVzt9Q (accessed 18th January 2012)).

Pan, Y., Scollon, S. and Scollon, R. (2002) *Professional Communication in International Settings*. Blackwell, Oxford.

Pauleen, D.J. and Yoong, P. (2001) 'Relationship building and the use of ICT in boundary-crossing virtual teams: a facilitator's perspective'. *Journal of Information Technology*, 16, 205–220.

Putnam, L.L. and Kolb, D.M. (2000) 'Rethinking negotiation: feminist views of communication and exchange' in Buzzanell, P.M. (ed.) *Rethinking Organizational and Managerial Communication from Feminist Perspectives*. Sage, Thousand Oaks, CA, 76–104.

Raiffa, H. (1982) *The Art and Science of Negotiation*. Harvard University Press, Cambridge, MA.

Robertson Languages (2007) 'About Robertson Languages International'. (Available at: http://www.robertsonlanguages.co.uk (accessed 29th August 2007)).

Sheer, V.C. and Chen, L. (2003) 'Successful Sino-Western business negotiation: participants' accounts of national and professional cultures'. *The Journal of Business Communication*, 40, 1, 50–85.

Tsang, E.W.K. (1998) 'Can guanxi be a source of sustained competitive advantage for doing business in China?' *Academy of Management Executive*, 12, 2, 64–73.

Tse, D.K., Francis, J. and Walls, J. (1994) 'Cultural differences in conducting intra- and inter-cultural negotiations: a Sino-Canadian comparison'. *Journal of International Business Studies*, 25, 3, 537–555.

Tuckman, B.W. (1965) 'Developmental sequences in small groups'. *Psychological Bulletin*, 63, 384–399.

Yeung, I.Y.M. and Tung, R.L. (1996) 'Achieving business success in Confucian societies: the importance of *guanxi* (connections)'. *Organizational Dynamics*, 25, 2, 54–65 (Autumn).

Chapter 14

Communication in perspective

'Torawarenai suao-na kokoro,' which means, 'Mind that does not stick.'
A favourite phrase of Konosuke Matsushita, founder of Matsushita Electric

Learning outcomes

By the end of this chapter you should be able to:

- make connections between communication practices and organisational strategy, drawing on the preceding chapters and other sources, including personal experience;
- recognise the unresolved challenges and paradoxes faced by organisations seeking to communicate 'effectively' in networked, multiple-stakeholder environments;
- appreciate the purpose of communication audits, and how they can be conducted;
- develop communication practices, and contribute to the development of communication strategies, that reflect the diversity and dynamism of today's organisations;
- formulate relevant questions and engage in informed argument concerning the wider communication issues raised in this book.

14.1 Introduction

The aim of this short chapter is to draw some useful conclusions, based on our review of organisational communication perspectives, principles and practices. The chapter also points to some continuing questions, regarding the themes that have been addressed in previous chapters. The opening quotation is from the Japanese entrepreneur and business leader, Konosuke Matsushita. These wise words have been cited by several management writers, including the international strategy specialist Kenichi Ohmae (1989: 132) and the pioneering knowledge management researcher Dorothy Leonard (1995: 29). They also encapsulate the core message presented in this text, which is that 'effective' communicators need to recognise the importance of remaining both flexible and critical, rather than simply sticking with established patterns and practices. Matsushita's words also echo the opening quotation from Chapter 1, where the architect and designer Walter Gropius celebrated the practical value of keeping your mind open to changing circumstances and new ideas: 'The mind is like an umbrella, it works best when open.'

This chapter is based around five questions, which are designed to encourage further reflection and debate. The themes draw on various parts of the text, but can also be seen as an extension of the discussion that was opened in Chapter 7. This chapter contains four cases; the first one introduces the concept of the communication audit, the second one illustrates implementation of multichannel customer engagement, and the third highlights the strategic importance of communication issues during periods of change. The fourth, and closing, case, 'Sequencing the human genome', brings together several ideas developed throughout the text. It tells the story of a dramatic communication 'race' involving rival public and private sector scientific teams as they struggled to publish the so-called 'book of life'. The practical exercises are replaced in this chapter by a number of discussion questions.

14.2 Five questions for organisational communicators

This section contains questions rather than answers. The questions have been selected on the basis that they pose some of the greatest challenges for those responsible for communicating in today's public, private and voluntary sector organisations. Each question is illustrated by practical examples, with references to practices described in previous sections, and is concluded with a topic for further discussion. The list of questions does not provide a comprehensive review of the text, nor is it presented in any particular order. The main criteria for inclusion are: that it addresses issues relevant to real organisations; relates to current communication practices; and demands the continuing attention of managers. (Note: You may wish to revise some of the questions, or to add others, in order to reflect your own experience.)

Question 1: How can we find out what we are communicating?

Throughout this text, we have been concerned with achieving two-way communication in organisations. This has revealed both the importance of interaction, and the practical obstacles to achieving it in practice. We began by considering some of the major barriers to communication, including a mixture of physiological, socio-cultural and political factors (sections 2.4 and 2.5). We also considered how organisations attempt to secure relevant feedback (section 6.2), and assessed the extent to which real dialogue can be achieved with multiple stakeholders (section 7.4) and through various channels. The **communication audit** is a formal assessment of the effectiveness of an organisation's communication systems and practices, which may encompass both internal and external communication. Communication audits have become more common in recent years, but follow a long-established tradition of managers seeking reliable feedback on the performance of their organisations (Downs and Adrian 2004: 6). Various techniques have been developed to collect and to evaluate the relevant evidence. Each has its strengths and weaknesses, and the best approach is generally to combine several techniques. The most popular technique is probably the survey questionnaire, which is circulated to an organisation's employees and, in some cases, to its external stakeholders (e.g. suppliers, customers and members of the local community). Questionnaires often comprise a series of statements and an associated Likert scale. The respondent is asked to mark the response that best reflects his or her experience (i.e. it relies on self-reporting of the respondent's personal perceptions). A survey originally developed in conjunction with the International Communication Association (ICA) is perhaps the most widely-used example (Downs and Adrian 2004: 124–138). Zwijze-Koning and de Jong (2007) argue that whilst such Communication Satisfaction Questionnaires are useful for gaining general insight into employees' perceptions of their organisation's communication practices, this approach is less appropriate for detecting specific communication issues and identifying solutions. Other common sources of evidence used by auditors include in-depth interviews, 360 degree appraisals (see section 6.3), and focus groups. A **focus group** is a qualitative research method used to explore a group of individuals' opinions on a particular experience, issue, product or service. It is normally facilitated by an independent consultant to allow for a more open exchange of ideas. Some audits may include a type of **social network analysis**, which investigates the pattern of connections between individuals, and groups of people within and between organisations. Auditors collect a mixture of quantitative and qualitative evidence in an effort to discover how (and where) information is flowing. By mapping these networks, auditors can highlight potential problem areas, such as 'bottlenecks' and obstacles (i.e. where the flow is restricted or obstructed). They may also identify important 'gatekeepers' (i.e. people who control access to information) and 'isolates' (i.e. people who are not getting access to information). Ruck and Welch (2012), who flag internal communication evaluation and improvement as being particularly important in times of increased financial strain, criticise this overemphasis on communication channels and processes, and recommend that audits focus on employee needs in terms of communication of content. Case study 14.1 illustrates the challenge of assessing communication practices and systems in 'real-world' organisations.

Topic for discussion: Consider the strengths and limitations of conventional communication audit techniques such as questionnaires and focus groups. Are they likely to be a useful indicator of how an organisation is communicating with its various stakeholders? How might you modify or enhance the audit process, in order to deal with issues raised in Case study 14.1 and in the previous chapters?

CASE STUDY 14.1

The communication assessment challenge

In this case study, researchers from the Engineering Design Centre, University of Cambridge, examine communication practices in three engineering companies, where teams of designers are engaged in extremely complex and costly development projects. The people involved in these projects are highly skilled and very well educated; they make use of sophisticated computer software packages to share knowledge and to support collaborative work. However, on further investigation, the researchers uncover some serious communication problems. The following extracts drawn from two longer research articles illustrate the challenge of assessing organisational communication and introduce some factors to consider when planning a communication audit.

Case study 14.1 (*continued*)

Hidden issues: the aerospace supplier

Anja Maier investigated communication practices at an aerospace manufacturing firm in the UK. Several methods were used. The daily work practice of a group of about 20 design analysts was observed, to better understand communication patterns throughout the design process. This functional group, working on stress analysis, thermal analysis, reliability, detail design and performance analysis, supported the project engineers across different projects, and also performed research into technological innovations. Interviews were conducted with higher management to get a 'top-down' view on important issues in and around engineering design practice. Additionally, a questionnaire was distributed to elicit the information needs of designers and design managers. Within the group, communication worked well, but it became apparent that several communication problems existed between different departments in the company. One was that the different disciplines used different terminology, for example at the interface between design and manufacturing. There was, furthermore, a problem of data transmission at the computer-aided design (CAD) and computer-aided manufacturing (CAM) interface. Another issue was that the company had gone through three phases of ownership change within six years. Relics, in the form of different corporate logos on shirts, cups, manuals, business cards and, more importantly, procedures were still visible. This exemplified a lack of an overall corporate identity, a problem that manifested itself in communication conflicts between the style of the 'old' and 'new' company. Having accumulated several communication issues, it became clear that there would not be one single solution to all. Instead, the need for a structured analysis of communication support was detected.

All too human: the engineering manufacturer

Claudia Eckert investigated communication problems at the consultancy wing of a UK engineering manufacturer. Methods used included semi-structured interviews with 15 designers, and two weeks of observation distributed over a period of two months. The group consisted of about 40 engineers housed in a beautiful building at the outskirts of a large city. The engineers all knew each other well and respected each other's technical competency. They had a canteen where fresh meals were cooked every day, a tearoom with unlimited free tea and coffee, a meeting room and picnic benches outside. Despite plenty of opportunities to converse informally, everybody agreed that communication did not work well in the organisation. Several knowledge management systems were purchased. Designers were encouraged to put their diaries on shared systems. In addition to that, a reward scheme was introduced for entries into a 'lessons learned' database. Yet communication did not improve. It quickly became clear that communication problems arose at a management and interpersonal level. The unit had a fierce technical director who did not like to manage. He introduced a three-tier hierarchy and communicated only with those on the top level. The only time he interacted with the engineers was to demand new work or to criticise. The people who reported to him were selected for their technical rather than managerial skills. In addition to that, workload differed enormously among the project teams, leading to envy between teams. Further acrimony was generated through the way hours were allocated to projects. Time could only be booked for funded projects, so that work on new projects or speculative work had to be assigned to existing projects. This not only destroyed any ability to account for work but also increased animosity between project teams. While everybody in the organisation was discontented with the communication amongst employees, they were well informed about what was going on. As the

Case study 14.1 (*continued*)

organisation was small, people understood the flow of information well and knew who needed which piece of information. However, there was no proactive information sharing. The computer technology they bought to enhance the information flow did not solve the problems they had, because the software tools supported aspects of their work that did not need supporting. Yet the group gave the explanation that the tools did not work because the problems did not go away.

Disappearing welding spots: the car body design process

Anja Maier investigated influences on communication at a large German automotive manufacturer. Design and development projects involve interactions among a multitude of stakeholders who work across functional, organisational, cultural, temporal, and geographical boundaries. Projects often require 'concurrent engineering', meaning that many tasks are executed in parallel. Concurrent engineering can speed up the process of bringing new products and services to market, but it also increases the need for effective communication in order to keep everything on track. Typically, the participants in the design project have different competencies, skills, responsibilities, interests, professional experiences, perceptions and viewpoints, and consequently see a given product, technological problem or process in a different way. Given these differences, it is crucial to actively promote good communication between the various stakeholders in order to achieve a well co-ordinated process and to avoid unproductive conflicts.

During the early phases of designing a new car body, different teams of engineers need to come together to specify key parameters: what is its size and weight? What kind of performance does it need to deliver? How do we ensure that it meets safety standards (e.g. 'crashworthiness')? How can we design it to allow for efficient, high-volume manufacturing? Members of the design team and the simulation team collaborate on questions of this kind.

One of their tasks is to agree on the number and location of the welding spots (i.e. the places where different parts of the car body are joined together). For example, unless the designers work closely with engineers from the production planning department, they may end up with welding spots that are out of the reach of welding robots. To ensure that the design is workable, the co-ordinates of each welding spot are recorded in a spreadsheet that is linked to computer files that detail how the sheet metal design of the car body is assembled. All files are available through the company's product data management (PDM) system. However, the audit exposed that this information was not being used directly by engineers in the simulation team who compiled these files for further numerical calculations, for example on 'crashworthiness'. The co-ordinates of the welding spots were sometimes vague and, without further cross-checking, were transferred into the numerical model generated with a technique called 'finite element method' (FEM) – a computer simulation technique used in engineering analysis. As a result, the design and simulation teams could end up having different assumptions about the way the different components connect with each other. After Simulation handed its analysis results back to Design, the welding spots were no longer contained in the geometry model of the individual component and the connection to the original definition of the welding spots could no longer be traced. Design focuses on details of the component or module; whereas simulation focuses on specific functions, which requires more than one component or module to be considered. For example, the design team might concentrate on the design of the door frame as a distinct component. In order to assess 'crashworthiness', for example, the simulation team needs to focus on the door and its interaction with the rest of the car body. Accurate

Case study 14.1 (*continued*)

information and visual representation of the welding spots – very important for the design team – is only one of the concerns for the simulation team. Lack of communication between the design, manufacturing and simulation teams in order to co-ordinate activities (obvious in this example) reflects the different understandings and goals of different groups – as well as a less efficient sequence of tasks in the new product development process overall. A better understanding of usage of different software tools, different formats of information visualisation, and detailed information needs of the teams involved, could improve the communication and design process.

There are many factors contributing to the problem of the 'missing' welding spots. Designers are tasked with the interaction with manufacturing engineers. Once the design task is finished, the design is handed over to the simulation engineers. The logic of the process, however, could be different. The welding spots might be identified after the analysis of the part, if they do not affect the design. In this case, the *overview of the sequence of tasks* could be revisited. Alternatively, it might be necessary to bring the simulation engineers into discussion with the manufacturing engineers and the design engineers earlier in the process, thus requiring a redefinition of the *activity at interfaces with the other party*. As this is a recurring problem it could be inferred that roles and responsibilities around the placing and recording of welding spots are not clearly defined. The problem might also be indicative of a deeper problem across these different groups, such as different *goals* and performance assessment criteria, and a different *vision* of the project at large.

The communication audit technique

Communication problems were uncovered by the researchers using the 'communication grid method' (CGM). This assessment method is based on the idea of a process assessment along with what are termed 'maturity grids' in quality management and software development. Levels of maturity are allocated against a number of factors influencing communication, such as terminology, information transmission, roles and responsibilities. Text descriptions in the cells of the individual grid sheets express different levels of maturity. Four design engineers and four simulation engineers were each interviewed for between sixty and ninety minutes. During the interviews the participants in the study were asked to score the current ('as is') and the desired state ('to be') of various factors influencing communication. Gaps between the current and desired states exposed areas for improvement. An ensuing group workshop described examples and potential causes and worked towards solutions exposed by the audit.

Real world examples like these illustrate the importance of gaining an understanding of the specific 'communication situation' in an organisation, before attempting to make changes to its communication systems and practices. If managers are going to intervene effectively, they need to have a sense of where processes can be influenced. This requires understanding of how factors are connected, so that their effort is not misdirected by attending to the symptoms while ignoring underlying causes. They need to be aware that 'a communication problem might be the outcome rather than the cause' (Maier, Eckert & Clarkson, 2009). In practice it may be possible for a group of managers to analyse and resolve a specific situation. However, the purpose of this research is to get a better *theoretical* understanding of factors influencing communication during the design process, and to produce communication audit tools that can be used more generally. As the authors have suggested, we need to develop communication assessment (or audit) methods that can help people to reflect, in both senses of the word: to mirror back perceptions about

---

Case study 14.1 (*continued*)

communication in industrial practice as well as to think about communication practices in a systematic way. In the remaining sections of these articles, and in related work, the researchers have outlined a method for the systematic assessment of communication, with a particular application to teams of designers working together (see the further reading section and the references for details).

Questions

1 Prepare a list of the communication problems identified in these case studies, and try to connect each problem to one (or more) communication barriers discussed in previous chapters. Remember that you may be observing the symptoms of a deeper (and possibly unobserved) set of causes.

2 Imagine that you are reporting to the senior managers of one of the companies featured in this Case study. Prepare a short (maximum 1,000 word) briefing paper, or a short presentation (maximum 5 minutes) summarising the findings, and your proposal for dealing with the issues identified.

3 Discuss the proposition that: 'All organisations have the same communication issues, so they can all be assessed using similar methods.' Consider the arguments for and against this proposition (Note: students working in groups could present their arguments in the form of a debate.)

Source: Maier et al. (2006), Maier et al. (2008), Maier, Eckert and Clarkson (2009), Maier et al. (2009) and Maier et al. (2012). Extracts reproduced with the kind permission of the authors and publisher. Case prepared by the authors, with acknowledgements to Anja Maier and colleagues.

Question 2: How can we make better use of new and emerging technologies?

The text has emphasised the importance of new technologies for the future of organisational communication. Chapters in Part II included several examples of organisations making creative use of new and emerging communication channels, including the creation of new internet-based ventures (Case study 7.3), internet-based stakeholder reporting (Case study 9.3), incorporating social media into advertising activities (Case study 10.3), online recruiting (Case study 11.3) and virtual team-working (Case study 13.2). We also saw how patterns of communication and collaboration are shaped by the established technologies (Yates and Orlikowski 2002), and identified examples of where emerging online communication practices pose challenges for organisations. For example, there is still a lack of agreed etiquette, or code, for e-mail communication (Case study 8.2) and organisations have faced severe criticism over misuse of text messaging when communicating with employees (Case study 8.3). We have also seen how social media tools can be used or misused by companies (see section 7.3). Other on-going challenges include efforts to create more accessible web-based communication channels (Case study 2.1), to combine traditional and emerging communication technologies; to maintain effective communication flows with virtual teams (Case study 13.2); to adapt to distance communication opportunities opened up by telepresence (Case study 13.5) and to avoid the more common abuses of presentation software, a phenomenon popularly known as 'death by *PowerPoint*' (Case study 12.2).

Discussion topic: Organisations of all kinds, including multinational corporations and large public and voluntary sector bodies, have had both 'good' and 'bad' experiences of applying new technologies for the purposes of communication. Which recent technological innovations do you think have had the biggest impact on organisational communication? Do you consider this impact to have been positive or negative for organisations and their stakeholders? What lessons might you draw from these experiences?

Now that you have considered these questions, read Case Study 14.2 which offers insight into the decision processes and practical steps taken by a multinational organisation in the early phases of harnessing social media to communicate with stakeholders.

CASE STUDY 14.2

Harnessing social media: engaging customers and employees online

Roberto Mastrota, eCommerce Director at 'Saporito', a multinational retailer specialising in authentic Italian food and drink, is excited. He's recently embarked on his latest project to use social media to engage with their customers. As well as the one-off and occasional customers that visit their shops and shop online via their website, they have a sizable hard core of regular shoppers who are very passionate about their Italian antipasti, groceries and wine. It is these people that Roberto hopes will be the early adopters of Saporito's social media and will establish the Saporito online community. And it is through this community that he hopes to open up a dialogue with customers, largely to get feedback that will enable Saporito to improve the service they offer. This should, in turn, result in increased sales to existing customers and attract new customers.

Roberto has reason to believe that his plans for multichannel customer engagement will be successful. Customer engagement via Saporito's website is already very impressive. The eCommerce team regularly post Italian recipes (the ingredients for which can be bought from their shops and online) and suggest wines to accompany the recipes. There is regularly updated information about the Italian regions from which the food and drink originate, including interviews with local producers. Customers frequently rate the recipes and wine, and post additional comments, including feedback to producers. The success of this project rests largely on Roberto's ability to involve the staff in Saporito's 490 Europe-wide shops. He already has evidence to suggest that they will be keen to cooperate. On the website there is a blog to which retail staff already contribute about 40%. Every shop maintains a webpage that store managers are responsible for updating with information about relevant local offers and events. This was established to support the notion that even a multinational organisation can make customers feel like they are receiving a locally-based service, from staff that are interested in them, their community and their retail needs. Furthermore, many of the trainee managers and staff in his shops are recent graduates with well-developed IT skills and lots of experience of communicating via social media.

He has already piloted the use of Twitter and Facebook. This involved arranging for staff in 10 branches of 'Saporito' to attend half a day of training in how to use social media tools. In order to ensure a level of cooperation he then set some minimum standards. For example, retail staff in each shop are required to make a minimum of one tweet per day and to provide a biweekly update of relevant, local events on Facebook. He was surprised to find that those shops in the large cities where he thought staff would be keen to communicate in this way were less engaged than retail staff in smaller, more rural locations. This could have been because they were less busy serving customers and had more time to tweet!

> **Case study 14.2 (*continued*)**
>
> Customer engagement is currently measured quantitatively by number of store page views, dwell time on each store page and, in the case of the shops piloting Twitter and Facebook, the number of tweets per shop, the number of followers attracted to the Twitter feeds and the number of 'friends' joining the Facebook groups. There is currently no monitoring of quality but Roberto knows that this is important if he is to attract and maintain customer engagement and communication. That said, they have sought feedback via online questionnaires from customers who took part in the social media pilot and have used this to develop their approach. Finally, Roberto has observed an unexpected outcome of this project: staff between stores, and indeed across Europe, are using these social media tools to communicate amongst themselves, to share ideas and to spread best practice. It seems that here is a staff development and motivational opportunity that he hadn't previously considered. But he will now . . .
>
> **Questions**
>
> 1 List the communication channels being used by Saporito to engage with their customers.
>
> 2 What are the factors suggesting that Saporito might successfully engage and communicate with their customers online?
>
> 3 What are the benefits to such organisations of harnessing social media as a communication channel?
>
> 4 How is customer engagement currently being measured? If you were tasked with conducting a communication audit, what methods would you use?
>
> 5 Imagine you were the eCommerce Director of a large retail organisation. Identify:
>
> (a) the approaches you might take to engage customers online
>
> (b) the strategies you would adopt to ensure employee buy-in and cooperation.
>
> *Source*: Case prepared by the authors. Saporito is a fictional organisation.

Question 3: How can we learn to communicate 'with emotion'?

Human emotion is a mysterious and powerful force, which can have a profound effect on the performance of organisations. Indeed, the success or failure of a strategic initiative can be determined largely by the emotional response of key internal and external stakeholders. Consequently, dealing with the emotional aspects of communication is both a demanding and a critically important managerial task. There is a substantial body of research on the role of emotion at work (e.g. Lewis and Simpson 2007, Planalp 1999). In this text we have considered the ways that emotion is used in persuasive communication (see section 5.3), and the role of 'emotional intelligence' in enhancing feedback (see section 6.6); we have also touched on the additional complexities posed by culturally diverse organisational settings, where there may be contrasting approaches to emotional expression (see section 2.5) (Kramer and Hess 2002).

Consider, for example, an organisation attempting to implement a new computer system across several sites, perhaps in different countries. Change management initiatives of this kind are bound to generate political tensions, as different factions promote their interests over those of others. People are also exposed to uncertainty, and may feel a lack of control over the process. Research suggests that the success or failure of such initiatives depends to a large extent on how ordinary employees perceive the change process, including the ways that they interact with others, and the socially-constructed meanings that emerge (Zorn 2002).

Discussion topic: What do you think are the main problems to be faced by managers as they attempt to 'handle' emotion across various communication channels? What are the most likely causes of these problems? How would you suggest that an organisation might enhance its capabilities in handling emotional aspects of its communication?

Question 4: How can our communication practices reflect increasing diversity?

The text has referred to many sources of diversity in today's organisations, including varieties of national and organisational culture, as well as differences in gender, and (dis)ability. This has been driven by several factors, including: the internationalisation of businesses, governmental and voluntary sector organisations; organisational responses to stakeholder activism; and the blurring of organisational boundaries (see sections 2.5, 7.3 and 7.4). Increasing diversity challenges many traditional communication practices. For example, organisations need to learn how to accommodate cross-cultural team-working; a requirement that is intensified by new technologies that enable virtual teams to engage in real-time working across continents and time zones (see section 13.7). While it has always been essential to consider the needs of the 'receiver', this task is complicated when the requirement is for interactive communication that can reflect the diversity of all those involved. For example, report writers and presenters need to pay particular attention to their use of language, and may have to make difficult trade-offs between creativity and clarity of expression in order to meet the needs of all stakeholders (see section 3.4 and Case study 12.4). Similar issues arise with non-verbal cues, such as the images used to reinforce promotional or campaigning messages, which may be appropriate for some audiences yet ineffective or even offensive to others (see sections 5.7 and 10.4). Even human gestures, such as those used in face-to-face interviews or negotiations, may need to be reviewed or modified (see sections 11.3 and 13.8 and Case study 13.3).

Discussion topic: Do organisations really need to adjust their communication practices to reflect increasing diversity? How can they engage in a meaningful dialogue with multiple stakeholder groups? What steps would you take to ensure that an organisation was better prepared to meet these challenges?

Question 5: How do communication practices relate to leadership and strategy?

The Irish writer George Bernard Shaw once noted that 'For every complex problem, there is a simple solution – that is wrong.' The underlying message in this text has been that organisational communication involves many complex problems, and that contrary to the optimistic words of many popular management books, these problems are rarely open to simple 'recipe book' solutions (see section 1.6). For example, we have seen how apparent barriers to communication between members of a committee may be symptoms of deeper structural problems in the organisation, or in its wider environment (see section 13.5). The solutions are also likely to reflect pragmatic compromises, which are far from ideal. For example, formal structures and managerial hierarchies are often the result of earlier compromises in the organisation (i.e. trade-offs between the competing demands of different actors). Furthermore, one set of demands, such as efficient day-to-day operations, may suggest different patterns of communication from other demands, such as stimulating creativity and innovation (see section 7.2). Organisations also develop their own distinctive cultures and sub-cultures over time, leading to the potential for misunderstanding and conflict at their boundaries. Given this complexity, organisational communication is often referred to as a key strategic issue, closely connected to the task of leadership. However, as we have seen, organisational leaders often face serious communication problems within their own top management teams (Hambrick 1995) (see section 7.2). In addition, there are major tensions between the decentralised approaches to communication indicated in recent stakeholder thinking, and the more unified messages associated with corporate communication (see Andriof et al. 2002, 2003, Kitchen and Schultz 2001) (see sections 7.3 and 10.6).

Discussion topic: What are your views on the argument that organisational communication is a complex phenomenon that should be treated as a key strategic issue? How can the leadership of an organisation seek to influence its communication practices? How would you deal with the tension between maintaining consistent messages and allowing parts of the organisation to engage in real dialogue with stakeholders?

The five questions we have discussed in this chapter highlight how challenging it is to achieve, and more importantly to maintain, effective organisational communication. The implication is that managers, in particular, must be willing and able to reflect on their existing practices and assumptions, in order to deal with rapidly-changing environments. Case study 14.3 looks at the challenges that managers face when they try to combine previously separate organisations through mergers and acquisitions (M&A). Kim Thomas interviews a number of key actors involved in this process of change, including consultants and managers of major corporations, to find out how it works and the kind of things that can go wrong (Thomas, 2007). Mergers and acquisitions are often complex and highly technical affairs, requiring a great deal of financial, legal and technical ground-work, sometimes referred to as 'due diligence'. However, as the writer discovers, more familiar *communication* issues often prove to be decisive in the success, or more commonly the failure, of these collaborative ventures.

CASE STUDY 14.3

Understanding the culture of collaboration: the art of joining different cultures

Mergers and acquisitions (M&A) provide a first-class opportunity to cut costs, increase profits and benefit from another company's knowledge and expertise. Yet surveys consistently show that a high proportion of M&As do not fulfil their objectives. One study of senior business leaders conducted by the Hay Group earlier this year found that only 9 per cent of mergers were judged 'completely successful' in achieving their aims. So what goes wrong? Dave Aron, research director at Gartner, the technology research firm, says that studies of realworld disasters, such as the 1984 chemical leak in Bhopal, have found that three conditions tend to prevail before a disaster happens: that it is not business as usual; there are tight timeframes, with no slack in the system; and that the people making the decisions

Case study 14.3 (*continued*)

are biased in a particular direction. He argues that these conditions are also present in M&As – providing plenty of opportunity for things to go wrong. Faced with those conditions, it is essential to have strong governance and clear aims. 'The most successful deals,' he says, 'are very clear about the primary goal. Is this about cutting costs through economies of scale? Is it about acquiring a specific capability or product and leveraging that through your existing channels?' The hardest kind of deal is the 'best-of-breed' merger with a competitor, which means bringing together two powerful management teams, merging two sets of IT systems and aligning two sets of working practices. 'The first important task is getting governance right at the macro and micro level because there are not natural decision-making bodies that span all the parties,' explains Mr Aron. 'You need to establish who is to be involved in decision-making, and what the lines of accountability are.' Carolyn Firstbrook, European head of strategy at Accenture, the consultancy, agrees that setting clear targets is crucial, and emphasises the importance of managing a tight process. 'In large complex deals,' she says, 'integration efforts are likely to involve hundreds, if not thousands, of employees and third party advisers around the globe. Co-ordinating and sequencing their activities correctly is a mammoth task that requires customised tools and experienced practitioners.' Not only do M&As involve making difficult decisions about complex issues at a time of change and uncertainty, they require those decisions to be made quickly. When fashion retailer Mosaic merged with Rubicon last year, Mike Wilks, the integration programme manager at Mosaic, had to make rapid decisions about which IT systems to retain if the benefits of the merger were to be realised. 'My job was to keep everyone's mind focused on the key dates that we need to get things done by, to protect those "go live" dates,' he says.

The key to achieving a merger's stated objectives – and to achieving them quickly – is to start planning even before the deal is signed, says Alan Jones, group HR director of Resolution, a life fund management company. Resolution expands through the acquisition of closed life funds, and was itself formed as the result of a 2005 merger between Resolution Life Group and Britannic Group. When Resolution makes an acquisition, it involves the key functions at the stage when the deal is being considered. The job of the human resources team, for example, is to look at every detail of the company being acquired, including terms and conditions, pension schemes and attrition rates. This careful pre-planning enables the organisation to 'hit the ground running' on the first day of the acquisition, says Mr Jones. When it acquired Abbey National Life, for example, early research found that, at the company's Glasgow call centre, more than a quarter of staff recruited were leaving within 12 months. By creating a strategy to deal with that problem, Resolution was able to halve that attrition rate within three months of the acquisition. Another frequent cause of failure, says Ms Firstbrook, is to underestimate the cultural difficulties in integrating two companies with very different working practices. When Hewlett-Packard (HP) acquired Scitex, a digital printer company based in Israel with 500 staff, it was taking over an organisation unused to big corporate practices.

'You're telling a fairly small, agile company, which doesn't invest a lot in processes or long-term planning, that they need to conform with necessary corporate processes that are totally alien to their culture,' says Pau Molinas, operations director for HP's graphics and imaging business. The danger is that morale will sink and people will leave the acquired organisation. In fact, says Mr Molinas, since the acquisition 18 months ago, only four of Scitex's staff have departed. Partly, he says, this was down to the goodwill HP had already established in its acquisition of another Israeli firm, and partly it was due to the hands-off approach HP took towards Scitex: 'It was a market HP didn't have a lot of experience in. We wanted them to have a lot of freedom when it came to investment decisions. So they

Case study 14.3 (*continued*)

were teaching us, and they appreciated that.' Cultural differences can even add value, says Ms Firstbrook. 'A merger offers a window of opportunity,' she explains, 'when all employees are expecting and prepared for change, to introduce new ways of working that neither side may have embraced in the past.' The important decisions that need to be made in the wake of a merger can risk antagonising staff on both sides. In each of the companies involved, people hold partisan views on which IT systems to keep. 'Everybody pretty much backs whatever is installed in their own business,' says Mr Wilks, 'which is why the process needs to be transparent. You need to involve the people both from IT and from the general business in this process of analysis, so once the decisions are made there is no suggestion that there has been a hidden agenda.' The principle of transparency applies not just to IT but across the board. Very often the acquiring organisation will bring in a third party to enable the process of decision-making to be more dispassionate and objective. Resolution, for example, uses Atos Consulting to advise on its acquisitions for this very reason. George McCormick, the US director of the Hay Group's M&A practice, gives the example of one acquisition when he worked for the purchasing company: 'We were able to interview executives in both firms, and we realised that the company being acquired had some very fine best practices. We said, "These are the ones you need to adopt long-term." They were shocked. But eventually it worked out.' Effective communication to all stakeholders (employees, customers, suppliers and shareholders) is an important part of making the process transparent. 'We have always told them how it is, good and bad: when we tell them information it is factual,' says Mr Jones, emphasising the need to keep existing employees well-informed as well as ones from the acquired firm.

Mr Aron agrees: 'Uncertainty is a killer in terms of strategy, operations and people's morale.' While e-mails and meetings are the traditional means of communicating news to employees, he suggests using social technologies such as blogs and wikis as well, because they allow staff to have their say, too. The trickiest question is: how do you know whether the merger or acquisition has been successful? Although many deals have disappointing results, it has to be remembered that a merger often happens when at least one party is already doing badly. 'Ideally, if you want to know if the deal is a success you should be measuring the business value compared to what would have happened if you hadn't done the deal,' says Mr Aron.

Questions

1 Read the article carefully and identify any important 'lessons' for managers.

2 Summarise each of these lessons in the left hand column of a two-column list, and in the right-hand column, note the implications (if any) for the way people communicate in organisations.

3 What does your list suggest about:

   (a) the importance of effective organisational communication?

   (b) what managers and other people working in organisations can do to ensure that it takes place?

4. Discuss (or debate) the following statement: 'Having a lot of people in your organisation with good communication skills is NOT enough to ensure that your organisation is communicating effectively.'

Source: Thomas (29 June, 2007). Copyright Financial Times Limited. Reproduced with permission. Commentary and questions prepared by the authors.

As we approach the end of *Effective Organisational Communication*, our final Face-to-face returns to the earlier topic of evaluating or 'auditing' communication. However, this time we are concerned with how you might assess (or perhaps it should be 'reassess') your own inter-personal communication skills. The scenario may be familiar to you, since it involves the sometimes traumatic process of applying for a job. We hope you have found the book to be useful and interesting and encourage you to keep reflecting on how to improve your own communication (and, when necessary, to provide the occasional piece of constructive advice to others – see guidance on giving feedback in section 6.6). We close by wishing you 'all the best' for your future efforts at communicating with, within and between organisations.

FACE-TO-FACE 14

'My communication audit', by Jane

'HAH! I just do not believe these people!' Jane pulled a face, sighed loudly and stared into her coffee cup. Her sister Sophie held her hand and tried to think of something encouraging to say. Spread out across the dining room table was an assortment of letters, each with a letterhead displaying the corporate identity of a major international company. Sophie looked at the spreadsheet that Jane had just printed out.

'Looking on the bright side,' Sophie said, 'You did manage to get three interviews – that's not too bad for a first attempt.'

'But I wrote more than 50 applications!'

'Well, that's true, though I suppose . . .'

'And not ONE single job offer! All three interviews were, like, "Thank you SO much for coming to see us Ms Whatsyourname, but we're really not interested.' Jane paused to wipe her eyes.' . . . I mean, what do they expect, BLOOD? What more can I do? I spent HOURS writing the same things over and over again in those application forms – it's so PATHETIC!' Jane let out another big sigh.

Sophie decided it was time to change the subject. 'So, anyway, at least you got a free trip to Paris!'

'Paris was good, but the interview was a nightmare; all these DULL people in expensive suits, asking really DUMB questions.'

'What do you mean, "dumb"?'

'Well, they kept asking me questions about their company – surely they know this stuff? – And "where do I see myself in five years' time?", stupid questions like that.'

'And how did you answer these questions?'

'Well, I TRIED to sound interested, and kind of made up something, basically.'

'Oh, right,' said Sophie.

Later that evening, Jane went out to get a take-away meal, and Sophie took another look at her sister's job applications. She noticed the following sentence in one of the replies, 'Thank you for your letter. Unfortunately we do not have any vacancies at present.' Another letter asked her to re-submit her application to the graduate recruitment office, which was based at a different address. When Sophie looked at some of the application

Face-to-face 14 (*continued*)

forms, she found that Jane had answered questions like, 'Why do you want to work for our company?' with exactly the same wording: 'I just want a fun job with a good salary and not too much stress.'

When Jane returned with the meal, Sophie poured her a drink and said, 'You know, I was just wondering about your job applications – would you like me to take a look and maybe give you a few suggestions?' Jane frowned, sighed loudly, and stared at her sister. 'OK, then,' said Sophie, 'let's leave it for now, and have our meal.'

Questions

1 If you were Sophie, what advice would you be giving to Jane about:

   (a) her written job applications?

   (b) her interview technique?

2 What additional questions would you want to ask Jane, in order to better assess the way she communicates?

3 Consider how you might use communication audit techniques to assess your own communication practices. This might be as an individual (as in Jane's case) or in an organisation where you have some involvement (e.g. a sports team or social club).

Source: Fictional case prepared by the authors.

Summary

- Organisational communication is a complex phenomenon, which is not open to simple 'recipe book' solutions. Effective communicators require an open and analytical mind that can draw on multiple perspectives in addition to their own immediate experiences.

- Organisations face important questions regarding their communication practices, including: how to find out what is being communicated; how to make better use of new and emerging technologies; how to communicate 'with emotion'; how to ensure that communication practices reflect increasing diversity; and how to relate communication practices to organisational leadership and strategy.

- Communication specialists have developed a variety of techniques for conducting a communication audit, which can help to diagnose problems and promote the introduction of improved practices and systems.

- Leaders of organisations need to face up to their own communication barriers; they need to be responsive to changing environments and willing to abandon long-established practices and assumptions in response to evidence and informed advice.

- While a great deal can be achieved using existing knowledge, effective communicators also need to be innovative, asking new questions and experimenting with novel approaches.

- Improving communication practices and systems can be demanding, but it is also very rewarding, helping you to achieve both organisational and personal goals.

Key Terms

communication audit 384   focus group 385   social network analysis 385

QUESTIONS FOR DISCUSSION

Reviewing an organisation's communication practices and performance

Select one organisation for detailed analysis, using the following questions as a guide. Your access to information may be restricted, but could include organisational websites, media reports, direct observation (e.g. as a customer) and interviews with employees or other stakeholders. If you are working with others, it would be useful to compare different organisations. Report your findings verbally, supported with six presentation slides or posters. In the case of presentation slides, you may want to summarise your key points in 'bullet point' format; the posters could be more elaborate, including a combination of text and graphics. For instance, you could include examples obtained from the organisation (e.g. sample web pages, promotional materials, letters, reports) to support your arguments.

1 What do you consider to be the main barriers to communication currently experienced by this organisation?

2 What is your assessment of the use of verbal and non-verbal communication in its efforts to communicate with the organisation's internal and / or external stakeholders?

3 How does the organisation make use of persuasive communication to achieve particular objectives? Try to find evidence that might indicate success or failure in this area.

4 What mechanisms does the organisation use to secure feedback from various stakeholders? Try to find evidence that might indicate effectiveness of these mechanisms.

5 How do you see communication practices as being influenced by formal structures (e.g. rules, regulations, hierarchies) and external relationships (i.e. links to other organisations)?

CASE STUDY 14.4

Sequencing the human genome – the communication 'race'

Background

Sequencing the human genome has been one of the great scientific achievements of recent times. The human genome has been called 'the book of life' and its three billion 'letters', contained within DNA, form our genetic instruction book. Sequencing the genome means decoding all the letters, in the right order. Researchers can use the genome sequence to understand disease, to gain new knowledge of the body functions and to search for new treatments.

In June 2000, the American President, Bill Clinton, and the British Prime Minister, Tony Blair, announced at a joint press conference that the draft of the human genome had been completed by two rival teams: a public consortium called the Human Genome Project (HGP) and a private company, Celera. In 2001, some months after this announcement, HGP and

Case study 14.4 (*continued*)

Celera published separate draft versions of the sequence in different scientific journals (New Scientist 2001). By the time HGP had published the final version of the sequence in April 2003, Celera had abandoned genome sequencing (Coghlan 2003). However, just five years earlier Celera's entry into genome sequencing had led to suggestions that the publicly-funded HGP should be closed down. This case describes the 'race' that developed between the public and private sector projects, and examines how communication affected the outcome.

The public sector rivals: the Human Genome Project

The Human Genome Project (HGP) formally began in 1990. It was a loose international collaboration, which still continues today. The single biggest partner was the UK's Sanger Institute in Cambridge, funded largely by the Wellcome Trust, a medical charity. It contributed about 30 per cent of the genome sequence. In the US, four government-funded laboratories contributed about 60 per cent of the sequence between them, while laboratories in France, Germany, Japan and China together provided the remainder. The key aim of the public project was not only that the human genome should be sequenced, but that all the data should be made freely available, without restriction. John Sulston was the director of the Sanger Institute, where he led the British team in their work on the Human Genome Project. Sulston was a scientist with a specialism in the genetics of worms; he was reluctant to become the identifiable figurehead for the HGP. He later wrote: 'I hadn't wanted to take a lead on the PR front for the simple reason that, judging by the usual standards in the scientific community, the human sequence was not my work' (Sulston and Ferry, 2002: 242).

The private sector rivals: Celera Genomics Corporation

Celera Genomics was founded in 1998 by Craig Venter, a long-established genetic scientist, and Perkin-Elmer, a company that manufactured the advanced machines needed for decoding the human genome. Celera was created for the purpose of sequencing the genome. The new company suggested it could complete the task more cheaply and quickly than the public project. Celera's strategy has been described as an 'attempt to privatise the human genome by sequencing it before the publicly funded Human Genome Project' (New Scientist 2002). The company's slogan at this time, 'Speed matters, discovery can't wait', reflected their emphasis on completing the project in advance of their rivals. Craig Venter was the president and chief scientific officer of Celera from its inception until January 2002. He proved to be a very talented communicator, with a gift for putting the Celera case to various audiences, including one highly influential statement that was delivered to the US House of Representatives in 2000 (Venter 2000).

The 'race' begins

By May 1998, HGP had been publicly publishing sections of the genome as they were decoded for several years. It was at this point that Celera announced its intention to sequence the human genome. From then onwards, the quest to sequence the whole human genome was widely perceived as a head-to-head competition between Celera and HGP. As *New Scientist* reported, 'Like it or not, 1998 was the year in which the genome project turned into a race' (New Scientist 1998). During the period 1999–2000, there were tentative negotiations between Celera and HGP to see if they could collaborate. However, these talks broke down over differences in their views about public access to data. From this point, there were reports that the race was becoming increasingly acrimonious.

This was a race that mattered very much to HGP. It feared that, if Celera was able to sequence the genome first, the company could patent the knowledge and prevent it being freely available. HGP did not believe it could guarantee winning the moral argument (i.e. that such knowledge should, by its nature, not be patentable), and decided that it must win the scientific race in order to put this knowledge in the public domain and make it impossible to patent.

HGP's communication challenge

HGP also faced a serious communication challenge. It needed to persuade its key stake-holders, and the world at large, that the public project was successful. HGP had to demonstrate that it was delivering good results and, ideally, that it was out-performing the private sector company. Above all, it was vital to convince the US government agencies, to ensure that they would continue funding the project. Support for the publicly-funded project was far from guaranteed. For example, after Celera announced its entry into genome sequencing, some US politicians began to argue that the public project was redundant and federal funding should cease (House of Representatives 2000).

From the start, HGP had formidable challenges in conveying its messages. Sulston and others believed that Celera consistently did a better job. As one of the American HGP scientists said, 'The public project was portrayed as labouring with a clumsy, bureaucratic, difficult-to-implement strategy, and these fast-moving folks in the private sector were going to run circles around us . . .' (quoted in Sulston and Ferry 2002: 184). One of the key problems for HGP was the political sensitivity around any attempts to criticise a private company in the US. For example, within a few days of the private-sector announcement, the UK-based Wellcome Trust announced that it would double the money it gave to the Sanger Centre. An official from the Trust stated, 'To leave this to a private company, which has to make money, seems to me completely and utterly stupid' (House of Representatives 2000). By contrast, the US response was much more conciliatory, with both of the major funding agencies welcoming Celera's initiative, while questioning its ability to deliver data in timely manner (House of Representatives 2000). This difference in approach persists today, as can be seen by the content of the UK and US HGP websites (Your Genome 2012, ORNL 2012).

Science by press release?

In his reflections on the 'race' John Sulston suggests that HGP and Celera were not competing on equal terms. He felt that Celera was not abiding by the scientific ethics that HGP held dear, in particular the convention that results are not announced until the work is completed and accepted for publication in a peer-reviewed journal (Sulston and Ferry 2002: 182). Echoing this point, an American HGP researcher accused Venter of engaging in 'science by press release' (House of Representatives 2000).

The genome project was breaking new ground in science, and using technologies understood by very few people. HGP and Celera were using different scientific strategies to try to decipher the genome and Sulston believed that Celera were making over-ambitious claims. For example, in January 2000 the company released a statement that gave the impression it had sequenced nine times as much of the genome as HGP. Sulston believed this was a deceptive comparison of different sorts of data, and in fact the true picture was that HGP had completed more than Celera, and that much of Celera's data came from the publicly available HGP database. However, once Celera had communicated its version of events, Sulston did not think he succeeded in getting his complex scientific rebuttal across, 'I tried hard to explain . . . to journalists, but not many got it and most thought it was sour grapes on my part' (Sulston and Ferry 2002: 241).

Case study 14.4 (*continued*)

HGP's communication lessons

HGP could be accused of being naïve about what was required to communicate effectively. For example, it took until early 2000 for Sulston to become the generally acknowledged figure-head. Sulston himself was more used to the discipline of science, where the system is geared to finding out the truth, rather than to public relations and journalism, where other factors need to be addressed. As Sulston says, 'I began to realise that presentation matters enormously, that nobody has time or patience to examine the facts for themselves, but rather takes up what is proffered most conveniently' (Sulston and Ferry 2001: 242). HGP also suffered from internal communication difficulties arising from its organisational structure, and a lack of specialist resources. 'We were all thrown back on our own resources to present the case as well as we could. We suffered from lack of co-ordination and lack of time' (Sulston and Ferry 2002: 242).

How it ended

The public project succeeded in its goal of ensuring that the genome sequence was put into the public domain and could not be patented. However, it did not feel the media reflected either the importance of its ethical position, or the quality of its science. As Sulston noted, 'The media myth of Celera being ahead of the game became firmly established' (Sulston and Ferry 2002: 241). Sulston's conclusion was that HGP won the scientific challenge, but came a distant second in its efforts to communicate. Furthermore, a combination of HGP's poor communication strategy and Celera's professionalism almost lost them the scientific chal-lenge too. If this had happened, the outcome for the human genome sequence, which is now freely available to the world, could have been very different. When the draft genome was jointly published in 2001, an editorial in *New Scientist* reflected on what might have been:

> 'Think about what would have happened if the Human Genome Project had been shut down . . . Celera would now have absolute power over the human genome. Ask yourself whether the com-pany would now be offering anyone free access to its data.' (New Scientist 2001)

Note: The website http://psci-com.org.uk/ is a guide to quality web-based resources on public engagement with science and technology. It offers free access to a searchable cata-logue of websites covering public engagement in science, science communication and the interpretation of science in society.

Questions

1 What do you consider to be the major communication challenges facing:

   (a) the Human Genome Project (HGP);

   (b) Celera Genomics;

   (c) both organisations.

2 Use examples from the case to contrast the communication strategies adopted by the two organisations, noting any changes that occurred during the race.

3 How might communication-related factors have contributed to the breakdown in negotiations between HGP and Celera?

4 Draft a set of guidelines (maximum 1,000 words) for scientists/science-based organisations on communicating with the media, politicians and the public.

Sources: Coghlan (2003), House of Representatives (2000), New Scientist (1998, 2001, 2002), ORNL (2012), Ridley (2006), Sanger Institute (2012), Sulston and Ferry (2002), Venter (2000), Your Genome (2012). Case prepared by Tina Fawcett and Richard Blundel.

Glossary

communication audit The communication audit is a formal assessment of the effectiveness of an organisation's communication systems and practices, which may encompass both internal and external communication.

focus group A focus group is a qualitative research method used to explore a group of individuals' opinions on a particular experience, issue, product or service.

social network analysis investigates the pattern of connections between individuals, and groups of people, within and between organisations.

Further reading

Huff and Jenkins (2002) is an edited volume, which exemplifies the links being made between communication-related concepts (in this case, managerial cognition), organisation theory and strategic management.

Hargie and Tourish (2009) and **Downs and Adrian** (2004) are accessible and comprehensive guides to communication audits, including many practical examples.

Lewis and Simpson (2007) is an edited text addressing the important (and often under-emphasised) topics of emotion and gender in organisations.

Sulston and Ferry (2002) tells the story of the human genome project from the perspective of one of the leading scientists, who headed up the public sector team.

Ridley (2006) is a 'popular science' guide to the human genome that shows how complex scientific information can be communicated effectively to a non-specialist audience. See also the further reading guide at the end of Chapter 7, which contains a number of useful references about the relationship between organisations, organisational strategies and communication.

Useful websites

Here are several websites which might be of interest to you. You might like to add some of your own too:

The International Communication Association is an organisation for professional specialists in various aspects of organisational communication, and indicates some potential areas for developing your interest in the subject. (Available at

http://www.icahdq.org/)

Many consultancy firms provide communication audit services, covering external and internal communication; following are a few examples of companies that feature case studies or samples of their work. (Available at

http://www.vervecommunications.co.uk/ communicationAudit.php
http://www.ewa.ltd.uk/case-studies/
http://www.guidestarco.com/Site/surveys_consulting/communications_audits/index.html)

References

Andriof, J., Waddock, S., Husted, B. and Rahman, S. (eds) (2002) *Unfolding Stakeholder Thinking: theory, responsibility and engagement*. Greenleaf, Sheffield.

Andriof, J., Waddock, S., Husted, B. and Rahman, S. (eds) (2003) *Unfolding Stakeholder Thinking 2: relationships, communication and performance*. Greenleaf, Sheffield.

Coghlan, A. (2003) 'First and only edition of the book of life'. *New Scientist*, 178, 2391–2419, 19 (April).

Downs, C.W. and Adrian, A.D. (2004) *Assessing organizational communication*. Guildford Press, New York, NY.

Hambrick, D.C. (1995) 'Fragmentation and the other problems CEOs have with their top management teams'. *California Management Review*, 37, 3, 110–127 (Spring).

Hargie, O. and Tourish, D. (eds) (2009) *Auditing Organisational Communication*. Routledge, Hove.

House of Representatives (2000) 'Hearing charter for Hearing on the Human Genome Project.' Subcommittee on Energy and Environment, US House of Representatives Committee on Science, Washington (6th April). (Available at: www.house.gov/science/ee_charter_040600.htm (accessed 14th August 2003)).

Huff, A. and Jenkins, M. (eds) (2002) *Mapping Strategic Knowledge*. Sage, London.

Kitchen, P.J. and Schultz, D.E. (2001) *Raising the Corporate Umbrella: corporate communications in the 21st century*. Palgrave, Basingstoke.

Kramer, M.W. and Hess, J.A. (2002) 'Communication rules for the display of emotions in organizational settings'. *Management Communication Quarterly*, 14, 1, 50–89.

Leonard, D. (1995) *Wellsprings of Knowledge: building and sustaining the sources of innovation*. Harvard Business School Press, Boston, MA.

Lewis, P. and Simpson, R. (eds) (2007) *Gendering Emotions in Organisations*. Palgrave Macmillan, Basingstoke.

Maier, A.M., Eckert, C.M. and Clarkson, P.J. (2006) 'Identifying requirements for communication support: a maturity grid-inspired approach.' *Expert Systems with Applications*, 31, 663–672.

Maier, A.M.; Eckert, C.M. and Clarkson, P.J. (2009). Towards managing team-interfaces: an exploratory elicitation of factors influencing communication. In: *17th International Conference on Engineering Design (ICED'09)*, 2009, Stanford, CA.

Maier, A. M., Kreimeyer, M., Hepperle, C., Eckert, C.M., Lindemann, U. and Clarkson, P.J. (2008) 'Exploration of correlations between factors influencing communication in complex product development', *Concurrent Engineering: research and applications 16*, 1, *37–59*. Sage Science Press, London.

Maier, A.M., Kreimeyer, M., Lindemann, U. and Clarkson, P.J. (2009) 'Reflecting communication: a key factor for successful collaboration between embodiment design and simulation'. *Journal of Engineering Design*, 20, 3, 265–287.

Maier, A., Moultrie, J. and Clarkson, P.J. (2012) 'Assessing Organizational Capabilities: reviewing and guiding the development of maturity grids'. *I E E E Transactions on Engineering Management 59*, 1, 138-159.

New Scientist (1998) 'The tortoise and the hare'. *New Scientist*, 160, 2165–19, 34 (December).

New Scientist (2001) 'Free for all'. *New Scientist*, 169, 2278–2317, 3 (February).

New Scientist (2002) 'Venter quits'. *New Scientist*, 173, 2327–2426, 7 (January).

Ohmae, K. (1989) 'Companyism and do more better'. *Harvard Business Review*, 67, 125–132 (January–February).

ORNL (2012) *Human genome project and the private sector: a working partnership*. (Available at: www.ornl.gov/sci/techresources/Human_Genome/project/privatesector.shtml (accessed 13th March 2012)).

Planalp, S. (1999) *Communicating emotion: social, moral and cultural processes*. Cambridge University Press, Cambridge.

Ridley, M. (2006) *Genome: the autobiography of a species in 23 chapters*. Harper Perennial, London.

Ruck, K. and Welch, R. (2012) 'Valuing internal communication; management and employee perspectives'. *Public Relations Review* 38, 2, 294–302.

Sanger Institute (2012) 'Communication and Public Engagement Programme'. Wellcome Trust Sanger Institute, Hinxton. (Available at: http://www.sanger.ac.uk/about/engagement/ (accessed 13th March 2012)).

Sulston, J. and Ferry, G. (2002) *The Common Thread: science, politics, ethics and the human genome*. Corgi, London.

Thomas, K. (2007) 'Understanding the culture of collaboration: the art of joining different cultures'. *Financial Times*, 29th June 2007. (Available at: http://www.ft.com/home/uk (accessed 29th August 2007)).

Venter, J.C. (2000) 'Prepared statement before the Subcommittee on Energy and Environment, US House of Representatives Committee on Science,' Washington DC (6th April). (Available at: www.house.gov/science (accessed 14th August 2003)).

Yates, J. and Orlikowski, W.J. (2002) 'Genre systems: structuring interaction through communicative norms'. *The Journal of Business Communication*, 39, 13–35.

Your Genome (2012). 'Wellcome Trust Sanger Institute's Your Genome, London'. (Available at: www.yourgenome.org (accessed 21st March 2012)).

Zorn, T.E. (2002) 'The emotionality of information and communication technology implementation'. *Journal of Communication Management*, 7, 2, 160–171.

Zwijze-Koning, K. and de Jong, M. (2007) 'Evaluating the Communication Satisfaction Questionnaire as a Communication Audit Tool'. *Management Communication Quarterly* February, 20, 3, 261–328.

Index